personal computing hardware and software basics

Edited by Raymond P. Capece,
Solid State Editor, Electronics

Electronics Magazine Book Series

McGraw-Hill Publications Co.
1221 Avenue of the Americas
New York, New York 10020

ELECTRONICS BOOK SERIES

Also published by *Electronics*
- **Microprocessors**
- **Large scale integration**
- **Basics of data communications**
- **Applying microprocessors**
- **Circuits for electronics engineers**
- **Design techniques for electronics engineers**
- **Memory design: microcomputers to mainframes**
- **New product trends in electronics, number 1**

Library of Congress Cataloging in Publication Data

Main entry under title:
Personal computing
(Electronics magazine book series)
1. Microcomputers. 2. Minicomputers.
I. Capece, Raymond P., 1952—
QA76.5P394 001.6'4:04 78-13996
ISBN 0-07-099925-2

Contents

Preface

Personal computing is now a reality. Anyone interested in computers, whether for programs to simplify daily work or simply for expression through graphics displays and synthesized sound, can afford his or her own computer. The machines are small but no less powerful than the computers of a decade ago that filled rooms with equipment—a small computer, in fact, contains hundreds of thousands of transistors. But their basic theory of operation is not as complex as one might expect.

No matter how deeply one wants to understand the workings of personal computers, this book provides an adequate basis. The material—selected from top trade and hobby magazines including *Electronics, Datamation, Mini-micro Systems, IEEE Spectrum, Byte, Interface Age, Kilobaud, and People's Computers*—is arranged by subject in order of increasing technical depth.

Part 1, "Introduction to Personal Computing," gives the history of the development of the hardware and of the field itself, and starts with a basic description of what the personal computer is.

Part 2, "Basic Computer Theory," gets into the hardware of the machines—processors, memory, input/output—and some basics of design.

Part 3, "Advanced Microcomputer Theory," describes the most popular microprocessors, which are at the heart of the personal computer.

Part 4, "Reviews of Personal Computers," evaluates some of the personal computers on the market today,

Part 5, "Software for Microcomputers and Microprocessors," describes and compares the programming languages and includes information on simplifying the chore of software generation.

Part 6, "Specifications and Other Useful Information," compiles general information like microprocessor specifications, glossaries, tables, and helpful hints.

—Ray Capece

Part 1: Introduction to Personal Computing

The term "personal computer" may be taken literally: it means a computer that's to be used by one person—whether for solving engineering problems, doing business accounting, or simply balancing a checkbook. But just how these computers differ from the big IBM machines that first come to mind with the word "computers" is explained in this introductory section—and what might be surprising is that the difference is not as great as one might think. In addition, this part discusses components, some of the equipment available and what each costs, and several of the interesting uses they are being put to.

Home computing: an introduction for novices

by James S. White

Welcome to home computing! The time has arrived for a computer in the home of almost everyone who wants one.

During the past few years, expensive, complex computers in industry and commerce have helped you by cutting costs and raising the quality of many products and services you use. Now, computers have been designed for home use and their prices have been drastically cut. Personal computers are available today at prices similar to other major household purchases.

Thousands of Americans are enjoying their own computers now. You can select a computer for your home, a computer that will be easy for you to use, even if you have no technical experience. This paper describes how you can benefit from your own computer.

Learning about computers can be a little confusing because many different kinds of things are sometimes called computers. A computer can not be consistently identified by its size, appearance, construction or use. None of these features are characteristics of computers in general. Computers are electronic devices built according to certain technical rules, which we won't discuss here.

However, all types of computers do have some common characteristics that make them different and much more powerful and helpful than many other things we use. We will discuss some common characteristics of today's popular types of home computers, characteristics that are important to computer users and that make computers especially helpful to us.

COMPUTERS ARE TOOLS

We use tools to extend our capabilities and to multiply our natural powers. We use tools to help us do things we can't alone, or so we can do jobs easier, quicker, or better than we can alone. Computers help us in all these ways.

MENTAL TOOLS

Computers help our minds. Rather than helping our muscles, as most tools do, computers multiply our intellectual power and capabilities. Computers are extensions of our minds. Computers are tools we can use for greatly increased mental achievement and enjoyment. Because our mental activities are much less limited in potential benefits than our physical activities, the helping potential of computers is much greater than the potential of other tools.

PROGRAMMABLE TOOLS

Computers follow people's instructions and do nothing unless instructed to do so. Computers are useful as extensions of our minds primarily because they faithfully do just as we instruct. Your computer will follow your instructions. Your computer's ability to follow a complex set of instructions and thus do just what you specify gives it power far beyond any other kind of tool. We don't know the limits of the ultimate potential of computers because we don't know the limits of the ultimate capacity of men and women.

If you examine a computer in detail, you see that it recognizes only a few instructions that can do only certain limited things. These instructions allow a computer to, for example:

1. Perform mathematical calculations
2. Store a large amount of information, and select a particular piece of information to meet a specific need
3. Evaluate a vast number of alternatives to determine the best solution to a question, even a question unrelated to mathematics.

However, the instructions a computer recognizes are so powerful and so varied that a person can combine them to instruct his computer to do almost anything as an end result.

A set of instructions you give to your computer is a *program.* When you instruct your computer, you are *programming* it.

A computer's program can be changed easily and quickly. A complete program can be changed in as little as a fraction of a second. However, the work or play of composing a program the first time usually takes a person several hours or longer.

CONTROL TOOLS

Computers can help us by controlling other tools and machines. A computer can cause a much larger tool to do something in a certain way and at certain times, as programmed. This capability extends the power of a computer far beyond the things it can do directly.

Our minds are control devices which control our muscles. We thereby control the most powerful of machines, the generation and use of power, and many natural events.

So, although computers function intellectually, their direct benefits extend far beyond the intellectual. By helping us to "work smarter," computers can be a way to physical accomplishment that is better than just working harder.

MACHINE TOOL

A computer is a machine. A machine is generally a tool that can operate by itself, doing a desired job, without always needing the personal control or constant attention of a person. A computer can follow its assigned program with little or no need for the further assistance of a person.

A machine used in a home is generally called an appliance. A computer can be a home appliance, a machine that can continue working to help us while we do things that are more useful or enjoyable.

VERSATILE TOOLS

Computers can be extremely vertatile. One computer can do, and be, many different things. A computer's versatility results from two other characteristics. The first is a computer's previously discussed programmability, the fact that you may instruct your computer to do whatever you want.

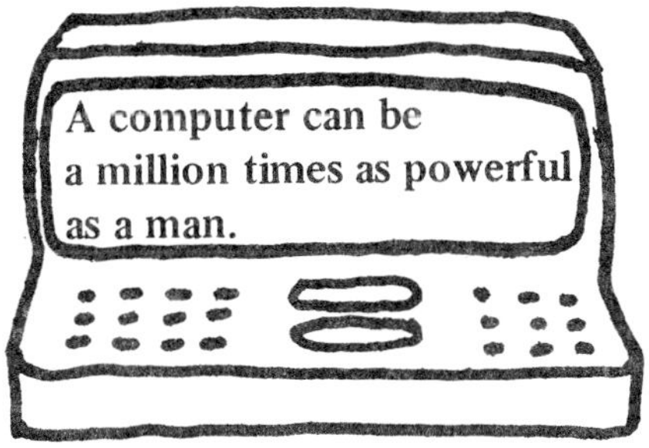

The second reason a computer is versatile is that it is a system. A system consists of various parts, each doing its own job. All of a system's parts operate together, supporting each other as do the various organs in our body.

A computer can be composed of a few or many different types of parts; each can have widely varying characteristics. The parts you choose to assemble your computer are those parts that together will give the resultant system the capabilities to best do what you want it to do, at a price you can afford. You can change these parts as you want your computer's capabilities to change.

The wide range of possible computer characteristics also results from the fact that a computer, as a control device, is often combined with other devices. A large variety of devices may be combined so the resulting system can have a wide variety of characteristics. A computer generally remains the key part of the resulting combination, so all these types of systems are often called computers.

Computers are so versatile that a computer can do, or control, any rational or mechanical process, activity, or happening. What a computer can do is essentially limited only by the skill and imagination of the person(s) who build and program the computer.

A particular computer must be equipped with the power and accessories appropriate for the job it will do. Power usually isn't a serious constraint; a computer that is half as powerful may just take twice as long to do a given job. Even computer accessories are usually versatile, and many can be used for a wide variety of different kinds of jobs.

PRECISE TOOLS

Computers can be perfect. A properly programmed and operated computer makes so few errors in end results that a computer mistake may never occur during years of doing a particular job. Computers do occasionally make mistakes, typically one in many millions of operations. However, computers can, and many do, check their own work so that a mistake is not given to a human user.

Most "computer mistakes" occur because computers do exactly as they are instructed. Many people find it difficult to give correct instructions to handle complex problems. The computer that follows incorrect instructions will produce an incorrect result, and is often incorrectly blamed.

FAST TOOLS

Computers are extremely fast. A typical home computer can do 500,000 of its basic operations per second. Home computers often move information as fast as physically possible—at the speed of light.

This great speed also gives computers great power. Because computers are so fast, they are very useful even for those jobs that they can't do efficiently. Computers just go ahead in their roundabout way, doing many, many operations to provide a useful result. A typical computer that must do a million operations to complete a particular job may be done in two seconds, which is often sooner than any alternative.

How powerful are computers? A computer can be a million times as powerful as a man. That's almost beyond comprehension, so let's consider an example.

The great pyramid of Egypt is generally accepted as the world's most costly single structure, in terms of man years. According to the most commonly accepted estimates, 100,000 men worked 20 years. In total, two million man years was required to do this job.

Building pyramids is out of style today. Our world is oriented towards numbers, such as dollars. So let's think about two million man years of working with numbers or calculations.

The first common home computers were delivered about two years ago. One of these computers, working for these two years, could have done calculations that would take one million men working with pencil and paper 24 hours per day, 365 days per year, for 2 years. You can buy such a computer, or one much faster, in your local computer store.

PERSONAL TOOLS

Despite their great power, computers can be personal tools. You can select your own computer to help you, and to expand your own capabilities. More than 10,000 Americans have their own computers; more than 100,000 Americans are using computers as personal tools, to make their work easier and their play more fun.

We should consider a couple of philosophical points here. Despite its great power, a computer can no more do anything by itself than can any other machine. Computers are constructed, and instructed, by man, as tools. A computer is and does only what it is made to be and do by man.

Further, as we plan to use computers, we should consider their strong and weak points, just as we do for other tools. For some tasks, computers can be a million times as powerful as man. In other of the many ways we can use computers, they will be much less than a million times as powerful as we are alone.

A COMPUTER IS:

Having reviewed outstanding characteristics of computers as they appear to users, we are now ready for a glimpse of some technical details. We have come to a fundamental question: What is a computer?

A computer is a *programmable electronic data processing system.* Computers have been called many other names, but this definition gives us a good start towards understanding computers technically. We'll consider the significant meaning of each word, except "programmable" and "system", which are discussed elsewhere.

Because a home computer is electronic, it is powered by electricity, generally from a 110 volt wall outlet, just as other electronic appliances are. Computers are solid-state electronics, so need relatively little power and are not likely to wear out soon or to need many repairs. Many parts of a computer are less likely to fail after they have been used for several months or years than when they are new. However, computers are very complex and some parts are not solid-state, so the availability of repairs should be considered when selecting a computer.

A computer works with *data,* or information. This characteristic is similar to the fact that our minds work with ideas, rather than the physical things our bodies work with. However, as previously mentioned, a computer can control almost any physical activity.

The data a computer works with must be objective and precisely expressed. Computers can't work with feelings or subjective ideas unless they are expressed objectively. Neither computer data nor computer results are ambiguous, despite the fact that their meanings aren't always obvious to all people.

All computer data is expressed in a very simple numeric code. Knowledge of this coding is necessary for the user who wants to understand the internal operations of a computer. However, a computer can translate its codes into words or numbers that you are familiar with, so computer codes need not be of concern to you. You can use today's computers without consciously learning any codes.

A computer processes data. Processing means changing, generally into a more useful form. A computer changes data it has been given into data that is more useful, or more fun, for its individual user. The processing a computer does is whatever its program directs it to do.

MICROCOMPUTERS

The type of computer generally used in homes is called a *microcomputer.* Most of the computers sold in local computer stores are microcomputers.

A microcomputer is a computer that is small in size and price. A microcomputer need not be small in power or capability. There is no exact definition that precisely distinguishes microcomputers from other types of computers, just as there is no commonly accepted rule that distinguishes a microskirt from a skirt. This paper discusses computers in general and emphasizes the characteristics of home microcomputers.

INPUT

To start a computer working you give it a program and data. Communicating these things to a computer is called *inputting.* The computer parts you use are called input devices.

You often communicate to a home computer in ways similar to some you use to communicate information and instructions to people. You can communicate to a computer by pressing keys, or buttons, on a keyboard that is very similar to that of an electric typewriter. Some lower cost computers have keyboards that are much like the keyboard of an electric calculator. All computer keys are electrical switches.

Other types of switches used for computer input are similar to the on-off light switches in your home. Computers with many switches of this type are best suited for the user who wants to know much about computers and work with them in intimate detail.

A variety of other types of input devices are used with home computers. Some computers can understand spoken words, but this capability is not yet common for home computers.

PROCESSOR

The key part of a computer is a processor. A *processor* is a group of electronic circuits which actually performs the calculating and the logic operations comprising a program. A processor performs the same functions for a computer that a brain (less its memory function) does for an animal.

The processor of a microcomputer is a microprocessor. This is a small electronic component, one kind of the wide variety of components called *chips.* A microprocessor is a small form of a processor. Microprocessors are widely used as control devices, in many kinds of machines besides microcomputers.

You may hear a microprocessor called a microcomputer or a processor called a computer. However, there are critical differences for the user.

A processor is a control element, a part of a machine that directs, by following a program, the rest of the machine to do whatever it is supposed to do. A microprocessor can be part of a calculator, part of a microwave oven, or part of a sewing machine. In none of these uses is a microprocessor a computer. Nor is the calculator or the microwave oven a computer just because it is controlled by a microprocessor.

A computer, or a microcomputer, is a complete machine, including all the parts and accessories needed to do whatever it is used for. A computer can operate entirely on its own, needing only a source of energy and, at the start, directions from a person. A computer is built so you can input your instructions to it, and so it can communicate the results of its processing to you.

MEMORY

A computer uses parts called *memory* to store, or remember, the programs and data that have been input and the results that perform the memory function are chips, similar to microprocessor chips. In many computers, memory chips are physically part of the processor.

A home computer can also remember information by storing it on a magnetic tape cassette, such as the type you use on a cassette recorder to record, and thus remember, music or words. A cassette recorder can also be an input device because you can use it to read into your computer programs that other people have written and recorded on their computers.

Another type of home computer memory device is a relatively expensive and powerful device called a floppy disc drive. This is a recording and playback device that uses a rapidly spinning disc about the size of a small phonograph record.

OUTPUT

The final common functional part of a computer is an *output* device, which a computer uses to communicate to you. The most common home computer output device is one you are quite familiar with — a TV screen, on which the computer displays words, numbers, and sometimes pictures. This screen can be that of a standard home TV, or of a specially de signed device.

Computers can also display their output by using lights that form numbers and letters as do the output lights on an electronic calculator. Computers can also use individual lights that are either off or on, and thus communicate to you the status of various processes and coded data. Computers can also communicate to you by printing on paper and, less commonly today, by "speaking" words.

INTERFACE

Many computers have several groups of electronic components, called *interfaces*, to allow the computer to communicate with devices not normally compatible with the computer. An interface is like a translator. You can, for example, buy an interface so your home computer can display data on a TV set you now have. Often some interfaces are built as part of a computer, while interfaces for less common input, output and memory devices are options.

POWER SUPPLY

Computers have one other part which the potential buyer should consider. A computer uses electrical power, but of a low voltage, similar to that used by electronic calculators and similar devices. This low voltage is supplied by a group of electronic components called a *power supply.* Probably you've used an "AC adaptor" to supply power to a device which normally uses batteries; a computer power supply has the same function as an AC adaptor.

A power supply is sometimes included as a standard part of a computer, is sometimes an extra cost item, and is sometimes not even available from some vendors. Also, a large microcomputer system with many accessories needs a more powerful supply than a small system, and perhaps more power than can be supplied by a computer as sold. Check before you buy.

PROGRAMS

A program is not usually considered a part of a computer because it doesn't exist physically, just as an idea doesn't. Programs are often called *software*, while the physically existant computer and accessories are called *hardware.* Software is essential to the use of a computer, and some types of programs are commonly purchased with the computer or as accessories. The availability of software should be a key computer selection factor for most potential users.

The most important type of program generally furnished by a computer manufacturer is a language translator. This program translates between your English language and the computer's machine language so your computer can understand the programs of instructions you communicate to it. This translator program may be called an *interpreter*, an *assembler*, or a *compiler.*

The most common English-like language used to program home computers is called BASIC. This is one of several languages, called *high level languages*, that are easy for casual programmers to use. BASIC interpreters are available for many computers. For some computers, more than one BASIC interpreter is available. Different BASIC interpreters vary in the number and the power of the instruction words they recognize and in the accessories and capabilities they require of the computers on which they operate.

Lower cost computers have no language translator programs, so you must communicate with them in machine language. Although such communication is educational for the user who wishes to understand how a computer works in detail, it isn't in an easy language for a person to use.

The other major category of home computer programs includes those that give a computer the capability to do whatever its owner wants. Some sources of programs of this type include:

1. The manufacturer and vendor of your computer
2. Other vendors
3. Program libraries, which loan or give copies of programs, at little or no charge
4. Friends and computer club acquaintances
5. Your own ideas —this is the type of program you can write yourself.

Although some programs will be easy for you to write, others could take several months of hard work. A discussion of the many factors affecting program procurement decisions and the decisions of which programs you should write yourself is beyond the scope of this article. A brief summary is that there are many ways you can get programs and many unexpected options and decision factors that may be involved. The availability of programs for doing specific jobs certainly can be a major computer selection decision factor.

USES OF HOME COMPUTERS

Having now covered the technical characteristics of computers, we are ready to consider some of the things they can do for us. Even though many people understand the immense potential computers have for helping in our homes, they still ask: What are home computers used for today? This is a reasonable question, and probably the most common one for a home computing newcomer. The answer is: Mostly for fun.

Although computers have proven that they have many other potential uses, the reason relatively few people are using computers for serious purposes is that most people can't seem to quit playing with their computer. I see nothing wrong with that. Work, for many people, should be done at work. Those who can spend most of their time at home for enjoyment seem to have achieved an important measure of life's success.

The most common type of home computer owner today is the builder, a craftsman or craftswoman. For these many people, understanding, building, or otherwise developing computers is an end in itself. These computer hobbyists are similar to the painter or woodworker whose enjoyment comes from creating, rather than using or possessing.

Computers are the world's most pliable media — you can make more things of a computer than you can make of clay, paint, or wood. Creating with computers can be extremely challenging, and success extremely rewarding, because the potential for creativity, mental and physical, is almost infinite.

Other people enjoy using computers for playing games. When used for games, computers are often somewhat like TV games, today's hottest consumer item. Unlike today's common games, which are very limited and rather quickly become boring, the variety of computer games can be almost infinite.

People with home computers can keep getting new games, sometimes for less than $1 each. Better yet, they can design and use games they create themselves. And these aren't just bouncing ball games. Home computer owners program and use their computers to play cards, space war, chess, and many other games. The really fun games are ones you never heard of because they can only be played with the help of the immense power of a computer.

But computers can be very practically useful, as proven by their use in, and great benefits to, almost all of commerce, industry, and medicine. Easily affordable home computers can be at least as powerful as many of those that are doing thousands of different jobs in business today.

Families use computers in home offices to keep records and to handle accounting chores. Some also plan stock and commodity futures buying and selling. Home businessmen use computers in many occupations.

Computers control heat and other environmental factors so an entire building, such as a home, is more comfortable and so energy is used more efficiently. Home security is another service, meeting an unfortunately increasing need, that computers are being developed to help supply.

Education is another of today's uses of home computers. As educational tools, computers are helping to teach subjects ranging from first grade addition to financial and engineering math, and a wide range of other subjects. Also, many people are using computers to teach themselves about computing, a field with considerable employment potential. In addition to vocational benefits, learning about computers is both enjoyable and practical because of the rapidly increasing role computers are coming to play in the everyday lives of each of us.

Many computer owners have talked of the great potential of computers for keeping track of kitchen supplies, planning menus and recipes, and for many similar household chores. For some reason, these uses seem to be like most household chores, they end up in a "tomorrow" category, even though their long range benefit can include considerable work savings.

Returning to fun applications, computers are used to catalog and control the playing of musical recordings. Computers are also used to make music. There is even a magazine devoted to the topic of computer music.

Electronic hobbies are another home computer application. When electric train layouts are so complex that parent and child together can't control them, computers keep the home railroad running smoothly. Some amateur radio hams make extensive use of computers in their hobby and have generally been the pioneers in home computing.

The list of what computers can do, of what you can do with your computer, can go on and on. Aside from hopefully giving you some more reasons for getting involved in computing, the preceding examples of computer uses should further support the idea that a computer can do almost anything.

HOME COMPUTERS TODAY

But a computer in your home? Lots of people have computers in their homes already. But keep in mind that these people are the pioneers. They didn't have to cut down logs with an axe to build their own cabin. But some of them have done as much pioneering in other ways. They have done the hard work. You can buy a prefabricated, ready built computer, ready to move in. However, there is plenty of wilderness left in computing. If you want to be a pioneer, there are many opportunities for you to go ahead into the unknown and develop techniques and products. And there are lots of people who will follow and much appreciate any real discoveries or progress you make.

This is one of the choices you can make as you look at today's computers, and as you decide how you will become involved in computing. You can buy the equivalent of 40 acres of wilderness, or a prefab in a subdivision, or many things in between. You can totally design and build your own computer. Or you can get one that you can plug in and have start immediately to work for you. There are many available options between these extremes. Your home computer can be what you want it to be.

ELEMENTARY COMPUTERS

You can get a very basic type of computer. This will be relatively inexpensive, costing between $100 and $250, generally less power supply. It won't have a fancy cover, and probably will have no cover at all. All the parts of this type of computer may be on one piece of plastic-like material called a printed circuit board, or just "board" or "card".

You will have to do lots of detailed work to program and use such a computer, especially because programming generally must be done in machine language. The power of this type of computer is limited — you can't easily add many accessories, nor can you easily connect such a computer to other devices to control them.

This type of computer is a good training device, an educational tool. The lack of fancy accessories means that you work directly with your computer, with little interference. Therefore, you can learn, by doing, much about the details of how a computer works.

EASY-TO-USE COMPUTERS

Some people don't want to work closely with a computer. They would rather have their computer follow their general instructions. Such people aren't especially interested in knowing the details of how a computer works. They would rather learn how to use a computer to solve a particular type of problem, control a particular process, or help them in a field unrelated to computing.

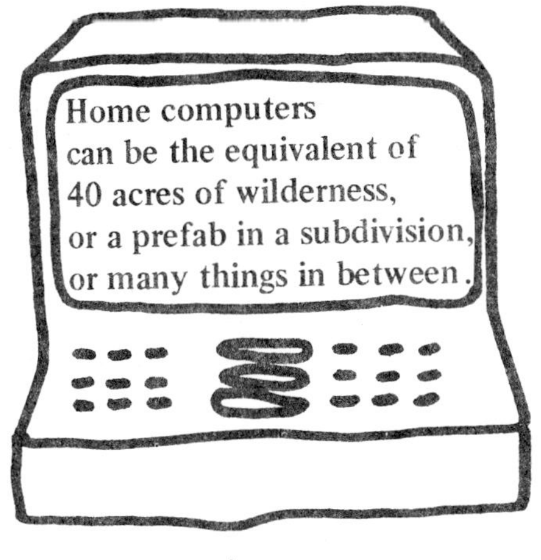

Computers designed for this type of user are available. One key characteristic of this type of computer is that you program it by using a high level language. As we discussed earlier, a high level language is easy for people to use.

These computers are generally built on several printed circuit boards which plug into guides and connectors mounted on the computer frame. Computer capabilities are changed by plugging new boards into appropriate spaces, as long as there is room available. For some computers of this type, especially "Altair bus compatible" or "S-100 bus" computers, many accessories are available that can be added. For other types of computers, only a few accessories are available. Consider what you may need and want.

Prices of computers in this category generally start at about $500. A system with enough power and accessories to use a high level language may cost $1000. The price of a full system, such as might be used for a business application, can easily reach $5000.

KITS?

Another primary choice when selecting your home computer is whether to purchase a kit of parts, or an already assembled computer. A kit, like the traditional model airplane, requires your work and time to put it together. A computer kit often takes from 50 to 200 hours to assemble; accessory kits generally require less time. Time requirements vary depending on your skill, the ease of assembly of the kit, and your luck in not encountering problems which can take many hours to diagnose and repair.

The major benefit of a kit is that it saves money. An assembled computing product generally costs from 30% to 50% more than a kit. Another benefit of a kit is the experience that assembly gives. However, the person who has so little experience that he would benefit probably would encounter considerable problem in assembling a working computer.

Most computing kits require skill and knowledge in electronics work, sometimes a considerable amount. The decision whether to build a computer kit is not one to be made lightly. Anyone, after he has enough skill, equipment, time, and expert help available, can build a kit. The amount of these resources required for assembly and successful use varies widely among kits. The quality of instructions provided also varies considerably. These are all factors to consider when selecting your computer.

HELP!

Although good instructions and the availability of expert help are essential to the novice kit builder, these aids are important to every computer user. Computers today are too complex to be understood completely by most people. Because computers have so much potential, appropriate understanding is very important for using a computer well. Because skill requirements vary widely among types of computers, a solution to the need for skill is to choose a computer which needs the amount and types of skill you have or plan to have.

A special resource to consider when evaluating sources of computer skills is the dealer from whom you buy your computer. This is the person from whom you will also probably get the several types of support you will need to use your computer and to keep it operational. A dealer who is knowledgeable about the equipment he sells, and is willing to share this knowledge, can be a great help in using a computer. So the decision of whether to buy from a dealer, and the selection of your dealer are both important home computing decisions.

CONCLUSION

After this quick overview, you probably are much more confused than when you started because you have learned a little and can better see how much there is to learn. At least you have some understanding of the fact that much information about microcomputers is new, even to the most knowledgeable and experienced persons. The knowledge you now have is greater than that of many other people. So go ahead: talk to owners of home computers and visit computer exhibits and stores. Most of all, have fun as you plan and learn about your new helper, your own home computer. ■

Everybody's doing it ('computing' at home)

by Don Mennie

Reprinted, by permission, from IEEE SPECTRUM, vol. 14, no. 5, May 1977, pp. 29-34.

Slavery is immoral, servants are expensive, and socio-political consciousness raising has given the family pet a monopoly on loyalty and obedience. Yet the human ego still longs to dominate a more productive, skilled, and responsible entity.

The microprocessor-based microcomputer seems destined to satisfy this need soon on a grand scale. Costs are down, applications are up, and a whole new cottage industry catering to amateur or "hobby" computing needs has emerged during the past two years.

Most of the products available from these very new but thriving businesses are kits, and much of the distribution is mail order (patience advised). But many urban and suburban dwellers will find that a suitable electronic serf is available off-the-shelf from a nearby "computer store," though the local phone book may not help much in locating an address. Chances are the retailer you want wasn't in business a year ago. Besides, store owners often opt for offbeat names like "Byte Shop," "Itty Bitty Machine Company," or "Kentucky Fried Computers." Some advertise in the "how-to" electronics/hi-fi press found on local newsstands, while others use the established amateur radio journals. Of course, the best references are the microcomputer hobby publications themselves. These are just as new as the products they describe, and may also be a little hard to find initially. Whatever your nearby opportunities, be sure and see p. 11 of this article for a review of several active, and apparently healthy, microcomputer periodicals.

From core to cassette

Fans of *Future Shock* will find that hobby computing makes a classic Exhibit A. Things are changing so fast that 1975 and early 1976 are now nostalgically referred to as "the good old days" by those who first recognized the potential of low-cost computing power responsive to a high-level language (machine can recognize a limited English vocabulary for simplified programming).

Language is certainly a key consideration here because, historically speaking, small bands of build-it-yourself computer fans have been around at least since the mid-1960s. For example, back in August 1966 some like-minded experimenters in Connecticut organized themselves as The Amateur Computer Society, constructing makeshift systems with scrap transistor logic boards and surplus core memory. Programming required finesse in machine or assembly language. Between the parts scrounging, debugging, and interfacing problems, only the skilled enthusiast made much progress.

However, change was in the wind. During the early 1970s the first microprocessors became a reality. The Intel Corp. started things rolling with its 4-bit 4004, followed closely by the 8-bit 8008. By late 1973, Intel was producing the 8-bit 8080 that enjoyed speed, packaging, and memory address advantages over the two earlier models. Of course, Intel was not looking to the amateur electronics market for business (at least not initially), and the original microprocessor pricing structure precluded such an alliance anyhow.

Meanwhile, an easily learned high-level language called the Beginner's All-purpose Symbolic Instruction Code (Basic) was getting heavy play through time-share terminals rented for computer-use instruction by many colleges and high schools. This new batch of programmers enjoyed software experiments (making up computer games), and they were essentially presold on having their own hardware should it ever become affordable.

Yet another group anxious for hands-on experience with microprocessors were (and still are) electrical engineers. Many soon recognized that microprocessor design experience would be important to their careers, but few could convince employers to allot company time and funds for the undertaking. Some took the plunge on their own, buying sample chips and setting up laboratory space at home for experiments.

The first entrepreneur to tap this growing interest on a significant scale was H. Edward Roberts, whose company, MITS (formerly Micro Instrumentation and Telemetry Systems), Albuquerque, N.Mex., had once been involved in the scientific calculator market. *Spectrum*'s calculator roundup of April 1974 counted MITS among the early vendors selling advanced personal calculators. As calculator prices tumbled, MITS, Bowmar, and many other assembler/producers lost out to the vertically integrated giants like Texas Instruments, Hewlett-Packard, and (later) National Semiconductor.

Mr. Roberts responded by designing a computer construction project—plans and parts available from MITS—based on the Intel 8080. MITS' kit, now known as the Altair 8800, was first described in a January 1975 *Popular Electronics* feature article. Reader interest was far greater than anticipated, and MITS was soon swamped with orders from turned-on computer fans.

Not long afterward, MITS' first competition arrived. Processor Technology, Emeryville, Calif., was probably the first company offering memory boards compatible with the Altair 8800. And the parade is far from over.

Among MITS' more succesful challengers (to date) has been IMSAI Manufacturing, originally a tiny consulting firm headquartered in San Leandro, Calif., that did occasional microprocessor design work. According to IMSAI director of industrial and commercial sales, Arnold Karush, about 18 months ago the example of MITS' success inspired a "we can do it too" attitude among IMSAI's engineering staff. Soon they had designed the IMSAI 8080, a microcomputer also based on Intel's 8080 microprocessor, and compatible with memory and interface boards designed for the Altair 8800. (This board compatibility, now a quasi-standard, is known as the Altair or S-100 bus.) IMSAI ads were loaded with adjectives like "commercial,' "rugged," and "heavy-duty." "Amateur" may have been the customer, but "professional" was the marketing strategy.

And for every IMSAI there were two dozen smaller (even part-time) operations hawking used teletypewriter terminals, CRT displays, memory boards, cassette interfaces, and floppy discs. (In fact, Parasitic Engineering, a tiny California-based firm, has as its total product line a noise surpression "fix" for MITS and IMSAI mainframe power supplies.) Similar growth was also triggered in the production of printed and recorded Basic software.

One of the success stories among this bumper crop of peripherals is Tarbell Electronics, Carson, Calif. Owner Donald Tarbell was part of the original Amateur Computer Society, and has since used his expertise to develop the Tarbell cassette interface. This is a printed circuit board that plugs directly into the Altair 8800 or IMSAI 8080 computer mainframe and allows an external audio tape cassette player to load prerecorded programs into the computer's random-access memory.

The Tarbell system works with an audio tone of 1500 Hz that is phase-shifted to encode data. This method withstands large amounts of wow and flutter and can operate sucessfully with most $40 audio cassette recorders. Mr. Tarbell told *Spectrum* that his encoding method is particularly sensitive to cassette frequency response. About 8 kHz minimum bandwidth is needed to avoid phase-distortion problems.

Another option open to hobbyists using tape for program storage is digital data recording. This offers a higher data density than audio recording, but requires a special cassette player and tape oxide formulation designed just for this purpose. One source of such equipment is the National Multiplex Corp. in South Plainfield, N.J.

With this system, approximately 8 volts (alterniatively positive or negative) are fed to a record head/resistor network, which causes the record head to saturate the tape. As the input signal swings alternately from +8 volts to −8 volts, the tape saturation polarity changes from north to south. The resistance values are carefully chosen to saturate the tape magnetically with about 30–40 percent excess, enabling the signal being recorded to write over any previous data (no erase head needed). This technique is termed the nonreturn-to-zero recording method since the tape is always saturated as a north or south magnetic pole.

Floppy disks are also available to the hobbyist, but at considerably more cost than cassettes. An example here is the Frugal Floppy, a complete floppy disk subsystem from iCOM, Canoga Park, Calif. It contains all the functional elements of iCOM's commercial FD360 but at reduced price ($1195 vs. $2350). The main advantages of floppy disk over tape cassette are high data density and speed, allowing random-access auxilliary storage.

However, computer speed is not really a problem for most hobby applications. For instance, loading an advanced Star Trek game program from cassette storage to a computer memory may take several minutes, but the hobbyist is in no desperate rush, and his expenses are not directly related to the computer time consumed.

Expertise: the time-shared peripheral

Broadly defined, there are essentially two types of persons presently active in hobby computing: the software professional who fancies owning a machine, and the hardware designer/experimenter who can build equipment but may lack programming experience. Often the two end up joining forces at a local computer club. Clubs by the hundreds have already been formed in the U.S., the largest being the Southern California Computer Society (SCCS). Despite its regional roots, the SCCS is really an international organization with worldwide membership. They are seriously considering a name change that would clearly reflect this fact.

With the local club as a social framework, hobbyists find it easy to trade equipment, share programs, or buy computer hardware in bulk to save money. Engineers in the group become the experts at unraveling kit instructions, rewiring used equipment, and inspecting homemade PC boards for solder bridges. Meanwhile, programmers who might have a bank or insurance company computer at their command by day help debug software or teach other club members the nuances of Basic, Fortran, and Cobol.

The kind of teamwork that's required so all computer hackers may benefit was amply demonstrated during *Spectrum*'s visit to the Computer Mart of New York. Owner Stanley Veit was putting one of his demonstrater mainframes through its paces, when problems developed with a peripheral floppy disk. Neither he nor his part-time counter man (EE student and computer-game whiz) wrestled with the problem for long, or seemed particularly concerned. Later, a hardware-oriented Computer Mart regular showed up and found the trouble (a dirty connector pin) within five minutes.

Mr. Veit was most helpful in giving *Spectrum* a candid look at just who is buying hobby computers. As he leafed through his order book, it became obvious that a lot of equipment is being purchased by schools, businesses, and even Government or military groups—the same crowd that (presumably) purchases commercial-grade minicomputers at $10k apiece. Asked for an explanation, Mr. Veit remarked that low price had appealed to educators, and he suspected that "destructive testing" of computer-controlled defense projects accounted for his sales to the Government.

Computers like bootstrapping too!

In principle, several of the popular hobby computing mainframes can be operated directly from a front panel of lights and toggle switches. This technique is tedious and not particularly easy to master, so most users opt for a keyboard and CRT terminal (including the necessary interface boards). However, these mainframes still need some manual prodding when first turned on before they are "smart" enough to accept a fresh program load—say from an audio cassette. This is necessary because the machine's volatile solid-state memory wipes clean each time the power is shut down.

One company particularly concerned with this situation is PolyMorphic Systems, Santa Barbara, Calif. Its Poly 88 microcomputer (also an 8080 microprocessor-based design) has no lights, no toggles—just one reset button and (naturally) a power switch.

The Poly 88's secret is bootstrap loading—a built-in read-only memory (ROM) that contains enough permanently stored information (firmware) to make the machine immediately usable every time it is powered-up. Of course, a keyboard, video monitor, and tape cassette must be available to load and execute programs.

A similar computer package and start-up capability is also available from Southwest Technical Products, San Antonio, Tex., whose SWTPC 6800 computer kit includes a ROM-stored mini-operating system, and from Vector Graphic, Westlake Village, Calif., producers of the Vector 1. Vector Graphic's start-up feature is part of a special PROM/RAM plug-in board.

Modifying a MITS or IMSAI product for instant-on is also possible using the BYTESAVER® from Cromemco, Los Altos, Calif. This plug-in compatible board is designed to transfer program content from the microcomputer's volatile random-access memory (RAM) to the board's programmable read-only memory (PROM) that retains information when the power is turned off. The BYTESAVER board can hold up to eight PROMS, allowing the convenient storage of Basic and programs written in Basic.

Make the hobby press your source for project construction details and software programs

A wealth of printed information awaits every computer hobbyist who wants construction projects or programming routines laid out in detail. Books are helpful as self-teaching aids and references, but the most up-to-date action takes place on the pages of over a half-dozen new magazines. *Spectrum* has obtained sample issues of each, and talked with the editors about what their respective publications are trying to accomplish. Here's what we learned:

- *Byte* ($12/yr, monthly, write *Byte* Publications, 70 Main St., Peterborough, N.H. 03458). This is the largest of the group, having been published as a commercial magazine since September 1975. Prior to this, editor Carl Helmers put out an informal newsletter for hobby computing enthusiasts. Contains a no-nonsense balance of "how-to" hardware and programming features along with background tutorial articles. The January 1977 issue includes a nine-page listing of regional computer clubs and newsletters.
- *Creative Computing* ($8/yr, bimonthly, write *Creative Computing*, P.O. Box 789-M, Morristown, N.J. 07960). Addresses the more intellectual and recreational aspect of hobby computing with articles on such subjects as catastrophe theory, computer art, and computational unsolvability, with more recent issues emphasizing applications and high-level software. Also contains cartoons, humor, and computer fiction. Hardware articles and reviews of equipment, books, and software comprise the balance.
- *Dr. Dobbs Journal of Computer Calisthenics & Orthodontia* ($10/yr, ten issues/yr, write *Dr. Dobbs* . . ., Box 310, Menlo Park, Calif. 94025). A kind of *Consumer Reports* for computer hobbyists, *Dr. Dobbs* carries no advertising. It also has no color pictures of professional line drawings, and is basically a forum and reference work. The contents are largely editorials, product and book reviews, readers' letters, and software programs. Editor James Warren was the organizing force behind the First West Coast Computer Faire held April 15–17, 1977.
- *Kilobaud* ($15/yr, monthly, write *Kilobaud*, Peterborough, N.H. 03458). Created by the same people who put out *73* for radio amateurs (publisher Wayne Green is also a founder of *Byte*). This magazine, with an index-cover format, could be mistaken for an *IEEE Transactions* at first glance. Articles run the gamut from building projects to game programs. Also included are editorials, letters, and industry news. Each page is laid out in four narrow columns, and in some sections the tiny type used is hard to read. Excellent technical content, however.
- *Interface Age* ($10/yr, monthly, write McPheters, Wolfe & Jones, 13913 Artesia Blvd., Cerritos, Calif. 90701). This publication emerged as a separate entity last year after its publisher dissolved a strained association with the Southern California Computing Society. The society's magazine, *SCCS Interface*, ceased publication for two months when *Interface Age* first appeared. *Interface Age* presently provides a balance of hardware and software features, many of particular use to the small businessman microcomputer user. The May issue features "free" software programming (for 6800 μP-based systems) on a thin vinyl phonograph record insert.
- *Personal Computing* ($8/yr, bimonthly, write Benwill Publishing Corp., 167 Corey Rd., Brookline, Mass. 02146). Here's a brand-new magazine aimed squarely at the nontechnical and novice computer user. Feature articles in the January 1977 premiere issue covered microprocessor operation, Basic language instruction, computer art, a computer show review, and an interview on computer crime. Though construction projects were noticeably absent from the first issue, the publisher has since merged with *Microtrek* and promises that hardware features will be prominent in future issues.
- *SCCS Interface* ($10/yr—includes SCCS membership, monthly, write Southern California Computer Society, Box 54751, Los Angeles, Calif. 90054). Contains projects, software, society news, interviews, editorials, new products, reader letters, and even a computer science fiction corner. Stresses short contributions over long features. Logo type is almost identical with *Interface Age* (thus some possible confusion). The SCCS claims membership advantages by providing support activities aimed at the computer hobbyist. These include meetings, seminars, publications, technical assistance, and the arrangement of group hardware purchases.

Several newly organized and revamped computer shows are also proving important to the hobbyist. A major event of this type is the 1977 National Computer Conference coming June 13–16 at the Dallas Convention Center. It will feature a personal computing fair.

Kits—here now and here soon

Simply to increase options and save money, most active computer hobbyists end up as kit builders. This can be rewarding or frustrating—depending on one's skills with a soldering iron and the manufacturer's effort to provide sufficient documentation. Some marketing experts predict that this situation is only a transitory phase, with hobby computing rapidly becoming personal computing. They say fully assembled "turnkey" computer systems will soon predominate (*à la* the cash-and-carry rigs of citizens band radio) with creativity largely confined to software applications. But for now, the electronics experimenter's opportunities are hardly limited.

Spectrum took a look through the poly bags, pc boards, parts lists, and instructions comprising several kits presently available at local computer stores, and concluded that an experimenter's skills are certainly required. There are no hand-holding checklists showing every part and connection. Often the best clue to final assembly is a schematic or logic diagram, not a detailed perspective drawing. Caution notes abound concerning voids, cracks, solder bridges, and static electricity.

Amazingly, store owners and manufacturers we polled report minimal problems with kit-building customers who jump in over their heads. There are the usual horror stories about certain individuals selling kits, getting into financial trouble, and leaving the market—all within a few month's time. Outright deception is rare. But one computer club official with whom we spoke about such problems reported a particularly bad experience. It seems many club members lost their investment recently during a bulk-purchase hardware transaction that was not conducted in a "prudent, businesslike fashion."

Perhaps the biggest news affecting anyone presently considering a hobby computer purchase will be Heathkit's initial market entry, an event rumored for the past several months. According to Louis Frenzel, Heath's director of computer and educational products, the official announcement will occur in June, followed closely by an advertising campaign and product shipments. Heath's

Microcomputers: from bare-bones to turnkey

				Supplied at System Price Quoted						
				Mainframe I/O					Memory	
Manufacturer	System	µP	Uses S-100 Bus	Front-Panel Switches and Lights	Keyboard and Interface	Video Display and Interface	Cassette Tape and Interface	Floppy Disk and Interface	ROM (Monitor and/or Bootstrap)	RAM
Apple Computer Inc. Cupertino, CA 95014	Apple-II	6502		n/a	X	I'face	I'face		X	4k
Computer Power & Light Studio City, CA 91604	COMPAL-80	8080A	X	n/a	X	X	X	*	X	16k
Cromemco Mountain View, CA 94043	Z-I	Z-80	X	X	I'face				X	8k
	Z-II	Z-80	X							
E&L Instruments Derby, CT 06418	MMD-1	8080A		LEDs	Octal entry				X	0.5k
ECD Corp. Cambridge, MA 02139	MicroMind I	6512A		n/a	X	I'face	I'face		X	8k
	MicroMind II	6512A		n/a	X	I'face	I'face		X	16k
Electronic Control Tech. Union, NJ 07083	ECT-100-8080	8080A	X	n/a					*	
	ECT-100-Z80	Z-80	X	n/a					*	
HAL Communications Urbana, IL 61801	HAL-Eight thousand	8080A		n/a	X	X	*		X	9k
IMSAI Manufacturing San Leandro, CA 94577	8080	8080A	X	X	*		*	†		
Intelligent Systems Corp. Norcross, GA 30071	Compucolor 8001	8080A		n/a	X	X	*	†	X	16k
	Intecolor 8001	8080A		n/a	X	X		†	X	4k
MITS Albuquerque, NM 87106	Altair 8800b	8080A	X	X			†	†		
	Altair 680b	6800		X	*	*	†		X	1k
Ohio Scientific Instruments Hiram, OH 44234	System pkg 1	6502A		n/a	X	X		X	X	16k
	System pkg 2	6502A		n/a	X	X		X	X	16k
PolyMorphic Systems Santa Barbara, CA 93111	POLY 88 Sys 16	8080A	X	n/a	X	X	X		X	16k
	POLY 88 Sys 6	8080A	X	n/a	X	I'face	I'face		X	16k
Processor Technology Emeryville, CA 94608	Sol System I	8080A	X	n/a	X	X	X	*	X	10k
Southwest Tech. Products San Antonio, TX 78216	SWTPC 6800	6800		n/a	I'face	I'face	I'face		X	4k
The Digital Group Denver, CO 80206	Z-80 Sys 1	Z-80		n/a	I'face	I'face	I'face		X	10k
	Z-80 Sys 3	Z-80		n/a	X	X	X		X	18k
Vector Graphic Westlake Village, CA 91361	Vector 1	8080	X	n/a		*	*	†	X	1k
Wave Mate Gardena, CA 90248	Jupiter IIC	6800		n/a	X	X	X	*	X	8k
	Jupiter IIIC	Z-80		n/a	X	X	X	*	†	8k

System Price ($)		
Kit	Assembled	Comments
n/a	1298	System includes color graphics capability. ROM: 6k bytes Basic, 2k bytes monitor.
n/a	2300	* Floppy disk available as an option. System includes extended Basic on cassette.
n/a	2494	Both systems use the 4-MHz version of the Z-80.
595	995	
422.50	600	Optional cassette tape interface and external hex entry keyboard available.
n/a	987.54	Especially suited for computer graphics. Has writable character generator, memory mapping.
n/a	1287.54	
320	500	* ROM bootstrap available as an option.
420	600	
n/a	under 1600	* Cassette tape available as an option. Machine can drive Teletype current loop. Includes RS-232 serial and parallel I/O.
699	931	* Multiple I/O board available. † Floppy disk available as an option RAMs: 4k static; 16k, 32k, 64k dynamic.
n/a	'2750	* Comes with dual floppy tape drive, interface, and 11k bytes Basic (ROM).
n/a	1495	† Shugart mini-floppy available as an option Both systems feature a color CRT terminal.
840	1100	* Serial I/O port is provided.
466	625	† Cassette, floppy disk are options.
n/a	2599	Pkg 1 video display is 64 characters across.
n/a	2499	Pkg 2 video display is 32 characters across.
n/a	2250	System 16 includes 11k of Basic on cassette
575	n/a	
1649	2129	* Floppy disk available as an option.
395	n/a	Peripherals: alphanumeric terminal, cassette, line printer, floppy disk.
895	1295	*System 3 supplied with four digital tape drives.
2045	2545	
619	849	* Available as peripherals. † Compatible with Northstar floppy disk.
2550	3500	* Floppy disk available as an option.
2620	3570	† ROM contains complete operating system. All systems employ wire-wrap assembly.

Many small new companies produce advanced microcomputers for the hobbyist. This is a cross section of popular products, *not* a comprehensive list of everything presently available. For example, none of the one-board evaluation kits sold for a couple hundred dollars by microprocessor manufacturers are included here. Also note that those microcomputers that are mentioned can often accommodate up to 64k of RAM (at additional cost), though only a fraction of this may be included at the system price quoted. The Digital Group's Z-80 System Three (below) is shown with an optional 96-character printer in addition to all the hardware items noted with its table listing.

marketing philosophy includes customer education, so Basic programming courses will be available for kit builders who need such instruction. Mr. Frenzel explains that documentation, not hardware design, has paced product introduction.

What does it cost; what does it do?

Like every other major electronics retailer, Heath was caught off balance by hobby computing's rapid evolution. Thus, the market initially remained a wide-open opportunity for new business ventures. But the shadow of Wall Street is not far off. Already MITS, the original hobby computing pioneer, has been purchased lock, stock, and franchises by the Pertec Computer Corp., a major supplier of commercial-grade minicomputers. Investors are taking the new market seriously, and rightly so.

Financially speaking, a hobby computer purchase is on par with the investment needed for many other leisure-time activities including photography, hi-fi/stereo, skiing, and sailing. The computer fan's bankroll should have solid middle class credentials since upwards of $2000 can easily be spent procuring the central processing unit (mainframe), memory, keyboard, and readout. And that's just a bare-bones system with enough capacity and programming flexibility to qualify as useful. "Extras," such as color CRT terminals, special interface boards, increased memory, and advanced software packages, can push the investment total much higher.

For instance, a very popular computer option is video display. The cheapest route is an interface board and low-power RF modulator wired to the family television set. This is the route taken by Apple Computer Inc., Cupertino, Calif. Its Apple-II features two color graphics operating modes and a "scrolling window" that can combine graphics and text as a programming aid.

Sharper character resolution can be obtained from a broadcast-quality video monitor. Such equipment is available from HAL Communications Corp., Urbana, Ill. HAL also produces a video display terminal that includes keyboard, video monitor, and 8080 microprocessor interface to achieve transmission and reception of ASCII code at standard data rates.

Those hobbyists seriously interested in color display and computer graphics are offered the Compucolor 8001, a stand-alone system from Intelligent Systems Corp., Norcross, Ga. ($2750). ISC's Compucolor 8001 includes a keyboard, a 48.3-cm (19-inch) diagonal screen that can display 3840 characters, and Basic 8001 language. Also available is ISC's Intercolor 8001 color CRT terminal with specific user options. Though ISC sells to the computer amateur (Compucolor line), its Intercolor products were originally designed (and priced) to compete in the commercial minicomputer market—long before MITS had sold its first kit. As a result, ISC units do not interface with the "hobby" S-100 bus, but do maintain compatibility with the RS-232 serial interface common to commercial minicomputers.

The well-documented willingness of small business and private individuals to spend significant sums for microcomputer hardware naturally raises the question, "why?" What practical applications justify the investment? *Byte* magazine attempted to answer this question recently based on a survey of its readership, and editor-in-chief Carl Helmers, Jr., presented the results, "A profile of the personal computing market," during an ELECTRO '77 show session on April 19. *Byte* asked for both "home" and "business" applications, and found the hobbyist concerned with software development, interactive keyboard games, graphics, household automation, personal data bases, and education. Professional interests related strongly to scientific, mathematical, and engineering areas: data analysis, simulation (modeling), data-base creation, and text processing.

It is probably unfair and inaccurate to attempt a precise, example-by-example definition of hobby computing based on applications because, as several *Spectrum* sources remarked, "hobby computing is all things to all people." The limitations—or, more accurately, ever-changing frontiers—are imagination, programming skill, and software availability.

Software has an enormous impact on the design of popular microcomputer hardware. A glance at the listing of microcomputer mainframes on p. 12 shows that the 8080A microprocessor is by far the favorite, even though there are many very fine competitive chips around. The reason is software availability. Since MITS, Processor Technology, and others started developing 8080 software very early, many excellent, proven programs are now available for 8080-based microcomputers. And maintaining access to this software pool is proving important to new microcomputer designs.

Carl Galletti of Technical Design Laboratories, Princeton, N.J., explains that Federico Faggin, inventor of the 8080 while at Intel and now president of the Zilog Co., developed his new Z-80 microprocessor to be software- (but not pin-) compatible with the original 8080. The Z-80 has double the instruction set of the 8080 (158 machine language instructions vs. 78). TDL was the first company to market Z-80 microprocessor boards compatible with the S-100 bus.

Where can I buy one?

Though mail order accounted for all of hobby computing's infancy, and still represents the only access to many of the smaller peripherals manufacturers, retail computer stores are becoming very important, both as marketing points and as education centers. Some—most notably the shops carrying MITS products—are franchises and, for obvious reasons, have a limited selection of competitive goods. Others are purely the handiwork of their owners, and as such are free to stock whatever they please. This independence also extends to location, sales tactics, and business hours.

For example, the Byte shop chain headquartered in California has resorted to AM radio advertising to draw nontechnical people into the ranks of potential customers, while alerting the general public to the growing microcomputer revolution. Other merchants depend on attractive showrooms in downtown business districts or suburban shopping malls. By contrast, Dennis Buckley, owner of Audio Design Electronics in New York City, doesn't want the merely curious shuffling through his premises. And it's not too likely they will. His shop is behind a locked door on the fifth floor of an old office building in SoHo. There are no signs for Audio Design Electronics at street level.

Mr. Buckley, a self-styled audio experimenter who has "retired" from hi-fi/stereo (as a business), now devotes his full effort to selling and servicing microcomputer hardware. He doesn't have the time or staff to demonstrate equipment and field questions for anyone but the serious hobbyist.

Customer education is the name of the game at Computer Power & Light Inc., Studio City, Calif., according to president Gene Murrow. His retail outlet actually contains a classroom area where neophytes are given language and programming instruction. The Basic class, which meets either two evenings a week for four weeks or once a week for eight weeks, covers the writing, documenting, and debugging of applications programs. Assembly language is taught on Saturday mornings for eight weeks and emphasizes the construction of flexible, well-documented machine language routines. This instruction is not free. There is a $100 fee that covers teaching, text material, and computer time, but $40 of this can be used as a rebate toward equipment purchases.

Not only a retailer, Computer Power & Light also manufacturers the COMPAL-80 microcomputer system. "It's designed for the second-generation hobbyist," explains Mr. Murrow. "COMPAL-80 is a fully assembled system—no soldering or debugging required."

Soon, something for everyone

As the example of Computer Power & Light illustrates, hobby computing need not remain limited to engineers, experimenters, and programming professionals. *Spectrum* solicited opinions on the near-future growth of the microcomputer market and got several interesting responses. One marketing director we polled (who wished anonymity) believes that a "continuing circle" of interest generated by schools, universities, and the hobbyists themselves will always keep new people coming into the personal computing world. He envisions every household having a "black box" computer, very much like a color TV in appearance, availability, and ease of operation.

Also seeing a strong relationship between television and computers is Raymond Borrill, head of Data Domain, Bloomington, Ind. He expects that intelligent video games will provide the key to a mass market for microcomputers.

Apparently ready to back predictions with hardware is Charles Peddle, a marketing executive with Commodore Business Machines, Palo Alto, Calif. He says Commodore will introduce its "PET" computer this summer at prices starting under $500. The PET is built around the 6502 microprocessor and will feature a built-in black-and-white monitor for graphics and text display. A turnkey product, PET will be mass-merchandised through television advertising and traditional outlets for consumer electronics hardware.

Naturally, the average consumer will be particularly partial to low-cost (under $500), readily available computers that are extremely easy to operate. Such hardware cannot be purchased yet, but the push in this direction is unmistakable. What's more, a first-round "shakeout" among the dozens of small new businesses presently serving hobby needs is expected soon. This should help identify those companies with sound financial underpinnings, truly innovative products, and the kind of leadership that can turn an intellectual pastime into a major commercial enterprise. ◆

Personal computing

by Portia Isaacson

Low cost personal computers are being widely used for business applications, mostly by small businesses. Computer stores commonly estimate that 20% to 50% of their dollar volume sales are of computers to be used for business purposes. Industrial process control, education, and hobby sales make up the remainder. This month's column will explore hardware and software configurations typical of low cost computers used in business applications. An exhaustive survey isn't intended, but rather a discussion of products typical of those available.

Typically, the small business application requires a central processing unit, memory, dual disc drives, a hardcopy printer, a BASIC interpreter, and a disc operating system. The central processing unit and memory form the nucleus of the processing system. A disc is required for random access or rapid sequential access needed in most applications. Dual discs are necessary for reasonable copying operations. A hardcopy printer generates reports, keeps permanent records, and prints forms. The BASIC interpreter and disc operating system allow development of applications in a reasonable higher-level language rather than assembly language. The photo above shows a personal computer system typical of those used in business applications. Table 1 lists the major components of the system with their approximate costs.

Central processing unit

The cpu in this configuration is a microprocessor. The 8080, with seven central registers, eight-bit wide data paths, eight-bit integer arithmetic, and an instruction execution time range of two to nine microseconds is the most common. The 8080 can address a maximum memory space of 64KB. The 8080 cpu is roughly comparable to the S/360 Mod 30 in terms of the data path widths, number of registers, instruction execution time, and maximum memory size. Several manufacturers of personal computers use the 8080, including MITS, IMSAI, Vector

Graphic, Processor Technology, PolyMorphic Systems, and the Digital Group. Recently a number of Z-80 systems have become available, offering improved execution time, extended addressing modes, additional registers, and block instructions. One company, Alpha Microsystems, now offers a 16-bit cpu in the AM-100 which is based on the Western Digital microprocessor and offers a substantial increase over the eight-bit cpu's.

Memory

A memory size of 32KB is sufficient for many business applications. In fact, the typical memory size found on a S/360 Mod 30 in a dp installation is 32KB. In personal computing systems, BASIC typically occupies 12 to 20KB of memory, depending on the BASIC, leaving the rest for the application program. Expansion to 64KB is possible if the application requires it. Although it is physically possible to place more memory in the card cage, only 64KB can be addressed at any one time. Memory management software to support the use of memories larger than 64KB is not available. The memory speed is typically 500 nsec access time, five times the speed of the S/360 Mod 30.

Memory is commonly available in 8K, 16K, and 32K byte boards. The respective costs are approximately $230, $400, and $800 for assembled and tested boards. Memory is available from all cpu manufacturers and also from many other companies. This very competitive environment guarantees the lowest possible price.

Discs

For most data processing applications, the most important decision will be the choice of a disc. As shown in Table 1, the disc is half the cost of the entire system. The performance ground rules are the same in low-cost computing as they have been for years. Data processing applications tend to be limited by the disc, which not only determines the amount of data that can be accessible at one time, but also determines the speed at which it can be accessed. Since the disc is largely mechanical, it will also be one of the least reliable components of the system. Another reason for caution in the selection of a disc is that in mixed vendor systems the system software comes from the disc manufacturer.

Floppy discs of the eight-inch and 5¼-inch variety are being widely used. Dual eight-inch floppy disc drives, which store 500 to 600KB total have an average access time of 35 milliseconds and a transfer rate of 30KB/second, cost about $3,000 including the controller. The eight-inch floppies are offered by numerous companies including MITS, IMSAI, and ICOM. Dual 5¼-inch floppy disc drives which store about 150KB, have an average access time of 30 milliseconds, and a transfer rate of 30KB/second, cost about $1,800 including the controller. Several companies offer the 5¼-inch floppies including ICOM, North Star, Polymorphic Systems, Processor Technology, and Southwest Technical Products. We can expect to see some significant increases in storage per dollar in the near future. In fact, Micropolis is already delivering 5¼-inch dual floppy disc drives which store 630KB total for $1,900 including controller. We also can expect to see hard discs for low

System Component*	Approximate cost
Card cage, cpu, and power supply	$1,000
Memory (32KB)	900
Hardcopy terminal and serial interface (30 cps)	1,650
Dual floppy discs and interface (256 bytes per drive)	3,000
BASIC	100
Disc Operating System	100
TOTAL	$6,750

*All components are assembled and tested.

Table 1. Typical small-business application configuration

cost computers. MITS presently offers a 10-million byte disc for $7,995. Alpha Microsystems offers the Calcomp Trident disc which stores 25 to 300 million bytes.

Printer and/or terminal

Most business applications need a hardcopy or crt terminal and a printer. For the most part printers or terminals have not been developed especially for the personal computing market; time-sharing terminals and low end minicomputer printers are being used. The computers use the serial RS232C standard interface for a terminal or printer. This is the same interface used by time-sharing terminals, minicomputer terminals, and some printers. Since any terminal or printer using the RS232C standard interface can be used with personal computers, a wide selection is available. The ones mentioned below typify the range of equipment available.

At the low end of printers useful in a business environment is an impact printer that prints on roll paper at 120 characters/second for approximately $750. The Digital Equipment Corp. DECWriter LA36 terminal accepts continuous forms, prints at 30 characters/second, and costs about $1,500. The Texas Instruments 810 impact printer prints 150 characters/second and costs $2,100. For word processing applications the Diablo terminal plots and prints at 30 characters/second and costs $3,000. If a printer is chosen, a crt terminal such as the Lear Siegler ADM-3A costing $900 also is needed. It's clear that the terminal and/or printer can be nearly the most costly component in the system. Since the printer is largely mechanical it may also be a source of maintenance problems.

Software

When comparing the capability of personal computers to larger computers and time-sharing services, the most obvious shortcoming of the personal computer is in the software area. There is a minimum amount of system software available and nearly no application software.

BASIC is the language of personal computers. Fortunately, many of the available BASICS have been extended especially for business applications. The added features include formatted input/output and disc file manipulation including random access, decimal arithmetic, string processing, subroutine parameter passing, and chaining of programs. The typical cost of a BASIC interpreter is about $100.

Macro assemblers also are available, but due to the very low level of the machine language these would generally not be useful for business applications. Should it be necessary, the BASIC interpreters usually will allow the execution of assembly language subroutines. FORTRAN recently has become available for about $700, but would probably not be the language of choice for business applications over business-extended BASIC.

Disc operating systems are available from the disc system supplier. These are typically a single user system featuring a minimal set of file maintenance commands such as copy, delete, build, and edit files. They also offer a text editor and usually an assembler and linker. At the high end, Alpha Microsystems offers a multitasking, multiuser, time-sharing operating system.

A few application packages are available. These include general ledger, payroll, inventory control, word processing, accounts payable, and accounts receivable. The prices vary greatly but $1,000 to $2,000 is a typical price for an application program. Application software packages are available from the personal computing manufacturers in some cases, but, for the most part they are offered by individual computer stores. Significant additional offerings may be expected soon—primarily packages for particular types of small businesses such as medical clinics, personnel agencies, real estate firms, lawyers, motorcycle shops, and astrologers.

Maintenance

Most businesses are very concerned about the maintenance service available with personal computing equipment. From the manufacturers the only available service is through the mail. If it breaks, you send it in, the manufacturer will fix it either under warranty or for a fee. Warranty coverage varies greatly, with three months to one year common on assembled products. This type of service will not be immediately acceptable to most businesses, but in some cases it may be satisfactory.

The answer to the maintenance service problem for most businesses is the computer store. Most offer maintenance service on the systems they sell, and most require that the equipment be brought to them for service. However, an increasing number of stores are willing to offer on-site service for businesses.

Computer stores may be expected to provide better maintenance service as the market becomes more competitive.

If you want to buy a large mainframe computer or a minicomputer, you call the manufacturer who sends out a salesperson. This same procedure is not applicable in the personal computing area. Low cost computers require a new method of marketing and servicing in order to keep the price of these services in line with the price of the equipment. The retail computer store has emerged to fill this need.

It is not necessary to buy all parts of a personal computing system from the same manufacturer. In fact, mixed vendor systems are the rule rather than the exception. It's quite common to buy the card-cage, power supply, and cpu from one manufacturer, the memory from another, the disc from a third, and the terminal from still yet another. With the obvious potential compatibility problems, it is clear that most businesses will need some knowledgeable assistance in planning the proper configuration for a particular application. The retail computer store offers this service for a very small charge or, in many cases, no charge.

Increasing business usage of personal computers

Several factors will contribute to the increasing business usage of personal computers. First, the new, much lower cost threshold for the feasibility of application will open many new application areas. Packages including hardware, software, maintenance, and training will be developed, primarily by computer stores, for particular types of businesses and business applications.

Next, the misconception, primarily by large business dpers, that personal computers are very small will be dispelled. Personal computers are not small; they are low cost. As noted previously, today's personal computer compares quite closely to the S/360 Mod 30, the dp workhorse computer of the late 1960s.

Another important factor will be the declining cost of disc storage. When disc storage capacity doubles for the same cost, as it has done recently in floppy discs, many new business applications become feasible.

The other major factor is maintenance and support. As computer stores provide better service, more businesses will be willing to computerize their applications. National service organizations specializing in personal computing equipment maintenance will probably emerge.

We can look forward to the rapidly increasing use of personal computers by businesses large and small. ❀

Personal computers mean business

by Lawrence Curran

More and more homes and even small businesses are putting out a welcome mat for the personal computer. The first computer designed specifically for the hobbyist emerged little more than two years ago and to everyone's surprise triggered the development of an entire new industry, complete with a crop of new small companies, retail outlets, trade shows, and magazines.

Just where the appeal of the personal computer lies is still something of a mystery. Some believe it caters mainly to the desire for more sophisticated video games, others stress its educational uses or its utility for handling financial and domestic chores. Already a few observers are speculating on the eventual rise of a mass market, with $300 black boxes reaching tens of millions of consumers through department stores.

Present products, though, appeal mainly to the technically minded who are prepared to make a larger initial outlay: $1,500 to $3,000 for a utilitarian machine or something under $1,000 for a hobby computer. Total sales last year neared $10 million—a figure that by 1981 could approach $60 million for mainframes alone, according to consulting company Venture Development Corp. of Wellesley, Mass.

Technological origin of all the excitement is of course the microprocessor. Some of the systems in private use are general-purpose microprocessor-based machines aimed at industrial or commercial users but low enough in cost—a few thousands of dollars—to appeal to some home users as well. Others are the usually one-board evaluation kits sold by microprocessor manufacturers for a basic $100 to $400 to promote their product among system designers but also being grabbed for private use through distributors. But many are kits made up of several circuit boards (and maybe a chassis, motherboard, cabinet, and terminal gear, too). These are sold, assembled or unassembled, mainly through computer-hobbyist stores.

In most kits, the microprocessor on the central processing board is an 8-bit device. Often the read-only memory that holds the computer's microcoded instructions also includes a monitor, to help with information input. The random-access memory varies from less than 1 to 8 kilobytes in size, though systems can generally be expanded to address 65 kilobytes (contrast the megabyte capacity of minicomputers).

As for programming, the simpler systems must be set up with machine language. Others include assemblers. But most suppliers are pushing Basic or some variant of that higher-level language. Program entry may be very simple, through switches or a 16-key keypad, or from a paper-tape unit or cassette recorder. Output is often on a light-emitting-diode display of hexadecimal digits or on a specially adapted television set.

Computer kits and evaluation boards appeal to two categories of user—the inveterate kit builder, for whom the assembly step is half the fun and utility a secondary consideration, and the electronics engineer or software sophisticate, who wants the system to do useful work and is willing to do some soldering, wire-wrapping, or extensive programming, though he may prefer an already assembled kit. Then there is a third category—the layman, who just wants a machine that will let him play more and better video games, keep track of personal financial records, or help him run a small business.

Whether, how soon, and how fast this last group will really grow is anybody's guess. A plausible parallel is with citizens' band radio, which boomed only after ham radio had been around for years. Doubt about the outcome is probably what is protecting the small companies that manufacture personal computers from serious onslaught by established microprocessor manufacturers, video-games suppliers, and even minicomputer makers. Even so, the threat is enough to have produced undoubtedly accurate predictions of shakeouts or consolidations among the newcomers, who are often underfinanced.

Others who stand to profit from the new industry are peripheral manufacturers, software suppliers, semiconductor distributors, and the host of new hobby-computer stores, which sometimes assemble and service equipment as well as sell it. Also available through these stores is a mushrooming library of technical books, which their readers may supplement with "how to" information gleaned from some two dozen specialized magazines and newsletters or through attendance at one of nearly 100 computer clubs.

Trade shows are springing up, too, and in June the National Computer Conference will give official recognition to the phenomenon. Its 1977 program will include a personal computing exposition, two whole days of sessions, and a computer-club congress.

Learning system. Seated at terminal of a Baby! I computer from STM Systems Inc., a teacher changes a Basic program to help a child learn multiplication tables. Computer is portable.

Hobby-computer makers supply a widening public

The company that really got the personal-computer business going is MITS Inc., Albuquerque, N.M. Computers had been put together at home before, of course, with microprocessor chip sets or single-board computers. But MITS' introduction of its Altair 8800 computer kit in January 1975 is the watershed from which a definable market flowed—$6 million of it last year in sales to MITS alone.

By now at least 50 more companies have started supplying hardware—both central processors and peripherals—to the private individual. Scattered throughout the country, they have names like Apple Computer Co., the Digital Group, Logical Services Inc., and Ohio Scientific Instruments. Significantly, Heath Co., the biggest kitmaker of all, is not yet among them, though there are unconfirmed but strong rumors that later this year it will offer kits based on the LSI-11 chip set made by minicomputer manufacturer Digital Equipment Corp.

But that may be the closest a minicomputer maker may come for some time to tangling with personal machines. Eventually, of course, this kind of firm might become very interested in attracting users like small businessmen with a small computer that they could upgrade later to a $20,000 minicomputer.

Closer competition

More immediate pressure on the young companies is being felt from the big semiconductor manufacturers, whose microprocessor evaluation kits are widely available from distributors. The possibility here is that as personal computers take off, firms like Intel or Motorola or Fairchild will integrate upwards, preventing the kit companies from expanding out of the hobbyist area into the commercial and consumer world. Indeed a move in this direction may already have been made by Commodore International Ltd., which could be planning to combine its merchandising expertise in the consumer calculator field with the microprocessor know-how of its recent acquisition, MOS Technology.

Awareness of this pressure is widespread among the personal-computer companies, but reactions vary. "We know the ultimate market will be a packaged, high-volume, low-cost consumer product," says Kerry Berland, marketing vice president of kit-maker Martin Research Inc. in Chicago, "and we'd like some of that market, but we have serious doubts that anyone who doesn't control the semiconductor process will make it there. So to survive we'll go to the hobbyist." Also among those aiming just at hobbyists are California companies IMS Associates Inc. of San Leandro, Polymorphic Systems of Goleta, and Processor Technology of Emeryville.

Others are broadening their base into the gap between personal systems and minicomputers, producing kits that can add enough extra memory, peripherals, and software to cope with small commercial and industrial applications. MITS is doing this, as are California's Cromemco in Mountain View and Gnat Computers of San Diego and New Jersey's Quay Corp. in Freehold and Technical Design Laboratories in Princeton, not to mention STM Systems in Mont Vernon, N.H. Moving in the reverse direction are Wave Mate Corp., Gardena, Calif., and Electronic Tool Co. in nearby Hawthorne, both of which started out in low-cost general-purpose industrial computers and are now attracting home users as well.

One or two are even daring to approach the nontechnical consumer. A Cambridge, Mass., firm, ECD Corp., sells a home computer called MicroMind that among its other talents can run games on a home television set.

Strictly for pleasure

The basic hardware offered to each of these three categories of customers is not so very different. In fact, the only difference Arnold Karush, IMS Associates director of marketing, sees between home computers and commercial/industrial models is that "the former is low-cost enough to be personally affordable."

IMS Associates, believed to be MITS' nearest competitor, is not yet taking MITS' public stance that it is interested in the small-business market. Instead, Karush believes home computers will be mainly devoted to video games, at least for the near future. The company began as a consulting firm five years ago, got a contract to design a computer, and decided to market its own, which it did with the first IMSAI 8080 a little more than a year ago. The machine, incidentally, uses the S-100 bus designed by MITS for its Altair 8800 and emerging now as the standard bus system in its field.

The $699 basic kit ($931 assembled) includes a logic and central-processing-unit board, 1,024 bytes of random-access memory, a front panel, and a 22-slot metal chassis. But Karush says a total system will cost well over $1,000, probably requiring another board with 4 kilobytes of memory ($139), a multiple input/output board ($195), and either the Lear-Siegler ADM-3 black-and-white video display with keyboard ($1,295) or a video interface board ($200) that connects to a home television set.

IMS Associates has also begun a franchised retail outlet chain—called Computer Shack—which Karush hopes will grow to 100 stores by October, probably selling 80% kits and 20% assembled hardware. According to Kilobaud, a publication serving the hobby field, more than 1,200 IMSAI machines have been shipped to hobbyists alone, and the formidable grapevine tuned in to personal computers has the company tabbed as an aggressive competitor with a quality product.

Processor Technology, Emeryville, Calif., introduced its 8080-based Sol line in April 1975. President Gary Ingram says the company plans to stay with the hobbyist, confident that smaller firms like his will be the only ones able to meet the after-sale needs of the user. Dealers say the Sol-20 kit is one of their popular sellers, providing just about everything but a display. It sells for $995 ($1,495 assembled), and its Basic 5 software is free, along with a lunar landing game.

Service is important. "Computer doctor" George Tate checks out ailing system at hobbyist store Computer Mart. His fee ranges from $75 for a board diagnosis to $500 for a system "cure."

Also still dedicated to the personal or hobby user is Polymorphic Systems, which sold only component boards for microcomputers before introducing its Poly-88 last summer. The 8080-based kit, which also uses the S-100 bus carries a $595 price tag.

Martin Research Inc., too, is after "the guy who wants to get his hands on," says Berland. His company's more recent machines are the MIKE 3, an 8080-based system that is sold in three-board ($395) and four-board ($495) versions, and a Z-80-based three-board system, the MIKE 8, introduced earlier this year. The latter sells for $495 and includes the CPU board, a console board with a calculator-type keyboard and six decoded LED digits and a programmable-ROM programming board. Additional memory and peripheral-interface boards are optional extras. Martin Research sells only a minimal amount of programming.

Also for profit

In contrast to this group, MITS is talking now about going after small businesses with systems carrying price tags as high as $14,000, which would put it in competition with such portable computers as IBM's 5100. About 80% of the 8,000-plus Altairs shipped through late 1976 went to hobbyists, but a MITS source says that portion of the business is leveling off as the company focuses more attention on small businesses. "We see the small-business market as the biggest," this source says, defining the personal-computer market as "people who never dreamed they could own a computer."

MITS has established a subsidiary to supply Altair users with software initially directed to the small-business-system applications. The first of these range in price from $1,200 to $2,500 and include a general ledger package, payroll, receivables and payables, inventory management, and word-processing package. As a result, the company is projecting a sales jump to $12.8 million this year. It is to be acquired next month by Pertec Computer Corp., the Los Angeles-based company, which will presumably provide financial stability and manufacturing expertise.

Cromemco, too, is beginning to develop software for business applications, though till recently, according to marketing manager Alice Ahlgren, the firm has been largely hardware-oriented. The company sells two microcomputers and a variety of peripherals. The older Z-1 system, built with Zilog Microcomputer's 8-bit Z-80 microprocessor, is a fully assembled $2,496 development system; the newer Z-2, at $595 in kit form or $995 assembled and tested, also uses the Z-80 board. About 60% of Cromemco's systems go to hobby stores, the rest to industrial users.

Quay Corp. in New Jersey is working both sides of the street by offering kits and finished hardware for hobbyist and OEM microcomputer systems. The 80AI Z-80-based personal system is compatible with the S-100 bus "because of the many peripherals and memories available to play on that bus," says Dick Maly, marketing vice president. But the company also has a system called 80MPS, which offers the OEM more memory than the personal computer and sells for $695 assembled and tested. Quay's personal computer is priced in kit form at $450, or $600 assembled.

New Jersey's Technical Design Laboratories also sells a Z-80-based microcomputer, the ZPU, for $269 as a kit or $325 assembled. The company is planning several

An educated public. Educational levels of users of personal computers are high. Of the group canvassed by Venture Development Corp., almost 70% had bachelor degrees or higher, with a third of their number holding masters' degrees.

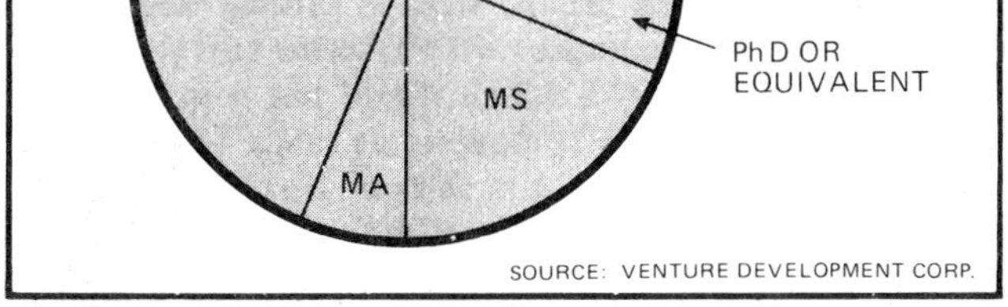

peripherals, and the ZPU is sold to home as well as commercial users. The only difference is in the software.

The Baby! I from the very new STM Systems Inc. is still in its infancy. STM has sold some of its Baby units, but is only now gearing up for production runs and soliciting dealers. Housed in an attaché case, Baby! I includes a 62-key typewriter-like keyboard, the 6502 microprocessor board and 4 kilobytes of memory, a 1,024-byte ROM monitor, and an audio-cassette interface. With the 9-inch-screen Panasonic monitor, that basic package sells for $1,170. Don Gunter, STM's vice president for marketing, says a total of 32 kilobytes of memory can be put in the 6502 set for less than $1,000. The Shugart minifloppy-disk drive, soon to be added, will provide 90 more kilobytes of formatted storage for a price of $850.

For profit and pleasure

The expansion in personal computers is in the other direction as well—from the industrial market to the consumer. California's Wave Mate got started in business to address the industrial market with a small computer, then took advantage of the Motorola 6800 in a wire-wrapped industrial-quality system—the $2,850 Jupiter IIC—that it is selling to home users as well.

Nearby, Electronic Tool Co. has experienced something similar. The company entered the small-computer business with general-purpose, low-cost systems for commercial-industrial use in the summer of 1975, only to find home users buying their hardware, too. Not only will ETC's Etcetera system accommodate the Intel's 8080A, Motorola's 6800, MOS Technology's 6502, or Fairchild's F8 as the main processor, but it also lets one operate as subordinate to the other. The company has four standard ETC-1000 system configurations, all assembled. They range in price from $830 for the beginner to a small-business system at $7,197.

As for products with direct consumer appeal, ECD Corp.'s MicroMind, the home computer that plugs into a TV set's antenna leads, loads its game programs into a MOS Technology 6512A microprocessor from a cassette recorder. Its $987 price for a fully assembled, encased unit includes an 80-key ASCII keyboard, the CPU board with 8 kilobytes of memory, and an I/O board that holds the power supply.

MicroMind's Basic language allows it to be used as an intelligent terminal, for computation, remote job entry or to run games, three of which are offered with the system. ECD already has more than 200 orders for it.

Possibly unaware of MicroMind's existence, Apple Computer Inc.'s Steven Jobs sees the hobbyist as "a latent home user, but no product exists for him to plop into his living room." Jobs is product manager at the Palo Alto, Calif., firm which last year sold 150 of its Apple I microcomputer boards built around the 6502 from MOS Technology. The $666 board also includes a PROM monitor, 4 kilobytes of dynamic RAM, video interface and power supply.

Apple II, which has the home-user grapevine buzzing, is scheduled for introduction next month. It will have up to 48 kilobytes of RAM on the same board and will be the first personal computer to include the Mostek 16,384-bit

RAM. An assembled but unencased board version will sell for $600. The company is at work on a music synthesizer to sell for about $200 as a peripheral for Apple II.

Focus on programmability

A good many hardware companies appear to bother little about the ease of programming their products—though users worry about it a lot. One of the exceptions is 12-year-old Southwest Technical Products of San Antonio, Texas. Before November 1975 the company sold kits of parts to be used in projects published in Popular Electronics magazine. It attributes much of its growth since then—to $4 million sales—to its introduction of the SWTPC 6800 computer system.

Motorola's 6800 8-bit microprocessor was chosen for this system, says Southwest president Daniel Meyer, because it eases software writing for the user. But recognizing that entering programs in machine code "is a little tedious," says Meyer, and that Basic has become the most widely used personal-computer language, Southwest also provides Basic as a high-level language. The $345 hardware kit for the SWTPC 6800 includes everything required for a system except an ASCII terminal.

Semiconductor manufacturers hesitate to commit themselves

Not yet competing directly with all these small systems companies, only one of which (MITS) expects to do more than $10 million of business this year, are all the multimillion-dollar semiconductor biggies. Still, National, RCA, MOS Technology, and GI, as well as Fairchild, Motorola, Signetics, AMI, TI, and Intel, have sales of single-board microcomputers that are of some consequence in the personal computer market. But it is difficult to get a handle on numbers. Sales are often through distributors, with the chief among them being Cramer Electronics, Hamilton/Avnet, and Semiconductor Specialists. Cramer itself offers "Cramerkits," specially tailored as single-board evaluation kits using the 8080, 6800, RCA's Cosmac unit, and TI's 9900.

National Semiconductor Corp. is addressing the personal computer market downward via the microcomputer path and upward through its consumer operation's programmable video games.

"I think the personal-computing market caught many of us flatfooted," says Phil Roybal, microprocessor marketing manager at National. "We've seen the numbers, made a few projections of our own, and we like what we see, but we're not quite sure how to approach it, and when. Be sure of one thing, all of us, all the semiconductor houses and microprocessor makers, will be in it one way or another."

A double thrust

National has also been making a serious effort to reach the non-electronics engineers with its 8-bit SC/MP microprocessors. The company has designed a high-level computer language specifically for SC/MP called NIBL, for national industrial basic language. Consisting of a simple, limited vocabulary of written English words in a rigidly defined grammar, NIBL has been placed in the public domain and is available free of charge. "We want to make SC/MP as easy as is imaginable to use," says Roybal.

While National's microprocessor group is focusing its

On display. A complete personal-computer system built around an IMS Associates 8080 machine is being shown here to a customer by Alan Tarsky at his store, Computer Mart, in Orange, Calif.

efforts on the hobbyist, the Santa Clara, Calif., company's consumer products division is looking at the consumer who wants a completely packaged low-cost personal computer, oriented toward entertainment, education, and simple bookkeeping tasks. Right now, National is bringing out an 8080-based programmable game terminal with many of the elements of full computer architecture, with options for add-on keyboards and game software in tape cassettes.

RCA Corp.'s Solid State division in Somerville, N.J., has two products using Basic language that are applicable to the home-computer market, although both are primarily design aids for the industrial market, where RCA's CDP 1802 microprocessor finds application. There is a $249 evaluation kit that includes 256 bytes of RAM on a board that will handle up to 4 kilobytes. The unit also offers terminal interfacing, which is handy because RCA plans to come out in May or June with a handheld terminal with a $150 teletypewriter-like interface, says William Dennehy, microprocessor product line manager.

RCA also offers the Microtutor, a completely assembled elementary computer that is programmed with switches. Priced at $349, it comes with a self-teaching manual and is "truly a beginner's microcomputer," says Dennehy. Coming shortly is Microtutor II, a new version that will do more but cost less.

MOS Technology's KIM-1 is a complete one-board evaluation system for the 6502. It sells for $245 and though Rick Simpson, manager of product support, claims KIM-1 is easy for a hobbyist to start with, he expects only 20% of the more than 9,000 units ordered to end up as personal computers.

The picture will change, though, with the introduction of a system, called PET for personal electronic transactions, packaged in a plastic case and looking like a conventional TV terminal. "Since it's aimed at the consumer market," notes Simpson, it will have a typewriter style keyboard and a place to plug in audio cassettes. PET will be distributed at retail stores for a price of $495.

General Instrument Corp.'s Microelectronics division, Hicksville, N.Y., also found itself in personal computers through its Gimini microcomputer, designed as a development system for the firm's 1600 family of 16-bit microprocessors. To achieve a stronger presence there, GI is developing a new system, Gimini Jr., that will be on the market in the second quarter at less than $1,000, in contrast with $3,000 for a Gimini system. The Gimini Jr., says Ron Stephens, general manager for GI's microprocessor line, "will be a high-performance home computer that will outsell the Gimini in the hobbyist market by 10 to 1. It's geared to that market."

On the fence

Some of the other major forces in the semiconductor microprocessor business are selling evaluation kits or demonstration systems mainly through distributors. These include Fairchild, Motorola, Signetics, AMI, Intel, and TI. Some of them are also playing it very close to the vest about future plans for personal computers. Undoubtedly, they're watching to see how much of a market evolves—and when.

Fairchild Semiconductor sells its assembled kit 1-A for $185 through distributors. The F8-based computer is being acquired by engineers for their personal use. "To that extent," says Donald D. Winstead, director of marketing for the Microsystems division, "we're in the hobbyist market."

Motorola Semiconductor is participating in personal computing with two kits, in addition to selling its 6800 processor and other chips to what it regards as a growing market in these systems. The MEK6800D-2, which the company introduced in February, is a two-board kit selling through distributors for $235 in quantity. The Educator 2 is just out this month and sells for $169.95 through retail computer outlets. Both kits are upwardly expandable and compatible with Motorola's Exorcisor development system.

At Signetics, in Sunnyvale, Calif., George Vaschel, manager of product support, sees the hobby-computer market alone reaching $15 million to $20 million by 1980 and says the company is "keeping a keen eye" on that part of the market. The Signetics 2650 kit, which includes RAM, PROM and interface circuits in its $155 price, is used in some video games. Those games are the vehicle Vaschel sees "for getting computers into the home," envisioning the day when the owner of a microprocessor-based game will buy a cassette that will also let him program the system for bookkeeping or for recipe storage.

Nearby in Santa Clara, AMI has recently completed an internal evaluation of whether to enter the hobbyist or home-computer fray. One of the conclusions, says Rob Pawsner, product manager for development systems, is that the hobbyist market is risky. Another is that the home market will be split into microprocessor-controlled appliances and general-purpose control systems. Meanwhile, AMI's 6800 MPS evaluation boards drift into use as personal computers through distributor sales. There are five such kits, ranging in price from $133 to $765.

Not talking

One of the biggest questions is what Intel will do in personal computers. Rumors abound that the Santa Clara microprocessor pioneer is about to enter the hobby market in a big way, but Intel officials are not commenting. "Obviously we're interested in home computers," says Don Bryson, strategic marketing manager in the microcomputer division. "We're interested in any market that uses Intel parts," he adds, but will amplify on that only enough to say it plans to expand in the hobby field. Intel is already involved in home computers with its SDK-80 design development kits and the MDS-80 microcomputer development system.

Texas Instruments, while it has nothing directed clearly at the personal-computer market, will announce a single-board microcomputer in the second quarter that could find use among do-it-yourselfers. Called the EVM-9900, it is an assembled evaluation board using the 16-bit TMS-9900 microprocessor that also includes erasable PROM, RAM, and RS-232 and teletypewriter interface circuits. The price will be about $400, with optional extras including a low-cost keyboard and display, keyboard interface and resident assembler.

Personal-computer owners brim with ideas for applications

Personal computers appeal to farmers, educators, music lovers, fuel-bill trimmers, household-chore haters, video-game players, but above all to people interested in learning more about programming. According to a survey taken by hobby-computer magazine BYTE, software development ranks first among the applications for which its readers use their machines, with interactive keyboard games second and interactive graphics third.

Swartz: software 'junkie'

"I'm a class-A software junkie—I collect code," acknowledges 26-year-old Robert Swartz. "Whenever a new piece of software comes out, I'll enter it, get it up and running, and fiddle with it." He works for Embosograph Co., his family's firm that manufactures point-of-sale displays in Chicago.

Swartz got hooked in college. He says, "There's nothing more engrossing than an interactive computer, and until now, that's only been available to people who get on time-sharing systems." Getting started three years ago was hard, he admits. "I first built a couple of clocks and a power supply, then I started a Mod-8," a development system from the now-defunct Microsystems International Ltd., he says. "At that time there was only one way to get parts, and that was to lie to distributors." Microsystems International promised that the 8008-based Mod-8 would be convertible upward to an 8080, "but MIL went broke, and I had to build my own conversion board," Swartz explains.

After building his Mod-8 system, Swartz put together a package on how to build, debug, and program it and sold copies for $20 each. With the proceeds he bought his present system, an 8080 CPU with dual floppy-disk drives, disk operating system, Diablo printer, teletypewriter, and CRT. It's worth "in the neighborhood of $10,000 today."

Chamberlain: farmer

Calculating the return on investment per acre on a farm: that job makes Thomas Chamberlain's Altair 8800 a small-business system. Besides being scheduling officer for the University of Massachusetts, Amherst, Mass., Chamberlain operates a farm in Ohio, which he owns with a brother and sister. Having a degree in systems analysis from New York University, the 60-year-old retired Army colonel decided to apply his knowledge to running the farm.

His computer is an Altair 8800. With it, he uses 32 kilobytes of memory, a floppy disk, teletypewriter and teletypewriter controller, plus a hardware disk loader and Basic as the language. Chamberlain taught himself how to program the machine, with the goal of improving the farm's profits by 20%.

Chamberlain estimates he has $6,500 in the Altair system, "and while I consider running the farm an avocation, I bought the computer as an investment." He is developing a data base that could include such things as what fertilizer to use to give the best yield per acre for a given crop. The system would also contain cyclical weather data and price histories on the commodities of interest from planting time to market time. He puts his true costs into the computer, along with commodities and weather histories, and the computer helps him decide when to sell or not sell.

Blaney: music-maker

It was to generate synthesized music that Robin Blaney two years ago decided to build a low-cost computer system—though as a 21-year-old college student, he has not yet been able to buy a synthesizer. "The $500 computer is a beautiful sell, but you have to buy so much more to have anything that works," he comments. "I have $2,000 to $3,000 invested, and I have scrounged for used equipment and bargains."

Blaney bought his IMSAI kit from Computer Mart, Orange, Calif., after shopping most computer-hobbyist outlets in the Los Angeles area. Its pledge of after-sale service was the convincer, he recalls.

At his home in Woodland Hills, Calif., Blaney also has a Lear Seigler "Dumb Terminal" built from a kit, Cromemco analog-to-digital interfaces and PROM board, a Tarbell audio cassette, approximately 30 kilobytes of memory, and Polymorphic I/O devices for computer-generated music. The software Blaney wrote in Basic.

To write a song, he punches notes into a plugged-in electronic organ keyboard, which are reproduced by an amplifier and read out on the terminal in real time, while also being stored in memory. Through an electronic synthesizer, however, his system could simulate sounds for any instrument.

Dilks: games player and teacher

For John Dilks, "the computer will be more important in education than the blackboard in a few years." He uses his system at home with his three children ranging in age from 5 to 12, to play games such as Hangman. He

Music man. Preparing to run a program on his system for generating electronic music, Robin Blaney flips control switches on his IMSAI computer and punches instructions into his Lear-Siegler terminal.

used a variation of Hangman to improve one of the children's spelling radically.

Dilks estimates he has about $2,000 invested in his IMSAI-8080-based system, which includes 14 kilobytes of RAM, 4 kilobytes of PROM, a tape-cassette interface board, and I/O board with two bidirectional ports. There is also a serial port that he uses with an 80-character-by-2-inch video terminal "picked up as junk," and a model 28 teletypewriter used as printer.

A Western Electric installer of electronic switching systems, Dilks also teaches adult educational courses at a Mays Landing, N.J., high school, using an E&L Instrument MMD-1 8080-based system.

Lavallee: fuel-saver

Ron Lavallee insists, "I'm not a computer hobbyist. I put my system together out of necessity." His personal solution to the national energy crisis is a vintage-1920 wood-burning stove—plus a heat-regulating system built around the $99 SC/MP kit from National Semiconductor Corp.

In January, when his neighbors in Hudson, N.H., lowered their thermostats to avoid a second month's gas bill of well over $100, he kept his six-room home at a toasty 75°. His December gas bill for heating, cooking, and hot water was only $29.

"The microprocessor increases the efficiency of a very inefficient stove," says Lavallee, who hauled the wood burner down from the Maine woods and installed it in November, just before the winter cold wave began. "When wood is loaded into the belly of the stove," he explains, "the fire flares up for a short time, then slowly burns down to embers until another log is thrown in. If the air from the stove's flue is regulated, the wood will burn evenly, generating more heat over a longer period."

A thermal sensor in the stove's stack pipe monitors the heat. To maintain the stack temperature within a specified range, the microcomputer periodically checks it, then opens or closes the flue damper via a stepper motor. "When the temperature does not rise to the control range after a certain number of openings, a low-wood alarm is activated," Lavalle continues. "The signal beeps once a minute until the stove is loaded again." He estimates that the computerized wood burner is 10% more efficient on very cold days and about 30% more efficient in above freezing weather.

An electronics engineer who designs machine control systems for Nashua Corp., Nashua, N.H., Lavallee built his system with odds and ends and a used motor.

Raskin: model-home owner

But the potential of the personal computer is perhaps spelled out most clearly by Jef Raskin. When he finishes building his 1,700-square-foot house in Brisbane, Calif., every room will have an RS-232 port, a parallel bus and coaxial cable strung behind the walls so Raskin can move his Poly-88 system into any room. The house is "designed from the ground up for music and computers," says the 34-year-old bachelor.

Energy saver. By heating his six-room New Hampshire house with a wood-burning stove raised to maximum efficiency by a SC/MP-based controller, Ron Lavallee has cut his monthly gas bill by $100.

A writer, electronics consultant, professional musician, hobby-airplane manufacturer, and photographer, Raskin holds both a master's degree in computer science, which he taught at the university level, and a philosophy degree. His living room creates a feeling of time warp: a 100-year-old organ, used by missionaries on door-to-door recruiting trips, sits next to a computer. In other parts of the room are another organ, a harpischord, an electric piano, bass cello, and a rack of recorders. Raskin plays them all.

Not that the computer controls his life. On the contrary, Raskin uses it to liberate him from mundane duties such as letter writing. The basic machine is a $150 Poly-88 with 48 kilobytes of memory. To it he has added a $3,700 printer, a $50 typewriter keyboard he uses for programming in Basic, an RS-232 interface, a cassette interface, and an interface that allows him to play programs on his home TV set.

Raskin plans to use 4 kilobytes of the memory to control a large $90,000 pipe organ (but which cost him much less after bargaining at a local convent). The concerts he holds there will be "computer-controlled:" the theater-type lighting he is installing will be run by computer; his coffee machine will automatically perk in time for intermission. He is currently developing a program to run his microwave oven. The solar-energy system that will run his house will also power the computer. □

Microcomputers: for fun and profit?

by Edward K. Yasaki

Adam Osborne knew nothing about the publishing business. He had a software company that specialized in business dp applications. But today, with the current rage in microcomputers, he's out of the software business and into a flourishing book publishing and distributing business—all centering on the personal or hobby computer. His book, *Introduction to Microcomputers*, sold to the tune of 50,000 copies in the first nine months and is expected to reach sales of 100,000 in its first year.

"The hobbyists are going to run the small software houses out of business very quickly," says Osborne in his new Berkeley, Calif., quarters. He explains that these tinkerers will continue to hold their jobs, programming at night

What started as a hobbyist movement has quickly grown into a serious business.

and over their weekends and producing, say, a payroll package for a moderate fee that covers their hobby expenses rather nicely. Systems houses, too, are vulnerable, according to him, unless they have a strong technical expertise or are entrenched in a particular market. "In fact the reason we got out of the business data processing (software). business a year ago was that I saw this coming."

Thus what started out as a hobbyist movement, offering tinkerers the chance to assemble a computer at home to play simple games, has quickly grown into a serious business. When those with assembled machines found a dearth of usable software, they quickly developed the facility to write their own. Some of them, with an eye on this burgeoning market, are evaluating various methods of distributing those programs at a price that is low enough to discourage the buyer from reproducing it for friends but high enough to return a profit.

Much is happening. The popularity of micros has spawned the development of a number of small and relatively low-cost peripherals like the minifloppy. Newly configured small business dp systems are already being talked about for use as remote processors in distributed computing systems.

Microcomputers have mass appeal, as the opening of the Computer Warehouse Store demonstrated last November. More than 2,300 people were said to have attended the affair, which included the giveaway of used computer equipment.

Faster micros are appearing with multiuser, multitasking, time-shared operating systems.

A field of Walter Mittys

It's almost as though everyone woke up the same morning with the secret aspiration to become a one-man systems house. For example, on the fringes of downtown Denver is the Computer Hut, run by a former cab driver. In its first three months of operation, the store had sold 15 systems, mostly to people who want to develop applications programs for a particular line of business. "I haven't sold one system yet to an end user," says proprietor Stephen Patterson. "But I will someday."

Dick Van Leer, general manager of the Computer Shack in Hayward, Calif., says he has a mailing list with 500 names, of whom only two or three can be considered pure hobbyists. Many, he says, talk like hobbyists, but their buying patterns suggest to him that they are developing systems for commercial applications.

Carl Burlin, sales manager for Computer Mart in Anaheim, Calif., says their business is split evenly among software people trying to learn about hardware, hardware people wanting to learn software, and people who know neither but would like to learn.

A large segment of the business of the Computer Warehouse Store in Boston, a division of Sonny Monosson's American Used Computer Corp., is comprised of students of computer sci-

Adam Osborne, who gave up his software company to become a publisher in the hobby field, claims that "the hobbyists are going to run the small software houses out of business very quickly."

ence, math, or economics who feel they can get more classroom work done with their own machines. Monosson, however, also counts small business people among his customers. One, for example, makes and installs burglar alarm systems and buys a cpu every week or two. And then there's a third category. "Some of them have this grand design," he says in describing them. "They're going to develop a software package to save the world and make a fortune. They really think it."

> Everyone woke up the same morning with the secret aspiration to be a one-man systems house.

Monosson, exhibiting still another departure from the typical computer store, offers a 20% discount to anyone who also buys a piece of used equipment from his inventory of peripherals. "For every cpu we sell," he says, "I think we end up selling two pieces of used equipment." Indeed his microcomputer catalog includes a used Olivetti replacement for the Teletype ASR 33 for $875 and a used Hazeltine 1000 crt terminal priced at $795.

A one-year guarantee on parts and labor on all assembled systems is provided by Computer Kits in Berkeley, Calif. The store, where some 60% of the customers are said to be noncomputer-types, also offers a three-month parts and labor guarantee on components purchased as a kit.

Pete Roberts of the same store says he is starting to see turnkey systems houses buying hardware from him. He says he has sold about 150 systems, large and small. A small system for business applications, available for $5,000, includes a 32K-byte Altair with one floppy, a Lear-Siegler ADM-3A dumb terminal, and Disc BASIC. The large systems he's selling for some $16,000 come with a 48K Altair, two floppies, a dumb terminal, 300lpm printer, and general ledger accounting software.

Roberts tells of a well-drilling company that is using such a system for its internal accounting, and planning now to add payroll and inventory to the system. Computer Shack's Van Leer has sold to a few real estate firms that say they have a property management system up—and then refuse to provide further details. Another is in the business of taking inventory for businesses and sees the need for a small processor. In businesses from accountancy to zoology, microcomputer retailers will tell you they have customers.

> A micro can offer a 30:1 price/performance advantage over an IBM 5100.

But small businessmen having micro-based systems up and running are still

Too young to be a hobbyist yet, this attendee of the Warehouse opening isn't too young to be as fascinated by the equipment as his parents are.

a rarity, according to Michael Levy of Jethro, a systems house in Wayland, Mass. He thinks many businessmen are buying machines for amusement and depreciating them as a business expense, a situation that will change as low-priced, turnkey systems become available.

"I have not seen an awful lot of present-day business applications," he

How about a speech recognition system for $249?

says. "But that doesn't mean that there aren't going to be a lot. I think there will, but the equipment hasn't caught up with it yet." He sees the need for low-cost random access storage and the wider availability of software. He mentions, for example, that a small system would be ideal for the instant-printing shop's use in job cost estimating, stepping the proprietor through the estimating job and providing reasonableness checks along the way.

Levy also tells of a minicomputer manufacturer that had visions of providing turnkey systems for the corner drugstore owner, until they found that the average drugstore has some 20,000 items in its inventory. Most of the items move off shelves so slowly that it isn't worth including them in an inventory data base. Statistically, Levy says, it's been found that in such examples 80% of the business comes from 20% of the inventory, so it is possible to get by with smaller storage capacities. Still, among people anxious to sell systems to that type of market, "I think there's a lot of glossing over of the difficulties."

A share of disaster

Levy worries that people will be developing systems for businesses with which they are totally unacquainted. "It's going to be an utter disaster," he says, for neither the vendor nor the buyer likes to document anything. Speaking of the owner of a small machine shop, for example, Levy says, "The last thing he ever wrote was his business card. That's why he went into business for himself. He'd rather tinker with a machine than write up a system." And neither the businessman nor the system developer will understand the other's business.

The small business market, nonetheless, will be significant. "The market for the $500 or $800 computer, when they're down to that, is going to be far more in small business than it's going

The microcomputer is not the equivalent of a mini.

to be for the hobbyist market," he says. But today there are still many manual systems that are better left manual.

Adam Osborne is publishing a series of three books with applications programs for business dp, and he also sees disaster ahead for systems developers. "I think business data processing applications represent one of the first things a lot of people are getting into. My advice to them is: 'don't.'" He feels that many people have the idea that because the hardware is cheap, the software will be equally cheap. "It will not. It will be more expensive," he says, "because you don't have the program development tools that you have on the mini system."

The typical micro-based system, he explains, might consist of $7,000 to $10,000 in hardware, considerably lower than the $25,000 minicomputer-based system. "However it's not going to take you long before the extra problems associated with programming such a primitive machine will consume the difference in price." Saying that one might spend $50,000 for software, "which you can easily do," he says a micro-based system might come in for $60,000, compared with $75,000 for a mini-based system. "And all of a sudden it's not such a big difference anymore."

Osborne cautions against the idea the microcomputer is the equivalent of the mini. "The average microcomputer can execute an assembly-language instruction every two to five microseconds," he explains. "And the assembly-

As the line for the First West Coast Computer Faire (April 16 & 17, San Francisco) illustrates, the market for the micro products is a nonhomogeneous group of hobbyists, businessmen, entrepreneurs, and others.

This scene from the Computer Faire strongly resembles many early Spring and Fall Joint Computer Conferences in the '60s.

language instruction doesn't do a heck of a lot. The average minicomputer is going to execute instructions at between one to two every microsecond, and each assembly language instruction will do as much as maybe half a dozen microprocessor instructions."

Success with toys and sharks

But the applications for these systems range widely, and speed may not always be critical. A hobbyist in the Chicago area is said to be using one to control his model railroad trains. A number of them purportedly are being used by investors for stock market analysis. A plastics maker has one in a production control system, and a rancher in the (formerly) lush San Joaquin Valley of California has a micro waiting for some water to come down an irrigation canal. A prospective buyer is looking to hook one up to his electronic organ so that he'll be able to get the computer not only to record what he has just played but also to make modifications to his performance. And the Computer Mart in Anaheim sold one to California State Univ. in Long Beach for shark research.

Paul Lamar, an automotive engineer and consultant, is developing a timing and scoring computer for automobile races, based on the MOS Technology 6502 microprocessor. Lamar, of Lamar Instruments in Hermosa Beach, Calif., used MOS Tech's Kim-1 computer with additional hardware to come up earlier with a road testing system for *Road & Track* magazine, a system that runs off a 12-volt battery. "The 6502 is probably the most underrated microprocessor there is," he says, ranking it on a par with the Zilog Z80. For real time applications, he claims, he'll be able to run the 6502 at up to 8 MHZ. (This would be equivalent to about two million micro instructions/sec, however, and Zilog sources say that even the follow-on product to the Z80 (the Z80A) can do only half that much.)

Applications for handicapped people are a prime interest of Dr. Robert T. Suding, director of research at the Digital Group, a Denver, Colo., vendor of hardware and software. He has developed a voice synthesizer linked to a keyboard, allowing blind programmers to know instantly what they have keyed. He is also looking into the Opticon system, a handheld optical character reader that scans text and produces a Braille readout. "One of the problems of the blind person is that only 10% know Braille," he says. So he wants to try linking a synthesizer to the Opticon too.

Suding, an amateur radio operator for the last 23 years, has used the micro to perform a number of ham radio functions, including the sending and receiving of Morse (telegraph) code, of Baudot (teletypewriter) code, and tv pictures. He adds that some have set it up for keeping logs and for satellite tracking.

"I have my processor programmed to run a solar-heated house that I'm designing up in the mountains," he adds. One of its functions will be to take into consideration the time of day and outside temperatures to direct heat on a room-by-room basis, even monitoring whether anyone is in that room. It will require several temperature sensors in each room, instead of one thermostat for the entire house. Another application is lawn monitoring and the watering of only that portion of the lawn that is dry. A third is surveillance, the processor being linked to smoke alarms and to electrical contacts at all windows and doors. Already available, he points out, are circuits that will work with dial and pushbutton phones to make a call to a neighbor or the local fire or police department. Of course one could program a sequential list of numbers to be called in an emergency.

Finally, Suding says he will use the computer to determine the required capacity of the solar panels he will be using, thus keeping to a minimum his original investment. And then the computer will control their operation so as to maximize efficiency.

Impacting education

In schools, too, microcomputers are expected to become almost as preva-

Getting Involved

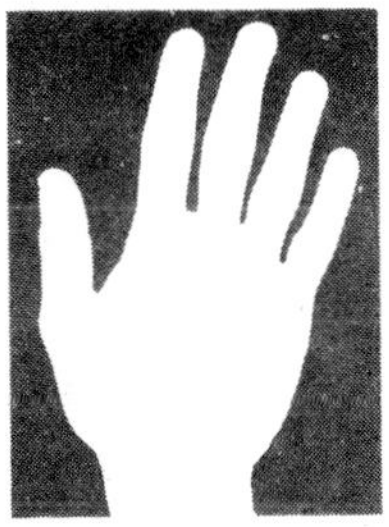

Can non-engineer members of the data processing community hop on the accelerating hobbyist bandwagon? The answer is a qualified, though optimistic, "yes." If you are a programmer, half the battle is won, especially if you know assembly language; luxuries such as high-level languages are not available on many microcomputers. If you know nothing at all about programming, you should probably consider getting a micro with BASIC to ease the transition. And if you have some electronics background, your entry into personal computing should be rapid and rewarding.

Those are our conclusions after several hours of assembling an SC/MP 16-bit microprocessor kit furnished by National Semiconductor, Inc. The kit is oriented toward engineers who are looking to familiarize themselves with microprocessor technology. After soldering seven resistors, eight capacitors, two memory chips, the microprocessor chip, a ROM chip, tty interface, timing crystal, and voltage regulator to a small printed circuit board, the SC/MP was ready to be attached to a Teletype terminal and exercised.

We didn't have a tty handy, so we may never know whether the SC/MP would have run—but it *probably* would have. The point is that hardware assembly is really more fun than work. All you must learn is how to solder pins spaced one-eighth-inch apart to a circuit board. It isn't too tough.

One of the tools recommended for assembling the SC/MP (and presumably any other microcomputer) is what's called a "solder sucker." This is used to remove excess solder and solder that's managed to reach the wrong places on the board. The device turns what would be a nearly impossible job into one which is only slightly challenging.

There is help available too. The owner of the local Byte Shop was helpful, for one. The electronics shop he recommended (for parts he did not have in stock) not only had books on how to get into personal computing, but also people behind the counter who could give assistance —people who had built kits before and even designed some of their own machines. Everyone seemed willing to answer questions, no matter how basic, and we felt they knew what they were talking about since they'd already done it.

So, roll up your sleeves (no nylon shirts or blouses, please—the static electricity is fatal to some components) and get busy building your own fun. —**Michael Cashman** lent as the electronic calculator. "I think microcomputers in general will have a tremendous impact on the educational system," says Dr. Alice E. Ahlgren of Cromemco. Another hardware developer, Cromemco has a computer that will support up to eight terminals. Based on the Zilog Z8 processor and operated at a 4MHZ rate, the computer has eight memory bank select switches that allow the user to partition portions of memory for each user. In June the firm had scheduled announcement of a 16K BASIC for use with the so-called Z-2 computer, which could make it appealing to schools.

Agreeing with Ahlgren is Don Inman, a former high school math teacher who now consults with schools that are looking to integrate the computer into the curriculum. Inman, the editor of a new publication for schools called *Calculators/Computers*, taught 30 teachers in the San Jose, Calif., Unified School District, which bought a single-board micro for each school, the idea being to teach some computer science courses in those schools. The teachers assembled the machines, then programmed them in machine language. In nearby Sunnyvale, too, the intermediate-level schools have Imsai computers, Lear-Siegler dumb terminals, and cassette interfaces for experimentation in math and reading instruction.

From this workshop, in the basement of Robert Suding's home, have come numerous designs for the products of the Digital Group.

Sunnyvale's elementary schools have introduced the electronic calculator under consultant Bob Albrecht, who visits schools weekly to put on demonstrations. Not restricted to calculator games, however, Albrecht has at his disposal a wide variety of calculators, all the way from the four-function to the programmable, as he works with students and teachers to bridge the gap between calculators and computers.

Inman, aware of the limitations of having but one microcomputer for an entire class, or even for one school, nevertheless prefers the micro to a terminal, citing the former's even more personal nature. He tells of a school in Modesto, Calif., where the math teacher who had had no previous computer experience assembled an Imsai computer, and then provided a plexiglass cover so that the students could see the components inside.

> Many people are willing to pay $200 to have their kid learn programming in front of the tv.

When the computer in the classroom catches on, he adds, "it's going to have to be a machine that's self-contained and not a kit." It must be turnkey, have BASIC or some such language on PROM or easily read in from a cassette. "I think we're getting away from kit building." He looks for the marketing of low-priced, packaged systems that emphasize applications, rather than programming. "That's where your mass market is," he says. "It's not with the computer buff or the teacher who has some knowledge," but instead with teachers who merely want to use it as a tool, like a typewriter. He explains that a reasonable price is $500 for a cpu, keyboard, minimum amount of memory, and the language on a ROM. "And the schools are going more to the display, rather than the hardcopy printer."

The do-it-yourself aspect does not appeal to all microcomputer buyers. Retailers often build the kits for the customer, as George Tate does for the Computer Mart in Anaheim, Calif.

No sooner said than done. In September, first shipments are expected of the Pet computer, an approximately $500 machine from Commodore Business Machines of Palo Alto, Calif. The self-contained Pet has a 9-inch crt, a full but compact keyboard that includes 64 graphics symbols, plus a cassette drive, 4K to 32K of RAM, an operating system on 4K of ROM, and an 8K BASIC on ROM.

Not only is the low price significant, but the machine also takes a major departure in its use of the IEEE 488 bus. The industry "standard" has been the bus structure pioneered by the Altair computer, called the S-100 bus, for which a large percentage of low-priced peripherals has been developed. Now Commodore has adopted the bus structure pioneered by Hewlett-Packard, facilitating the interfacing of the Pet with lab instruments.

In addition to lower priced micros, however, there are also a number of faster micros available which are closing in on the minicomputer territory. Alpha Micro Systems in Irvine, Calif., has a multitasking time-shared system with a BASIC compiler, hardware floating-point, and a number of bells and whistles. A 64K system with text editor, line printer spooler, passwords, and two floppy disc drives sells in the neighborhood of $7,000. It uses a 16-bit microprocessor chip set from Western Digital.

Low prices can be found in peripherals too. At the First West Coast Computer Faire in San Francisco a 180 cps bidirectional printer available in kit form for $995 was shown. "About three years ago something like that was being sold for $5,000 or $10,000, if you could get it at all," noted Hal Singer of Lompoc, Calif. "And I think we can still see the price of an item like that going down to $200 or $300."

How about a speech recognition system, including the hardware and software, for $249? That's available in kit form from Heuristics Inc., Los Altos, Calif. Or a voice synthesis system for less than $400? What about Lear-Siegler shipping 250 to 300 kits monthly of its dumb crt terminal to retail stores, some 20% of total output?

And things no one's thought of

What happens when the mass merchandisers like Sears, J.C. Penney, and Heath Co. enter this market is still open to discussion. But enter they will. Tom Munnecke, president of Metasystems in Riverside, Calif., sees a large Christmas boom arriving this year, similar to what happened with video games last season.

> Hardware manufacturers are entering the market unaware of the "software vacuum" that exists.

"I think the rumblings will begin at Christmas (if not a mad rush)," says Munnecke, who is preparing an introductory book on the subject for September publication. "But I think it's going to turn the data processing world upside down." He cites the Pet computer, saying it offers a 30:1 price-performance advantage over the IBM 5100.

Less certain of this immediacy is Computer Mart's Carl Burlin, who thinks the large retailers will have to offer a packaged product, one that can be plugged in and made to run with little additional effort by the buyer. "It's not a packaged product yet," he says. "I'd say they're a good three years away."

Publisher Adam Osborne draws an analogy to the sales of hi-fi/stereo equipment. Department stores sell packaged systems, but the sophisticated shopper still goes to a hi-fi specialist where one can buy a receiver from one manufacturer, speakers from another, and a turntable or tape from still a third. "I see Sears getting into the type of product that you can package and sell and then forget about," he says. That includes things like video games or devices to hang onto the tv set for specific applications.

He can foresee, for example, a keyboard for the tv set that enables the user to work with BASIC, something that could be packaged today for $400. "And for the kind of volume that Sears could support, it could quite easily sell for $200. There are a lot of people willing to pay $200 to be able to have their kid learn computer programming at home in front of the tv set."

Software, indeed, is lagging behind the hardware, and Munnecke thinks hardware manufacturers like Commodore and Heath are entering the market unaware of the "software vacuum" that exists. The problem is compounded, he adds, by an incompatibility in language support. Munnecke, who is a member of the MUMPS language development committee, says, "MUMPS is the saving grace because its operating system, file management system, and application language are all wrapped up into one standard language." He says the language would be suitable for micros, and feels it would be an answer to all this incompatibility.

Accordingly, he is working on a MUMPS operating system for the micro. Concerned that the vacuum will be filled by "two-bit" software companies springing up in people's garages, he adds, "It'll certainly be 'buyer beware' for some time in the software area." Others who are similarly critical of BASIC are carrying banners for other languages, such as PILOT, APL, FORTRAN, and FORTH.

> "We're going to see about 10 processors in the average home in about three years."

"What interests me is that people are using computers, regardless of what they're being used for," says Computer Kits' Roberts. He sees a significance in people becoming acquainted with the technology. "Back into the hands of individuals has come this immensely powerful tool." He likens it to the early days of scientific discovery when one didn't need expensive equipment or tools to study science, and looks to the day when people will begin writing programs to do things others haven't even thought about.

Tom Munnecke, also drawing upon history, sees an analogy with the Gutenberg press being viewed initially as a Bible-making machine. He says people are looking at the computer as a . . . well, a computer, rather than a "whole new level of intelligence" that will reside in homes.

The Digital Group's Robert Suding asks his visitor how many motors there might be in an average home. "You start counting and you'll find about 50 motors. We're going to see about 10 processors in the average home in about three years." He cites their use in microwave ovens, sewing machines, the washing machine, automobile, and lawn control system, not including those for the hobbyist's use.

He talks, for example, of a programmable sewing machine that the homemaker can lead through the process of, say, making a new stitch. Once performed correctly, she'll be able to make a perfect stitch every time. But more significantly, so will everyone else in the family. And the same applies to baking something in a programmable oven.

"We're very primitive in the way we do things right now," he continues. "There are some exciting times coming up in the next five years." ✲

A Consumer Product in Japan

More than 30,000 copies of a $2 paperback on microcomputers were sold in the first three weeks in Japan, indicating the recent surge of interest there. The author, Prof. Toshiaki Yasuda of the Tokyo Electrical Engineering Univ., can see 100,000 copies being sold by the end of this year, in only the first nine months since its debut.

According to the author, the largest computer club in Japan was formed only nine months ago and already has some 6,000 members. He figures there are about 10,000 kit builders there, half of them in it for kicks and the other half hoping to make a business out of some aspect of microcomputing.

The former newspaper reporter is no newcomer to the technology. He says he saw his first Intel 8008 microprocessor chip at a Tokyo electronic components store back in 1972. It was one of the initial 20 of the 8008 chips shipped to Japan. He bought it for the equivalent of about $300, spending the summer months acquiring the supporting circuitry and assembling it at home, where it continues to operate. Four months later, he adds, the same 8008 chip was priced at $160. His machine has only 128 bytes of RAM; he says he then couldn't afford to buy more memory than that.

Yasuda, considered one of the two top microcomputer gurus in Japan, the other being a Tokyo Univ. professor, has four or five systems at home that he has assembled, putting to use the knowledge that came with his bachelor's degree in electrical engineering.

Pushing the use of BASIC for a Japanese population reliant on FORTRAN and COBOL is Prof. T. Yasuda of Tokyo, one of that nation's two microcomputer gurus.

He says that the most popular processor is the Nippon Electric TK-80, of which 8,000 have been sold in kit form alone. That processor sells for about $300, including 512 bytes of RAM and 768 bytes of ROM.

To show the degree of popular interest in the devices, he adds that computer kits first showed up in computer stores and in electronic supply shops such as those where the founders of Sony Corp. bought vacuum tubes and other components to begin their business. Now the kits are being sold in major department stores too. They've become a consumer product in Japan. ✲

Home computers versus hobby computers

by Alan R. Kaplan

Less than three years ago, a computer in the home was unusual enough to warrant coverage in the general press. Today, there are more than 20,000 general purpose computers in American homes, and their number is increasing by over 40% per year. Also, where there were only a handful of manufacturers in 1975, there are now approximately 75 producers of kit-form and assembled microcomputers for home use, and their products are distributed by over 300 retail stores.

Clearly there is an enthusiastic and growing population of computer hobbyists. But are we seeing the leading edge of a true consumer market? Will the growth peak as it has for other hobbies, like amateur (ham) radio? Or keep going as it has for CB car radio?

Even if the growth peaks at a hobby level, the microcomputer market may surge to 15 times its present size (to as many as 300,000 units installed in five to eight years).

On the other hand, if the computer in the home becomes a consumer product, the numbers get very big very fast. There are some 75 million households in the U.S. If only one of every 25 purchased a home computer at $500 (which now looks like too low a number for what can be offered, but which will help keep the results conservative), then revenues would exceed those now generated by all mini systems suppliers put together.

Actually, it is likely that both of these things will happen, that there will be a hobbyist market and a home computer market. We know something about the former, and we've at least gone far enough into researching the latter to be able to guess at what a computer will have to be and how it will have to be priced before a home-computer consumer market will be established.

Who are the hobbyists?

The hobby computer market as it exists today was born in January 1975, when *Popular Electronics* published a cover story on MITS Inc.'s hobby computer, the Altair 8800. Experimental "home-brew" systems were in use well before then, however, and several computer buffs had even purchased commercial systems for home use. At the end of 1975, almost one-fourth of all hobby computers were either adapted from kits intended for industrial prototyping, built from "scratch" around microprocessors and MSI components, or assembled from commercial subsystems. Then, as now, hobbyists were a sophisticated, highly motivated lot.

> Nearly two-thirds of today's hobbyists are programmers, technicians, or engineers.

Statistics on the backgrounds of computer hobbyists provide further evidence of the gulf between them and the general public. A mid-1976 Venture Development Corp. survey of over 1,500 hobbyists revealed that nearly two-thirds were directly employed as programmers, technicians, or engineers, and that nearly three-quarters of hobby computer owners used computers on the job. (See Fig. 1.)

Thus, hobbyists have not only been exposed to computers, they appear to be quite knowledgeable in their use. 40% of self-described computer hobbyists—people who all called themselves "hobbyists" but slightly more than half of whom did not own their own computer at the time of the study—considered themselves above the novice level in both hardware and software. (See Fig. 2.)

Some of the most surprising results of the VDC study concern the nature, rather than the level, of hobbyists' software expertise. It was found, for example, that almost as many hobbyists knew Digital Equipment PDP-8 and PDP-11 machine languages as the assembler on the most popular hobby microprocessor, the Intel 8080.

Similarly, the study found that almost as many hobbyists cited experience with FORTRAN as with BASIC, even though BASIC is available as an interpreter and so far is the only higher level language in general use among hobbyists. These data further support the contention that, unlike the general public,hobbyists have had considerable direct experience with computers.

The distinction between today's hobby computer user and tomorrow's home computer user becomes most meaningful where it influences their respective product interests. In the case of hobby computers, the desiderata are variety and flexibility. A cursory glance through any of the dozen or so hobbyist publications quickly impresses the reader with the strong "do-it-yourself" appeal of the advertisements for everything from board connectors to custom interfaces. Yet it is just this impression that home computer makers will strive to avoid.

Although an end-user, the hobbyist mentality is more akin to that of the oem. He (or she) is a systems builder, a designer of unique systems. By virtue of the sophistication noted previously, the hobbyist is usually capable of assembling at the chip level, always capable of customizing at the board level, generally required to configure at the subsystem level, and invariably forced to seek out (and/or develop) software

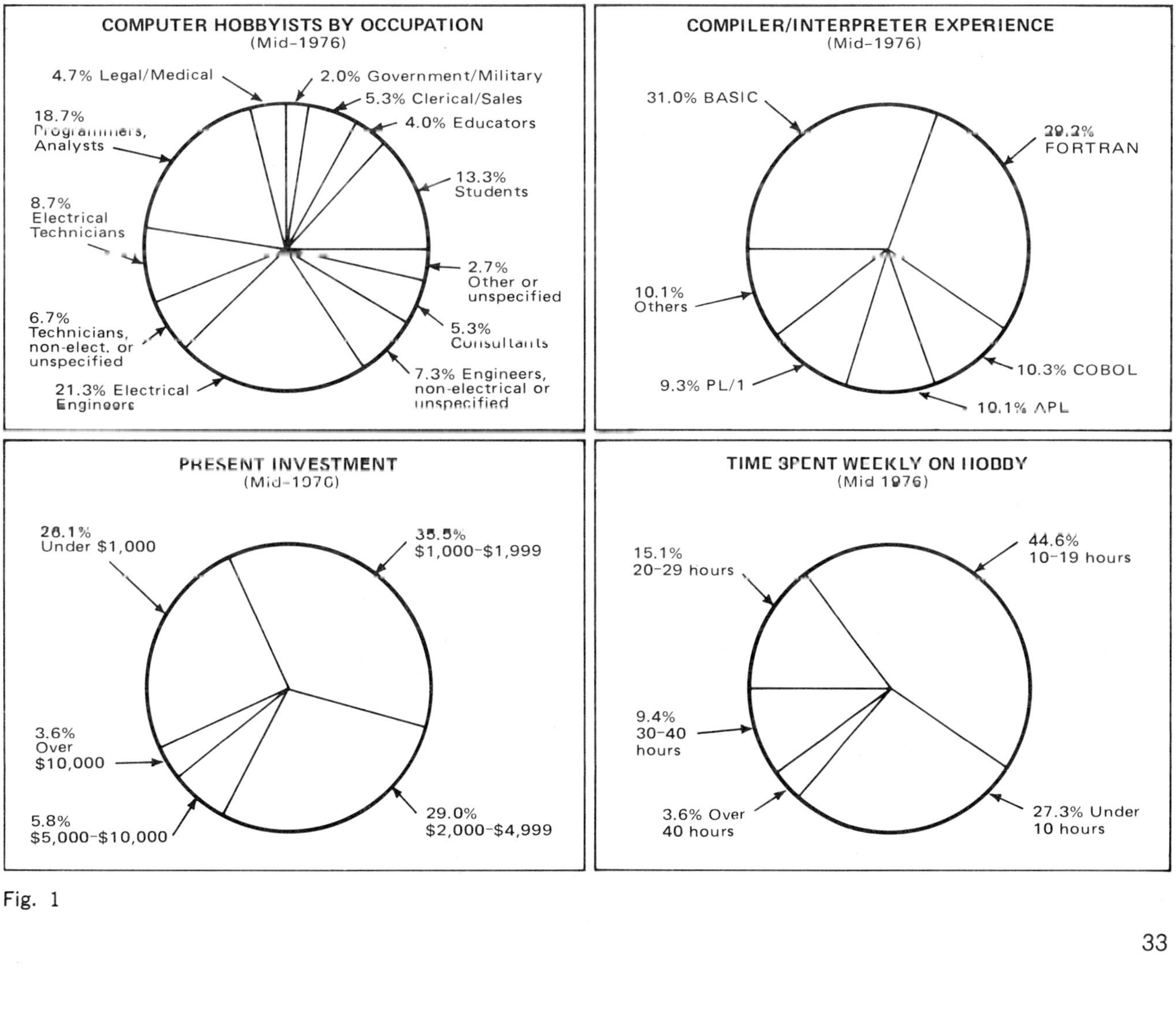

Fig. 1

beyond that available from his "mainframe" vendor.

General consumers, on the other hand, can barely be expected to customize, much less design, any significant part of their systems. The general consumer will be a classic end-user. His system must be preassembled and ready to go. Whereas hobby computers may or may not be provided with (or configured for) higher level languages, the general consumer's home computer will be required to interact immediately with the user via an interpreter prestored in ROM. Unlike hobby systems, for which the expression "includes I/O" usually refers only to the signal interface, home systems will be required to include the I/O device itself, together with the cables, sockets, controller, software drivers and everything else necessary simply to "insert plug *A1* into socket *A2* and press *'Run.'* "

Home computer users will, of course, have a range of selectable options. They will be able to choose their peripheral mix, memory size, and applications software. But the relative ease required to implement these options will impose on them a much higher degree of integration. In contrast to hobby computers, which feature variation and flexibility, home computers must stress modularity and simplicity.

More than one-third of the computer-owning hobbyists have invested over $2,000.

Analyses of hobby computer usage indicate that the hobbyist "does to learn" more than he "learns to do." That is, his prime motivation is educational rather than functional. Nonetheless, his commitment, both in terms of dollars and time, is significant. More than one-third of computer-owning hobbyists have invested over $2,000 in their systems, and nearly 10% have invested at least twice that amount! While $2,000 may not seem impressive, it represents more than 10% of the annual income of the majority of hobbyists, and more than 20% of the income of 20% of them.

Hobby systems are used in as many ways as their commercial counterparts. Even the most sophisticated areas of artificial intelligence have hobby parallels. For our purposes, however, we can classify all hobby applications into one or another of the eight specialized areas illustrated in Fig. 3, which presents the application data acquired from VDC's survey of hobbyists. Fig. 3 further includes a "Non-Specialized, Development" category representing systems that at the time of the survey were intended mainly for internal study and experimentation or were still being assembled.

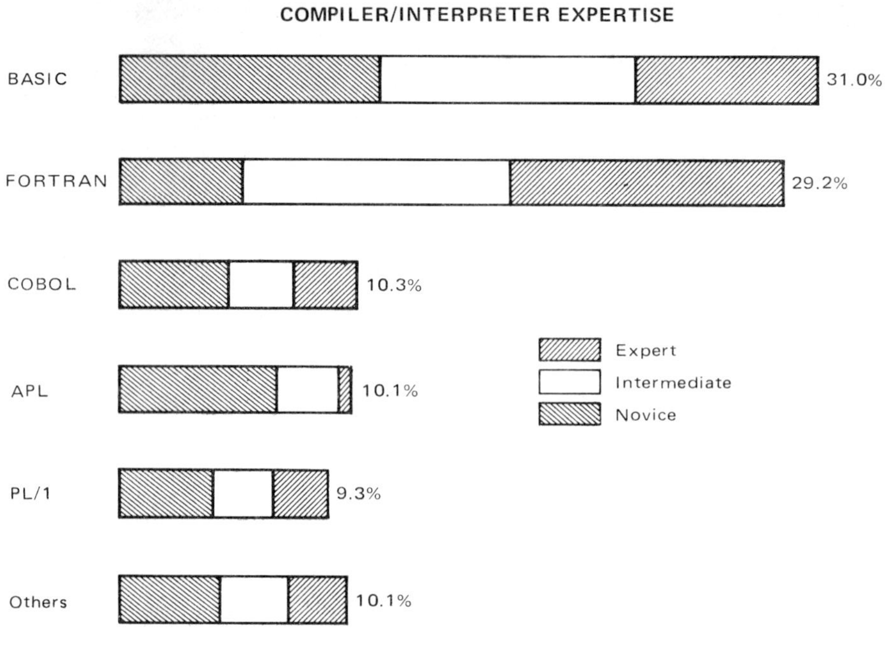

Fig. 2

A central characteristic of hobby computers is that they are rarely dedicated to one application, a natural corollary of the "do to learn" philosophy. On this point, hobby computers differ from "real world" systems, but, as we shall see later, are not expected to differ from home systems even though general consumers will be of the "learn to do" variety. Of the seven specialized applications shown, only two, "Games" and "Real-time," were found to include users who had totally dedicated their systems, and those dedicated systems accounted for only 3% of all hobby systems noted.

Who will the consumers be?

With this application data from hobbyists in hand, VDC then sought to determine general consumers' level of interest in a potential home computer. The method used was the "focused group session." This technique, commonly employed in consumer market research on new products, consists of assembling small groups of consumers for participation in a highly structured but informal question and answer session during which the interviewee, rather than the interviewer, establishes the price and specifications of the subject product. Most of the interviewees were college graduates employed in professional and/or academic careers. Ages ranged from 23 to mid-fifties; income from approximately $12,000 to over $40,000.

The sessions were conducted in

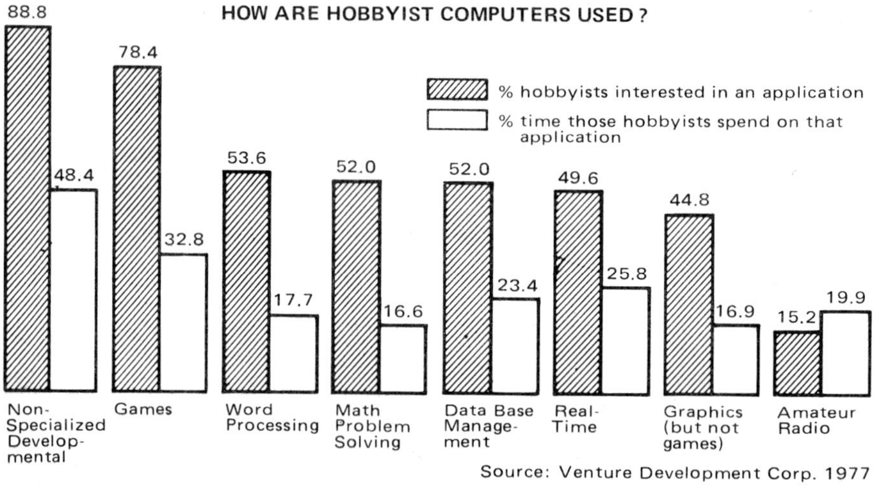

Fig. 3. Hobbyists claim already to be involved in, or plan to be involved in, a variety of interesting applications. How they spend their machine time, however, may reflect very different interests. For example, the 49.6% of the group who claim to be interested in real-time applications spent only 25.8% of their time on them—the remainder may have been spent on games.

three parts, beginning with the interviewer asking, "Would you consider purchasing a small general purpose computer for personal use in your home, and if so, what would you use it for and how much would you pay for it?" The general responses were: first, an expression of familiarity with the fact that hobby computers are available; second, an expression of ignorance concerning the ways hobby computers are used; third, skepticism that the interviewee would have a practical application unrelated to his or her vocation that would justify the investment in time and money. Estimates of

There is presently no hobby system under $2,500 capable of doing what a consumer would want.

the cost of a home computer ranged from $500 to $2,500, with the average about $1,500.

The second part of the session began with the interviewer stating, "Among the general tasks that a home computer would be likely to perform are calculations, records management, text editing, and games. How much would you pay for a system capable of performing these tasks?" At this point the interviewees were able to suggest some examples of several of the general tasks mentioned, typically in the form of, "Do you mean by 'calculation' it will do my income taxes?" or, "I would consider any machine that would help with my typing." Usually, however, the subjects asked for specific examples of the general tasks mentioned, such as, "How would I (or "Could I") use a computer for____?" Estimates of cost began to reflect the subject's own interpretation of the applications mentioned, such as, "I wouldn't pay more than *X* dollars for a machine that could____."

The third part of the session began with a lengthy dissertation by the interviewer on specific applications, such as filing and retrieving addresses, entertaining and educating children, producing and correcting typed text, cross-indexing personal book and record collections, monitoring home security and environmental systems, etc. At this point most subjects were very interested and quite positive. Estimates of prices they were willing to pay began to be based on multiple applications, and were well above those offered in the second part of the session. Ease of use and ability of the system to perform as described became more important issues than price. The statement, "I'm not (or,"I don't want to have to be") a computer programmer (or engineer)" was made often.

Focused group data are rarely conclusive, but the sessions did reveal some clear patterns among potential home computer buyers to reinforce the thesis that what we have now in the hobby computer is a long way from what is needed for tomorrow's "volkskomputer." Consider, for example, that:

1. There is currently no hobby computer system below $2,500 capable of *immediate* general consumer interaction for any of the "practical" applications noted above. None is available (although some are offered!) in assembled form with integral I/O and operating systems applications software (other than games), and sufficient internal memory (at least 8KB of RAM) to perform any but the most primitive "practical" applications.
2. Although a great deal of hobby software is freely available, some of it quite good, almost all of it is either recreational, or developmental in the form of assemblers, interpreters (such as a 2K "Tiny BASIC"), editors, diagnostic routines, and utilities. "Practical" applications software is rare.
3. Hobby documentation is unsatisfactory even for hobbyists. It would be totally unacceptable to general consumers. This point is very important, and also happens to touch on the one similarity mentioned earlier between the hobbyist and the potential general consumer: neither is likely to dedicate his system, although for different reasons.

The hobbyist becomes involved in many applications because he is primarily a learner—he is willing to invest considerable time in education, which for him is a form of recreation. Conversely, the home consumer will be a doer. He will justify his dollar investment by distributing it over several applications, but he will resent investing any more "learning" time than the absolute minimum necessary to perform those applications. He has made it quite clear that he does "not want to have to be a programmer or engineer."

4. Although hobbyists find the reliability of their systems to be acceptable, giving that factor an average rating of 3.8 on a 0 to 5 scale, it is doubtful that general consumers would be as charitable. For the hobbyist, mean time to failure (MTTF) is not as important as mean time to repair (MTTR). He rarely sees his application as critical; he is typically a "regular" at computer stores and a member of at least one hobby computer club, both of which serve for parts and information; and he is capable of performing most of his own maintenance.

General consumers, however, *will* see their applications as critical, cannot be expected to diagnose or maintain their own systems, will resent frequent trips back to their vendor, and can be very demanding when they perceive that their right as a consumer to a product that performs exactly as advertised has been violated. Thus the hobbyist is prepared to react to a short failure cycle for participating in the repair cycle; the general consumer is not.

What's coming

The hobby computer, then, has not yet developed to the point where it poses any truly popular potential. Simply because hobby computers are found in homes does not make them "home computers" any more than are the Digital Equipment PDP-8s and used IBM 1620s that have also been purchased for home use. The hobby computer is, rather, a repackaged industrial microcomputer without the specialized software and peripherals backing vital for general consumer acceptance.

On the other hand, the hobby computer has given us a preview of what promises to become the most important home development since the roof. Hobby computer manufacturers, undercapitalized and inexperienced in mass markets, have sparked the interest of every consumer electronics manufacturer and mass retailer. It will be from these companies that we can expect to find a home computer, and their participation is imminent.

What we have seen so far is only the emergence of a fast moving but small and parochial market. What we are about to see is the machine that has changed our lives become a part of them. ✻

Part 2: Basic Computer Theory

The way that computers are put together is referred to as architecture, and just as any building may be thought of as an elaboration of floors, walls, and ceilings, so, too, do all computers share a fundamental structure. This section introduces the fundamental components of computer hardware and describes how they interact to get the job done.

The focus is on microcomputers—so named because they're built around a complex integrated circuit called a microprocessor. It is the microprocessor that has made personal computers portable and affordable. Indeed, microcomputers have affected various aspects of traditional computer systems—and an article in this part addresses the problem of getting those involved in traditional data processing to think at the "micro" level.

Much of this section is devoted to memory, one of the most significant parts of a computer. The job of a computer memory may be simply the storing of data in an organized, retrievable manner, but there are many different types, and each has its own niche in a hierarchy that it is extremely complex. The picture is further complicated by the changes in cost and speed that memory devices undergo each year as technology improves. Moreover, memory makes up a great deal of a computer's total hardware, and often the bulk of its cost.

An introduction to the world of home computers

by Roger Edelson
Reprinted by permission of INTERFACE AGE Magazine from the Feb. 1978 issue.

Depending on how you may use a computer, your view of what a computer is will be different. Those of you who use a company computational facility by means of job submittal cards do not really see the computer. All that is seen is a window into which a job is submitted, and from which the result is obtained. At the other end of the spectrum is the circuit designer whose responsibility is one small function block of the computer and never sees the computer as a problem-solving machine at all.

Obviously, most of us fall somewhere in between and would like to understand the computer as manipulative machine which may be applied to various problems. It is to this end, or basically the view of the home or small-business computerist, that these articles are addressed.

To most of us the computer will be a variegated assemblage of circuit boards, chassis, and input/output devices. In order to use these assemblies, we will have to take a look at what they are and how they interact.

Let's start by taking a look at the general architecture of a stored-program computer—which is the real name of the beast with which we are dealing.

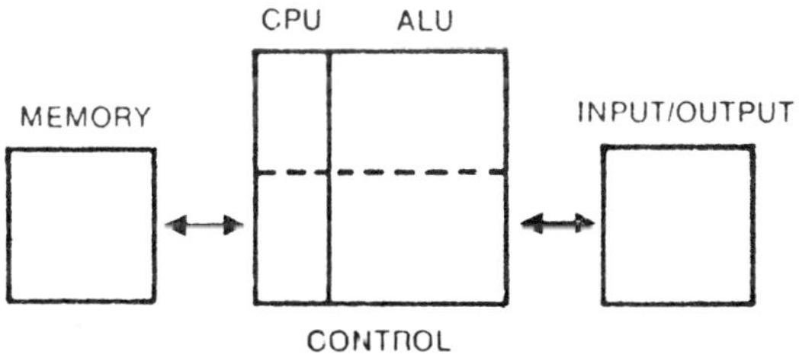

Figure 1.

Pretty simple—huh! This diagram does not actually represent the typical microcomputer with which we shall be dealing because it does not show the typical bus structure. Actually, with the exception of the input/output device all of the major elements (CPU and memory) could be placed on one chip. In some of the newer control-oriented machines they are. In the type of machines with which we are usually involved this is not practical because of the limitations to expansion. Prior to the advent of microcomputers and solid-state memories a much larger piece of real estate was required. As a historical note, the Univac 1, which was built out of vacuum tubes in 1950 and filled a room, had less computing powers than most of today's microcomputers.

Let's take a somewhat more detailed look at the various pieces which make up the microcomputer block diagram. In this article the look will be basically an overview with subsequent articles examining each section in considerable detail. We shall begin the overview with the CPU—the central processing unit.

The CPU is the essential heart of the microcomputer system. With the advent of the single-chip CPU (in essence a whole computer on a slice of silicon), home computing came of age. The basic function of the CPU is to perform calculations, memory handling, and various logical functions. The CPU of a typical microcomputer generally contains one or more accumulators which are used to store data retrieved from memory. It is in the accumulator register that the data fetched from memory are operated upon. The accumulator also serves as a holding point prior to returning data to memory. It might be possible to obtain a word from memory, operate on it, and return it directly to memory in an instruction cycle, but the additional significant amount of logic required to implement this operation would be substantial. The CPU will also have a register which stores the address of the data in the memory. The size of this register will determine the extent of the memory that can be directly accessed by the CPU. (Other schemes can be used to extend this address field.) In most of the CPUs we shall be concerned with, the memory size will be 65,536 words—equivalent to a 16-bit address field. In many CPUs this register is also called the data counter.

The CPU must also have a place for storing the instruction to be implemented. This is called the instruction register. The CPU will always interpret the contents of the instruction register as an instruction. On the other hand, the CPU does not care what the bits of data stored in the accumulator represent. They can be either instructions or data.

Another register is always required, the program counter. The program counter is assumed to always refer to a program memory word and specifies the next location from which the instruction will be taken.

Most CPUs also contain one or more index registers, which may be used to store data or a memory address for use in indexed-mode memory addressing. Again, most modern CPUs feature a register called the stack pointer. The stack pointer indicates the next available location in an external transient storage area, usually the lower address of the system memory. The stack and stack pointer are used to modify the memory-addressing technique in a manner called implied memory addressing.

Almost all of the CPU chips which we shall cover in a subsequent article are bus-oriented devices. By this we mean that the data (usually 8 bits) are transferred both into and out of the CPU by one set of eight lines through the use of bidirectional drivers. The same is true for the address bus—usually consisting of 16 lines as necessary to handle the 64-K memory space. Many of the CPU chips also have a control bus structure for some of the specialized control functions necessary. Figure 2 illustrates the implementation of the typical microcomputer bus structure.

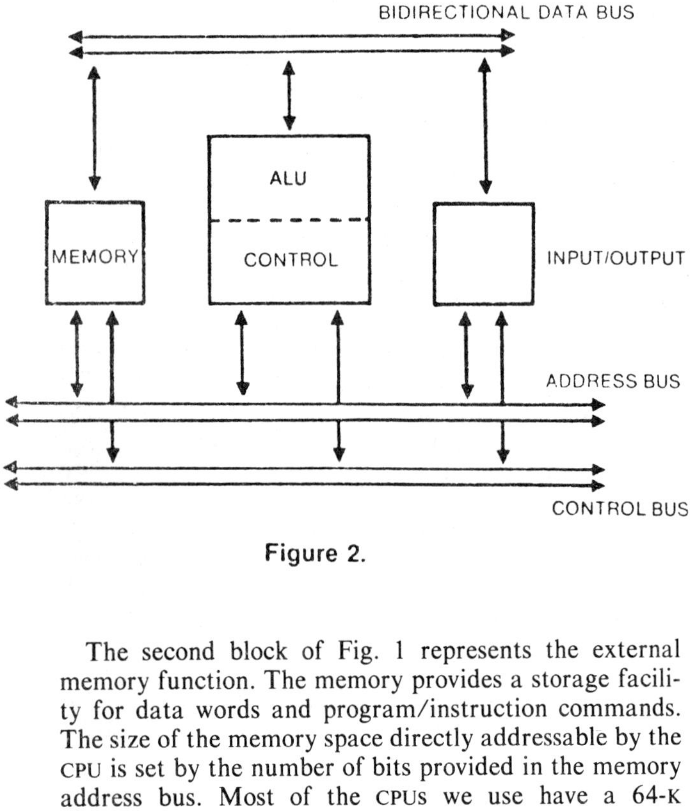

Figure 2.

The second block of Fig. 1 represents the external memory function. The memory provides a storage facility for data words and program/instruction commands. The size of the memory space directly addressable by the CPU is set by the number of bits provided in the memory address bus. Most of the CPUs we use have a 64-K memory address capability. This can be expanded by the use of additional mass storage devices which access the CPU through the input/output function. The memories available range in both function and technology used to inplement the particular function. RAM stands for random-access memory, which usually is the working memory of the computer. This style of memory may be either written into or read from under program control. Depending on the technology used, the information may be lost upon reading (i.e., magnetic cores) or retained in storage after a read (semiconductor memories are an example). Again, depending on the technology used, the memory may be volatile (information is lost when power is removed) or nonvolatile. Semiconductor memories with some exceptions are an example of a volatile memory, and magnetic cores are nonvolatile.

ROM refers to read-only memory. This type of memory is nonvolatile but can only be read from. ROM is preprogrammed during the factory manufacture by the selection of an appropriate mask. Some memories are programmable in the field—PROMs, programmable read-only memories. Some of the technologies used to implement PROMs allow one write operation only—the device then becomes a ROM. There are technologies which allow data stored in a PROM to be erased and new information written. In most of the available devices the erasure is done by ultraviolet light. There are other devices that can be erased electrically. Most of these devices are limited to single thousands of bits. On the high end of the spectrum are the mass-storage memories which are usually used as peripheral devices. In this category we will find tape recorders, paper tape, disks, both rigid and floppy, bubble memories, etc. In a later article all of the various competing memory technologies will be examined.

The input/output function provides the communication between the CPU and the outside world of peripheral devices, i.e., readers, punches, displays, keyboards, etc. Without some I/O function there would be no way to access the computer nor to obtain the results of a computation. The I/O function is also used to provide access to additional mass memory devices such as floppy disks, and magnetic-tape recorders. Most of the I/O peripheral devices are not hung directly onto the bus structure because they have data rate requirements much slower than the CPU and its associated memories. Instead one of the communications interface adapter chips is used. Also, since many of the peripheral devices interchange data serially (a bit at a time), rather than in parallel (8 or 16 bits at a time), some provision must be provided to convert the parallel data transfer from the CPU to a serial string at the rate required by the peripheral device.

Tying all of these functions together is the Program. It is the program which tells the computer what tasks to perform and details how each of the various functions is to be used. □

Microcomputer overview

by Carol A. Ogdin

The prospect of $25 computers captures the imagination of clever system designers. The potential uses are so far-reaching that new applications are being announced more quickly than most designers ever thought possible. Following the trend of the decades, technology will continue the downward spiral in computer cost from multi-million dollar monsters to $10,000 table-top minis to $1000 computer-on-a-card micros. The result will be to make the computer an even more important element in our daily lives. Already, specialized computers may cost under $20 in certain uses. Just as one-chip computers rival the power of the digital computers of the 1940's, the future may reduce today's large-scale data processing systems to mere hand-held devices . . . and such devices may cost a mere $20. Today's microcomputer is merely another point on a continuing trend, but this instant must be understood to be able to exploit technology now and in the future.

The potential for microcomputer applications has already outstripped even the most inventive minds. Systems designers have found more new uses for micros than any semiconductor vendor ever dreamed possible. And each of those new ideas stimulates another inventive designer . . . and the end of the computer era gets pushed further and further into the future.

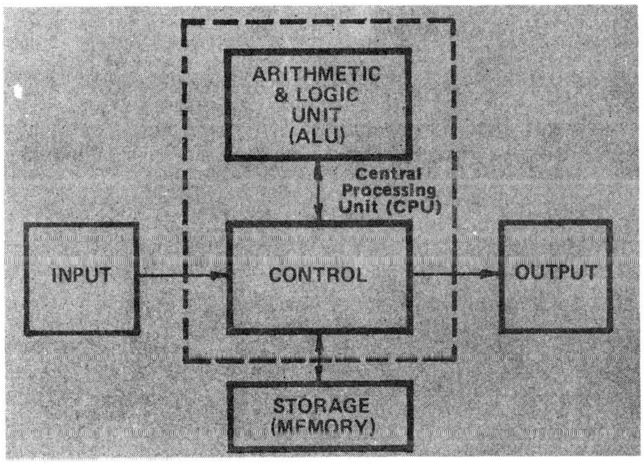

Fig. 1.1.

But what is a micro? How is it used? Is it merely a cheap replacement for a conventional computer? Can designers wait for the technology and the software support to mature? Indeed, the advent of the micro poses more questions than it answers. While new applications abound, the shape of complex questions that would have been irrelevant ten years ago is becoming clear. Will arrays of thousands of micros all connected together form the basis of architecture in the future? It is possible.

While a micro may be treated simplistically as "just another computer," it is foolhardy to slavishly retain that notion. The mind boggles at the concepts microcomputers permit designers to realize. The fact is, though, that micros are being used successfully by thousands of companies as just another system component. Those designers are finding that the micro has opened up wider opportunities for profitable ventures, but at the cost of changing traditional techniques and at the cost of learning more about the fundamentals of computers themselves.

Industry and professional periodicals now carry dozens of articles on microcomputers and their applications each month. Most of these assume the reader is knowledgeable about digital circuitry and proficient in programming. But in fact, most system designers have little direct experience with the electronics inside the hardware, and this is especially true of designers who emerge from a systems software background. These professionals are accustomed to fitting together compatible CPUs, memories, and peripherals to solve a problem. Problems that can not be solved with off-the-shelf building blocks are often deemed "unsolvable." These designers will find that some change in their behavior will be essential in the coming years.

That is what this course is all about. To be economically competitive, more and more systems will incorporate micros. System designers who understand micros now will leap far ahead of less enlightened colleagues who remain aloof from the new sources of computing power. This series will explain the background and principles needed to select and apply microprocessors and microcomputers. Our course is unique, however, in that it assumes the reader is comfortable with software and systems, but has virtually no background in digital electronics.

A MICRO DEFINED

A microcomputer looks, architecturally, like any other computer (Fig. 1.1). What distinguishes a micro from other computers is the intrinsic power inside each of the five functional boxes. It is a moving target. What large-scale computers used to do, minis now handle. Similarly, micros have begun to supplant minicomputers in many applications. Advances in semiconductor technology have made all this possible (Fig. 1.2).

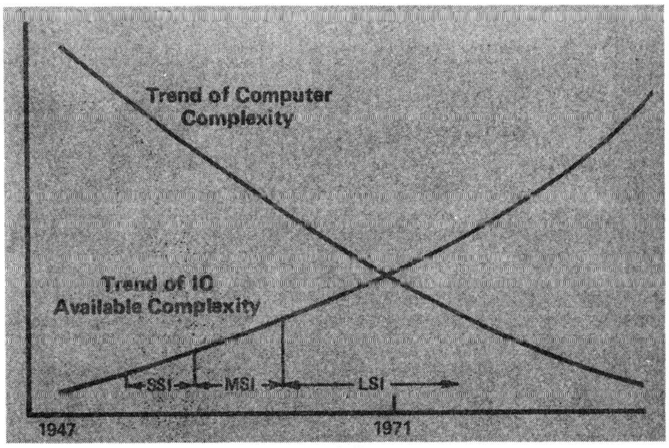

Fig. 1.2.

In the earliest days of computers, a central processor was made up of banks of thousands of vacuum tubes. Reliability was measured in mere hours between failures, and the cooling plant was often larger than the computer itself. Then, fortuitously, the transistor was invented. Compared to tubes, transistors require less power, generate almost no heat, are much smaller and more reliable. Early data processing computers incorporated thousands of them in each mainframe.

In computers of the 1950's, the transistors, diodes, resistors, capacitors, and other components were mounted on printed-circuit (PC) cards – phenolic or fiberglass cards from which copper had been selectively etched to leave patterns of wires between holes where the components were inserted. A typical 5-in. square card might have contained a dozen transistors and a hundred other parts and cost about $100. A card might have contained a single flip-flop, for example, and several thousand cards were required to build each computer.

In the early 1960's, semiconductor makers created a whole new technology. By fabricating dozens of transistors together on a single small silicon chip, using the same fabrication techniques used for single isolated transistors, a whole flip-flop could be integrated. Such integrated circuits (ICs) cost about $1 each, and computers are still built using them. Several of these ICs can be mounted on a single printed circuit card. The card, as before, may still cost $100, but it may now contain all the logic necessary for the arithmetic-logic unit of a CPU.

Soon, improved fabrication processes enabled even more complex circuits to be created in a single IC. While the earliest devices had a complexity equivalent to about ten transistors, the new circuits had complexities on the order of 100 to 1000 transistors. The new technology was called medium scale integration (MSI), and the older technology was labelled small-scale integration (SSI). Now, the complexity of a computer's ALU could be reduced to a mere handful of ICs.

Many of today's minicomputers are manufactured on a single printed circuit card with a hundred or so MSI circuits. The CPU may cost a few thousand dollars, but only part of that cost can be attributed to parts and manufacturing. Support software and documentation account for most of the sale price.

Simultaneously with the developments in semiconductors, computer architects were showing that computers no longer had to be complex. By stripping out the logic required in floating-point arithmetic, sophisticated input/output control schemes, and other little-used features, engineers could design simpler and simpler computers. These two trends merged in 1970.

Not content to stop on the achievements of MSI, semiconductor companies started producing large scale integrated (LSI) circuits, with complexities in excess of 1000 transistors. The simplest computer required about that many. In 1971, Intel Corp. delivered the first microprocessor, the 4004. All the logic to implement the CPU of a tiny computer was put onto a single silicon chip less than 1/4-in. square. It now sells for $5. That design was soon followed by another Intel product, the 8008, which boasted eight-bit wide registers and the ability to refer to 16K bytes of memory.

These early devices were slow and limited, but they were useful computers; several tens of thousands of them are still shipped each year. More recent products, such as the popular 8080, have overshadowed these early versions, however.

When the central processing unit (CPU) of a computer is implemented in a single, or very small number of, integrated circuits, we call it a *microprocessor.* When a computer incorporates a microprocessor as its major component, the resulting configuration is called a *microcomputer.* When the entire computer, including CPU, memory and input/output capability, is incorporated into a single IC, we also call that configuration a microcomputer. To distinguish between the two microcomputer types, we call the latter a *one-chip microcomputer.*

WHY USE A MICRO?

If micros are merely computers on a chip or two, why all the fuss? Because the total cost of the parts to build a very complex computer can be very little indeed. In fact, in many applications, the cost of peripheral devices far outweigh the cost of the computer and its memory. Thus, for those applications that require few expensive peripherals, the cost of computation can be very small, and this, in turn, opens the door for an entirely new class of low-cost computer applications. Today, entire computers are being installed in microwave ovens, telephones, and gas pumps, and whole new markets are opening up for micro-based products such as consumer games.

At the same time, traditional applications can be handled less expensively and more reliably. As a result, micros are found in transaction terminals, process control interfaces, and new peripheral device controllers in large computer systems. The concept of distributed computing is spurred by the inexpensive availability of minis and micros – indeed, many of the less expensive minis take advantage of micro technology internally.

Cost is the final determinant in the choice of a micro, and in many applications, the micro is *not* the lowest cost alternative. If the application is a traditional bookkeeping job with no novel peripheral devices to be handled, the microcomputer may be a poor choice. New software will be required and commonplace interfaces developed to support such an accounting system. These development costs can be so large as to dominate the entire system cost. Although the micro looks cheap, especially when the CPUs cost $25 each, it can be one of the most expensive ways to go. The use of a micro is justified only if the development expense can be amortized over a large number of units, or if the application requires unique features inherent in microcomputers.

Successful applications abound:

- Several telephone equipment suppliers have created PABXs around micros. The systems are more reliable, easier to maintain, easier to upgrade, and yet cheaper than competitive equipment that are based on more traditional ICs.
- Micros have been used as sophisticated controllers in applications that range from outer space to the ocean bottom. In one case, a micro controls a data collection buoy that records water flow, temperature, and pollution, and then radios that data to a satellite.
- Most of the new self-service gasoline pumps are microcomputer controlled. By replacing mechanical counters, the product's longevity, reliability, and durability have all been increased.
- The majority of computer terminals introduced in recent months include a microcomputer as an internal controller. In addition to reducing costs by replacing all the traditional logic with a single computer, the terminals can be custom programmed to have unique features.
- While minis have been used to off-load the "front-end" communications tasks on large centralized computer systems, micros, in turn, are being used to off-load the detailed communications chores from the mini so that it can handle more traffic. This detailed communications handling is now performed by a phalanx of micros, each handling one channel.
- Distributed systems with computers controlling discrete parts of a manufacturing or refining installation are popular, replacing racks full of electromechanical logic and increasing reliability and ease of maintenance.

WILL MICROS DOOM THE MAXI?

Micros are much too small for many applications, such as an airline reservation system that requires multiple access to a common data base. These require the facilities of a large centralized system. However, the terminals of such systems will eventually incorporate micros, as will communications controllers, disk file managers, and operator's console. In sum, the impact of micros on the big machines, especially large centralized computer systems, is that large systems will decline in number but increase in power.

Minicomputers will not be hurt at all. In fact, mini usage should increase as micros are installed in distributed sys-

SYSTEMS

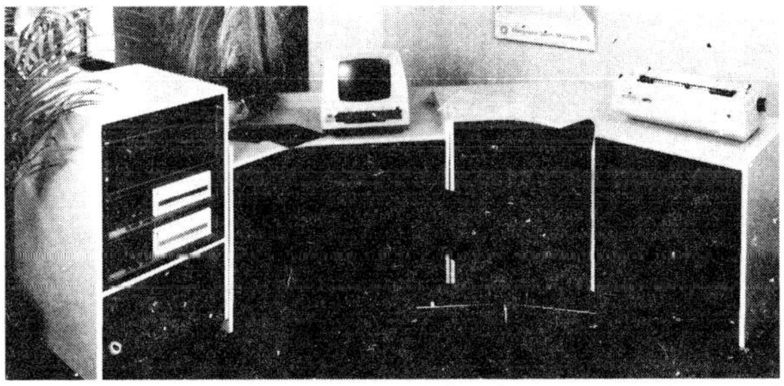

DEVELOPMENT SYSTEMS

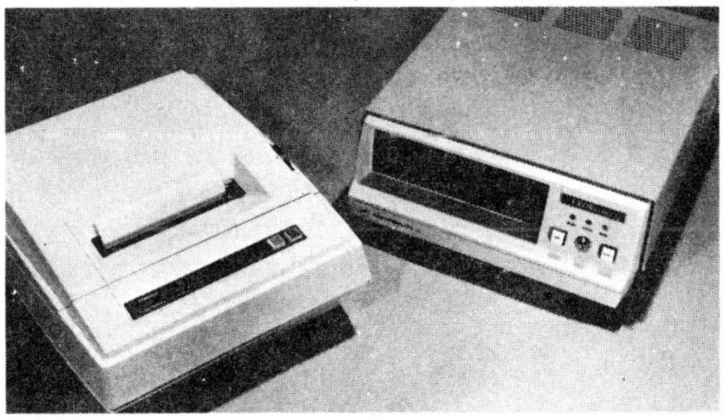

SBC's

KITS

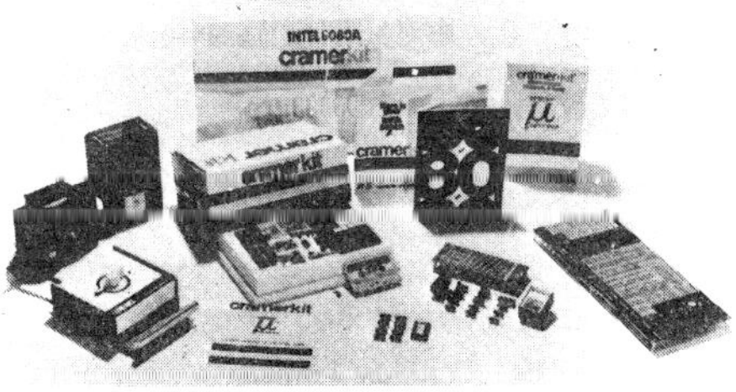

CHIPS

CUSTOM

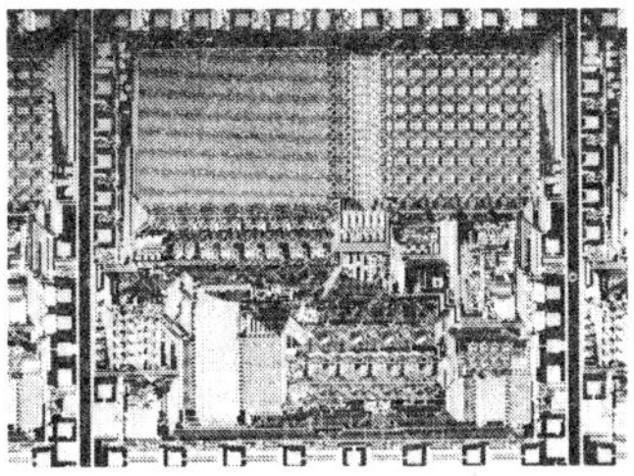

tems. The mini will tend to act as a system or network controller, with micros out at the ends of the "tentacles" of the net. In time, however, there will be trend away from putting all software on one large central computer.

MORE THAN A CHIP

Trade literature tends to treat the individual microprocessor IC as *the* major component. The microprocessor itself, however, represents but a small part of the system. In most configurations, the CPU chip represents less than 10 percent of the total cost. The rest is in memory and interface electronics to get inputs and produce outputs. That, in turn, may be less than half the total installed cost by the time power supplies, packaging, and cooling are added to the list. Often, a $25 CPU chip is the heart of a $1000 computer subsystem.

The microcomputer media available include (Fig. 1.3):

1. Prefabricated microcomputers, configured much like minicomputers that have their power, packaging, and cooling pre-installed. Examples include the PCC Altair 8800b and DEC's PDP-11/05.

2. Development systems, converted to end-application use, like Motorola's EXORciser, or Intel's MDS 800.

3. Single-board computers (SBCs), or modular card sets, from which you can configure virtually any size computer. The DEC LSI-11, Intel SBC 80 series, or Pro-Log's PLS series of cards are typical products.

4. Kits, from which custom designs can be adapted. Kits are available from Heathkit, semiconductor makers, and electronic parts distributors.

5. Custom designs, based on popular microprocessors such as the 8080A or 6800.

6. Custom, high-volume, one-chip microcomputer systems – Fairchild's F8 or Texas Instruments' TMS 1000 series, for example – which have program, data storage, input and output on one or two chips, along with the CPU.

Engineers are naturally inclined to want to design a unique computer. For certain applications, that may be the best choice. But for a person with limited experience or during initial prototype stages, it may not be the wisest move.

One popular tool is the prototype microcomputer system that is specifically designed to support software and hardware development efforts like the Intel MDS 800, Motorola EXORciser, and Rockwell Assemulators. Costs range from $3500 to $20,000, depending on peripherals.

Most semiconductor companies are in the low-end mini business with their proprietary lines of single board computers and other card sets. These prototyping systems usually are sold separately, and are especially useful if production volumes are low. The Intel SBC-80/10 is probably the most popular of these computers with several smaller companies, such as Pro-Log and muPro, all having viable offerings.

Kits are an inexpensive way to get started in microcomputers, but they do require some skill with electronics. While the more sophisticated kits, because of their documentation, can be built by a user with little electronics background, maintenance may be nearly impossible to buy. If the application calls for some unique power or space requirements, a kit is often the way to solve the problem quickly. Starting with a schematic that is known to work, an experienced digital designer can modify the design to

◀ *Fig. 1.3. Microcomputer media available to the system designer range from custom designed processor chips to full-blown microcomputer systems. The products illustrated here are: (from bottom to top) the Texas Instruments TMS1000 processor chip; the Intel 8080A processor in a 40-pin DIP; the Cramer Electronics 8080A microcomputer kit; the Intel SBC-80 single board microcomputer; the Motorola EXORciser microcomputer development system; and the Pertec Computer Corp. Altair microcomputer system.*

suit specific needs, then use the parts within the kit to fabricate the product.

The most exotic approach, of course, is to design your own computer. There have been so many successful designs marketed and published, however, that few applications are really unique enough to warrant the extra engineering expense. An organization planning its first microcomputer application probably should not seriously consider this alternative. It is much better to use a set of prototyping cards to prove that the software and hardware first can be made to work, then redesign the CPU, memory and input/output interfaces to reduce the manufacturing cost. Furthermore, development of a unique computer solely for economic reasons can not usually be justified below production quantities of about 250. As semiconductor prices continue to fall, that quantity level will rise.

Only the very highest volume users of micros are in a position to take advantage of custom-made, one- or two-chip microcomputers because of the added development cost that must be passed along that is acceptable if amortized across thousands and thousands of units, but not acceptable if applied to a couple of hundred units. Some semiconductor vendors will not even accept orders for less than 1000 pieces because of the expensive fabrication steps required to permanently "etch" the program into the chips.

The choice among these different media that can be used must be based on economic considerations including both development and total manufacturing costs. Systems designers with a background in large-scale computers or minis tend to minimize development costs out of habit. In micros, however, the prospect of saving a few dollars worth of parts in each of hundreds or thousands of units can often justify significant increases in development budget to reap those savings.

SKILLS REQUIRED

Designers of mini-micro systems are becoming aware of their background limitations. The digital designers are finding that software is an indispensible tool, and the programmers are learning that lack of knowledge in electronics may be disastrous to successful project realization. There are several books and numerous magazine articles designed to teach programming skills to digital designers (the principles are very similar to other kinds of logic design), but there are very few "short courses" in digital electronics for programmers and analysts, outside the formal electrical engineering curricula. This is unfortunate, because the separation between successful and unsuccessful micro projects often depends on the clever selection of the hardware/software boundary. When individuals remain content with their own skills and refuse to learn new ones, they tend to be myopic and protective of their designs. Thus, a digital designer without programming experience may tend to design circuitry using a minimum number of parts, while a software designer may tend to overdesign software without an appreciation of the essential hardware features. This is why microcomputer designers having both hardware and software knowledge are in great demand today. Prudent managers look to experienced minicomputers interface designers with both hardware and software skills as the pool of future micro designers.

Without a complete laboratory that may cost several tens of thousands of dollars, these skills can not be effectively harnessed. Since there are few off-the-shelf interfaces between common micros and popular peripherals, some electronic development will almost always be needed. If neither the equipment, nor the people with the skills are available, the first design should probably be sent outside to a competent consultant or design group. Look for a designer with experience in hardware and software in this application area, rather than one with just any kind of micro design background. ■

Computer architecture

by Carol A. Ogdin

System designers have tended to remain aloof from the detailed workings of digital computers, leaving this aspect of system design to electrical engineers. Management has perpetuated the dichotomy by encouraging the use of high-level languages and other productivity tools to minimize development costs.

The advent of microcomputers, however, demands a new attitude toward hardware. The economics of many micro applications, for example, are such as to make the practice of "bit fiddling" an essential activity during system development.

Traditionally, introductory literature on computers has taken great pains to avoid discussions of their internal operations, especially those of the registers and buses. But to be able to exploit the novel features of microcomputers, the system designer must fully understand their principles of operation. Unlike large-scale computers, which operate with standard peripherals and hence do not require special interfaces, most microcomputers are used in applications where some custom interface circuitry design is essential. Hence, the system designer who can not communicate effectively with the electronics designer, will not be able to make significant contributions to the application's development.

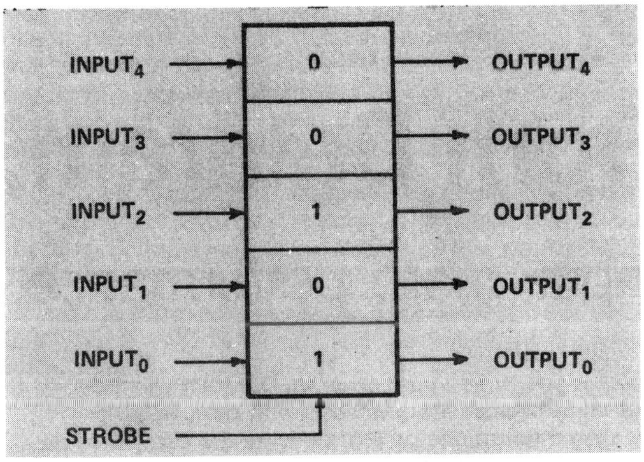

Fig. 2.1.

UNDERSTANDING NEW COMPUTERS

Every designer has been faced at one time or another with the problem of trying to understand how a new computer works. With micros, this problem is exacerbated because there are so many different types to choose from, and the number is increasing constantly.

In analyzing a new computer, most designers begin by studying the reference manual to see what instructions and registers are available and how they operate. Few designers, however, look past the "programmer's registers" that are used to hold data in between instruction executions. By looking for the registers that are used in program *control,* the designer can find new features, many of which require more than one instruction to invoke and are not, therefore, usually described in the reference manual itself.

REGISTERS AS BUILDING BLOCKS

A *register* can be thought of as a "box" to store data. An idealized register is shown in Fig. 2.1. It consists of some medium to store one or more bits of data, an input route, output route, and a control signal to specify when the register is to be loaded from the input. In modern digital computers, each register bit-cell is composed of electronic or magnetic circuitry that can "capture" and retain the Boolean states, one or zero. The register inputs and outputs are wires that are at one of two voltage levels; usually, the higher voltage level signifies the logical *one* state.

Every computer is made up of a set of registers, and of pathways between the registers. A typical example is shown

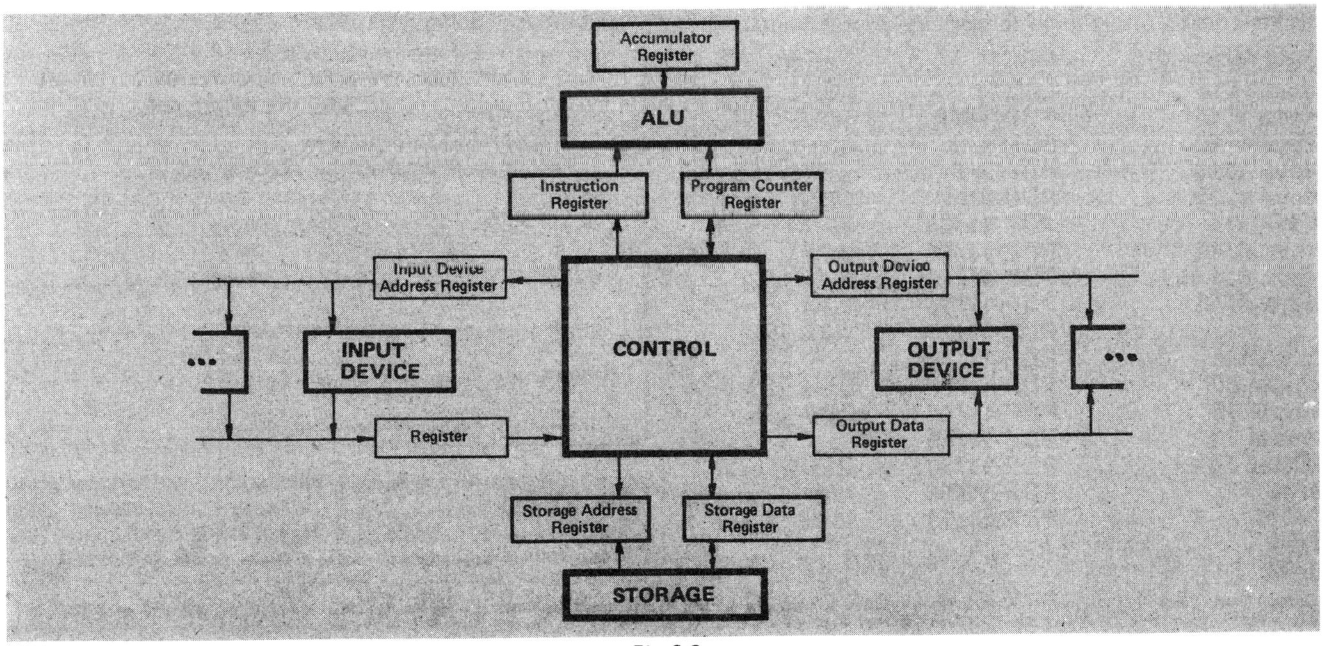

Fig. 2.2.

in Fig. 2.2. This basic model illustrates precisely how the various operations in a computer's repertoire are carried out. Instructions are executed by transferring data from one register into another. The control of register transfers is the function of the control section of the central processing unit. Indeed, the internal operation of the control section, itself, consists of even more detailed sequential register transfers.

In a contemporary computer, instructions are alternately fetched from central storage and executed. The fetch portion of the instruction cycle is a good example of register transfer principles at work.

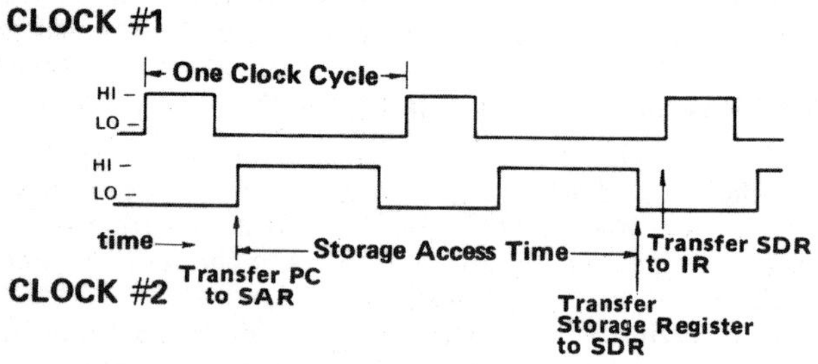

Fig. 2.3.

At the start of the instruction cycle, the control section (see Fig. 2.2) transfers the address of the next instruction from the program counter register to the storage address register. The storage address register is then fed through a complex set of address decoding logic to produce a single control signal to the memory register that contains the next instruction. The instruction is then transferred from memory into the storage data register (SDR). Finally, the control section transfers the instruction from the SDR into the instruction register. Now, the control unit enters into the execute phase of the instruction cycle, during which yet another series of register transfers carries out the instruction.

Register transfers take place over time. It is imperative that the source and destination registers coordinate the times at which they send and receive data to prevent erroneous transfers. All this coordination is performed by the master clock signals that are distributed throughout the computer. (A clock is an electronic circuit that produces one or more square waves like those shown in Fig. 2.3.) Although a system designer need not know in detail how clock signals relate to each other, he should at least know how the relationships can be varied to achieve cost-effective memory and input/output interfaces. The time between the instant the program counter is strobed into the storage address register, and the instant the data in the storage data register is transferred into the instruction register, for example, must be greater than the access time of the storage subsystem. By increasing this interval the designer can use slower and hence less expensive memories, but at the penalty of a reduction in the throughput.

The designer should also know something about how the master clock, itself, is controlled, since the amount of "jitter" in timing computations done in software can be directly affected by the precision of the clock's reference. Most clocks are precisely controlled at some fixed-frequency by a quartz crystal. However, in many microcomputer applications, the clock is controlled by a less-expensive, but much less precise, resistor-capacitor timing circuit. As a result, execution time may vary by as much as 20 percent from the nominal rate. Virtually all prefabricated microcomputers and single board computers employ crystal controlled clocks. Many computer-controlled games, on the other hand, employ simple resistor-capacitor timing circuits instead. Such devices do not require precise timing, and the elimination of the expensive crystal leads to tremendous cost savings when the games are mass-produced.

TYPICAL REGISTERS

Most computers provide a set of registers to be used by the programmer. Some are used for data manipulation; others are devoted to the control of the program itself. The registers available on the 8080, today's most popular microprocessor, and on the 6800, its nearest competitor, are

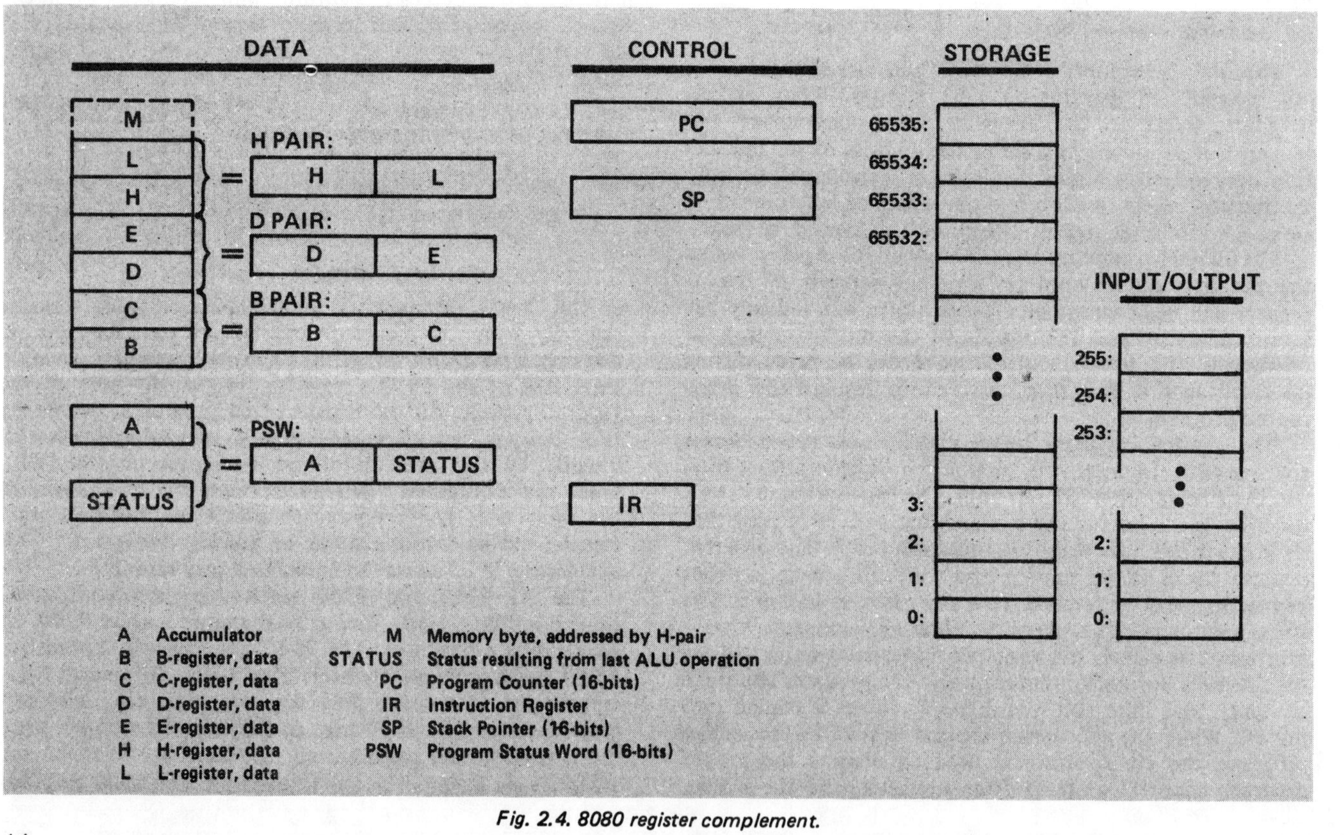

Fig. 2.4. 8080 register complement.

listed in Figs. 2.4 and 2.5, respectively. There are numerous subtle differences between these computers, even though each operates on eight-bit data words and can access 64K bytes of memory. The easiest way to distinguish between the different services each offers is to study the complement of registers available, and the kinds of transfers allowed between them.

The 8080 belongs to the one-address architectural class of microcomputers. Most instructions that refer to memory refer to a single location. In instructions that refer to two operands, the other operand is one of eight eight-bit data registers, designated A, B, C, D, E, H, L, and M, respectively. (Some instructions assume that one operand is in the A-register, which is also called the accumulator, and hence do not explicitly specify a register.)

Pairs of these eight-bit data registers are treated as sixteen-bit registers by certain instructions. The B- and C-registers are called the B-pair; the D- and E-registers, the D-pair; and the H- and L-registers, the H-pair. These three sixteen-bit registers are not separate registers, but are merely alternate ways of referring to the same data.

A typical 40-pin IC, the Intel 8085 with protective cap removed and the circuit inside exposed. (Intel Corp.)

The eighth register in the 8080 set, the M-register is not actually a separate, physical register. When an instruction refers to the M-register, the contents of the H- and L-registers are treated as the address of the instruction operand. The reason for using a register pair to hold the indirect memory address is that memory may consist of up to 65,536 bytes, and that requires a sixteen-bit address.

The 8080 also employs a special sixteen-bit register, called the program status word (PSW), that consists of the A-register and eight status bits. These status bits indicate the interrupt status and the results of the most recent ALU operation. The program status word can be saved during interrupt service and then restored to resume the interrupted program.

The control registers of the 8080 are the program counter (PC, 16 bits), the instruction register (IR, 8 bits) and the stack pointer (SP, 16 bits). The instruction register's function needs no further explanation, except to note that all instructions have eight-bit operation codes. The program counter needs to be sixteen bits wide, of course, so that instructions can be fetched from any memory location. The stack pointer is also a memory referencing register. When a subroutine is called, the next two bytes below the address specified by the stack pointer receive the program counter's contents, and then the subroutine's address is copied into the PC. When the subroutine returns control to the calling program, the stackpointer is used to retrieve the proper program counter contents from memory, and the calling program then resumes execution.

The input/output register file is an array of 256 bytes, each of which may be made up of a set of wires for making external connections. Like memory locations, these registers need not all be installed in a given configuration.

The Motorola 6800 has a smaller register complement (Fig. 2.5) than does the 8080, but it employs a more elaborate addressing scheme. The data registers include two accumulators, but no temporary data storage registers. The program counter, stack pointer, and instruction register are all conventional like the 8080's. The 6800's index register (XR), however, does deserve special mention. Although the 8080's sixteen-bit register pairs (BC, DE, and HL) do permit references to storage, they are not true index registers. To access an adjacent storage location, the register holding the storage address must be modified. In the 6800, on the other hand, the index register is added to the address portion of an instruction to yield an effective memory address. Thus, different storage areas can be referred to without having to modify the addresses in registers.

The 6800 differs from the 8080 in another way, too. There are no input/output instructions, so there is no separately addressed suite of I/O data registers. In the 6800 architecture, I/O is performed through memory locations in a fashion similar to that on the PDP-11. Since the total number of memory locations reserved for I/O is small, it has negligible impact on storage capacity. In fact, in many 8080 designs, the input/output instructions are ignored in favor of "memory-mapped" I/O.

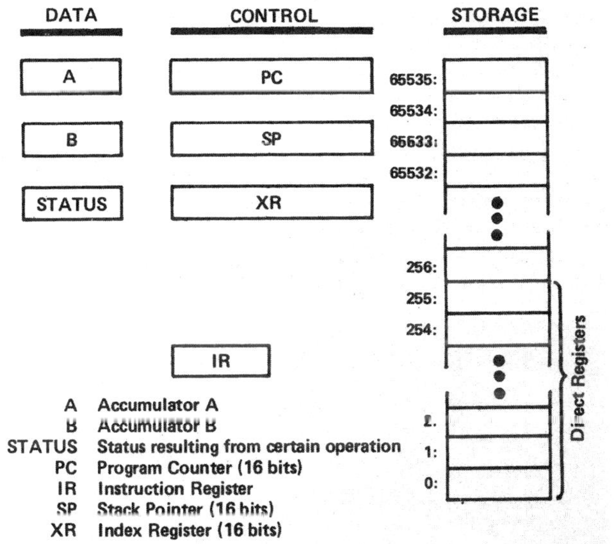

Fig. 2.5. 6800 register complement.

The Texas Instruments 9900 microcomputer departs radically from the kinds of architecture described above. For one, it is a 16-bit rather than an 8-bit computer. In addition, few of the 9900's registers are actually part of the CPU chip itself. All the registers that programs operate on (Fig. 2.6) are located in main storage and are addressed indirectly by the contents of the workspace pointer (WP). Since the workspace pointer's contents can be changed at the same time the program counter's are, both the subroutine and its data space can be quickly "swapped." This enables the 9900 to service interrupts very rapidly.

The TI 9940 and 9980 single-chip microcomputers, though architecturally similar to the more mature 9900, do have subtle differences. The 9940, for example, has only a 13-bit wide program counter. The major difference, however, is the convention used for communicating with off-chip memory. The 9940 uses an I/O-oriented scheme, since most applications require only the on-board EPROM and RAM arrays included in the IC package. The 9900 employs a sixteen-bit wide data bus, and a fifteen-bit address bus;

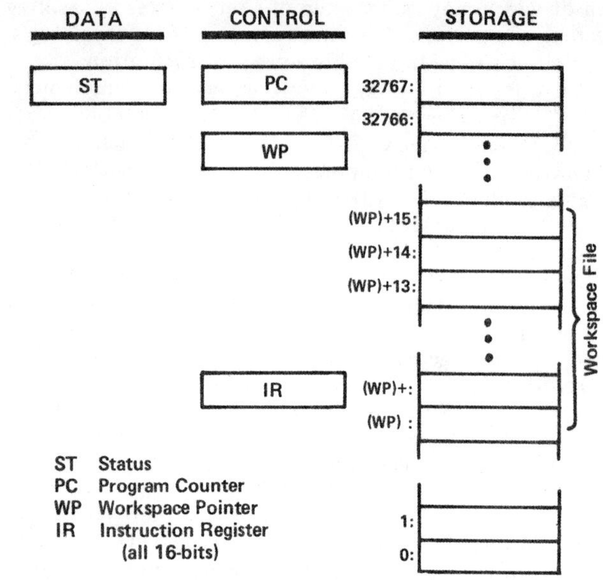

Fig. 2.6. 9900 register complement.

these two buses alone account for 31 of the 64 pins on the 9900 IC. The 9980 by multiplexing the sixteen-bit data words on an eight-bit bus, sacrifices speed for a reduction in package size. And although the 9980 has a sixteen-bit program counter, only fourteen of those bits are sent out on the address bus. As a result, the entire 9980 is contained in a more familiar 40-pin package.

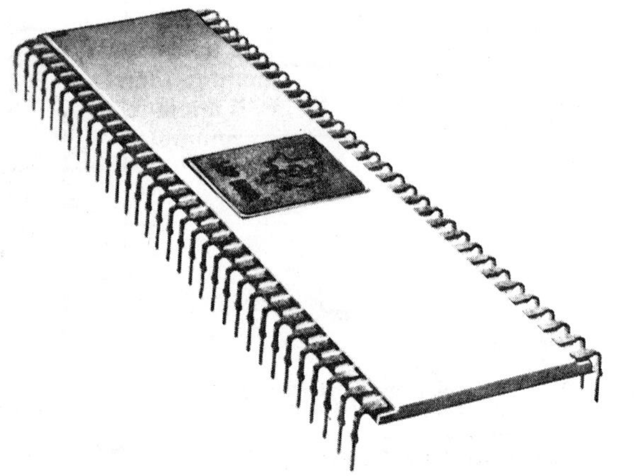

A 64-pin package with pins spaced in two rows, 0.6" apart. The TI 9900.

ADDRESSING SCHEMES

Another important difference among computers that register transfer models reveal is the difference in the addressing modes used. Each addressing mode can be described as a sequence of register transfers. Indirect addressing of memory via the 8080's H- and L-register pair, for example, involves referring to the nonexistent M-register. This in turn causes the contents of the H- and L-registers to be sent to the storage address register in the storage subsystem. Similarly, when indexing is used to refer to memory on the 6800, the second byte of the instruction is added to the contents of the index register (XR), and the sum is then sent to the storage address register. When an addressing mode seems particularly strange on a new computer, working out the register transfers required to implement it is usually the best approach to understanding it.

The various addressing schemes used on the 8080 and the 6800 are shown in Fig. 2.7. Normal direct addressing requires that instructions be three bytes long. The second and third bytes of the instruction supply the full sixteen-bit ad-

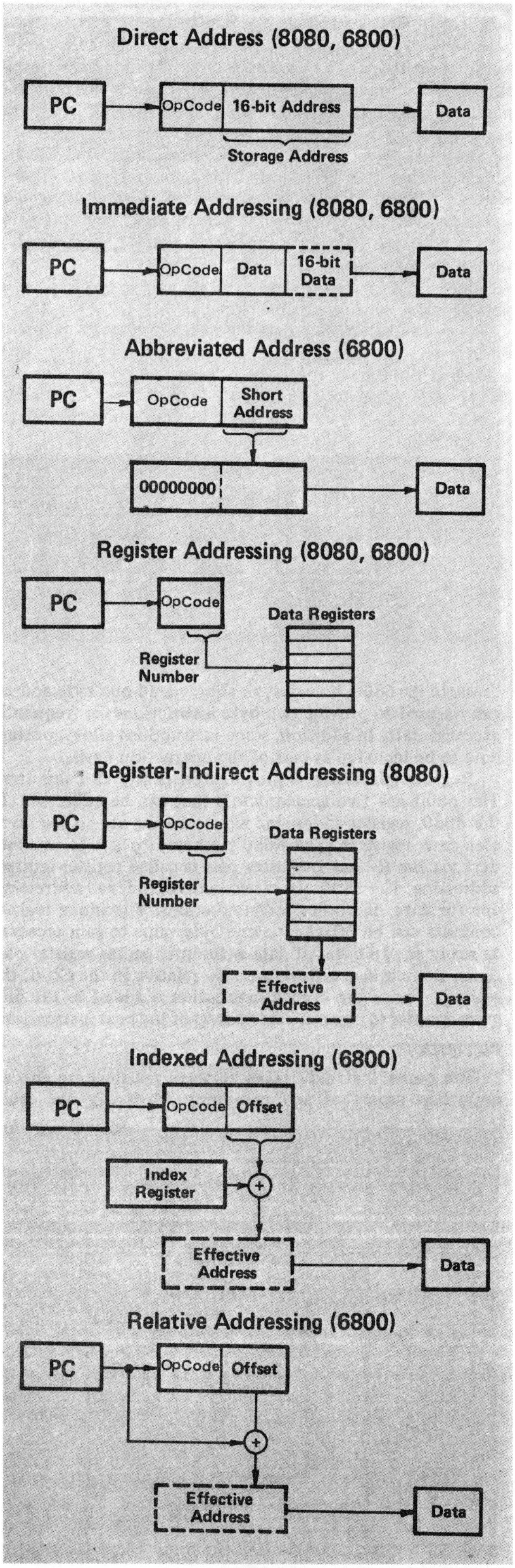

Fig. 2.7.

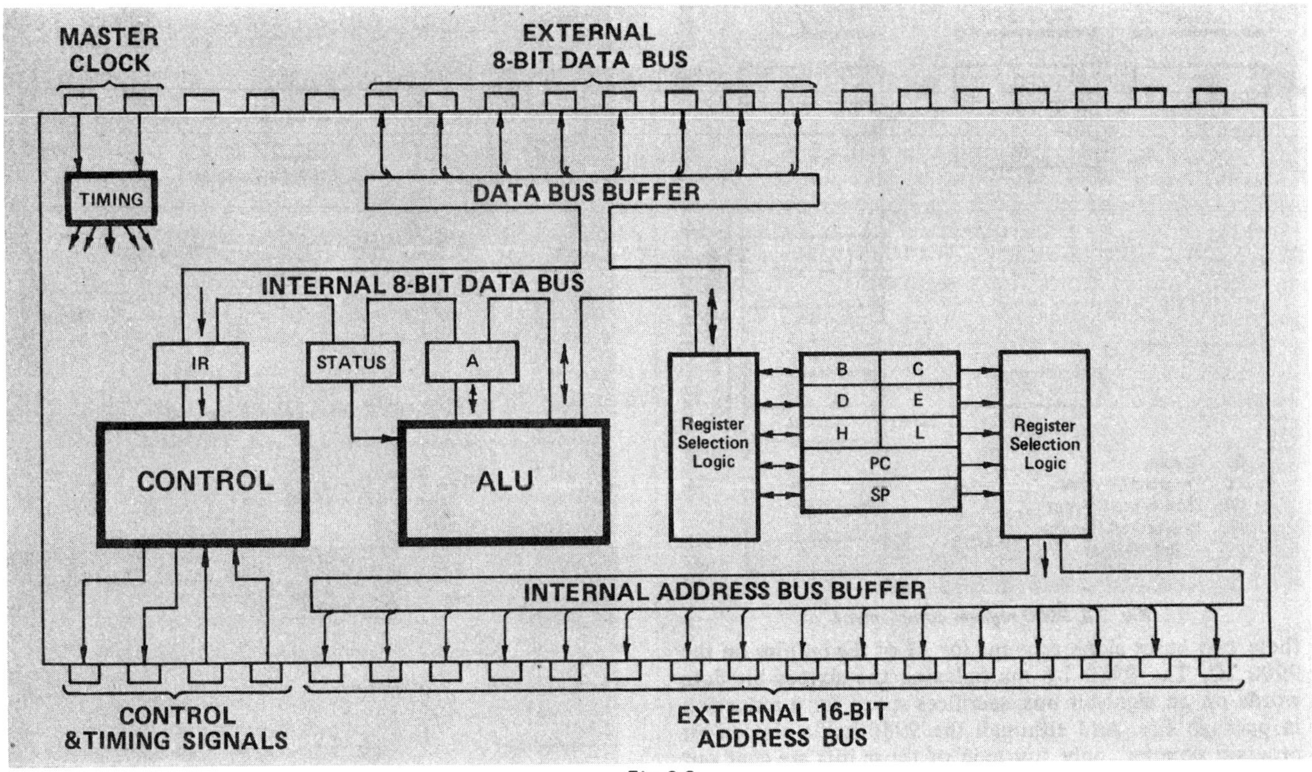

Fig. 2.8.

dress. In the 6800, however, an abbreviated one byte address can be used to provide two-byte instructions for frequently accessed data. In addition, some instructions allow constant data to be included as part of the instruction itself.

Register addressing is provided on nearly all computers. The 6800 has two accumulators that can be addressed. In the 8080, register addressing selects among one of the seven real data registers. The 8080's scheme to get at memory data via the H- and L-register pair is called register-indirect addressing. The 6800 offers two kinds of indexed addressing, one for data, the other for instructions. The index register contents can be offset by a one-byte value to gain access to as many as 256 bytes of data without changing register contents. Branch instructions are also relative in the 6800: the second byte of the branch instruction is added to the program counter to compute the address of the next instruction.

PATHWAYS

The paths that data takes between registers are also an important aspect of any computer. Obviously one could design a system with wires between each pair of registers that need to communicate. However, the number of such pathways would be astronomical. Real estate on the 1/4-inch square piece of silicon that holds the typical microprocessor is a valuable commodity; therefore, the space occupied by inter-register wires is minimized by using a bus scheme (Fig. 2.8). Each register communicates with an internal bidirectional bus. At any given moment, only one register is sending information on the bus, and usually only one register is receiving it. At the end of the transfer period, the data that was in the source register will have been copied into the destination register.

All this detailed internal operation takes place in less than a microsecond. Using an external two-phase clock and the contents of the instruction register, the various pathways to the registers are opened and shut in precise sequence to achieve the desired data transfer.

There are three main external communications pathways on a microcomputer: the address, data, and control buses (Fig. 2.9). The address bus is used to select the memory or I/O registers involved in a register transfer. The transfer itself takes place along the data bus. The control bus carries signals that specify the direction in which the data is to be transferred (to or from memory, for example) and the times at which to start and stop a transfer.

In most microcomputers, the address bus is sixteen bits wide to accommodate a 64K-byte memory address space.

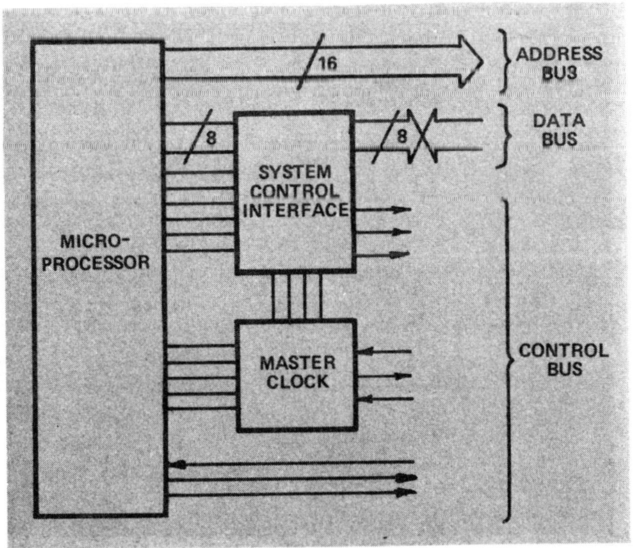

Fig. 2.9.

Table 2.1.
Typical signals found on microcomputer control buses.

MEMR	specifies a memory read operation
MEMW	specifies a memory write operation
INT	notifies CPU of pending interrupt
INTA	acknowledges interrupt to CPU
DMAREQ	requests access to memory for DMA
DMAOK	notifies controller that DMA is permitted
PAUSE	notifies CPU that memory or I/O is not yet finished
HALT	notifies system that CPU has halted
RESET	resets all control registers to zero

Table 2.III.
Some selected register transfers for the 8080.

SOURCE REGISTER \ DESTINATION REGISTER	A	B	C	D	...	DE	HL	SP	PC
A		MOV B,A	MOV C,A	MOV D,A	...	—	—	—	—
B	MOV A,B		MOV C,B	MOV D,B		—	—	—	—
C	MOV A,C	MOV C,B		MOV D,C		—	—	—	—
D	MOV A,D	MOV B,D	MOV C,D			—	—	—	—
⋮			⋮		⋮			⋮	
DE	—	—	—	—			XCHG	XCHG SPHL XCHG	XCHG PCHL XCHG
HL	—	—	—	—	...	XCHG		SPHL	PCHL
SP	—	—	—	—		XCHG LXI H,0 DAD SP XCHG	LXI H,0 DAD SP		LXI H,0 DAD SP PCHL
PC	—	—	—	—	...	CALL $+3 POP D	CALL $+3 POP H	CALL $+3 POP H SPHL	

The data bus is as wide as the basic word length of the computer. Thus, eight-bit micros, like the 8080 and the 6800, employ eight-bit wide data buses, and sixteen-bit micros, like the TI TMS9900, use a sixteen-bit data bus.

When you consider how greatly micros differ in their architectures, it is amazing how similar their control buses tend to be. The control bus signals listed in Table 2.I, for example, are used in virtually every microcomputer system.

ANALYZING THE CPU

All computers operate alike, but this does not seem to make learning a new computer any less of a chore. Nonetheless, to evaluate candidate microprocessors for a particular job, the designer must first understand how they operate, and the best approach to this task is to go about it systematically. First, make up a table listing all of the computer's instructions. Fortunately, most micros have eight-bit operation codes, so the table can be short. A section of such a table for the F8 microprocessor is shown in Table 2.II. It relates the various eight-bit F8 operation codes to their assembly language representations. In most cases, the programmer will note some regularity in the table, such as in column 3 in Table 2.II. Such regularity can reveal the power of the various instructions. Table 2.II, for example, reveals that the "DS" instruction on the F8 is very powerful because the operation code itself incorporates some of the address or data bits.

Table 2.II.
Part of an operation code table for the Fairchild/Mostek F8.

Least significant four bits \ Most significant four bits of OpCode	0	1	2	3	4	5 ...
0	LR A,KU	LR DC,H	LI ii	DS 0	LR A,0	LR 0,A
1	LR A,KL	LR H,DC	NI ii	DS 1	LR A,1	LR 1,A ...
2	LR A,QU	SR 1	OI ii	DS 2	LR A,2	LR 2,A
3	LR A,QL	SL 1	XI ii	DS 3	LR A,3	⋮
4	LR KU,A	SR 4	AI ii	DS 4	⋮	
5	LR KL,A	SL 4	CI ii	⋮		
6	LR QU,A	LM	IN aa			
7	LR QL,A	ST	—			
8	LR K,P	COM	PI aaaa			
9	LR P,K	LNK	DC iiii			
A	LR A,IS	DI	NOP			
B	LR IS,A	EI	⋮			
C	PK	POP				
D	LR PO,Q	⋮				

Next, create a table summarizing the register transfers possible on the computer being analyzed. Table 2.III gives such a summary for the 8080. Along each axis, the table lists all the registers to which the programmer may have access. Each entry in the table lists the instruction or sequence of instructions that will transfer data from the specified source register to the specified destination register. Here again, such a table can show up capabilities and deficiencies in the computer's architecture. The 8080, for example, lacks an instruction to transfer the stack pointer into the H- and L-register pair so that the stack address can be operated upon. A two instruction sequence, however, can accomplish the transfer, as shown in the shaded block in Table 2.III. The designer may, in fact, never need to transfer data in this particular sequence. But the exercise of working out such examples helps one to understand a new computer.

Some transfers that seem attractive may not be possible even with multi-instruction sequences. Usually this is true, if the source and destination register are unequal in size. On the other hand, the designer may have left out some capability. In the 6800, for example, the index register can not be loaded from another register – only from memory, a fact you will not discover until after programming has begun, unless, of course, you have previously made and studied a register transfer table. ■

Systems-on-a-chip

Reprinted with permission from *Mini-Micro Systems*, May 1976.

The revolution in full flower

by Dan M. Bowers

In our Technology Profile on Microprocessors and Minicomputers, January and February of 1975, we likened the present time period to the era a dozen years ago when (relatively) inexpensive, fast, I/O oriented minicomputers appeared on the scene and revolutionized our industry, wiping out and creating whole subindustries, such as digital logic modules and minicomputer systems houses, in the process. We predicted (as indeed, we have been predicting since mid-1973) a period of violent and traumatic upset during 1975-1977, a period which will offer more business opportunities than at any time since the mid-1960s.

In this Technology Profile we revisit the revolution to find it in full flower. We shall examine the effects thus far upon the various parts of our industry, study the options now available to the user, and, as usual, predict where the revolution will lead, based on the more specific insight which another year has made available to us.

The computer-on-a-chip is at the heart of the new revolution, but we are now seeing many more systems on the chip than just the computer – memories, modems, I/O units, A-D and D-A. We therefore have a revolution due to the *System-on-a-Chip,* hence the general title of this Profile.

The scope of the revolution is unlimited; however, we shall limit our Profile to the areas which are currently experiencing the greatest impact (mini/microcomputers, peripheral equipment, communications, storage), and the systems-on-a-chip that are at the heart of the revolution (microprocessors, modems-on-a-chip, ROMs, RAMs, D-A and A-D, I/O adapters, the CCD).

MICROPROCESSORS ARE EVERYWHERE

Before the advent of the microprocessor, the programmed logic array parade (PLA), which was a one-chip, complex, logic unit, was used in some digital systems to replace acres of discret logic. Also, the read-only memory (ROM) began to be used more than a decade ago as a mechanism for replacing large amounts of sequential logic circuitry. The concept now known as ROM-control was known a decade ago as firmware, and had its real beginnings with the first introduction of IBM's System/360 in 1964. There is nothing really dramatically new about present systems, except the considerably greater number of circuits which can be placed on a single monolithic chip.

We observed last year that the primary impact of microprocessors, RAMs and ROMs, etc., is not in the low-cost of replacement of standard hardware, but in the new methods of operation which they make possible, such as super-intelligent-terminals, peripherals-with-a-processor, intelligent modems, intelligent instruments,etc. Distributed intelligence is the new watchword, centralized processing is on the way out. We envision entire networks of communications devices, terminals, peripheral equipment, etc., without the presence of a central processor in the usual sense: microcomputers in each of the peripheral equipments will perform, in a dispersed manner, the functions now allocated to the central computer. Modular central processors, modular programs which can be executed in any of many different subprocessors, and many other new ways of processing are being developed, and an entire new set of hardware tools is being presented to us, and the old software, systems, procedures, etc., are fast becoming obsolete.

Last year we observed that the first equipment manufacturers to take advantage of the microprocessor's capability were in the instrument field; intelligent, microprocessor-controlled instruments were commonly available a year and a half ago. In the past year we have seen the emergence of microprocessor-controlled printers, terminals, and disk controllers; remote control of traffic signals, remote and unattended communications repeaters, the "intelligent disk" – in short any function which was previously performed by TTL logic can be performed by the microprocessor. It is strictly an economic tradeoff to determine whether the cost is less using the microprocessor, and this is usually determined by the complexity of the function to be performed, and the number of TTL chips that would have been used to perform it. In the case of the microprocessor controlled printer, for example, the microprocessor is used for such functions as control of chains, synchronization of printed characters with the rotation of the chain, code conversion, input/output control, etc.

These applications are entirely separate from the use of the microprocessor as a computer in the conventional sense. There is clearly much activity in that direction as well, and the microcomputer, which is a combination of the microprocessor, memory and I/O chips to produce a complete processor equivalent to the minicomputer that we have been using for years, is now seriously challenging the conventional minicomputer industry. We have predicted for some time that the conventional minicomputer manufacturers are in the same position as the manufacturers of digital logic modules were more than a decade ago; they must adapt their products to the new technology, or find some other business in which to make a living.

OTHER SYSTEMS ON A CHIP

The impact of other LSI chips is equally important. Semiconductor RAM has been available for many years, and each year the economic tradeoff between semiconductor storage and conventional magnetic (e.g., core) storage for high speed memories moves further toward the advantages of semiconductor memory. The charge-coupled device (CCD) appears to be the first serious challenger to the long dominance of magnetic surface storage for mass and archival memory. Modems on a chip will seriously impact what has become a substantial business, packaged modems.

It is, as we said, a real live revolution, and no element of the industry will escape unscathed. Companies which do not presently have plans encompassing both the technological development of new products taking into consideration the swift advance of technology, and a comprehensive business plan will not survive the next several years.

THE GARAGE SHOP PHENOMENON

Having been among the leading practitioners of garage shops for a decade, we will be the last to denigrate these small, hustling operations, which represent capitalistic enterprise nearly at its purest, and in its most exciting form. The system on a chip provides, as we said last year, opportunities for the astute, brave, and the daring (and even the foolhardy) to begin their own business on a shoe string. We estimate that there are presently more than 100 companies actively promoting products, companies and products which were unknown or nonexistent a year and a half ago.

Microcomputers can be manufactured by any company which can buy the basic chips and put them on a PC card, supplying such software, service, etc., as their expertise provides. Microcomputer peripheral controllers offer similar opportunities, and there has long been a group of small companies providing specialized controllers and interfaces using the old technology. Microcomputer development systems are all the rage. There are dozens of companies giving seminars, offering training courses, and offering consulting services in the business of learning to use the microprocessor; some of these even have more knowledge and experience than those whom they purport to teach.

Few of these shops will survive in their present form, because the nature of the revolution, while it presently encourages the development of small operations, is such that two years hence the business will shake out into substantial companies competing in each of the segments of the industry – processors, software, peripherals, etc. After the revolution has thoroughly shaken the technology, solid companies will again have the advantage as the small computer industry pursues the vast new markets which have been opened during the period of the revolution. At that time, the usual virtues of sound financing, expert marketing, efficient manufacturing, and astute management will again outweigh the expertise of the development engineering departments.

What, then, is the future, for today's small enterprises, the epitome of capitalism, the brave and venturous souls, etc.? Many will be acquired by larger companies which see that the quickest and frequently the cheapest way into this new era is to bring in the people and the organization that are already organized and familar with the new technology. Unfortunately, many of the established companies will continue with their "we can do it better than anyone" philosophy, and will miss the boat. More than half the garage shops will go "down the tubes," but then this is the usual fate of approximately that many new businesses. Few will combine among themselves to make larger companies, because they are presently geographically dispersed, their technological capabilities overlap considerably rather than complementing one another, and they also are highly endued with the we-can-do-it-better philosophy.

IN OUR PROFILE THIS MONTH

We begin our profile this month with a brief review of the nature and capabilities of the microprocessor, courtesy of Roy Twitty of National Semiconductor Corp. Following that, and following all of Mr. Twitty's and our glowing words about the potential of the microprocessor, we present a caution, "Beware the Microprocessor," by Donald McDonald of Technology Marketing, Inc. Finally, we present some unique ideas for future systems and equipment, by Marty Jarosz of Northeast Services.

The LSI microprocessor

by Roy Twitty

Similar to the central processing unit (CPU) of a computer, a **microprocessor** manipulates data by interpreting and executing coded program instructions. This general purpose data processing device is contained on large-scale integrated (LSI) circuits, which are produced by means of metal-oxide-semiconductor (MOS) technology.

A microprocessor consists of an accumulator, an arithmetic-logic unit, a scratch-pad read/write memory, a register and decoder for instructions, a program counter and address register stack, a timing and control section, a parallel data and input/output bus, and a controller for input and output of data.

When the microprocessor (CPU) is incorporated as a CPU in a working system along with a data-storage memory, a program memory, and input/output (I/O) circuitry, it is called a **microcomputer**. Some firms produce complete microcomputers – CPU, data-storage memory, program memory and input/output circuitry – on one or two MOS-LSI circuits. The tendency in such cases is to call the unprogrammed circuits a **microprocessor system**, which term is also used to describe unprogrammed multi-circuit sets that include memory and I/O options.

MICROCOMPUTERS

The microcomputer is a smaller version of a minicomputer,

which is generally a more powerful computer based on bipolar transistor-transistor logic (TTL) semiconductors. The terms "micro" and "mini" refer not to limitations in performance, but rather to physical size. Both "micro" and "mini" computers can be made nearly as powerful as large computers that cost many times more.

An MOS-LSI microcomputer costs one-half that of a mini; it requires far less power (a fraction of a watt); it is far smaller (an 8 by 10 inch circuit board versus the size of a typewriter); and it can be equipped with about the same memory capacity. While the mini processes data faster, the micro is sufficiently fast to handle manually-fed data, which is all that is required for most computer terminals, cash registers, industrial controllers and instrumentation.

The microcomputer consists of three sections:

1. The microprocessor, or data processor (CPU), which contains the basic control logic, the circuitry for decoding instructions, and logic circuits for processing arithmetic functions.
2. Memory circuits: one type for storing data, and another which contains the microcomputer's program instructions. The data-storage unit is known as a random-access memory (RAM), or read-write memory. Program instructions are contained in a read-only memory (ROM), which is permanently encoded with information that tells the microcomputer what to do.
3. Input/output (I/O) LSI devices or circuitry used to interface the microcomputer with keyboards, displays and other peripheral equipment.

The integration of semiconductor and computer technologies in MOS-LSI microcomputers provides many features unavailable in some big computers. One example is a register stack that allows the CPU to be interrupted quickly to handle short subroutines. Others are the ability to handle serial input-output functions directly from the CPU, or to build controller functions into input/output circuits so that peripherals can be handled independently of the CPU.

Integration of technologies also permits the "architecture" (the arrangement of CPU, memories, I/O devices and auxiliary components) of microcomputers to be varied according to their intended use. One form of architecture may facilitate arithmetic operations for lengthly numerical analysis, while another architecture may emphasize input and output operations for control and monitoring applications.

MICROCOMPUTER CAPABILITIES

Basically, microcomputers are classified by the number of bits that can be handled at one time. The smallest and least expensive can handle a block of four bits. Machines in this category include FIPS (Four-bit Integrated Processing System) made by National Semiconductor Corporation, the 4004 by Intel, and the PPS-4 and PPS-4/2 from Rockwell International.

Eight-bit microprocessors, such as National's SC/MP and IMP-8, are the most popular type for general control applications. National popularized the "bit slice" building-block approach to larger processing capability by connecting four-bit devices in parallel. In the IMP-16, four 4-bit slices are connected together to form a machine of 16 bits, which is the word length used by most minicomputers. A complete 16-bit microcomputer, known as PACE (Processor And Control Element), in the form of a single integrated circuit was recently introduced by National, and is an economical substitute for a minicomputer in many applications. The longer word length for instructions and addressing provides higher overall throughput and simplifies the programming.

MICROCOMPUTER APPLICATIONS

The microprocessor portion was first developed for use in sophisticated calculators, and to replace the inflexible circuitry known as "hard-wired logic." The greatest future impact of microcomputers will probably not be in the low-cost replacement of standard hardware, but rather in the new methods of operation which they make possible. The largest market for microcomputers will be found in new applications that were once technically impossible or which could not be justified economically. In five years, new applications could encompass as much as 70 percent of sales.

The microcomputer market in 1975 accounted for almost $100 million in sales, a figure that would obviously be much higher were it not for the economic recession of the nation. This year, the market is expected to exceed $180 million, and by the end of the decade, factory sales could reach from $350 to $500 million. By 1983, microcomputers will be a $1 billion business.

Although the application of microcomputers is more evolutionary than revolutionary, their use will be pervasive by the end of the 1970's, and almost everyone will be affected by them in some way. There will soon be one in every new car, and in a few years, they will enter the home. They will be able to communicate via telephone or television to provide stock market reports, newspaper items, local library services, special entertainment such as games of strategy, and control of systems in the house from the lights and lawn sprinklers right down to the coffee pot. They will make it possible to phone a department store, scan selected merchandise via TV, order the items, and be billed automatically at the bank. The microcomputer will soon be in the hands of a new generation of designers who will be trained to regard it as a simple device, much as today's engineers look at semiconductor components or commodity products.

Beware the microprocessor

by Donald McDonald

When it comes to incorporating a computer function into a piece of equipment, many designers start by asking "How can I use a microprocessor?" That's the wrong question. It proposes a solution before the problem has been defined.

Instead, designers, engineering managers – and indeed top corporate line executives – must go back to basics by first asking "What is it I'm trying to accomplish?" Only when that question is properly and fully answered can appropriate decisions be made.

Thus a warning for everyone concerned, from executive to designer: *don't be fooled by the apparent ease with which a microprocessor can be selected and implemented in a product.*

At Technology Marketing, Inc., we have encountered

many misconceptions among both line executives and designers regarding the use of microprocessors. The misconceptions include overestimating the capabilities of microprocessors in general and underestimating the complexities involved in their use; they also include a lack of understanding of the differences among the available microprocessors in function and performance as well as the support available and required from the supplier during development.

This leads to problems from two different sources. Most designers like to use the latest technology available, and many are intrigued by the idea of the microprocessor, which often sounds like a great solution to their problem when they read about it. Similarly, corporate executives can easily succumb to the glamour of a "computer on a chip" and direct their engineers to use it without fully understanding the level of expertise needed to design one into a system and attain the required cost and performance goals.

The potential trap is that it is equally or more complicated to design using a microprocessor as it is to incorporate a minicomputer into a system. When a minicomputer is to be used, an executive will generally recognize the degree of complexity involved, and will either hire computer experts or retain the services of a skilled computer engineering firm. But the microprocessor appears so simple, those precautions are too often overlooked.

All too frequently the equipment manufacturer finds late in the game that he is locked in with a microprocessor that has insufficient capability, or throughput that limits system performance. He may then discover he needs far more software, ROM, main memory or supporting components than anticipated. In some instances, a company ends up spending three or four times as much in development costs than they had budgeted without achieving a satisfactory design in terms of either performance or cost or both.

Unless a designer has very detailed experience with a microprocessor, he can fall into a very insidious trap – the amount of code needed to implement specified functions can be excessive. The designer may not discover this until well into the design process – in fact, the program may even be into prototype production before it is discovered that, with all peripherals online and the data loaded, the system throughput is inadequate.

The pain of bailing out the design at this point can be excruciating. It may mean adding considerably more memory than planned, or investing in a large-scale software development program. Even then, the finished product is likely to be an unhappy compromise that disappoints the designer and his management.

At TMI we're not against microprocessors. Properly used, they are a very cost-effective solution to a broad range of applications and we have used them in several designs for our customers.

But they're not a panacea. It's a mistake for an executive to order the engineering department to use a microprocessor unless the department has the requisite level of computer experience. If you're intent on using one, make sure the right people are assigned the design task, and keep track of the development program so you know early enough if the microprocessor and the way it is being used are appropriate for the job.

Minicomputers-microcomputers-peripherals

by Marty B. Jarosz

In the past five years, manufacturers have gone from $3000 mini CPUs to $20 micro CPUs. In simple control situations – hardware replacement, small RAM/ROM memory requirements, and non-peripheral applications – these advancements have been great cost savers. But in many applications, the real cost saving can be less than 10 percent!

Why has technology been spending most of its effort in an area that accounts for less than 10 percent of the "real" total cost? Let's look at a typical mini system, consisting of a CPU, 6K memory, DMA, power fail restart, chassis, power supply, control panel, teleprinter interface, real-time clock, autoload, 16-bit I/O interface, high-speed paper tape reader/punch, moving head disk, and printer. What has pricing done on this typical system in the past four years? See Table 1.

Let's look at these items individually.

- **CPU/2K**. This has been one of the areas that the greatest price decreases have been obtained. It is now possible to pay 500 times the CPU cost for a single peripheral interface. The real problem is that the CPU never accounted for more than 10 percent of the total cost; therefore, if completely eliminated, the total savings can not be more than 10 percent.

- **Memory**. This too has shown remarkable price decreases. The problem here has been that as price per bit decreases, memory requirements increase and they seem to increase to the square of the dollar decrease.

- **Chassis/Power Supply**. These prices have stayed basically the same. This is due to the fact that as technical advances have been made, component cost has increased.

- **Control Panel**. These prices have stayed basically the same, but in some systems have actually increased in cost.

- **DMA, PF, TTI, RTC, AL**. These prices on CPU options have also decreased, but in many cases only because manufacturers are doing in memory what had previously been done with hard-wired circuits.

TABLE 1 – Recent Minicomputer Price History

	1972 (%)	1973 (%)	1974 (%)	1975 (%)
CPU with 2K Memory	$ 2500 (8)	$ 1125 (4)	$ 900 (3)	$ 650 (2)
4K Memory	2200 (6)	1525 (5)	550 (2)	550 (2)
Chassis	300 (1)	275 (1)	100 (.5)	100 (.5)
Power Supply	400 (1)	375 (1)	375 (1.5)	375 (1.5)
Control Panel	225 (.5)	225 (1)	275 (1)	275 (1)
DMA	300 (1)	Incl.	Incl.	Incl.
Power Failure Restart	350 (1)	250 (1)	Incl.	Incl.
Teleprinter Interface	150 (.5)	100 (.5)	100 (.5)	150 (.5)
Real-Time Clock	350 (1)	225 (1)	Incl.	Incl.
Autoload	400 (1)	175 (.5)	50	50
16-Bit Digital I/O	500 (1)	500 (2)	500 (2)	500 (2)
Paper Tape Reader/Punch	5800 (18)	5700 (20)	5600 (21)	5600 (22)
Moving Head Disk	13000 (40)	13000 (45)	13000 (50)	12000 (48)
Floppy Disk (Dual)	NA	NA	NA	4300
Printer	5500 (17)	5500 (18)	4950 (18)	4950 (20)
	$31,925	$28,925	$26,400	$25,200

NOTE: (%) Denotes approximate percent of total cost

• **16-Bit I/O.** These items are the money makers for manufacturers. In many cases the only time prices have been decreased is when competition from peripherals systems houses or build/buy decisions have forced competitive pricing.

• **Paper Tape Reader Punch.** This unit has been fairly stable at a cost of 18 to 22 percent of the total system.

• **Moving Head Disk System.** For an item that can account for 40 to 50 percent of the system cost, the only improvements have been to increase storage for the same cost. Do we really need 10 megabytes of storage at $13,000 on a $20 CPU?

• **Printer.** Prices have been stable and in some cases, there have been speed increases for no or little real cost increase. A slow printer can account for 17 to 20 percent of the cost of a typical system.

As shown, costs will go down on some items. The only problem is, if these items were obtained *free,* the most that could be eliminated is 10 percent of the total systems cost.

Let's look at the remaining 90 percent cost area and their functions.

1. **SLOW SERIAL STORAGE** – Program Load
   – Input Output Storage
2. **MASS STORAGE** – Random Access
   – Batch Access
3. **PRINTER** – 10-60 Characters
   – 100-300 Lines Per Minute
4. **SYSTEM INTERFACE** – Serial
   – Parallel
   – High Speed
   – Low Speed

THE FLOPPY DISK AND CARTRIDGE TAPE

We believe that two peripherals, which were announced in the past few years, are outstanding. They are the floppy disk – developed by IBM (which is *not* known as a mini or miniperipheral manufacturer) and the 3M cartridge by 3M (again, 3M is *not* known as a mini or miniperipheral manufacturer). The single quantity price of both these units is approximately $700 for a drive with read/write and motor control electronics. As we attempt to lower pricing on our $20 CPU, $400 power supply/chassis, $600 memory, $5600 low-speed serial input/output, $13,000 random access memory and $5000 printer, let's ask ourselves, "Does the world need another storage media pioneer?" What the mini/micro world may need is a way to use *present media,* but in lower cost ways.

THE PAPER TAPE PROBLEM

Let's examine the $5000 paper tape reader/punch: Most mini/micro manufacturers use this media for distributing programs, updates, diagnostics, because its cost is low and it can be mailed and handled easily. Mini/micro users have used paper tape for program loaders, data input/output, variables, etc. Can this $5000 300-character input, 75-character output (with no error checking) be replaced? We believe it can and will: a $5000 low-speed peripheral does not make sense on a $20 CPU.

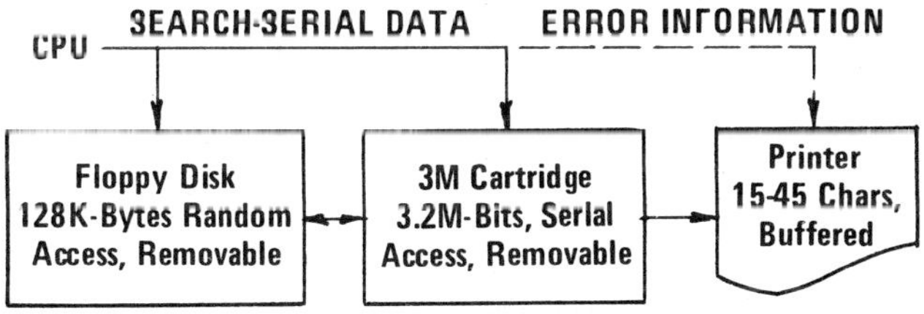

Fig. 1 : Mass Storage and Printing System

For an idea as to a good solution, let's look at a little history. When Mohawk Data Sciences came out with their key-to-tape unit, a disadvantage was that with a keypunch program cards could be loaded in 5 to 6 seconds, but with the MDS units 160 characters must be keyed in to accomplish the same thing. MDS solved this problem at *no cost* by recording programs on 2 foot strips of 1/2-inch magnetic tape and reading the programs into the unit with two key strokes.

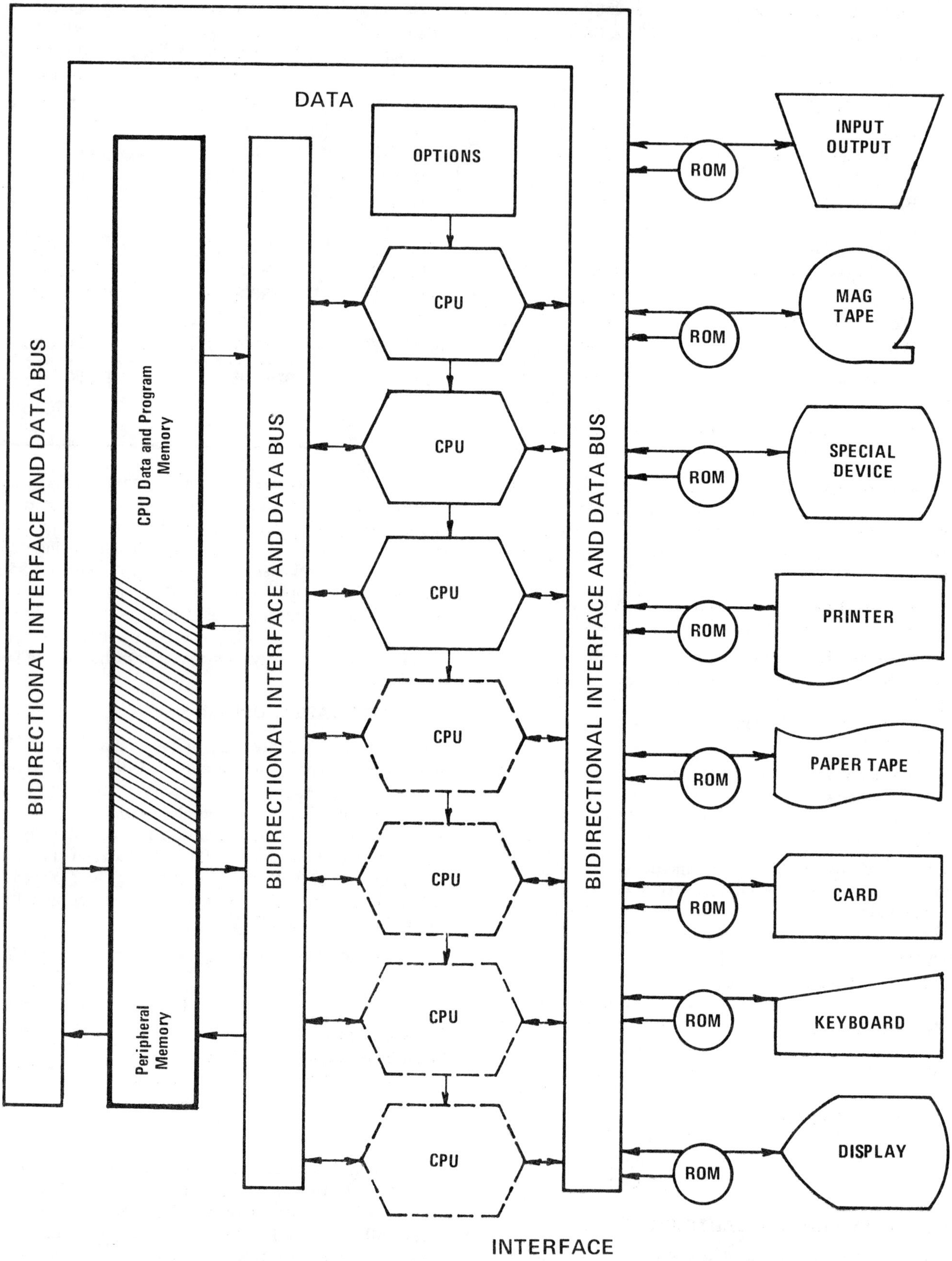

Fig. 2 : The Multiple CPU System

How much paper tape is usually read at one time — 4K words, maybe 16K words? Each 4K would take approximately 30 seconds on a 300-character reader, more than 15 minutes on a 10-character per second reader. We believe the solution is a magnetic tape strip micro/mini reader/writer, with specifications:

- Single-track read/write
- 4.8-ips tape speed
- 200-bpi recording density
- 9600-bps transfer rate
- Length Variable with 4K words less than 40-inches

We believe that such a magnetic strip reader/writer will easily outperform paper tape equipment for 1/20 the cost — a $300 peripheral for a $20 CPU.

DISK MEMORY

Most mini/micro manufacturers use cartridge disk as a massive (10 million 8-bit bytes) random access storage. It is so massive that many users store all programs, updates, diagnostics, and even games on it, and in most cases still have a large percentage of storage area vacant. Can this $13,000, 10-megabyte random access device be replaced? We believe it can and will: a $13,000 peripheral does not make sense on a $20 CPU.

We suggest that a random access mass storage peripheral for mini/micros should consist of the combination of a 128K byte mini floppy disk, random access, removable medium, and a 3.2M-bit 3M cartridge serial access, removable medium. (See Fig. 1.)

The specifications would be as follows.

Random access unit

- 128K-byte storage
- 11-msec access per track
- 167-msec latency per revolution
- 250-kHz transfer rate

Serial access unit

- 3.2-million bits storage
- 30-ips read/write speed
- 90-ips for word/reverse speed
- 48kHz transfer rate

The cost of such a dual system, with R/W, control, and interface: about $4000.

PRINTERS

A printer is one way of putting in usable form the results of the operations of the mini/micro computer. In many cases

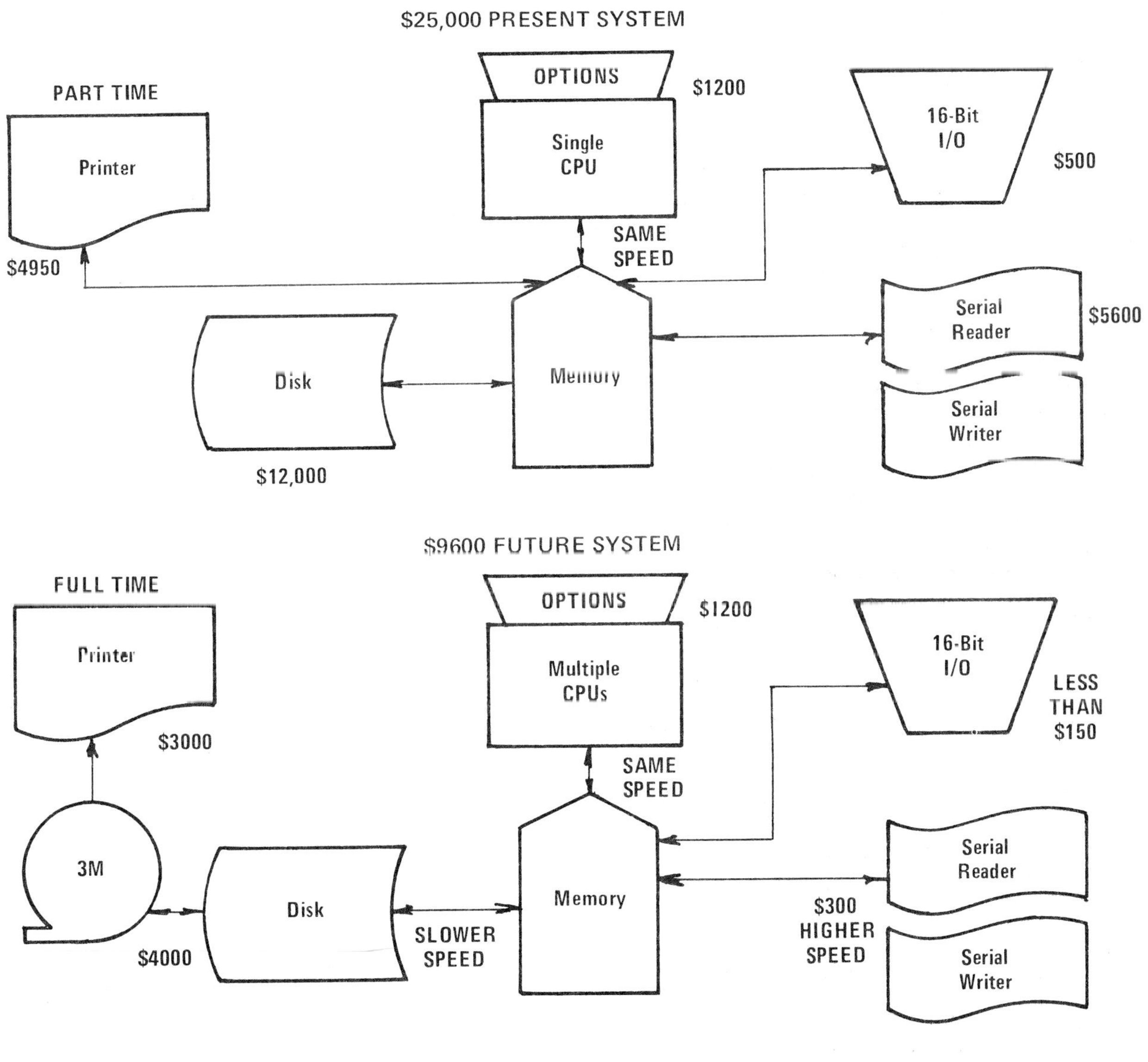

Fig. 3 : The Old and New Systems

this unit operates less than 10 percent of the time. The problem is that when the information being processed is ready, it must be sent to the output device. Therefore, most printers are used for a small amount of time and print at a much faster rate than is really required, but for only short periods of time. Can this $5000 (100-character per second, 80 column) printer be replaced? We believe it can be and will: a $5000 part-time peripheral does not make sense on a $20 CPU.

Offline printing has been an accepted operation for many years in large computer systems, requiring only a $10,000 computer tape drive and a $40,000 high-speed printer. We can add a printer to our micro/mini mass storage system, (See Fig. 1.) using an RS-232-compatible offline printer, on demand of the 3M storage device, with buffered carriage return and line feed. 3M-to-printer operation would be available when 3M is not in staging to floppy disk. The complete cost would be about $3000.

THE INTERFACING PROBLEM

Interface cards ranging from $500 to $2000 are used to logically tie a foreign device to the I/O bus of the computer. The interface card does the logical start, stop, handshaking, and data transfers that are required. Can this $500 to $2000 interface be replaced? We believe that this concept must also come to pass, ince a $20 "smart" CPU can not afford a $500 to $2000 "dumb" interface for each and every part-time device.

We suggest that a system would internally have multiple $20 microprocessors working on data and interfacing, as shown in Fig. 2. From the low order end, as many "data" micro-CPUs as required would be working on internal functions doing basically the same operations as performed by today's normal CPUs. Working from the high order end, these micro-CPUs would be working as "interface" micro-CPUs. Under emergency conditions, "data" micro-CPUs could be interrupted to perform "interface" micro-CPUs functions or vice versa. Dedicated ROM would be microprogrammed to handle all interface requirements; ROM-to-interface-micro-CPU assignment would be on availability, starting at most significant micro-CPUs. The cost, of interface, microprocessor, ROM and cable would be less than $150.

We believe that selective microprocessor/ROMs/cables could easily out perform hard wired interfaces, for 1/3 the cost, resulting in a $150 interface for a $20 CPU.

THE NEW MINI/MICRO SYSTEM

Let's look at our old and new system (See Fig. 3.):

	Present	(%)	Future	(%)
CPU/Memory	$ 1200	(5)	$ 1200	(12.5)
CPU Options	950	(4)	950	(10)
16-Bit Digital I/O	500	(2)	150	(1)
Serial Reader/Writer	5600	(23)	300	(3)
Mass Storage	12000	(48)	4000	(41)
Printer	4950	(20)	3000	(31)
	$25,200		$9,600	

The future of high performance minis and/or micros are secure. But, for the best growth, we must stop running with "logic technology" and look at the true costs and where they lie with each mini/micro system. The time may come when a system is designed with peripherals, cables, ROM, and interfacing microprocessors – AND – a multiprocessing CPU may be available at NO COST! ■

Storage devices—or, memories are made of this

by Roger H. Edelson
Reprinted by permission of INTERFACE AGE Magazine from the March 1978 issue.

In considering memory technology and applications, one of the fundamental problems that comes to mind is the fact that the various technologies and applications overlap. This makes it difficult to characterize a particular memory technology into any specific category. For instance, it is possible to build either volatile, non-volatile, or permanent memories out of semi-conductors, and magnetic memories. While non-volatile memories may be either destructuve or non-destructive depending on the particular element. Table 1 is the breakdown of categories that I will use for these articles.

First it is necessary to define the terms used in the category table before we can begin to discuss the memories themselves. *Permanent Memory,* one which can not be easily altered once the contents have been stored. *Non-Permanent Memory,* one whose contents may be altered by the user and new contents can be stored. *Volatile,* a memory whose contents will become unreliable once power is removed. *Non-Volatile,* a memory whose contents remain stored when the power is removed. This does not, however, mean that the memory cannot be erased. *NDRO (Non Destructive Read Out),* a memory whose contents are not altered when those contents are accessed by the using device. *DRO (Destructive Read Out),* a memory whose contents are disturbed by the reading process.

Static and *Dynamic* are two terms whose meaning is dependent upon the particular technology used.

MAGNETIC DEVICES

A *dynamic memory* is one in which the magnetic medium, and its supporting structure, are moved physically to produce a signal describing the contents. A *static magnetic memory* is one in which no physical movement of the magnetic element, and its support must be moved.

SEMI-CONDUCTOR DEVICES

When referring to semi-conductor memories, a *static memory* is one whose contents will remain stable so long as power is applied. A *dynamic semi-conductor memory* is one in which the contents slowly fade away unless constantly rewritten, or refreshed.

PERMANENT MEMORIES

Let's begin our memory survey with a look at the various *permanent memories.* Punched paper tape and Hollerith (IBM) cards are two examples of a *permanent memory.* Both are easy to load and fairly easy to read. Barring accident, the contents will remain unchanged. If an error is made in storing contents in either of these media, corrections can be made with tape and a manual punch. Hardwired memories, such as diodes, or wired transformers (cores), are not as prevalent as the paper memories, but they are generally less accident prone. In particular some very compact, highly reliable *permanent memories* have been built using the wired core-transformer element.

The semi-conductor *permanent memories* either configured as a ROM (Read-Only Memory), or as a PROM (Programmable Read-Only Memory), are probably the devices most of us think of when we hear *permanent memory.* Various semi-conductor technologies can be used to produce a ROM or PROM, and we will discuss these in depth in a later article. The ROM version can be built by having the factory pre-program the device, after manufacture but before shipment to the user. A ROM may also be constructed by having the contents set up during the manufacturing process by means of the metallization mask. These devices are called mask-programmable ROMs. They provide the lowest cost method of fabricating a semi-conductor *permanent memory,* but you had better be very sure of the memory contents before you commit to a mask programmable device. The cost of the mask is not cheap. Also, these masked devices are selected when a large quantity of memories is to be purchased.

NON-VOLATILE MEMORIES

By far the most varied branch of memories is the devices which make up the *non-permanent memory* technology. To ease our consideration of this group we will divide it into volatile and non-volatile memories. The volatile branch contains some of the more exotic members of memory devides, so let's begin our discussion with the non-volatile devices. Until recently almost all non-volatile memories used a storage based on a magnetic element. Semi-conductor technology has changed this picture, but we shall still begin with the *magnetic memories.* Basically, all magnetic memories depend on the fact that if a magnetic element is placed in one position, it will remain with its north and south poles in that direction, until the orientation is changed by the application of another external field. This simplistic statement neglects domain walls, and other more esoteric components of magnetic theory, but for our purposes is a sufficient working rule.

The major differences between *magnetic memories* occurs in the method used to sense the orientation of this magnetic dipole. In destructive read out (DRO) memories the dipole orientation is sensed by always attempting to change its direction to a previously estab-

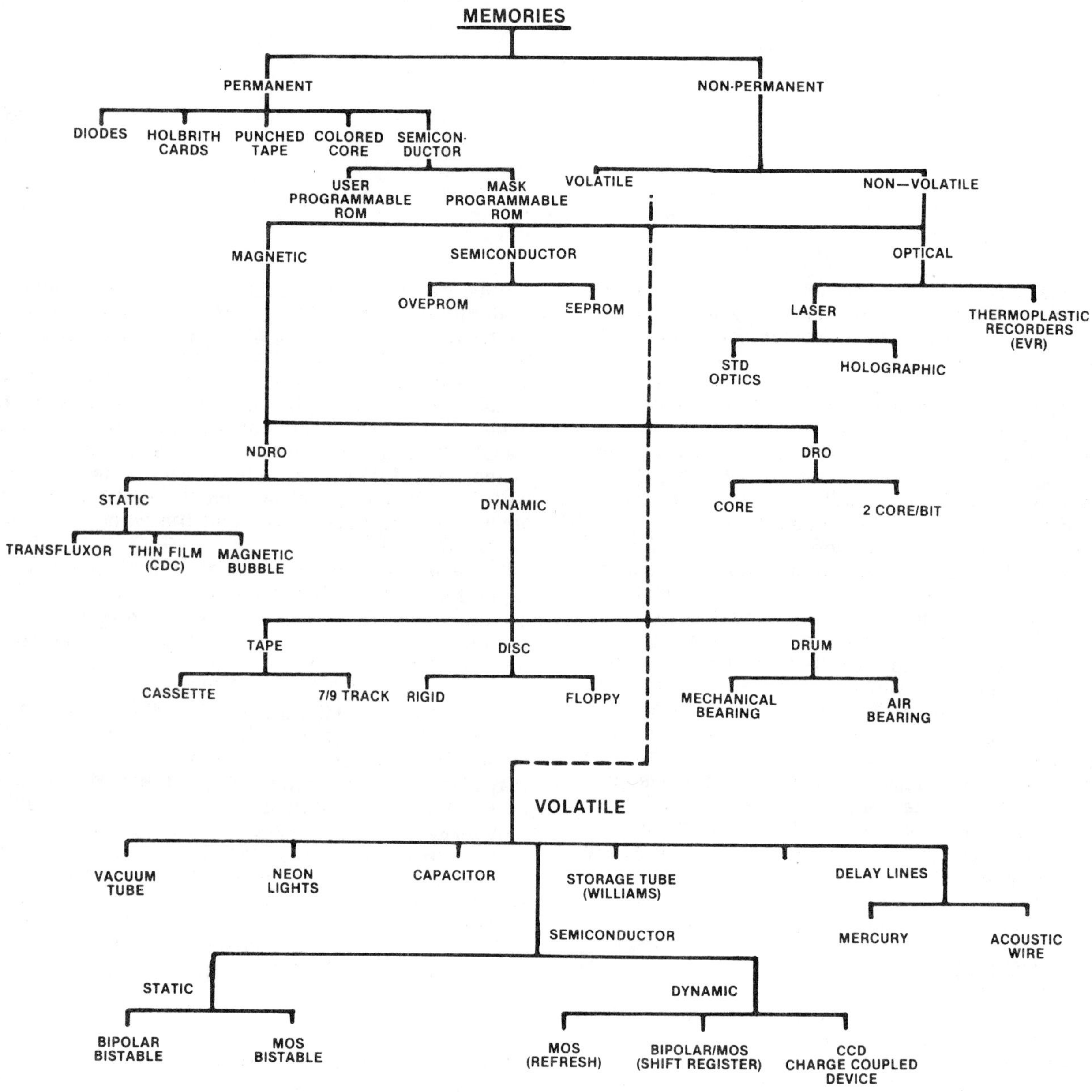

Table 1.

lished rest direction. If the dipole were oriented opposite to the rest direction, a signal will be generated when the dipole is flipped. Should the orientation be identical to the rest direction, no output signal will be generated, as no magnetic lines of flux are generated. However, in this case, the contents of the memory are altered by the application of the field which reverses the direction of the magnetic dipoles, storing one state of information.

All single hole per core magnetic elements are in the DRO class. These types of core memories can be further classified, depending on the methods used to address the individual elements, and the number of cores per bit. If we add one more hole to the core, and orient it so that the axis of the two holes are orthogonal (right angled), a device is formed which is capable of being used as an NDRO, non-destructive read out, memory.

The non-destructive properties of this device are due to: A sensing field, applied through one of the holes, can provide information on the direction of the magnetic dipoles, around the orthogonal hole. This is accomplished without disturbing the stored dipoles direction. This device is called a *transfluxor.* The *transfluxor* is one of a class of magnetic NDRO memories that is static. In other words, the *transfluxor* does not have to be physically moved to produce an output signal, only the store field is partly rotated.

Another static magnetic NDRO, much the same as the *transfluxor,* is a thin-film memory produced by CDC. To form this memory element two different magnetic films are sputtered onto a glass substrate. One film is made up of a hard magnetic alloy (one that is difficult to re-orient). The other film is a softer alloy and is placed over the hard film. Information is stored by setting the hard film into the appropriate direction. The soft film tracks the dipole direction of the harder alloy. The stored information is sensed by providing a field just strong enough to flip the soft film, but the hard film retains its orientation. If the soft film changes direction, an output signal is produced indicating the storage of same data. After the sensing field is removed, the soft film will revert to the orientation stored by the hard film. As might be expected, this device does have an upper limit on the number of reads (greater than 10^6). Basically, this is a very reliable NDRO memory. However, it is extremely expensive to produce.

Another magnetic, static NDRO that is just now starting production is the magnetic bubble memory. This memory operates by the propagation of magnetic domain bubbles through a medium. It is a bulk-storage device that will rival magnetic tapes in a few years. As the technology is just being refined and developed, the prices of this element should begin to drop rapidly in the next two to three years. Also the availability will increase. Currently, the only commercially available devices are being produced by Texas Instruments.

The more familiar magnetic NDRO memories are the dynamic, or moving medium, types. In this class we find the magnetic tapes, disks, and drums. All of these memories depend on moving the magnetic dipole physically, rather than rotating the dipole magnetically. The theory of operation of these devices is similar to the generator or alternator in your car.

Magnetic tapes may be either cassette or the larger 7/9 track types. Information may be recorded either in an audio (analog) form or digital format. Many different types of storage techniques have been developed to increase the density of the recording information, and the reliability of the recording.

The disk storage elements may either be rigid, or the more familiar floppy (flippy) types. Again, various different methods are used to optimize this technology.

The magnetic drum is no longer widely used as a memory device. Magnetic drum memories have been built with fixed head to drum spacing, or with heads which flew on an air cushion over the drum surface. The drum bearings are normally the mechanical type which we are all familiar with. However, there have been some drums in which an air-bearing was used to reduce the friction, and consequently the driving force. As might be expected, a great deal of difficulty was experienced in making an air-bearing drum operate reliably.

Returning to the general class of non-volatile memories, there are at least two other technologies that allow constructin of a non-permanent non-volatile memory, optical or semi-conductor.

Optical based memory systems usually depend on the storage of information in a thermoplastic medium. An optical device was built by Motorola, using this technique for the storage of video information. The technology never caught on, and surplus units may be found for only about $100 for interested experimenters. These units will read only, using a small scanning oscilloscope with photocell output.

Permanent memories can also be built using optical based techniques. Either a scanning oscilloscope, or a laser can be used as the addressing element. The information can also be stored in conventional films or in holographic records.

More familiar to microcomputer buffs are the non-permanent non-volatile memories, using semi-conductor based technology. These are the EPROMs (erasable programmable read only memories). EPROMs are programmed by applying an overvoltage which sets internal charge layers. The erasable EPROMs found in the typical home computer are usually 1702 or 2708 types, which are erasable through the application of ultraviolet light. In many applications, a system is designed and debugged using UV-erasable EPROMs. The EPROMs are then replaced with ROMs in the production phase. Another device, manufactured by at least three companies, is an electrically erasable EPROM (EEPROM). Nitron (a division of McDonnell Douglas Corp.), Burroughs and NEC Microcomputers, Inc., produce a device of this type.

VOLATILE MEMORIES

That about covers the non-volatile, either permanent or non-permanent, memory devices. We will now turn to the volatile memories, of which the semi-conductor types comprise the largest and most familiar class. However, before looking at the more familiar volatile semi-conductor memories, let's review some of the stranger types that have been used in past computer systems.

One type of device that enjoyed great usage during the begining of the digital computer era was the Williams storage tube. With this memory, the information was stored as a light spot on the face of an oscilloscope. The tube was built as a storage scope, using a flood gun and a storage mesh just behind the face plate. Electrical interaction maintained the light, or non-light, condition of the phosphor. The contents of the memory were dynamically refreshed to prevent the ultimate deterioration with time.

Delat lines were also used to store information; with mercury ultrasonic, or long wire acoustic lines being popular. These devices can be considered to act like short tape loops with the exception that the information must be continually recycled.

Capacitor arrays have also been used to build memory systems. These offered some advantages in that they were a little easier to read and write than magnetic cores. However, their volatility and large size make them impractical for most uses. Because of their low cost and bi-state characteristics, neon lights have also been used as memory elements. One had to, in all cases, use the devices containing a small amount of a radioactive substance, because lamps without this source of radiation would exhibit different characteristics when subjected to varying degrees of light.

Vacuum tubes arranged as bistable elements were used for a long time as memory elements. An interesting problem occurred in these memories. The cathode emission characteristics of the tube would change drastically if the tube were in the "OFF" state for a long period of time versus the characteristics associated with the "ON" state. The problem would manifest itself by unreliable memory operation. The cure was to arrange for some period of time when all tubes would be "ON."

Originally, semi-conductor memories were just copies of the vacuum tube flip-flops. The major advantages of semi-conductors were low power (no filament), small size, higher reliability (both physically and electrically), and ease of construction. Additionally, semi-conductors more closely approached the perfect switch. Consequently, their off and on states were more easily distinguished. Semi-conductors did suffer from problems due to high temperature environments and speed.

The advent of integrated circuits ushered in the true ability of semi-conductor memory elements. At first tens, then hundreds, of flip-flops were placed on one chip. At last an element had been found that could compete with the core memories. The first integrated circuit memories were static types based on the flip-flop. It was later found that charge could be stored for a considerable length of time in the high dielectric of a MOS transistor. This led to the development of the high capacity *dynamic semi-conductor memories.* These memory elements need a continual refresh cycle, to maintain the content. Because of this characteristic, *dynamic semi-conductor memories* have a non-zero error rate. For many applications, this is significant. As a result, military systems are generally built using only static memories because of this problem. In home computers, the slight error rate can usually be tolerated, or reduced, using parity error checking techniques.

The newly emerging field of *charged-coupled devices* is now offering memories with the highest storage densities of any non-permanent semi-conductor element. At present 16K bit *CCD serial memories* are available, and 64K bit devices are on their way. These devices are usually organized as groups of parallel recirculating serial shift registers. This organization maintains a low average latency time (access time to any given bit in the memory), with a reasonable output decoder structure. The readout is non-destructive and the refresh circuitry is usually provided on the chip. To move the charges along, a four phase clock is generally required, somewhat complicating the drive circuitry.

That completes our Cook's tour of the quite prolific memory world. Next month, we will delve somewhat deeper into the organization and technology of the memory devices generally favored by the home and small computer enthusiast. □

Memories remembered

by Roger Edelson
Reprinted by permission of INTERFACE AGE Magazine from the April 1978 issue.

We will begin this month's discussion with a view of core memory principles and operation. Core memories store binary digits, without consuming electrical power, by virtue of the fact that they can be put into two different states of remanent magnetization. The two states of remanence are produced by applying magnetic fields of opposite polarity with sufficient strength to saturate, or nearly saturate, the material. Figure 1 shows these two possible states on the hysteresis loop of a typical square loop material. The fact that the store information will remain in the core with no application of power, once the initial state of remanence has been established, accounts for the non-volatility of this memory system. The reason for using a rectangular loop material can be seen from a glance at the typical B-H loop presented in Figure 1. Once a sufficient magnetic field (H_m) has been

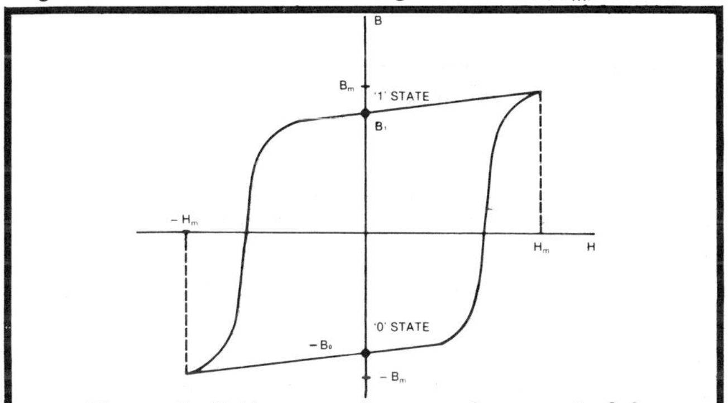

Figure 1. B-H curve of square loop material.

applied, the magnetic flux will attain a level of B_m. When the field is removed the flux level will move to B_1. Subsequent applications of a field H_m will move the flux level to B_m and back to B_1. The core will remain in this remanent flux state so long as a reverse field sufficient to switch the flux is not applied. When a field of $-H_m$ is applied, the flux will move of a level of $-B_m$ and move to $-B_0$ when the field is removed. If the core has a sense winding on it, a considerably larger voltage will be produced by the flux change from B_1 to $-B_0$ than will be produced when the flux changes from $-B_0$ to $-B_m$. It is this voltage that is sensed to indicate the presence of a stored "1." Because the core must be switched to the "0" state when being read, this type of memory is referred to as a *Destructive Read-Out (DRO)* memory. In a real life memory the voltage from the disturbed cores, (those with "0's") and the lead inductance produces a significant voltage as shown in Figure 2. As the "0" output

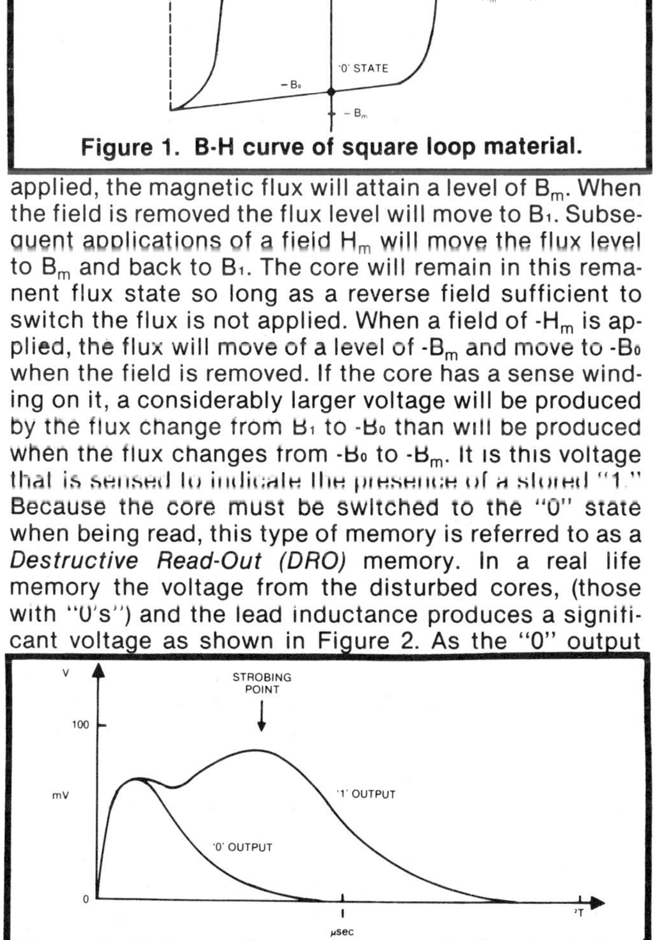

Figure 2. Output voltage of sense winding in a plane array of cores.

cores and the inductive voltages peak earlier in time than the "1" voltage, it is possible to obtain a greater "1" to "0" discrimination by evaluating the signal at some delayed time.

Besides their small size, one of the advantages of magnetic cores is the ability to easily wire up these devices to store large amounts of data. Figure 3 shows a

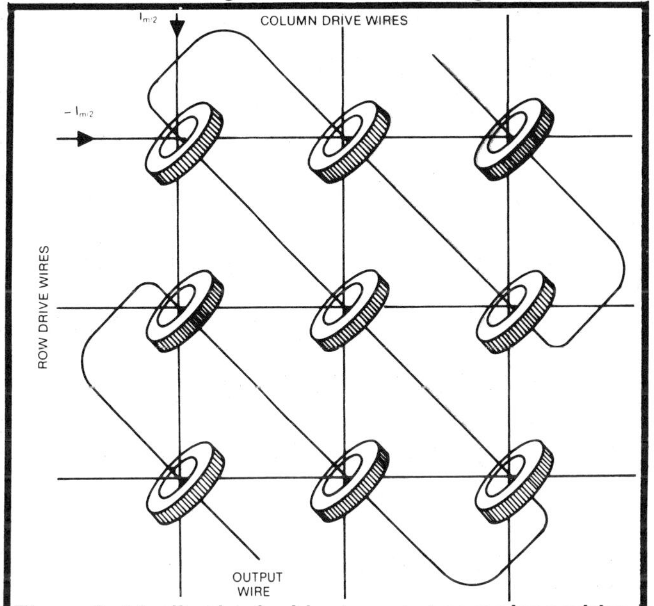

Figure 3. Idealized coincident current core plane wiring.

simplified diagram of the principle of a coincident current matrix store. In this design, a current ($I_m/2$) sufficient to produce half of the switching field, (H_m), is applied to the one each column and row drive wire. The core present at the intersection of the selected row and a "1" would be stored. The other cores, which are threaded by only one energized wire, receive only half this magnetic field strength and are substantially unaffected, although they are said to be disturbed. When reading, the currents are reduced and the output voltage is sensed by the additional output line threading each core. This figure shows a plane of only one digit of nine words. There will have to be as many planes as there are digits (bits) to be stored.

A more common method of wiring a coincident current drive matrix is shown in Figure 4, and the interconnection of these planes in a stack is shown in Figure 5. This wiring method uses a more complex pattern for the sense winding in order to affect a greater cancellation of the output of the disturbed cores and minimize the inductive coupling to the drive wires. When the planes are connected in this fashion, it is necessary for some trick to be used to keep from storing the same bit state in all the planes. The fourth winding called the digit, or inhibit, line performs this function. When information is being written into the cores a pulse of current equal, but opposite, to the half-write current in either the X or Y line is applied to very plane were a "0" is to be stored. This prevents the flux in the selected core from exceeding $H_m/2$, so the attempt to write a "1" is in-

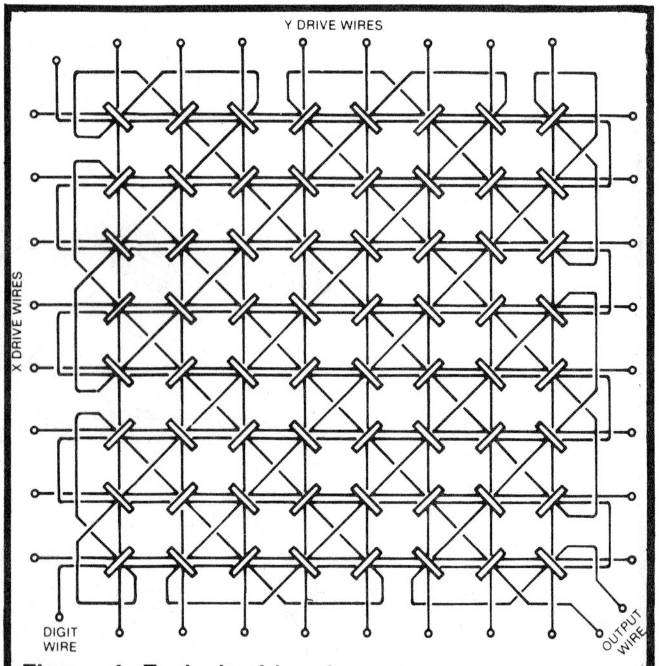

Figure 4. Typical wiring for coincident current with digit/inhibit.

hibited. Information in the other cores in the plane will be unaffected by the digit pulse as it will reduce the drive experienced by cores on the selected row and column to zero, while the remainder of the cores will receive a half-current pulse in the opposite direction.

More complex systems can be constructed using additional cores for eitehr selection or storage. Systems using the additional cores for switching exhibit less dependence on the coincident current tolerances at the cost of higher drive currents and more complexity. A two-core per-bit system using both cores for storage allows faster operation at the cost of increased complexity. In the main, almost all practical core storage systems are constructed using only one core per bit; as faster speeds were required, they were achieved by decreasing the core size.

The possible practical arrangements of the cores and core planes is reasonably limited and well known. The success or failure of the storage system really depends on the design of the drive, selection, and sense circuitry. It is in this arena that the ingenuity of the circuit designer plays an important role. The selection circuits developed are too numerous to catalog here, but some of the problems that must be solved are: 1) high drive currents, 2) variation of drive requirements with temperature, 3) large back voltages from the effect of the core inductances, and 4) fast switching speeds. In almost all new core stores the function of the sense circuitry is provided by an integrated circuit sense amplifier. The advent of these devices has greatly simplified the life of the core memory designer.

Another way to use information stored in the square loop of a magnetic material is to move this magnetized medium under a sensing head. With this method the change in flux, which produces a voltage output, is accomplished by physically moving the magnetized area rather than switching the flux. For this reason the stored flux remains at the same state as it was prior to the read operation and the device is a *non-destructive readout memory.* This is the principle behind the magnetic recording on all moving memories: tape, disks, or drums. The magnetic medium selected is based on cost, system access time, and complexity considerations. Tape storage usually has the longest average latency time with disks falling between the tape drives and the magnetic drums. Complexity and cost appears to be the inverse of the latency time. Drums saw great utility in military aircraft systems because of their ruggedness and high storage capacity, coupled with a reasonable access time. The more common approaches for the micro/minicomputer field are tapes (either cassette or 7/9 track) and floppy disks.

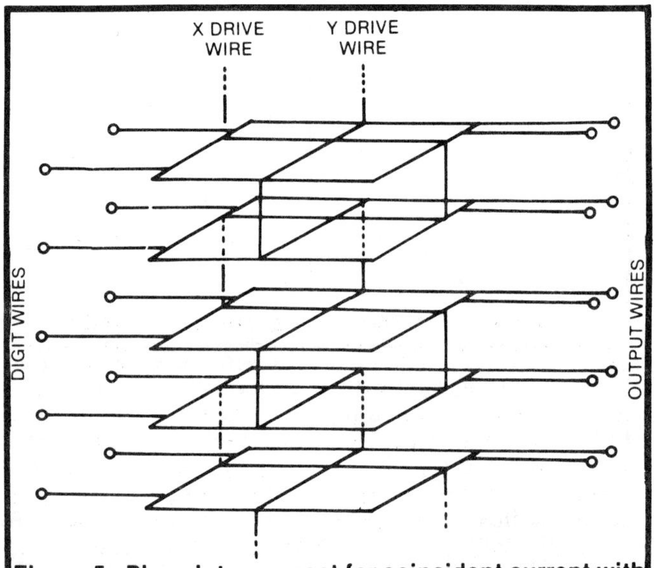

Figure 5. Plane interconnect for coincident current with digit plane.

No matter which type of store is selected, it is necessary to select a recording method for providing information as to the data being stored. Nine of the most popular recording methods are shown in Figure 6. Any method could be used with any recording medium, but in practice certain systems work better with a particular storage device. Cassette recorders, because of their lack of speed, accuracy and the use of less than optimum tapes, require a method which overcomes these limitations. The Kansas City Standard has achieved wide usage with some systems which employ better drives, using either Manchester or a modification of the NRZ system. Most drum systems used wither NRZ or Manchester, with

Manchester being the preferred system because of its self-clocking nature. The 7/9 track tape drives use NRZ for the lower character densities, and use Phase Encoding or Manchester at higher character densities. Floppy disks can use either NRZ or the Phase Encoding Manchester method. Let's look at each system briefly:

Double-Frequency Recording (DFR), is an inherently self-clocking scheme which is immune to wow and flutter. It does not have the magnetic drift and bit packing problem of NRZ, but requires a high bandwidth.

Frequency Shift Keying (FSK) is used in most modems, (Modulator-Demodulator), data transmission systems because of its noise and amplitude rejection. However, it is very speed dependent. It does provide a very good tape drop-out rejection because of the number of flux reversals per bit. This system is found mostly in high quality instrumentation recorders.

Non-Return-To-Zero (NRZ) system, and its brother NRZI (NRZ Inverted), have the current in the head in one direction for a "1" and in the opposite direction for a "0." In NRZI the magnetic flux is reversed at every "1" and is left unchanged for "0's." This system requires an extremely high bandwidth, it must go down to almost dc because of the lack of flux changes for "0's." It also suffers from bit packing problems due to the shift of the "1" output peak, depending on the previous information, and from baseline shift. It is not self-clocking and must have an additional clock track and read/write head.

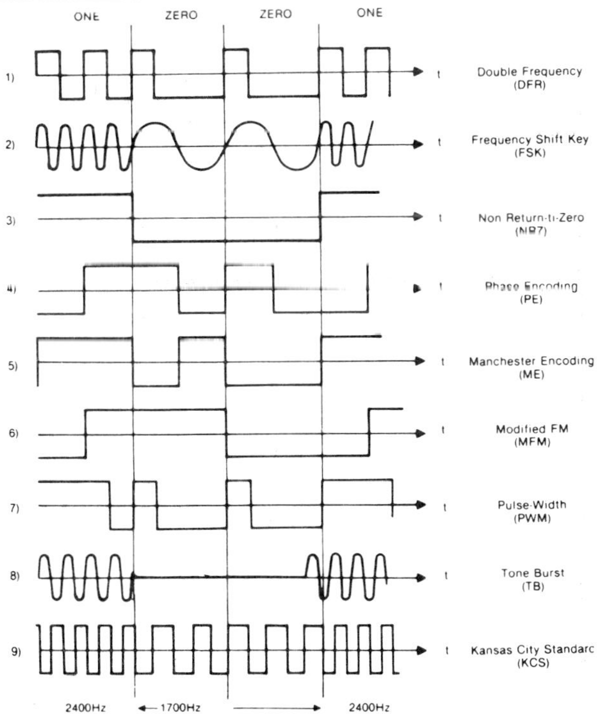

Figure 6. Popular Recording Methods.

Phase Encoding (PE) and *Manchester Encoding (ME)* are two manifestations of the bi-phase recording technique. In an effort to overcome the limitations of NRZ a scheme was developed in which there was at least one flux change for each recorded bit, be it a "1" or a "0." The state of the information determines the direction of the flux change and hence the polarity of the output signal. In PE the flux change occurs in the middle of each bit cell and in ME it occurs at the beginning of each bit cell. Both methods are inherently self-clocking; there is at least one flux change per bit with ME being easier to generate and decode. The required frequency of bi-phase recording is equal to twice the bit rate.

Modified FM (MFM) was developed in an attempt to reduce maximum of two flux reversals per bit of bi-phase. This system requires the addition of a data encoding device to place the flux reversals according to the following rules: A 1 is defined as a flux reversal at the center of the bit cell and a 0 as a flux reversal at the beginning of the cell *except* when preceded by a 1. In that case no flux reversal occurs during the bit cell for a zero. The system is self-clocking and can pack twice the data that can be recorded with bi-phase. A companion scheme M^2FM (Modified Modified FM) uses a more complicated encoding algorithm in order to reduce bit shifting problems.

Pulse Width Modulation (PWM) is a scheme to adjust the width of the recorded flux to correspond to a 1 or a 0. It is a patented process which is self-clocking and noise and amplitude-level tolerant.

Tone Burst (TB) is an extremely simple scheme for recording data; a 1 is recorded as a burst of tone while a 0 is blank. It is not self-clocking and is extremely sensitive to amplitude level and noise.

Kansas City Standard (KCS) is the most popular system in the home computer market. It is a mixture of Manchester, FSK and Tone Burst. An 8-cycle burst of 2400 Hz is used to record a 1 and 4-cycle burst of 1200 Hz is a 0. A phased-lock loop can be used to produce a 4800 Hz clock from the recorded data. This system is reasonably independent of speed variations, and relatively insensitive to amplitude variations and noise. The use of multiple flux reversals per bit limits the packing density, but reduces the possibility of tape drop outs.

With the exception of bubble-memories, (which will be covered much later), this completes the survey of magnetic storage techniques. We have not covered the detailed design and formating specifications of the tapes or disks because they are somewhat device or controller dependent. Basically you can have it IBM's way and be compatible with the rest of the world, or you can use your own format for increased storage but be restricted to your own system, or similar systems.

Next month we will take a look at the semiconductor memory field, with coverage of RAMs, ROMs, PROMs and EPROMs.□

More memories

by Roger Edelson

Reprinted by permission of INTERFACE AGE Magazine from the May 1978 issue.

This is the third article in this series to discuss memories. The heavy emphasis placed on memory is due to the major role this subsystem plays in the small computer system, both from a cost and size viewpoint. Until the advent of the semiconductor memory, the small computer user had no really viable means of providing the short term memory function required by almost any computer application. As mentioned in an earlier article, numerous schemes were tried including used core planes, tape loops, delay-lines, etc. The problem with all these attempts was that they were not available to a large proportion of the possible users, and they were only suitable for the more knowledgeable tinkerers.

Speaking of delay lines, I just came across a 1968 model desk calculator that uses a magnetostrictive delay line for its entire memory. The line stores 408 bits organized as 5 registers of 68 bits each and 1 register of 68 bits. The single register portion of the line circulates five times as fast as the five-register segment, making it more available to the calculation logic. This is achieved on a single line by intermixing the single register with the storage of the five registers as shown in Figure 1.

This is a unique method of solving the memory problem; unfortunately the line is packaged in a box 7x4x1½ inches. The electronics which includes two write amplifiers, a read amplifier and address decoding, takes up a full card. With the presently available semiconductor memories, this storage function could be implemented with about three chips. You can see why semiconductor memories have replaced almost all other competing devices for small-to-medium size fast-access applications.

The first semiconductor memories were bipolar devices fabricated using S-R (Set-Reset) flip-flops with the addition of addressing structures. The basic memory cell of such a device is shown in Figure 2. As can be seen, cross-coupled NOR gates are used to form the flip-flop, which is only accessible when the word line is high. The output of the flip-flop is gated on to the "0" line for reading. An early organization of this type of memory resulted in a 64-bit RAM (AM29700) shown in Figure 3. $D_{0\text{-}3}$ are the data input lines and $O_{0\text{-}3}$ are the data output lines. WE controls the write/read operations and the CS line is used to provide for memory expansion. A device built like this, using Schottky technology is capable of a 17ns access time.

Sixty-four bits on a chip, while representing a significant advance over previous storage densities, still did not meet the needs of the microcomputer industry. At this point MOS technology began to flex its muscles with the development of static and dynamic memories. Both types of memory serve the same market and were developed at about the same time. The static devices have the edge in ease of use and speed, while the dynamic types lead in the power-cost function.

Figure 4 is a diagram of the basic static cell — a six-transistor flip-flop formed of depletion mode devices. Data is stored as charge on the gate of either Q_3 or Q_4, the cross-connected transistors. Devices Q_2 and Q_5 function as high-value load resistors. It is interesting to note that it is easier to fabricate resistors as degerate active devices (two terminal MOSFETs) than to add the extra process steps necessary to form a passive resistor. For this device, we will use the convention that if Q_3 is "ON" then a "0" is stored in the cell, and if Q_4 is "ON" then a "1" is stored. If Q_3 is "ON" it holds the gate voltage of Q_4 low enough to keep device Q_4 "OFF" and the cell will hold that state. Transistors Q_1 and Q_6 form switches which connect the cell to the data read/write lines when that particular row has been selected.

Column selection is done with the data lines. Figure 5 shows the organization of a typical 1024 words x 1 bit memory (Intel 2102A), and Figure 6 shows a more detailed view of the internal data path. Note how the column select line actually selects the write buffer and a read output gate.

For a read operation, a sense amplifier connected to both I/O "0" and I/O "1" outputs of each column detects the state of the selected storage cell inthat column. If Q_3 is on, then Q_4 is off, and when Q_6 is turned on (ROW SELECT) current will flow in the I/O "0" line. Current will flow in the opposite line (I/O "1") if a "1" is stored in the cell.

To set the state of the storage cell, a write buffer controls the level of the I/O lines. If it is desired to write a "1" then the I/O "1" line is taken to approximately V_{cc} while the opposite line is held low (V_{ss}). This action will

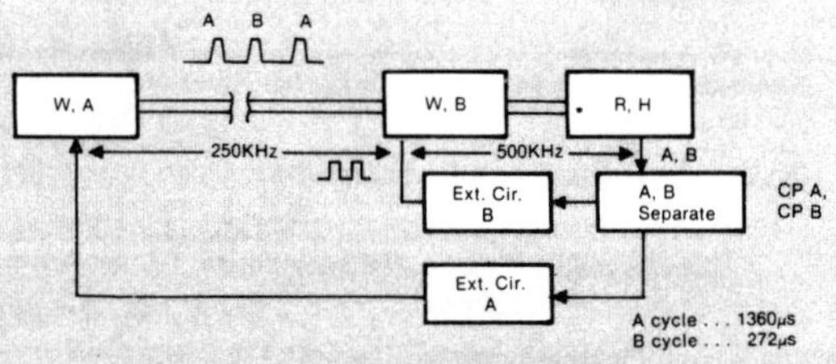

Figure 1. Delay Line Circuit.

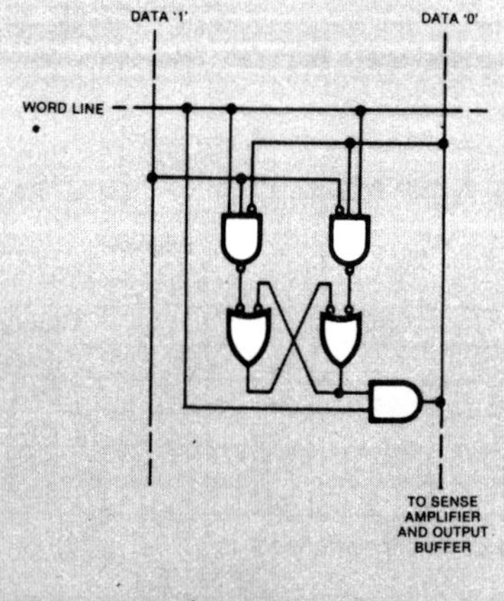

Figure 2. Basic Memory Cell.

override the previous state of the storage cell and the new information will be stored. A chip enable line is shown which gates both the internal data busses, allowing easy memory expansion.

A newer entry into the RAM field is the static memories utilizing the C-MOS (complementary-metal-oxide-semiconductor) process. One-kilobit devices are available with access time under 350ns and supply currents of less than 100 microamperes. In these memories, the load devices are replaced with P-channel devices. Static RAMs can be built as either synchronous or asynchronous devices. Asynchronous devices will allow an address change at any time with no loss of data, while synchronous memories must have a clock pulse to disable the chip during address changes. Figure 7 shows the block diagram of the Intersil IM6523, a 256 x 1 Asynchronous RAM.

The ability to store charge on a capacitor for an appreciable time is utilized in the MOS dynamic RAMs. The storage cell of a typical dynamic RAM (in this case the Intel 2107B) is shown in Figure 8 along with its associated Input/Output circuitry. This is a 4096 word x 1 bit memory organized using a 64 x 64 memory array. The overall memory organization is shown in Figure 9.

Operation of this memory is dependent upon proper design of the sense amplifier. This device not only senses the small voltage changes when the cell is read, but it then latches to the appropriate state to provide a logic level output and rewrite the data back into the cell. The data sense/latch (S/A) is shown in Figure 10. It should be noted that this memory is of the inverting type — that is, the data output at the output pin is the logical inverse of the data written into memory. The operation of the memory depends on the level of the voltage stored by capacitor C_{STG} — if it is above V′ a logic "1" will be outputted, and if the stored voltage is below V′ then a logic "0" will be read.

Consider first a read operation where the storage capacitor C_{STG} is discharged (node 1 is at V_{ss}). Before the chip enable line is brought high, the bit sense lines will be at a level of V′ due to the on condition of transistors Q_1. When the address lines have stabilized, the proper column select line is brought high. This turns on device Q_2 and the storage capacitor is electrically connected to the bit sense line. The charge on the storage capacitor is then distributed between C_{STG} and $C_{I/O}$ (the parasitic capacitance of the bit sense line). Since the parasitic capacitor is much larger than the value of C_{STG} (also a parasitic capacitor), the voltage change of the bit line will be very small.

The sense/latch amplifier is a cross-coupled pair of transistors. The voltage level V′ is such that both devices will be in their active regions, and the circuit will act as a very high gain regenerative amplifier. Therefore, if the left bit line is lower than the right bit line, Q_3 will conduct more heavily than Q_4. This operation is regenerative and very quickly the amplifier will latch-up with bit-sense-left going to V_{SS} and bit-sense-right going to nearly V_{DD} (V_X). Note that during the read operation the previous contents of the cell are destroyed and the read operation is effectively a destructive read. The action of the sense/latch amplifier is such that the information is automatically rewritten back into C_{STG} and therefore the process is transparent to the user, who in effect sees an NDRO device. A write operation is identical to the rewrite portion of the read cycle. In the case of a "write," the new information just overrides the state of the sense/latch and the desired logic level is written into the cell.

Since the information in a dynamic RAM is stored in a capacitor, it is subject to a voltage change because of leakage currents caused by parasitic resistors. For this reason the data must be constantly rewritten, or refresh-

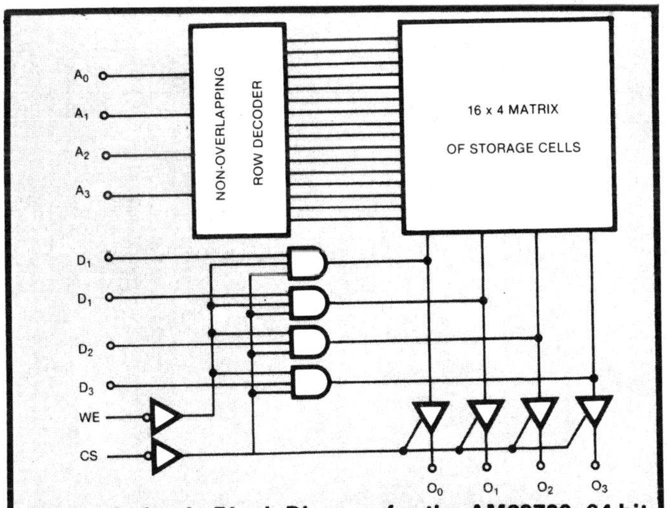

Figure 3. Logic Block Diagram for the AM29700, 64-bit.

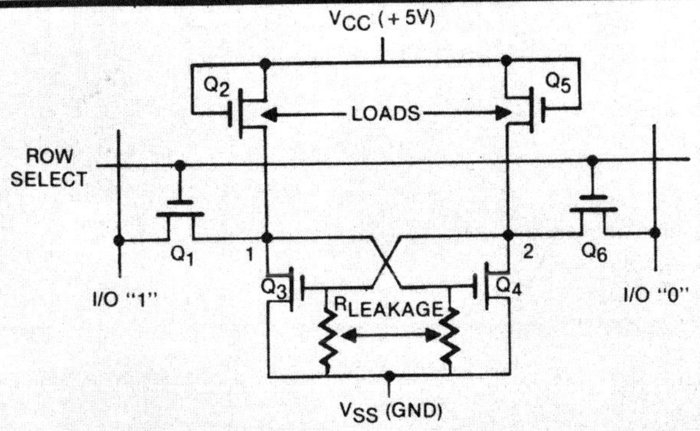

Figure 4. Basic MOS Static Memory Cell.

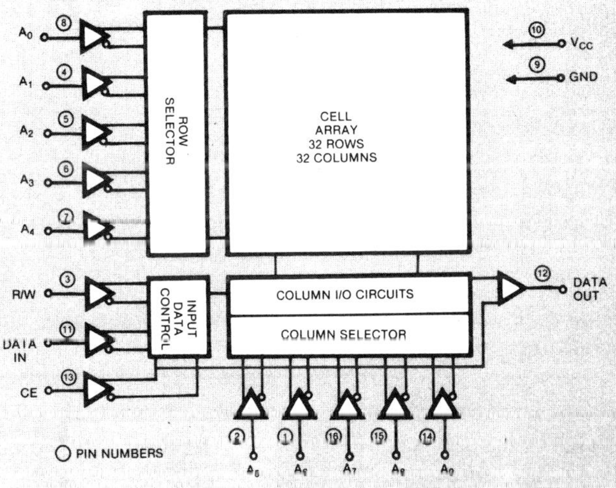

Figure 5. 2102 Block Diagram

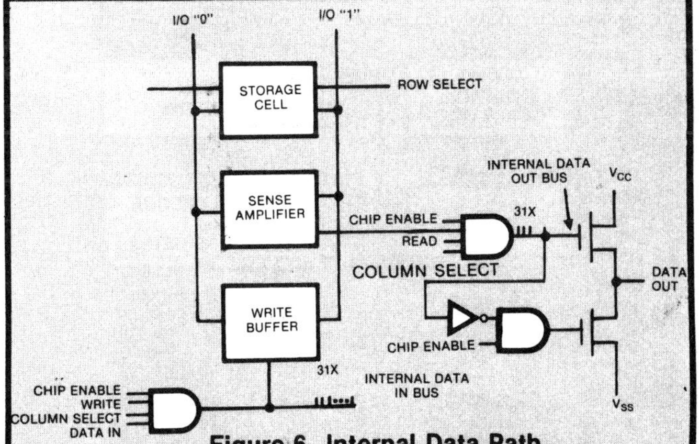

Figure 6. Internal Data Path.

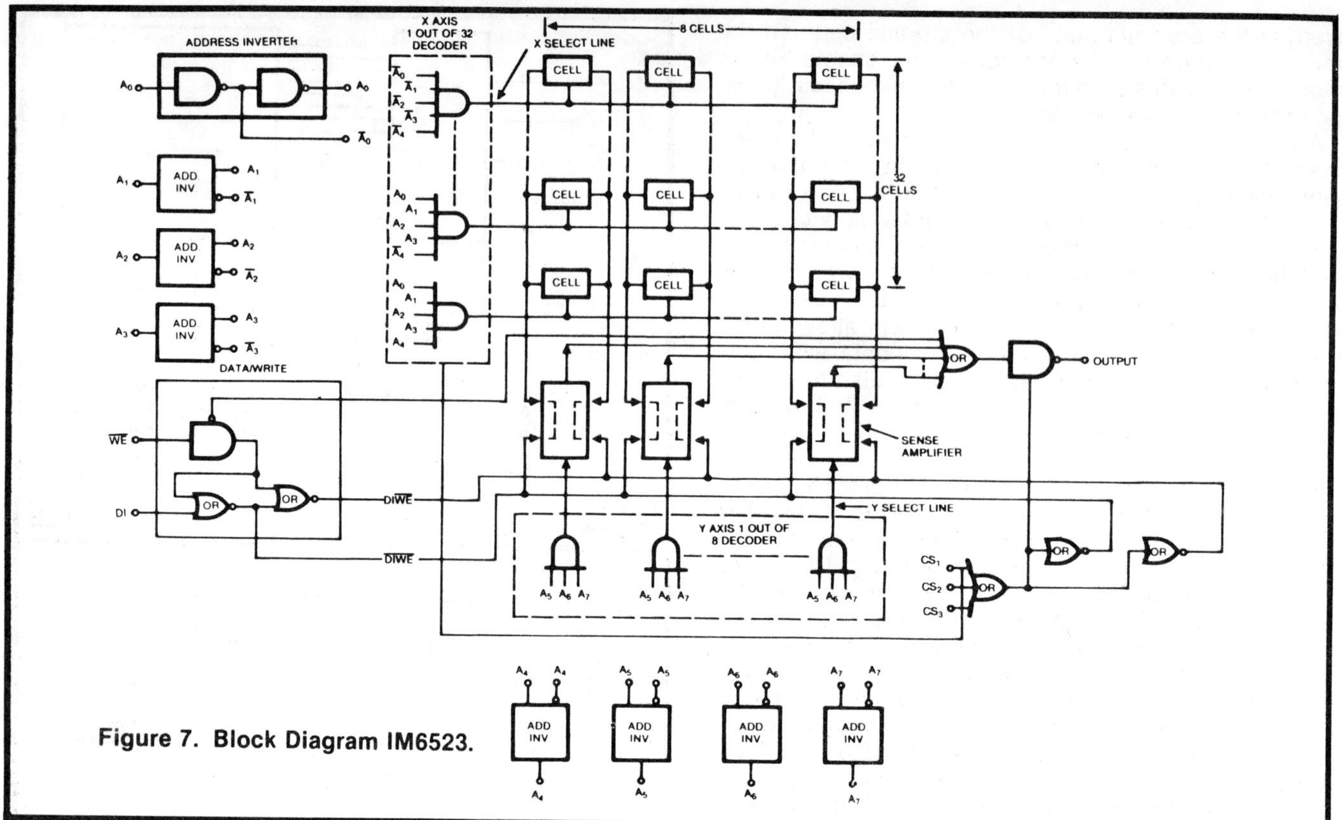

Figure 7. Block Diagram IM6523.

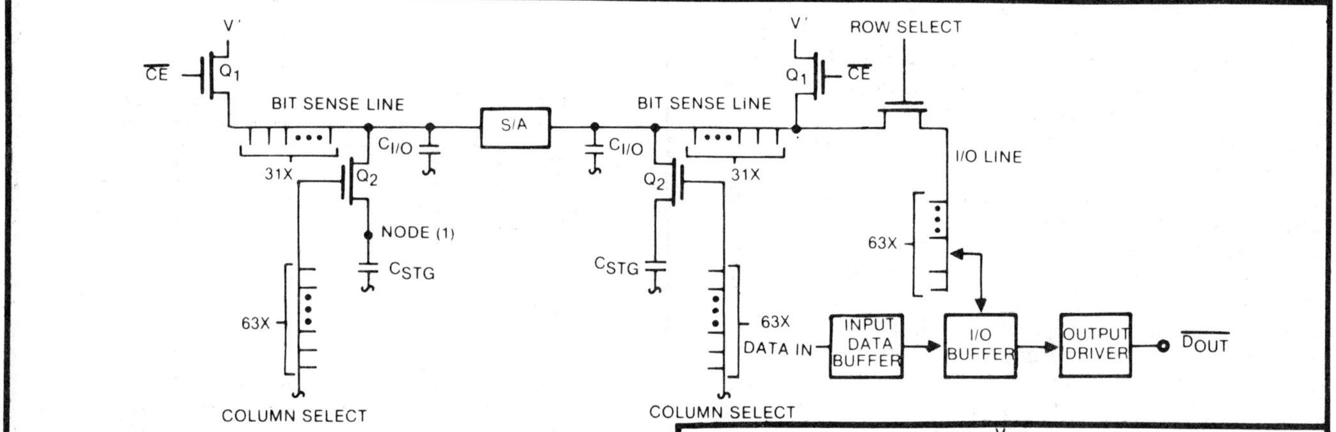

Figure 8. 2107B Memory Cell and Associated I/O Circuitry.

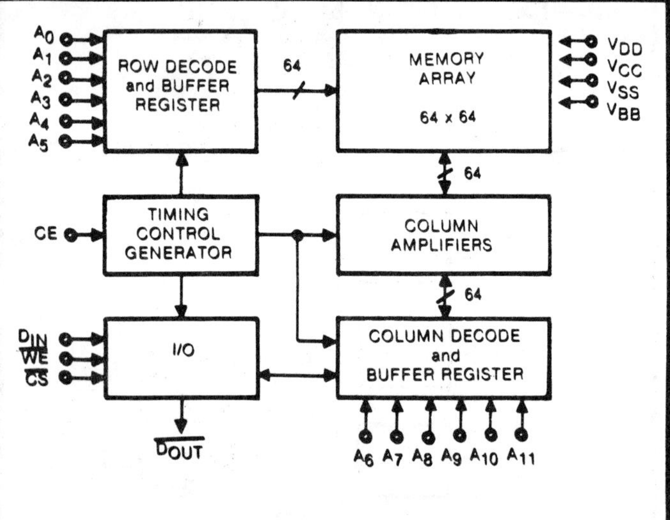

Figure 9. 2107B Block Diagram.

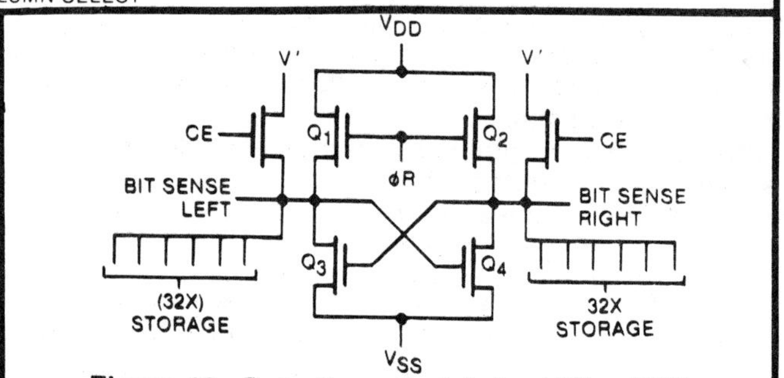

Figure 10. Data Sense/Latch Amplifier (S/A).

ed. This can be done by either a read cycle, a write cycle, or a read-modify write cycle. As each column has a sense/latch amplifier, the easiest way to accomplish this refresh is to perform one read cycle on each of the 64 row addresses. For the 2107B, the maximum refresh time is 2 ms. In earlier memory subsystem designs, the refresh cycle was done by halting the MPU. This would introduce delays into the computer operation, or would cause flashes or gaps in a video field. Later designs accomplish refresh during states of the MPU when memory access is not required — cycle stealing. The Z-80 provides a dedicated control to implement this transparent refresh.

The dynamic RAM provides high storage densities because of the small substrate area required by the storage cell. The storage capacitor is a parasitic element and therefore does not add to the real estate. The disadvantage is a somewhat higher subsystem complexity over static memories. The dynamic memory also provides a power saving over the standard static MOS memories. The C-MOS devices challenge the power dissipation superiority of the dynamic devices, but at a significantly higher cost. As the state of the art matures, various memories process improvements will provide increased storage densities with lower power and costs.

Figure 11 shows the organization of the Intel 2117 memory. This is a 16K word x 1 bit memory with 150 ns access time and a power dissipation of only 465mW. The same basic memory organization can be used to produce a read only memory (ROM) or a programmable read-only memory (PROM). Figure 12 shows the block diagram of the AMI 56834, a 512 x 8 bit uv erasable and electrically reprogrammable memory. This device provides for bulk erasure of the memory by exposing the chip to ultra-violet light through the transparent lid. After this bulk erasure, a new pattern may be stored.

Other types of PROMs can be built by using fusible Ni-Cr links. Once a fusible link PROM has been written, the pattern cannot be erased, although additional logic "1"s can be placed over any logic "0".

Other types of memory organizations may be designed using semiconductor storage elements, among them FIFOs (First-In-First-Out) buffer registers, 16 bit (4 word x 4 bit) register files, and a 4 word x 2 bit content addressable memory. This later device provides the novel capability of data association, where the memory can be searched for a word to match a specific word. Actually matching may be done a bit basis, further expanding the applications may be done on a bit basis, further expanding the applications of this unique element. Figure 13 provides a logic diagram of this device, the Signetics 8220 CAM element. □

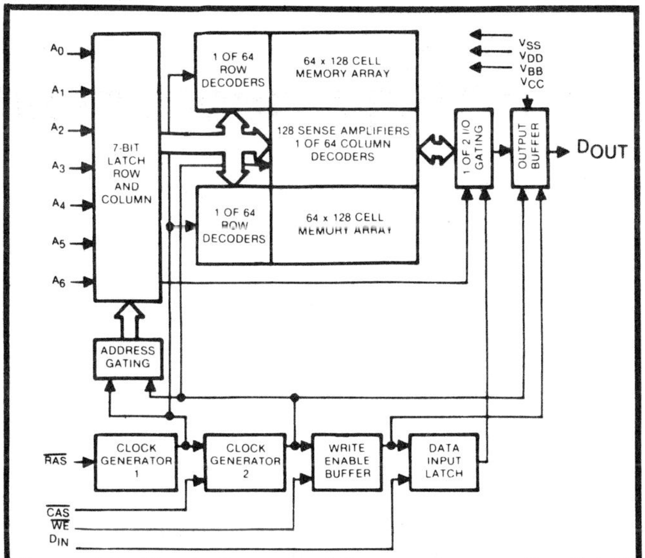

Figure 11. Block diagram of "second generation" 16K RAM. 2117 family.

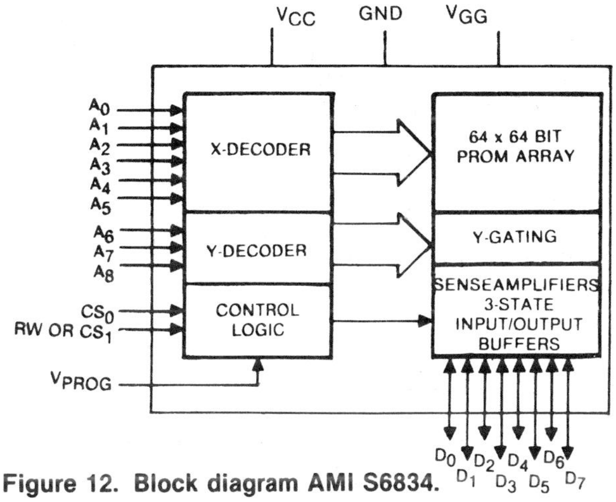

Figure 12. Block diagram AMI S6834.

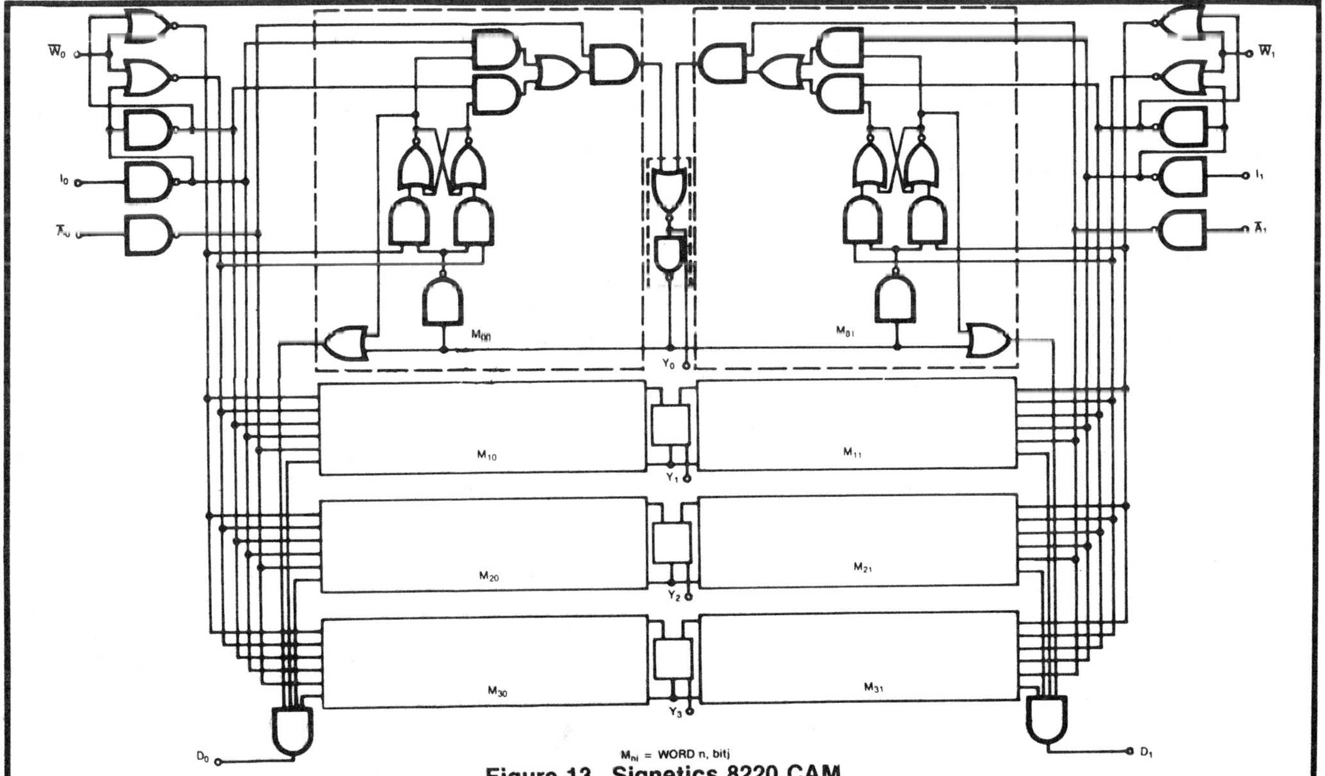

Figure 13. Signetics 8220 CAM.

Acquiring microcomputer skills

by Carol A. Ogdin
Reprinted with permission from *Mini-Micro Systems*, Sept. 1977.

It is said that a cook is as important to the outcome of a stew as is the recipe or the quality of the ingredients. And so it is that a successful microcomputer design project is more than a judicious mixture of hardware and software. Indeed, a microcomputer project entails a different set of skills than those used in traditional computer applications, and knowing what these are is an important first step to concluding a project on time, within budget, and to specifications.

Such prerequisite skills are supplied by four distinct disciplines:

- Applications and system design
- Hardware and electronics design
- Software design and programming
- Project management

Such designs are usually characterized by an overabundance of external logic to implement functions that had best be done in software. Input/output hardware, for example, may contain so many extra capabilities that the processor spends more than 99 percent of its time waiting on external events.

In other cases, a cost-conscious designer may go to another extreme: his hardware is so primitive that the software cannot possibly cope with all of the tasks. Furthermore, a designer who lacks software experience tends to underestimate program storage.

Similar problems also occur when software people design microcomputer systems, even though electronics people fre-

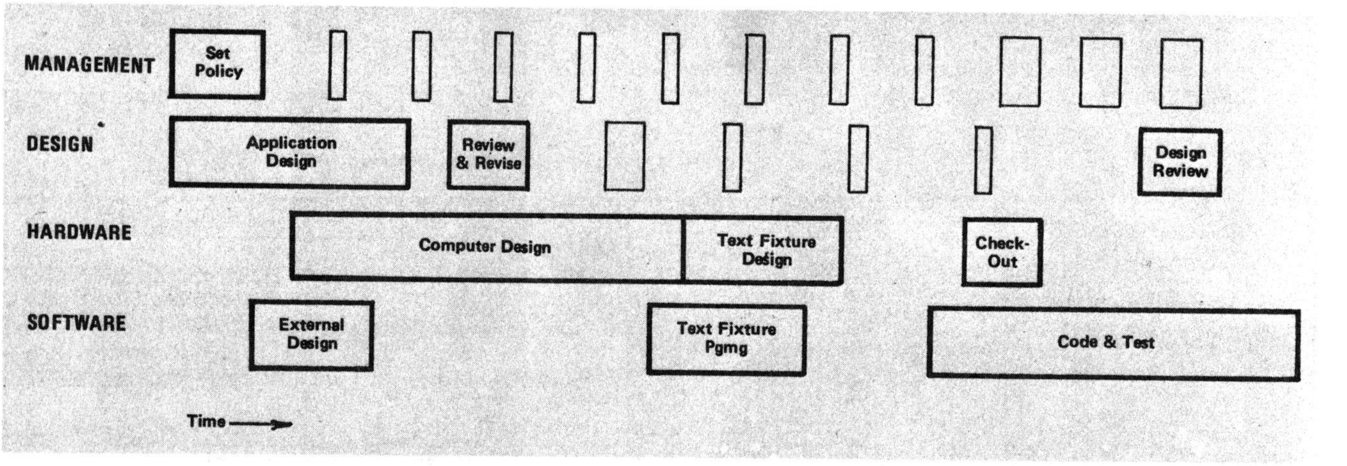

Fig. 1. Stages in a micro systems project.

Many successful microcomputer projects are completed by a single designer who possesses all of these skills, though usually to different levels of proficiency. Early microcomputer applications tended to be implemented by a "converted" digital electronics designer, but the designer's lack of software experience often biases the product to emphasize hardware solutions.

quently assist them. General system timing and input/output interfacing often take a serious beating, though the designer may devise a brilliant software system and estimate storage needs precisely. For example, some microcomputers can operate either at their maximum rated clock speed *or* with maximum capacity memories, but not both. A system designer is in for a rude surprise when his entire software design has to be scrapped because he is unaware of the trade-off.

In the micro field, so-called interdisciplinarians that know how to work with both hardware and software are essential. Such people, however, are rare, and the educational system, unfortunately, is not geared up to impart such breadth of skills. Electrical engineers are not exposed to software design in sufficient depth, and computer science majors do not study circuitry. Even the new college-level microcomputer courses do not fill the bill: To earn an inter-

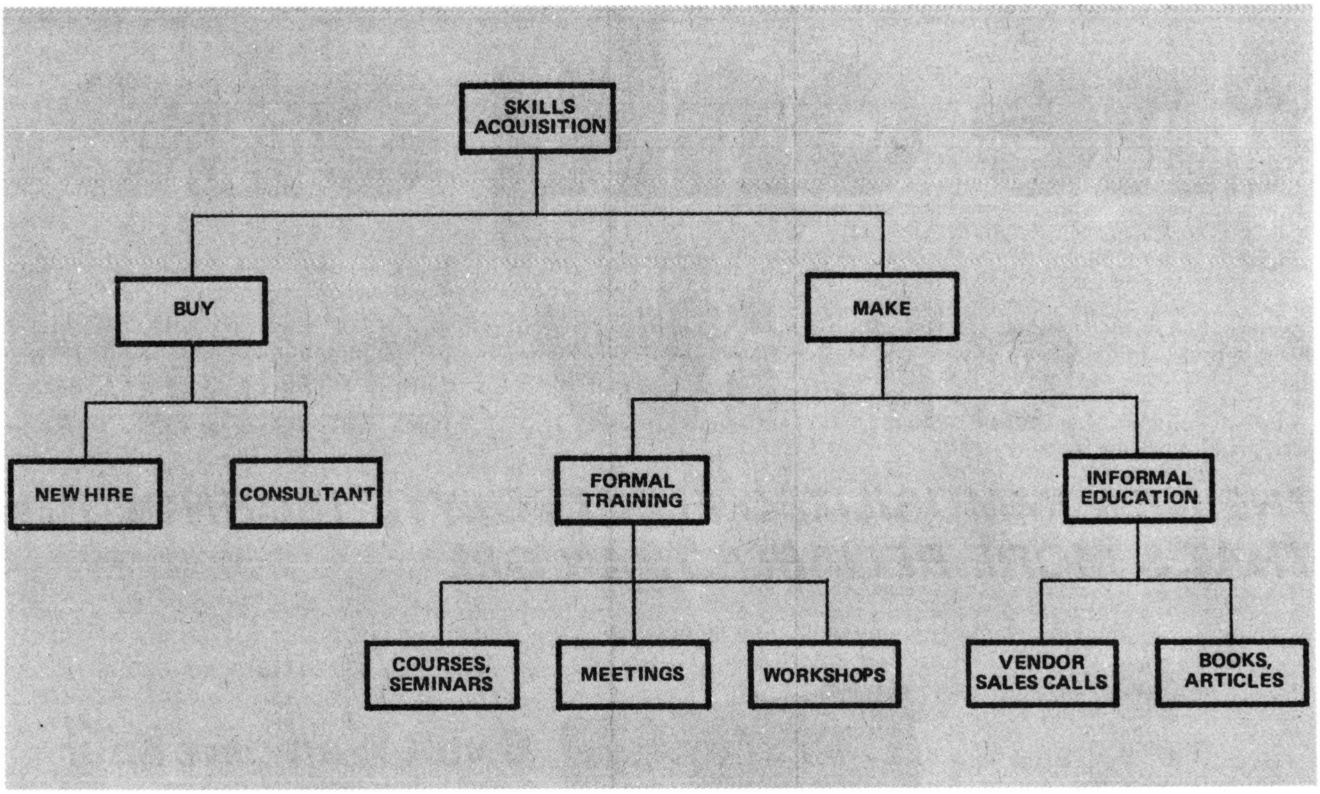

Fig. 2. Skill acquisition Hierarchy.

disciplinarian title takes a lot more than 100 hours of course studies in digital electronics or software design.

TEAM SIZE

Despite the hurdles, all of the software/hardware skills outlined above must be brought to bear on a micro system project – whether the design "team" be a single individual or a group of experts. But when it comes to project management and control, it makes all the difference in the world whether the design "team" be a single individual, or a few people, or a large group.

If all required skills reside in one individual, such as a chief programmer, then the remainder of the team need merely be a support staff.

"A designer who lacks software experience tends to underestimate program storage."

On the other hand, if no such superperson is on hand, then only a balanced team can prevent either hardware or software experience from dominating a design. This can be particularly difficult to accomplish where a two-person team contains a software expert and hardware expert; Then a separate manager may be necessary to serve as an arbiter. Otherwise, whoever of the two experts is not placed in charge will feel slighted.

Thus, the ideal "team" seems to be either a one-person operation or a four-member team where no member need be dedicated to any one microcomputer system project on a full-time basis. Indeed, each person that represents one of the major skill areas will come into the picture and exit from it as he or she is needed (Fig. 1). During the first few weeks, everybody must be involved and cooperating – the applications and systems expert, software programmer, and hardware designer. This is the design phase where most of the critical decisions are made, and a common understanding of goals among the team workers is essential.

The complete absence of any misunderstanding, which is automatic in the case of the one-man "team," indeed enables a project to succeed eventually, even though implementation difficulties arise. This is because the product has a single coherent design, such that any design changes are easily made.

"Only a balanced team can prevent either hardware or software experience from dominating a design."

But a lone person cannot handle projects that are too complex. A group effort is necessary. Here, each team member must appreciate and value the skills and contributions to be offered by other team members. At the very least, software people must understand hardware design principles, and hardware people must know software engineering principles. Otherwise the project is likely to suffer because constant squabbling and even subtle sabotage results.

That is why a design and development team must also have a competent leader whose decisions will be accepted as essentially final by the members. Otherwise, acrimonious debates will arise even over the most trivial issues. At some point, a team leader must be strong enough to make an arbitrary decision – and then to make it stick.

ACQUIRING THE SKILLS

The alternatives for acquiring the necessary microsystem design skills to carry out a project are limited. Typically, a project manager faces a make-or-buy decision. The advantages to hiring experienced personnel are clear. A person can be chosen because he or she has relevant experience to apply to the problem immediately. But a manager taking the new-hire approach had best be prepared to spend lots of

TO GET STARTED

Self-education via the resources of vendor literature and products, good books, and trade publications is the most direct and least expensive method to improve one's skills. Microproduct vendors are eager to help a beginner to learn about their wares, and an indispensable starting point is a technical manual on each device of interest. For example, the Intel 8080 and Motorola 6800 user manuals are both comprehensive *and* concise. Furthermore, applications engineers at these companies can answer questions that are not covered in the literature. The test equipment companies also make available an informed sales cadre. Software types can get demonstrations of logic analyzers, oscilloscopes, and other paraphernalia to acquaint themselves with hardware.

Several sources now offer self-education workshops that typically include a small microcomputer, often in kit form, and an educational text. It is wise to skim the text before committing to the course to make certain that the text is intelligently written and is at the appropriate level. Some so-called evaluation kits assume too much knowledge on the part of a beginner. In addition, microcomputer learning aids tend to assume some knowledge of electronics on the part of the user as well as a minimal exposure to computers and software. This means that to use these tools effectively, a software designer has to acquire a basic know-how in digital logic that will enable him to read a schematic diagram. Many types of digital logic "trainers" are on the market, and these can supply such necessary background.

The hardware designer wanting to learn about software, on the other hand, will find that the self-teaching tools on the market are quite adequate for learning about computer architecture, program coding, and checkout. But such commercially-prepared texts seldom treat the difficult issues of software design (precoding), documentation, and other important software activities.

money and at least a few months on recruitment. Microcomputer experience is in great demand and salary levels are high – $20,000 at least. Moreover, an employer may have to shell out a recruiting firm's 20 percent finder fee, relocating expenses, travel costs, and so on. Nor can a project manager be certain that a new-hire will mesh nicely with other members on the design team.

The other approach, engaging a consultant or design service firm, turns out to be the least costly way to acquire any of the missing skills, unless the people are needed on a permanent basis to serve a series of projects. Any such arrangement should name the specific individual(s) that are to be assigned to the company. Consultants are expensive, of course, and a manager should be certain that he gets the talent that he contracts for. A consultant may even be able to supply some of the specialized equipment that he has acquired through other work, such as a logic analyzer or development system.

CREATING SKILLS

If a company's employees are highly motivated, though limited in experience, exposing them to a carefully structured training program may impart all the necessary skills. This approach is the least expensive and the most gratifying for the company and its employees, though such a training program typically takes several months to get under way. A warning: Sending employees to the various professional meetings as a quick solution is tempting, but attendees need to have some initial knowledge to find such a meeting useful. Team members can better be brought up to speed quickly through participation in a three-to-five day "cram" course, such as those offered by microcomputer vendors, colleges and universities, and commercial firms.

The cost to attend anyone of these are strikingly similar, and a cram course succeeds or fails primarily on the strength of the instructors. To check on instruction quality, a manager should talk to the principal instructor personally. Inquire about his background and teaching experience, or else track down former attendees at the course and ask them for an appraisal. A reputable course operator will gladly refer you to past participants from your local area. Another, more leisurely, approach is to put company engineers through formal college programs.

Course emphasis will also vary depending on who is behind the program. Semiconductor company courses cover only the specific products made by that vendor. These can be good courses, however, if a specific microprocessor or supplier is already chosen, even though such courses can be paid sales pitches in a sense. Participants are often given advanced information on forthcoming products as well as insights as to tricks and techniques on how to work with specific chips. On the negative side, however, no vendor will reveal the quirks and deficiencies of a product.

The three-day courses are a good training vehicle for a multi-member team. Each participant will be exposed to the problems faced by the other team members and the interdisciplinary coverage should especially help to identify weaknesses in the team abilities. Nonetheless, each participant should do some preparation beforehand, otherwise much of the value of the course will be lost. A discussion of a microprocessor's status bus clocking, for example, will go over the head of a software designer who has no background on the subject.

As for one-day courses of the type offered by professional society local chapters, these are best regarded as introductory overviews useful to project managers, applications analysts, and system designers. These key professionals have no need to understand electronic details or software structure. In essence, a participant will come away with a knowledge of the jargon and how the functional parts of a microcomputer system fit together.

WORKSHOPS

An important alternative to a cram course is the so-called "workshop" where participants acquire hands-on experience and practical skills – compared to courses and seminars that emphasize cerebral design activity. The most successful workshops seem to be those intended to teach the rudiments of software to digital designers and electronics technicians. This is a worthwhile goal, since these hardware types must be able to create small programs to test the hardware during fabrication, even if a high-powered software expert is part of the team.

Still other workshops familiarize a participant with the design and implementation of digital circuitry. Such a course entails expensive equipment and curricula development – too expensive for commercial training ventures – so college-sponsored courses seem to offer the most value.

Retail computer stores are yet another education outlet, especially on hardware. Some stores, to supplement their income, conduct relatively inexpensive how-to courses. For a basic introduction on software and hardware implementation, these sessions are quite adequate. The opportunity to interact in a small group and with a knowledgeable instructor in a hands-on setting can compensate for the lack of a rigorous presentation.

Conventional college courses on software and electronics should also be considered by the designer who wants to become an interdisciplinarian. These may take a year or more to complete, but a student is more likely to retain the knowledge acquired than when taking a condensed course. The better college courses combine classroom education, homework, and laboratory experience. A software designer who needs to know how to design simple digital electronics circuits, but finds that the microcomputer courses assume too much initial knowledge, should supplement the formal work with a careful reading program plus some special tutoring by one of the college instructors. The electronics designer who wants to learn software, on the other hand, should have little difficulty uncovering a course aimed specifically at digital designers who have limited software experience. However, entry-level courses should be followed-up with advanced courses on data structure and program structure.

Professional meetings are yet another way that a professional can catch up on technical state-of-the-art. The IEEE, for example, offers a variety of programs – as do the National Computer Conferences and the three major electronics shows – Electro on the East Coast, Wescon on the West, and Midcon in the Mid-West. They all offer extensive programs, but the exhibits are often more educational than are the technical papers. The panels and discussion groups are especially rich sources of practical information. Other meetings include the two annual COMPCONs (computer conferences) sponsored by the IEEE Computer Society and the personal computing conferences and shows that are proliferating throughout the country. ■

SELF-STUDY DIRECTORY

Short Seminars

Integrated Computer Systems, Inc., 4445 Overland Ave., Culver City, CA 90230

Infoscope, Inc., 160 Tices Lane, E.Brunswick, NJ 08816

National Engineering Consortiou, Inc., 1211 W. 22nd St., Oak Brook, IL 60521

Brief Workshops

American Institute for Professional Education, Carnegie Bldg., Hillcrest Road, Madison, NJ 07940

Wintek Corp., 902 N. 9th St., Lafayette, IN 47904

Retail Stores

(Check local telephone directory for the following)
Byte Shop
Computerland
Heath Company
MicroSystems

Periodicals

Byte ($12/yr), 70 Main St., Peterborough, NH 03458

Creative Computing ($15), P.O. Box 780-M, Morristown, NJ 07960

Dr. Dobbs' Journal ($12), P.O. Box E., Menlo Park, CA 94025

Interface Age ($10), 13913 Artesia Blvd., Cerritos, CA 90701

Kilobaud ($15), 1001001, Inc., Peterborough, NH 03458

Microprocessors ($67.60), 527 Madison Ave., Suite 1217, New York, NY 10022

ROM ($15), Route 97, Hampton, CT 06247

Professional Societies

Association for Computing Machinery, 1133 Avenue of the Americas, New York, NY 10036

Institute for Electrical and Electronic Engineers (IEEE), 345 E. 47th St., New York, NY 10017

IEEE Computer Society, 5855 Naples Plaza, Suite 301, Long Beach. CA 90803

Digital Training Products

E&L Instruments, 61 First St., Derby, CT 06418

Heath Company, Benton Harbor, MI 49022

Microprocessor Training Products

E&L Instruments, 61 First St., Derby, CT 06418

Heath Company, Benton Harbor, MI 49022

Iasis, Inc., 815 W. Maude Ave., Suite 37, Sunnyvale, CA 94086

Integrated Computer Systems, Inc., 4445 Overland Ave., Culver City, CA 90230

Home-Study Courses

National Radio Institute (Computer Electronics Course) 3939 Wisconsin, Ave., Washington, DC 20016

BOOKS

To Acquire Systems Skills:

An Introduction to General Systems Thinking, by Gerald M. Weinberg, Wiley-Interscience, 279 pp.

To Aquire Management Skills:

The Psychology of Computer Programming, by Gerald M. Weinberg, Van Nostrand Reinhold, 1971, $9.50.

The Mythical Man-month, by Frederick P. Brooks, Jr., Addison-Wesley, 1975.

To Acquire Hardware Skills (read in given order):

Computer Hardware and Software, An Interdisciplinary Introduction, by Marshall D. Abrams and Philip G. Stein, Addison-Wesley, 1973.

Computer Hardware Theory, W.J. Poppelbaum, Mac Millian, 1972.

TTL Cookbook, Don Lancaster, Howard W. Sams & Co., 1974, $8.95. (See also the CMOS Cookbook by the same author.)

Designing with TTL Integrated Circuits, Edited by Robert L. Morris and John R. Miller, McGraw-Hill, 1971, $12.50.

To Acquire Software Skills:

Standardized Development of Computer Software, by Robert C. Tausworthe, Prentice-Hall, 1977.

The Art of Computer Programming, by Donald Knuth, Addison-Wesley, 1975

Vol. I. Fundamental Algorithms, 1968, $20.95.
Vol. II. Seminumerical Algorithms, 1969, $19.95;
Vol III. Sorting and Searching, 1973, $21.00.

(Warning: Many examples cited in these books relate to the large-computer environment and citations of technology are often woefully out-of-date.)

Making the transition to micros

by Carol A. Ogdin
Reprinted with permission from *Mini-Micro Systems*, Oct. 1977

- **Programming a microcomputer is just like programming more traditional machines.**
- **Programming a microcomputer is totally unlike traditional programming.**

The two observations are clearly contradictory, but each is true in a way. Much of the fundamental task in programming remains the same no matter what the computer, but the subtleties differ. Programmers experienced on large-scale computers are appalled at first upon finding that the micro does not come with a sophisticated real-time multiprogramming operating system. Later, after they understand the application domain of micros, their attitudes change. They come to appreciate the tight man-machine interaction during micro software development and the creative potential that this fosters.

"The essential differences in hardware between large systems and micros come into play in memory design and interface circuitry."

The initial stages – requirements analysis, system design, input/output design, and general external design of system features – are the same for all computers and are oriented to defining the needs of a user. But afterward, when the external design is transformed into the reference specification, and when coding, translation and testing are carried out, the programmer must be constantly aware of how micros differ from other kinds of processors.

Most important is knowledge of computer architecture and fundamental operation at a level beyond that traditionally required of programmers. To know that the CPU has registers, for example, is not enough. A programmer must know the cycle-by-cycle operation of the underlying computer to ferret out hardware/software interface bugs.

Programmers with a maxi system background tend to lose the internal motivation to exorcise as many bugs as possible through good, solid design and painstaking, thorough testing. Instead, they seek to rush programs into development, hoping to snare bugs in the initial months of program use. But to work with micros, the programmer must shake this attitude that inherently permits the development and delivery of faulty software. Instead he must embrace the viewpoint that delivered software must be highly dependable. The prudent programmer would do well to make that metamorphosis now, through the adoption of top-down design and the principles of structured or systematic programming, in order to survive in the micro environment.

UNDERSTANDING HARDWARE

From the programmer's standpoint, the essential differences in hardware between large systems and micros come into play in memory design and interface circuitry. In a conventional system, core memory is commonly used. Core is non-volatile: Its contents are not erased when power is shut off. But for micros, data is usually stored in integrated circuits called random-access memory (RAM). The volatility of the RAM can have a significant impact on the "hot start" capability of reliable real-time software. Unless batteries are used for backup to main power, there is simply no way to keep critical information in storage when power is removed.

"Interface documentation, no matter how well written, is often not even suited to the needs of the programmer."

A program design for a microcomputer system may also be very much affected by a clever hardware designer who dreams up an exotic architecture to save a chip or two in the final product (box). But this can backfire when the programmer sets out to write some rudimentary input/output routines. He discovers just how "naked" the microcomputer really is. Channel Command Words are missing, and the computer might not even have a basic direct memory access capability. Typically, all input/output data transfers are handled byte-by-byte through the computer's accumulator. Sometimes the arrangement can be still more primitive: Serial input/output to a teletypewriter terminal, for example, may require the program to issue each bit of out-

HARDWARE VS. SOFTWARE TRADEOFFS

Many of the programmer's treasured assumptions about computer architecture will be challenged when he is exposed to microcomputers. For example, to save a chip in the electronics, the hardware designer may require that programs consist of no more than 4K bytes, spread throughout memory as shown in Fig. 2.

Notice the arrangement of the four leading address bits:

$$(A) = 14 = (1110)_2$$
$$(B) = 13 = (1101)_2$$
$$(C) = 11 = (1011)_2, \text{ and}$$
$$(D) = 7 = (0111)_2.$$

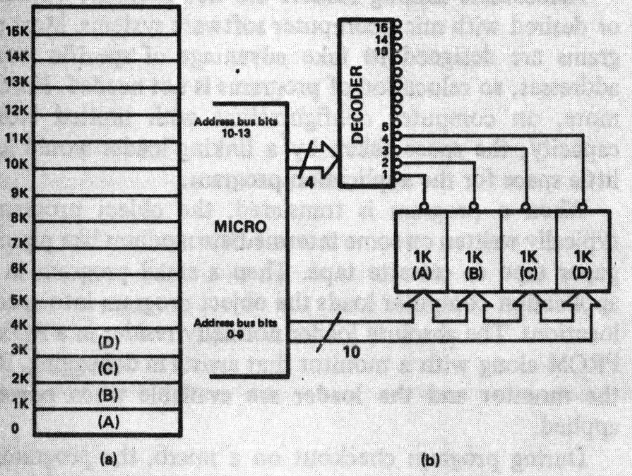

Fig. 1. Traditional computer systems design uses a decoder on the address bus to allow various units of storage to be addressed contiguously.

Each group consists of three ones and a zero. The four most significant address bus bits can be wired directly to the memory parts; when one of those bits is at zero, the affected memory part will respond. Not only is the storage arrangement fragmented into three sections (parts A and B form one contiguous section), but there is no memory at location zero. This could make coldstarting of the program difficult if the program counter is reset to zero when power is applied. The difficulty is alleviated in the more familiar arrangement shown in Fig. 1, where a decoder is used. This allows the programmer to address memory locations in the interval 0-4K.

Hardware designers continually propose novel solutions, which the clever software designer has to consider and accept or reject. The storage arrangement described here looks clumsy, but that is not a reason to discard it.

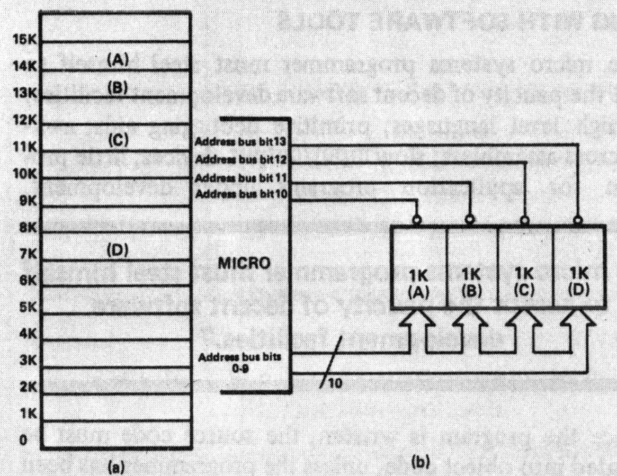

Fig. 2. An inexpensive design may eliminate the memory decoder, but then the programmer must be more concerned about where storage actually lies in the address space.

Consider the impact on the costs of programming. It may be possible to build a fancy relocatable assembler to help create programs for the odd storage arrangement in Fig. 2, depending upon how the program exploits the loader's features. Still, subroutines must be designed to fit within the various noncontiguous blocks of storage. If the total production volume for systems is very low, say, below 20 or so, the savings in electronics and power consumption, on the order of $2.00 per decoder, is negligible; the additional programming effort will outweigh those savings. Then the design of Fig. 1 will prevail. However, if thousands of copies of the system will be produced, each additional decoder in the design must be purchased and installed in quantities of thousands. Then the engineering and manufacturing savings of the configuration in Fig. 2 will undoubtedly be worth the additional software effort.

put individually, interleaved with sequences of instructions that do nothing but waste time in order to control timing of the communications link.

Interface documentation, no matter how well written, is often not even suited to the needs of the programmer. When interfaces are constructed out of the new specialized logic devices, the programmer is usually offered little more than the manufacturer's manual on the part to use as a programming aid. The manual is meant for an electronics designer, not a programmer. Cryptic descriptions of the important features and functions must be read carefully before the programmer can create software to control the input/output devices.

Many applications for microcomputers are implemented on one-of-a-kind configurations. Novel interfaces between the computer and the peripherals may be devised to save implementation time or eventual production costs. These exotic lashups may cause the programmer no end of aggravation because of inadequate documentation.

Interfaces built out of common ICs should be well documented and explained so that the micro programmer does not have to understand the circuitry. But to be most productive, a programmer must learn enough about electronics, TTL, and CMOS to follow a schematic diagram; then he will not constantly need an electronic designer at his elbow to answer questions. The skill comes rapidly to the bright programmer, though the going is tough at first. After about a year, he can read a digital schematic and an assembly language program with equal facility. Of course, hardware designers can do a great deal to help. They should describe input/output devices, storage arrangements, and special features without resorting to block diagrams or schematics. They should be encouraged to use tables to describe input/output device number assignments instead of showing a block diagram of the decoding scheme.

"Because of the unique interfaces, I/O programs for micros must be written in assembly language."

Because of the unique interfaces, I/O programs for micros must be written in assembly language. High-level languages have elementary input/output capabilities for typical computer terminals, but if the input device is a phototransistor that measures impinging light, a high-level language usually can not provide a mechanism for direct access. Instead, the programmer has to write an assembly language subroutine that conforms to the calling conventions of the high-level language processor. Indeed, he may have to write the entire program in assembly language if no high level language is available or if a high-level language produces very inefficient code.

LIVING WITH SOFTWARE TOOLS

The micro systems programmer must steel himself to accept the paucity of decent software development facilities: Few high level languages; primitive debugging aids; awkward cross-assemblers; slow input/output devices; little protection for application programs under development.

"The micro systems programmer must steel himself to accept the paucity of decent software development facilities."

Once the program is written, the source code must be translated into object code, unless the programmer has been hardy enough to write in hexadecimal. If the program is written in a high-level language, a large-scale data processing system or minicomputer may be required for cross-compilation. Even Intel's vaunted PL/M language is supported by an expensive special computer, the Intellec Development System. On the other hand, to translate a program written in assembly language, the assembler may be native to the computer or a similar kind of microcomputer, or it may be a cross-assembler residing on a separate computer.

A separate computer is used for translation, unless the application computer configuration can accept the programmer's language directly. Some fairly small assemblers can be "plugged into" a small microcomputer during development and removed before the product is shipped. There are interpreters, notably for Basic, now available in read-only memories. The interpreter coexists with the applications program throughout the productive life of the system, and the programmer deals with the computer as if its native language is Basic. Of course, the programmer who works directly in hex does not need to use an additional computer, since no translation is required.

Relocatable linking loaders are not normally furnished or desired with microcomputer software systems. Most programs are designed to take advantage of specific storage addresses, so relocation of programs is not needed. Furthermore, on computer configurations with limited storage capacity, the space taken by a linking loader would leave little space for the application program.

When a program is translated, the object program is typically written on some intermediate medium like punched paper tape or cassette tape. Then a small program in the application computer loads the object program into specific locations. The absolute loader normally resides in a ROM or PROM along with a monitor that assists in debugging. Both the monitor and the loader are available when power is applied.

During program checkout on a micro, the programmer interacts with a monitor program, typically smaller than 1024 bytes. It offers the capability to read an object program into read-write memory for trial execution; it accepts the commands necessary to selectively dump and alter the contents of memory to correct bugs; and it recognizes a command to transfer control out of the monitor and back to the program under test. Control is transferred to the monitor automatically during power-up, or whenever the RESET button is depressed.

With such primitive tools, testing and debugging is a serious challenge. The mediocre programmer, accustomed to relying on lots of large-scale software to isolate the bug, will find it almost impossible to work with micros. Should a fault occur, there is no operating system to intercept the bug and print out a trace-back and dump for the programmer to study. No one has yet built sophisticated software systems for micros that can identify bugs in terms of the original source code statements.

"The programmer in transition to micros may have to refresh old knowledge of basic physics and then read some of the newer books on the market."

Retranslating and reloading the program is an arduous process with the slow peripheral devices on micros. The programmer spends a lot of time writing patches to the code. In an average day, the programmer will track down and repair a dozen or more simple bugs, and each fix will require some modification of the object program. The program will be retranslated once or twice a day. Every so often, when the program is stored in RAM for easy patching, the program will wipe itself out, necessitating reloading and reposting of all the patches to date.

HELP IS COMING

But help is on the way; new tools and techniques are coming. The logic analyzer is such a tool. The programmer will be required to make a front-end investment of time and effort to learn to use the analyzer effectively, but the effort will be well spent. New software tools are being developed, too. Taking advantage of the one-man, one-machine environment, new packages are being created that "disassemble" the object code in the computer's memory to display the assembly language equivalent on a CRT. The RAID program furnished by Electronic Module Corp. allows the programmer to interact with an 8080 at the assembly source language level. The user can step through the program under test; as each instruction is executed, the CRT display changes, showing the next several instructions in sequence. A more primitive history-only trace that displays instruction execution, in symbolic form, is offered in the Tektronix 8002 Microprocessor Lab.

LEARNING THE ROPES

To learn how to live in this new world, the programmer in transition to micros may have to refresh old knowledge of basic physics and then read some of the newer books on the market. Since the subject of digital circuit design is so embedded in the electrical engineering curriculum, most engineering schools offer a wide range of courses. Even if the programmer does not have time to attend classes, the books are generally quite readable, though it helps to have a digital designer handy to answer questions. Most programmers will have no trouble following the self-study books and videotapes offered by the Texas Instruments Learning Center.

Still, there is no substitute for hands-on experience. The programmer should start by studying the microcomputer's underlying architecture. If it is based on one of the popular microprocessors, the programmer should study the computer manual to gain a feel for typical programs. Then the programmer should acquire several pages worth of program that are understandable, and read that code. Next, he should write programs for all of the primitive input/output interface ports. The programmer will gain some direct experience in working at the elementary level demanded with micros, and he will be able to judge the lucidity of the documentation and the utility of the interfaces themselves.

"The programmer new to micros is often tempted to try to define and implement an entire input/output control system."

At the same time, problems may crop up that software can not solve, and the electronic design can be modified before it is "frozen." The hardware design, for example, may make impossible demands upon the software, such as invoking a subroutine that executes for one millisecond more than 1000 times a second.

The program that results from this initial effort can be used to exercise the peripheral devices and input/output ports during hardware checkout. The engineers and technicians will appreciate this software, especially if they have no programming experience of their own.

The programmer new to micros is often tempted to try to define and implement an entire input/output control system (IOCS). Some even try to implement real-time schedulers and task oriented operating systems. The experienced users of micros tend to shy away from anything so complex. Why have a 3000-byte overhead when the entire application program runs to the same size? In general, such systems are as hard to program as the native input/output facilities of the micro, and the latter approach leaves more room for creative interfaces and software solutions.

BAD PROGRAMMING'S HIGH COST

Software reliability, long a subject of conferences and papers, is extremely important to micro system programmers. Software failure – that is, the unpredicted behavior of some part of the system – may have catastrophic effects. When a micro, for example, controls a chemical process in a petroleum refinery, a small bug can cause loss of life and property.

Even on simple economic grounds, the reliability of programs becomes an important issue. If a product is manufactured in 1000 copies, and each read-only memory (ROM) costs $20, a bug in ROM-resident software will cost $20,000 in parts alone, and the vendor will be forced to wait several weeks until corrected ROMs are fabricated. In addition, tens of thousands of dollars will be spent to replace the parts in already installed equipment. In such a situation, it is easy to project a per-bug cost in excess of $100,000 that far and away exceeds the original development cost. ■

Part 3: Advanced Microcomputer Theory

Really getting into the hardware of microcomputers means getting to know the microprocessor chips that are at the heart of them. Though as many as 50 different microprocessors exist, only a handful or so are truly popular. This section includes technical articles on their architecture. But it takes more than just one chip to build a computer, and with today's levels of circuit integration, all the additional chips—memory, input, output, and control—can fit on one printed-circuit board. Thus the board-level computer has been born. Most personal computers are really simply one-board computers that are boxed up and have a keyboard and display added; this part also takes a look at how those boards are put together.

Designers gain new freedom as options multiply

After 18 months of calm, in which microprocessor manufacturers have consolidated the designs of their first general-purpose families, a second big wave of activity has begun. This time, however, it reaches a more sophisticated level.

Urged on by savvy users, whose concern is with system design rather than chip architecture, the manufacturers are introducing second- and third-order refinements aimed at boosting microcomputer capacity while lowering system cost. At the same time, they are rushing new devices to market to extend the microprocessor performance range both at the low end, where existing chips present an overkill solution, and at the high end.

Four trends are emerging. First, established families are being enhanced. System throughput is being increased and instruction sets enlarged as manufacturers turn to new metal-oxide-semiconductor processing and improved central-processer architecture. Input/output power, too, is being increased with new sets of programable I/O chips.

Second, the new 16-bit single-chip processing units are heading upwards. What they are aiming for is the high-performance end of the microprocessor market, where precision arithmetic and large memories must be accommodated.

Third, the one-chip controllers, as their name implies, contain enough computing power to handle many stand-alone controller functions on their own. On the same chip as the central processing unit sit control read-only memory for program storage, random-access memory for data storage, and input/output registers for system manipulation.

Finally, there's a host of single-board microcomputers, beguiling alternatives to the do-it-yourself approach of buying just the chips.

All these developments are changing the microprocessor universe. In order to graph this change, Fig. 1 charts the various family types against the applications spectrum.

Clearly, the 8-bit system covers the most ground, being used in many more different designs than either the 4- or 16-bit devices. Indeed, the 8-bit word seems just about right for most of today's microcomputer systems, in contrast to the 16-bit words that are the staple of minicomputers.

How much overlap there will be between powerful 8-bit general-purpose systems and the 16-bit high-performance systems is still to be determined, especially in large-memory process-control applications. The current wisdom is that the 16-bit families will remain primarily on the high-performance end of the application spectrum for several years, since the 8-bit families are so well established.

Besides, enhanced 8-bit microprocessors are coming along that are faster and can handle 16-bit word data anyway, making it easy for a user to upgrade his 8-bit system to a 16-bit design without much additional investment in software. Moreover, the use of single-chip controllers in distributed processing systems boosts the performance of 8-bit designs by taking much of the burden off the central processing unit and, in many cases, by making it unnecessary to move up to a higher-capacity 16-bit CPU system.

Meanwhile the multichip 4-bit systems—the earliest microprocessors to appear—are feeling increasing pressure from the minimum-chip system designs. Rockwell's PPS-8/2 and PPS-4/2 two-chip systems, Fairchild Semiconductor's F-8, National Semiconductor's SC/MP, and Electronic Arrays' 9002 can all handle many of the jobs formerly done by the 4-bit Intel MCS-4 or Rockwell PPS-4 but often with fewer packages and at lower cost. Moreover, the single-chip 4- and 8-bit microcontrollers already mentioned will increasingly eliminate the need for multichip 4-bit designs.

Puts it all together. Activity in microprocessors is fast and furious, as manufacturers make available a wide range of products, from low-cost microcontroller chips to powerful, general-purpose families and boards. This 16-bit microcomputer is from Data General.

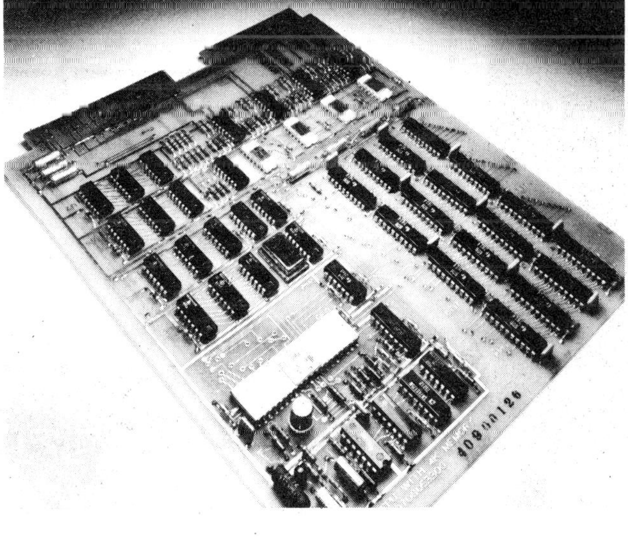

The 8-bit mainstream

In the 8-bit microprocessor applications spectrum, Intel Corp.'s 8080 family, with its enhanced 8080A CPU, Motorola Semiconductor's 6800 family, with its enhanced 6800D CPU, and Rockwell's PPS-8 family currently rank one, two, and three in popularity among users. The 8080 system is being used in a wide range of industrial process controls, games, intelligent data terminals, and so on. The 6800 has found its greatest penetration in data-communications terminals and instrumentation. The PPS-8 has found strong acceptance in skid-control automotive designs, as well as in other high-volume systems. All are second-sourced—the 8080 by AMD, TI, NEC, and Siemens, the 6800 by AMI, and the PPS-8 by National.

What makes these chip families so suitable for general-purpose applications is the centralization of their computing capabilities—an orientation borrowed from minicomputer architecture. Unlike many newer designs, such as the F-8, which distributes its computing power among its family of devices, the 8080, 6800, and PPS-8 concentrate that power all on a single chip. In effect, their central processing units act as their own peripheral controllers, using generalized bus lines to manipulate external memories, interface chips, and input/output chips.

These CPU chips are well equipped for their job. Both the 8080A and 6800D have a 16-bit address bus, an 8-bit bidirectional data bus, and fully TTL-compatible control outputs. Besides supporting up to 65 kilobytes of random-access memory, they can address a large number of peripheral devices, providing for practically unlimited system expansion.

Moreover, both CPUs show a considerable improvement in architecture over the preceding generation of 8-bit designs. The 8080, for example, contains a 16-bit stack pointer that controls the addressing of an external stack located in memory. The proper instructions can initialize this pointer to use any portion of external memory as a last-in/first-out stack, so that almost unlimited subroutine nesting becomes available. The stack pointer in addition allows the contents of the program counter, the accumulator, the condition flags, or any of the data registers to be stored in or retrieved from the external stack.

The 8080's stack control instructions also permit multilevel interrupts. The current program or "status" of the processor can be pushed onto the stack when an interrupt is accepted, then popped off the stack after the interrupt has been serviced, and this can be done even when the interrupt service routine is itself interrupted.

Where the two families differ is in several of the system requirements. The 6800's single 5-volt power supply contrasts with the 8080's ±5 V and 12 V supplies. The 6800 timing is quite simple. All instructions are executed in two or three cycles, which are identical in length. Control outputs are real-time signals instead of look-ahead instructions. Moreover, in the 6800 system, separate I/O instructions are unnecessary since memory locations can house either I/O or memory data.

On the other hand, the 8080 has more powerful instructions, with stronger branch and interrupt capability. It can interface with a wide variety of peripheral devices. It has tremendous software support, such as an in-

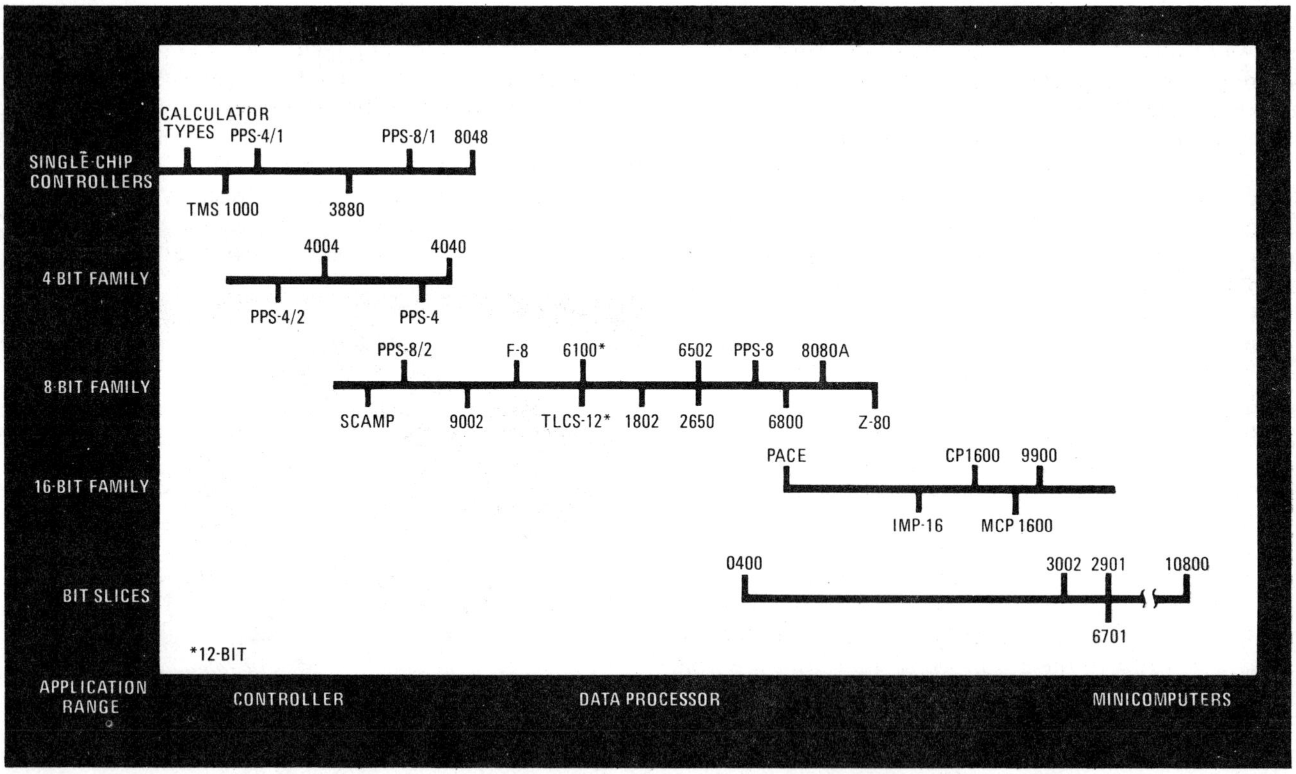

1. The universe. The 8-bit microprocessor families cover most ground, being found in everything from peripheral controllers to powerful data-processing systems. The 4-bit systems handle the smaller controller jobs, while the 16-bit chips and bit slices rise to minicomputer work.

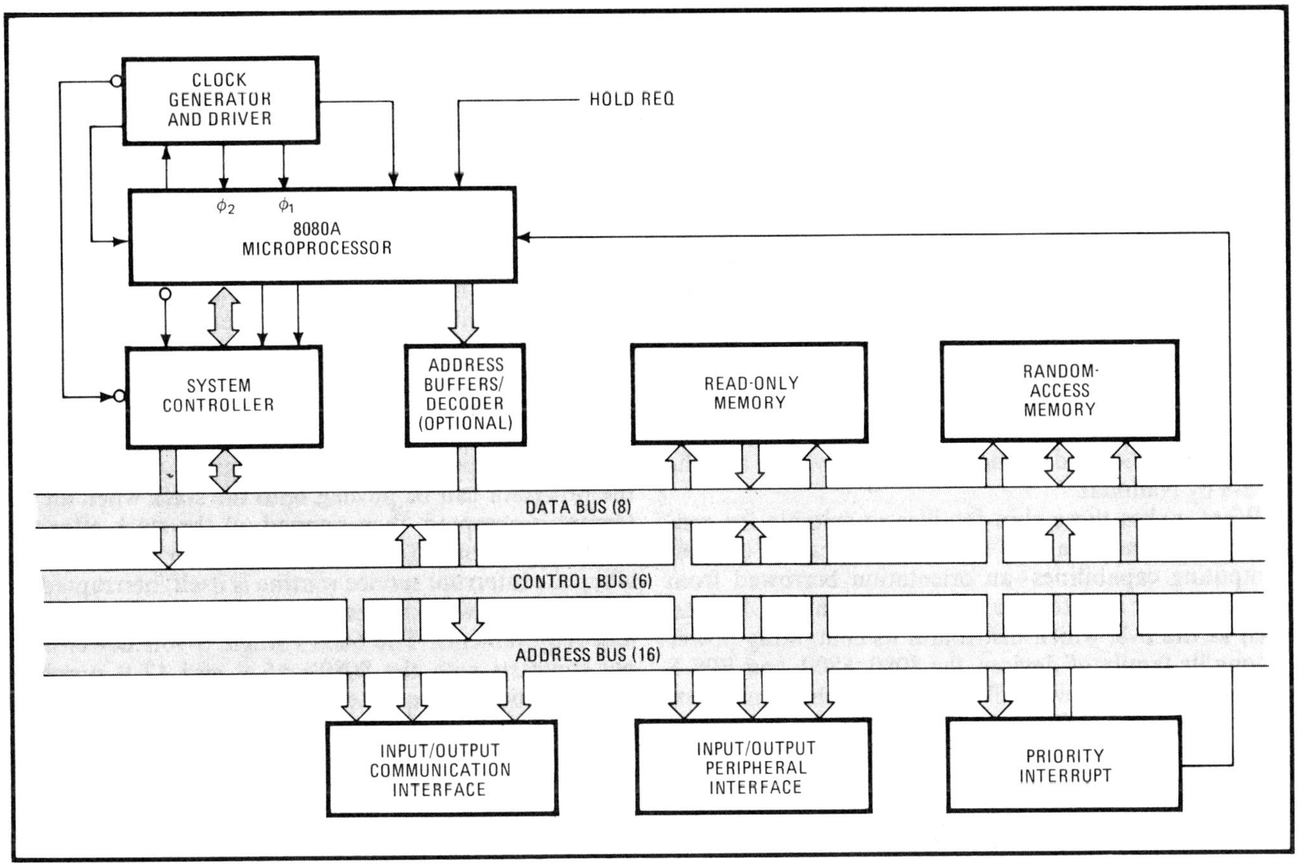

2. The 8080. Intel's 8080 system can produce dozens of peripheral and I/O device configurations. Because all devices connect to a system bus, hooking up parts into complex configurations becomes quite straightforward once the instruction program has been developed.

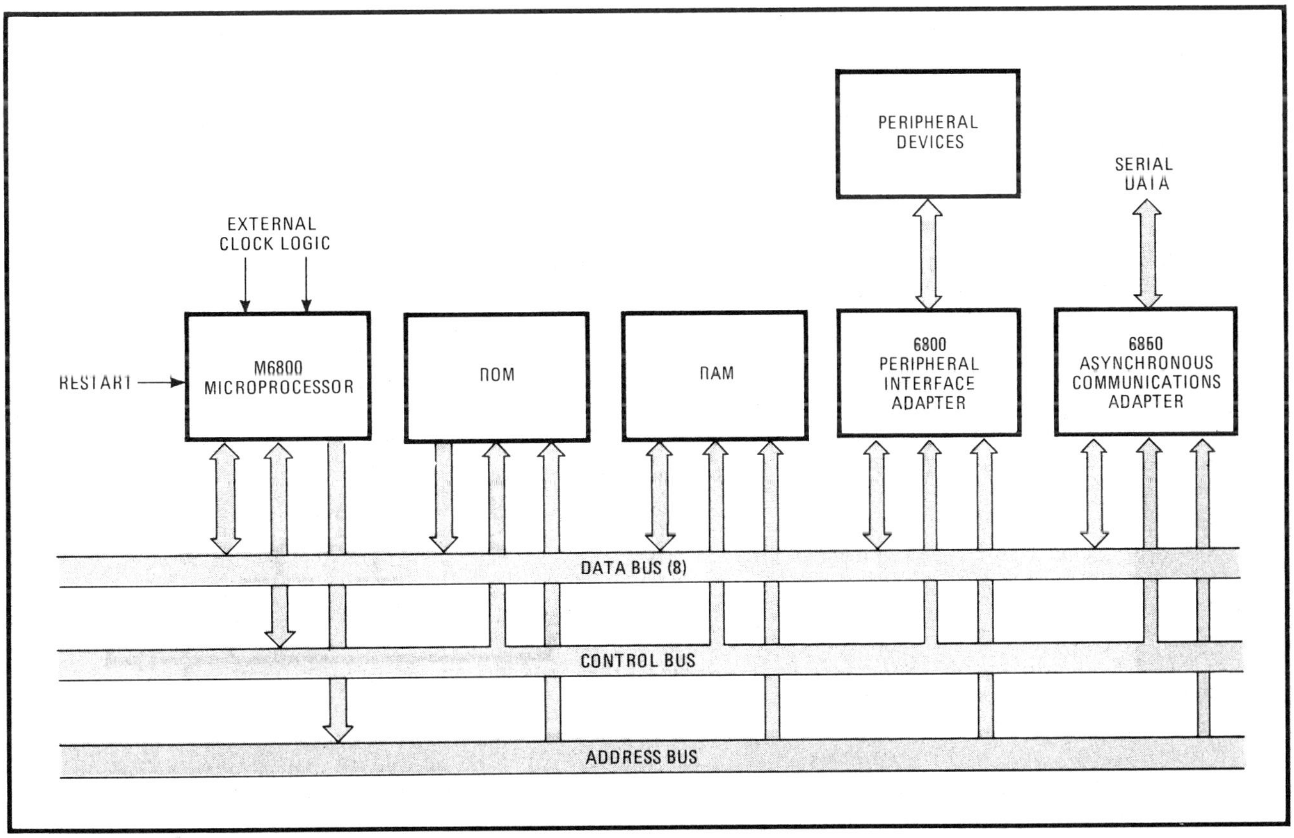

3. The 6800. A Motorola 6800 system, also designed around a central bus, keeps the package count to a minimum by using powerful peripheral devices, such as the peripheral interface and communication adapters. System works off standard ROMs and RAMs.

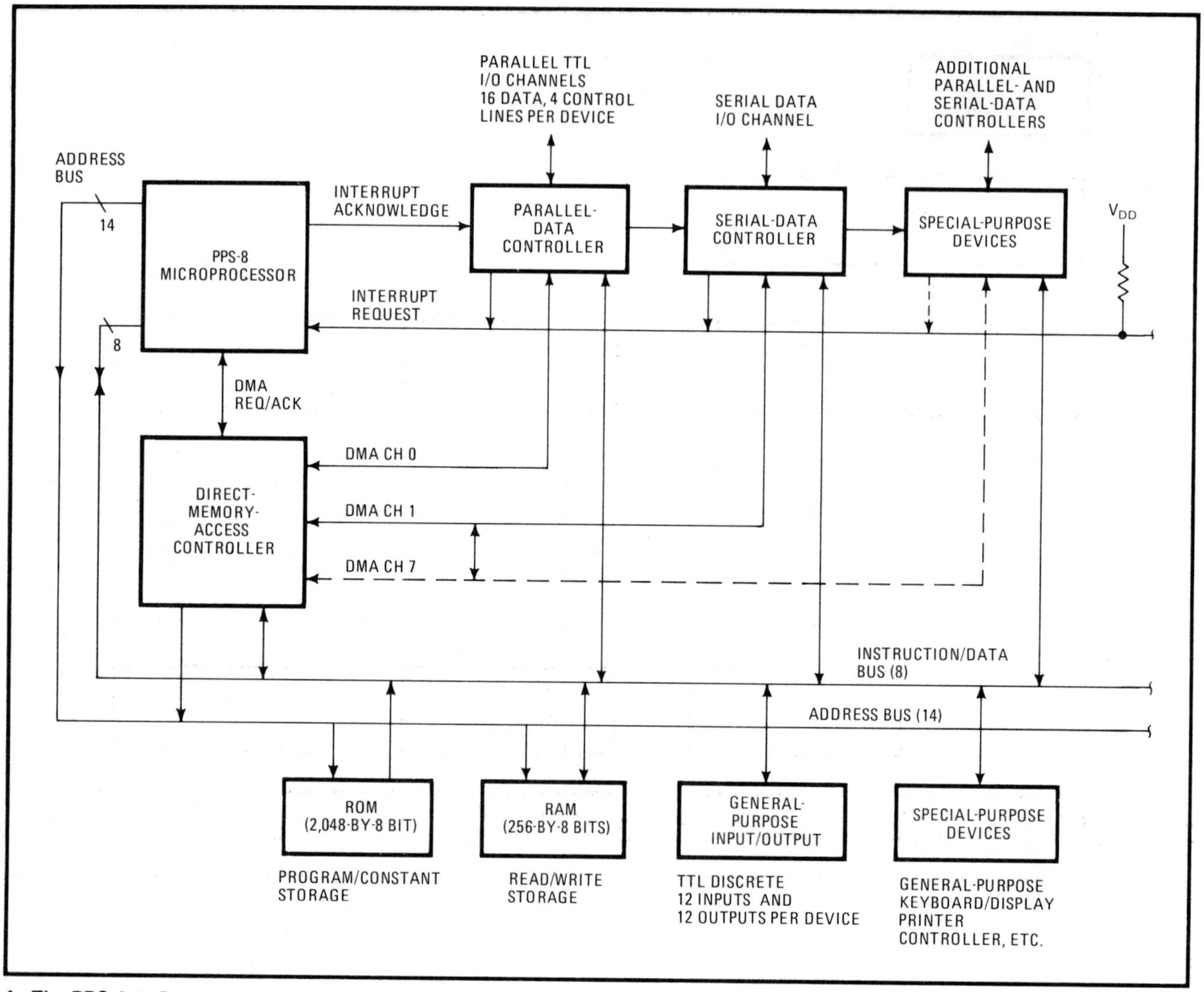

4. The PPS-8. In Rockwell's PPS-8 microcomputers, general-purpose input/output, ROM, and RAM chips again hook up directly to address and instruction data buses. Family contains a direct-memory-access controller and parallel and serial I/O data channel modules.

circuit prototype developing system and a large library of user-generated instruction programs. All this accounts for the 8080 system's overwhelming success.

Rockwell's PPS-8 differs from both the 8080 and the 6800 in the basic architecture of its CPU. Its CPU chip has an arithmetic/logic unit, a control unit, accumulators, and address registers, laid out much as in the 8080 and 6800, but interlinked quite differently from either the 8080 and 6800 families (see Figs. 2, 3, and 4). For example, the program and data memories in a PPS-8 microcomputer system have completely separate and parallel address spaces, so that a memory address may legitimately identify two different memory locations—maybe a byte of program memory containing an instruction code and a byte of data memory containing binary data. This double-duty memory address accounts for the PPS-8's high throughput, even though it is built with p-channel MOS technology.

A unique feature of the PPS-8—its clock signals—adds to its flexibility. These signals serve for both synchronization and control. The four-phase clock generator transmits two clock signals to every device in a system, and every device contains logic to decode them, interpreting the contents of the data and address buses in different ways during different phases of a machine's cycle. As a result, the CPU can program a wide variety of peripheral devices—if the user is willing to learn his way around the clocking scheme.

While the CPU or microprocessor chip is the central controlling element in a microcomputer system, just as vital are the ROMs, RAMs, and various input, output, and interface circuits that make up the balance of the design. Figures 2, 3, and 4 illustrate typical system configurations for the 8080, 6800, and the PP-8: these, the most established general-purpose microcomputer systems, have highly-developed system components that hook up directly with the CPU on simple bidirectional bus lines.

The bus line configuration of the 8080 and 6800 families generally has become the model for most 8-bit systems. Its three bus lines—a data bus, a control bus, and an address bus—handle all elements of a system. Standard ROMs, which store the program data in the form of lookup tables, are hooked up by connecting the ROM's output lines to the data bus and input lines to the address bus. RAMs get their data written from CPU com-

AVAILABLE MICROPROCESSORS

Type No.	Technology	Address Capacity (bytes)	Manufacturers* and Comments**
4-bit			
4004	p-MOS	4-k	Intel
4040	p-MOS	4-k	Intel (National)
PPS-4	p-MOS	4-k	Rockwell (National): SV
PPS-4/2	p-MOS	8-k	Rockwell: CC, SV
PPS-4/1	p-MOS	—	Rockwell: CC, SV, RAM on chip
TMS-1000	p-MOS	8-k	Texas Instruments: SV, MP
8-bit			
EA 9002	n-MOS	65-k	Electronic Arrays: SV
F-8	n-MOS	65-k	Fairchild (Mostek): CC
8008-1	p-MOS	16-k	Intel
8080 A	n-MOS	65-k	Intel (AMD, TI, NEC, Siemens)
8048	n-MOS	2-k	Intel: 512-bit RAM on chip
6502	n-MOS	65-k	MOS Technology — other versions are available with lower address capacity
5065	p-MOS	32-k	Mostek
6800	n-MOS	65-k	Motorola (AMI): SV
SCAMP	p-MOS	65-k	National: CC, SV
1801	C-MOS	65-k	RCA: 2-chip CPU
1802	C-MOS	65-k	RCA
PPS-8	p-MOS	32-k	Rockwell (National): SV
PPS-8/2	p-MOS	32-k	Rockwell: CC, SV
2650	n-MOS	32-k	Signetics: CC, SV
300	TTL-S	8-k	Scientific Micro Systems
Z-80	n-MOS	65-k	Zilog: SV
12-bit			
6100	C-MOS	4-k	Intersil (Harris): SV, CC
TLCS 12	n MOS	4 k	Toshiba: MP
16-bit			
CP1600	n-MOS	65-k	General Instruments: MP
MCP-1600	n-MOS	65-k	Western Digital: MP, MC
IMP-16	p-MOS	65-k	National: MP, MC
PACE	p-MOS	65-k	National: MP
PFL-1600A	n-MOS	65-k	PanaFacom: MC
TMS-9900	n-MOS	65-k	Texas Instruments: SV, general-purpose registers in memory
Bit slices			
2901	TTL	65-k	Advanced Micro Devices (Motorola, Raytheon): MP
9400	TTL	65-k	Fairchild: MP, SV
3002	TTL	512	Intel (Signetics): MP, 2-bit slice
6701	TTL	65-k	Monolithic Memories: MP
10800	ECL	65-k	Motorola: MP, CC, ECL
SBP0400	I^2L	65-k	Texas Instruments: CC, MP

NOTES
*Developing manufacturer listed first.
**Key: MP — microprogramable
ECL — emitter-coupled logic
TTL — transistor-transistor logic
I^2L — integrated injection logic
SV — single voltage
CC — clock on chip
MC — multi-chip central processing unit

Assessing microprocessors

Making comparisons between the available microprocessors on the basis of data sheets is a very tricky business. Even a simple specification like cycle time can be highly misleading. In most cases cycle time by itself tells you practically nothing—you must know how many cycles are needed to execute what instruction. For example, some microprocessors boast cycle times as low as 1 microsecond but require multiple cycles to execute even the simplest instructions. Others list longer cycle times but require fewer cycles to do the same instruction.

Nor does it help too much to compare execution times of simple instructions. Often the time to do a fetch or a register-to-register ADD has little relation to the time required for executing more complex instructions, like calling in a subroutine on the basis of various bit settings.

Even more misleading is ranking CPU complexities in terms of numbers of registers, or I/O ports, or whether the chip has built-in direct memory access, and so on. Many powerful microprocessors, such as TI's 9900 expel all the general-purpose working registers from the CPU chip and locate them in external RAM. But the chip is more powerful than most CPUs with multiple general-purpose registers. Likewise, a minimum-chip system design, such as the F-8, has computation logic distributed over two or three matched chips, so just looking at the CPU doesn't begin to show the capability of the system.

The instruction set is another area that lends itself to vendor specmanship. Repertoire size alone has little meaning, unless you know how the supplier is counting instructions. Are multiple, closely related instructions counted as one or as many? What instructions are included? And the various types of instructions that differ only in their "if" conditions, how are they counted?

That's why this microprocessor chart is kept fairly simple. Breaking down the chips by word length gives an idea of a processor's range—but only a rough one, since the efficiency of doing anything certainly does not depend on word length alone. The technology is broken out only because knowledgeable users feel more comfortable knowing what's in the device, but it too has to be related to design—whether processing is done serially or in parallel, and so on. (All things being equal, devices built with n-channel MOS are faster, smaller, and easier to interface than those built with p-channel MOS, whereas devices built with bipolar technology are faster and can do more but are larger and cost more to build than MOS LSI devices.)

As for address capacity, obviously the more memory that a chip can access, the larger the system that can be implemented. But again, watch out. Some processors can access large amounts of memory directly. Others need external devices to reach large bytes of memory.

Another area that concerns users is alternate sourcing In general, the alternate sources of microprocessors are proving well able to satisfy customers' demand for multiple-sourced devices. For instance, AMD's 9080A series claims speed and power specifications that in some respects exceed Intel's 8080A specifications, and AMI undertook considerable process development in building its version of Motorola's 6800 family. Mostek Corp. has done a nice job supplementing Fairchild's F-8 support and applications effort. Then too, there is the National/Rockwell technology exchange that made their respective microprocessor families available to each other.

mands that travel on the address bus, and their data is read out to the CPU on the data bus. Peripheral interface circuits receive their inputs on the control and address bus and return their data outputs on the data bus. Thus, this bidirectional bus system is the conduit serving all members of the microcomputer family. New interface and peripheral chips, regardless of their complexity, will use these bus lines, ensuring a user a simple and well-formulated method of upgrading his basic system with more powerful I/O and peripheral chips.

The dedicated 8-bit types

Unlike the general-purpose 8-bit systems, which generally use at least a dozen chips, Fairchild Semiconductor's F-8, also supplied by Mostek Corp., and National Semiconductor Corp.'s SC/MP families were designed to realize controller-type systems with the fewest possible chips at the lowest possible cost. Both families can dish up useful designs with just two chips, although the F-8 is a more powerful system, readily expandable into memory-rich designs.

The dissimilarities of these two devices stem from dissimilar design philosophies. The Fairchild F-8 designers chose a configuration that is quite unlike the CPU orientation of minicomputers. Instead they distribute process and memory control throughout the system. The F-8 therefore works best where two or three of its powerful family members can do the job standing alone, without a large number of external memory (although they can be added if necessary).

Because they interact so intimately, a designer must be familiar with the functions of the F-8 chips. Besides the CPU chip, there's a programable storage unit, which provides read-only memory plus various logic functions—it combines with the CPU to form a complete microcomputer if so desired. A dynamic-memory interface chip links the first two chips to either dynamic or static RAMs storing data, and a static-memory interface is for use with state RAMs only. Finally, a direct-memory-access chip implements the direct-memory-access logic in conjunction with the dynamic-memory interface chip.

Because various logic functions are distributed among the four peripheral chips, the CPU contains only the arithmetic/logic unit, the control unit and instruction register, the logic associated with interfacing the system bus with the I/O control signal, and the accumulator register. It does not contain memory-addressing logic, memory-addressing registers, stack pointer, program counter, and data counter, all of which reside in the companion memory and memory interface chips.

This configuration has both advantages and disadvantages, the chief advantage being that fairly powerful systems can be implemented with remarkably few chips.

Moreover, the lack of memory-addressing logic on the CPU chip itself means that no address lines are needed on the system bus, and the 16 address signals, which CPU-oriented systems need to interface with the bus, can instead be used for two 8-bit I/O ports on each

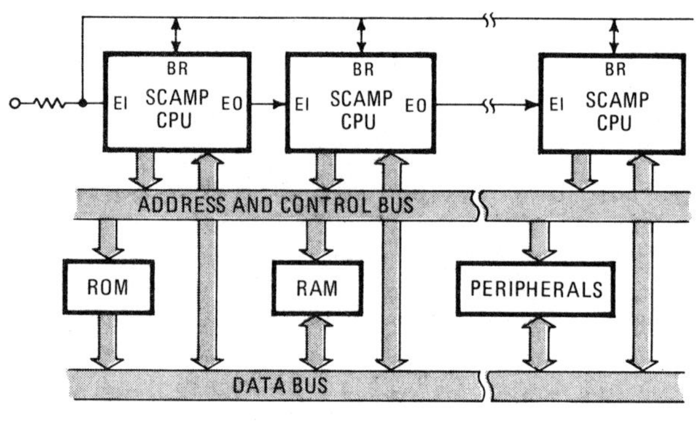

(a)

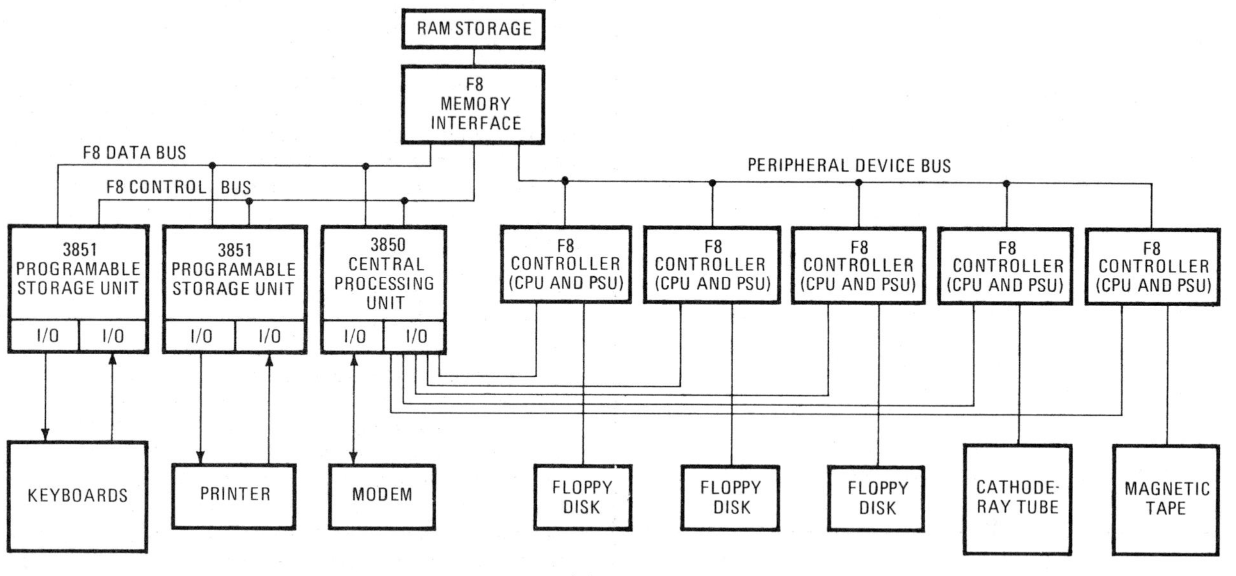

(b)

5. Efficiency experts. SC/MP and F-8 carry off the prize for minimum-chip multiprocessor systems. This SC/MP configuration (a) from National daisy-chains several microprocessors along one bus. The Fairchild F-8 disk controller has five F-8s operating as distributed processors. F-8 systems can readily be expanded to handle a wide variety of peripheral control and complex data communications applications.

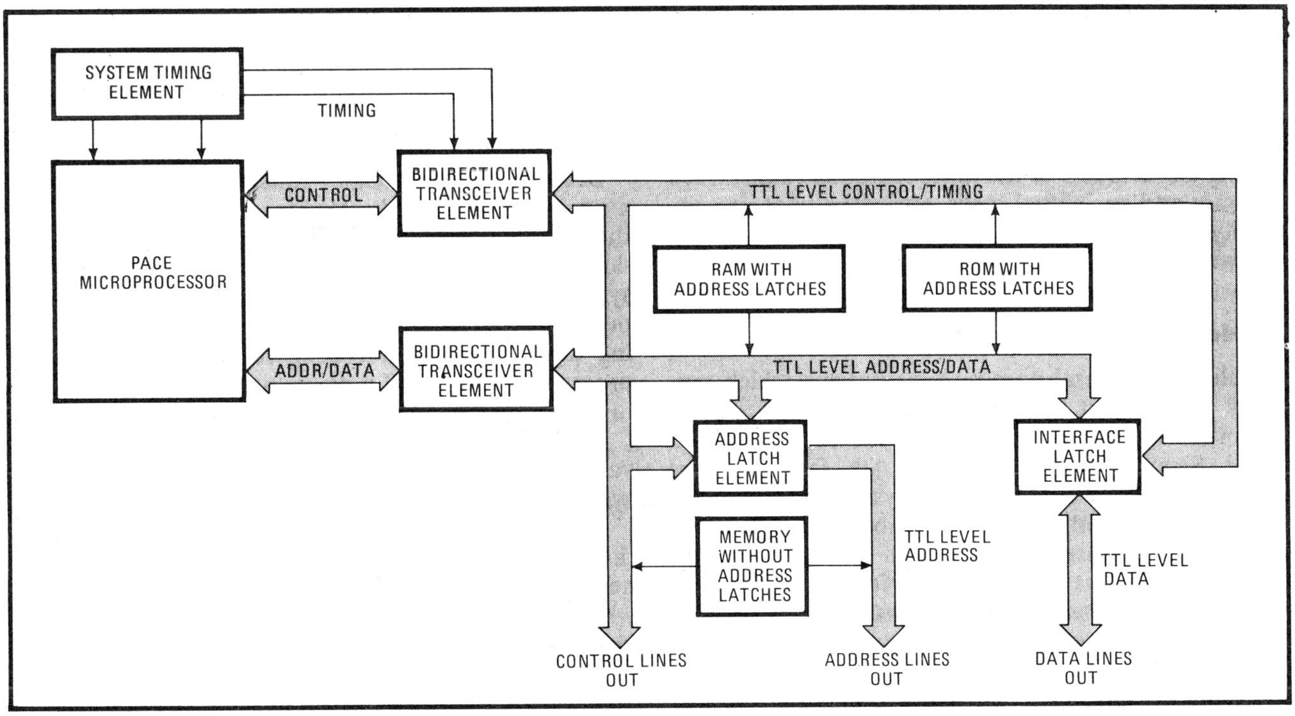

6. Relating. National's 16-bit PACE system reaches the TTL world with transceivers that interface directly with any RAMs or ROMs designed with on-chip address latches. Standard memories can also be used if an 8-bit address latch element is included.

device. Better yet, the place on the CPU chip formerly occupied by address registers and memory-addressing logic can now accept 64 bytes of random-access memory. It is this on-chip RAM that makes an F-8 minimum two-chip configuration functionally useful.

Now for the disadvantages. Because of the removal of memory-addressing logic from the CPU chip, external memories can no longer be connected directly to the system bus, which no longer has address lines, and the family's other devices must be used. Of course, this is easily done with the memory-interface devices, but the extra packages do add to the cost of the design. Worse yet, this memory-addressing logic must be duplicated if more than one memory device is present.

On the other hand, SC/MP (pronounced Scamp) centralizes its computing capabilities in the CPU, just like the 8080 and 6800 families, so that systems can be configured with standard memories directly. The SC/MP chip can handle up to 4 kilobytes of memory with no additional logic or interface packages. Systems requiring more memory are also possible: a five-chip system, handling up to 65 kilobytes of RAM, would consist of the SC/MP, a two chip bidirectional transceiver, an address latch, and a buffer.

Internally, SC/MP is a programable 8-bit parallel processor. It contains one 8-bit accumulator, four 16-bit pointer registers (one of which is dedicated to the function of program counter), an 8-bit status register, and an 8-bit extension register. On-chip timing circuits eliminate the need for external clocks, and TTL compatibility allows easy interfacing with other system components.

Architecturally, SC/MP, again like the 8080 and 6800 families, employs a unified bus system, to which the central processing unit, memory, and peripheral devices are each connected. The common data bus enables memory-reference instructions to reference peripheral devices. In addition, SC/MP architecture provides serial data and control streamlining under software control and has built-in programable delay.

Both the SC/MP and F-8 families lend themselves to multiple processor systems. In SC/MP, the bus configuration is responsible, allowing many SC/MPs to be tied to the bus for daisy-chain operation (Fig. 5a). When one SC/MP stops transmitting or receiving, it notifies the next SC/MP in line that it may take over.

The F-8 CPU chips can serve either in a multiple processor system or in two-chip peripheral controllers subordinate to a multichip processor-based system, such as large point-of-sale terminals. The floppy-disk controller shown in Fig. 5b contains five F-8s working in conjunction with floppy disks, a magnetic-tape unit, a cathode-ray-tube display, a keyboard, printer, and modem. While the low-speed devices (the keyboard, printer, and modem) can be adequately handled by the programed I/O structure, the other, high-speed devices require separate F-8 CPUs and programable storage units.

The 8-bit newcomers

While established suppliers of microprocessors have recently come out with upgraded products—most notably the 8080A and 6800D—newcomers to the field are trying to gain entry with still higher-performance versions of the earlier devices. A good example is Zilog Inc.'s Z-80 chip. In a tribute to the success of the 8080, designers at the Los Altos, Calif., company have based their design on it, but have added more data-processing and instruction-handling capability. At the same time, they have tried to simplify the system configuration along the lines of the 6800.

For example, the Z-80 is heavily CPU-oriented, like

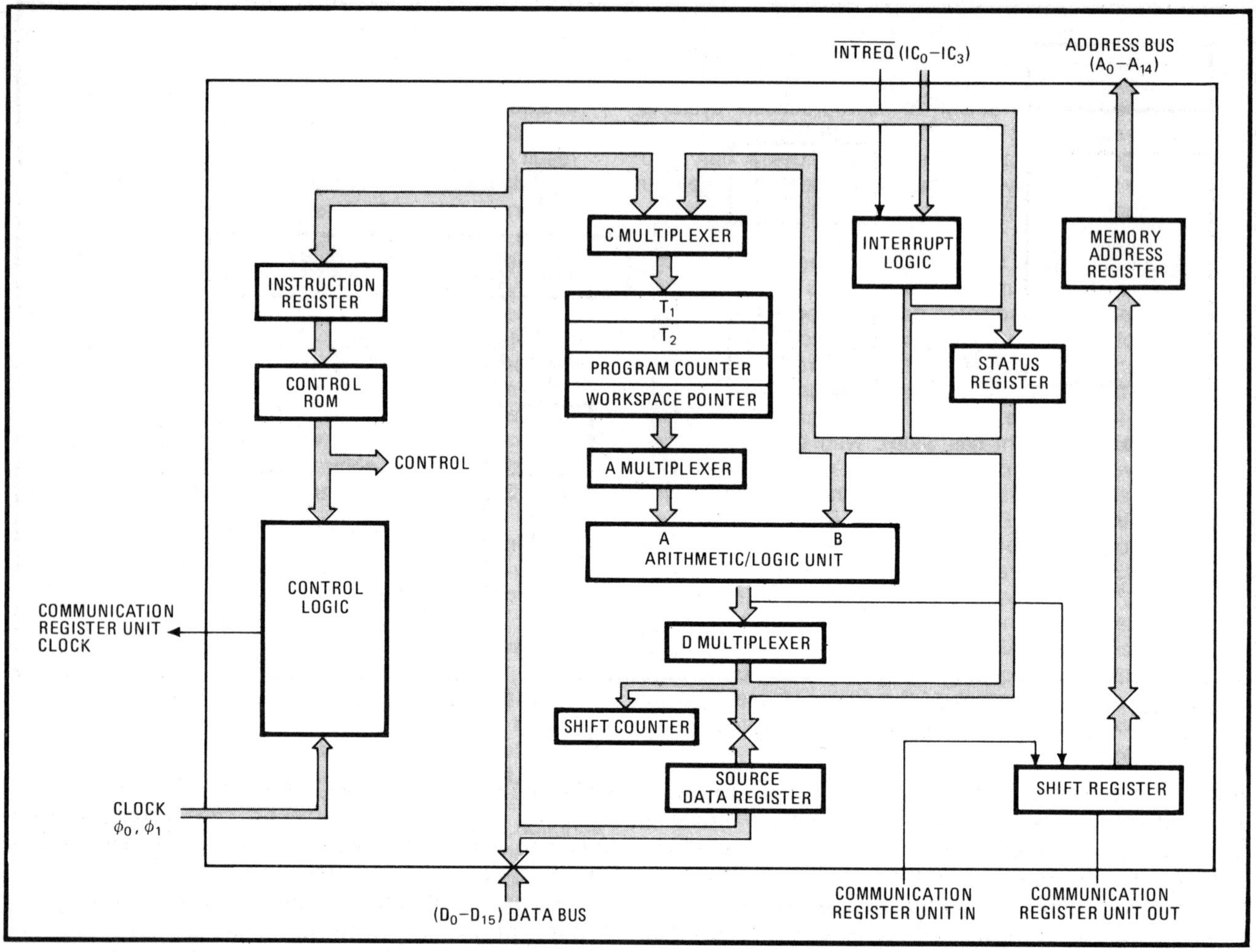

7. Thinking big. Texas Instruments' 9900 16-bit microprocessor has full 16-bit data bus and 16-bit ALU on chip but exiles all general-purpose registers to external RAM locations. A wide range of interrupt capability is included, making the chip very flexible.

the 8080A, and is completely compatible with 8080A software. But thanks to depletion-mode technology, it, like the 6800, has a single-phase clock on the chip and requires only a single 5-V power supply.

The Z-80 can handle 158 different instructions and, like the 8080A and 6800D, has an internal 16-bit-wide data bus. Unlike them it contains both an 8-bit and 16-bit external address bus, so that it can process either 8- or 16-bit words in one cycle.

Architecturally, the Z-80's CPU chip resembles the 8080A, where general-purpose registers perform basic computation operations and special-purpose registers perform various program operations, such as program counting and stack pointing. Also as in the 8080A, the CPU contains the accumulator and flag registers.

The Z-80's block of general-purpose registers has a distinctive feature: it consists of two matched sets of six 8-bit registers. Now a programer can use them individually, as 8-bit registers, or in tandem as 16-bit register pairs, depending on whether he is handling 8-bit or 16-bit words. Moreover, the programer may select one set of registers for a single exchange command while using the other set for the rest of the sequence. This saves interrupt time—and is especially useful in systems that require a fast interrupt response—because there's no need to transfer the register contents to an external stack during the fast-cycle interrupt or subroutine processing.

As for the Z-80's special-purpose registers, the program counter and stack pointer function much as they do on the 8080A. The program counter holds the entire 16-bit address of the current instruction just fetched from memory, and the stack pointer keeps track of the 16-bit address of the current instruction. An external stack memory, organized as a last-in/first-out file, allows simple implementation of multiple level interrupts, unlimited subroutine testing, and simplification of many types of data manipulations.

Like the Z-80, another recently introduced microprocessor that takes cognizance of established 8-bit general-purpose designs is the 9002 from Electronic Arrays Inc., Mountain View, Calif. But unlike the Z-80, which is being supplied with its own set of dedicated support devices, the 9002 has been conceived as a stand-alone digital process controller that can interface with standard peripheral chips through an 8-bit parallel TTL-compatible data bus.

The 9002 timing and control signals allow a user to bring the chip together with any bus-oriented peripheral devices he may choose. Examples are: Motorola's 6820 peripheral interface adapter for general-purpose controller applications; the asynchronous communications interface adapter and low-speed modem for

Learning about microprocessors

In approaching the design of microprocessor systems, the first requirement for the novice is to learn the specialized jargon. The basic terms defined below can help. They are followed by some advice on the next steps in an education in microprocessor theory and applications.

Central processing unit: a group of registers and logic that form the arithmetic/logic unit plus another group of registers with associated decoding logic that form the control unit. Most metal-oxide-semiconductor devices are single-chip CPUs, in that the registers hold as many bits as the word length of the unit (the 8080 and 6800, for example, are 8-bit devices and thus the basic registers are eight bits wide). With bit-slice devices, however, central processing units of any bit width can be assembled essentially by connecting the bit-slice parts in parallel. Externally, a bit-slice device will appear to be a coherent single CPU capable of handling words of the desired bit length.

Register: logic elements (gates, flip-flops, shift registers) that, taken together, store 4-, 8-, or 16-bit numbers. They are essentially for temporary storage, in that the contents usually change from one instruction cycle to the next. In fact, much of the microprocessor's operation can be learned by studying the registers, which take part in nearly all operations.

Accumulator: a register that adds an incoming binary number to its own contents and then substitutes the results for the contents.

Program counter: a register whose contents correspond to the memory address of the next instruction to be carried out. The count usually increases by one as each instruction is carried out, since instructions generally are stored in sequential locations.

Instruction register: storage for the binary code for the operation to be performed. Usually this instruction represents the contents of the address just designated by the program counter. However, the contents of the instruction register or the program counter may be changed by the computations. This, of course, represents one of the key ideas of a stored-program computer—instructions, as well as data, can be operated upon and subsequent operations will be determined by the results.

Index register: some memories are organized by index number (the contents of the index register). The address of the next instruction may be found by summing the contents of the program counter and the index register. Increasing the index register by one will cause the processor to go to a new section of memory.

Stack pointer: a register which comes into use when the microprocessor must service an interrupt—a high-priority call from an external device for the central processing unit to suspend temporarily its current operations and divert its attention to the interrupting task. A CPU must store the contents of its registers before it can move on to the interrupt operation. It does this in a stack, so named because information is added to its top, with the information already there being pushed further down. The stack thus is a last-in first-out type of memory. The stack-pointer register contains the address of the next unused location in the stack.

Flag: usually a flip-flop storing one bit that indicates some aspect of the status of the central processing unit. For example, a carry flag is set to one when an arithmetic operation produces a carry. A zero flag is set when the result is zero. These flags aid in interpreting the results of certain calculations. Others are sometimes provided to permit access by interrupt request lines—for example, if a CPU is engaged in the highest priority of calculation, it may set all status flags to zero—which, loosely translated, means "don't bother me now." If only some of these flags are set, then only certain interrupt lines will be able to get through according to their priority.

Direct memory access: a technique that permits a peripheral device to enter or extract blocks of data from the microcomputer memory without involving the central processing unit. In some cases, a CPU can perform other functions while the transfer occurs.

In going beyond these definitions, an engineer will probably find that there's not an abundance of good basic information on microprocessors. However, the gap is filling.

Certainly, a first source on the details of a particular product is the manufacturer's product descriptions. Some of them are quite readable. Most provide easily understood introductions to the microprocessor, with just enough information to get started. Best known are Intel's "8080 Users Manual," Motorola's mammoth "Microprocessor Applications Manual" and 6800 System description, Fairchild's "F-8 Circuit Data Book," Signetics' 2650 manual, Rockwell's microprocessor family descriptions, and the descriptive literature National puts out on SC/MP, PACE, and IMP-16 families.

Independently produced sources also are available, but they're of varying quality. A useful one is a monthly publication on a variety of microprocessor subjects called "New Logic Notebook," edited by Jerry L. Ogdin of Microcomputer Technique Inc., 1120 Reston International Center Office Bldg., Reston, Va. 22091. A monthly compilation of microprocessor news and product introductions is a newsletter called "Microcomputer Digest," P.O. Box 1167, Cupertino, Calif. 95014.

One of the best books is a paperback called "An Introduction to Microcomputers," from Adam Osborne and Associates, 2950 Seventh St., Berkeley, Calif. 94710. It has a compact tutorial section on basics, followed by good comparisons of key families.

Then there's "Microprocessors," first volume in the Electronics Book Series. It is a compilation of all the original articles on major microprocessor designs that appeared in this magazine—from the first 4004 to today's complex 8- and 16-bit designs. It also contains detailed design and application material. It's available for $8.95

A good source of basic information is the independent seminars that are becoming widely available. One of the most successful is Integrated Computer Systems' three-to-five-day courses held across the country. A schedule is available from David Collins at ICS, 4445 Overland Ave., Culver City, Calif. 90230.

An opportunity for hands-on experience is the suppliers' seminars. These are manned by applications specialists who travel around regularly, offering a good review of a particular microprocessor line. Finally, there are the courses offered by the IEEE and the universities.

communications-controller applications; or any of Intel's new programable interface devices, such as the programable peripheral or communications interfaces. This means that a system designer can use the 9002 as a powerful controller chip, managing the operation of any TTL-compatible peripheral device.

The 9002 designers also picked the best features of existing processor designs. The CPU combines the on-chip 64-byte scratch-pad RAM of the F-8, the push-pop subroutine stack of the Intel 4040, the simplified timing concepts of the PPS-4, the straightforward peripheral addressing techniques and single 5-V-supply requirement of the 6800, and the general-purpose registers of the 8080.

To these borrowed features the 9002 adds some purely its own. It contains a seven-level subroutine stack for multiple interrupt capability and eight 12-bit general-purpose data registers. With its 64-byte scratch-pad memory it can handle many stand-alone controller jobs without requiring additional RAM. Moreover, one of the 9002's internal flags allows the user to perform either 8-bit binary arithmetic or packed binary-coded-decimal arithmetic (dual 4-bit operands) with built-in, automatic decimal correction. To choose, he simply sets the flag in one state or another. This is useful for peripheral controllers where CRT displays need BCD data.

With all this computing power, ample control signaling, and on-chip RAM capability, the 9002 can realize many fairly powerful designs with only two or three packages. For example, a controller can be built with the 9002, a 1,024-by-8-bit ROM, such as the EA 4700, and two Intel 8212 peripheral interface chips, or else it can be built with the 9002, a 2,028-by-8-bit ROM, such as the EA 4600 and Motorola's 6820 PIA chip.

C-MOS: another choice

Another enhancement of an existing device is RCA Solid State division's single-chip version of its 8-bit C-MOS microprocessor. Designated the 1802, the chip is three times faster than the old two-chip design, has one third more instructions—a total repertoire of 91—and costs less. This came about thanks to RCA's new silicon-gate process that yields C-MOS devices almost half the size of metal-gate designs and also increases transistor switching speed. As a result, a C-MOS microprocessor becomes as fast, cost-effective and flexible as today's p- and n-MOS microprocessors.

To illustrate, the 1802 has a cycle time of 1.25 microseconds and takes only one or two cycles, plus a fetch cycle, to execute any instruction. This gives it an instruction time of either 2.5 or 3.75 microseconds that puts it well in the speed range of either the 8080 or 6800. Moreover, with its 91 instructions, it is as powerful and as flexible. Yet RCA designers were careful to retain the architecture of the two-chip design, so that the 1802 is software-compatible with its predecessor.

What distinguishes the 1802 CPU from other 8-bit designs is its separate instruction and address registers. The address data is placed in an array of sixteen 16-bit scratch-pad registers, each of which can point to either data or program. That means that a user is not forced to provide an address with each memory reference instruction—something he must do with other processors.

What it costs

Like all semiconductor chips, microprocessor prices are coming down. Here's a rough guide to how much it costs to do some typical jobs at today's prices (in appropriate volumes):

Job	Number of packages	Cost
General-purpose minicomputer emulation	30 and up	$1,000
Dedicated minicomputer	20–30	600
Process controllers	15–20	400
Smart terminal (i.e. communications, etc.)	10–15	300
Complex general controllers (i.e. traffic lights, medical, machine tool, etc.)	10–15	200
Complex peripheral controllers, industrial	10	150
Point-of-sale terminals	10	150
Games, instruments, etc.	5–10	75
Simple controllers, hobby gear, appliance control	1 or 2	10

As address pointers, individual scratch-pad registers in the array are selected by any one of three 4-bit registers, so that the contents of any address can be directed to any one of three destinations. As data pointers, the 16 scratch-pad memories are equally flexible. They can be used either to indicate a location in memory or as pointers to support a built-in direct-memory-access function.

The only other C-MOS microprocessor is Intersil's 12-bit device. By using the same software as the PDP-8A, the device lets users of that popular computer implement their systems in low-power easy-to-use C-MOS technology. The 40-pin package has an instruction capacity of about 40, can access 32-k bytes of external memory, and can control 64 I/O parts. For the 1600, Intersil plans to supply a complete set of C-MOS peripheral devices, such as C-MOS ROMs, RAMs, and UARTs.

Two n-channel 8-bit microprocessors that have begun to make headway for general-purpose applications are the Signetics Corp. 2650 and the MOS Technology Inc. 6500 family of microprocessors. The Signetics part, available only in sample quantities about a year ago, lately gained momentum—especially in Europe, thanks in part to Philips' recent acquisition of Signetics.

The 2650 is a single 5-V parallel 8-bit binary processor capable of performing 75 instructions in a machine cycle time of 2.4 microseconds, which puts it in the same general class as the 8080 and 6800 families. The chip can address up to 32 kilobytes of external memory (compared to 65-k for the others). But its ability to execute variable-length instructions makes it somewhat more efficient, since a one- or two-byte instruction may often be used for memory addressing. Moreover, most instructions require only 6 of the first 8 bits, so the remaining bits can be used for the register field.

MOS Technology's family is unique in that it includes a number of software-compatible microprocessor chips differing primarily in the amount of memory they can address. The 40-pin 6502 can handle 65-k bytes of

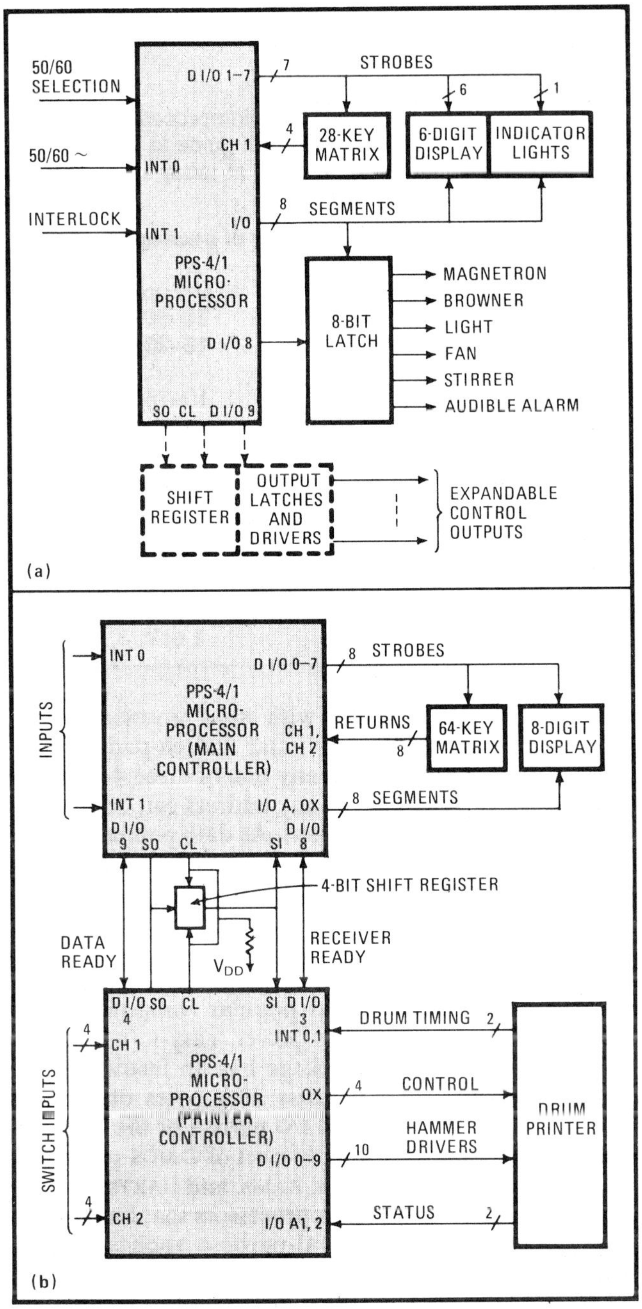

8. Independence. Rockwell's PPS-4/1 handles many controller jobs almost by itself. Microwave oven controller (a) needs only an 8-bit latch to drive the high-current oven gear. Two PPS-4/1s (b) handle more complex systems like cash registers.

memory, as well as a large number of real-time interrupts, putting it in the class of the 8080 and 6800 families. For smaller systems, there's the 6503, a 28-pin device capable of addressing 4-k bytes while accommodating two interrupts. The 6504, also a 28-pin package, can address up to 8-k bytes of RAM and handle one interrupt, and the 6505, a 28-pin package, can address 4-k bytes with one interrupt.

All the chips are single 5-V depletion-load devices with on-chip clocks that operate with very fast 1-microsecond cycle times. Moreover, all can handle 55 instructions, have 13 addressing modes, contain true indexing capability, and come with direct memory access. And, since all the parts use the same software, they allow a user to tailor his microprocessor selection to the size of his system.

Recently, MOS Technology has announced several peripheral chips that work directly with the processor chips. There's a combination RAM/ROM chip (6530)—the first to incorporate RAM, ROM, I/O, and an interval timer on a single chip. It contains 1-k byte of ROM, 64 bytes of RAM, and two 8-bit bidirectional peripheral interface ports. The timer is programable from the CPU and has interrupt capability. Two other versions have no ROM but twice the RAM content.

The only single-chip 8-bit bipolar microprocessor on the market is the SMS 300, from Scientific Micro Systems Inc., Mountain View, Calif. A recently introduced version cuts the original cycle time by 20% to 250 ns, so that the device can now, for example, directly control double-density floppy-disk units.

More performance

The 8-bit microprocessor has undoubtedly caught on—it fits many of the controller and medium-sized data-handling jobs that formerly went by default to minicomputer designs. But the 8-bit word length can be a handicap for large systems, where big bytes of memory must be processed, or in high-performing data-acquisition systems where speed and high resolution are needed. This is where the 16-bit microprocessor comes in: its 16-bit words reach external memory locations two bytes at a time, while its long words can easily accommodate the 10-, 12-, and 14-bit converter resolution that's standard for most systems.

National Semiconductor Corp. was the first semiconductor manufacturer to recognize the value of the 16-bit systems. In fact, the industry's first microprocessor above the 4-bit level was National's IMP-16, introduced in 1973 and still a viable product today. (The company is redesigning the IMP-16 with bipolar technology for ten times faster performance.) Though among the most powerful and flexible, the IMP does, however, need rather a large number of chips to implement most systems—the CPU alone uses five. The company therefore began working on a single-chip version of IMP, producing another industry first—the one-chip 16-bit PACE.

The first 16-bit CPU on a chip

PACE is software-compatible with IMP and retains many of its features. Like IMP, PACE provides 16-bit instruction and address processing plus a choice of either 8-bit or 16-bit data processing. In addition, many CPU-related operations, for which IMP needed external TTL packages, are included in the 40-pin PACE chip—for instance, status and control registers, instruction branching, interrupt logic, and clock generation (although some clock logic is still needed). Thus, a six-chip PACE system, including a ROM for program control and four 1,024-bit RAMs with on-chip latches for data storage, can run a powerful data-processing terminal containing 16-kilobits of program storage and 4-kilobits of data RAM. Such a terminal would previously have needed either dozens of TTL packages or, in an 8-bit microprocessor-based design, longer programs, more memory and more interface chips.

Indeed, because its 16-bit capability can process two 8-bit words at a time, PACE can supply faster throughput to many designs now using 8-bit microprocessors. Moreover, a 16-bit system can work with shorter programs using less memory. Clearly, a user must analyze all system requirements—program length, memory, and peripheral functions—before he can be certain whether an 8- or a 16-bit design is better for his purposes.

For example, in complex, high-speed, data-processing terminals or in large point-of-sale and industrial process-control systems, an 8-bit CPU system may require double-precision arithmetic to attain the necessary data accuracy. Moreover, in 8-bit designs, multiple registers must be provided if 16-bit memory addresses and multiple accesses to memory are used to fetch multibyte instructions.

Besides PACE, National supplies a set of matched LSI chips that hook onto a TTL-compatible PACE bus system. A typical PACE system is shown in Fig. 6. Included in the family are a system timing element, for generating the clock signals, and a bidirectional transceiver element, for converting PACE's p-channel MOS signals to the TTL levels required by the TTL bus line. (These level converters will be eliminated in n-MOS versions of PACE that are in development.) Since the address and data lines are multiplexed on the PACE CPU, there are also an interface latch element, actually an 8-bit-wide demultiplexer that selects and retransmits data outputs, and an 8-bit address latch element, which does the same demultiplexing job for the address outputs. These system-matched components, together with external ROM and RAM, form the PACE 16-bit system. No TTL parts are needed for most system designs.

Designed for power

An even more powerful 16-bit microprocessor is Texas Instruments Inc.'s 9900, which was designed for TI's minicomputer division and is now available on a microcomputer board or as a lone chip. Its use of advanced n-channel processing results in very fast (3-megahertz) clock operation, and its minicomputer-like CPU design results in efficient register-to-register computation and direct memory-to-memory data transfer.

This method of handling data permitted the 9900 designers to remove from the chip all general-purpose registers, along with their associated 16-bit parallel buses (Fig. 7). Their functions are instead assigned to locations in external RAM, and room is made available for several powerful special-purpose registers—accumulators, pointers, index registers and the like.

This configuration has several advantages. For one, the incorporation of working registers in memory produces a memory-to-memory architecture that makes for very flexible programing. For another, the beefed-up special-purpose or housekeeping registers enable the CPU to handle up to 17 interrupts, 15 of them external plus two pre-defined ones. (Four bits in the status register store the priority of the interrupt currently being serviced.) Also, seven addressing modes are available.

Finally, the 9900 has separate address and data bus lines, so that external demultiplexing devices are not needed, unlike in the PACE system. The chip operates efficiently with standard memories and many standard peripheral circuits, whether TTL-compatible MOS packages or standard TTL circuits.

Clearly the architecture of the 9900 is fundamentally different from most 8-bit general-purpose processors, including the 8080 and 6800. Whereas the 8080 employs conventional stack architecture, with the program and data spaces in external memory, the 9900 puts not only the program and data spaces but also the general-purpose registers in external memory. There are two basic advantages to such an architecture, especially for large systems. First, the number of workspace register files is not fixed, as it is on the 8080. Second, interrupt handling can be very fast, since all data used in program execution is contained in memory.

Another 16-bit microprocessor gaining in popularity is General Instrument Corp.'s CP1600. It's a more conventional general-purpose CPU that can handle instruction cycles about as fast as the 9900, but keeps its working registers on the CPU. These eight 16-bit registers operate either as accumulators or as memory stack pointers, in this respect behaving very much as in RCA's 1802 8-bit design.

A strength of the CP1600 is its sophisticated interrupt system which yields fast service but has low hardware and programing overhead. Both interrupt servicing and priority programing within the CPU are handled by stack processing on command from the stack pointer.

Finally, in the 16-bit area, the Western Corp. MCP 1600 microprocessor, which originally was designed for DEC's LSI-11 microcomputer, is also available as an independent device. Like the other 16-bit chips, it is an n-channel MOS device that can be microprogramed for control applications, or programed to emulate most minicomputers. It differs from the other 16-bit designs by its use of three matched LSI chips to make up the processor: a data chip (1611B), a control chip (1612B), and a ROM program chip.

The three chips are interconnected by an 18-bit microinstruction bus that provides bidirectional communications between them for address and instructions. An additional data-access bus uses a 16-bit port for communicating with memory, input/output devices, and other system components.

The one-chip controller

Even while microprocessor manufacturers are moving up into the 16-bit minicomputer region, others are extending the technology in the other direction to the stand-alone controller. These new self-contained single-chip controllers provide the cheapest solution to a host of small control applications—in appliances, low-cost instruments, such as digital thermometers, and gear that requires a minimal amount of data processing, such as calculators, gas pumps, cash registers, and scales. Since the level of performance required is not too high, even a single low-cost chip can contain enough CPU, program ROM, data RAM, and I/O capability to handle most small-to-medium controller applications on its own. TI and Rockwell already have 4-bit controller chips on the

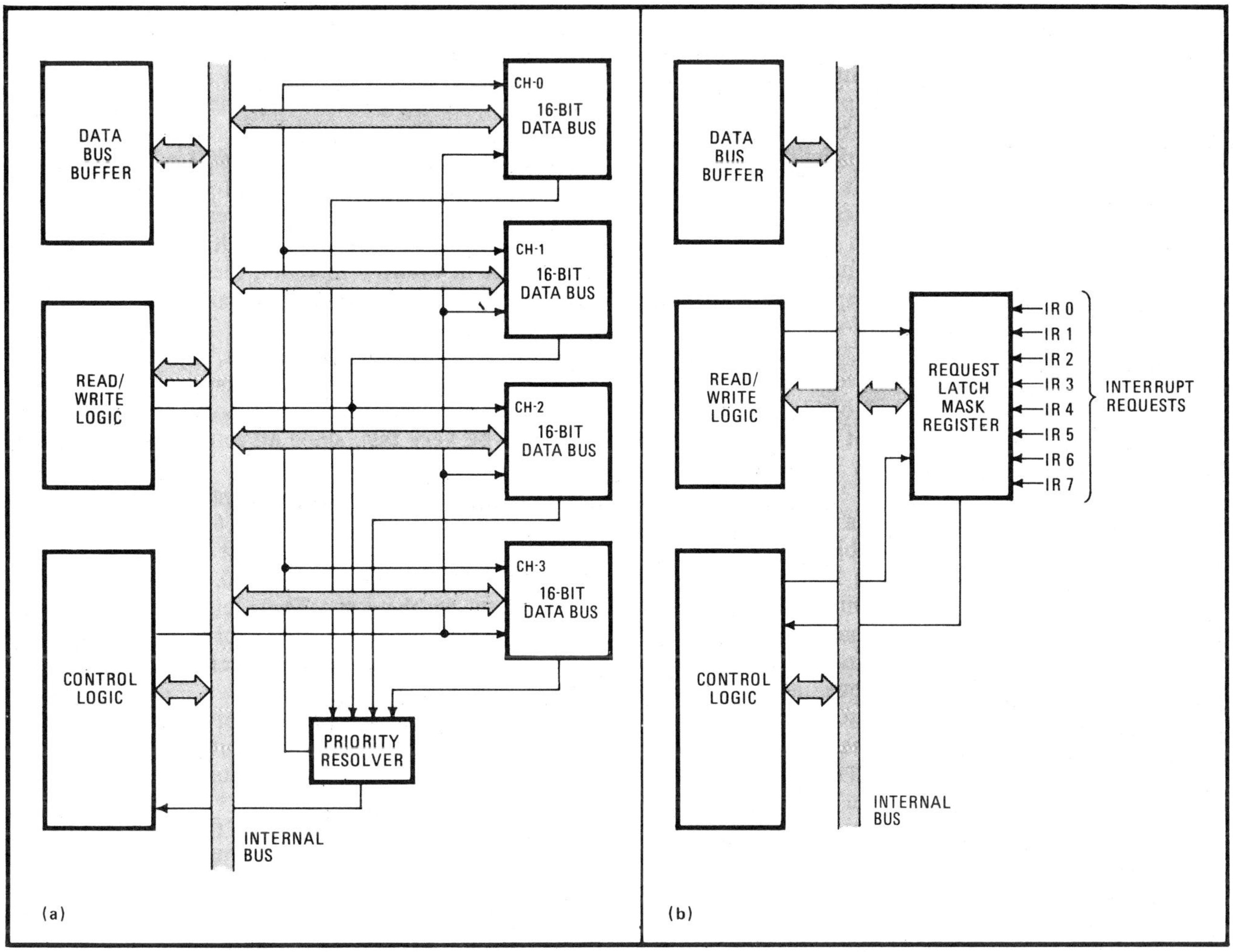

9. New talents. Programable peripheral circuits are extending the capabilities of CPU-oriented microprocessor systems and at the same time simplifying them. The programable interrupt controller (a) can handle up to eight vectored priority interrupts, while the programable direct-memory controller (b) can access or deposit data directly from or into memory. Intel makes both for use with its 8080 family.

market, and other manufacturers are expected to announce 4- and 8-bit designs shortly.

But bear in mind, there is an overlap here. Clearly minimum-chip microprocessors, like the F-8, SC/MP, or the 9002, could be used to implement controller systems. But their processing power might be wasted in too small an application—they're better in configurations of at least two and usually three or more chips.

The first single-chip processor to have been designed specifically as a stand-alone controller is Rockwell's PPS-4/1. Several of these small microcomputers can also act as peripheral controllers in large systems, such as point-of-sale and communications terminals, to take the load off the central processors.

Each PPS-4/1 chip contains 10,752 bits of read-only memory, 384 bits of random-access memory, and 31 input/output ports. That's more on-chip I/O capability than is available on the single-chip 4-bit controllers originally developed for calculators. Also adding to the chip's versatility is a large set of 50 instructions and compatibility with Rockwell's older general-purpose PPS-4 and recent two-chip PPS-4/2 systems.

In more detail, the PPS-4/1's program memory is a 1,344-by-8-bit mask-programable ROM while a 96-by-4-bit RAM provides data, parameter, and working storage. Data is processed by the chip's accumulator, functioning as the primary register, and five-register arithmetic/logic unit, which, together with a carry register, combine to perform either binary arithmetic or decimal arithmetic.

The efficiency with which such a chip can serve a controller is illustrated in Fig. 8. The microwave-oven controller (Fig. 8a) needs in addition to the PPS 4/1 only an 8-bit latch chip for the oven's mechanical controls—blowers, stirrers, and so on. A 28-key matrix supplies the controller inputs, while the strobe signals from seven of the chip's data output channels operate the 6-digit display and indicator lights. The eighth data output runs the latch. One interrupt line provides real-time clock inputs for accurately measuring cooking time, and the other interrupt provides an interlock input for turning off the oven when the door is open.

The cash-register design (Fig. 8b) shows how two or more controller chips work in one system. Here one PPS-4/1 operates as the main controller, the other operates as the printer controller, and the two communicate over any of the input/output lines, helped by a 4-bit serial shift register tied to the serial I/O lines of both chips.

A more ambitious (and more expensive) single-chip design is Intel's soon-to-be-available 8-bit microcontroller, the 8048. The Intel chip will contain all the elements of a microcomputer—CPU, program ROM, data RAM and I/O. But it will be both more powerful, because it contains an n-channel 8-bit ALU for handling over 80 instructions, and more flexible, because its on-chip control ROM is programable and alterable by the user. (Intel will also supply an unalterable version.)

The chip's PROM, a 1,024-by-8-bit configuration, is similar to the company's recently introduced 2708 erasable read-only memory, which the user can erase with ultraviolet light. Erasability has distinct advantages. Not only can a system designer program his ROM on the bench as his design progresses, but he may update or change that program at any time afterwards without exchanging one chip for another.

Besides the ALU, data registers, and PROM, the chip contains a 512-bit static RAM for scratch-pad data handling, a programable interval timer, and I/O channels. Moreover, it can address up to 2,048 bits of external RAM. Thus, a designer can use either the 8048's own 64 bytes of RAM in stand-alone controller applications or an external 256 bytes of RAM in more complex systems.

Besides being useful as a stand-alone controller, the 8048 works well as a peripheral controller in 8080 distributed processing systems. The powerful 8080 CPU chip acts as the main microprocessor, handling the central computation and providing the control signals needed to run the peripheral controllers and programable I/O and interface circuits. In point-of-sale systems, for example, several 8048s would provide the control logic for cash registers, credit-card validators, and inventory accounting, while the 8080 would handle the number crunching and central processing operations.

While Intel alone will offer a field-programable 8-bit controller, other suppliers are developing mask-programable devices. Rockwell, for example, will soon have a one-chip software-compatible controller (PPS-8/1) for its PPS-8 product line, and National is developing a single-chip SC/MP system. Fairchild will offer a one-chip 3860 controller for its F-8 line. Fairly typical of this class, the 3860 will have 2 kilobytes of ROM, 64 bytes of RAM, 32 I/O ports, interrupt capability, programable timer, clock circuit, and power reset.

The bottom line: calculator types

Texas Instruments led the way in making the TMS 1000—originally developed for its line of programable calculators—available as a stand-alone microcontroller. Now other calculator firms, such as Rockwell and National, are preparing calculator-type controller chips. Generally smaller and cheaper than the more powerful stand-alone 4- and 8-bit controllers, they work best in slow-input equipment, like keyboards or clocks.

But the TMS 1000 is still quite powerful. Introduced about 18 months ago, the p-MOS device is in heavy demand as a high-volume low-cost 4-bit serial controller. Several software-compatible versions are available: a 28-pin TMS 1000 with 1,024 bytes of ROM and 64 bytes of RAM; a 40-pin TMS 1200 with more I/O; the TMS 1070 and TMS 1270, which have high-voltage output capability for directly driving displays, and the TMS 1100 and TMS 1300, which have twice the memory of the others. TI also plans enhanced n-channel versions.

National's line of 4-bit calculator-type controllers will start at the high performance end with the MM7581 and 5782 chip set. The first chip has 2-k bytes of ROM, ROM address and control logic, and some I/O; the second chip contains the ALU, a programable-logic-array instruction decoder, a 160-by-4-bit RAM, some RAM registers, and a serial I/O port. A lower-priced single-chip combination, the MM5799, will offer 1,536 bytes of ROM and 96 by 4 bits of RAM, and last in line will come a very low-priced MM5734, with less memory.

Rockwell's calculator-like controller line is aimed at applications below the capability of its single-chip PPS-4/1 controller. Coming soon is the A76XX, which will have about half the PPS-4/1's ROM and RAM capability and a slightly smaller instruction set. It is intended to sell in the $5, high-volume range.

I/Os with intelligence

While microprocessor suppliers are answering the call for lower-cost controller chips on the one hand, they are also satisfying the demand for more I/O and peripheral flexibility in general-purpose systems. Rockwell, for example, has paid close attention to I/O and peripheral support. In its PPS-8 family, besides the CPU chip, clock generators, and memory modules, there are a general-purpose I/O chip, parallel-data, serial-data, direct-memory-access and printer controllers, a telecommunications data interface, as well as a general-purpose keyboard/display and floppy-disk controllers, the last compatible with IBM's floppy disks. Again, all work directly on CPU control at system clock and voltage levels.

Motorola and Intel have been actively adding power and flexibility to their general-purpose I/O and peripheral devices. Since these chips can operate at TTL voltage levels, they will undoubtedly find markets outside of those of their families, especially with the new bus-oriented n-channel microprocessors.

The peripheral devices in Motorola's 6800 system have found wide acceptance in the industry. Included are the peripheral interface adapter, the asynchronous communications interface adapter, and the low-speed modem. Working with the CPU (or MPU, as Motorola calls it), ROM and RAMs, all on a single 5-V supply, these peripheral chips can implement many systems with a minimum of packages.

Intel's new 8080 peripheral devices have stirred interest because they are all software- or I/O-programable. These programable chips complement a large number of I/O devices, both TTL and MOS, that already are available, including an 8-bit I/O port, one-of-eight decoders, a priority interrupt control unit, and a 4-bit bidirectional bus driver.

Two of the programable chips are already available: a peripheral interface and a communications interface. Three others are coming: a programable interval timer, DMA controller, and interrupt controller (Fig. 9). The interrupt controller can handle eight levels of requests, and is expandable to configurations of up to 64 levels. The interval timer is actually a group of three indepen-

BIPOLAR MICROPROCESSORS COMPARED				
Parameter	AMD Am2900	MMI MM6701	Intel 3002	TI SBP0400
Slice width	4 bits	4 bits	2 bits	4 bits
Functions of arithmetic logic unit	8	8	about 6	16
Number of microcode control inputs	9	8	7	9
Working registers	17	17	11	9
Two-address operation	Yes	Yes	No	No
Independent shift and arithmetic	Yes	Yes	No	Yes
Cycle time (register to register, read, modify, write)	100 ns	200 ns	150 ns	1,000 ns
Technology	Low-power Schottky	Schottky	Schottky	I^2L
Power dissipation (4 bits)	0.92 W	1.12 W	1.45 W	0.13 W
Pin connections (4 bits)	40	40	56	40

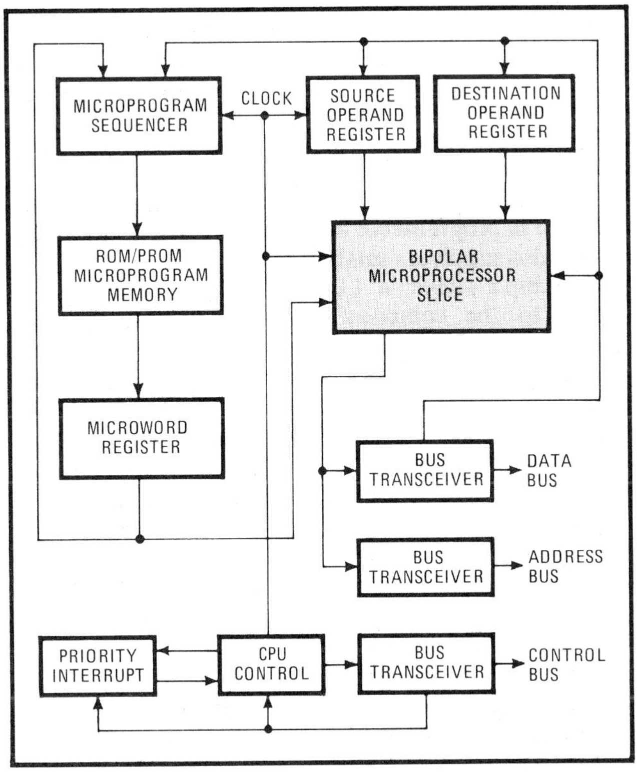

10. However it's sliced . . . In AMD's 2900 family of high-performance bipolar chips, the 4-bit processor slice is the key element in minicomputer configurations. The powerful 11-chip system can handle 16- or 32-bit-wide words for data-processing equipment.

dent 16-bit counters driven simply as I/O ports—instead of setting up timing loops in system software, a programer can now satisfy his system timing requirements with a single chip.

Bit slices and microcomputer boards

While the MOS single-chip microprocessors are dominating control and data processing in small, medium-performance systems, the bipolar processor slices are taking on the tough process-control and high-speed controller jobs now handled by minicomputers.

Unlike MOS designs, a bipolar bit slice is only a section of a central processing unit. It is not intended to operate alone. A 16-bit computer design requires eight 2-bit slices or four 4-bit slices for the CPU, plus a host of peripheral input and output packages. These are usually standard TTL circuits, which are not available in low-cost LSI form and therefore add considerably to the cost of the system. Finally, bit-slice-processor designs generally require a lot of external memory—up to 64 kilobytes and more—and memory is expensive. In fact, a typical minicomputer CPU using the slice technique may need 15 packages costing about $300.

Nevertheless, bit-slice activity is humming along, with several families already on the market:

- For stand-alone controls and minicomputers there's TI's integrated-injection-logic low-performance 4-bit processor slice. This chip, with 1,500 gates operating at delays of 25 nanoseconds, works with TI's existing family of TTL LSI processor parts. In addition, a 4-bit Schottky TTL slice is to be introduced shortly, increasing speeds into the 1-to-10-nanosecond range.
- For high-speed processors and fast minicomputers there are the 2-bit and 4-bit Schottky TTL slices produced by a growing number of bipolar-circuit manufacturers (Fairchild, AMD, MMI, Raytheon, and Intel). These generally emulate existing minicomputers.
- Finally, there are the highest-performing emitter-coupled-logic processor slices for the control of big mainframe memories. Motorola has already announced a 4-bit ECL processor slice using its ECL 10K technology.

All this performance and flexibility do not come free. Bit-slice microprocessor designs are considerably more expensive than those built with MOS microprocessors.

The major asset of the bipolar LSI families is their processing power, which is far greater than that presently available from MOS microprocessors. By packing their processing power on several matched LSI chips, they are easily expandable to 16-bit or even 32-bit word lengths, and they can be microprogramed to handle the most powerful high-level instruction sets available.

No matter how different each new bit-slice system may appear, certain circuit blocks are common to them all. Besides the processor slice itself, there are the functions of control register, timing, slice-memory interface, and carry look-ahead. The control register always contains the logic necessary for microprogramable control. It includes a 2- or 4-bit-wide data path, which can be expanded to larger words, plus enough storage and logic to address and control the memory circuits. It can also handle status, branching, and interrupt functions.

In the arithmetic/logic-unit block, the computational logic sits side by side with data routing paths and the input/output ports that handle the control-register inputs and memory outputs. The timing function ties the other functions together by providing the various clock phases needed to drive all parts of the system.

But the systems generally differ in capability and speed (see table on p. 91). Almost in dead heat are the AMD 2900 and MMI 6700 designs. More points go to the AMD system, which can operate twice as fast off less power. Nevertheless, with 17 working ALU registers and two address operations, both systems offer the digital designer a large measure of high-quality design capability at very reasonable costs.

AMD's 4-bit slice is typical of processor-slice architecture, since it includes a high-speed ALU, a 16-word-by-4-bit two-port RAM (to handle the two-port address configuration), and all the associated circuit blocks for shifting, decoding and multiplexing. Crucial to the layout is the 9-bit microinstruction word-decode block that selects the ALU source operands, the required ALU function, and the ALU destination registers. Thus configured, the microcontroller can be cascaded either with full look-ahead logic capability or with ripple carry. Also, it has three-stage outputs, and it can provide various status flag outputs directly from the ALU.

Double address operation is made possible on the CPU chip by the two-port RAM and an ALU fast enough to handle concurrent input sequences in turn without slowing up the system. Essentially, any of the 16 words of the RAM can be read from one of its ports under control of the address field input selector. Meanwhile, data from the other port is being read with the same code. Both data groups then appear simultaneously at the RAM port output for ALU processing.

Only 11 AMD chips are required to implement a typical central processing unit (Fig. 10). Four distinct data-processing functions are needed—the microprocessor slice, the I/O bus interface transceivers, the microprogram control, and the CPU control, including priority interrupt—plus whatever main memory is needed. These 11 chips replace about 200 TTL packages.

Motorola's ECL 4-bit-wide CPU chip design is sliced parallel to the data flow so that it, too, is fully expandable. The advantage of this approach is that the system can be extended both laterally to any bit length in increments of 4 bits and vertically. This kind of ECL pipe-line design achieves very high data throughput—rates of under 50 ns.

Configured somewhat differently from the Schottky TTL units, the slice contains a mask-programable latch network, the ALU, an accumulator, the shift network, input and output bus controls, and associated interconnections. This configuration copies most mainframe controller designs built with hardwired ECL packages.

To build or to buy?

Of course, engineers do have an alternative to putting together their own microcomputers from what might be a bewildering array of competing devices. For a reasonable cost (considering the design time, assembly, and testing), packaged microcomputer boards are available from essentially three types of sources:

- Semiconductor companies themselves are offering prototype boards and single-board microcomputers and microprocessors. Most notable examples are Intel's 8-bit SBC 80/10 and Texas Instruments' 16-bit 990/4 based on the 9900.
- Minicomputer manufacturers, growing concerned about the impact of the microprocessor on their low-end OEM business, have extended their lines downward. Their major weapons in this battle will be the quantities of development software that they have built up over many years and their ability to offer customers the option of moving upward to more complex systems while still maintaining software compatibility.
- Independent manufacturers of logic modules, such as PCS Inc., Flint, Mich., Pro Log Corp., Monterey, Calif. and Control Logic Inc., Natick, Mass., are offering microcomputers based on popular types of microprocessors (mostly the 6800, 4040, and 8080). There is also a host of smaller manufacturers who, having designed a microcomputer for internal use, have decided to try the microcomputer business. (With a microprocessor, almost anyone can call himself a computer manufacturer—and some of these companies will survive.)

There are many cost factors that may escape an engineer's notice in his flush of enthusiasm to get into microprocessor system designing. Besides extra hardware, he should also consider cost of software development, prototype test, incoming inspection, documentation,

The let's-get-acquainted kits

An alternative to either buying microprocessors and designing your own system or buying fully packaged microcomputer boards is to buy an evaluation parts kit. They're available from all the semiconductor manufacturers as well as many independent sources. You can use them to familiarize yourself with a device before committing to it, and they can even be used for short production runs.

The kits typically include a CPU chip, a programable ROM chip, a RAM chip, I/O interface devices, additional circuits to complete the computer, and a printed-circuit board. Some semiconductor vendors also offer self-teaching aids, such as RCA's Microtutor, MOS Technology's KIM-1, and Texas Instruments' learning module. Such units will help an engineer learn machine language.

Another type of source is an electronics distributor. Cramer Electronics, for one, commissioned Microcomputer Technique Inc., Reston, Va., to design a set of parts kits called Cramerkits. Present versions use some of the most popular microprocessor types: several manufacturers' 8080s, Motorola's 6800, Texas Instruments' 9900, RCA's 1802, and Mostek's F-8.

11. Minicomputer maker's answer. Digital Equipment Corp.'s LSI-11 is a microcomputer built around custom MOS LSI chips. A member of the PDP-11 family, it runs the standard software.

production equipment, and special test equipment.

What an engineer must decide is whether he can do the same design job, and manufacture, test, and support his own microcomputers for less than he would have to pay for someone else's microcomputer. Intel, for example, sells its SBC 80/10 for $295 in quantities of 100 (single units are $495). Included, at that price, are the 8080A CPU, 1 kilobyte of RAM, sockets (only) for 4 kilobytes of ROM, two 8255 I/O devices allowing 48 programable I/O lines, and interfaces (an 8251 serial interface device for a programable communications line and interfaces for an RS-232 peripheral or a teletypewriter, plus clock circuitry and TTL circuits that are needed to complete the computer).

Texas Instruments, which has been in the minicomputer business for years, put it all together late last year when it sprung its 9900 16-bit microprocessor, and at the same time announced the 990/4 single-board microcomputer based on the 9900. For $512 in quantities of 50, the 990/4 has the following major features: 8 kilobytes of memory, sockets for 2 kilobytes of programable ROM or static RAM, and I/O interfacing through its communications register unit (CRU).

On the minicomputer front, Computer Automation Inc., Irvine, Calif. was an early entry with its Naked Milli, the LSI 3/05, built with TTL Schottky circuits. Although it does not use a microprocessor *per se*, its cost puts it in the same ballpark with many of the other one-board minicomputers. The CPU is built on a standard RETMA half-board and sells for $295 in single units. With 1,024 bits of memory on another half board, the cost comes to about $400. Computer Automation is proudest of its I/O interfacing scheme, which uses microprogramable circuitry to tailor the I/O lines to any type serial or parallel peripheral device.

Digital Equipment Corp.'s LSI-11 is a 16-bit mini built around four MOS microprocessor chips custom-manufactured for DEC by Western Digital Corp. (But the Maynard, Mass., firm will probably soon begin its own production of the chips to serve as its own second source.) The LSI-11, at $634 in 100 quantities, has a 4-kiloword RAM, a parallel I/O bus port, and other CPU circuitry on an 8.5-by-10-inch board. Aside from having the full weight of DEC's reputation behind it, the LSI-11 also has the full range of PDP-11 software going for it. More than about 20,000 PDP-11s of various sizes are in use, and it is a familiar computer in many OEM plants.

The latest minicomputer manufacture to slip in a one-board computer at its low end was Data General, Southboro, Mass. For its microNova, Data General is making its own 16-bit n-channel microprocessors in its Sunnyvale, Calif., semiconductor facility. As a member of the Nova family, the microNova runs all the already developed software. With 4 kilowords of memory, it sells for about $570 in 100 quantities. Data General also says it will sell the microprocessor and memory chips separately, but this does not necessarily put the company in direct competition with semiconductor manufacturers. Users will likely first buy the complete boards. Later, when the volume justifies it, or when a different form factor is needed on the printed-circuit boards, the user will buy the chips, and assemble and test his own boards, still maintaining software compatibility.

At the other end of the microcomputer spectrum lie boards produced by the independents. Pro Log, for example, says it has the only logic processor system priced below $100 (it's $99 in quantities of 500). The system, PLS-401A, is a 4004-based system that includes a crystal clock, 80-character RAM, 16 lines of TTL input, 16 lines for output, and sockets for 1,024 words of memory. Pro Log essentially spans the Intel microprocessor line, offering computer boards with the 4040, 8008, and 8080, but it also has a 6800 board. □

In switch to n-MOS microprocessor gets a 2-μs cycle time

by Masatoshi Shima and Federico Faggin

☐ The first microprocessors borrowed many desirable architectural features from minicomputers—but not their speed. The 8-bit Intel 8080, however, achieves typical execution times of 2 microseconds, which are comparable to those of many of today's minis.

In so doing, it improves on the speed of its predecessor, the Intel 8008, by an order of magnitude or more, and, since it also adds 30 new instructions to the 48 shared with the 8008, it can be considered the start of a second, more powerful generation.

The key to both improvements is the shift from the 8008's p-channel MOS technology to n-channel MOS. Indeed, the decision to develop the 8080 was taken about 18 months ago, as soon as high-volume production of silicon-gate n-channel devices was feasible. The goal was a single-chip central processing unit (CPU) compatible with but markedly superior to the earlier 8008. The 8080's characteristics were to include:

- A 10:1 speed improvement over the 8008.
- None of the known limitations of the 8008 (such as interfacing problems and lack of multiple interrupts).
- Improved functional capability plus retention of all

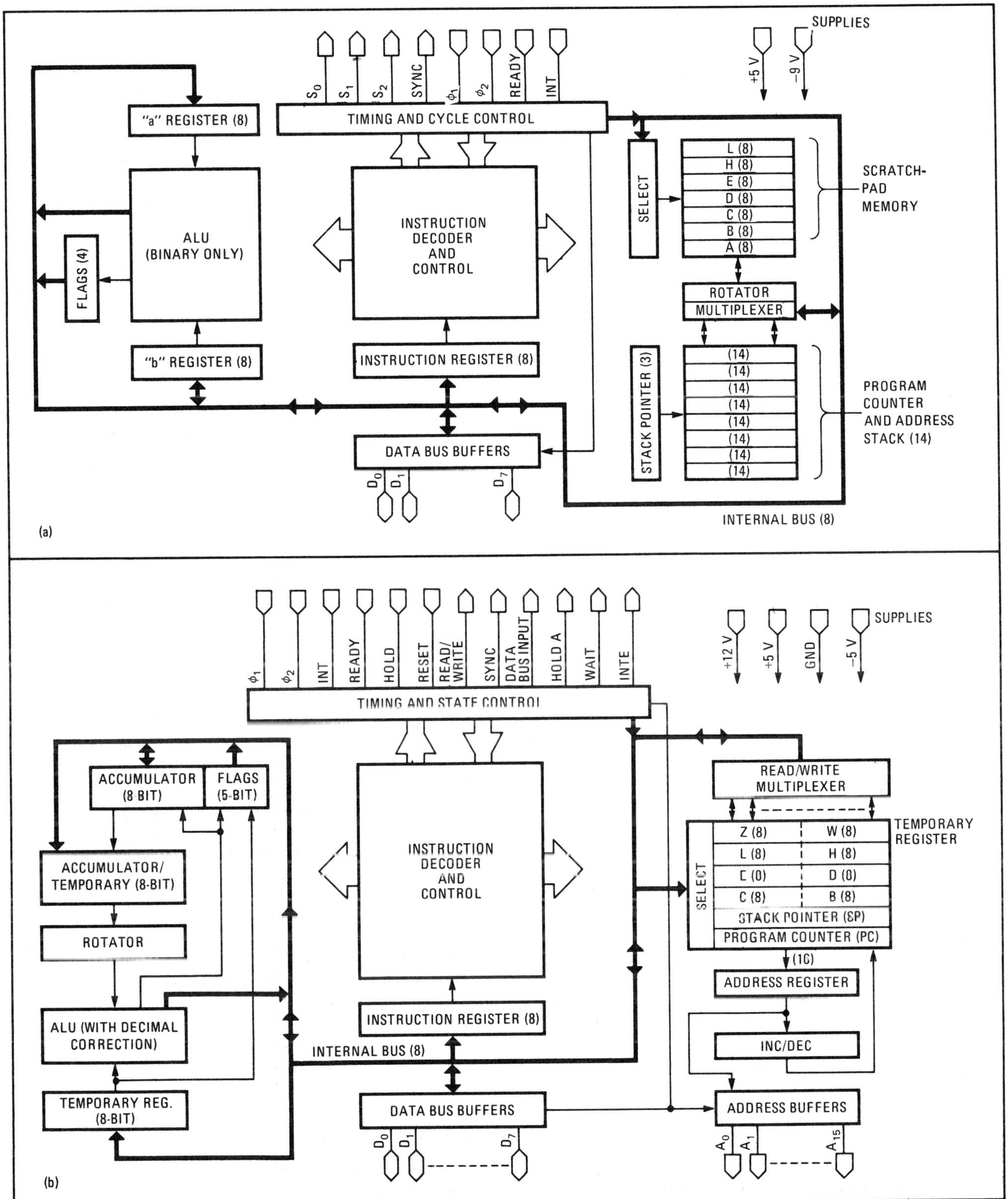

1. Comparison. Intel's earlier single-chip microprocessor, the 8008, has a separate scratch-pad memory and address stack (a). In the 8080, these have been combined into the six 16-bit registers (b). The accumulator has been moved into the arithmetic and logic unit, avoiding the use of the internal bus for data transfers between the scratch pad and the ALU during arithmetic and logic operations.

of the various features and instructions of the 8008.
■ Economic feasibility—a small chip and conventional packaging.

If the higher mobility of electrons versus holes were the only difference between the n-channel and p-channel technologies, only a 2.4:1 improvement in speed could have been expected. But n-channel's lower threshold allows use of a 5-volt supply for internal logic, with a 4:1 improvement in speed-power product.

There are other contributions to higher speed. The higher substrate concentration of the n-channel starting material, combined with the lower supply voltage, allows channels to be shorter than with p-channel technology, so that input capacitance is lower and size smaller. Finally, lower junction capacitances and lower resistivities of diffusion and polysilicon areas, which result from the n-channel process and the use of substrate bias, reduce the interconnection time constants by a factor of four—and, in logic circuits of this type, one of the limiting speed constraint lies in the electrical properties of the interconnections.

The interfacing requirements were simplified because n-channel technology allows a big reduction of the power dissipation of individual output buffer circuits, so that the 8080 could be packaged in a 40-pin package to include 30 buffers as against the 12 of the 8008. In the 8008, each output buffer sinks two low-power TTL loads (440 microamperes) for a total dissipation of 250 milliwatts. Eight of the 8008 buffers are shared (time-multiplexed) for addresses and data outputs, reducing the number of package pins but increasing the complexity of the interface. The 8080's 30 output buffers, on the other hand, are six times faster, sink 1.9 milliamperes each, and dissipate a total of 150 mw. The 100 mw saved was used to improve the speed of the internal circuits (a 40-pin ceramic package allows a maximum dissipation of about 750 mw, so the power budget was limited).

The layout effort took 18 man-months because it required great care to minimize parasitics and to optimize signal flow for increased speed and smaller size. The result was a 165-by-191-mil chip that is smaller than

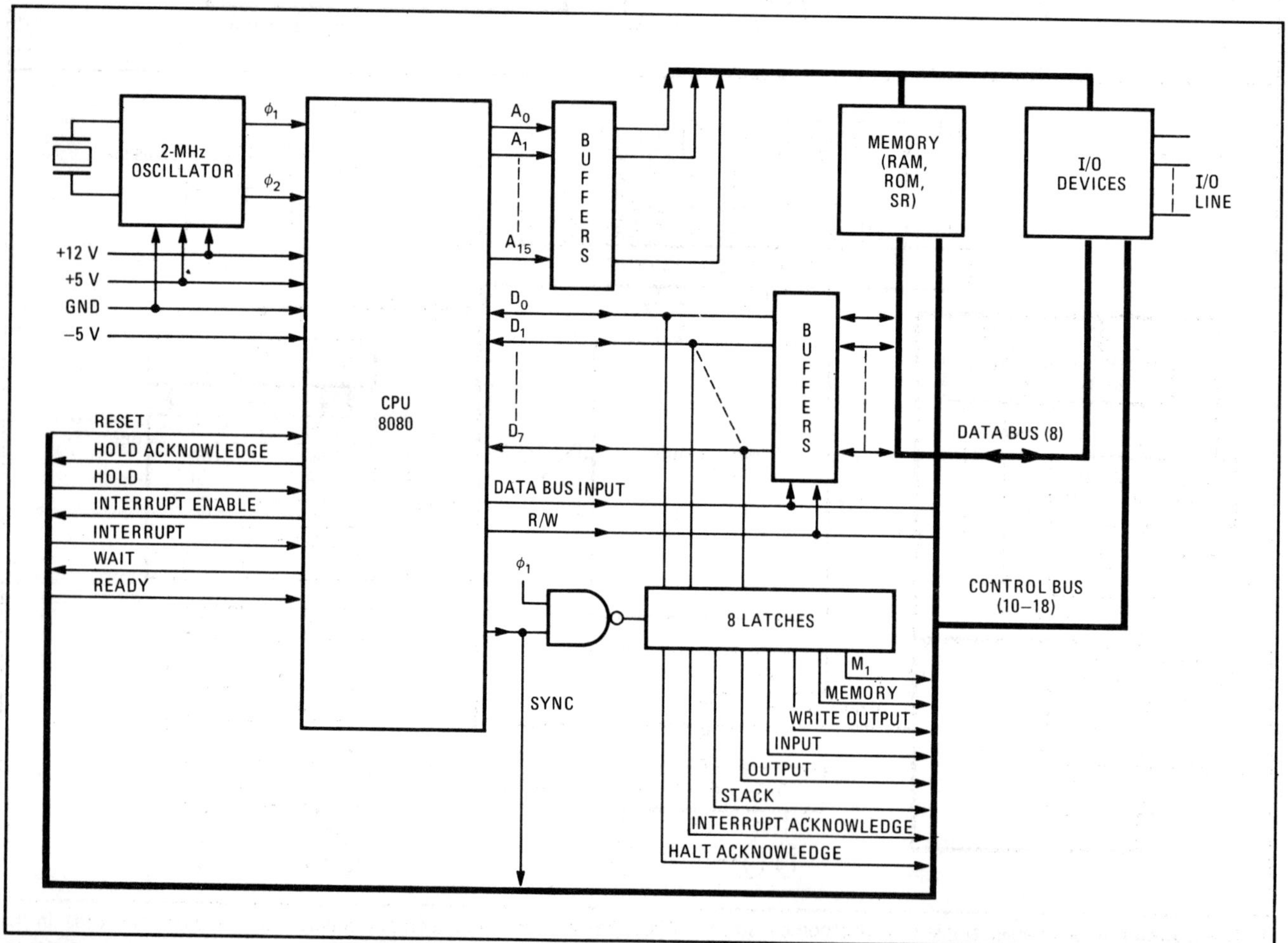

2. 8080 at work. When connected in a microprocessor system, the 8080 requires only six external TTL packages, as against the 20 needed by the 8008. The address bus can access up to 64 kilobytes of memory and up to 256 input and 256 output ports.

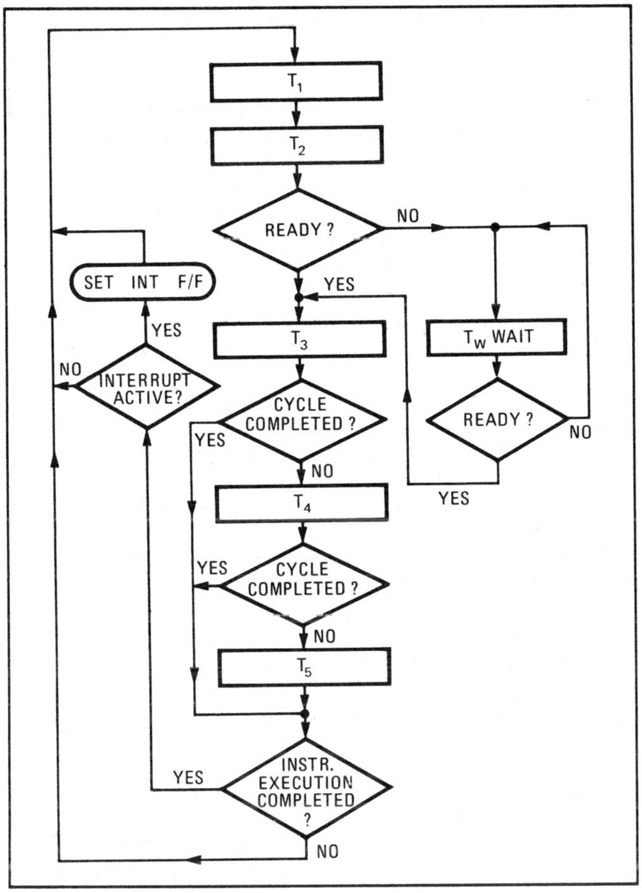

3. State diagram. A typical machine cycle requires three to five states. The operation is basically as follows: during T_1, the content of the internal address register is sent to the address bus; during T_2, READY is tested; during T_3, data is transferred between the CPU and memory or I/O devices; T_4 and T_5 are used when necessary to complete the instruction execution; and finally, the circuit goes back to T_1 for the next machine cycle. Only after the last state of the last machine cycle is the interrupt request line tested.

many of today's single-chip calculators. Great effort went into both logic and circuit design minimization, as a result of which the complex functions of the 8080 were implemented in only about 5,000 transistors.

The effectiveness of a CPU can be measured by its execution speed and memory storage requirements for a representative class of practical benchmark programs. The real improvement in performance is highly dependent on specific applications. If the 8080 had only the same 48 instructions as the 8008, it would handle the same problems about eight times faster (and five times faster than the 8008-1, a high-speed version of the 8008). However, with the 30 new instructions, the 8080 offers speed improvements on the order of 10:1 to 20:1 with smaller storage requirements—from 95% to 70% for an equivalent program written for the 8080.

The internal organization of the 8080 is shown in Fig. 1b, while Fig. 1a shows the same detail for the 8080.

The most important change concerns the internal memory organization. The 8008 has separate memories: an address stack—eight 14-bit registers which comprise one program counter storing the current effective address and seven others that store the addresses of nested subroutines—and a scratch pad, which contains the 8-bit accumulator and six additional 8-bit registers used for memory addressing and temporary storage of operands. In the 8080, these memories have been combined into a single internal 16-bit-wide memory with paired 8-bit register organization. The 8080's program counter and stack pointer, also each 16 bits wide, replace the 8008's internal address stack.

The 8008 has an internal 3-bit stack pointer, which gives the user up to seven levels of nesting of subroutines. The 8080's 16-bit stack pointer can address up to 64 kilobytes of external stack memory, providing essentially as many nesting levels as needed.

The 8080's accumulator and its associated circuitry have been moved into the arithmetic logic unit (ALU) section, to speed up the operation of the processor (data transfers between memory and ALU on the internal data bus are therefore not required for arithmetic and logic operations). Notice that the 8080 memory is double-ended—information can be transferred from the internal bus 8 bits at a time, while 16-bit transfers can take place from the address register.

Extra benefits

This organization yields a number of other new features for the 8080. The most important are:

- New instructions allow the contents of any register pair (B-C, D-E, H-L, or ACCUMULATOR-FLAGS) to be quickly stored and retrieved by being "pushed into" or "popped from" the top of the external memory stack. This is a fast way to save the machine status (the contents of the registers) when an interrupt occurs and then restore the status after the interrupt has been serviced. The stack can also be used as an extension of the internal registers.
- Other new instructions allow easy manipulation of addresses and the memory stack, since the registers B-C, D-E and H-L, and STACK POINTER can be incremented and decremented with 16 bits in parallel.
- The temporary register pair W-Z can be used as a program counter to hold a direct address to quickly load or store H-L or ACCUMULATOR. Also possible are double precision additions between any register pair and H-L.
- Fast, parallel transfers of H-L to PROGRAM COUNTER or STACK POINTER are now possible with a minimum amount of internal control logic.
- The addition of decimal correction to the ALU section enables binary and BCD arithmetic to be performed at about equal speeds.
- The addition of many new, easy-to-use control and

The 8080's inputs and outputs

The Intel 8080 takes four control inputs and generates six control outputs:

SYNC—output; a synchronizing signal that indicates the beginning of each memory cycle.

DATA BUS INPUT—output; a signal that indicates when the data bus is in the receiving mode, i.e. when data is expected by the CPU.

READY—input; a signal to the CPU that valid data is available. If not activated, the CPU enters a WAIT state.

WAIT—output; a signal that acknowledges that the CPU is in the WAIT state.

WRITE—output; a signal that tells the memory and output devices that valid data from the CPU is available on the data bus.

HOLD—input; a signal used by an external device to request access to the CPU address and data bus. Request is granted upon completion of memory access and it is acknowledged on the HOLD ACKNOWLEDGE output pin. The CPU address and data buses become floating (in a high-impedance state), but internally, the CPU completes the execution of the current memory cycle. After that, the CPU idles for as long as HOLD is active. HOLD and HOLD ACKNOWLEDGE can be used for DMA (direct memory access) control and in multiprocessor applications.

HOLD ACKNOWLEDGE—output; signals acknowledgment of the HOLD state.

INTERRUPT REQUEST—input; the interrupt input is sampled at the end of the current instruction cycle and if the internal software control interrupt enable flip-flop is set, it initiates the interrupt servicing sequence.

RESET—input; a signal that clears the content of the program counter so that program execution will start from location zero in memory.

INTERRUPT ENABLE—output; a signal that displays the status of the interrupt enable flip-flop.

The CPU also provides eight status bits on the data bus at SYNC time:

HALT ACKNOWLEDGE—a response to the HALT instruction.

INTERRUPT ACKNOWLEDGE—follows the acceptance by the CPU of an interrupt request.

INPUT CYCLE—indicates that the address bus holds the address of an input device.

OUTPUT CYCLE—indicates that the address bus holds the address of an output device.

MEMORY READ—indicates that the data bus will have data coming from memory.

M_1—indicates that the current cycle is for fetching the first byte of an instruction.

STACK—indicates that the address bus holds the push-down stack address.

WRITE OUTPUT—indicates that the data bus will have data for memory write or for an output operation.

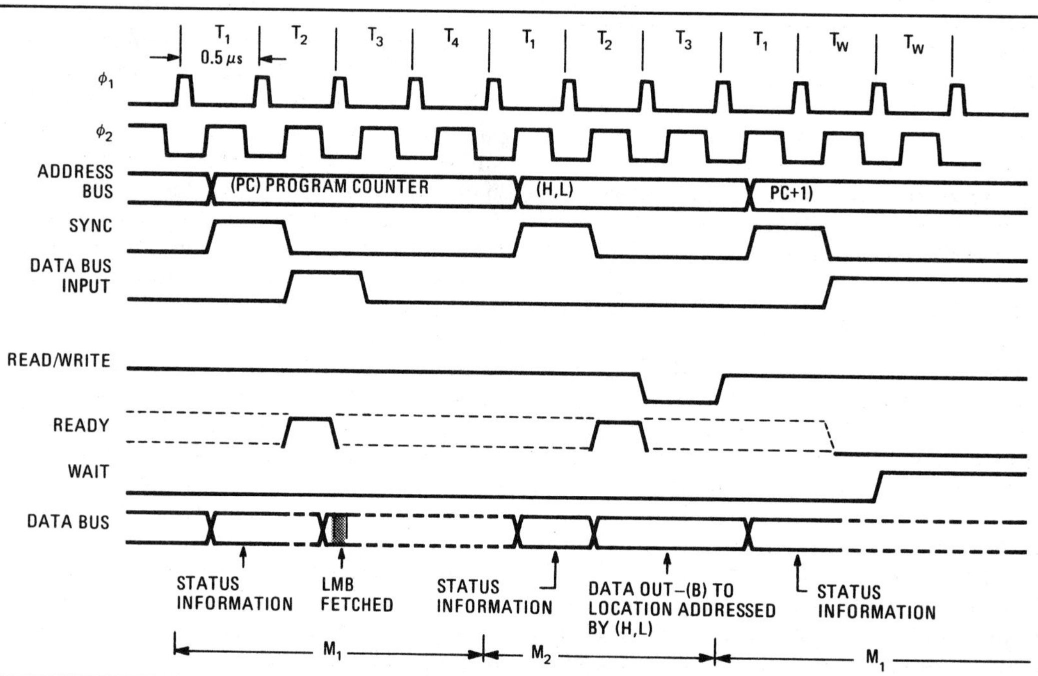

4. Timing. The instruction LMB (load the content of register B into the location addressed by the contents of registers H and L) requires two machine cycles (M_1 and M_2). During M_1, the address bus holds the program counter contents, and during M_2 it holds the contents of the H-L register pair. DATA BUS INPUT shows when the CPU expects data from the data bus. WRITE shows when data from the CPU is available on the data bus. READY shows that valid data is available to the CPU. The bottom waveform shows the corresponding data-bus actions.

status signals simplifies interfacing, allows direct memory access, and helps in program debugging.

Figure 2 shows how the 8080 interfaces with outside chips to make a microprocessor system. An external crystal-controlled oscillator supplies two non-overlapping clocks, ϕ_1, and ϕ_2. Buffers interface to external address and data buses, and a gate and eight latches set up status bits during sync time. All inputs and outputs are TTL-compatible, with the exception of the two clocks, which require +12 V. A memory and the input-output devices complete the system.

The amount of external interface logic necessary to implement any system depends on that system's complexity. The minimum requirement is six packages of conventional TTL (the 8008 needs at least 20).

External signals are organized on three buses. An address bus with 16 lines addresses up to 65 kilobytes of memory and up to 256 input and 256 output ports. A bidirectional eight-line data bus carries data to and from memory and I/O ports. A control bus synchronizes

COMPARING THE GENERATIONS

	INTEL 8008	INTEL 8080
Technology/threshold voltage	p/1.5–2.5 V	n/0.8–1.4 V
Supply voltage	+5, –9 V	+12, +5, 0, –5 V
Number of pins on package	18	40
Number of interface chips	20	6
Number of instructions	48	78 (48 + 30)
Instruction execution speed	12–22 μs	2–9μs
Internal memory type/number of bits	dynamic/100 bits	static/101 bits
Chip size (mils)	124 x 173	164 x 191
RAM size/speed (typical systems)	256/1 μs	1,024/500 ns
ROM size/speed (typical systems)	2,040/1 μs	1,006/600 ns

the CPU, external memory, and I/O devices, and also has the job of handling interrupts, direct-memory-access (DMA) controls, and CPU status information.

Instructions in the 8080, as in the 8008, use one, two, or three bytes of storage. Each instruction requires from one to five machine (or memory) cycles for fetching and execution. Machine cycles are called M_1, M_2, . . ., M_5. Each machine cycle requires from three to five states—T_1, T_2, . . ., T_5—for its completion. Each state has the duration of one clock period (0.5 microsecond). There are three other states (WAIT, HOLD, and HALT) which last one to an indefinite number of clock periods, as controlled by external signals. Machine cycle M_1 is always the operation-code fetch cycle and lasts four or five clock periods. Machine cycles M_2, M_3, M_4, and M_5 normally last three clock periods each.

To understand the basic operation of the 8080, let's refer to the simplified state diagram shown in Fig. 3, starting at cycle M_1 and state T_1.

During T_1 the content of the program counter is sent to the address bus, SYNC is true, and the data bus has status information pertaining to the cycle that is currently being initiated. T_1 is always followed by another state, T_2, during which the condition of the READY input is tested. If READY is true, T_3 is entered; otherwise, the CPU will go into the wait state (T_w) and stay there for as long as READY is false. READY thus allows the CPU be synchronized to a memory with any access time and to any I/O device. Also, by controlling the READY line, the user can single-step through his program.

During T_3, the data coming from memory is available on the data bus and is transferred into the instruction register (during M_1 only). The instruction decoder and control sections then generate the basic signals to control the internal data transfers, the timing, and the machine-cycle requirements of the new instructions.

At the end of T_4, if the cycle is complete, or else at the end of T_5, the 8080 goes back to T_1 and enters machine cycle M_2, unless the instruction required only one machine cycle for its execution. In such cases, a new M_1 cycle is entered. The loop is repeated for as many cycles and states as required by the instruction.

It is only during the last state of the last machine cycle that the interrupt request line is tested and a special M_1 cycle is entered, during which no program-counter incrementing takes place and INTERRUPT ACKNOWLEDGE status is sent out. During this cycle, one of eight possible single-byte calls will be sent to the CPU by the interrupting device.

Execution times

Instruction state requirements range from a minimum of four states for non-memory referencing instructions, like register and accumulator arithmetic instructions, up to a maximum of 18 states for the most complex instructions—such as XTHL (exchange the contents of registers H and L with the content of the top two locations of the stack). At the maximum clock frequency of 2 megahertz, this means that assembly-language instructions can be executed in 2 to 9 μs.

As an example of 8080 timing, Fig. 4 shows the timing diagram for the one-byte, two-cycle instruction LMB (load the content of register B into the memory location addressed by the contents of registers H and L). This example also illustrates the timing when a WAIT state is entered after the execution of LMB. Notice that seven states (a total of 3.5 μs) are required to fetch and execute the LMB instruction. The same instruction would require 28 μs by the 8008, 17.5 μs by the faster 8008-1.

Though this example demonstrates an 8:1 improvement in speed over the 8008, the real impact of the new 8080 will not be as a replacement for the 8008. The 8008 has, after all, adequate speed for a large number of applications. The 8080 will be used in new systems that were not feasible before because the first-generation microcomputers were not powerful enough. □

N-channel MOS technology yields new generation of microprocessors

by Link Young, Tom Bennett, and Jeff Lavell

□ The great promise that programable LSI circuits have for all kinds of control applications is fulfilled in the second generation of microprocessors, such as Motorola's and Intel's 8-bit devices. These new n-channel MOS chips have many more instructions and need much less in the way of costly systems circuit support than did the first wave of 4- and 8-bit p-channel systems. Their level of computing power is also high, and they are versatile and easy to use.

The n-channel metal-oxide-semiconductor microprocessors are completely self-contained. They are designed to work directly with a minimum number of memory and peripheral support chips, all of which are supplied in coordinated families to allow them to operate off the same voltage and power-supply conditions as the central processor chip.

A typical set contains the CPU chip, a random-access memory for fast scratch-pad logic control, a read-only memory for storing the system's program parameters, and a set of input and output chips. These input/output chips enable the CPU to control a large variety of industrial and communications equipment: process and manufacturing control systems, peripheral and terminal hardware, parameter-control systems of all types—from microcomputers in the automobile to control systems

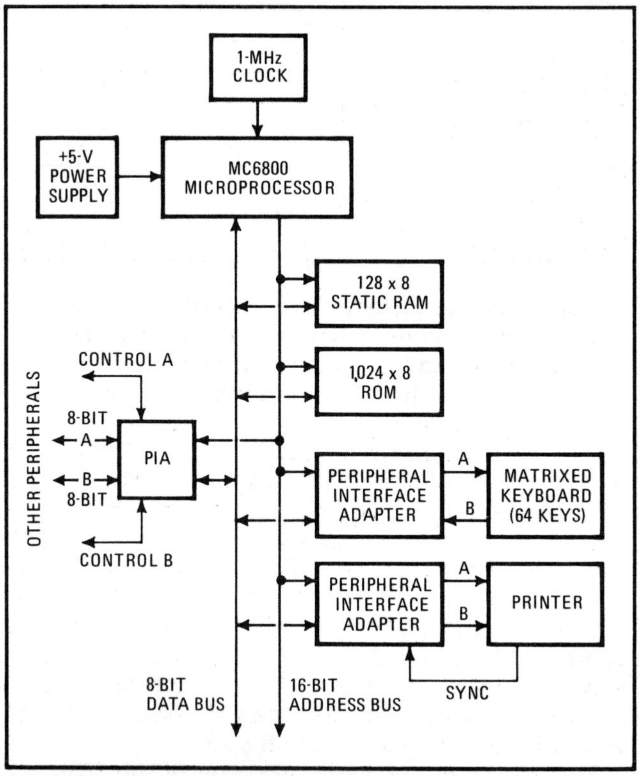

1. Eight-bit family. Motorola's M6800 family of components is organized around the concept of the parallel data bus. Consequently, all memory and peripheral interface adapter (PIA) chips are simply designed to hang on its CPU's eight bidirectional data lines.

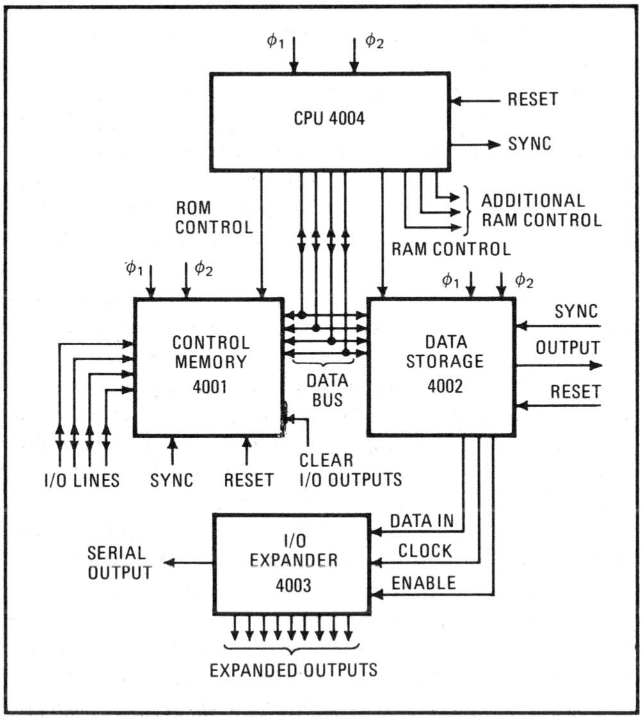

2. Basic computer. One of the first microcomputer chip sets to have been fabricated comes from Intel. Called the MSC-4, it consists of four simple LSI blocks and provides 45 instructions with an instruction cycle time of 10.8 microseconds.

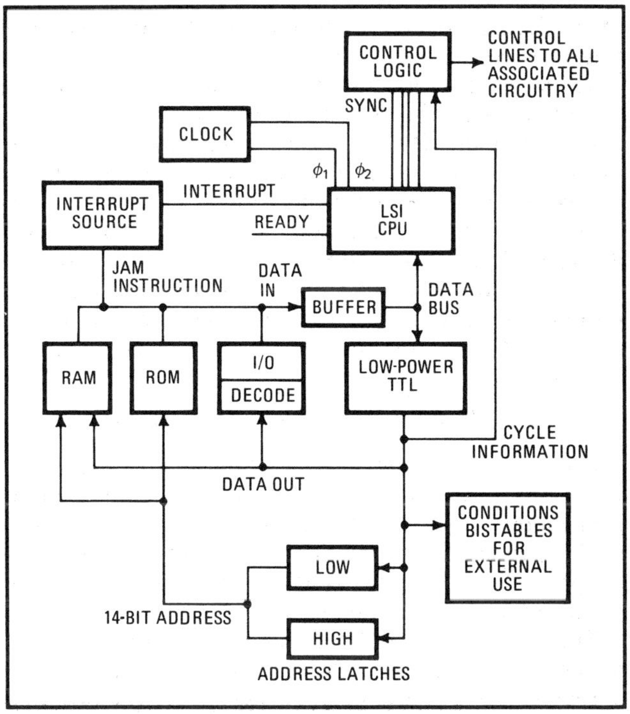

3. Heavy duty. The first 8-bit microcomputer system, Intel's MSC-8, can interface with over 16,000 8-bit words of read-only, random-access, or shift-register memory. Its drawback: substantial external circuitry is needed for most applications.

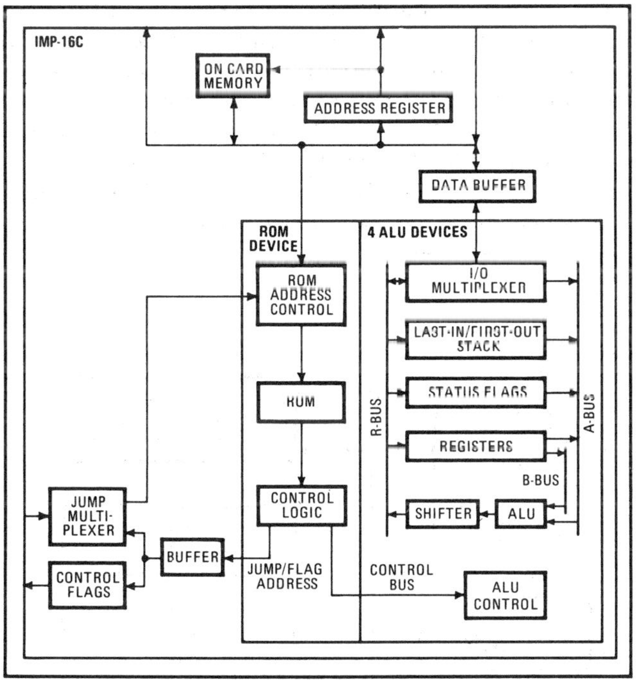

4. Sixteen bits on a board. National's IMP-16 architecture supplies a full 16-bit minicomputer capability on a single pc board. Microprogramable ROMs control the four 4-bit arithmetic logic units that do the processing. Four- and 8-bit versions are also available.

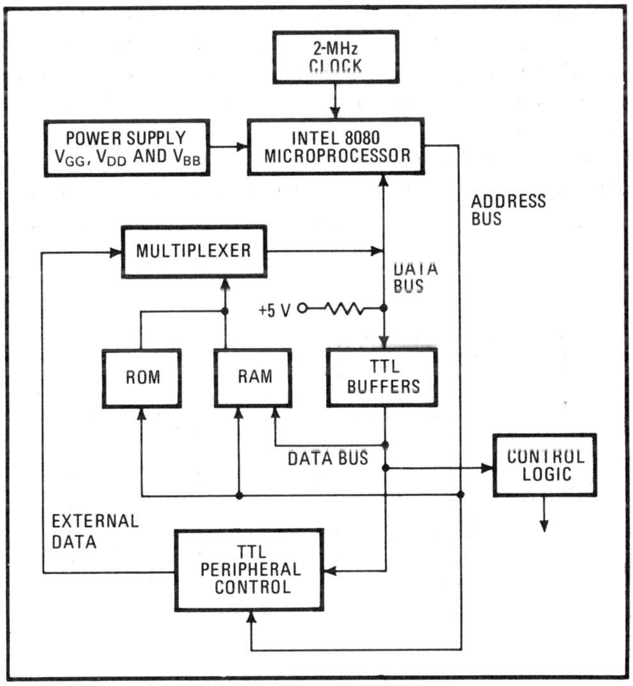

5. Straightforward. The new n-channel microprocessor chips make designing microcomputers simply a matter of choosing a family of matched components. This Intel 8080 system, for example, requires only a half a dozen standard products.

for traffic lights—and anywhere else that random-logic computer control needs optimizing.

These second-generation n-channel units expand considerably on the system benefits offered by the first microprocessors. Over 70 instructions may be available, as against about 40 for the largest p-channel unit. As few as four packages are required to build a complete 8-bit microcomputer. Moreover, in the Motorola family, the M6800, TTL compatibility is achieved with only a single +5-volt power supply, instead of the usual three supplies. Therefore, board space, package count, and component costs are reduced, even while system capacity is increased.

Other benefits to the system

Consequently, as with all microprocessor system designs, board layouts are simplified. The complex interconnections required for large numbers of conventional ICs are replaced by ROMs. The only interconnect wiring on printed-circuit cards runs between the various address and data buses and input/output devices.

The cost savings are not limited to direct circuit component costs but they extend to other, related, system hardware costs. Connectors can be decreased in number, cabling can be simplified, the card cage can be reduced in size, and so on. Associated indirect costs also fall, of course, since assembly takes less time, documentation is simpler, and maintenance is easier.

Equally important to cost savings in hardware systems is the ability of system engineers to build a proposed design quickly. No hardwire logic need be simulated, optimized, or breadboarded. The logic design portion of the cycle now becomes the manipulation of functional building blocks, where the control sequence takes the form of writing a software program into an external ROM. Breadboarding consists of interconnecting a few LSI packages.

Design changes, too, are simply a case of modifying the control program, in contrast to designing and laying out the logic afresh. The various microprocessor manufacturers offer the use of simulators, so that most of the design can be verified even before it is committed to hardware. This all cuts at least 90% from the design time.

The numerous instructions and system versatility despite the very few packages stems directly from the organization of the new CPU chips. For example, the MC6800 chip is organized around the popular parallel data bus concept (Fig. 1), so that all the memory and peripheral interface chips simply hang on the MC6800's eight bidirectional data lines (16 address lines are provided). Up to 10 LSI chips can be directly attached to the bus for operation up to 1 megahertz. To drive still more peripherals, a bipolar extender can be added.

This direct access to a variety of interface and peripheral equipment, obtained with a minimum of packages (see "The M6800 microprocessing family," p. 104) is a tremendous advance on many of the early microprocessor chip families—even though the first single-chip microprocessor was introduced just two years ago.

Intel's MCS-4 and MCS-8 and Rockwell's PPS-4, which all used p-MOS silicon-gate technology, were excellent starting points, in that they were self-contained sets of circuits requiring no external logic. In the 4-bit MCS-4, for example, the CPU, random-access memory, and read-only memory interfaced optimally as a set (Fig. 2). However, these first microprocessors had major limitations. Selecting correct memory locations required complex address logic: 12-bit addresses needing three 4-bit words had to be multiplexed onto the CPU's input

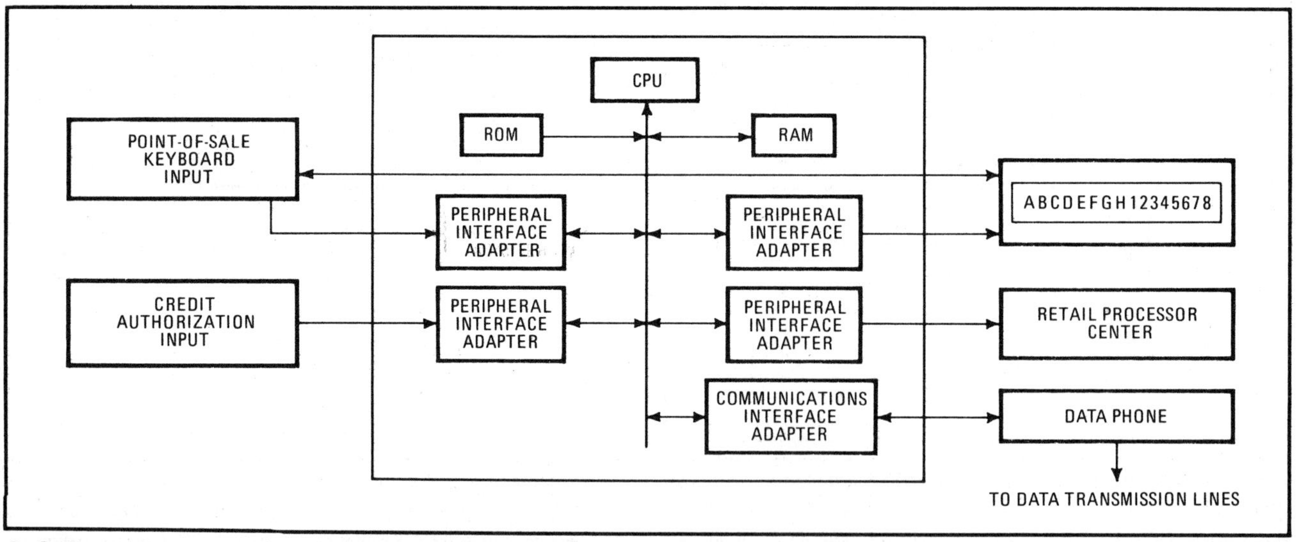

6. Selling well. With microprocessor design techniques, systems such as this point-of-sale installation are capable of being implemented with only five or six circuit blocks, which are designed to work directly with the basic CPU family.

matrix. All instructions operated on complex 4-bit data signals, as did even simple word fetches for each instruction. Still more restrictive was the fact that input and output access was serial, not parallel, limiting the number of peripherals that could work with the CPU. Instruction speeds were also slow—it could take 80 microseconds to execute one—and power-supply requirements were complex and costly.

For larger systems, the 8-bit MSC-8 microprocessor chip set (Fig. 3) could be used, but it was not a self-contained system, requiring external TTL for any application. It was, however, quite powerful: the 8008 CPU of that system can interface with 16,384 8-bit words of read-only, random-access, or shift-register memory. It was also quite economical to build: all communication between functional units and the CPU is carried out over the single 8-bit data bus, a sync line, a ready line, an interrupt line, and just three status lines. Its low cost, together with its respectably fast instruction execution time of 12.5 microseconds, makes the 8008 microprocessor still very useful for moderate-performance systems in point-of-sale terminals, credit-card verifiers, calculators, and other keyboard-addressed applications.

It does, however, fall short of being a useful general-purpose microprocessor chip set, primarily because, unlike its 4-bit predecessor, the MCS-4, it is not a system of compatible parts. Indeed, it requires many small-scale packages to build even a moderately powerful system—a simple modem hook-up would need about 50 TTL packages, increasing circuit board area and systems costs.

Another problem is addressing it. True, its 18-pin package saves board space, but it must be multiplexed both for address and data on common input/output pins, which in the end lengthens excessively the time it takes to execute an instruction. Not only that, the need for seven control registers on the CPU chip makes it difficult to manage the logic cycles, limiting subroutines and creating problems in programing and interrupt handling. Finally, its outputs are compatible, not with standard TTL, but with rarely used low-power TTL, so that circuits are needed to boost voltage level in most applications.

Most of these problems were overcome with National Semiconductor's IMP-16 (Fig. 4), a 16-bit microprocessor set that for the first time provided full mini-

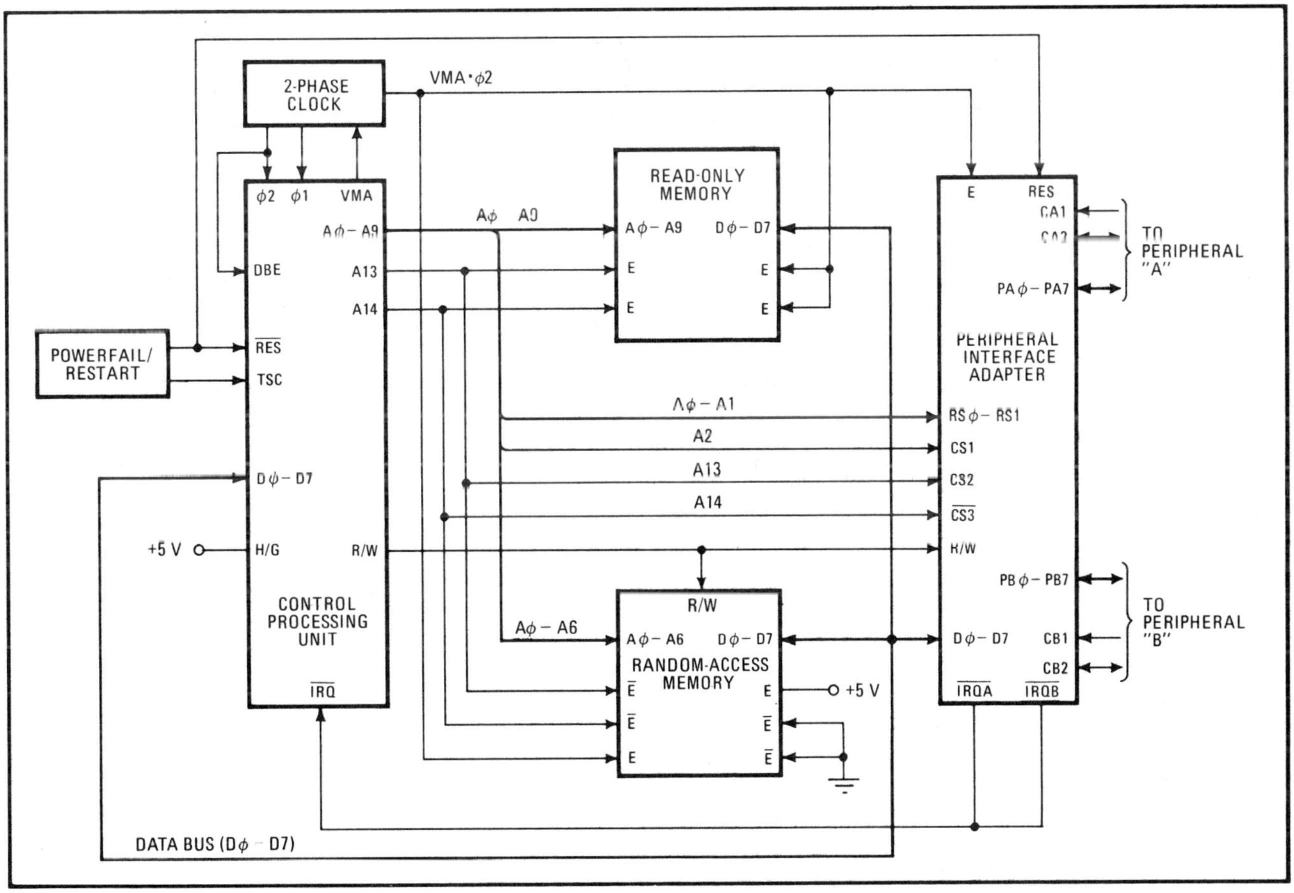

7. At a minimum. The minimum M6800 system configuration contains four functional blocks but can be expanded to 10 modules of memories, I/O adapters, and even additional CPUs on the same data bus with no external interface packages.

computer CPU capability on a single board. Designed to operate on both ends of the MCS-8 performance curve, this p-channel microprocessor unit is central to a family of systems with typical execution times of 4.5 to 10 μs for a system and 9 to 18 μs for a 8-bit system. Although it gained wide strong acceptance for many 16-bit minicomputer applications, it has been less used for 8-bit systems because the designer is forced to use microprograming—a far more complicated task than the programing techniques required for any of today's 8-bit microprocessors. (Because of this, National has now designed 4-bit and 8-bit versions of the basic IMP system.)

The problem then from a design point of view is how to incorporate the maximum system flexibility into an 8-bit unit, make it self-contained, have it offer a large variety of instructions, but nevertheless require the fewest possible external parts. Motorola's newly announced MC6800 microprocessor set and Intel's 8080 are examples of just such a system (Fig. 5). Using implanted n-MOS silicon-gate technology instead of slower p-MOS and operating from a single clock, each is based on a single 40-pin package containing a CPU chip that's far more versatile than previous microprocessor products. (For details of the 8080, see pp. 94–99.)

The M6800 family

The M6800 microprocessor set incorporates many of the qualities of the 8080, but exhibits additional flexibility because it requires fewer external circuits to implement most control and communication systems. The fact that the family can operate from a single +5-V power supply immediately reduces system cost by about $20 over a typical 8080 system, which needs three power supplies. What is more, the peripheral memory and input/output logic adapters, instead of needing external logic packages, have been designed so that they

The M6800 microprocessing family

The family comprises five chips: a single-chip central processor unit, a 128-by-8-bit static random-access memory, a 1,024-by-8-bit read-only memory, and one from each of two groups of input/output interface circuits—a peripheral interface chip designed to provide a buffer to terminal and peripheral systems, and a communications interface adapter circuit for interfacing communications hardware. They all operate from one 5-V power supply, and for many applications require far fewer interface packages than other microprocessor sets.

Basis of the M6800 family is the CPU chip (MC6800) packaged in a 40-pin DIP (see figure). Built with ion-implanted, n-channel silicon-gate technology, this chip contains all the functions required for multi-instruction processing: an arithmetic and logic unit, instruction decode and address registers, an instruction register, all of the clock and logic circuits required for timing, and a full complement of data-bus input and output matrices and address bus drivers.

The equivalent of about 120 MSI TTL packages, the chip provides 72 self-contained basic instructions that have decimal and binary arithmetic capability. The variable-length instructions include double-byte operations (such as increment or decrement, load, store and/or compare) and have tri-state outputs, two-accumulator capacity, and enough registers to provide seven addressing modes. A typical instruction time is under 5 microseconds, and there is direct memory access on the chip. Up to 64 bytes of memory can be addressed in any combination of RAM, ROM, or peripheral registers.

All other members of the set (see table) have been designed specifically to work directly with the CPU chip from the same 5-V power supply. The peripheral adapter (MC6820) is a bidirectional unit with two parallel 8-bit outputs that can either drive two peripherals or, if tied together, provide a higher throughput. The adapter can interface with Teletype and display terminals, with cassettes and test equipment, with keyboards and control panels, and even with large computers for time-shared expansion of computer capability.

The communications interface adapter (MC6850), on the other hand, couples the processor to most standard modems for communications with other computer systems via telephone lines. For still more system flexibility, it's possible to use without adapters not only the static RAM and ROM in the table but other memories, too.

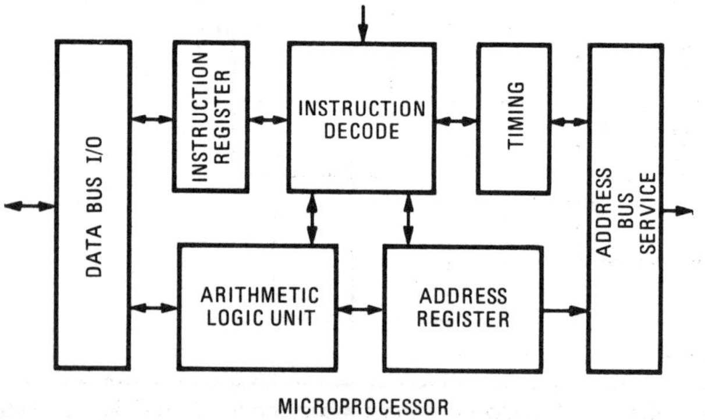

MICROPROCESSOR

MICROCOMPUTER FAMILY OF CIRCUITS
8-bit microprocessing unit
128-by-8 static random-access memory
1,024-by-8 read-only memory
Peripheral interface adapter
Asynchronous communications interface adapter
0–600-b/s low-speed modem (compatible with Bell 100 series)
Quad, bidirectional data/address bus extender

can work directly with the chip containing the CPU.

The smallness of the package count is dramatically illustrated by the comparison of the breadboard, engineering model, and final chip design of an MC6800-type CPU (see photograph on p. 82). The breadboard, a gate-to-gate implementation of the CPU employing basic gates and flip-flops, needs five 10-by-10-inch boards containing 451 packages. The engineering model is a functional implementation of the design and made extensive use of MSI logic packages and programable ROMs to reduce package count to a mere 114, packed into a single 10-by-10-in. board by means of today's most effective hardwire logic techniques. Yet all this is replaced by the single 40-pin package containing the CPU chip. The example epitomizes the impact LSI chip design is having on the implementation of complex computer functions.

The new n-channel microprocessors go still further, by addressing themselves to other parts of the system as well. For the families of circuits are designed to minimize assembly costs by reducing the number of ancillary parts necessary to realize a design.

Consider the block diagram of a typical small terminal, a generalized point-of-sale terminal (Fig. 6). Since every CPU needs several peripheral interfaces, one key to cost-effective designs with a microcomputer lies in the input/output interface.

Indeed, anything that has to interface with a microcomputer ought to be compatible with the data-bus arrangement and with the particular addressing scheme. Moreover, this bus-compatibility requirement holds good for not only in the input/output area but in the memory area as well. Consequently, since a microprocessor is a word-oriented system, more and more word-oriented memories are beginning to appear.

The M6800 family is directed at just these system needs. It includes flexible input/output adapters and word-oriented memories, in addition to the basic microprocessing unit, as indicated in the minimum system configuration of Fig. 7. This system can maintain its 1-MHz level of operation even when expanded to 10 modules (memories, input/output adapters and additional CPUs) on the principal data bus, with no external interface package.

In order to handle applications that require 1-MHz operation with more than 10 modules on the data bus, bus extenders are provided. For systems that do not require 1-MHz operation, up to 30 modules can be added to the data bus without requiring bus extenders—for example, more than 20 modules can be added to the data

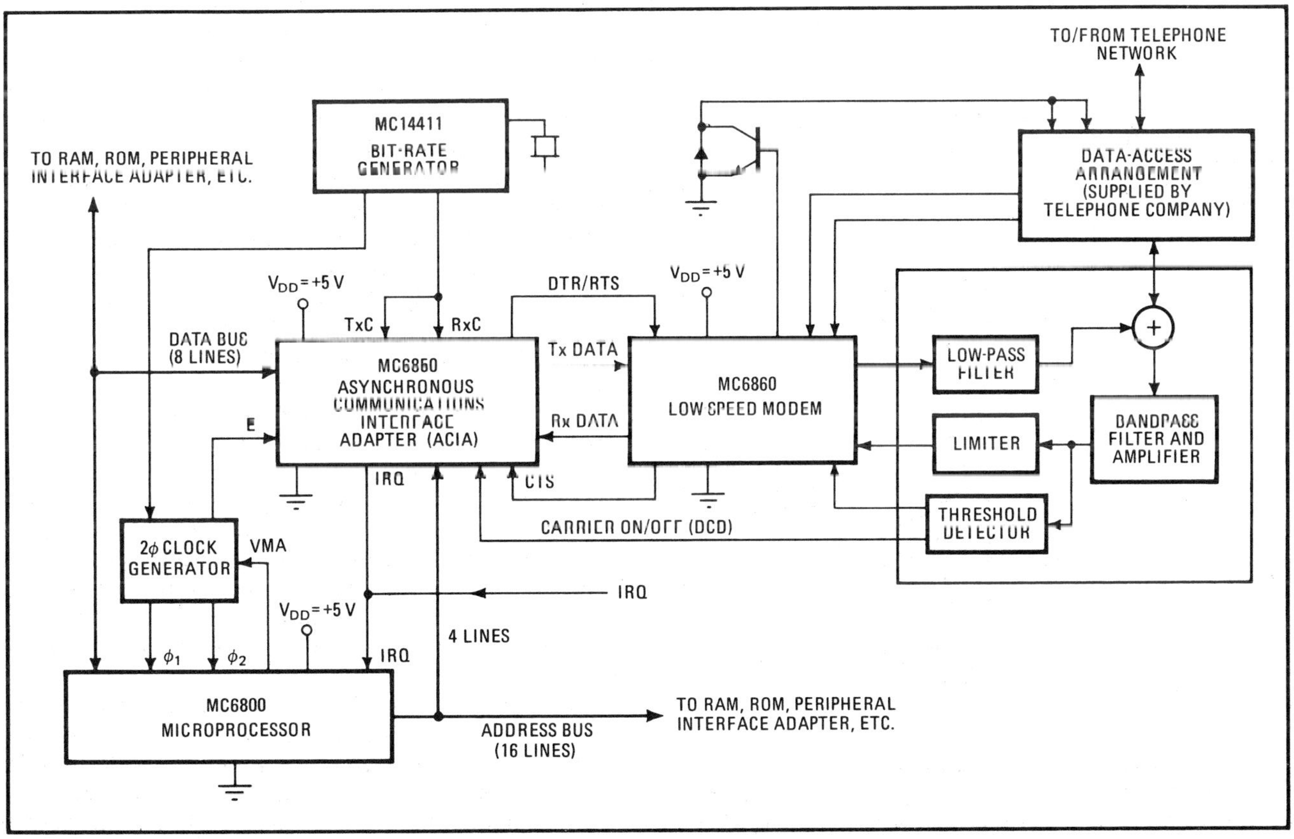

8. Communicating. A boon for communications systems, this microprocessor setup can be implemented using standard communication interface adapters (CIAs). These adapters' function is to give the CPU system access to any standard modem.

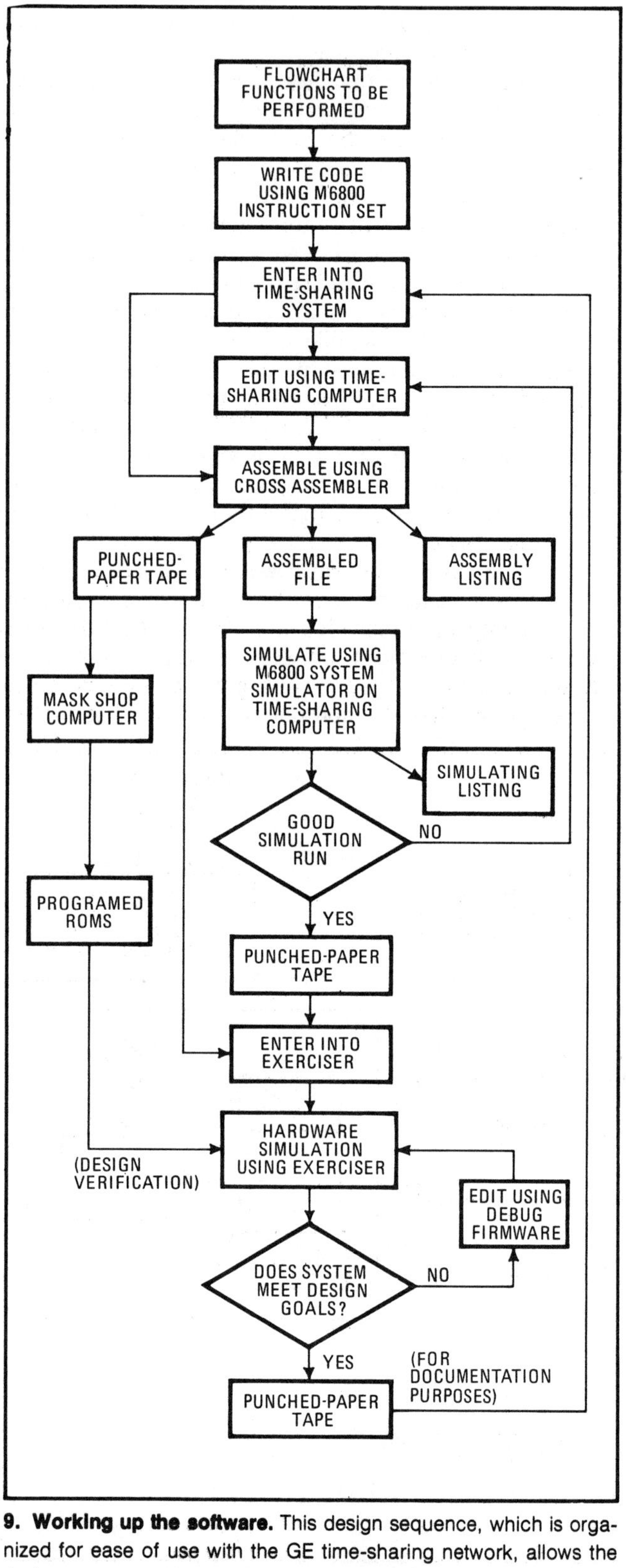

9. Working up the software. This design sequence, which is organized for ease of use with the GE time-sharing network, allows the designer to enter his specific program, which is then simulated on a cross assembler resident in the GE computer.

bus in a design for a typical 500-KHz control system.

Another example of how few packages are necessary with microprocessors is given by a typical modem communications system (Fig. 8). Here the asynchronous communication interface adapter performs the basic serializing/deserializing function required to interface the modems with the CPU. It also provides such additional logic capability as start, stop, and parity compensation. It can be used with a line driver/receiver for high-speed data transmission up to 5,000 bits per second, or with standard modems like the single-chip Bell 100 Series low-speed modem. Significantly, the 116 TTL and modem packages formerly required by this system are here replaced by only seven packages. The assembly costs alone are reduced by as much as two thirds.

Using the microprocessor

Most microprocessor manufacturers supply the software required to program their devices in a form usable with readily available computer systems. The software programs for the MC6800, for instance, are currently available on the ubiquitous GE time-sharing network. A designer might use them in the sequence shown in Fig. 9. Working with the GE edit program, the designer enters his specific applications program, which is simulated on a cross assembler resident in the same host computer. The cross assembler checks for obvious errors and violations and indicates them to the designer.

After the program has been assembled, the designer has two choices—to go to hardware directly, or to simulate his system by making use of the large GE host computer containing all the parameters of the particular system. If he chooses to simulate and his program works, he can then go to the hardware stage. If his program does not run, the simulator will pinpoint his problem areas, and he can modify his program and go through the loop again. This process can be continued until the designer is completely satisfied with his program.

In addition, exercisers, hardware, and programs are provided by many manufacturers to verify breadboard operation. In the system that is described in Table 1, the designer chooses the cards required to breadboard his system, plugs them into the machine, cables the input/output cards to his various peripherals, reads his program in through the TTY, or equivalent, network that interfaces to the debugging card. His program is contained in the read/write memory until it is debugged.

Then, in the debugging stage, a panel switch enables the flexible RAM to look like the appropriate ROM. If his program does not run, the exerciser will help him find out why and enable him to modify the program.

It's estimated that exercising aids like the off-the-shelf software and the Motorola Exorciser can save the designer from six to 12 man-months by providing him

TABLE 1

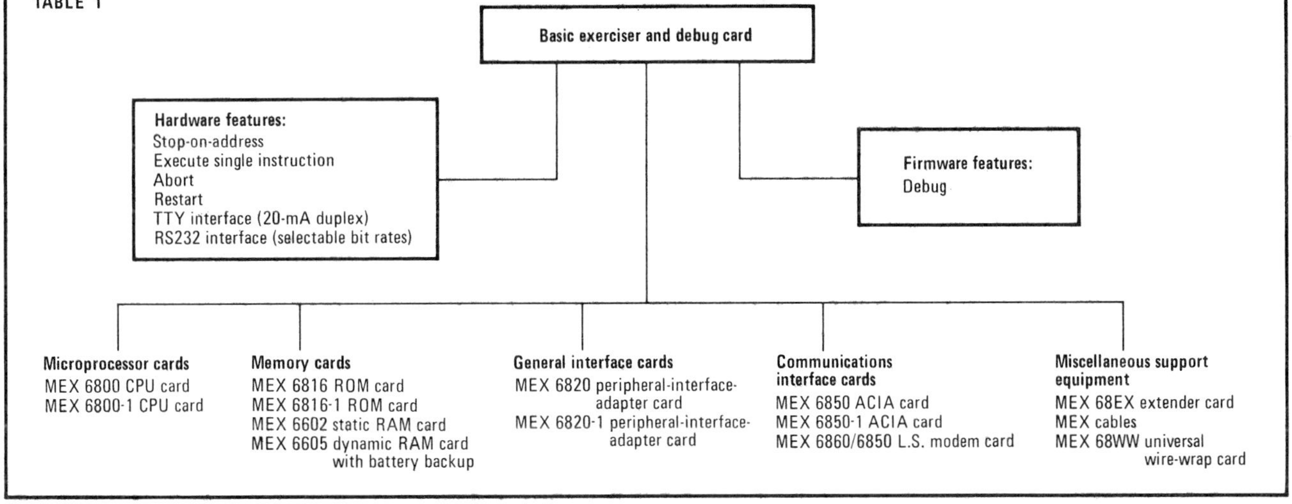

with a convenient method of communicating with the microcomputer.

Systems that are based on microprocessors are cheaper to manufacture, require shorter design cycles—and are also easier to modify or upgrade. The personality or function of the system, being determined by a master control program stored in a memory, is changed simply by modifying that program.

In the case of market testing, systems can be adapted in the customer's own environment to meet his needs better. For the first time a manufacturer has the capacity to make his product smarter and add features at any instant simply by expanding his master control program. A whole range of products becomes potentially available by simply adding LSI modules with their associated features.

System flexibility mostly depends on the new type of memory used, and here the choice is rich. For example, an inexpensive, volatile read/write buffer memory could be used in conjunction with a cassette or a floppy disk for very low-cost systems requiring moderate speed. For faster systems, such as modem interfaces, ROMs, programable ROMs, or even dynamic RAMs with battery backup could be used. In this area, the emerging 4,096-bit RAMs appear to offer the best speed/cost tradeoff. □

Z-80 chip set heralds third microprocessor generation

by M. Shima, F. Faggin, and R. Ungermann

□ The Z-80 microcomputer chip set represents as big an advance as was made between the 8008 and 8080. Throughput of the Z-80 is two to five times that of its predecessors, yet it needs only half to a quarter of their program memory.

The set's central processing unit has 158 instructions, including all 78 of the 8080A, and executes each of these instructions in an average of 1.5 microseconds. It also streamlines the handling of input/output operations and interrupts.

Because of the large instruction set, programs for the Z-80 will be shorter, so that they will require less preparation time as well as less memory. More convenient yet, the device is software-compatible at the machine-code level with the widely used 8080A, so that 8080A users can not only understand and master the Z-80 quickly, but can design it into new systems with comparative ease.

The chip set is an integrated family of CPU and

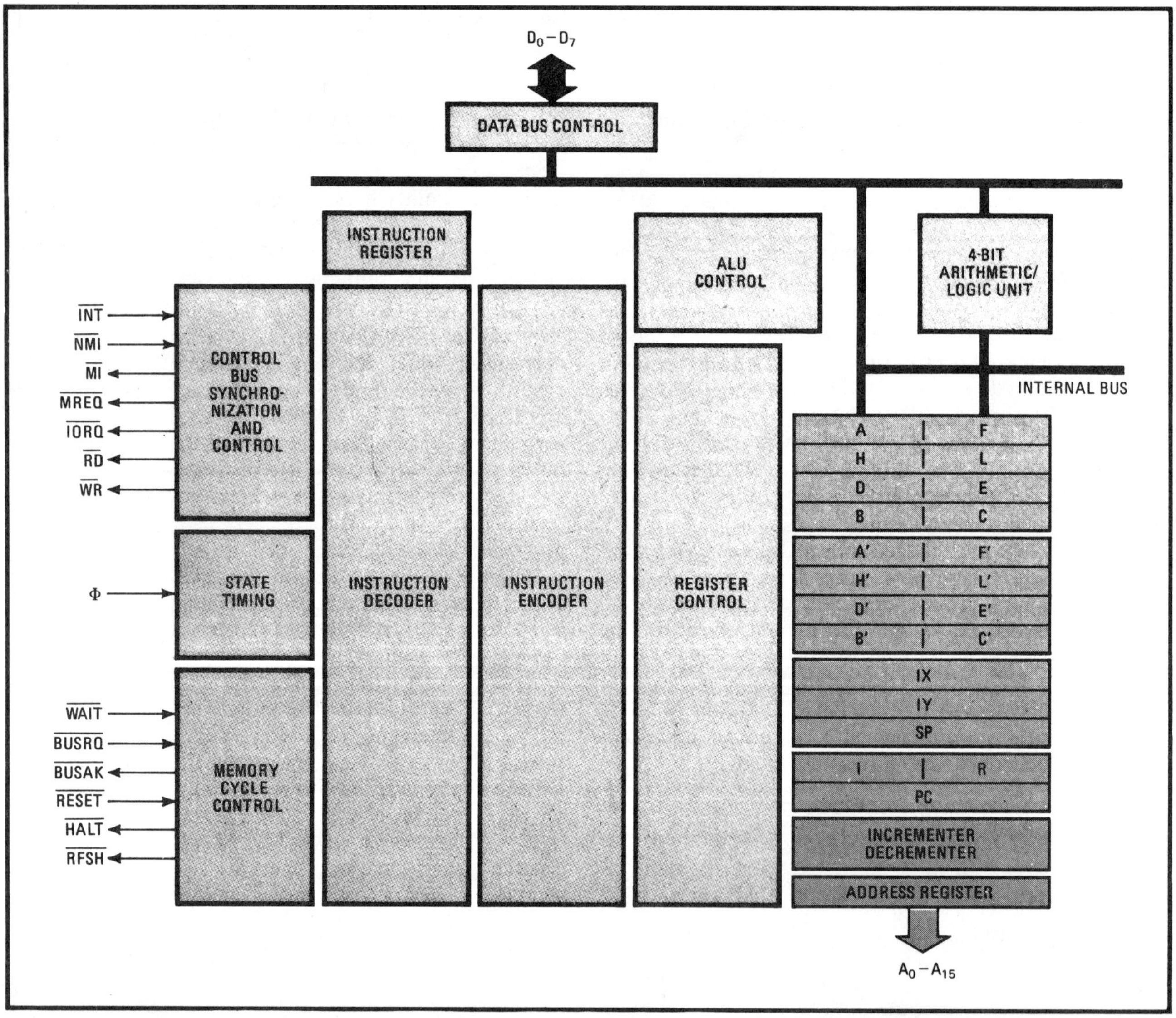

1. Central processor. The Z-80 CPU chip has a bank of 8- and 16-bit registers (right) that allow it great flexibility in such functions as handling interrupts. The device has an 8-bit data bus and a 16-bit address bus, and it employs a single-phase clock signal (ϕ).

Lines of control

The Z-80 has three types of control buses: system-control, CPU-control, and CPU-bus-control.

The system-control signals are:

$\overline{M}_1$ (machine cycle 1)—the current machine cycle is the operation-code-fetch cycle of an instruction.

$\overline{\text{MREQ}}$ (memory request)—the address bus holds a valid address for a memory-read or a memory-write operation.

$\overline{\text{IORQ}}$ (input/output request)—the address-bus holds a valid I/O address for an input or output operation. An IORQ is generated during M_1 to indicate an interrupt acknowledge.

$\overline{\text{RD}}$ (memory read)—the CPU wants to read data from memory or an I/O device.

$\overline{\text{WR}}$ (memory write)—the data bus holds valid data to be stored in a memory address or I/O device.

$\overline{\text{RFSH}}$ (refresh)—the lower 7 bits of the address bus hold the refresh address for dynamic memories.

The CPU-control signals are:

$\overline{\text{WAIT}}$ (wait request)—the address memory or I/O device is not ready for a data transfer. The CPU will continue to enter wait states as long as this signal is active.

$\overline{\text{INT}}$ (interrupt request)—a signal generated by an I/O device. The request will be honored at the end of the current instruction if the internal software-controlled interrupt-enable flip-flop is activated.

$\overline{\text{NMI}}$ (nonmaskable interrupt request)—an interrupt with higher priority than $\overline{\text{INT}}$. It forces the CPU to restart to memory location 0066H independent of the status of the interrupt-enable flip-flop.

$\overline{\text{RESET}}$—this signal is used to initialize the CPU.

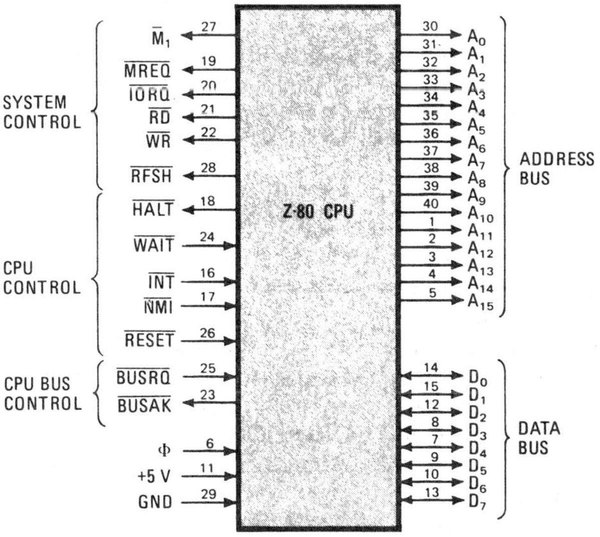

$\overline{\text{HALT}}$ (halt state)—the CPU has executed a HALT instruction.

The CPU-bus-control signals are:

$\overline{\text{BUSRQ}}$ (bus request)—used to request the CPU address and data buses, as well as $\overline{\text{MREQ}}$, $\overline{\text{IORQ}}$, $\overline{\text{RD}}$, and $\overline{\text{WR}}$, to go to a high-impedance state so that other devices can control them.

$\overline{\text{BUSAK}}$ (bus acknowledge)—the tristate buses are in their high-impedance state following a $\overline{\text{BUSRQ}}$.

peripheral controllers that uses a single 5-volt supply and a single-phase, 5-V clock. The metal-oxide-semiconductor CPU chip, built with n-channel depletion-load silicon-gate technology, has about 8,500 transistors in an area of 179 by 192 mils, for a density of about 133 gates per square millimeter. In comparison, the AMD Am9080—the smallest of the 8080 types—has a density of 102 gates/mm^2. The circuits in the Z-80 use static logic, and thus a user may step through every clock cycle while debugging system designs.

The Z-80 CPU is packaged in a standard 40-pin dual in-line package. These pins, apart from those used for the power supply, ground, and clock (ϕ), are organized into three buses. A 16-line address bus provides the address for memory (up to 65,536 bytes) and I/O data exchanges. A bidirectional 8-bit data bus serves for data exchange with memory and I/O devices. A control bus is subdivided into system-control, CPU-control and CPU-bus-control elements (see "Lines of control").

The importance of the registers

The heart of the CPU (Fig. 1) is its set of registers, which are built into a 208-bit on-chip static random-access memory, containing 13 words that are each 16 bits wide. The chip also contains the other blocks necessary to its operation—arithmetic/logic unit, instruction register, and logic for various control and timing functions. To understand the operation and the innovations in the Z-80, however, one must look closely at its array of registers.

There are two independent 8-bit accumulators (A and A′) with associated 8-bit flag registers (F and F′). The accumulator holds the result of 8-bit arithmetic or logic operations, while the flag register indicates specific conditions for the result of operations on words of almost any size—1, 4, 8, or 16 bits. The programer can work with either set of accumulators and flag register simply by invoking a single exchange instruction (EX AF, AF′).

There are two sets of six general-purpose 8-bit registers (B, C, D, E, H, L and B′, C′, D′, E′, H′ L′). Since the programer can call either set into action with a single command (the instruction for the exchange-register set, EXX), there is rapid-context switching following interrupts. Instead of being forced to store the contents of all the registers in an external random-access memory, the programer can simply deactivate one set without destroying its contents and switch to the other set to service the interrupt. The registers can operate as single 8-bit units or as 16-bit pairs, BC, DE, HL, and so on.

Each of the index registers, IX and IY, contains a 16-bit base address to point to a region of external RAM from which data is to be stored or retrieved. Each indexed instruction specifies an 8-bit signed-2's-complement displacement that is added to the base to calculate the effective address.

The stack pointer is a 16-bit register that contains the address of the top of the stack stored in external RAM. The external stack is a last-in, first-out file, allowing simple implementation of multiple-level interrupts.

There are two special-purpose registers, I and R, which

aid interrupt and memory-refresh operations, respectively.

The I register is used in one of the chip's three different programable interrupt-response modes. It holds the upper 8 bits of the address of a memory pointer, while the interrupting peripheral controller supplies the lower 8 bits during the interrupt-acknowledge cycle. The CPU then makes an indirect call to the memory location pointed to by the 16-bit address. With this method, the interrupting device will cause the CPU to push the program counter into the stack and go to the beginning of the previously stored required service routine, which can be anywhere in memory.

The R register contains the current memory-refresh address. Its content is sent out to the address bus during the second half of each operational code-fetch cycle (M_1 cycle), together with the memory-refresh-control signal ($\overline{RFSH}$). The content is automatically incremented at every M_1 cycle to refresh a new portion of memory. With this technique, the Z-80 CPU interfaces to dynamic memories with practically no hardware overhead.

Finally, there is a conventional 16-bit program counter, which holds the address of the instruction being fetched from external memory.

The extra instructions

The CPU can execute 158 instruction types with a total of 696 different operational codes. As mentioned, the CPU includes all 78 instructions of the 8080A CPU (a total of 244 op codes) and, since the compatibility is at the machine-code level, it can execute 8080A programs stored in a read-only memory without needing changes in the ROM pattern.

Among the new instructions are the block-transfer and block-search instructions. With a single instruction, a programer can transfer a block of information from one region of memory to another region or search for a single character in any block. Other instructions allow block transfers from I/O devices directly to any internal register or to any region of memory. Although this differs from direct-memory-access transfers in that it ties up the CPU during the block transfers, it can serve as a form of DMA in relatively low-speed applications, since it transfers one byte in about 8 microseconds.

There is a full set of rotate-and-shift instructions applicable to any register, rather than just to the accumulator, as in second-generation microprocessors. There are also byte-manipulation instructions, useful in word-processing applications, and bit-manipulation instructions that allow the CPU to set any bit in any memory location or any register. The addressing modes offer programers more flexibility than any of the second-generation microprocessors (see "How the Z-80 addresses memory," p.112)

The matter of CPU timing

The CPU executes instructions by stepping through a set of basic machine cycles. Thus an instruction cycle is a combination of one or more of the following basic cycles: op-code fetch; memory read or write; I/O-device read or write, and interrupt acknowledge.

Each memory cycle lasts from three to six clock

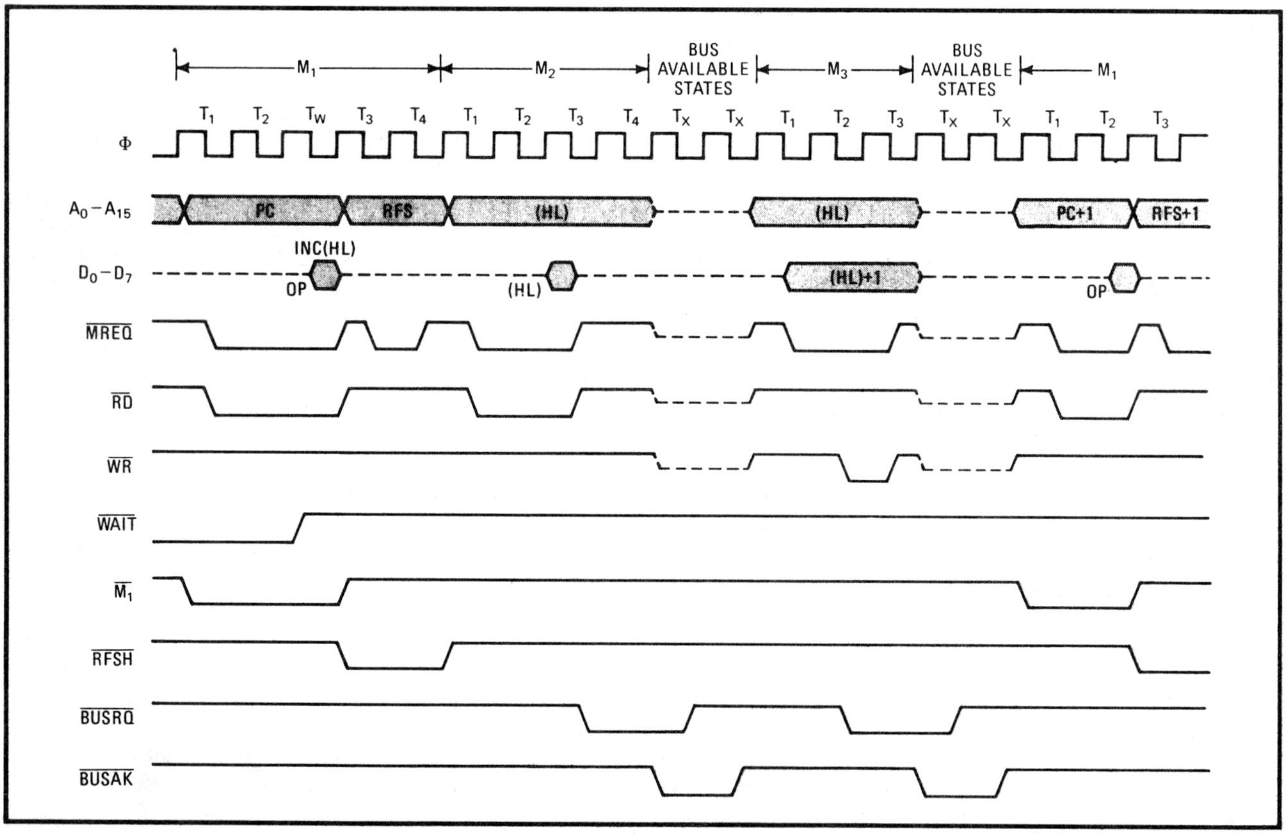

2. Timing counts. During the execution of an instruction—in this case, increment the memory location designated by the content of register HL—note that the refresh address is put out on the address bus while the central processing unit is interpreting the op code.

periods, which are 0.4 μs each for the standard-speed version (higher-speed versions with 250-nanosecond cycle times will soon be available). However, a memory cycle can be lengthened by two control signals: wait request ($\overline{\text{WAIT}}$) and bus request ($\overline{\text{BUSRQ}}$). $\overline{\text{WAIT}}$ allows the designer to synchronize the speed of external memory or peripheral devices to the CPU's speed by introducing extra idle states (wait states) into a machine cycle. $\overline{\text{BUSRQ}}$ allows external devices to have access to the address, data, and control buses. The CPU will complete its current machine cycle and then float its buses for as many cycles as required by the external $\overline{\text{BUSRQ}}$ signs.

An example of CPU timing is shown in Fig. 2 for the case of execution of the INC (HL) instruction—increment the content of the memory location addressed by the content of HL. For illustrative purposes, it is assumed that a wait state is requested during the M_1 cycle and that $\overline{\text{BUSRQ}}$ is active during M_2 and M_3 period.

During the M_1 cycle, the op code is fetched from memory and decoded during clock times T_3 and T_4. At the same time, while the CPU is fully occupied with the op code, the refresh-counter contents are placed on the address bus along with a refresh-control signal. Thus a totally transparent refresh of the memory occurs during

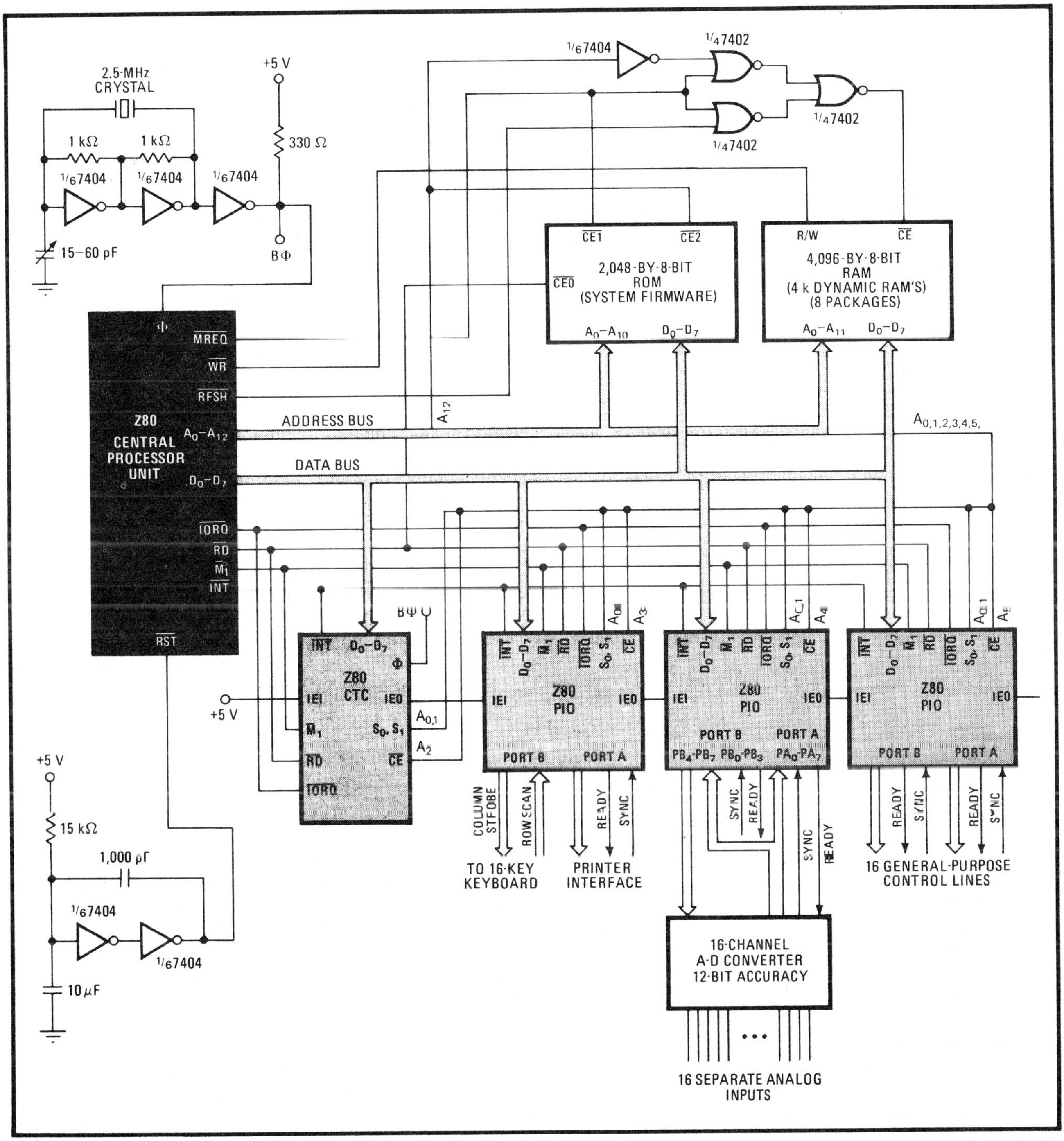

3. Process controller. To handle peripherals, three programable parallel I/O devices (PIOs) are added to the Z-80 CPU. On the PIOs, the IEI and IEO pins form a daisy-chain interrupt-control structure, with the device closest to the CPU having the highest priority.

How the Z-80 addresses memory

One of the advantages of the Z-80 is the variety of addressing modes available. Listed below are some of them, including an example of each mode.

Immediate [LD E, n]—load register E with 8-bit value n.

Immediate extended [LD HL, nn]—load register HL with the 16-bit value nn.

Modified page zero [RST 48]—call to location 48.

Extended [LD DE, (nn)]—load DE with the contents of memory locations (nn) and (nn+1).

Indexed [ADD (IY+d)]—add the content of memory location (IY+d) to the content of the accumulator (d is an 8-bit signed-2's-complement value).

Relative [JR e] or [JR kk, e]—jump from the current program-counter location to a new location offset by an amount indicated by e, the signed 8-bit quantity. This allows jumping up to +127 or −128 locations. A condition code, kk, may also be added to the instruction for conditional jumps.

Register [INC B]—increment the content of register B.

Implied [NEG]—negate the content of the accumulator (2's complement).

Register indirect [LD (DE), A]—load location addressed by the content of DE with the accumulator's content.

Bit addressing [SET 4 (HL)]—set bit 4 of memory location addressed by HL.

Stack addressing [PUSH IX]—push the content of register IX into the stack.

Since many instructions include more than one operand, two types of addressing modes may be employed, one to specify the source and one to specify the destination. The Z-80 CPU is provided with many such addressing combinations:

LD C, (HL)—load register C with the memory content addressed by HL.

LD (IX+d), B—load memory location (IX+d) with register B

LD (IY+d), n—load memory location (IY+d) with the value n.

EX (SP), IX—exchange the contents of the top of stack and register IX.

SBC HL, BC—subtract the content of BC from HL, which then will contain the result of the operation.

OUT (C), D—send the content of register D to the peripheral device addressed by the content of register C.

LDDR—move a string of data from one area of memory to another. At the beginning of the instruction, HL points to the top of the source string, DE points to the top of the destination string, and BC holds the string length.

INIR—move a block of data from the peripheral whose address is the content of register C to a memory area addressed by HL. At the beginning of the instruction, C points to the peripheral, HL points to the bottom of the memory block, and the content of register B represents the block length.

this time without slowing down the processor.

During cycle M_2, the data from the memory location pointed to by register pair HL is read from memory. This four-cycle operation has been extended two clock periods by an external device that requests the bus for a DMA cycle during the T_4 time periods. During cycle M_3, the incremented data is written back into the memory.

A versatile system

A set of peripheral controllers allows the implementation of a wide variety of systems, ranging from simple controllers to sophisticated computing systems. There are four of those building blocks.

- The Z-80 PIO is a programable circuit that allows parallel communication between the CPU and peripheral devices such as printers, plotters, paper-tape readers and punches, keyboards, and many other peripherals.
- The Z-80 CTC is a programable counter/timer circuit that contains four independent interval counter/timers and allows easy control of practically any electromechanical system, as well as several different communication protocols.
- The Z-80 DMA is a programable circuit that may be used where there is a requirement for fast direct memory access. However, note that the memory-to-I/O block-transfer instructions in the CPU will allow many applications to do without a DMA channel if the transfer rates are less than 125 kilobytes per second.
- The Z-80-SIO is a programable circuit that allows easy interface with most serial communications protocols.

A key feature of these peripheral controllers is the interrupt structure. They can be daisy-chained together to form a priority structure that allows nested interrupts to be handled by the CPU with no hardware or software overhead. Using the interrupt mode, the requesting controller will cause the CPU to go to the beginning of its service routine. At the end of its service routine, a special instruction—return from interrupt—is recognized by the controller, and this allows controllers with lower priority to interrupt the CPU and allows the CPU to automatically resume service routines interrupted by a higher-priority device.

In the example of a small Z-80-based process-control application in Fig. 3, the peripheral devices consist of a 16-key keyboard, a printer, a 12-bit analog-to-digital converter interfacing 16 analog lines into the system, and 16 discrete system-control lines. Three Z-80 PIOs handle the interfaces to the external I/O devices. For each peripheral device, the CPU merely configures a PIO for the required interfacing.

On the peripheral devices, two pins—the IEI (interrupt enable in) and IEO (interrupt enable out)—form a daisy-chain interrupt-control structure where the device closest to the CPU has the highest priority. Here, this device is the CTC, which performs all timing functions to avoid software timing loops. The complete computer requires only 14 circuits, nine of which are memory—2,048 bytes of ROM and 4,096 bytes of RAM.

In such systems, the Z-80's requirement of a single power supply and single-phase clock significantly eases the system design. And, since the CPU carries on-chip memory-refresh circuitry, standard memory chips may be selected. Thus, the Z-80 extends the range of cost-effective applications for MOS microprocessors. □

Third-generation microcomputer set packs it all into 3 chips

by D. W. Sohn and Andrew Volk

☐ To take full advantage of the microprocessor's talents, designers usually need a long shopping list of additional chips: series and parallel input/output devices, an interrupt controller, a timer, and read-only and random-access memories. One way to pare that shopping list is the MCS-85, the third-generation three-chip microcomputer system based on the 8085 microprocessor.

Incorporating all these functions into a three-chip set that requires only a single 5-volt supply represents a substantial reduction in package count—plus an improvement in system design throughput of as much as 50% over 8080-based systems. The addition of features such as higher speed, a more sophisticated interrupt arrangement, simple serial I/O lines, and a multiplexed address/data bus significantly improves system performance. Yet, despite all these refinements, the MCS-85 group retains 100% software compatibility with 8080-based systems.

Because all the chips in the group are multiple-function devices, the component count in any system design is reduced. The group comprises the 8085 central processing unit, the 8155 RAM, I/O, and timer, the 8355 mask-programmable ROM, and the 8755 electrically programmable ROM. Both of the 16,384-bit ROMs feature

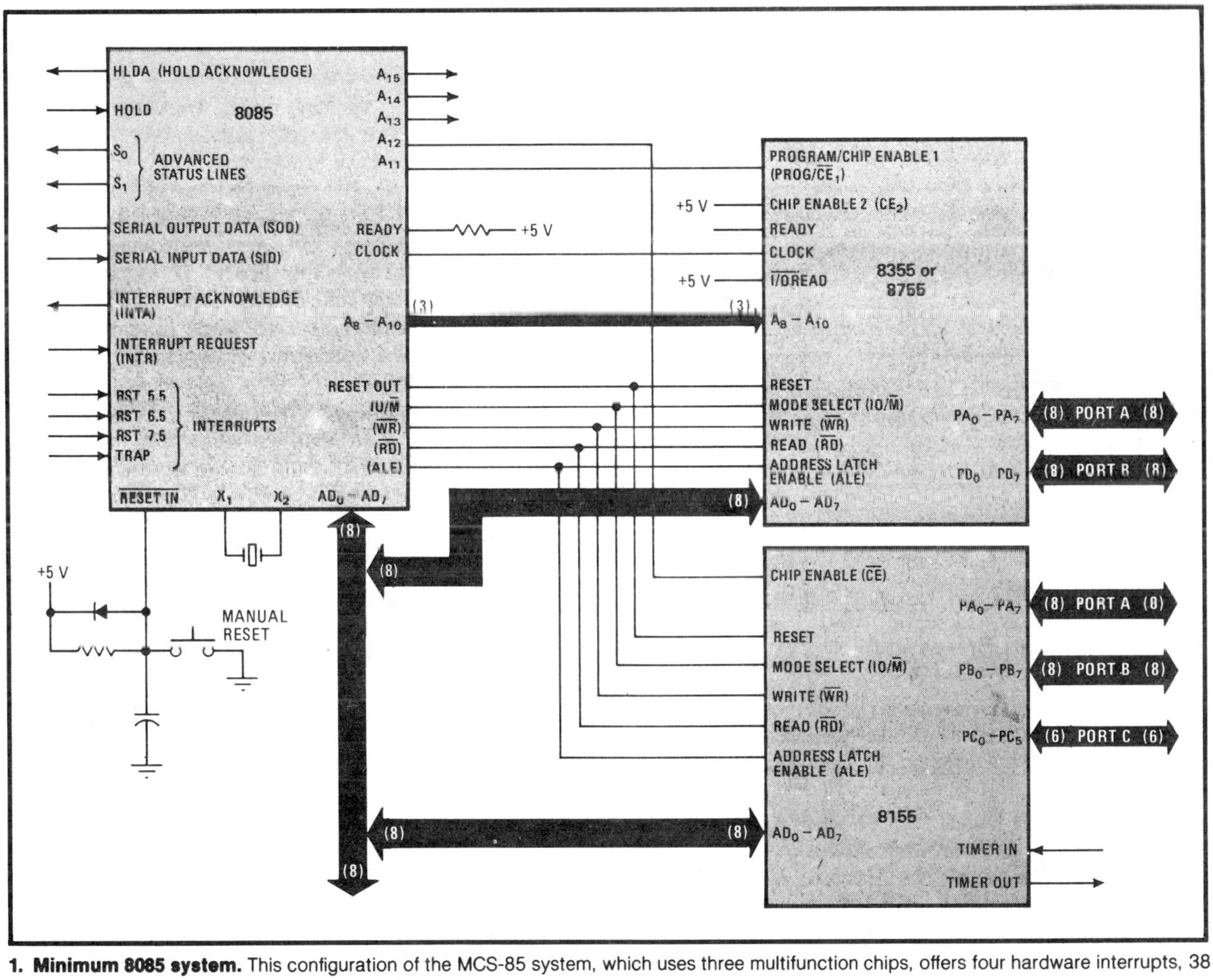

1. Minimum 8085 system. This configuration of the MCS-85 system, which uses three multifunction chips, offers four hardware interrupts, 38 I/O lines, a serial I/O port, and a 14-bit timer. Power requirement is a single +5-volt source, and overall system speed is 3 megahertz.

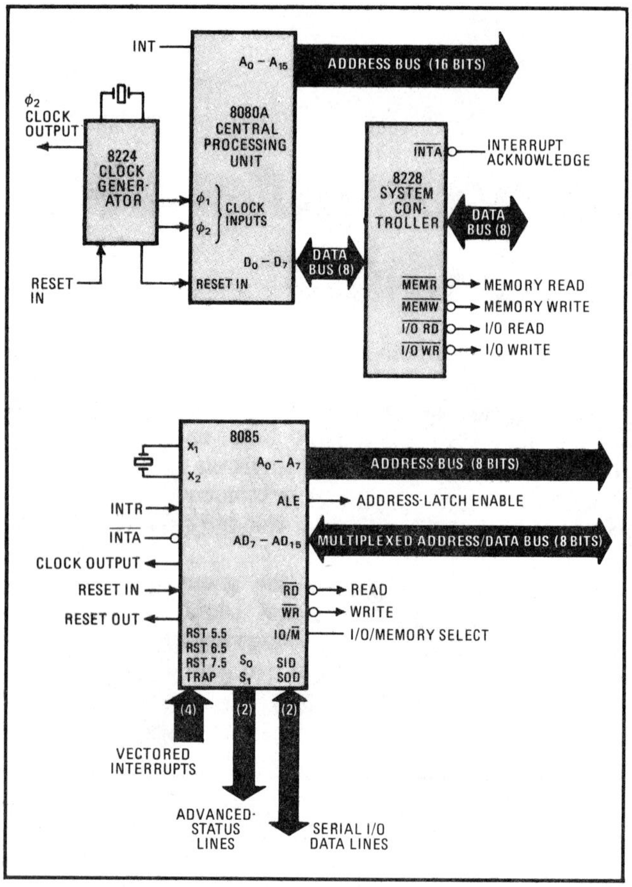

2. CPU groups. The third-generation 8085 chip comprises all functions of the three-chip 8080 group: clock generator, system controller, and CPU. The power of the system is increased by the addition of advanced status lines, hierarchical interrupts, and a serial I/O port.

TABLE 8085 RESTART INTERRUPTS

Interrupt	Restart address (hexadecimal)
RST 0	00_{16}
RST 1	08_{16}
RST 2	10_{16}
RST 3	18_{16}
RST 4	20_{16}
*** TRAP**	**24_{16}**
RST 5	28_{16}
*** RST 5.5**	**$2C_{16}$**
RST 6	30_{16}
*** RST 6.5**	**34_{16}**
RST 7	38_{16}
*** RST 7.5**	**$3C_{16}$**

* New hardware interrupts

I/O capability, and either may be teamed with the 8085 and 8155 to build the minimum system of Fig. 1.

As well as fulfilling all the functions of the 8080, the 8085 assumes the roles of clock generator, system controller, interrupt controller, and serial I/O port. It is specified for operation at 3 megahertz, a speed previously attained only by the 8080-1 (selected devices proven to operate reliably at 3 MHz). More importantly, improvements in CPU-to-memory synchronization permit a much faster overall system speed.

Combining data and address buses

The 8085's multiplexed address/data bus combines all the address and data bits onto 16 lines. This scheme, which frees seven pins, helps make possible the inclusion of the chip's additional features.

In the multiplexing scheme, the lower 8 bits of the 16-bit address are timeshared with the 8 data bits on lines AD_{0-7}. The address latch enable (ALE), a control line unique to the 8085, latches the lower eight address lines into peripheral devices. At the beginning of each machine cycle, the CPU sends out all 16 bits of address along with the ALE output. Upon command from the ALE, the lower 8 address bits are latched into any of the memory components or into an external latch for interfacing with standard memories.

During a write cycle, data appears on lines AD_{0-7} in the next clock cycle after latching of the 16 address bits. During a read cycle, which has identical timing characteristics, the data appears on the AD_{0-7} bus from a peripheral unit. The symmetry of the read and write control lines, as well as the elimination of eight lines on the bus, substantially eases system bus design.

No waiting for this bus

Speed limitation is a serious problem in designing an optimal system bus. In most cases, the CPU can handle data faster than the memory can deliver it. Such a disparity necessitates the insertion of a wait state in each memory-access cycle. For example, the 8080-1 operating at 3 MHz requires only a 310-nanosecond access time with no buffer between CPU and memory. With two levels of buffering, each specified at 30 ns, the system bus requires an access time of $310 - (2 \times 30)$ ns $= 250$ ns. Since standard ROMs have an access time of 450 ns at best, a 200-ns wait period must of necessity accompany each memory access.

The 8085 eases the synchronization problem between CPU and memory by relaxing its access time requirement by almost 50% while preserving the throughput. At a clock speed of 2.0 megahertz, the 8080-1 has an access time requirement of 570 nanoseconds, while the 8080 has a time of 1,025 ns. At 2.5 MHz, the times are 425 and 775 ns, and at 3.0 MHz, they are 310 ns and 575 ns. The net result is an overall increase in system speed without a wait state for memory access; in fact, the 8085 has no wait output pin, unlike the 8080.

8085 vs 8080

The basic internal architecture of the 8085 is similar to that of the 8080. The register file and arithmetic/logic unit in each are almost identical. The major differences are in the timing, control, and address/data bus circuits.

Figure 2 compares the basic functions of the three chips that make up the MCS-80's CPU group and the multifunction 8085. Besides requiring only a single +5-V supply (versus the +5-V, −5-V, and +12-V requirements of the 8080), the 8085 has integrated all the functions of the 8080 CPU, the 8224 clock generator, and

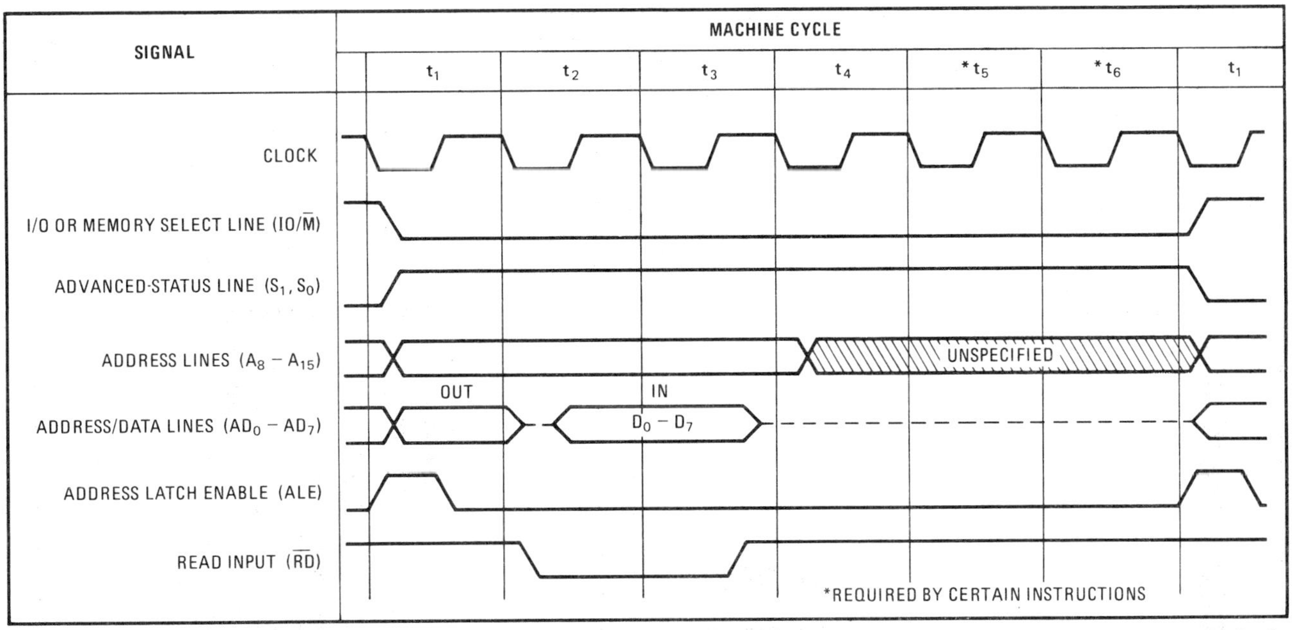

3. Basic bus timing. At the onset of the bus transfer cycle, the 8085 first sends out address over AD_{0-7} and A_{8-15}, and status over the S_0, S_1, and $IO/\overline{M}$ lines. The lower 8 bits of address, AD_0-AD_1 are static only for the first clock cycle t_1; after t_1, they transfer data to or from the CPU.

the 8228 system controller—plus a simple serial I/O port and new hardware interrupts that are integrated into a hierarchy with the restart instructions (software interrupts) carried over from the 8080.

The 8085's built-in clock generator can be used with a crystal or an RC or LC network, or it can be driven directly from an external source. The clock generator, running at twice the basic CPU frequency, provides a two-phase, nonoverlapping internal clock signal. One of the phases is buffered and is available as an external clock output equivalent to the phase-two transistor-transistor-logic output of the 8224 clock generator in the MCS-80 family.

The 8085 also provides a Schmitt action reset input, which effects power-on reset with the addition of only one resistor and one capacitor. And it provides lines for advanced status information describing the bus transfer that will be executed within the forthcoming cycle—as well as including the bus controller functions delegated to the 8228 in the MCS-80 system.

Bus timing

Compatibility with the MCS-80 system dictates that the 8085 must have the same basic bus timing structure. The timing of one machine cycle for a fetch instruction is shown in Fig. 3. At the onset of the bus transfer cycle, the 8085 sends out the address and status information. The status is indicated by the advanced-status lines S_0 and S_1, and by the mode-select line $IO/\overline{M}$, which determines whether the cycle is for I/O access or memory access. These three lines give complete information on the type of transfer. The upper 8 bits of address go out on lines A_{8-15} and remain static throughout the transfer. The lower 8 address bits, which go out on the address/data bus, remain stable only for the first clock cycle, t_1. Afterwards, the bus is used for data transfer to or from the CPU. Because the signals on lines AD_{0-7} are transitory, the ALE line must strobe the address into the internal address latch of the 8155 or into an external latch such as an 8212.

Following transmission of the address on lines AD_{0-7}, the data bus is ready for data transfer. In a read cycle (such as instruction fetch, memory read, or I/O read), the data bus goes into its high-impedance state at the start of the second clock cycle, t_2, just like the 8080 bus. At the same time, the read line goes low to indicate that the bus is available and that data is expected from the peripheral device. The 8085 reads the data on the bus during the third clock cycle, t_3, and the read line then goes high to indicate the end of the transfer cycle.

In a write cycle, the 8085 sends out the data to be written at the start of t_2, and the write line goes low at the same time. The write line returns high 1½ clock cycles later. The data is then held for another half cycle until the next transfer cycle provides the new address.

Unlike the 8080, the 8085 provides no data-setup time to the leading edge of the write signal. Although setup time is needed for dynamic memory components, it is not required for the Intel static memory family.

The power of the 8085 is further enhanced with hardware interrupts and simple serial-I/O capabilities. Four restart-interrupt input pins—RST 5.5, RST 6.5, RST 7.5, and TRAP—have been added to the eight software interrupts of the 8080. None of the new interrupts requires external logic to insert an instruction during interrupt. A mask register permits any or all of restarts 5.5, 6.5, and 7.5 to be blocked out with software and thus go unrecognized. To interrupt the processor, these interrupts must be both enabled (interrupt-enable flag = 1) and unmasked (mask bit = 0). The TRAP interrupt, however, is unmaskable and can interrupt independently of any enable or mask bit.

All four new interrupts execute an internally fetched restart instruction when recognized. The internal restart causes the program counter to remain in place on the stack and also causes branching to one of four fixed

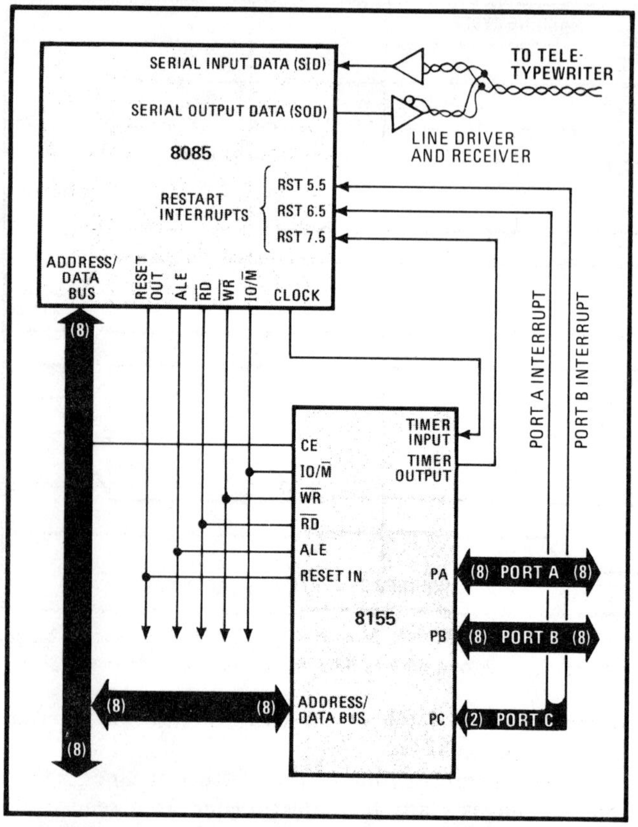

4. Serial interfacing. A teletypewriter interface demonstrates the utility of serial input and output data lines (SID and SOD). Hardware interrupts (RST 5.5, RST 6.5, and RST 7.5) on the 8085 are used by port C to facilitate handshaking of ports A and B.

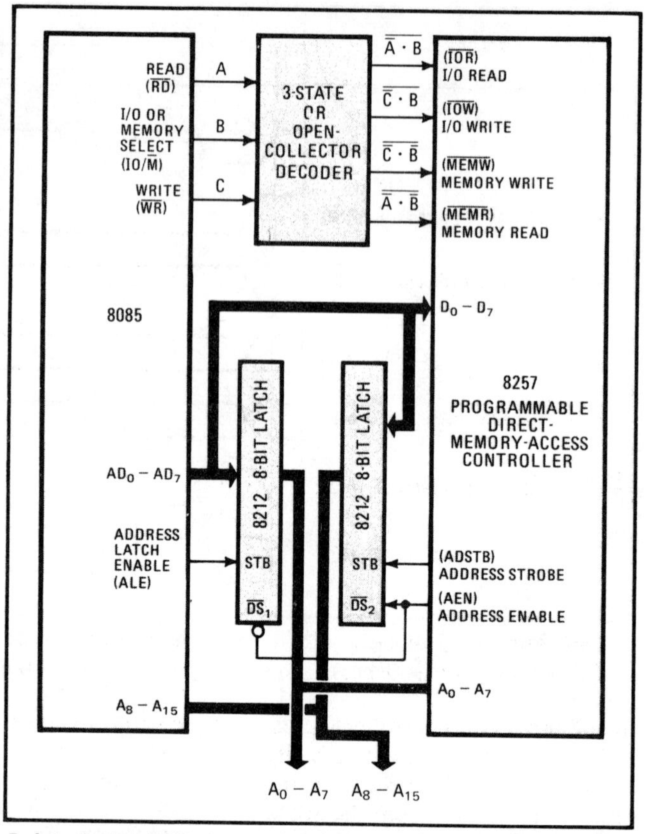

5. Interfacing DMA. Most peripherals in the 8080 family connect to the 8085 without the need for interface buffers. The 8257 direct-memory-access controller requires two 8212 8-bit latches for demultiplexing and a control-line decoding scheme.

locations. The table shows these locations and their relationship to the software restart instruction locations.

Two of the interrupt pins—RST 5.5 and 6.5—are high-level-sensitive like the interrupt-request line (INTR), also found on the 8080. The RST 7.5 input, however, is rising-edge-sensitive, and therefore only a pulse is required to set it. The TRAP input is both edge- and level-sensitive—it must go high and then stay high to be recognized. This ensures that another request can only be generated if the TRAP input returns low and then again goes high and remains high, thereby avoiding any false triggering caused by noise or logic glitches.

Interrupt hierarchy

An especially useful feature of the five interrupt inputs is that they are arranged in a fixed priority that determines the order of recognition when more than one is pending. The hierarchy, from lowest to highest priority, is INTR, RST 5.5, RST 6.5, RST 7.5, and TRAP.

The setting and reading of the masks for the restart interrupts are executed by two instructions: read interrupt masks (RIM) and set interrupt masks (SIM). The masks are initially set to a high level by the reset-in pin. The SIM instruction uses the contents of the 8085 accumulator to program the mask of a specified interrupt. It can also be used to reset the edge-triggered input flip-flop of RST 7.5. The RIM instruction reads the contents of the mask register back to the accumulator. It also reads the status of the interrupt-enable flag and any pending interrupt requests.

The 8085's serial lines permit simple I/O manipulation. The RIM instruction reads the serial-input-data line, and a SIM instruction writes on the serial-output-data line. Figure 4 shows how the interrupts and serial lines of the 8085 can be configured in a minimum system for communication with a teletypewriter.

8155 RAM plus ultra

The 40-pin 8155 has a 2,048-bit static RAM, 22 I/O pins (organized in three ports), and a binary countdown timer programmed by a 14-bit word. The bus of the 8155 allows it to interface directly with the 8085.

The RAM section is organized as 256 8-bit bytes. The 400-ns access time of the memory allows full-speed operation with no need for wait states, given the relaxed access-time requirements of the 8085.

The I/O section of the 8155 comprises the timer and three ports. The timer does one-shot or continuous counting and produces a pulse or square-wave output, as dictated by programming. It will also start and stop on command, and once stopped, its contents can be read through a count register.

Each of the 22 pins of the three I/O ports can be programmed for input or output. In addition, the 6-bit port C can assume the role of control port, thereby allowing the 8-bit ports A and B to operate in a hand shaking mode—that is, PC controlling PA and PB.

The chip-enable, read, write, and mode-select pins

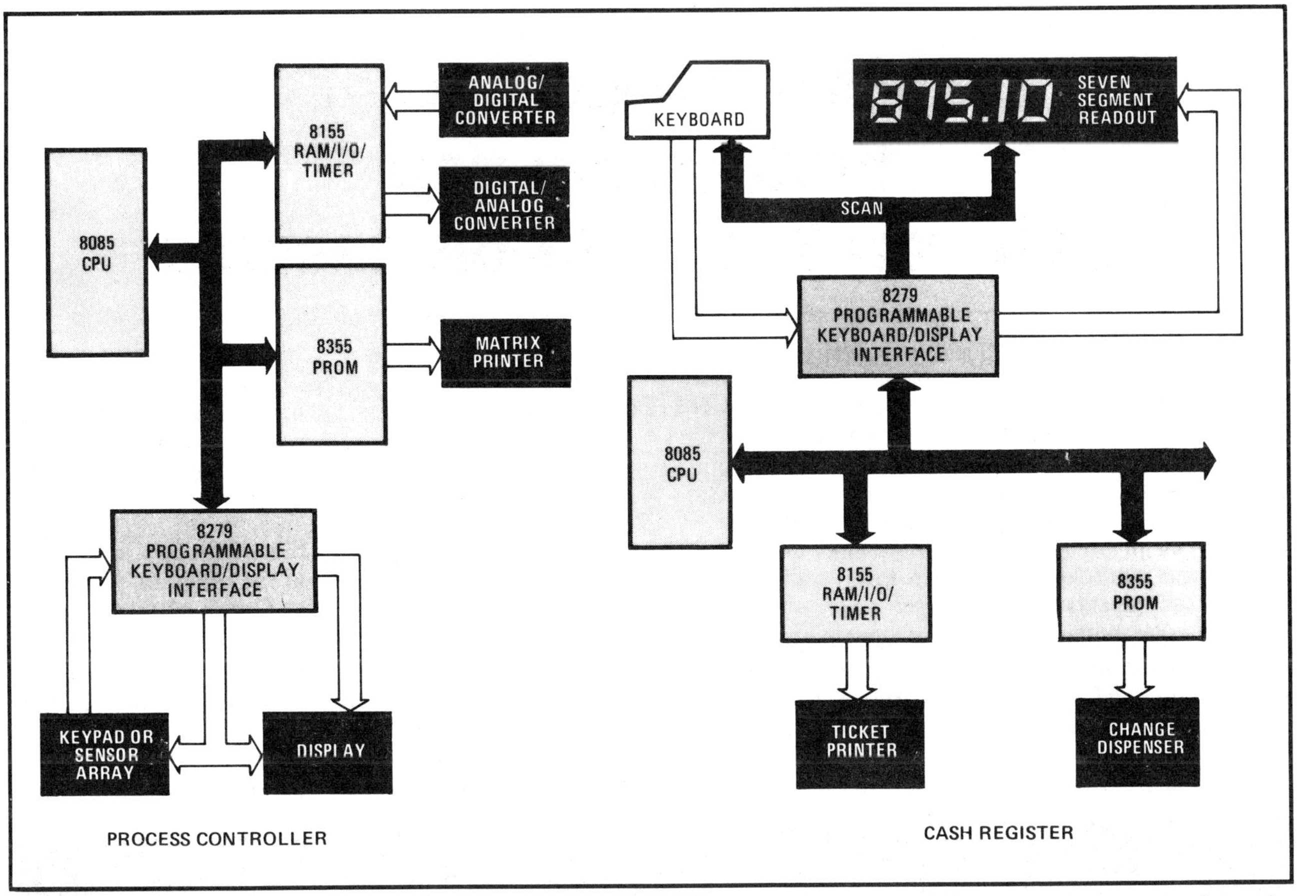

6. Typical applications. The high level of integration in the MCS-85 group makes possible low-chip-count arrangements of complex functions, such as a process controller and a cash register. Both applications use the 8279 programmable keyboard/display interface.

direct the reading and writing of RAM and I/O. There is no access to the 8155 unless the chip enable is active (CE = 1). The mode-select line (IO/$\overline{M}$) determines whether the access is to the RAM (IO/$\overline{M}$ = 0), or to the I/O section (IO/$\overline{M}$ = 1). Once the mode of the chip is selected, the read and write commands determine the direction of data flow.

The mode-select pin of the 8155 need not be connected to the mode-select pin on the 8085, as is depicted in the system configuration of Fig. 1. Connecting it to the 8085's address line A_{15}, for example, permits memory mapping of the I/O section.

The 8355 mask-programmable ROM, and the 8755 erasable PROM are organized as 2,048 8-bit bytes. Both ROMs have programmable I/O sections, organized as a pair of general-purpose, 8-bit ports. Each pin is individually programmable as input or output. Like the 8155, the ROMs have a maximum access time of 400 ns, so they also interface directly with the 8085 without wait states.

To allow the use of the ROMs with higher processor speeds or on a heavily buffered bus, an automatic wait-state generator is included on each chip. With $\overline{CE}_1$ low and CE_2 and the address-latch enable high, a ready output pin goes low. If the ready pin on the 8355/8755 is connected to the ready pin on the 8085, the clock input prevents the ready from going high until the rising edge one clock cycle after ALE. This guarantees one wait state from the 8085.

Two chip-enable inputs, the mode-select line, and the write are in charge of direct access to the 8355 or the 8755. To select the chip, $\overline{CE}_1$ must be low and CE_2 high. The ROMs can be read with read low and mode-select high. Writing is only possible on the I/O ports, using write control. Memory-mapped I/O may be implemented in the same manner as with the 8155 by tying the ROM's mode-select pin to one of the 8085's memory-selected lines (such as A_{15}) instead of its mode-select pin.

Programming the 8755 is similar to that of the 2708 erasable PROM, but is now much more efficient. Whereas the 2708 required as many as 100 pulses per cell to deposit the information, the 8755 can be programmed bit by bit with only a single 50-millisecond pulse required for each cell.

Compatibility with the 8080 family

The peripherals of the MCS-80 family will also work with the 8085, and most of these circuits require no interface buffers. The 8257 direct-memory-access controller is an exception, requiring a pair of 8212 8-bit latches and a control-line decoding scheme (Fig. 5).

Expansion of the MCS-85 system is easily accomplished with the MCS-80 peripherals and MCS-85 memory components (or a combination of standard memories if 8212 latches are added). The MCS-85 family, with its high level of system integration, lends itself well to the design of complex arrangements, such as the process controller and the cash register in Fig. 6. Both have a lower component count than ever before. □

8086 microcomputer bridges the gap between 8- and 16-bit designs

by B. Jeffrey Katz, Stephen P. Morse, William B. Pohlman, and Bruce W. Revenel

□ The Intel 8086, a new microcomputer, extends the mid-range 8080 family into the 16-bit arena. The chip has attributes of both 8- and 16-bit processors. By executing the full set of 8080A/8085 8-bit instructions plus a powerful new set of 16-bit instructions, it enables a system designer familiar with existing 8080 devices to boost performance by a factor of as much as 10 while using essentially the same 8080 software package and development tools (Fig. 1).

The goals of the 8086 architectural design were to extend existing 8080 features symmetrically, across the board, and to add processing capabilities not to be found in the 8080. The added features include 16-bit arithmetic, signed 8- and 16-bit arithmetic (including multiply and divide), efficient interruptible byte-string operations, and improved bit manipulation. Significantly, they also include mechanisms for such minicomputer-type operations as reentrant code, position-independent code, and dynamically relocatable programs. In addition, the processor may directly address up to 1 megabyte of memory and has been designed to support multiple-processor configurations.

How it is done

The 8086's improved performance stems from a combination of process and architectural enhancements. It is the first microcomputer to be fabricated with the silicon-gate H-MOS process which gives the device 4-micrometer scaled-down metal-oxide-semiconductor

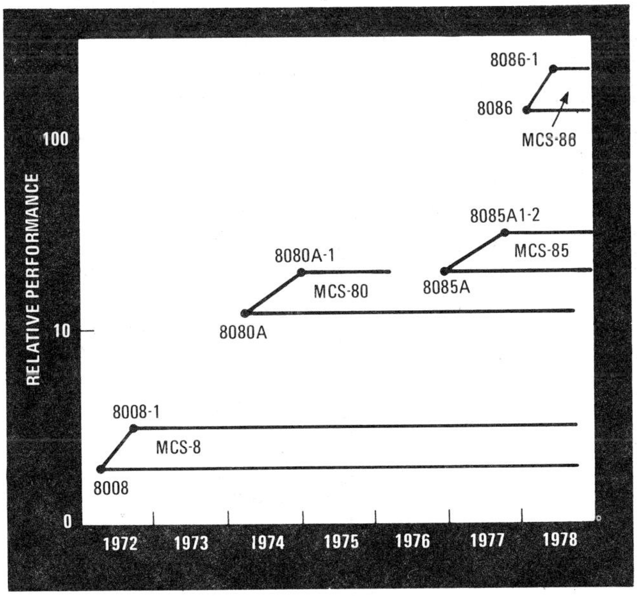

1. Next generation. Thanks to a faster MOS process and a generous number of powerful 16-bit instructions, the new 8086 attains a level of performance that is an order of magnitude higher than that of medium-range 8080-type microcomputers.

transistors and on-chip biasing that make it operate faster and more reliably.

The chip's general characteristics are listed in the table. With this high-performance MOS technique, typical on-chip gate propagation delays of 2 nanoseconds are as short as those obtained from costly Schottky transistor-transistor logic. This results in extremely fast internal clocking rates: 5 megahertz (200 ns) on standard chips and 8 MHz (125 ns) on selected chips. That is faster than any one-chip central processing unit now available. Since four CPU clock cycles correspond to approximately one memory cycle, the 8086 is much more efficient in accessing memory. Indeed, memory chip selection for the 8086 requires devices that cycle in 500 ns to 800 ns and access data (address to data-in valid) in a matter of 295 to 460 ns.

The H-MOS process also produces denser circuitry. The entire 16-bit data and microprogrammed control structures use 29,000 transistors integrated onto a die about 225 mils square. Many less complex peripheral chips that use large-scale integration are larger. The smallness of its die means that the high-performance 8086 will decline in cost as production experience with it grows, just as happened with the 8080, 8080A, and 8085.

An enhanced architecture

The architectural enhancements of the 8086 stem from a powerful register structure, increased memory address capability, almost unlimited levels of interrupts, and powerful input and output interface circuitry.

Unlike the 8080/8085 CPUs, the 8086's registers can process 16-bit as well as 8-bit data. The block diagram of Fig. 2 shows two register files. The general register file handles the 16-bit arithmetic/logic unit's instruction routines. It contains four 16-bit general data registers that are also addressable as 8-bit registers, two 16-bit memory base pointer registers, and two 16-bit index registers. All data manipulation instructions apply to all registers; certain addressing modes imply specific registers. All told, twice as many general-purpose data registers are provided as on 8-bit CPU chips. Complex arithmetical capability, very flexible memory addressing, and high computational throughput are the result.

The second bank of registers is designated the segment register file and extends the chip's addressing capabilities. It can address 1 megabyte of memory, in contrast to the 65,536-byte capacity of the 8080/8085. In this file, address relocation values for up to four 65-kilobyte program or data segments are stored in four 16-bit segment registers. The chip can control a full 65 kilobytes of address space for input/output ports.

Control and timing

The control and timing functions of the chip are extensive. A reset sequence control automatically establishes a clean machine environment, where during an interrupt much of the software overhead is performed by the CPU hardware. A multiprocessor lock facility enables the 8086 to share resources with a number of CPUs and peripheral controllers in large multiprocessor configurations. More important, though, are the independently controlled bus-interface unit and execution unit (Fig. 3).

The bus-interface unit maintains an optimized 6 byte fetch-ahead instruction queue. The queue is a technique found in larger computers for overlapping the execution and fetching of instructions. The bus-interface unit keeps the memory busy fetching words from the instruction stream, provided other system elements are not using memory cycles. The execution unit extracts bytes from the queue and executes them fast enough to eliminate dead time between instruction fetches. As many as two single-byte 8086 instructions can be executed within the time for one memory cycle in a fully overlapped fashion. The net effect is much improved performance for the same system bus bandwidth and memory speed.

Since the execution unit functions in parallel with the bus-interface unit's activities, it is largely unaffected by direct-memory-access operations, which also occur on the system bus—except, of course, when it requires a memory cycle for data itself.

Simulations of a wide variety of benchmark programs have indicated that six bytes is the optimum length for this instruction queue. Typical 8086 programs average two bytes per instruction, and their timing is somewhat execution-unit-bound—or to put it another way, the queue is usually nearly full. A smaller queue would be self-defeating, since it tends to make the timing instruction-fetch-bound. A larger queue, on the other hand, would aggravate the effect of wasted fetches of unused queue bytes when program branches occur.

Again, the 8086 processor performs 16-bit arithmetic, so the address objects that it manipulates in memory are 16 bits long. Since a 16-bit quantity can address only 65 kilobytes, additional mechanisms are required to build enough addresses to handle a 1-megabyte memory space.

This is done as shown in Fig. 4, where the 8086 memory is treated as an arbitrary number of segments, each at most 65 kilobytes in size. Each segment begins at an address that is evenly divisible by 16—the low-order 4

SUMMARY OF THE 8086'S GENERAL CHARACTERISTICS		
Process	H-MOS, scaled n-channel depletion-load silicon-gate (same as 2147 RAM)	
Transistors	29,000	
Package	40-lead Cerdip	
Supplies	5-volt, ground	
	Standard	Selected
Clock frequency	5 MHz	8 MHz
Memory cycle time (4 clocks/cycle)	800 ns	500 ns
Access time at pins (address to data-in valid)	460 ns	295 ns

bits of a segment's address are 0s. At any given moment, therefore, the contents of four of these segments are immediately addressable.

The four addressable memory segments are called the current code segment, the current data segment, the current stack segment, and the current extra segment. These segments need not be unique and indeed may overlap. The high-order 16 bits of the address of each current segment, called the segment address, is held in one of the four dedicated 16-bit segment registers (see Fig. 2). Bytes or words within a segment are addressed using 16-bit offset addresses within the 65-kilobyte segment (Fig. 5). A 20-bit physical address is constructed by adding the 16-bit offset address to the 16-bit segment address, complete with its four low-order zero bits.

Of course, some programs may be designed not to load or manipulate the segment registers, and they are said to be dynamically relocatable. Such a program may be interrupted, moved in memory to a new location, and restarted with new segment register values.

The instruction set

Several 8086 instructions may manipulate the four segment registers that make up the relocation register file. Most of the rest of the 8086's instruction set operates with the general register file, which contains two main sets of four 16-bit registers, as well as the 16-bit instruction pointer and the pair of 8-bit status flag registers (Fig. 6). The accumulator, base, counter, and data registers make up one set of general registers, the pointers and index registers the other set. The 8080 register set (shown tinted) is a subset of this structure.

The 8086 instruction set can address operands in several different ways. In general, operands in memory may be addressed either directly, with the 16-bit offset address, or indirectly, with base (BX or BP) and/or index (SI or DI) registers added to an optional 8- or 16-bit displacement constant. Here, if BX is used as the general-purpose data-base pointer, then the BP register may be used as a stack frame marker for efficiently supporting stack management in block-structured high-level languages like PLM-86. PLM-86 is an extension of the high-level PLM languages developed for the earlier 8080 and 8085 devices.

This two-operand technique allows memory or any

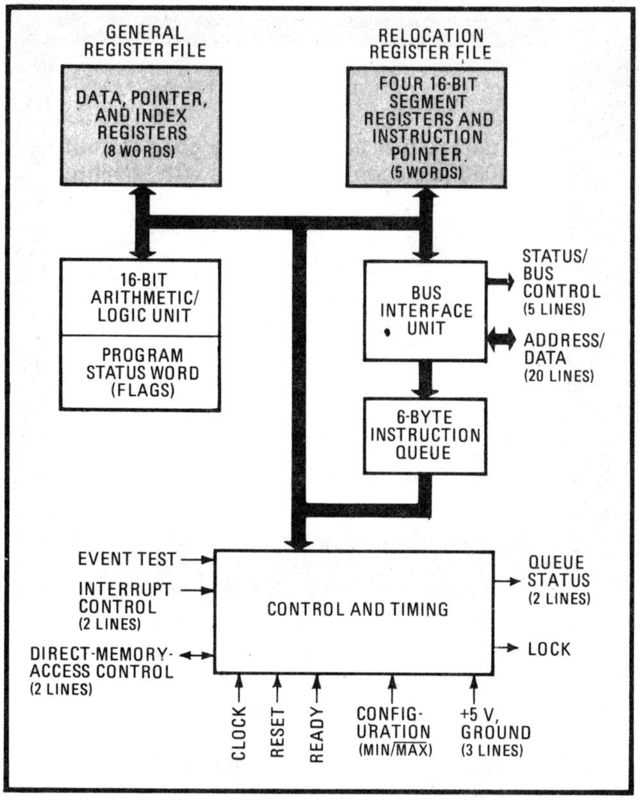

2. More processing power. The 8086 register structure is 16 bits wide internally. Additional pin functions can be supplied by time-multiplexing some pins (such as the address and data pins) and by strapping others to change the signal meaning.

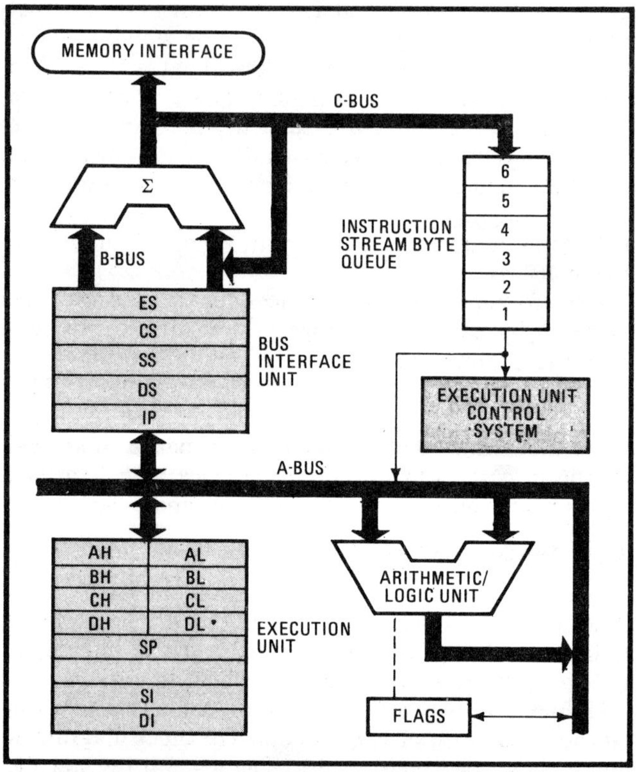

3. Processing data. The 8086 has two independently controlled units: the bus-interface unit (BIU) maintains a fetch-ahead queue of instructions, which the execution unit (EU) performs. Throughput is enhanced because the BIU keeps the memory as busy as possible.

How the string-manipulation primitives operate

A typical data-format translation is a good illustration of how the 8086 microcomputer iterates with primitive, one-byte operation to produce a complex string operation. The procedure is highly efficient, as the example will show.

Suppose an input driver must translate a buffer of EBCDIC characters into ASCII and continue transferring characters until one of several different EBCDIC control characters is encountered. Suppose also that the transferred ASCII string is to be terminated with an end-of-transmission (EOT) character.

To do this, source index register SI (see Fig. 6 in text) is initialized to point to the beginning of the EBCDIC buffer. Destination index register DI is then initialized to point to the beginning of the buffer for the reception of the ASCII characters. Next, base register BX is made to point to an EBCDIC-into-ASCII translation data table residing in memory, and count register CX is initialized to contain the length of the EBCDIC buffer (which might possibly be empty). The translation table, incidentally, should contain the ASCII equivalent for each EBCDIC character plus perhaps ASCII nulls for illegal characters. The EOT code is then inserted among those entries in the table, wherever it corresponds to the desired EBCDIC stop character.

The table shows the 8086 instruction sequence that will implement these events. It makes the efficiency of the 8086 in performing such complex operations quite obvious: the entire body of this loop requires only seven bytes of code.

```
         JCXZ     Empty     ;skip if input buffer empty
Next:    LODB     Ebcbuf    ;fetch next EBCDIC character
         XLAT     Table     ;translate it to ASCII
         CMP      AL, EOT   ;test for the EOT
         STOB     Ascbuf    ;transfer ASCII character
         LOOPNE   Next      ;continue if not EOT

Empty:
```

register to serve as one operand and either a register or a constant within an instruction to serve as the other operand. In these cases, the results of the two-operand operation may be directed to either of the source operands, unless one is an in-line (immediate) constant. On the other hand, single-operand operations are applicable uniformly to any operand in register or memory, with the same exception for immediate constants.

Within this instruction technique, the 8086 supplies several variations of the four basic arithmetical operations (add, subtract, multiply, and divide). Both 8- and 16-bit arithmetical operations and both signed and unsigned arithmetic are provided, standard 2's complement representation being used to distinguish signed values. In this context, addition and subtraction can be both signed and unsigned, with flag settings to distinguish between the signed and unsigned operations.

With the aid of its correction operations, the 8086 can do this arithmetic directly on unpacked binary-coded representations of decimal digits or on packed decimal representations. Standard logical operations, shift, move data, etc., are available to both 8- and 16-bit operands. Other instructions support the movement of 32-bit address objects called pointers, which consist of a 16-bit offset address and segment base address.

Also provided is a group of one-byte instructions that, besides performing various primitive operations to manipulate byte and word strings, can each be performed repeatedly when provided with a special prefix. The single-operation forms are then combined to form complex strings of operations, with their repetition controlled by special iterative operations. The effect is to create tight, efficient loops for performing subroutines (see "How the string-manipulation primitives operate," above).

For handling program flow, two basic varieties of calls, jumps, and returns are provided—one that transfers control within the current code segment, and one that transfers control to an arbitrary code segment, which then becomes the current code segment. The 8086 supports direct and indirect transfers, both of which make use of the standard addressing modes. Intrasegment calls and jumps specify a self-relative displacement, thus allowing position-independent code.

In all, 16 conditional jumps are provided to support all common program-controlled interrupt structures. Both signed and unsigned relationships can be tested, as well as parity, overflow, and sign conditions.

Many interrupt types

In an interrupt sequence, an interrupt signal prompts the transfer of processor control to a new location in a new code segment. The 8086 memory structure supplies a 256-element table that contains pointers to these interrupt service code locations. Each element is four bytes in size, containing an offset address and a segment address for the service code location. Each element of this table corresponds to an interrupt type, and there are 256 interrupt types, or enough for even the most heavily interrupt-driven applications.

The 8086 has the ability to detect program inconsistencies, such as errors in division or overflow conditions, by means of a one-byte instruction that causes an interrupt if the condition occurs. The internal interrupt instructions transfer the program's execution control to a checking sequence by means of operations like those done during external interrupts. Both the internal and external interrupts perform a program transfer by pushing the flag register onto the stack and then making an indirect call (of the intersegment variety) to the service routine.

Multiprocessing mechanisms

Besides handling a large variety of interrupts, the 8086 CPU has mechanisms for sharing resources and controlling access to those resources in multiprocessor applications. Such mechanisms are mostly provided by software operating systems but do require some hardware assistance. This is where the bus-locked output comes into use.

Labeled lock in Fig. 2, the output works like this. The 8086 has a special one-byte prefix that can be attached to the front of any instruction. This prefix then compels the processor to assert a bus-lock signal for the duration of the operation caused by that instruction. Meanwhile, external hardware, upon receipt of that same signal, is prohibiting other bus masters from bus access during the period of its assertion.

The instruction most likely to have such a prefix attached to it is "exchange register with memory." A simple software lock may be implemented with the following code sequence:

```
Check:  MOV   AL,1       ;set AL to 1
                           (implies locked)
 LOCK   XCHG  Sema, AL   ;test and set lock
        TEST  AL, AL     ;set flags based on AL
        JNZ   Check      ;retry if lock already set
                         ;critical region
        MOV   Sema,0     ;clear the lock when done
```

System configurations

A wide variety of system configurations can be built around the 8086 CPU. For small systems, where minimal external circuitry is needed, the 8086 may be strapped into a minimum mode, in which the microprocessor itself provides all bus control signals. In larger or Multibus systems, the strap pin may be set to the maximum mode, and the same control-signal pins take on the functions required to operate the 8288 bus controller.

For really big systems, the MCS 86 family of components includes several new Schottky bipolar support components that maximize the CPU's ability to control many external memory and peripheral chips. There are inverting and noninverting octal latches and octal bus transceivers, a clock controller/ready synchronizer, and a bus controller that makes the 8086 compatible with the 8080 family's Multibus timing and control protocols.

The latches and transceivers have three-state controls and separate strobe or direction signals. To ease system design, they are packaged in 20-pin packages with a uniform pinout. The bus side of the parts is capable of sinking 32 milliamperes of output current for driving a wide assortment of peripheral equipment.

The clock chip includes an oscillator circuit, a Schmitt-trigger-reset detector/driver, and a ready-synchronizer circuit. The chip's latch, which captures the asynchronous ready signal from the system or Multibus, prevents output glitches or metastable conditions in presenting the signal to the CPU within the required timing constraints. The bus controller, used when the CPU is strapped to maximum mode, generates Multibus command signals as well as control signals for the address latches and data transceivers that are used in buffered systems.

The multiplexing technique used by the 8086 CPU for address and data resembles the one used on the 8085. Each processor bus cycle consists of at least four clock

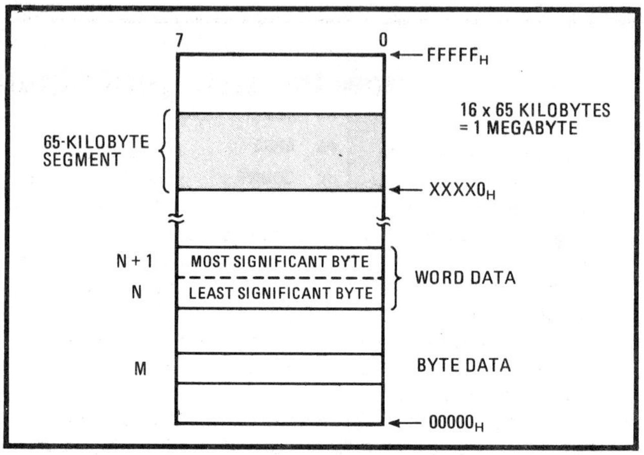

4. Memory organization. While the 8086 is made up of a sequence of 8-bit bytes, any two consecutive bytes may be paired to form a 16-bit word. Such words are grouped in four immediately addressable memory segments totalling 1 megabyte.

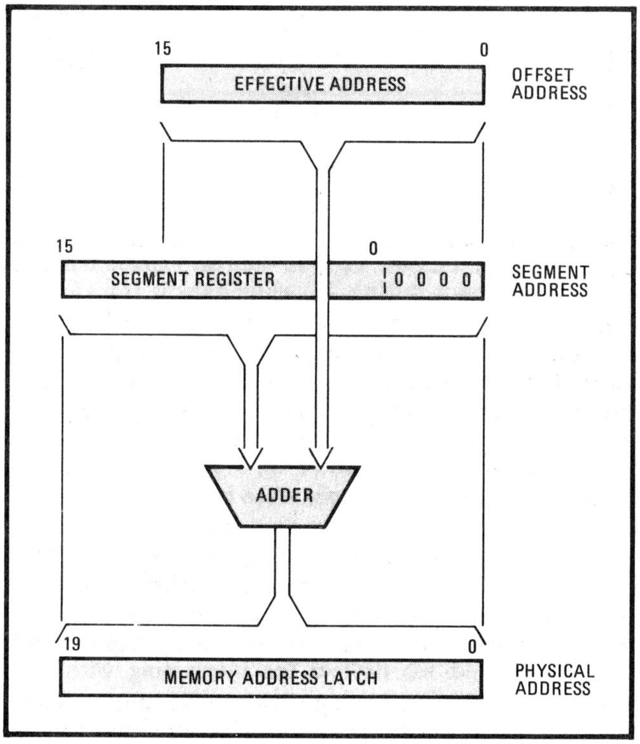

5. Addressing it. The 8086 memory can be thought of as an arbitrary number of segments. A byte or word within a segment is addressed with a 16-bit offset address. Adding the offset address to the 16-bit segment address creates a 20-bit physical address.

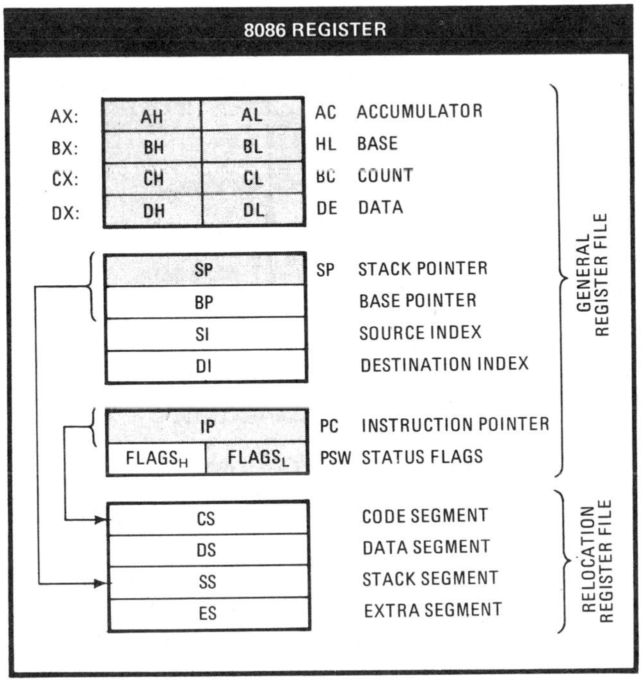

6. The registers. The 8086 register model consists of two main sets of four 16-bit registers, as well as the 16-bit instruction pointer and the pair of 8-bit status flag registers. Tinted areas indicate the subset of the registers that are to be found on the 8080 microprocessor.

cycles—T_1, T_2, T_3, and T_4. The address signals emerge from the processor during T_1, while data is transferred on the bus during T_2, T_3, and T_4. During the read operations, T_2 is used primarily for changing the direction of the multiplexed bus, and T_4 is used for terminating the present bus cycle and preparing for the start of the next bus cycle. If the addressed device gives a not-ready indication, wait states (TW) are inserted between T_3 and T_4. Each inserted wait state has the same duration as a clock cycle.

Some sample systems

In a minimum mode system of the kind shown in Fig. 7a, the 8086 generates the control signals used by the memory and I/O devices for interacting with the address and data buses, as well as a timing signal for latching the addresses emitted during T_1. In this configuration, as noted earlier, the access times required of memory and I/O devices for the 5-MHz 8086 are roughly 430 ns from receipt of address and 205 ns from receipt of read or write enable. These times are about 265 ns and 130 ns respectively for 8-MHz CPU operation. The difference between these figures and those in the table takes the addition of the address latch into account.

In the larger buffered configuration (Fig. 7b), the 8086, in its maximum mode, generates coded status information during T_1 on only some of the pins needed for producing minimum-mode control signals. Here, all that is needed is enough coded information to push an 8288 bus controller into generating Multibus-compatible control signals and timing signals for addressing latches and data transceivers. The minimum-mode control-signal pins can now take on additional functions, such as extra direct-memory-access control and bus-locking capabilities for use in multiprocessor operations.

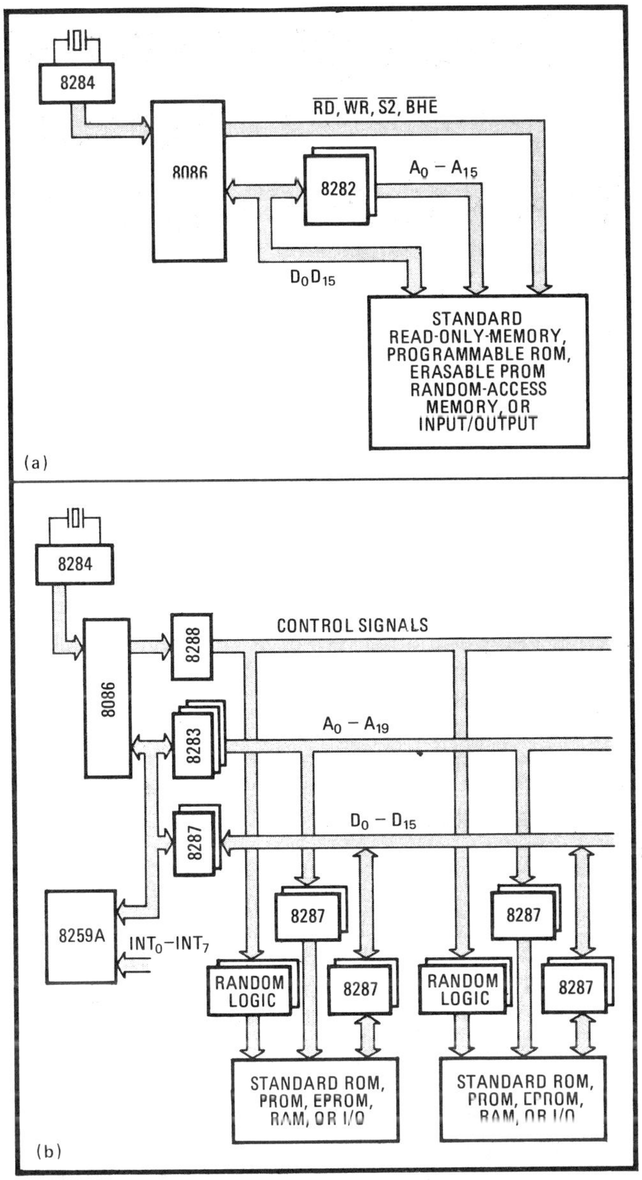

7. Systems. When operating in the minimum mode, the 8086 needs only 11 components to form a complete system, including clock, 2 kilobytes of RAM, and 4 kilobytes of ROM (a). By adding support components, very large systems (b) can be configured.

In buffered systems the required memory and I/O access times for 5-MHz CPU operation are 395 ns from receipt of address and 290 ns from receipt of read command. These times are respectively about 230 ns and 150 ns for 8-MHz CPU operation.

The bottom line of all system design is performance. Initial studies have indicated that on average an 8086-based system will perform about an order of magnitude better than an 8080A-based one. Depending on program type, execution speeds 7 to 12 times faster than 8080A speeds can be expected. At the same time, the program is typically 10% to 25% shorter. However, while there exists an 8086 instruction mapping for every 8080 instruction, and while 8080 programs may be easily transferred to the 8086, maximum 8086 efficiency does require the rewriting of certain routines. □

16-bit processor performs like minicomputer

by Alan Lofthus and Deene Ogden

☐ While most 8-bit microprocessors can be used for peripheral controllers and small-to-medium data handling systems, their processing and data-acquisition capabilities often face the system designer with unsatisfactory alternatives. For larger configurations, which accommodate big blocks of memory or handle fast, high-precision data, the designer has to push the 8-bit system beyond its most comfortable performance level or else turn to full-blown general-purpose minicomputers that could well represent an expensive overkill.

The new TMS 9900 microprocessor changes all that by offering data-processing performance and 16-bit precision of a minicomputer at a microprocessor-system cost. It can be used even in highly dedicated cost-sensitive applications. In addition, the 9900 allows the user a natural upward growth, since it is a member of a software-compatible family of computers that includes the microprocessor itself, the 990/4 microcomputer, and the 990/10 minicomputer.

Of the single-chip, 16-bit processors available, only the 9900 offers 3-megahertz cycle times and the minicomputer-type architecture that makes the central processing unit extremely efficient. Its 16-bit words can reach large blocks of external memory two bytes at a time and can easily accommodate the needed 8-, 12-, 14-, and 16-bit converter resolutions.

Unlike the 16-bit chips built with the p-channel,

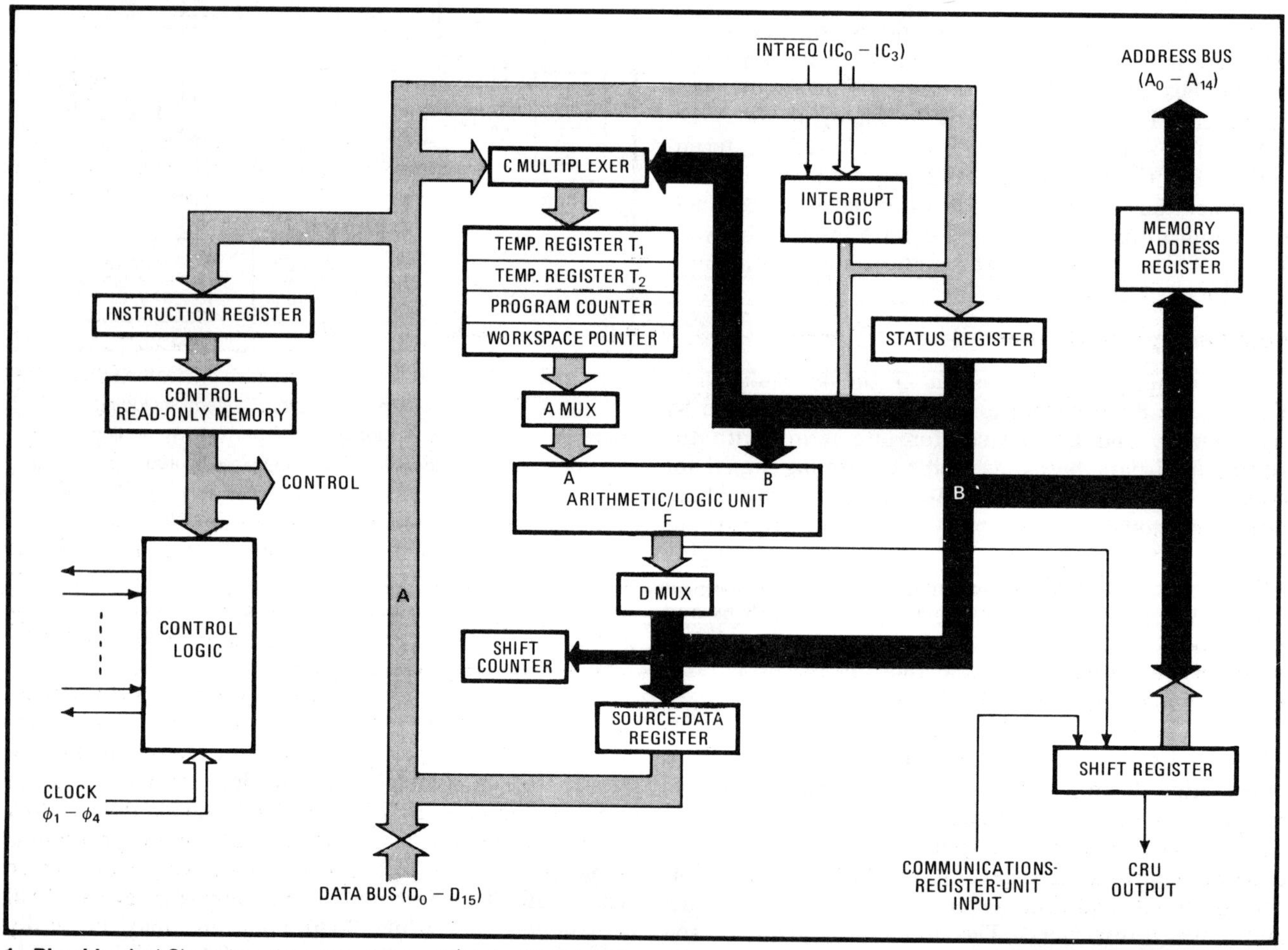

1. Big chip. An LSI version of a minicomputer CPU, the 9900 handles addresses on the 15-bit address bus (labeled B) and data on the 16-bit data bus (labeled A). Interrupts are handled on the interrupt request line and four code lines; I/Os by the communications register unit.

metal-oxide-semiconductor method, the new device uses n-channel silicon-gate technology. This accounts for its high speed and results in transistor-transistor-logic input and output levels that work directly with standard memory and I/O packages. No special memories or chips for system interfacing are needed.

Many features

The chip has full 16-bit capability on both address and data buses. Since both are full-capability parallel busses, access to 16-bit words is in one fast cycle.

There are no general-purpose memory registers in the central processing unit. All data goes directly from memory to the chip's arithmetic/logic unit or to special-purpose registers for interrupts, data status, etc. and then back to memory again. Forgoing on-chip, general-purpose registers gives extremely efficient data transfer and makes room for sixteen 16-bit general purpose registers in memory that greatly add to the CPU's capability and flexibility. Since all data processing resides in external RAMs, register capacity is not limited by the processor's on-chip register data. And putting all data in memory saves time during interrupts or subroutines since no CPU register data must be saved.

The interrupt capability has 17 vectored interrupts: two predetermined and 15 determined by the system designer in software. The device is almost as flexible as a minicomputer for general-purpose data-processing jobs.

Separate, nonmultiplexed data-, address-, and I/O-bus structures mean that no external multiplexers are needed to distinguish bus use. Moreover, the chip is fully compatible with all data inputs, outputs, and controls operable from standard TTL signals. Thus, it can operate with all standard RAMs, read-only memories; I/Os, and peripheral TTL circuits. Its 16-bit competitors need special peripherals.

Many of the set of 69, 16-bit instructions are two-operand instructions containing source- and destination-operand address information in one line of code. An example of the savings here is that the STORE and LOAD commands of other machines become simply MOVE in the 9900. The instructions are further enhanced by the seven addressing modes available for use on random-memory data, or formatted memory data such as character strings or tables.

In short, the 9900 is particularly well suited for interrupt-driven, real-time applications with large memory requirements where fast processing is required. Its 3-MHz instruction cycle, together with its powerful instruction set, gives the designer a true third-generation microprocessor for today's designs, especially in high-speed data-handling and process control applications.

The 9900's architecture

The configuration of the chip (Fig. 1) is basically a large-scale integration of a minicomputer CPU. The memory addresses (upper right) are applied to the 15-bit address bus B by the memory address register, while the 16-bit data bus A (left) serves as the memory data input and output. The interrupt interface consists of an interrupt request line, INTREQ, and four interrupt code lines, IC_0 to IC_3.

The input/output interface is usually accomplished through serial I/O ports designated as the communications register unit, or CRU, (lower right), which ties all I/O circuits implemented in this manner to a general-purpose on-chip shift register for control by the chip. The remaining miscellaneous control clocks and power signals (lower left) complete the functional elements.

The heart of the 9900 is the arithmetic/logic unit. During any machine cycle, it can receive one of two input signals on one of the two independent buses. The input on data bus A comes from the four-tiered, 4-by-16-bit register file with a program counter keeping track of the instruction sequence, a workspace pointer keeping track of external memory spaces, and two temporary registers, T_1 and T_2, used for short-time storage during instruction execution.

The second input to the ALU is the B bus, which can be driven by such various working registers as the source-data register, shift register, and status register. The bus also goes to the register file through multiplexers A and C, which jump the instruction in progress during interrupt operation.

The ALU output F, through the D multiplexer, also

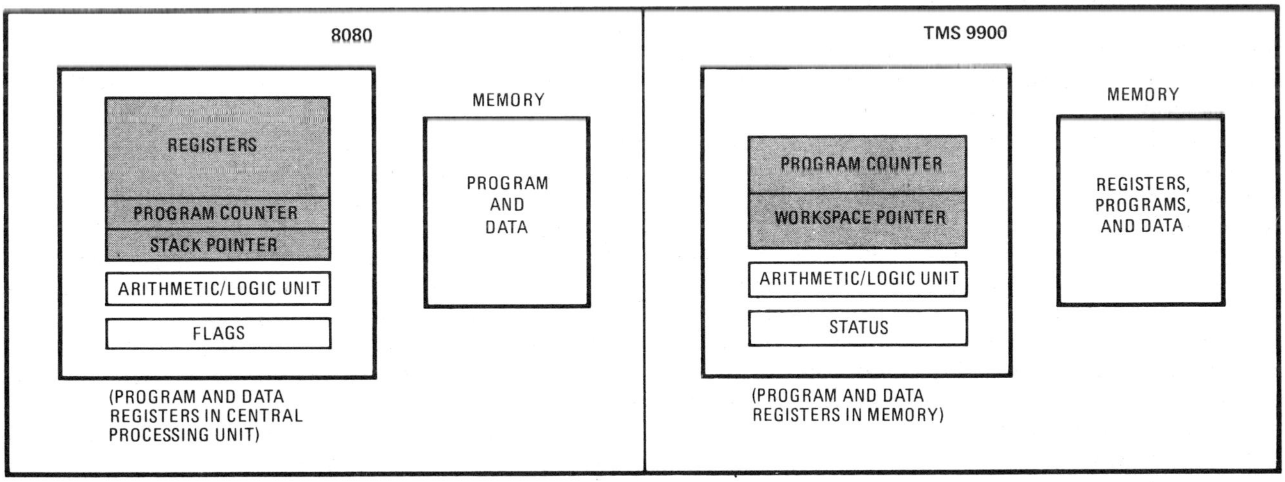

2. Makes the difference. While the 8-bit 8080 microprocessor reaches external memory with a conventional, stack architecture, the 9900 uses external memory for program and data spaces, as well as general-purpose registers organized as a 16-by-16 register file.

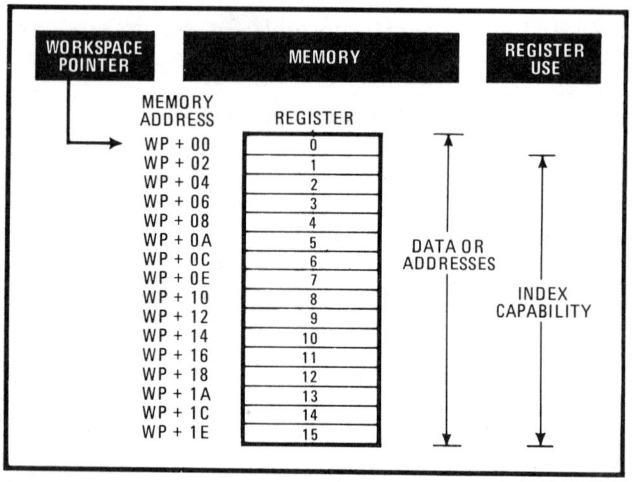

3. Pointers. The workspace pointer automatically generates memory addresses. Here it points to the first workspace register. The CPU reaches any register within the active register field by doubling the register number and adding it to the pointer.

drives the B bus and, for example, can feed either the shift counter, used with the shift register during shift, multiply, divide, and CPU instructions, or the source-data register, which is used to drive the data bus output lines, D_0 through D_{15}.

How it works

An instruction execution consists of four sequences that occur in the control ROM of the chip. The first sequence is the instruction-acquisition phase, in which the value of the program counter in the register file is passed through the ALU, the D multiplexer, and into the memory address register. During a memory-read cycle, the instruction moves from the data bus to the instruction register, which then initiates the remaining three sequences: source-operand derivation, destination-operand derivation, and execution.

The two derivations are control-ROM sequences that acquire instruction operands based on the type of instruction and the addressing mode. The operand addresses are generated from the values in the workspace pointer, along with the contents of the incoming instruction, while the source data, destination data, and destination address are stored in the source-data registers, T_1 and T_2. The instruction is executed using the source and destination data, and the result is stored in the external memory location specified by the destination address.

During execution, the LOAD and INTREQ inputs are checked to determine if an interrupt is pending. If INTREQ is active, then a 4-bit code is generated on the interrupt code lines and compared to the appropriate status-register data to determine whether the interrupt has sufficient priority to be accepted. If it is accepted, a vector address, generated in the ALU by the interrupt logic, goes to the memory-address register to initiate the interrupt sequence. If no enabled interrupts are active, the program counter is incremented by two to point to the next instruction, and the instruction acquisition sequence is initiated again.

How the 9900 machine architecture compares with the popular 8080 8-bit microprocessor is shown in Fig.

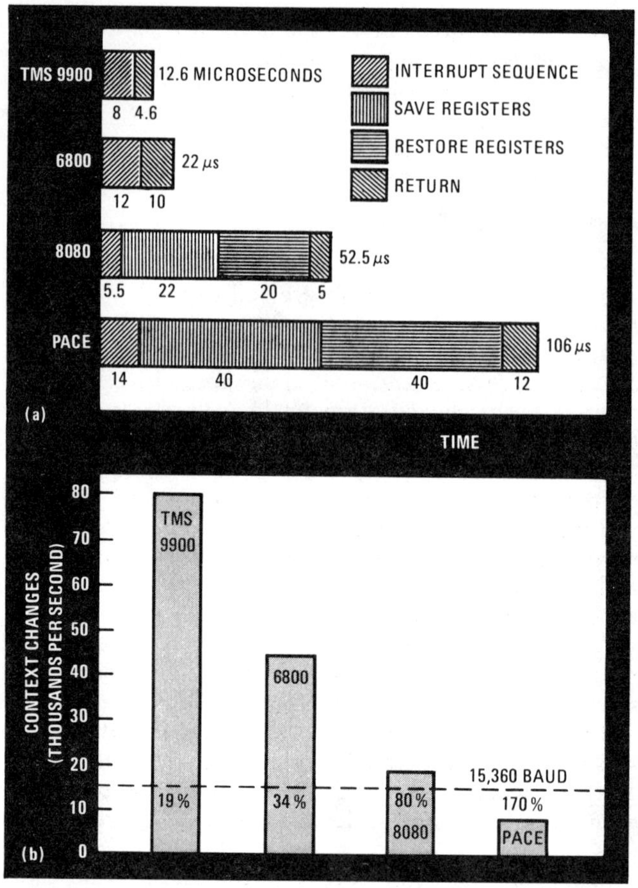

4. Low overhead. The 9900 keeps the interrupt overhead low (a) compared to other designs. Even for applications requiring a very high level of interrupt capability—above the line in (b)—the 9900 has over 80% of its processing time left over for useful routines.

2. The 8080 employs a conventional stack architecture with a register file, program counter, stack pointer, ALU, and flag register. The program and data spaces reside in external memory. The 9900's CPU consists of the program counter, workspace pointer (or register pointer), ALU, and status register, which is similar to the 8080 flag register. The new device's external memory provides program and data spaces and general-purpose data registers organized as a 16-by-16 register file.

Big jobs

For the big jobs, the memory-oriented 9900 architecture has significant advantages. Since the register file resides in main memory, the number of workspace registers is limited only by memory size. Thus it can handle a large quantity of data unlike the 8080, which handles only what the on-chip register file can accommodate.

The architecture of the 9900 also allows the programer access to three internal registers: the program counter, workspace pointer, and the status register. Thus, the fact that the data registers are located in memory is completely transparent to the user. A programer, for example, can specify any register, and the device generates the actual memory address with the workspace pointer, as shown in Fig. 3.

Memory access is organized so that all 16-bit memory addresses specify the location of one byte of data. Thus,

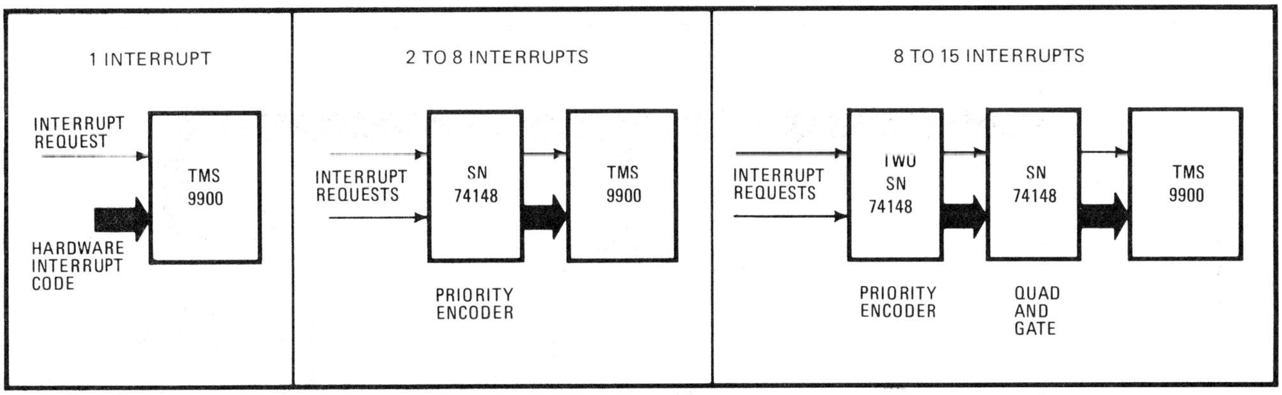

5. It's easy. Although the 9900 has a powerful interrupt capability, it's easy to work it. One interrupt requires no external hardware. Less than eight require one priority encoder, while eight to fifteen interrupts need only an additional quad AND package.

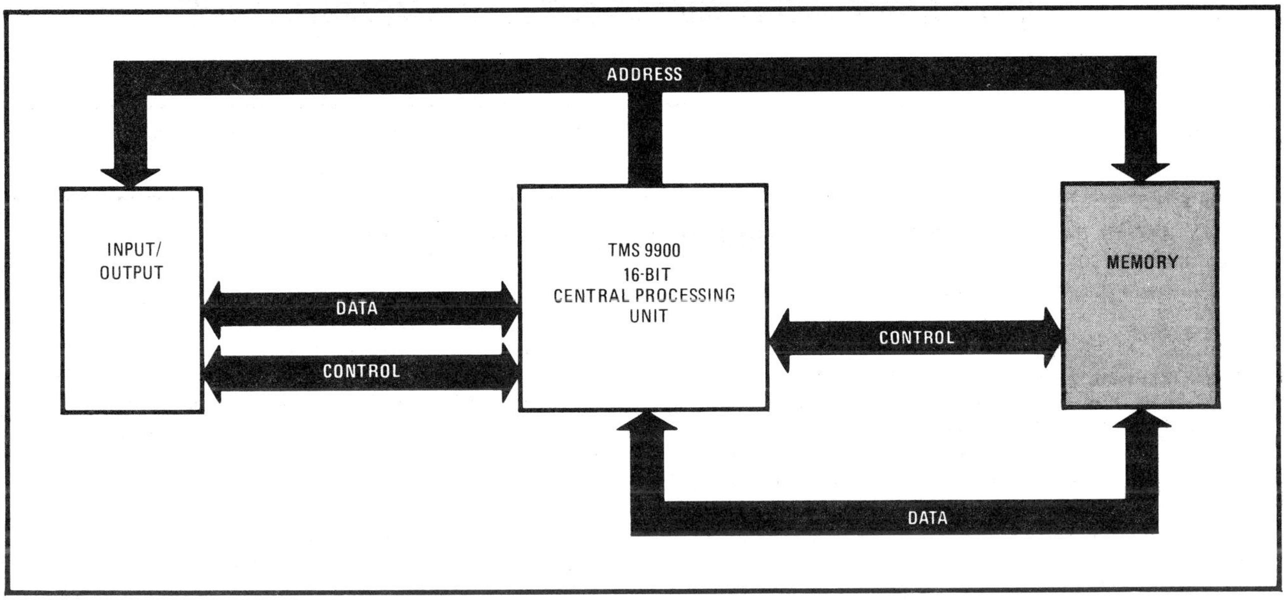

6. System bus. The system bus is simplicity itself. For memory there are completely separate address, control, and data lines. For I/O there are separate control and data lines. Moreover, all standard memory and I/O packages can be accommodated without interfaces.

the memory space for a system is 65,536 bytes, organized as 32,768 by 16 words.

Since each access to memory results in a 16-bit word, or two 8-bit bytes, the memory address bus requires only 15 bits specifying 32-k words. The 16th, least significant, bit is maintained inside the chip's working registers and specifies the byte which the CPU must use during instruction execution. Note that, during byte operations, the integrity of the unused byte is maintained, but, at the completion of the instruction, the two bytes merge and return to memory. This means that the instructions automatically control operations.

Handling context switches

The memory-to-memory organization handles context switches efficiently and rapidly. In standard minicomputer language, a context switch is a program-environment change that occurs as the result of an interrupt, a subroutine call, or a special software "trap" instruction referred to as an extended operation.

During interrupts, the exchange of data in the active registers proceeds very smoothly. The contents of the program counter, workspace register, and status register of program A are all automatically stored in registers 13, 14, and 15, respectively, of the B workspace register. Then the CPU obtains the locations of this register file and of the interrupt subroutine from the 2-word vector in lower memory space reserved for that interrupt. The return instruction moves the three A program linkages back into the processor, returning it to program A.

Figure 4a shows the effects of this typical operation on interrupt overhead for each of four microprocessors. In most processors, this overhead time consists of four sequences: CPU interrupt sequence (done automatically by its hardware); storage of the interrupted data in the CPU registers, called save registers, (done by instructions at the beginning of the interrupt subroutine); restore registers (done by instructions at the end of the interrupt subroutine), and return instructions. Since all the 9900's operations reside in external memory, there is no on-chip active register data to save or to restore. This cuts the total interrupt overhead time to only 12.6 microseconds, or ½ to 1/10 that of other popular designs.

Figure 4b shows why this speed becomes important to the system. Clearly, the 9900 can efficiently handle interrupts with the greatest percentage of processing

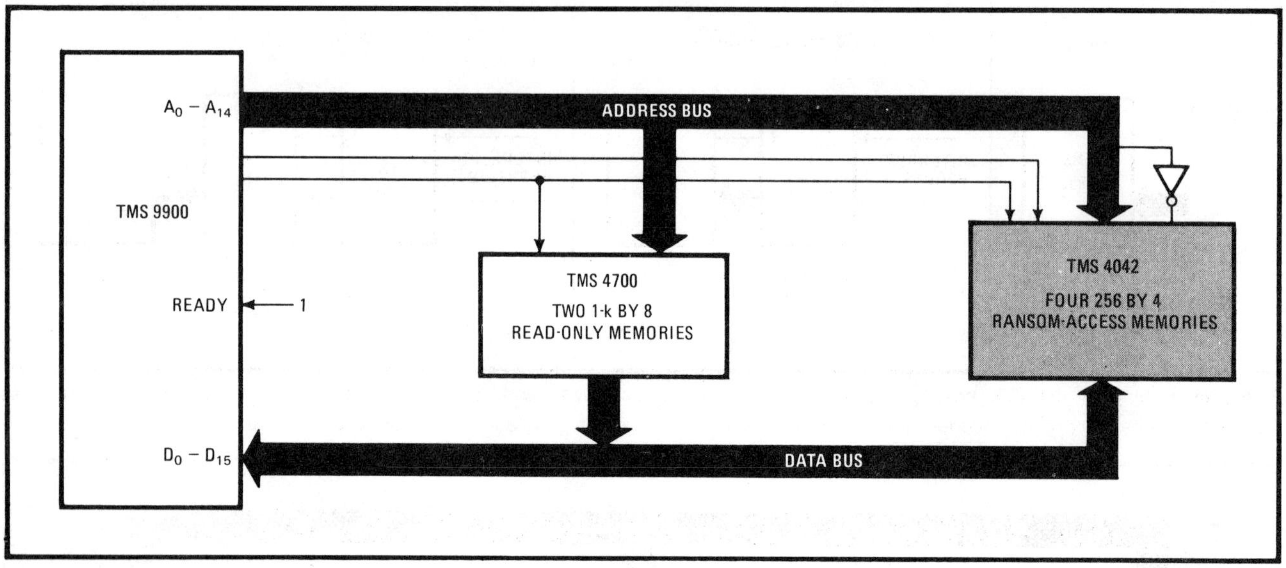

7. Getting ready. For small memory systems, say, 1,024 words of read-only memory and 256 bits of random-access memory, the ready line on the 9900 CPU can be tied high so that gates or buffers are not needed on the control, address, or data lines.

Pitting the 9900 against the competition

A benchmark test, pitting the 9900 against the 16-bit PACE system and the 8-bit 8080 and 6800 systems, compared performance on the execution of instructions. Six programs were used, with comparisons made in program memory requirements, measured in bytes, assembler states or lines of code, and execution times.

Results for the separate programs were added together (bottom, left), showing that the 9900 saved at least 20% on program memory requirements, used at most 56% as many assembler statements, and executed instructions at least 42% faster.

The input/output handler program is an interrupt-driven routine that brings in a character from a modem, tests for an end-of-line character, outputs the character on a cathode-ray-tube terminal, and returns control to the main program.

The character-search routine searches a table of 40 characters anywhere in the memory for a specific character. It generates the address of the matched character, or, upon failure, a zero address.

The computer-go-to routine tests a control byte that has one true bit. That bit's position determines which of eight table vectors controls transfer.

The vector-addition routine adds two N-dimensional vectors from anywhere in memory to generate a third N-dimensional vector. Both 8- and 16-bit precision routines are provided. N was 20 in the test.

The shift-right-5-bits routine shifts a 16-bit word right by 5 places, with zero filling on the left.

The move-block routine moves a block of 64 characters to another location. Both start and destination blocks can be anywhere within memory.

Also shown (below right) are the 9900's execution times for sample instructions. Although a simple register-to-register add is slower than with some current microprocessors, the device's ability becomes clear in the more advanced instructions, such as indexed-to-indirect add, multiply, and divide. All of these require many instructions in other processors for the equivalent function, while they require only a single instruction with the 9900.

	Program memory requirements (bytes)				Assembler statements				Execution time (microseconds)			
	9900	PACE	8080	6800	9900	PACE	8080	6800	9900	PACE	8080	6800
Input/output handler	24	38	28	17	9	14	17	7	71	154	79	49
Character search	22	24	20	18	8	10	9	8	661	1636	760	808
Computer go to	12	12	17	14	5	5	11	8	98	352	145	145
Vector addition: $A_N \leftarrow B_N = C_N$ (16)	20	30	29	46	5	14	20	22	537	2098	1098	1866
Vector addition: $A_N \rightarrow B_N = C_N$ (8)	20	32	23	40	5	15	14	22	537	2108	738	936
Shift right 5 bits	10	6	19	20	3	3	12	9	22	56	137	81
Move block	14	18	16	34	4	9	9	16	537	1750	1262	2246
Totals	122	160	152	189	39	70	92	92	2464	8154	4219	6131

Instruction	Execution time (microseconds) (Clock rate is 3 MHz)
Branch	
Register to register	2.67
Add (words/bytes)	
Reg. to reg.	4.67
Indirect to indexed	8.67
Multiply	
Reg. to reg.	17.33
Divide	
Reg. to reg.	41.33
Shift (left/right)	
1 bit	4.67
8 8 bits	9.33
Move data (words/bytes)	
Reg. to reg.	4.67
Reg. to directory/index	7.33
Load communications register unit (reg. to CRU)	
8 bits	12
16 bits	17.33
Store CRU (CRU to reg.)	
8 bits	14.67
16 bits	20

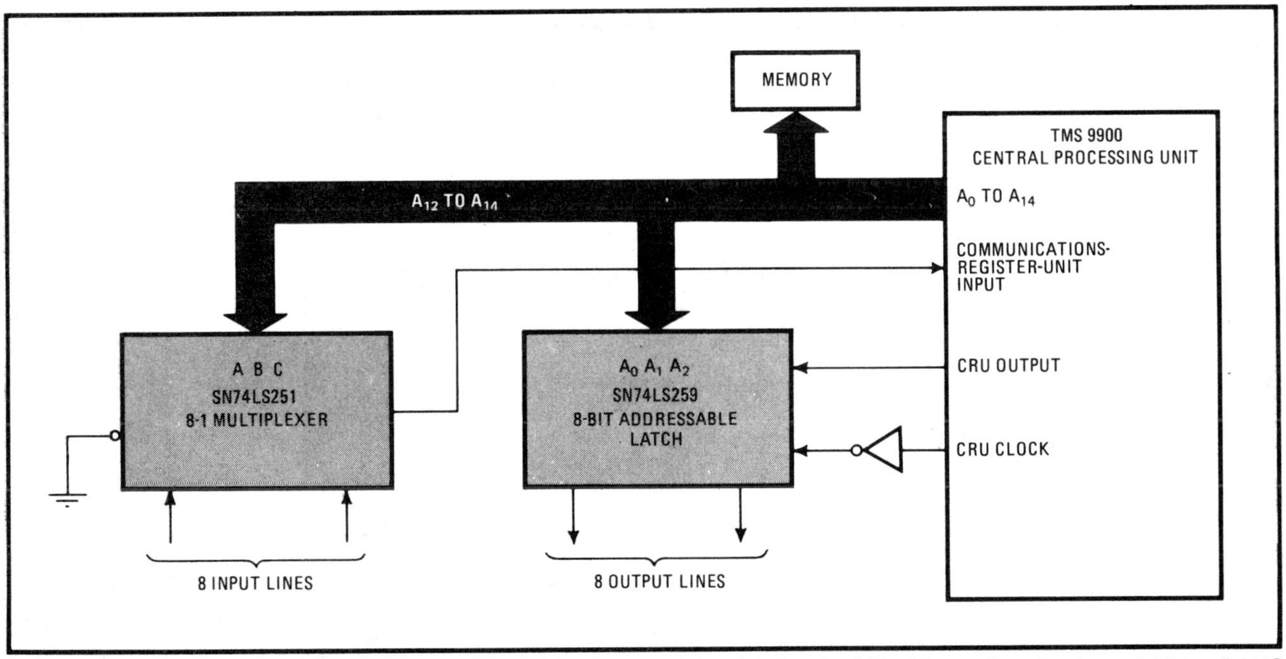

8. The interface. The special communications-register-unit interface port gives interface flexibility. The configuration for an 8-bit parallel I/O transfer requires only two standard TTL packages, compared to the LSI interface chips with most other processors.

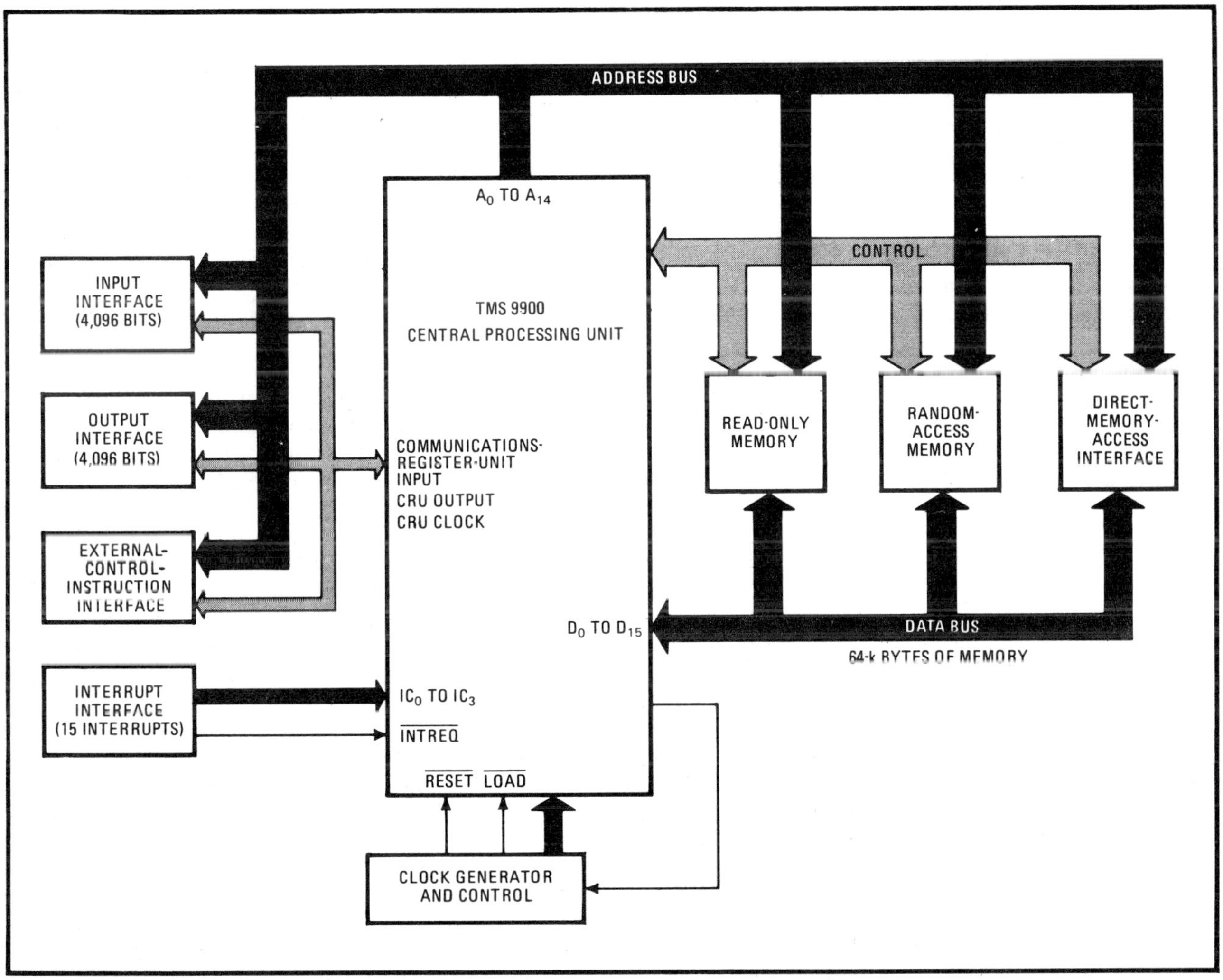

9. The system. The 9900 CPU can handle a powerful minicomputer-type system configuration. Here 64-bytes of RAM and maximum I/O capability are accommodated, yet the entire system has only nine circuit blocks, including direct memory access.

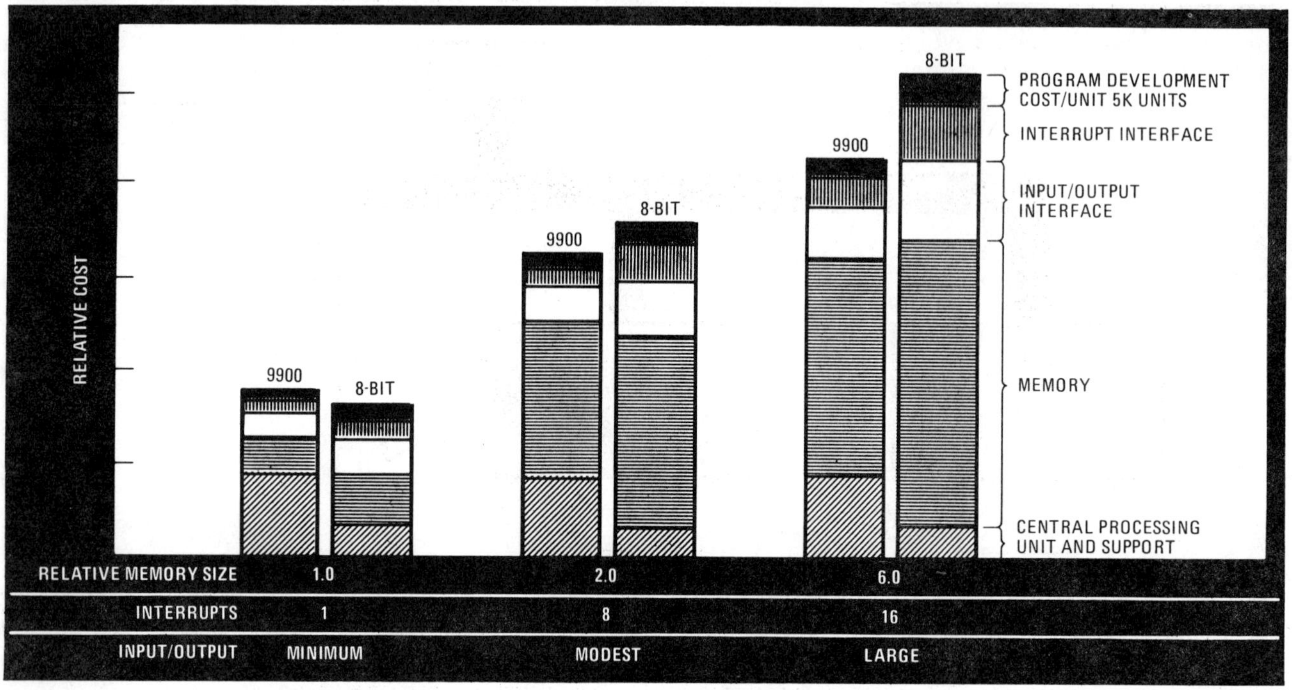

10. Value. For large configurations, although the CPU costs may be higher for the 9900 than for the 8080, the 9900 system costs considerably less thanks to the efficiency with which it handles large amounts of memory, I/O, and interrupts.

time remaining. As an example, the dotted line indicates a very high interrupt rate, where 16 cathode-ray tubes are performing data concentration at 9600 baud. Even in this application, the chip has over 80% of the processing time left to perform useful routines.

Taking interrupts in stride

The simple, cost-effective interrupt structure, (Fig. 5) includes 17 vectored interrupts arranged in priority. There are two zero-level, nonmaskable interrupts for handling the reset and load functions. The rest are available for external use. For single-interrupt applications, no external hardware is needed, and the interrupt request signal is directly connected to the CPU. For systems with two to eight interrupts, a single SN74148 priority encoder is needed, and for more than eight, two SN74148s plus a SN7408 gate package are needed.

The last 4 bits of the chip's status register provide a code that constitutes a masking level for interrupt operation. The CPU uses this mask, which is under program control. If the level is at, say, 8, the program allows interrupt levels 0 through 8 and disallows 9 through 15.

Then, if level 5 is requested, the 9900 will start the interrupt sequence at the completion of the instruction being executed. It will automatically move the mask to level 4, one step below. This effectively masks out lower interrupts and allows higher ones. During the return instruction, the previous status-register value changes the mask level back to 8. This sequence, which continues until all interrupts are processed, allows fully nested interrupts with no polling.

The 9900 microcomputer system

The key to the simplicity of a 9900 computer system (Fig. 6) is the completely separate address, control, and data lines to the memory, as well as the separate control and data lines to the I/O devices. This interfacing is simpler than with the 8-bit systems that have shared busses.

Included among the control signals are READY and WAIT, so that mixed memory speeds are allowed. For example, if the access time of the memory is 500 nanoseconds or less, the ready line can be tied to logic high, and the processor will never have to wait for the memory. Moreover, in a small memory system such as a 1,024-word ROM and a 256-word RAM (Fig. 7), the ready line can also be tied high, and neither gates nor buffers are needed on any input lines.

Three methods of I/O interface capability exist. In addition to the DMA conditions mentioned above, there are what is called memory-mapped I/O capability, which is similar to other microprocessors, and the CRU interface port, unique with the 9900.

This CRU structure makes it extremely easy to interface with I/Os. It can directly address up to 4,096 each of input and output bits and handles data transfers over serial I/O lines. Thus it is a simple, easily expandable, nonmultiplexed interface that hooks up directly with most types of I/O devices. Moreover, with special CRU instructions, it is possible to manipulate a single bit or multiple bit transfers through the port.

The interface logic required for, say, an 8-bit parallel I/O transfer (Fig. 8) is very simple, utilizing standard, low-cost TTL packages. Comparable interfacing for other microprocessors often requires special MOS-LSI circuits, which are more expensive.

Figure 9 shows the entire system capability of the 9900, and Fig. 10 shows how it compares in cost with typical 8-bit systems. Although the CPU costs may be greater, the savings in memory, I/O, and interrupt-interface circuitry on the system level can be significant, compared to a typical 8-bit system. Of course, the larger the memory system required, the greater the savings. □

Single-board computers

by Carol A. Ogdin
Reprinted with permission from *Mini-Micro Systems*, July 1977.

The dramatically low price on a CPU chip often seduces a systems builder into believing that he can devise an entire computer system inexpensively. However, unless that engineering expense can be amortized over a few hundred units, any designer taking recourse to a chip cannot win economically. Instead, the single board computer turns out to be the most cost-effective solution.

Indeed, in the multi-faceted world of the micro, the new single-board computer that incorporates a CPU, storage, and input/output interfaces on a single printed circuit card has begun to shine brightly. And there is a good reason for the glow: An SBC offers an inexpensive, yet expandable, way to computerize a product with minimal engineering effort. Often, the only remaining steps necessary to implement an application are to add wires to the input and output signal points, a power supply, and software.

A single board computer can also come in a "boxed" configuration that contains an enclosure, power supply, and additional memory cards. Such systems now begin to look like low-end minicomputers, especially when you take into account peripheral devices that can be linked to these microcomputers. There are differences, however. Generally, to use an SBC, a computer systems builder needs to know more about electronics than for a minicomputer application, since he, himself, must arrange many of the input/output terminations. Moreover, the software support available on an SBC is still much less than that provided by most minicomputer vendors.

VENDORS ABOUND

Single board computer vendors abound. They come from the ranks of the semiconductor makers that are integrating upward, minicomputer makers that are integrating downward, and newly-emerging independent companies. (Whether the independents will eventually be squeezed out is anybody's guess!) In any case, the advent of the SBC traces back to the early months of the microprocessor revolution when the semiconductor companies rediscovered an old principle: A customer needs to be supported with software and other aids before large volume orders can result.

The earliest transformation began with the Intel MCS-8 development system, which is something akin to a single-board computer based on the 8008. The MCS-8 accommodated 2K bytes of PROM, 1K of RAM, and a few input/output ports. User dissatisfaction with the system, however, prompted Intel to engineer what was to become the very successful Intellec MDS-8, later upgraded to the MDS-80 to be used on the 8080.

WHERE THE SBC FITS

The SBC fits into a niche between two extremes: Modular families that contain a CPU, memory, and I/O devices on separate cards at one end and the boxed microcomputer, or even minicomputer, at the other end. Microprocessors and microcomputers are usually more convenient than minicomputers when custom interfacing or design is necessary. The ideal SBC application arises when applications bear a general resemblance to one another and are relatively simple to implement with software and minimal additional hardware. Moreover, if production runs are to be very small, even one-of-a-kind, it will be difficult to justify economically any approach other than an SBC. An SBC can also be easier to maintain and require less staff training. The software and interfacing may also be applicable to another, similar job, in the future, and by using one SBC model in all applications, spare parts inventory in case of failure can be kept to a minimum.

But, there was still room for improvement. The MDS series requires separate cards for the CPU, program storage, data memory, and I/O. So Intel recently came up with a true single-board computer – the SBC 80 series that comes in two basic configurations:

- The SBC 80/10 has 1K bytes of RAM, provisions for up to 4K bytes of EPROM (or compatible ROM), and 48 programmable input/output lines. It also incorporates the interfaces for a terminal.
- The SBC 80/20 is a superior variant of the same card; it offers twice as much RAM, interval timers, more interrupts, and a shared system bus arrangement.

Also, the 80/20 has a shared system bus arrangement that is novel and that ameliorates a major problem in current computer design. All memory, input/output, and CPU modules intercommunicate on a single bus in most mini- and microcomputers, such that only one device can drive the bus at a time. Thus, in a high-speed data transfer application, a device may "hog" the bus. This deprives the CPU of efficient and frequent references to storage and slows program execution.

But now with the two-bus layout on the 80/20, as many as 16 devices can share the master bus, and instruction

A first SBC: The Intel 80/20 includes 4K PROM (right edge), 2K RAM (eight chips left of PROMs), CPU, and the control and I/O logic on a card 6-3/4 in. by 12 in.

fetches can proceed on the bus internal to the card at the same time. For example, a high-speed peripheral on one card can transfer data to, or from, memory on another card without any need to suspend the execution of instructions by the CPU so long as instructions are fetched from the storage on the SBC. Different users can now transfer data at any speed; fast devices can take advantage of high data transmission speed and slow devices can exploit the SBC's simplicity.

Other companies have begun to develop SBC-compatible subsystems, and this is one measure of the SBC's popularity. Burr-Brown and Analog Devices, for example, have introduced multi-channel analog-to-digital converters on SBC-size printer circuit cards that simply plug into an SBC bus, just as any Intel card does. Similar novel interfaces and specialized memories soon will become available from other sources. In addition, Intel recently announced an upgraded board based on the higher-speed 8085.

This Intel SBC is an OEM "boxed" configuration that includes a card cage, power supply, and case.

Other semiconductor makers, too, have developed product line extensions to their basic microcomputer. Motorola uses its EXORciser cards, for example, as the basis for its 6800 Micromodule family. The Monoboard Microcomputer 1 includes the 6800, 1K RAM, sockets for 4K of EPROM, and 60 input/output lines.

Zilog has undertaken one of the most ambitious efforts in the field. Its Z80-MCB microcomputer board includes the Z80 CPU, sockets for 4K of EPROM program storage, and 4K of RAM. And though the Z80-MCB has only 20 input/output bits compared to the Intel 80/20's 48 bits, the device has a clock that is 50 percent faster than the Intel device, though the anticipated 8085 SBC should eventually eliminate this Zilog advantage.

As the semiconductor companies integrate vertically into computers, the minicomputer makers, sensing a market erosion by the micros at the low-end of the business, integrate downwards by either building or buying microprocessor chips to turn out simple computers as well. And by basing the architecture on a well-established minicomputer line, such single-board computers immediately became endowed with an impressive array of software and peripheral devices.

The DEC LSI-11 at 8-1/2 in. by 10 in., though relatively large, does give 16-bit performance, plus limited I/O capability via inter-card bus lines.

The Digital Equipment Corp. LSI-11 that is based on the PDP-11 instruction set is the most popular of this genre. Its heart is a custom four-chip microprogrammed microprocessor, plus an extra socket on the board that permits insertion of optional microcode, and one preprogrammed ROM that implements fixed- and floating-point arithmetic instructions. The single board includes a 4K-by-16 RAM, a lone 16-bit parallel I/O port, and additional control logic.

The LSI-11, however, does have a big drawback. It lacks a PROM, and this means that a program must be loaded into storage each time the power is applied. DEC's claim that the LSI-11 has a 16-bit input/output is also questionable because that port is also the 16-bit bidirectional address and data bus. As a final drawback, DEC chose to implement a unique bus on the LSI-11, so some PDP-11 sophisticated peripherals are incompatible, such as high-speed line printers, large disks and graphics plotters. It is on this last point that Data General's SBC upstages DEC's LSI-11. The Micronova board is compatible with all of the Nova line so that all DG peripherals can be directly connected. The Micronova specs include 1K-by-16 PROM, 4K RAM, and 32 bits of input/output on a single board, all based around a one-chip implementation of the popular Nova computer line.

"An SBC offers an inexpensive, yet expandable, way to computerize a product with minimal engineering effort."

While the big vendors slug it out using voluminous advertising space to battle for market share, many smaller companies have introduced specialized SBC-like products. Relative newcomers, like Imsai, Pro-Log and The Digital Group, have all introduced products that could be used like an SBC. The systems, however, tend to lack product breadth. Most of the smaller firms do not offer a wide range of peripherals nor extensive software, because their products were initially intended to be used by the hobbyist who does not yet demand the extensive support that industry does.

CAN AN SBC BE MODULAR?

The single-board computer also offers relief from the cost disadvantage inherent in modular card families. As soon as microprocessor chips became available, vendors began to market such card families as modular sets. In such a modular system, the CPU and supporting logic occupy one card, another card is likely to contain only RAM chips, while yet another holds only PROM. These families enable a systems builder to configure a variety of computer systems, though they tend to be somewhat expensive: Each individual card must have the extra components necessary to intercommunicate with the other cards in the series, and that adds to cost.

In an SBC, however, the EPROM, RAM, input/output ports, CPU and central control logic are all placed on a single board, and this eliminates the board-to-board logic interconnections. This also leads to greater reliability, since the entire computer can be manufactured as a single unit. Before leaving the factory, the SBC can be subjected to complete functional testing.

"Other companies have begun to develop SBC-compatible subsystems."

Nor do SBC advantages stop here. A systems integrator is not limited by the self-contained package. He can add more memory and also input/output circuitry that comes on separate cards. The scale of integration thus accounts for the difference between an SBC and the more generalized modular card families. An SBC can be reduced to a single board in some applications, while a modular card set requires some minimum number of cards that must be interconnected to achieve an SBC's basic functional capability.

An SBC, moreover, can offer a systems integrator even greater design flexibility. Most semiconductor companies that make an SBC also offer compatible CPU-only cards that when combined with the other SBC expansion cards can be configured into a modular system. The Motorola Monoboard Microcomputer 1, for example, can be replaced by a CPU module card that is the same size as the Monoboard version and fits the same slot. However, it lacks memory and I/O interfaces. What is the meaning of all this? With an SBC, a systems integrator can have his modularity cake and eat it, too.

INTERFACING TO THE WORLD

A single-board computer is seldom the only computer component in a system, of course, and interface control logic, level-shifters, and driver/terminators, are typically additional components that need to be implemented. An SBC, however, usually does not have any space so that logic can be added to the board; therefore, any such addition must be done "outboard," meaning that access is necessary to a general purpose circuit card that can be fitted with ICs and discrete components.

Motorola monoboard, Microcomputer 1, is 6 in. by 9-3/4 in. having 8K ROM, 1K RAM, CPU and I/O, and control logic.

At this juncture, a designer had better proceed cautiously. Once he has selected an SBC, he has also chosen a card format as well, since no interchangeability exists among SBC product lines made by the different vendors. Once the SBC is fixed, a designer is "stuck" with that entire line, even in those few cases where the SBC cards can be supplemented by off-the-shelf hardware from traditional packaging sources. The warning is clear: Before committing to buy, a designer ought to be certain that a wrappable or otherwise modifiable card exists on which his special logic can be implemented.

"Newcomers, like Imsai, Pro-Log and The Digital Group, have all introduced products that can be used like an SBC."

Interface complexity is another important consideration, too. A designer adopts an SBC in the first place because he doesn't want to have to learn the arcana of bus interface logic. In such an instance, he will restrict his choices to just those cards available in a family. However, if his interfacing requirements are unusual, those cards may be difficult to work with, and such interfacing problems should be investigated before they arise. But there is a rub: Direct comparison among vendor offerings are almost impossible, since none of the inter-card interface buses are compatible. Some insight into the likely ease or difficulty is all that can be gleaned.

But some rule-of-thumb guidance can be offered. In general, the computer made by a semiconductor company tends to be simpler to interface than that made by a minicomputer supplier. To prove this, simply compare the number of wires on the control bus. The minicomputer style is likely to have twice as many signals to be controlled. In addition, the chip makers offer another advantage: They tend to make all necessary IC interfaces, while a designer could get boxed into a difficult corner by the limited IC interfacing that is available on minis.

"The SBC computer offers relief from the cost disadvantage inherent in modular card families."

But an SBC made by a minicomputer vendor may offer greater potential efficiency, and this can throw the decision in the mini's direction. An SBC from a minicomputer company offers other advantages, too, especially since the microcomputer software from the semiconductor companies in no way comes up to a mini's standard of performance. Most semiconductor companies have not learned a basic industry lesson. They continue to implement minimal software and introduce unique languages. Some of their efforts are laughable, such as providing languages purported to be like Basic, but so far removed from any accepted convention. If a designer wants a real-time operating system, he will simply have to go to a minicomputer company. The same reasoning holds if a designer wants to use a fully implemented popular high-level language, like Fortran and Basic.

A Motorola microcomputer comes in a "boxed" configuration, too.

On the other hand, minicomputer companies have not yet caught up to technology's leading edge. Because the minicomputer maker is oriented to maximizing throughput, it has ignored the relatively slow but conceptually powerful EPROM. Instead, the mini vendor uses a fusible-link ROM for bootstraps, but seldom for whole programs. Thus, when power fails on an LSI-11 or Micronova, a program must be reloaded from tape or disk.

In addition, the mini makers generally offer a core storage module – something that a semiconductor company would find heretical. With each step forward in semiconductor technology, the minicomputer vendor does not necessarily change a product configuration, so their products become stodgy over time. But they also remain constant, unlike the product outpouring from the semiconductor houses. The PDP-8, introduced by DEC in the mid-60s, is still a big seller. Semiconductor companies have still to learn that customers who have long-term problems do not appreciate gratuitious changes. ■

Part 4: Reviews of Personal Computers

Although it won't be long before new manufacturers join in making personal computers, the units now on the market exhibit all the basic features and capabilities likely to be offered for some time. The product reviews in this section, though of varied depth, give a good idea of the capabilities of some of the more popular microcomputers. But as in other things, it's the extras that often really make a unit. All manufacturers are continually adding peripheral devices and plug-in capability that take the machines into far more powerful realms.

The Radio Shack TRS-80: an owner's report

by Dan Fylstra

Photo 1: A view of the complete TRS-80 computer with the Radio Shack supplied video monitor and audio cassette recorder, supplied courtesy of Radio Shack. Priced at $599.95 for a 4 K byte version, this personal computer includes a BASIC interpreter and cassette interface software in 4 K bytes of read only memory. This is a BASIC only machine. The user cannot gain access to the machine language of the Z-80 processor which runs the BASIC interpreter.

Dan Fylstra
22 Weitz St #3
Boston MA 02134

Photography by Dan Comly

On August 3 1977, the Radio Shack division of Tandy Corporation announced its entry into the personal computing market with the TRS-80 microcomputer. The move held special significance for the personal computing industry, for with parent company sales of nearly a billion dollars and over 6000 retail stores including 500 overseas, Radio Shack is in a unique position to help bring personal computers to the average man or woman.

The TRS-80 is an "appliance" computer, preassembled and warrantied with a built-in BASIC language interpreter, and at a price of under $600 it will be affordable by many new personal computing enthusiasts. But $600 still represents a major investment for most of us, and it's desirable to know as much as possible about the detailed specifications of a computer before buying one. If you're contemplating purchase of one of the "appliance" computers now on the market, this review should be helpful to you in making your evaluation.

I ordered a TRS-80 the day after Radio Shack's press announcement, and hence I received one of the early units without a complete user's manual or any technical information on the TRS-80's provisions for expansion. Radio Shack has announced plans to introduce several significant hardware and software extensions to the basic TRS-80, some of which may become available before this article appears in print. As you read this, bear in mind that it was written in late October 1977, based on the somewhat limited information available at that time.

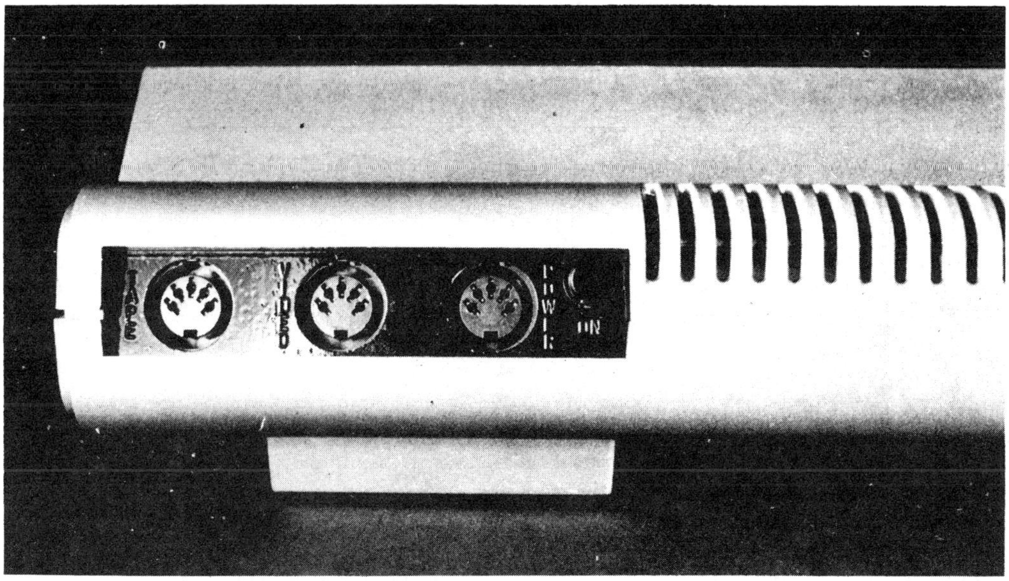

Photo 2: This back view of the TRS-80 processor unit shows the three 5 pin DIN type connectors used to attach the power supply, video monitor and cassette recorder. DIN connectors are commonly used in the audio component field, and are available at most Radio Shack retail outlets. If the complete system of photo 1 is purchased, all necessary cables are supplied.

General Specifications

Photo 1 illustrates the complete TRS-80 package, consisting of the keyboard which houses the microcomputer and memory, a video monitor, an audio cassette recorder and a power supply. The keyboard unit measures 16.5 by 8 by 3.5 inches (41.9 by 20.3 by 8.9 cm) and is very portable. The entire package including the video monitor and cassette recorder is a lot to carry, but I did take the entire computer with me on one half mile walk from the Boston home of Radio Shack to my apartment.

The components of the TRS-80 are easily plugged together using standard 5 pin DIN type audio connectors and cords which are supplied with the complete package. Jacks for the power supply, video monitor and cassette recorder are mounted on the back side of the keyboard unit, as illustrated in photo 2. For the experimenter, the DIN type plugs and jacks are available (you guessed it) as a stock item in most Radio Shack stores.

The video monitor and cassette recorder are standard items, and if you already own one or both of these you can probably use them with the TRS-80 to save on your investment. I actually bought only the keyboard unit for $400 and attached it to a Radio Shack CTR-35 cassette recorder which I already owned, and a Hitachi TV set modified for direct video entry using the Pickles & Trout kit. My home setup is shown in photo 3. The cassette recorder you use should have "earphone" and "auxiliary input" jacks and a "remote" jack for starting and stopping the cassette drive motor. The connection cords for the cassette recorder are supplied with the keyboard unit. The video monitor or TV set should accept a direct video signal (EIA standard, 75 ohm input) rather than a radio frequency (RF) signal generated by a modulator in order to provide the bandwidth required for the TRS-80's display. For the prospective buyer who doesn't already own this sort of equipment or who doesn't possess the special skills needed to modify a TV set, the complete TRS-80 package includes the video monitor and cassette recorder.

Inside the TRS-80's keyboard unit are 4 K bytes of read only memory containing Radio Shack's Level I BASIC interpreter as well as software to control the cassette recorder and display screen, and 4 K bytes of programmable memory which holds the user's BASIC program. The eight integrated circuit chips inside the unit which provide the 4 K bytes of programmable memory can be replaced by higher density memory chips to provide 8 K or 16 K bytes of memory inside the basic keyboard unit. Similarly, the two chips which provide 4 K bytes of read only memory can be replaced by higher density chips to provide 8 K or 12 K bytes of read only memory, enough to hold a much more powerful BASIC language interpreter and disk operating system which are said to be planned for later introduction.

Radio Shack has priced separately every component and memory option in the TRS-80 system. The microcomputer with keyboard and 4 K bytes of user memory is $399.95; the video monitor is priced at $199.95; and the CTR-41 cassette recorder is $49.95. These components can be purchased as a complete package deal for $599.95. An additional 4 K bytes of programmable memory for a total capacity of 8 K is priced at $99.95, while an additional 12 K bytes of memory for a total capacity of 16 K is priced at $289.95. For planning purposes it is important to note that there is no "trade-in allowance" on the lower density memory chips if the user decides to expand to the higher density chips. Thus it would not make sense to order the TRS-80 now with 8 K bytes of memory if the owner later intended to expand to 16 K bytes (which will probably be necessary to support the future disk operating system) since the total outlay for 16 K bytes of memory would then be $389.90.

BASIC programs in memory are stored in character form rather than encoded form, but abbreviations for most of the BASIC keywords are provided to save space. Thus you can write P. instead of PRINT and G. instead of GOTO, and thereby save a considerable amount of memory space since these keywords occur so frequently in a large program.

The TRS-80 is based on the Z-80 microprocessor, but this fact is really only important from the standpoint of designing and implementing the computer's read only memory software. At present the TRS-80 user is "insulated" from the hazards (and pleasures) of programming the Z-80 directly, since the BASIC interpreter is automatically activated when power is turned on, and there is no way at present to drop into machine language.

Display Screen

The TRS-80 includes a 12 inch (30.5 cm) black and white, high resolution video monitor which presents 1024 characters, arranged in 16 lines of 64 characters each. (The display is said to be "software selectable" for 32 or 64 characters per line, but no documentation is available at this writing on how the selection is made.) The display is memory mapped (ie: continuously read out of a section of programmable memory separate from the BASIC program and data memory), and is easily controlled from BASIC for both alphabetic and graphic displays.

Built-in software provides an underline cursor and automatic scrolling from the bottom of the display. The keyboard includes four keys to move the cursor in any direction, but present software supports only the "cursor left" key which deletes the character

Photo 3: The author's home setup showing the TRS-80 processor unit with its keyboard, connected to an ordinary Hitachi television set modified for direct video entry using a kit from Pickles & Trout, POB 2276, Goleta CA 93018. This setup permits conventional program reception on the television and saves about $100 over the price of the complete Radio Shack system; but it requires some electronics skill in order to modify the television set.

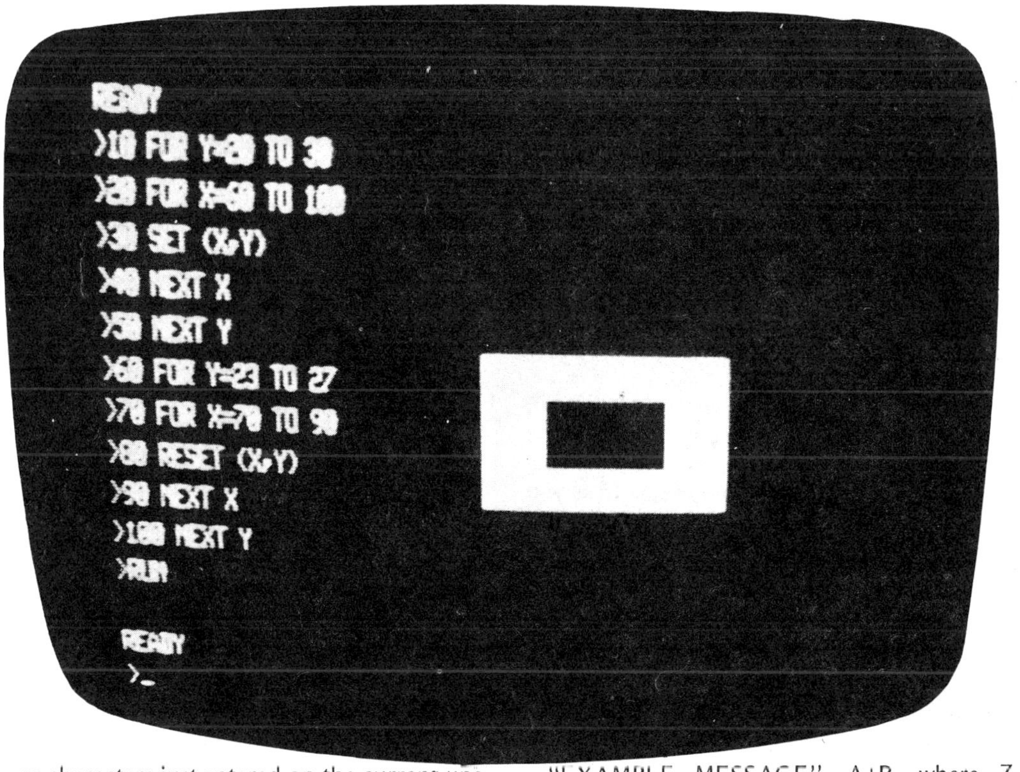

Photo 4: An illustration of the use of the TRS-80's graphics capabilities. The BASIC program shown on the screen created the square and cutout by using the SET and RESET statements to turn points on and off. This illustrates the arbitrary way in which text and graphics can be interspersed on the display.

or characters just entered on the current line. (The cursor can be moved to arbitrary positions under BASIC program control, as described below.) The "cursor up" key is used to continue a line by line listing of a program which has already filled the display screen. Another key is provided to clear the screen.

Character Set and Graphics

The TRS-80's character set consists of 58 characters including upper case alphabetic and various numeric and special characters. In addition, each character position on the screen is divided into six tiny squares, two across and three down, and each of these squares can be set on (white) or off (black) under program control. Thus graphic displays with a resolution of 128 by 48 points can be created on the screen.

The BASIC language features for controlling the graphic display are especially convenient. A point can be turned on with a statement of the form SET (X,Y), where X ranges from 0 to 127 and Y ranges from 0 to 47, or turned off with the statement RESET (X,Y). The function POINT (X,Y) can be used in an IF statement to determine whether a particular point on the display is currently on or off. Besides the graphic point addressing, the 1024 character positions on the screen are numbered sequentially from left to right, line by line, and the cursor can be set to an arbitrary position with a statement such as PRINT AT Z, "EXAMPLE MESSAGE", A+B, where Z varies between 0 and 1023. Thus displayed messages, which can be interspersed with graphics, are easily placed at any position on the screen. Finally, the CLS statement in BASIC can be used to clear the screen.

Photo 4 provides a simple illustration of the use of the TRS-80's graphics capabilities. The BASIC program shown on the screen created the graphic display by first filling in a solid square with the SET statement, and then blanking out the inner square cutout with the RESET statement. A variety of simple pictures could be drawn in this manner. The TRS-80's graphics features are especially convenient for plotting data or mathematical functions, due to the ability to address single points on the display.

Keyboard

The TRS-80's keyboard includes 53 keys with the standard spacing and arrangement used on a typewriter keyboard. It is well-suited for touch typing and will be quite familiar to the experienced user of the Teletype terminals found on timesharing systems and minicomputers. The keys are of the mechanical contact type, and they have a reasonably good "feel" and seem quite reliable in use. A BASIC program can read numeric quantities and character strings from the keyboard with the INPUT statement, which allows a message to be displayed at the same time, as in INPUT "ENTER STARTING VALUE";X.

Data Types	Real numbers (eg: A) and two string variables (A$ and B$), each up to 16 characters long.		
Arrays	One array variable, A (subscript), with one dimension. The array is as large as the entire memory remaining, after allowing for the program and ordinary variables.		
Precision	Six significant digits for real numbers.		
Speed	Executes the loop 10 FOR I=1 TO 10000, 20 NEXT I in about 22 seconds.		
Statements	LET	GOTO	REM
	READ	IF ... THEN	RUN
	DATA	FOR ... TO ... STEP	CONT
	RESTORE	NEXT	NEW
	PRINT	GOSUB	LIST
	INPUT	RETURN	
		ON ... GOTO	
		ON ... GOSUB	
		STOP	
		END	
Operators	=	=	
	+	< >	
	—	< =	
	*	> =	
	/	<	
		>	
Built-in Functions	ABS	MEM	
	INT	TAB	
	RND		
Other Features	CLOAD	CLS	PRINT AT
	CSAVE	SET	INPUT#
		RESET	PRINT#
		POINT	

Table 1: A brief summary of the features and performance of Radio Shack Level I BASIC, as available in the TRS-80.

Cassette Drive

The cassette drive interface can be used with any reasonably good audio cassette recorder, as outlined above. Data is recorded at a rate of about 250 bits per second. The recording method is designed to be reliable but does not employ any data redundancy or error correction capability. At first I had some trouble recording and playing back programs, but my results improved considerably when I set the tone control to zero. Like most cassette interface systems, the TRS-80 can get hung up searching for a signal on the tape that it never finds. A reset button near the expansion connector can be used to halt the cassette loading process, but afterwards memory may contain some "garbage" from the partially loaded program.

A problem frequently encountered when using audio cassette recorders with personal computers is that when a long program recorded on cassette is being read into memory, you don't know whether the computer is reading properly or has been unable to find the recorded program. The TRS-80 lets you know what's happening while a cassette is being read by flashing two asterisks on the screen when a program is found, and alternating between one and two asterisks while the program is being read. The TRS-80 also starts and stops the cassette drive motor automatically through the "remote" jack, but this means that you must remove the "remote" plug in order to manually rewind or fast forward the tape. This inconvenience is a necessary consequence of using a separate, standard audio cassette recorder without a manual motor control override implemented through operating system software.

Operating System

The TRS-80's operating system controls the cassette interface in response to commands and BASIC language statements. You simply type CSAVE to write the BASIC program currently in memory onto a cassette, and CLOAD to reload it later. The saved programs are not named and the CLOAD command will always load the next program it finds on the tape, but you can save several programs on the same cassette and find them later by writing down the settings of the tape index counter on a piece of paper. Also provided are PRINT# and INPUT# statements in BASIC which let you write and reread the values of program variables on cassette. Although Radio Shack plans to offer a second cassette interface, the syntax of the PRINT# and INPUT#

statements does not provide for references to different cassette units, so use of a second cassette drive will probably depend on support from "Level II" BASIC, which Radio Shack is said to be readying for future release.

Radio Shack Level I BASIC

Table 1 summarizes the features and performance of the Level I BASIC interpreter built into the TRS-80. The BASIC language features provided are somewhat limited, as might be expected in view of the fact that the BASIC interpreter and operating system fit in only 4 K bytes of read only memory. 26 possible variables can consist of one letter, but not a letter followed by a digit. Two string variables, A$ and B$, are provided and can be used in INPUT, PRINT and assignment statements, but string values cannot be compared. One singly dimensioned array variable, A(subscript), is provided, and all memory space remaining after the BASIC program and ordinary variables are allocated to this array. Each element of the array, a real number of up to six significant digits, takes four bytes of memory. Users requiring multiple arrays such as B(I) and C(J) must simulate by writing, for example, A(I) and A(10+J). Multiple dimensions may be simulated with expressions such as A(I+10*(J-1)), so having one array is obviously better than having none at all. Addition, subtraction, multiplication and division are provided but exponentiation is omitted, since this would require the EXP and LOG functions for exponentiation of real numbers.

Presumably Radio Shack's Level II BASIC, said to be due for release in early 1978 according to current expectations, will include a much more comprehensive set of BASIC language features. In the meantime, Level I BASIC can be used effectively for many computer games and for business applications with straightforward arithmetic calculations such as payroll (see below). But you can't plot a sine wave unless you write your own sine calculation subroutine.

Expansion

Radio Shack has announced plans to offer a variety of expansion options for the TRS-80, but very little detailed information on them is available at the time of this writing. Photo 5 shows the expansion port built into the TRS-80 which reaches the outside world through a small flip-up opening in the case. This 40 pin card edge connector no doubt includes the address and data bus, input, output, read, write, interrupt and interrupt acknowledge signals from the Z-80 microprocessor. A cable can be run from this connector through various peripherals and a memory expansion unit. In all probability Radio Shack will use a daisy chaining arrangement which permits a single cable to be run from device to device. (Each device in the daisy chain would either accept an IO request or interrupt acknowledge signal, or pass the signal on to the next device.)

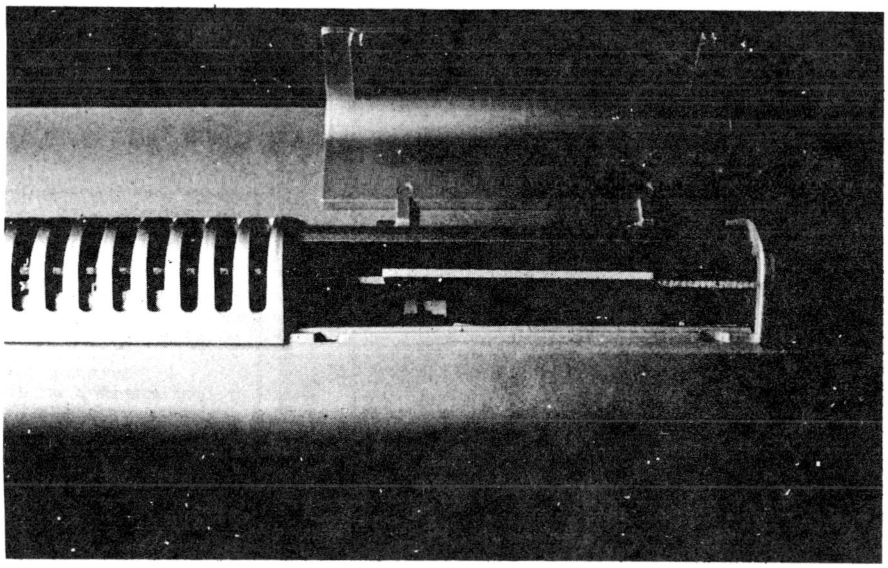

Photo 5: The TRS-80's expansion port, a 40 pin card edge connector which includes the address, data and control buses. This connector reaches the outside world through this flip-up opening on the back of the processor's case.

Peripherals for the TRS-80 currently foreseen by Radio Shack include a second audio cassette recorder interface, a printer reliable enough for business applications for about $1500, a smaller printer for less demanding individual applications for about $700, and a floppy disk drive also for about $700. Other planned options include a memory expansion unit and a modem to connect the TRS-80 to a timesharing or data communications system. Perhaps most significantly, however, Radio Shack has announced plans to offer an interface to the Altair (S-100) bus, which would provide access to the many memory and peripheral cards offered at competitive prices by other manufacturers.

Software

When the TRS-80 was announced, Radio Shack also introduced five small application software packages on cassette, all of which are designed to run on the basic TRS-80 with 4 K bytes of programmable memory. The first of these is a pair of game programs for blackjack and backgammon, which is included free with every TRS-80 computer. The display produced by the backgammon program is shown in photo 6. The program rolls the dice and maintains the board for two players, but does not provide for a 1 person game against the computer.

Other applications include a "kitchen" package which is said to provide menus, conversion tables, a directory and message center for $4.95; a "personal finance" package, apparently for checkbook balancing, for $14.95 including seven cassettes; an "education" package which provides drills in addition, subtraction and multiplication for $19.95 including three cassettes and a teacher's guide; and a "payroll" package for $19.95. The payroll package, which has been demonstrated to many interested businesspeople at trade shows, seems to require most of the 4 K memory for the program and handles just 15 employees on the basic TRS-80, but will handle 100 employees with 8 K of memory, and 300 employees with 16 K.

BASIC programs potentially useful with the TRS-80 can also be found in a number of books. Users will have to modify any such programs to fit the features of Radio Shack's Level I BASIC. In particular, variable names will have to be renamed and array references may have to be modified. And of course the total number of variable names used must be kept within Level I BASIC's limits. But this may still be easier than writing the programs from scratch.

Additional application packages are said to be planned for future release. The larger applications will probably require extended BASIC and a floppy disk. Also said to be in the works are an assembler, text editor, disk operating system and possibly compilers for other programming languages. It is not clear whether all this software will be developed in-house or will be obtained from outside sources. Some software undoubtedly will be developed by Tandy Advanced Products, another division of Tandy Corporation; Radio Shack also is thought to be negotiating with other software developers. In any case an enormous amount of effort will have to be invested in the development of this software.

Overall it seems that Radio Shack is aiming its application software and peripheral support primarily at the small business market, although applications for education, entertainment and home use are also clearly contemplated. Many related services, such as custom tailoring of application software and training of clerical staffs, will be required to meet the needs of small businesses, and perhaps knowledgeable hobbyists and small systems developers will be able to fill this need.

Availability and Delivery

When first announced, the TRS-80 was difficult to obtain like almost every personal computer. I ordered one on August 4 1977 and picked it up at my local Radio Shack store on October 11. The delay would have been even longer but for the special efforts of the store manager, Steve Lambert, who called me when another customer cancelled his order for a unit that had arrived at the store. In time, however, the TRS-80 should be among the most widely available personal computers, due to Radio Shack's widespread retail distribution and considerable manufacturing capacity.

At present you can order the TRS-80 at any Radio Shack store by placing a deposit of $100, which can be charged to a major bank credit card. The units generally are not stocked at the stores, although this is planned as the supply permits. When ordered the unit is delivered to the local store from Radio Shack headquarters in Fort Worth TX, where the TRS-80 is produced, with a planned order to delivery cycle of 30 days. Some stores have a demonstration unit on display. *[We recently saw one for example, at the Radio Shack store in Keene NH, not exactly America's biggest town ...* **CH***]*

A major problem for Radio Shack is the education of store managers who will have to answer questions from customers on the TRS-80. The managers of the first 100 stores to receive the computer were flown to Fort Worth for a special training session, and this sort of training effort may well be necessary in the future. But with Radio Shack's profit incentives for store managers, it is a safe bet to predict that the TRS-80 will be effectively merchandised.

Warranty and Service

Service has always been a problem in the personal computer industry, and because of the complexity of the product and the possibility that the user will misinterpret some peculiar but correct action of the computer as a failure, service is likely to be a problem for Radio Shack as well. In anticipation of possible servicing problems, Radio Shack apparently has tried to make the TRS-80 as foolproof as possible. The inability of the user to drop into machine language is a good example of this approach. Similarly, the plastic case of the keyboard unit is sealed, and the warranty is voided if the

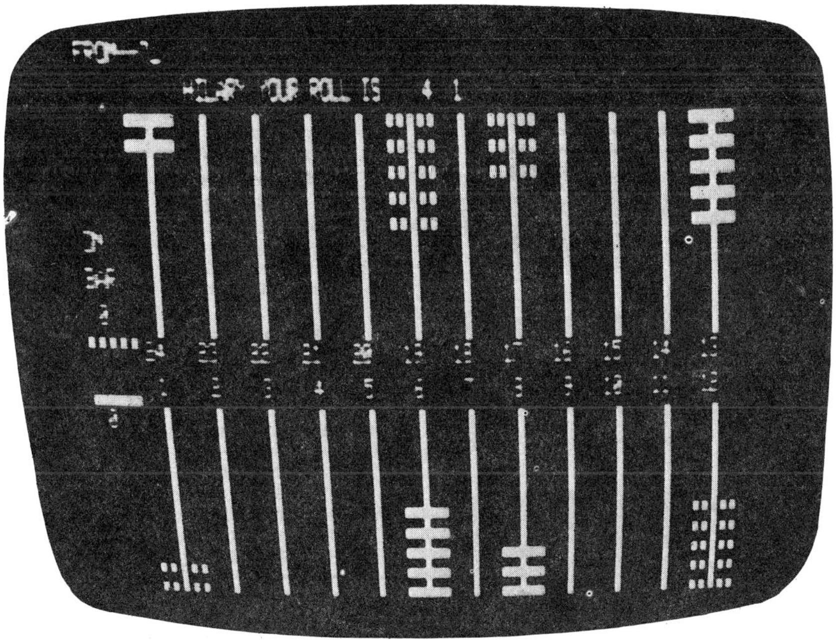

Photo 6: The display created by Radio Shack's backgammon game program, which is included free with every TRS-80 computer. This demonstration program acts as the dice roller and scorekeeper for the game, but makes no attempt to replace the two human players.

user opens the case.

The user can return the unit to a local Radio Shack store, which will ship the unit to a service center and receive it and notify the user when the repairs are complete. Initially all servicing will be done in Fort Worth, but it is planned that regional service centers will handle the TRS-80 eventually. This servicing practice also applies to the removal and insertion of memory chips when the user wants to upgrade to a larger (8 K or 16 K) memory.

Conclusion

Like other "appliance" computers now on the market, the TRS 80 brings the personal computer a good deal closer to the average consumer. It is as easy to plug in and turn on as a TV set or a stereo system, and should be usable for a wide variety of interesting games, calculations and educational drills. With a floppy disk and a printer it should be suitable for some business applications. Its BASIC language is somewhat limited at present, but this should be remedied when Radio Shack Level II BASIC is finally available.

The TRS-80 is not the only alternative for the aspiring personal computer user, but it is a strong contender. If you are thinking about a purchase, compare its features against other offerings along all dimensions, including capabilities, software, warranty and service, and expansion possibilities. Talk to owners of the TRS-80 and other personal computers, and think about what you intend to do with your own computer. I hope that this review article will help you in your evaluation.■

Commodore's PET

by Phyllis Cole

Commodore's PET is a self-contained, factory-assembled unit that contains a 6502 microcomputer, keyboard, CRT display (40 columns, 25 lines), 1000-baud tape cassette, and memory. For $595 you get 4K of user memory (or 8K for $795) plus the 14K needed by an 8K BASIC interpreter, a 4K operating system, a 1K diagnostic routine, and 1K machine language monitor. The PET's expanded 8K BASIC contains strings, integers and multiple dimension arrays. It has high precision (10 significant digits), floating point numbers, and direct memory access through PEEK and POKE.

The system weighs 44 pounds, is 16.5 inches wide, 18.5 inches deep and 14 inches high – about the size of a portable TV but a somewhat more awkward shape to handle. The 73-key calculator-style keyboard is upper case only; a calculator style numeric keypad is included. The 64 ASCII characters are available without using a shift key; the shift key makes 64 graphic and reverse field characters accessible from the keyboard. The graphic characters can be used to play games, plot, or draw pictures.

In late July, a motley crew interviewed Chuck Peddle, father of the PET, at Commodore. The interview panel included True Seaborn and Dennis Allison of IEEE's Computer *magazine, Don Inman and LeRoy Finkel of* Calculators/Computers, *stockbroker Jon Krass, vice president of E.F. Hutton and Company, and yours truly, Phyllis Cole of* People's Computers. *Here are some facts to add to the many rumors that are floating about.*

THE MARKET

Q: Chuck, how does Commodore view the PET's place in the computer field?

A: The major philosophical difference between what Commodore has attempted and anything that's happened until now is that we've tried to make a product that is merchandisable by a normal retailer to the ultimate consumer. That's why the PET has the built-in CRT, the built-in cassette, and the lower-cost, calculator-type keyboard. For a sale to be made by an inexperienced retail clerk to an inexperienced customer the unit has to have immediate perceived value. The only way to have immediate perceived value is for the unit to do something the customer wants as soon as it's plugged in. People have been taught that computers are difficult to operate, that computers are things to be afraid of, not things to get warm and friendly and cuddly with. Therefore, what we've tried to do is to package the unit in such a way that it's as close to warm and friendly as we can get it; but it has perceived value as a thing that does something.

The analogy between the way the PET will be marketed and the stereo market, I think, is very, very close. In K-Mart stores stereos are sold by retail clerks who have no real understanding of the product. We expect the PET will be successfully sold in a similar fashion.

Q: Does such an approach presuppose some mass-media advertising?

A: Oh, absolutely. It is our opinion that the Average American Public has no concept that personal computing is here. News about personal computing is starting to break in the media, but it has got to be mass-advertised and mass-merchandised. We expect to spend a significant amount of dollars relative to the size of our corportation on advertising, such as television, that is non-traditional for the hobbyist market.

Q: Does that mean you're going to go into retail marketing directly?

A: We're already in retail marketing directly. The Mr. Calculator stores are a legitimate test market. That doesn't imply that we're not dealing with dealers – we are. At the same time, there will be at least one major retailer handling the product on a nationwide basis simultaneously.

Q: You're thinking about September delivery?

A: That's to the mass retailer. We will not necessarily have the PET to smaller retail stores at that time.

Q: How do computer stores fit into your marketing plan?

A: We feel that the two types of stores are complementary. Stereos became something you could buy in the discount stores, but you still have the specialty stores. So we feel that the well-financed dealer who understands how to do specialized merchandise is going to be a very profitable guy. As a matter of fact he is going to take over, if you want a better analogy than stereo, exactly the same place as the appliance sales store did. He is going to service his community.

Q: Do you see that analogy as going further, do you see this becoming an appliance that is going to be widely used?

A: That is our goal. We're doing everything we can to make it happen. In other words, the product's technical direction and marketing direction is to be a consumer item, with a secondary strong market emphasis on small business applications. But in addition to that, it is our intention to find ways to make this product quite useful to insurance salesmen, doctors, real estate salespeople – the classic professionals, people who have money, but more than that, people who are considered 'thought leaders' in their community. Suppose all the doctors and all the insurance salespeople put the PET in their offices and start to use it. Because they've used it in the office, they're familiar with the product, and now can use it in their home. Next Mr. John Q. Public, who buys things because doctors have them, will in fact start buying the product.

Q: What about the area of education?

A: We're using three approaches to the educational market this year. First, we're trying to support development of innovative programs for schools by educational 'thought leaders.' Second, anyone planning to use the PET in a course this fall will get a high priority allocation. Third, we're setting up a royalty program to pay royalties for software developed for the PET.

We also plan to demonstrate the PET at teacher education seminars and we're encouraging educators to write programs for both the home and school. Even though it's too late to sell to schools this year, we expect some action immediately.

As professional educators start writing and trying out PET programs in schools we'll negotiate royalty agreements with the authors, then mass-merchandise the materials directly to the consumer.

Q: Can you give any price estimates on the educational packages you'll be selling?

A: The first year out, we are going to be able to get $20 for a decently packaged product. After that, I think the volume package is going to drop down to the $10 range.

Q: What can we say that is going to encourage people to write programs for the PET?

A: Suppose we had *really good* educational home programs right now, aimed at re-educating adults on how to compute interest rates, that kind of practical thing. I think such programs would sell rather quickly. But frankly, the aspect of education I consider most important, far broader than teaching children, is adult education. Everyone is missing

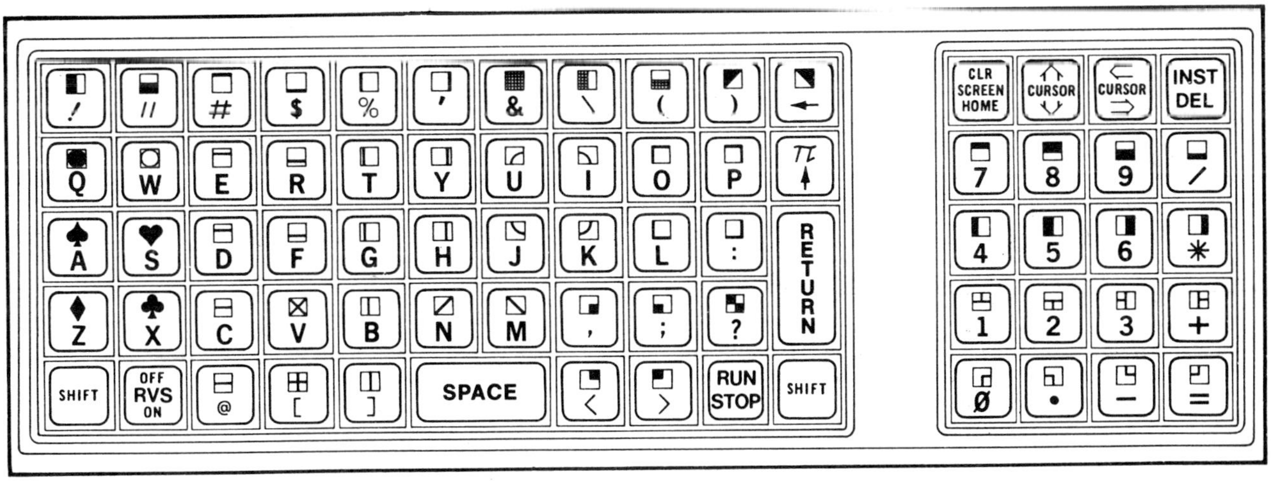

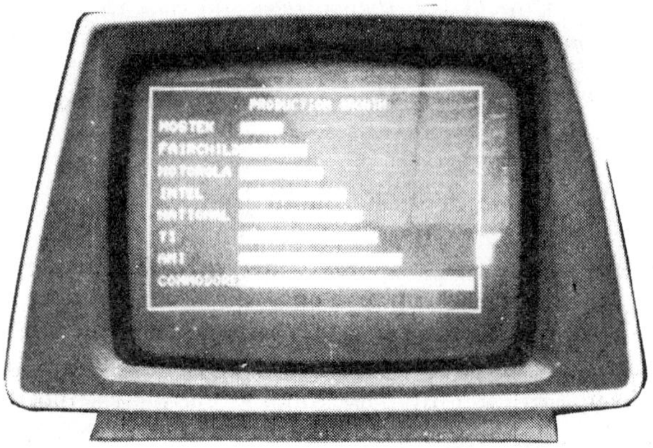

this fine market, educating the individual. We won't neglect that area: that is where the PET can be truly revolutionary.

Q: What sales volume do you expect to attain by Christmas?

A: By the Christmas period we will be manufacturing 5,000 a month in the United States; not long after that we'll be at the same production level in our Japanese plant.

Q: Are you doing all your manufacturing in the U.S.?

A: Nobody in the United States makes black and white CRTs anymore, you have to buy those things out of Taiwan. Cassettes are not made in Japan anymore, the only place to buy cassettes is out of Hong Kong and Korea. The semiconductors are, of course, made in this country, transported to Asia to be packaged, and transported back. The keyboards are Japanese, and will continue to be because the Japanese tend to do a very good job in that area. The housings, PC work, and assembly work will all be done in the United States for the U.S. market, in Europe for the European market, and in Japan for the Japanese and the Far East market.

Q: Are you going to make a very heavy marketing thrust in this country and then hit Europe or will both markets be tackled simultaneously?

A: You can't do it simultaneously. We have already opened Europe up with the Hanover Fair and we got very positive response. We will probably start selling in Europe after the first of the year.

Q: A year from now, who will be your competitors?

A: There'll be Tandy's Radio Shack, TI, a major U.S. games company, a European company, and a Japanese company competing with Commodore.

Q: What do you think of Radio Shack's TRS-80 computer?

A: Well, if you want to do calculations forget the computer and buy yourself a $30 scientific calculator. And Radio Shack's computer has only a 4K BASIC and no file system, so I don't think the system has what it takes to be classed as a real computer.

SOFTWARE

Q: What can you tell us about software distribution?

A: We are setting up either a division of the company or another company to publish software, most often on a royalty basis. We will only sell on a royalty basis software which has been *installed* and *tested* in a *financially rewarding environment.* In other words, the product has either got to have been installed in a scholastic situation or in some type of retail environment; the software publisher will test market programs strictly for the home. And we don't even talk to people until they've met those particular tests.

Q: What are the ranges on royalties for PET software?

A: We're going to try and make the successful author a good financial deal based on what the market for the particular product is. We have to set the prices of the cassette fairly low, because otherwise you get a high rate of theft. That means that the royalty percentage is fairly low, but hopefully it's compensated for by the fact that the volume is significantly higher.

Let's talk about the person who is writing programs for small businesses, particularly specialized applications. We'd like to see that author make a *better* than good living by writing three program packages a year.

Q: Can you tell us what software projects are currently in the works, either in house or out of house?

A: The answer is no, I can't. Not because I'm trying to avoid it, it's just that there are a whole series of software projects which people have started outside because of our official non-recognition. We do, by the way, offer an internal service where we will tell people that other people are working on similar products. Interested people should contact Terry Laude?eau.

Q: What about software repair?

A: Which kind? If it is operating systems software, you buy what you buy. And there will be no warranty: the unit does what it does. But we've done some fairly extensive testing to see that that is acceptable. We actually went out and hired an outside consulting firm who came in and audited the PET. They ran an extensive set of benchmarks and tried to in fact break it using standard software breaking techniques. In other words they got into the system, saw that it worked to spec, outside spec, inside of spec. We also went to the June '77 National Computer Conference (NCC) and said 'all come, try to break it,' but no one could.

One interesting measurement is the number of problems found in the last month: zero. And that's with people playing with it, trying to break it.

Q: Who developed your BASIC?

A: Rick Wyland at MicroSoft wrote the PET BASIC. We climbed on the backs of all the MITS users who had problems, all of the 6800 users.

Q: Are you going to stick with BASIC as your primary language?

A: We did some things to BASIC in the I/O area to make BASIC a lot more flexible for growth. We designed the machine and software so the first-time user could walk up to the machine and operate it comfortably, and so the novice programmer could program. But we did the I/O structure for the sophisticated programmer. I think you'll find that with intelligent peripherals (which is the *only* kind Commodore will build), that you'll find that the structure is going to let you do a lot of I/O things.

We have a logical file structure operating system that really lets you operate at the logical file level; it lets you get in and play with that IEEE bus, right down to almost anything you want to do on it.

I want the business systems analyst who wants to write a good program using our floppy and our printer to be able to feel very comfortable sitting down and writing a well done program, where he doesn't feel that the language is inhibitive. And if I have done that, then I have met my goal.

Q: Are you going to come out with any materials supporting the machine language on the 6502?

A: We'll have an assembly language manual. There is a monitor which is currently not in the software; it will be available on tape.

Q: What about text editing?

A: We have a string editor and we have some editing capability already in it. Now the question is whether or not that's a legitimate text editor; I think more work needs to be done.

ADD-ONS

Q: Do you have any dates or costs of a printer for the PET?

A: We are negotiating with the printer manufacturer, we expect adapting our program to take a month or so. We hope to show the printer at WESCON, in September, and make it available to customers shortly thereafter.

Q: Will the printer be capable of handling PET graphics?

A: We'll do graphics to the extent that we can, but the CRT and printer use different sizes of dot matrices for printing characters.

Q: What are your plans for floppy discs for the PET?

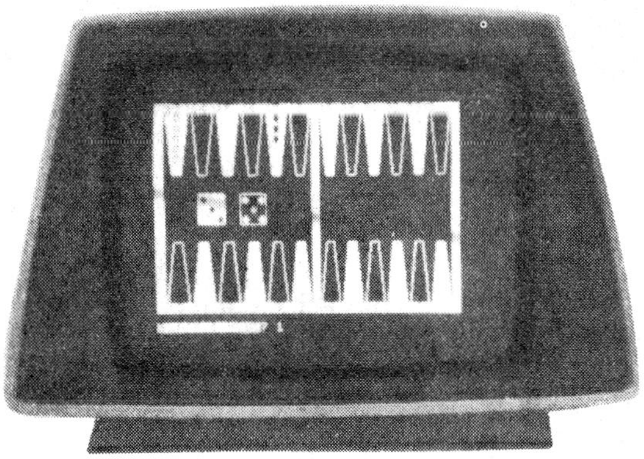

A: We're negotiating with two mini-floppy companies right now, but few mini-floppy manufacturers can come close to meeting the demand we foresee. So we're going to wind up coming out with a traditional mini-floppy, priced high, for those people that need it, and then get to work developing a low cost mini.

Q: Do you have any plan for when you would like to bring out your low priced mini-floppy?

A: Yes, as soon as I can get it designed and into production. If we could come out with a really low cost product it would blow the mind of the world!

Q: While we're discussing peripherals, is there anyone that is making IEEE bus peripherals that are price compatible with the PET?

A: In terms of price compatibility, what do you want? If you're talking about a consumer application then at this point the answer is no. But we expect to see other companies producing price compatible PET peripherals.

Q: I have the impression that a color bit-map display is low on your list of priorities, compared to the mini-floppy and the printer. Is that right?

A: Yes; first we want to provide support for the small business. Second we want to give people traditional computing capability, such as disk sorts and the ability to print. In addition to the printer and mini-floppy a third peripheral will be something that is an interesting, fun type of thing. And I have my own choice for that which I think has higher priority than a color display.

Q: What is involved in adding more memory to the PET?

A: There's a box for memory expansion; it is brought out the side, and you plug in a connector. Commodore will sell the box. In that box you can put APL if we sell it, or any memory expansion that turns you on.

Q: What is involved in adding and replacing ROM's?

A: For a short time the ROM's are on sockets until we are satisfied with their performance because they are fairly new components. But after that, replacing the ROM means un-

soldering and soldering, you don't want to do that. That's why we brought the bus out: do your outboard stuff outboard. This is not a unit to be tinkered with. By the way, you'd blow the built-in diagnostics out of the water the minute you change ROM's.

Q: Is Commodore interested in facilitating use of the PET over personal computer networks?

A: Yes; we want to provide a straightforward way to provide communication facilities for the PET. And that doesn't mean using an RS232 interface. Eventually we'll come out with a box equipped with what's needed.

Q: What if I want to hook on my own keyboard to the PET?

A: That would be very difficult. You'd have to get into the guts of the software, and it was not intended that you be doing that. By making the PET a consumer item, by making it so any TV repairman can fix it, we really have cut down your ability to screw with it. I hate pushing my competition, but if you really feel like you have to get in and mess around with your computer, buy an Apple.

Q: What's the PET II going to be?

A: PET II will be a higher priced product, with dual cassettes built in and a fullsized keyboard; it will be aimed at the small business market in particular, and will be priced accordingly. By the way, one of the tests we're running is a keyboard laid out not like a typewriter keyboard at all. Literally we are going to lay the keyboard out abcdefg and see what happens.

Q: Why did you choose the IEEE 488 bus?

A: The PET is not a *product*, it's the beginning of a *sales opportunity*. In order to make that real, you need standardization: my electrical plug has got to plug into all electrical outlets. There were four alternatives: we could go IBM compatible bus, which was kind of ridiculous; we could go S-100 bus, which was ill conceived and is very expensive; we could create our own, but that meant getting everyone to agree with us to promote standardization; or we could choose the 488. We chose the 488 IEEE bus because it was the best alternative: it was developed by many good people who put a lot of time and effort into trying to define a plug compatible standard.

Q: Can the PET operate as a slave as well as a master?

A: No, it's a master only.

SERVICE

Q: Will service contracts be available?

A: Not from the factory, but yes they will definitely be available, just like you were buying a TV. We put a great amount of attention into that trying to make the PET easily serviceable.

Q: Do you think we're likely to see price competition between service contractors?

A: We've set the unit up so that it can be repaired by the individual repairman, so I think you are going to see the same factors evolve as in television service.

Q: Will the service manual be available to retail customers? If so, for how much?

A: Yes, but the price hasn't been set yet.

Q: What about board replacement or trade-in costs?

A: All of the traditional things that you would expect to be able to do relative to a consumer appliance will be available. But we haven't set prices yet, they really have to wait. Remember, we had to pick a price in order to get out in the market and start talking. We need to get a little more product history before we start setting such prices; but there will be board repair centers.

Q: If I go down to Mr. Calculator and buy a PET and three weeks later my kid puts gum in someplace or pours syrup down it, what happens?

A: Your retailer or his subcontractor will fix it. Everyone who retails our product must be capable of servicing it before he introduces it; that's one of the requirements. That's true for all retailers, large and small. A retailer cannot have the product unless they can service it.

Q: Who is going to train retail service personnel?

A: Commodore will initially train service people, then the retailers themselves will take it from there. We'll be conducting service schools in late August and early September.

Q: What about a PET user's group?

A: We will try to set that up probably using some of the Hewlett-Packard conventions. That seems to have worked out fairly well for them, but we foresee the local retailer playing a major role in interfacing between Commodore and consumers.

THE RETAILER

Q: Could you say some more about the role of the computer retailer?

A: Computer retailers are a sociological phenomenon more than anything else. They're the places where the consumer can go to tell of troubles and get advice. And of course, the social experience of trading information is fine for the retailer, who sells a $5, $10, or $15 item at every turn.

A large department store won't provide the facility for letting you try out programs before buying them or for test marketing your programs. That's where the retailer comes in.

I think the retail channel is going to be the commmunication vehicle for users. Your local merchant is the person closest to the problems of users, who is capable, has a reason to do business with the customer on an individual basis, and is in a position to recommend software for Commodore's royalty program.

A retail distribution channel is developing for all of the products that can be dreamed of by the next five years. And that retail distribution channel is not a flim-flam-thank-you-ma'am type of market. Automobile dealers are substantial members of their community. They are valued people, they make a lot of money, they belong to the appropriate country clubs, and they're valued members of the community. We would like to see computer dealers acquire equal social status.

PURCHASING A PET

Q: What instructional materials will accompany a PET?

A: We've written an instruction manual; we also hope to provide an interactive instructional tape to teach the consumer how to use the PET and to introduce programming in BASIC.

Q: Are educational discounts available?

A: Commodore has traditionally found a way to sell to the educational community at a price that is favorable to education. But we haven't set a program up yet, and probably won't get to it this school year.

Q: Does that mean that anyone in education wishing a system now should send in $595?

A: Yes, that's right – or $795; plus 6% sales tax in California. And quite frankly, if you're a dealer, that's the way you get PETs too. We're not discriminating in that respect, there are some dealers that want to get started on writing software or getting their act together and so forth, and they're paying, retail.

Q: What about discounts for quantity orders, say buying clubs or computer clubs or anything like that?

A: Commodore has been a traditional mail order house, and the mail order house will probably still sell mail orders, but aside from that, we sell to retailers. So if your local club can convince your local retailer to give them a discount, then you should do that. But you should understand the corollary to that. People want to become dealers in order to get a discount, and that just doesn't happen with us.

Q: Suppose a retail dealer wants to be a PET dealer. Today he would like a commitment from Commodore – 'In October I'd like to be a PET dealer.' What's he do?

A: For now, Sam Bernstein's handling it, but the only way we even talk to dealers right now is with cash deposits up front. We're not trying to be difficult, we're just saying that if you want to do business with us, you must have financial stability; to measure that, we want your money.

Q: Is the fastest way to get a system to send Commodore a check?

A: It's the only way, right now. However we encourage people to wait and do business with their local retailer. For those wishing to order a system now, orders will be filled in 90 days and are FOB Palo Alto, or money will be refunded. Checks should be made payable to Commodore and sent to:

Commodore Business Machines, Inc.
901 California Ave.
Palo Alto, CA 94304

Our PET's first steps

by Phyllis Cole

We have a PET or perhaps I should say a PET has us – at any rate, the relationship is pleasantly symbiotic. The 'we' of this article is not an editorial we, it refers to members of a group of computer professionals – including your editor – who have purchased a PET as part of a project aimed at integrating personal computers into the daily routines in a local school.

Our group chose a Commodore PET for four reasons:

1) At the time, it was the only announced system that the school could afford.
2) Its integrated package (display, keyboard, and tape unit in a single cabinet) was easier for a child to manage than separate components would be.
3) Its quality BASIC featured strings, arrays, floating point, graphics and linkage to machine language subroutines.
4) It was manufactured locally – a big help, since we knew we would be receiving an early production model.

Our PET Stumbles. On Monday, October 4, we picked up PET number 54. When we turned it on we found that 1K of the 8K was taken up by tape buffers, the program stack and other system requirements, leaving only 7167 bytes for us. We soon found two errors caused by inadequate checking during production: a memory chip was flaky and 5 keys on the keyboard weren't making contact. Other 'problems' turned out to be:

a) nobody told us to remove the transparent packing tape from the key tops – when it began to peel, we feared plague had set in.
b) we did not understand certain features and conventions of the system since minimal documentation accompanied early systems.

Our Pet Goes to the Vet. The following day we swapped PET 54 for PET 57: we've been up and running almost constantly since then.

It took about two days to get used to the PET's calculator style keyboard, but get used to it we did. We came to accept the small size of the keys, their closeness, their arrangement, and the way contact with them must be made. In the short time that we've had the machine it has been extremely reliable. Three times in our first 80 hours of use the processor stopped – reputedly due to voltage drops in our power lines. This is the one disadvantage of not having a front panel – we had to power on and off to restart, thus losing the program in memory.

Our PET Starts to RUN. The PET has a number of nice features – we've space to mention just a few. You can get lower case displayed (instead of 26 of the graphic characters) by doing POKE 59468,14. Most versions of BASIC will STOP if you type just a carriage return for INPUT. This annoying behavior, particularly irritating to kids, can be bypassed in PET BASIC by using GET C$, which accepts a single character from the keyboard. Input and output are facilitated by the status word ST, logical device numbers and a WAIT command. Last but by no means least is the fact that the vast majority of error messages are not only comprehensible but even useful!

The on-screen editor that comes with the PET is the nicest one we've seen on a small system. For those unfamiliar with on-screen editors, here's a brief example: suppose you type in a BASIC program, run it, and get an error message which indicates to you that you typed 'Y' where you meant to type 'X'. Assuming that the text is still on the screen, you can move the cursor to the 'Y' then type 'X' and press RETURN: that line will be automatically recompiled. Now move the cursor to the word 'RUN' which you typed before, press RETURN, and the program will be executed once again.

Our PET Speaks. PET BASIC is Microsoft's latest, and is very similar to other microcomputer BASICs. Much available software should be easily converted for use on PETs. The BASIC seems to have very few bugs, and the ones that do exist are not encountered in simple programs. For those of you who want to get a head start on learning it, I recommend Jerry Brown's *Instant BASIC* ($6 from the PCC Bookstore) which deals with an almost identical dialect.

Dancing in the Dark. The temporary documentation provided with early systems contains only a brief summary of commands. By November 1 an instruction tape should be available. We have had to explore the system on our own, with an occasional assist from Commodore.

Files on cassette tapes can be accessed by name, but the file system is not quite so complete as those on more expensive micros such as Processor Tech's SOL. Since minimal software documentation has been distributed, we had to experiment alot before we could read data files reliably. By the way, we've tried out a variety of 'low noise' audio cassette tapes – differing brands, quality, and prices – and had good luck with all of them.

PET's Got Rhythm. With the aid of the PET's built-in timer, we timed most of the instructions on our unit. Based on these results, it is a simple matter to speed up the frequently executed portions of programs. Some of our results are printed in the timing table that accompanies this article. We consider the numbers to be reasonably accurate since they predicted within ±5% the benchmark program timings printed in 'BASIC Timing Comparisons' by Tom Rugg and Phil Feldman in the October 1977 *Kilobaud.* By the way, PET BASIC came in about 4th fastest out of the 30 BASICs examined by Rugg and Feldman.

Jumping for Joy. Was it worth getting an early system despite potential bugs and limited documentation? Yes – otherwise we most likely would have had to delay implementing our school program until September 1978. Besides, we're having great fun! And having a computer at home is a fine way to reduce – we're too busy PETting to eat or sleep. So far we have got running a PILOT interpreter, a number of PILOT programs, a tape file utility, and a drawing program. The drawing program (written by another member of our group) is presented below.

TIMING TABLES

BASIC STATEMENTS AND I/O

construct	*approx. time (millisec)*
FRE	1 to 10
PEEK, POKE	1
TI$	3 to 4
TI	1
GET	1 to infinity
POS	1
PRINT X or PRINT	15 to 19
PRINT X$;	14+LEN(X$)/2
READ X and DATA 3	9
REM	0.2 to 2
RESTORE	0.3
TAB	2
SPC(N)	1+0.6*N
FOR I=. . .NEXT I	4.0+(1.6 each)
STEP	1.3
IF	0.4
GOTO or GOSUB	1.1
ON A GOTO or GOSUB $L_1, \ldots, L_M$	0.5+(0.3*A) +(0.2*M)
RETURN	0.9

Using colon, :, saves 0.6 over new line.
SAVE or LOAD
15 sec + (2 sec per 100 char)
i.e. 500 baud

STRING FUNCTIONS

function	*approx. time (millisec)*
+	0.5+(0.2 per char)
ASC	1
CHR$	1.2
LEFT$, RIGHT$	3+(0.025 per char)
LEN	0 to 8
MID$	4+(0.025 per char)
STR$	7 to 10
VAL	1.3
=, <>, <, <=, >, >=	3 to 4

ARITHMETIC FUNCTIONS

function	*approx. time (millisec)*
ABS	0.6
ATN	42
COS	27
EXP	27
INT	1.2
LOG	23
RND RND(−1)	1.0
RND(0)	0.9
RND(1)	4.1
SGN	1.1
SIN	25
TAN	50
user FN	2.4

cont'd

DRAWING PICTURES ON THE PET

The PET has a set of 64 graphic characters, plus their 64 reverse video (black on white) counterparts. It also has cursor control keys. One might expect to be able to draw a picture simply by running the cursor around and pressing graphic keys. Although possible, it is quite awkward in practice, because the graphic characters and some, but not all, of the cursor controls require the shift key to be held down. It is rather like trying to thread a needle while running the 100-yard dash.

If you have tried to draw on a PET, you will appreciate the program below. It makes it possible for a human being with one or more fingers to draw pictures for entertainment. There is no provision for saving the pictures on tape, although that could be added quite easily.

Type the program, check it for errors and SAVE it on tape before attempting to RUN it. An erroneous POKE could be disastrous.

The Target. The program treats the screen as a grid of cells, 40 across and 25 down. When it starts, it blanks the screen and displays a large round dot character (the 'drawing symbol') in a cell near the center. That cell is the initial 'target' cell. A white square blinks at you occasionally to let you know where the target cell is.

To draw a picture made of dots, use the program's target-motion keys. They are not the same as the PET's cursor keys. Instead, the digit keys 1 through 9 are used to make the target move one cell in any of eight directions.

7	8	9
4	5	6
1	2	3

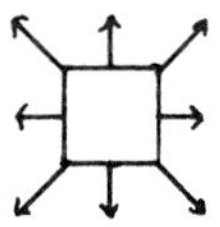

Pretend the target cell is on the '5' key. To move it left, press '4'; to move it up and right, press '9'; and so on.

Whenever the target moves, it will inscribe the drawing symbol in its new cell. In a few minutes, you should get proficient at drawing a picture with dots.

The Drawing Symbol. When you are tired of dots, press any graphic key on the left side of the keyboard. Shifting is not necessary. The graphic character on the key will become the new drawing symbol. It will be inscribed in the target cell.

Press RVS, and the color of the drawing symbol will be reversed. Subsequently chosen drawing symbols are not affected.

To erase, make SPACE be the drawing symbol. The reverse SPACE draws white stripes. DEL erases the target cell without changing the drawing symbol. You can 'un-DEL' using the '5' key.

ARITHMETIC OPERATORS

symbol		approx. time (millisec)
↑	0↑B, 1↑B	0.3
	2↑B	32
	else	50 to 100
/	0/B, A/1	0.5
	else	2 to 5
*	0*B, A*0	0.4
	else	1.5 to 3
+		0.3 to 1
−		0.3 to 1
=, <>, <, <=, >, >=		0.7
AND, OR		1.7
NOT		1.4

VARIABLES AND CONSTANTS

item	approx. time (millisec)
A, A$, A=, A$=	0.7 to (0.7+nv*0.1) nv = no. of variables in program
AA, AA$, AA=, AA$=	0.2 more than above
A%	0.3 more than A
A%=	0.6 more than A=
999	1 per digit
.999	0.7+(4.2 per digit)
E16	0.2+(0.4*exponent)
E-16	0.2+(3.0*exponent)
"ABCDE"	(0.6 to 0.7)+(0.02 per char)
M(I,J, . . .)	(1 to 1.5)* (no. of subscripts)

TIMING PROGRAM

```
100   N=300
200   T1=TI
300   FOR I=1 TO N
400   REM PUT TEST CONSTRUCT HERE
500   NEXT I
600   T2=TI
700   FOR I=1 TO N
800   NEXT I
900   T3=TI
1000  PRINT 1000*((2*T2-T1-T3)/(60*N))
1100  END
```

MEMORY USAGE (IN BYTES)

BASIC 1028 (I/O buffers, tables, etc)

each statement

- 4 for line number and following space, regardless of the line number
- 1 for each BASIC keyword
- 1 for each other character, including RETURN

each variable with a value assigned, regardless of spelling or value takes 7 bytes; for string variables, add the length of the string

each array (N.B., size includes 0th element) take f*(size+1)+(2 per dimension) where f=5 for floating point arrays, f=2 for integer arrays, and f=3 for string arrays.

The system slows down noticeably when memory is nearly full.

Other Features. You can draw with the graphics on keys 1 - 9 by SHIFTing. These are the only keys in the program affected by SHIFT.

To move the target without changing the picture, get rid of the drawing symbol by pressing either of the CRSR keys, then use the digit keys to move the target. When you are ready to draw again, press a graphics key or RVS.

When you want to admire your drawings without the screen blinking at you periodically, press RETURN. Then, to make the target cell blink again, type any other key; '5' is a good choice.

To start a new picture, press CLR. To stop drawing so you can do something else with your PET, first press RETURN and then press STOP.

Have fun! □

	1 REM PET DRAWING PROGRAM
	2 REM COPYRIGHT 1977 "PEOPLE'S COMPUTERS"
	3 REM PERMISSION TO USE, NOT TO SELL
Initializes constants.	10 P1=59409: P2=52: P3=60
Sets timing for blinking.	20 WH=50: BL=53: WT=5
Puts 'SHIFT-Q' center screen.	30 Y=12: X=20: GR=ASC(" ") AND 127
Cleans screen.	40 PRINT " "
	50 GOTO 2300
Looks for keystroke.	100 GET C$: IF C$="" GOTO 3000
Keystroke to unshifted ascii.	150 C=ASC (C$) AND 127
Checks target blinked off.	200 IF FL>=WH THEN GOSUB 4000
RETURN causes long blink.	250 IF C=13 THEN FL=−1.0E8: GOTO 100
Reset short blink.	300 FL=WH−WT
Handles number key.	400 IF C$>="1" AND C$<="9" THEN 1700
Handles graphic key.	450 IF C>=32 GOTO 1000
DEL blanks target cell.	500 IF C=20 THEN POKE L,32
Handles RVS.	600 IF C=18 GOTO 1200
Handles CRSR.	700 IF C=17 OR C=29 THEN GR=−1
CLR-HOME causes restart.	800 IF C=19 GOTO 30
	900 GOTO 100
Encode symbol for display.	1000 GR=64 OR C
	1100 GOTO 1300
Reset drawing symbol.	1200 IF GR<0 THEN GR=PEEK(L)
Reverse drawing symbol.	1250 GR=(128+GR) AND 255
Lines 1300–1500 display the symbol in the target cell.	1300 POKE P1, P2
	1400 POKE L, GR
	1500 POKE P1, P3
	1600 GOTO 100
Lines 1700–2200 move the target in the direction indicated by the number key.	1700 X=X+C+1−3* INT((C+2)/3)
	1800 IF X<0 THEN X=0
	1900 IF X>39 THEN X=39
	2000 Y=Y+1−INT ((C−49)/3)
	2100 IF Y<0 THEN Y=0
	2200 IF Y>24 THEN Y=24
Locates new target.	2300 L=32768+40*Y+X
Checks for drawing symbol.	2400 IF GR>=0 GOTO 1300
Lines 2500–2700 blink the target if there's no symbol to draw.	2500 GOSUB 4000
	2600 FOR DL=1 TO WT: NEXT DL
	2700 GOSUB 4000
	2800 GOTO 100
Lines 3000–3020 blink the target while you're not doing anything.	3000 FL=FL+1
	3010 IF FL=WH THEN GOSUB 4000
	3020 IF FL=BL THEN FL=0: GOSUB 4000
	3030 GOTO 100
Lines 4000–4020 reverse the color of the target cell.	4000 POKE P1, P2
	4010 POKE L, (PEEK(L)+128) AND 255
	4020 POKE P1, P3
	4030 RETURN

What are the advantages and disadvantages of the TRS-80 versus the PET?

Commodore's Chuck Peddle replied:

For people who like to put things together, it's an advantage that the TRS-80 is a modular system – Commodore deliberately chose to produce an integrated package. The TRS-80 keyboard is comparable to a typewriter keyboard, which wasn't designed for doing control functions. The difficulty in doing control functions has been overcome by adding special keys to control input/output devices. Commodore has tried to match the multi-key functions available on the more expensive intelligent terminals so as to give more keys in the same space. We'll let the market decide which is better.

The fact that the TRS-80 RAM is expandable up to 16K inside the unit (although I don't know whether such an addition requires an additional power supply) may be seen as an advantage. Commodore allows a 4K PET to be expanded to 8K. The real issue will come in comparing the memory extension boxes.

A UL listing of the PET will be secured by Commodore as soon as full production is reached, as per requirements of the Underwriter's Laboratory.

The software approaches are different on the two systems. The PET has built-in software – such as its editor, extra graphics, and full file system – to make the system easy to use. The PET operating system doesn't depend on a floppy disk for expansion. The PET has more graphics, and the graphics are more easily controlled than those on the TRS-80. Commodore and Radio Shack see the market in two different ways. A potential buyer needs to read the specifications of a PET and try one out in order to decide whether the significantly larger amount of software available on the PET means something to him as a person. I feel that the claims for the TRS-80 are misleading relative to their ability to store and manipulate data and files. I think that a user should really evaluate his need for data handling before buying any product in the computer field. It's not the number of tapes that make good software. It's what can be put in a program and what the program can do that has to be measured. Sometimes multiple low-cost or free items indicate a problem and not an opportunity.

Radio Shack's Don French replied:

I think that they're totally different type systems. They have a $795 8K system and our 16K system costs only $889 – a $94 difference. They have a different BASIC from ours, and they have a nonstandard keyboard. Our extended BASIC, which will be available by the end of the year, will do more than their 14K total system does. It's basically because of the differences in the Z-80 and the 6502. The 6502 has a faster instruction set at the same clock speed, but the Z-80 has a more memory-efficient instruction set, which means that you can provide a more powerful processor in memory size, which means that you can provide the same program in less memory with the Z-80 than you can in the 6502. It's just a trade-off in the type of system you want to design. Commodore chose the 6502 because it's made by a division of their company; Tandy Radio Shack chose the Z-80 just because we thought it was a more powerful unit.

The TRS-80 is listed with the Underwriter's Laboratory and the PET is not, which means that schools can buy our system, and some schools may not be able to buy a PET. You must have a UL listing to sell assembled electronic equipment in some areas, such as Los Angeles, Sacramento, and Oregon. In part we delayed introduction of our system until we acquired our full UL listing.

The TRS-80 is a two-piece system. Ours has a real keyboard on it, which means that with our system you don't have to buy the video screen. Many hobbyists have monitors already, and can use our $399 system directly with their own monitors and cassette recorders.

As for advantages of the PET over the TRS-80, there will be none as soon as we come out with our Level II BASIC. People owning a 4K system can replace chips to update to Level II BASIC at a cost of slightly over $100. The PET does have the IEEE bus, if you classify that as an advantage, but there's a very limited market for that type of bus structure.

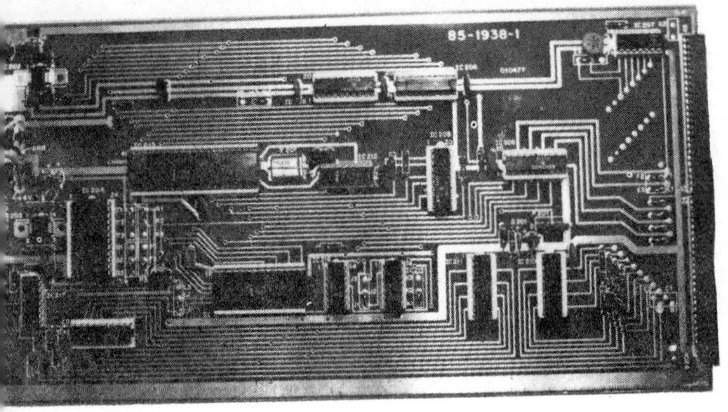

PHOTO 1 The H8 CPU board. 50-pin connector socket is at right; voltage regulator heat sink/card support bracket is at left.

PHOTO 2 The H8 power supply. Capacitor is covered with a shield after installation (see Photo 3). Slide switches at left select 120V/240V and regular/low-voltage operation.

A buyer's and builder's guide to the Heathkit H8 system

by Richard S. Arnold

Reprinted by permission of INTERFACE AGE from the June 1978 issue.

INTRODUCTION

The announcement last summer, and arrival last fall, of the Heathkit H8 microcomputer system have generated a great deal of speculation, discussion and controversy. This article will give you my analysis of the pros and cons of the H8 versus other popular microcomputer systems and a description of my experience in building this system. A separate article will cover what I feel are the strengths and weaknesses of the system in home, hobby and business applications.

THE H8 SYSTEM

The Heathkit H8 is an 8-bit general purpose microcomputer. It is housed in a black cabinet with a gray face; the cabinet measures 16"W x 17.5"D x 6.5"H. The basic computer includes the front panel/monitor and CPU cards, the mother board and power supply, and in that configuration weighs approximately 21 pounds.

The H8 uses an 8080A microprocessor running at 2.048 MHz. The CPU board (Photo 1) is supplied fully assembled and tested. Seven priority vectored interrupts are available, and DMA capability is included.

The H8 has a 10 amp power supply (Photo 2) which operates at either 120 or 240 VAC (switch selectable). An additional switch allows operation at normal or reduced input voltage. The power supply can handle 32K of RAM and 3 I/O cards in addition to the CPU and front panel cards. Cooling is by convection, rather than forced-air fan. The power supply uses a 77,000 μf filter capacitor for ripple-free DC output.

The motherboard (Photo 3) runs vertically along the right side of the cabinet. Ten slots are provided; the front panel and CPU boards occupy the first two, and the last slot is reserved for an expansion connector. Seven slots are thus available for memory, I/O and other cards.

Cards are mounted in the computer at an angle of about 30° back from the vertical; female connectors on the cards insert onto the male pins extending outward from the bus. Each card is additionally supported on its left-hand side by screws connecting it to the bottom of the cabinet and to a support bracket running along the top of the cards (Photo 4). The left edge of each card consists of a full-length aluminum heat sink, with screwholes at the top and bottom for mounting; each card contains its own on-board voltage regulators. The result is a very strong mounting system, which also provides very good heat dissipation.

Most boards are etched on both sides, most are solder masked, and all are fully screened with component designations. Sockets are provided for all IC's.

The H8 uses a 50-line bidirectional bus (see Figure 1). This bus is not compatible with the S100 unidirectional bus used in the Altair, Imsai, and other systems.

The H8 contains a resident monitor in 1Kx8 ROM. The monitor supports the front panel (Photo 5), which contains four status LEDs, nine 7-segment LED displays, and a 16-key keyboard.

The four status LEDs are labeled ION, MON, RUN, and PWR. The ION LED indicates that the CPU is accepting interrupts. The MON LED indicates that you have control from the front panel. The RUN LED indicates that the CPU is in a run condition. The PWR LED indicates that +5 volts is present at the front panel.

The nine 7-segment LED displays and the 16-key keyboard allow you to display, input and alter the contents

PHOTO 3 The H8 motherboard. Front panel connects to P1; CPU board plugs into P2. P10 is reserved for an expansion connector.

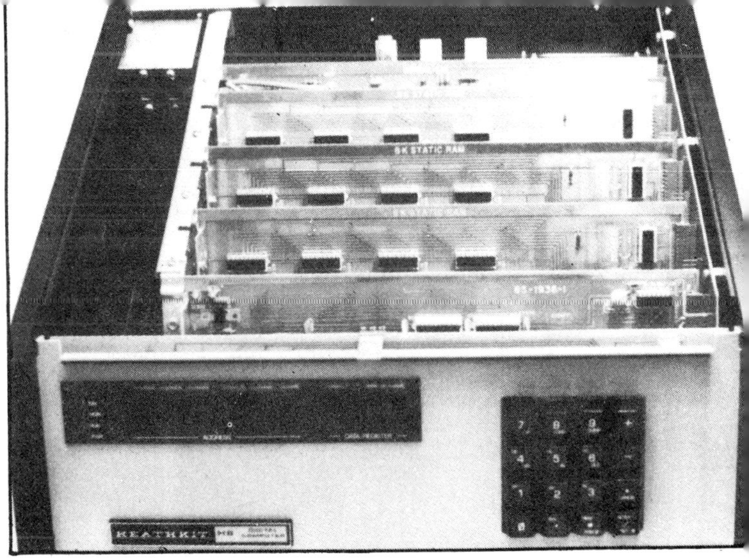

PHOTO 4 The completed H8 with top cover removed. The CPU, three 8K RAM boards, and the serial I/O and cassette interface boards are installed from front to back. Card mounting bracket is at top left.

of registers, the program counter, the accumulator, and any memory location. Data and addresses can also be displayed during input from tape. The front panel also allows you to load and dump to and from memory, and control input and output ports. Additionally, it allows monitoring of tape loads and dumps, resetting the computer, and executing programs. A CRC check is automatically performed during loads from tape.

You can single step through a program via the front panel keyboard, incrementing and decrementing memory locations as desired. An automatic repeat function allows you to step forward or backward at a 2.5 Hz rate if desired. A program may be stopped during execution, and control returned to the front panel monitor, without destroying information in the CPU registers or the serial and parallel ports.

A built-in speaker provides a useful audio signal. A short beep verifies each key stroke; a medium beep verifies successful address or data byte completion, and a long beep verifies a master reset or indicates an illegal command.

The nine 7-segment LEDs display address and data information in octal formal (Photo 6). Sixteen-bit numbers, such as memory addresses, are displayed as two 8-bit numbers in offset octal. Thus, the binary number 11 111 111 is displayed as 377, and the binary number 11 111 111 01 111 111 is displayed as 377 177.

Full keyboard debounce logic is provided. While a program is being executed, only the RST (reset) and RTM (return-to-monitor) keys will operate. Both of these commands require the simultaneous pressing of the indicated key and the 0 key, a nice feature to prevent inadvertent halting or destruction of a program. While a program is running, apart from these two commands the program itself may fully utilize the keyboard.

The sophistication of the front panel/monitor makes it very useful in debugging and modifying programs. It is a well-thought-out compromise between a front panel with nothing but power and reset keys versus one with rows of toggle switches and LEDs, it offers features not available with either of these other approaches.

Software is supplied with the H8 at no additional cost in audio cassette form. It is also available in paper tape form for an additional $20. An extended version of BASIC is available in cassette or paper tape form for an additional $10.

The assembly manual for the H8 is, as you would expect from Heath, very detailed and well organized. Also included are a separate operating manual for the H8 and a comprehensive reference manual for the various items of system software.

H8 ACCESSORIES

At this writing, Heath has three stand-alone accessories available: the H9 video terminal, the H10 paper tape reader/punch, and the H36, which is the DEC Writer II keyboard printer terminal. As I only have experience with the H9, which is described below, the other two peripherals will not be discussed.

Three H8 accessory cards are also currently available from Heath: a RAM board, a parallel interface board, and a serial I/O and cassette interface board.

The RAM board (Photo 7) is available in a 4K configuration, and can be expanded to 8K with a separately avail-

Pin	Signal	Pin	Signal
49	+ 8V	24	GND
48	+ 18V	23	MEMW
47	+ 18V	22	$\overline{02}$
46	$\overline{\text{ROM DISABLE}}$	21	I/OW
45	$\overline{A}$	20	RDYIN
44	$\overline{A}$	19	M1
43	$\overline{A}$	18	$\overline{D}$
42	$\overline{A}$	17	$\overline{D}$
41	$\overline{A}$	16	$\overline{D}$
40	$\overline{A}$	15	$\overline{D}$
39	$\overline{A}$	14	$\overline{D}$
38	$\overline{A}$	13	$\overline{D}$
37	$\overline{A}$	12	$\overline{D}$
36	$\overline{A}$	11	$\overline{D}$
35	$\overline{A}$	10	$\overline{D}$
34	$\overline{A}$	9	$\overline{INT}$
33	$\overline{A}$	8	$\overline{INT}$
32	$\overline{A}$	7	$\overline{INT}$
31	$\overline{A}$	6	$\overline{INT}$
30	$\overline{A}$	5	$\overline{INT}$
29	$\overline{RESET}$	4	$\overline{INT}$
28	MEMR	3	$\overline{INT}$
27	HOLD	2	18V
26	I OR	1	GND
25	HLDA	0	GND

Figure 1. The H8 50-line bus. Pin numbers correspond to those at each location along the motherboard (see Photo 3; pin no. 49 is at the top. Heath has reserved the right to change the designations of pins 8, 9, 18, 24, 25 and 27.

able chip set. The RAM board uses TMS-4044, 4Kx1 static chips. Maximum access time is given as 450 nsec. All inputs are 1 TTL load or less, the data out lines are fully buffered, and a full complement of bypass capacitors is included. Memory address assignment is selected by a jumper, along 8K boundaries. Like all H8 cards, each memory board contains its own voltage regulators. Current requirements are .75 amperes for 4K and 1.25 amperes for 8K.

The parallel interface board has three independent parallel ports, each with eight bits input and eight bits output plus universal handshake capability. Maximum transfer time is given as 390 μsec.

The serial I/O and cassette interface board (Photo 8) is used to connect the H8 to serial devices such as the H9 video terminal and also to one or two cassette recorders. The serial interface operates at data rates from 110 to 9600 baud, selected by jumper. Output levels, selected by jumpers, can be set to either 20 MA current loop or RS-232C compatible levels. The on-board USART can be programmed for 5- through 8-bit character length, one, one-half or two stop bits, and odd, even or no parity. The cassette interface data rate is jumper-selectable to 300 to 1200 baud. Recording and playback utilize the BYTE/"Kansas City" format. Control lines are provided for remotely starting and stopping two separate cassette units to allow separate recording and playback if desired. An on-board LED test circuit is provided for adjusting the PLL synthesizer and space detector in the cassette interface circuit.

Heathkit recommends, and will only assure proper operation of the cassette interface and the H8 software with, a Heath-supplied cassette recorder. This recorder is a GE model 3-5121; you may be able to purchase it elsewhere at a price less than the $55 quoted by Heath.

THE H9 VIDEO TERMINAL

The Heathkit H9 video terminal (Photo 9) is designed to match the H8 computer in appearance and performance. However, the H9 is a stand-alone peripheral, and can be used with any computer or in a time-sharing system.

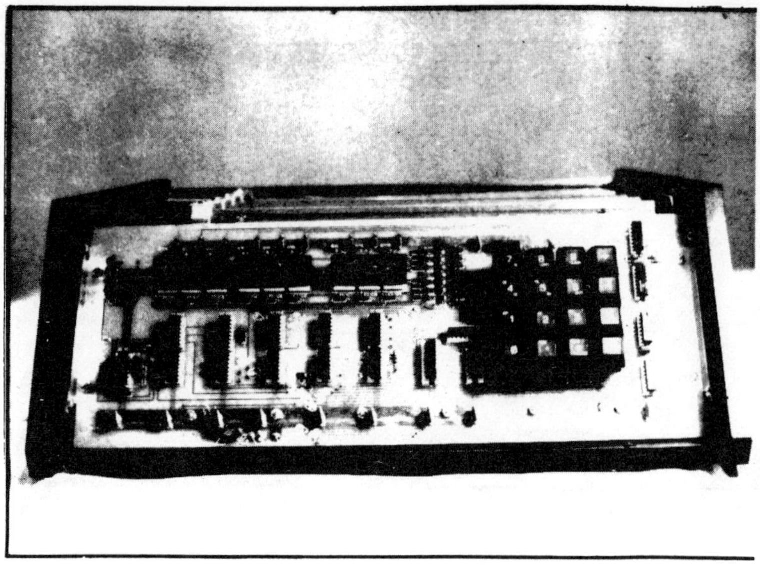

PHOTO 5 The H8 with front panel removed to show the front panel card.

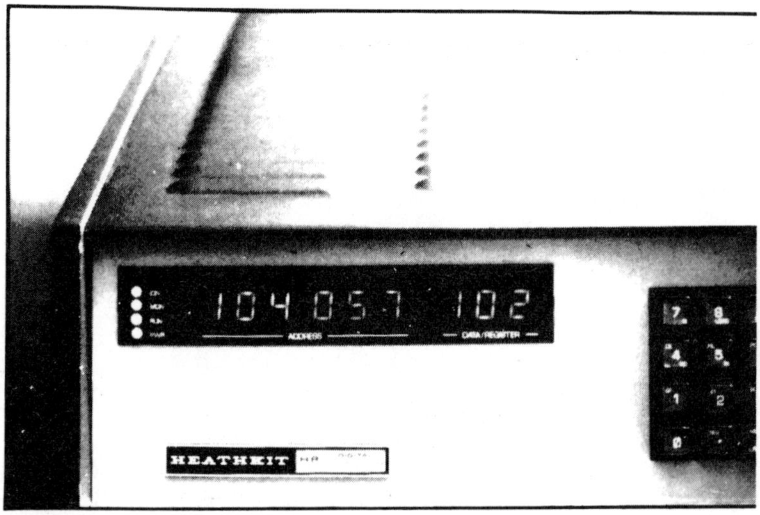

PHOTO 6 The H8 front panel display LEDs. RAM location 104 057_8 has contents 102_8.

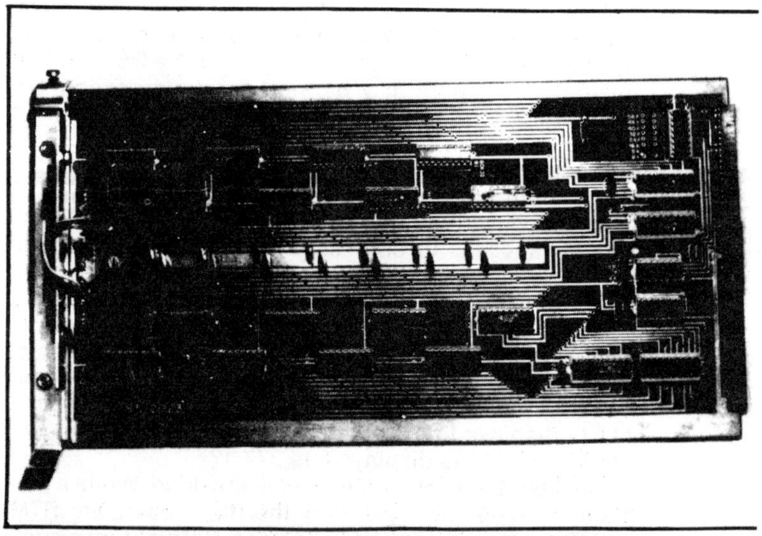

PHOTO 7 An H8 RAM board with 8K of static chips installed. Note bypall capacitors and double voltage regulators. Address selection jumper is at upper right.

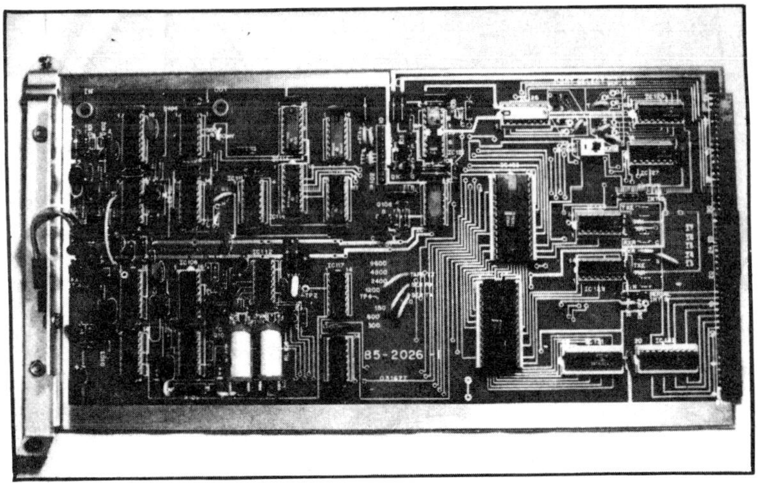

PHOTO 8 The H8 serial I/O and cassette interface board. Note the multitude of jumpers, described in text. The LED used for alignment is to the right of the second IC from the top in the left hand row.

PHOTO 9 The completed H9 terminal. Keyboard follows standard layout. Most special function keys are in the top row.

The H9 is housed in a black high-impact plastic cabinet with a gray faceplace surrounding the keyboard. The terminal measures 12½"H x 15⅝"W x 20¾"D; it weighs a hefty 32 pounds. The power supply is designed to operate from either 120 or 240 VAC. The dual primary windings of the power transformer may be wired in parallel for 120-volt operation or in series for 240-volt operation during construction of the kit.

The 12" diagonal CRT has 12 kV on its anode and provides a clear, bright display. There is no noticeable flickering and focus is uniform across the screen.

A jumper on the H9 video circuit board can be connected to select one of three separate display widths (normal, wide, and extra wide). The wide and extra wide settings are provided for use in low line voltage situations; the normal setting will provide the correct display width under normal circumstances.

Centering of the display is accomplished by rotating the centering magnets on the CRT yoke. The adjustment is not overly critical, and I was able to achieve a very good compromise between centering and linearity with little difficulty.

Potentiometers are mounted on the video circuit board for adjusting the focus, brightness and height of the CRT display. It is necessary to remove the cabinet shell to make these adjustments. If the height of the display is too great, the dots that form individual characters become more apparent, and thus a compromise has to be reached between display size and the sharpness of the characters.

The brightness and focus of the display are interrelated, and adjusting one will probably necessitate adjusting the other as well. Too bright a display will, over long periods of time, become tiring on your eyes; there also is a hazard of burning the CRT phosphor. When initially adjusting the display brightness, I was concerned that the CRT mask (which is attached to the cabinet shell and thus is not in place during adjustment) would significantly reduce display brightness when installed; this proved not to be the case.

Three display formats are available with the H9, switch selected from the keyboard. The usual format is 12 lines of 80 characters. A "short form," of four 12-line columns of 20 characters each, is useful when programming in assembly language or when writing BASIC programs that have short statements. A "plot" mode is also available. In this mode, a single line of text is displayed four times, once on each of the four bottom lines of the screen. The screen area above the bottom four lines is divided into 128 scan lines. A dash, one character wide, will appear above each of the characters displayed in the bottom four lines. The vertical position of the dash is proportional to the binary value of the 7-bit ASCII code for that character. Control characters, as well as standard letters, numbers and punctuation characters, will generate a dash at the appropriate position. In this mode, the cursor movements associated with different control characters do not take place. For example, a RETURN does not generate a return of the cursor but instead causes a dash to appear in the plot 13 lines above that location in the text.

The video terminal will display, and the keyboard will transmit, upper case alphabetic characters only. The display uses a 5x7 dot matrix; the cursor is a non-blinking underline appearing under the next space to be displayed.

The H9 keyboard is a 67-key ASCII keyboard. It contains the standard 52 ASCII keys, five cursor control keys and ten special function/mode keys. Keys are provided to move the cursor up, down, left, right and home. Unlike the others on the H9, these keys are not fully debounced, which is annoying. Additional keys erase the text from the current cursor location to the end of that line, erase all text on the screen and home the cursor; change the display format from 12x80 to 4x12x20 (short form); select whether or not the cursor automatically goes to the begining of the next line after a full line of text is typed; and select whether the display is to be scrolled upward after the first twelve lines of text are displayed. A REPEAT key will repeat the function of another key at a preset rate (3.7-, 7.5-, 15-, or 30 cps; jumper selectable). If the baud rate that has been selected is less than the repeat rate, the repeat function will operate at the slower rate. Additional keys are provided to transmit an entire page, select full or half duplex mode, take the terminal off line, and place the terminal in the PLOT mode.

If the screen has been filled, but the SCROLL key is not pushed in, the cursor will return to the start of the page location and blink. Until the page is erased or the SCROLL key is pushed in, all external inputs are disabled and data can only be transmitted out of the terminal by the keyboard. This feature, when used in conjunction with a paper tape reader/punch, allows program tapes to be reviewed quickly. The reader/punch can read the tape at its maximum speed, and after the last line has been written onto the display screen the tape will be stopped automatically. After the operator has reviewed the contents of the screen, pushing the ERASE PAGE key will cause another full page of data to be input automatically.

The terminal has a built-in audible tone generator to take the place of the old Teletype bell.

A baud rate key on the keyboard operates in conjunction with a switch on the rear panel to select the baud rate at which the terminal operates. When the key is pushed in, operation is at the rate set by the switch on the rear panel. This rear panel switch selects either 300 baud or a baud rate preset by an internal jumper. When the keyboard is released, the terminal operates at 110 baud.

The H9 contains a 1Kx8 RAM for storage of the characters to be displayed. This limits the display to the 12x80 format; however, there is room on the H8 RAM board for an additional 1Kx8 of RAM. This indicates that, hopefully, Heath will provide a retrofit in the future to expand the display to a 24x80 format. This would be a useful addition, particularly in word processing applications. A welcome companion modification would be the addition of lower case capability.

The H9 is interfaced to the computer via the terminal's internal serial interface. The H9 I/O circuit board can be wired via jumpers to operate in an RS-232C or TTY (20mA current loop, active or passive) mode. Word lengths of 5-, 6-, 7-, or 8-bit lengths can be jumper selected, as can be a parity bit (odd, even or none).

If a paper tape reader is in use, the reader control is not to be accomplished by connecting the reader to the parallel I/O of the computer, the tape reader can be connected to the H9 and controlled by it.

The connecting terminals on the rear panel of the H9 (and the H8 as well) are unique to Heath, not the 22-pin EIA standard terminals. The H9 is supplied with a very detailed assembly manual and a separate comprehensive operating manual.

COMPARING THE H8 WITH OTHER POPULAR MICROCOMPUTER SYSTEMS

By this point you should have a general idea of what the H8 has to offer. Now let's compare it with other popular microcomputer systems currently on the market.

By necessity, I will only discuss what I feel are the major characteristics of the H8 and its competitors. Some of these will surely seem more important than others to different readers, and I am sure I have left out someone's favorite criterion. Within the limits of my time and expertise, I'll be happy to correspond with anyone concerning any point I've slighted or omitted.

The key word here is "compromise." The H8, like every microcomputer, is indeed a compromise in almost every facet of its design and operation. Perhaps a good deal of the controversy over the H8's departure from the designs of other manufacturers stems from a lack of recognition of this fact. With that in mind, let's analyze the major points of comparison.

THE H8 BUS

As surely every reader knows by now, the H8 uses a 50-line bus. This is incompatible with the S100 bus used in most other 8080A systems. Heath spokesmen have stated that the S100 bus is an older design, has many unnecessary signals, is noisy, has timing problems, and is expensive to implement because of the circuit board edge connectors involved. Rather than get into that controversy, I'd like instead to explore the impact of the H8's unique bus from a practical perspective.

Using a computer with a non-S100 bus means, today, that you are relying heavily on the primary manufacturer. You can't as readily look to secondary sources for special circuit boards, replacement boards if the primary manufacturer isn't around, or lower priced boards which perform the same functions as those supplied by the primary manufacturers. This may mean higher costs (because of the lack of competition), delays in obtaining certain capabilities (because the boards aren't available from any manufacturer), and increased down time (because equivalent boards are not on the market).

In short, before deciding to purchase any non-S100 bus computer, you should look very carefully at the level of support you can expect to obtain for the system. This means support from the marketplace in general — both the primary manufacturer and also present and anticipated second sources.

There are today over half a dozen major non-S100 microcomputer systems on the market. Some have been around longer than others; in the case of the more established ones, we are already seeing a growth in the second-source market availability of circuit boards and peripherals designed to be compatible with these computers. Indeed, at this writing there are already second-source suppliers of both memory boards and CPU/floppy disk units specifically designed to be compatible with the Heath bus. Given Heathkit's size, its tradition of user support, the number of current and projected H8 users and the still-explosive growth of the microcomputer market, there seems little doubt but that the number of second-source suppliers (and the variety of H8 compatible boards and peripherals) will continue to grow. Heath itself is planning to introduce a floppy disk (H17) in June and additional accessory boards later.

Their motto is "We won't let you fail" . . .and they mean it. The service turnaround time I've experienced has been excellent . . .

Whether or not the S100 bus is now or continues to be the "standard of the industry" can be a topic for lively discussion. The point here, however, is whether the H8 bus will be supported by Heath and others. I feel that it already is being adequately supported, and will continue to be.

DOCUMENTATION AND SUPPORT

Heath's well-deserved reputation for superb assembly manuals and documentation has continued with its entry into the microcomputer field.

The assembly manuals carry "step-by-step" instructions to the extreme. If anything, the instructions are so detailed as to invite skipping over the more obvious steps. (This can be a mistake — believe me, there is a reason for Heath's going to the expense and trouble of spelling things out the way they do.) The manuals include schematic diagrams, circuit descriptions, troubleshooting guides, X-ray views and section-by-section test procedures. In addition, you can call Heathkit for help, either at the factory or at one of their over 50 retail sotres, and if it comes to it take the kit back in for diagnosis and repair by Heath technicians. Their motto is "We won't let you fail," and from what I can tell they mean it. The service turnaround time I've experienced has been excellent, and in each case the technician has made sure I understood what the problems were. This level of support is a far cry, regrettably, from that provided by many other microcomputer manufacturers.

Upon opening the H8 carton, the first thing you'll see is a notice: "The H-8 Computer requires a minimum level of programming knowledge and accessory equipment to be fully utilized. Before unpacking and commencing assembly, please review the manuals. If you find the H-8 is not suitable for your purposes at this time, the kit may be returned prepaid for credit or a refund by contacting Heath Company. . ." In other words, Heath has taken the remarkable step of inviting H8 purchasers to carefully analyze the system's assembly, operation and documentation, *after they've bought the kit,* to see if it's what they want. If it's not, they can return it (before it's unpacked and assembled, of course) for a full refund!

Microcomputers are high-technology products. Just because you've built a stereo tuner, and fixed it with a VOM, does not by itself qualify you to build and troubleshoot a unit of this complexity. Your success in building a system, debugging it, putting it to use in your intended applications and deriving any educational benefits in the process are in large part a function of the documentation and support provided by the manufacturer and retailer. In these areas, Heath and its H8 have to be viewed as the benchmark.

COST

A 16K H8/H9/cassette system can be purchased for approximately $1,500, depending upon whether you order by mail or purcahse the system at one of Heath's retail stores. While this does not make the H8 the cheapest microcomputer available, its price does compare favorably with other equivalent systems. A typical savings is $400-$500.

At the moment, Heath accessory cards are somewhat more expensive than equivalent cards available for S100 systems from second-source suppliers; for example, a Heath 8K RAM card currently costs $235 by mail and $250 from a Heath retail store. Again, however, second-source suppliers ar already beginning to undercut these prices; a 12K RAM card is, at this writing, being offered for the same $235 price. This same trend has occurred with respect to other systems, and should become even more pronounced as more small manufacturers begin to make H8 boards available.

HARDWARE

The H8, of course, uses the 8080A CPU. "Newer" microprocessors, such as the Z80, are available, and some commentators have questioned Heath's use of the "older" 8080A

Rather than depating the merits of one CPU versus another, I will simply point out that these newer CPUs probably will be made available configured for the H8 bus. Indeed, one supplier already offers the Z80 on a card for the H8

Heath's circuit boards are not particularly dense. As with the 12K RAM board already on the market, we can expect Heath and/or others to make better use of the space available on each circuit card.

RAM address assignments, and most I/O options, are selected by jumpers rather than switches on the H8 and H9 cards. Although this may be less convenient, it is less expensive. As a practical matter, most users will not be changing these jumpers very often if at all. I feel that Heath made the right compromise here between cost and convenience. Why pay for features you're unlikely to use?

One area where Heath may have compromises incorrectly is in the front panel knobs for the H8 and H9. The knobs are blank, and the builder has to attach pregummed paper labels to them. While probably less expensive than supplying knobs which are already marked, this approach results in a less professional appearance.

One minor annoyance when using the Heath-recommended cassette recorder is that the remote motor control cable from the H8 has to be disconnected to allow the cassette to be rewound. Upon completion of a load or dump, the H8 software automatically turns the recorder motor off. This can be remedied by modifying the recorder or cable to install an override switch. Another solution, and the one I use when running in BASIC, is to type in the VERIFY command from the terminal. This reactivates the recorder without destroying the program and allows the tape to be rewound.

All Heathkit software employs "command completion." This feature examines each character as it is typed on the console keyboard. When sufficient information is received . . . the command is . . . completed.

The connecting cable between the H8 and H9 is, if assembled per the Heath manual, only 4 feet long. I haven't tried operating with a longer one, but at the H8/H9 600 baud interface standard a lengthier cable would seem to be feasible.

SOFTWARE

Heathkit supplies without charge a complete software package with the H8. This package consists of the "PAM-8" panel monitor, the "BUG-8" console debugger, the "TED-8" text editor, the "HASK-8" assembly, and the Benton Harbor BASIC. Extended Benton Harbor BASIC is also available at a cost of $10. This software was developed for Heath by the Wintek Corporation.

All Heath software products which use a console terminal include a console terminal driver module which is located in RAM beginning at 040 100 octal. Similarly, all tape handling is accomplished through a common tape handling package. Figures 2 and 3 show the memory and I/O maps for the H8.

All Heath software is supplied on distribution tapes. Each item of software can be user-configured and then dumped, as configured, to a tape which should be used on a day-to-day basis.

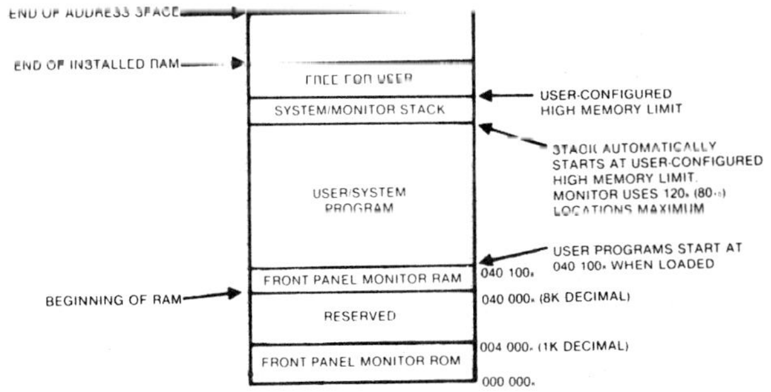

Figure 2. A map of the H8 memory. The high memory limit may be user-configured to coincide with the upper end of installed RAM, or may be set lower to reserve RAM for user-specified applications.

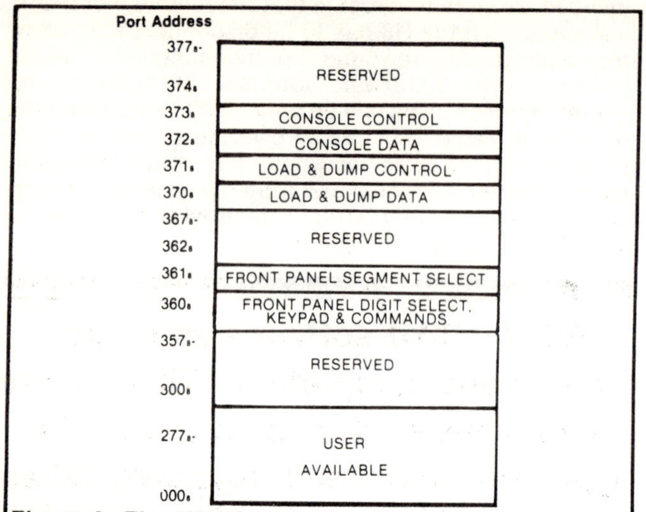

Figure 3. The H8 I/O port map. Ports 000 through 277 (octal) may be utilized by the user as desired.

When a master tape is loaded, the user can configure the software as follows:

1. Determine whether or not a new line is automatically to be generated when the print head or cursor moves past the last column of the terminal.
2. Determine what character (normally CONTROL H, 00008 decimal) generates a backspace.
3. Determine the width of the console terminal as seen by the software, e.g., the maximum number of characters per line.
4. Set the high memory limit. This enables the user to reserve a portion of high memory which won't be used by the software. When you install additional memory in the H8, be sure to reconfigure your software tapes!
5. Determine whether or not the software should input and output lower case letters, e.g., configuring the only software to work with upper/lower case or upper case only terminals.
6. Set the number of nulls which are to be inserted by the software following a carriage return. Slow terminals may require several pad characters; video terminals and many teleprinters will require none.
7. Determine what character (normally 127 decimal) generates a RUBOUT.

Following configuration, a memory image dump to tape of the configured product can be made under terminal control. Software patches are readily inserted by loading a configured or master tape, altering memory contents through the H8 front panel monitor, and then dumping the memory image containing the patches onto a new tape. Heath supplies patches for using an ASR console as the main load/dump port and using a 110-baud console terminal such as a teleprinter (which requires an extra stop bit on the ASCII character sent by the H8).

All Heathkit software employs "command completion." This feature examines each character as it is typed on the console keyboard. When sufficient information is received to uniquely identify one particular command, the command is automatically completed. For example, in BASIC, the letters LOA are sufficient to uniquely identify the command LOAD, and after the A is typed, BASIC supplies the letter D and a trailing space. This is a fine feature for the beginner and also for someone who is intimately familiar with all the commands. For those people, this feature saves time. However, everyone else winds up losing time typing backspaces to correct such statements as LOAD D. Heath does not anticipate issuing patches to disable this feature because it is so embedded in the software.

The PAM-8 panel monitor permanently resides in ROM located in the lower 1024 bytes of memory (000 00 to 004 000 octal). It also uses the first 64 bytes of RAM (040 000 to 040 100 octal). The H8 front panel is assigned I/O ports 360 and 361. PAM-8 contains the fundamental tape loading routines which are used to load all other software. The software manual includes a full listing of the source code for the panel monitor and also the console driver.

Upon power-up, PAM-8 automatically determines the upper limit of continuous RAM (without destroying memory contents) and passes control to the front panel. A program can then be loaded from tape by pressing the LOAD key on the front panel keyboard. When a successful load is completed, a short beep will sound. Program execution then occurs upon pressing the GO key.

The BUG-8 console debugger allows the user to write, load, execute and debug machine language programs in the H8 in octal, decimal or ASCII format working through a separate keyboard/CRT console terminal. The contents of memory locations and the CPU registers can be examined and altered, break points can be set and cleared, programs can be executed (in single steps if desired), and programs can be loaded from and dumped onto magnetic or paper tape. The BUG-8 resides in 3K of RAM, starting at 040 100 octal. The breakpointing feature allows the user to execute several instructions in a program and then return control to the console debugger for analysis and/or modification.

The TED-8 text editor is designed primarily to prepare source code for use by the HASL-8 assembler. However, it can also be used to prepare and edit any textual material such as reports and manuscripts. The TED-8 requires approximately 4K of RAM plus 200 additional bytes of working space. An H8 with 8K of RAM therefore has room for approximately 300 lines of a well-documented program or approximately 175 lines of solid text. A compression technique is used to reduce the amount of buffer used by blanks.

The text editor does not appear to have the capability of processing text in upper and lower case simultaneously. When used with the H8 terminal, this is not a deficiency since the H9 operates in upper case only. However, users with U/L case terminals cannot use the TED-8 as supplied for report writing and word processing. Hopefully, Heath will remedy this deficiency in the future.

The HASL-8 (what a name!) two-pass assembler runs in approximatley 8K of RAM. It assembles the source listings generated by the TED-8 text editor; however, the text editor and assembler are not linked together, and (unlike the case with the H11 software) no linking program is supplied. Therefore, the programmer must often go back and forth from one to the other, which is time-consuming and can be annoying.

Benton Harbor BASIC, and Extended Benton Harbor BASIC, are interpreters requiring 8K and 12K of RAM respectively. Both BASICs accept real and integer numbers and also recognize exponential notation. Integers must lie in the range of 0 to 65535; real numbers must lie in the range of approximately 10^{-38} to 10^{+37}. Both BASICs are internally floating point with approximately 6.9 digits of accuracy. Printout is in decimal form if the number lies in the range 0.1 to 999999; otherwise the exponential form is used. Truncation to six places will occur if necessary. Numbers may be positive or negative. Multiple statements are allowed on one line.

Both BASICs include a "command mode" of operation. This allows entering statements without line numbers, which are executed immediately upon receipt of a carriage return. The command mode allows the H8 to be used as a calculator and provides a simple way to test and debug programs.

Extended Benton Harbor BASIC has a number of additional features:

- Faster Operation
- Character string manipulation
- Subscribed variables and subscripted string variables
- Exponentiation
- Automatic generation of program line numbers
- Single-command deletion of blocks of lines of program statements
- Selective clearing of named variables, arrays or user-defined functions
- Turning the hardware clock on and off (to increase execution speed approximately 11%)
- Controlling the size of a print zone
- Controlling the front panel (LED display)
- Setting up a GOSUB routine which is automatically entered upon typing CONTROL-B on the terminal
- Display of amount of free memory and the amount of memory used for text, variables and arrays, FOR loops, GOSUBs, STRINGs, and working space
- Listing of one or a specific group of program lines
- Delaying program execution for a specified length of time
- Returning the maximum or minimum value of a series of expressions
- Returning the tangent of an argument.

Extended Benton Harbor BASIC also generates more explicit error statements and additional error statements pertaining to its unique features.

A new version of Extended B.H. BASIC, which should be available by the time you read this, will include GET, PUT, FLOAD and FDUMP commands. This version will allow the use of separate data files, a most desirable feature.

Both BASICs monitor user spelling. As a command is typed, invalid letter combinations are rejected and a terminal bell is rung.

Although some B.H. BASIC commands are a bit different from most other BASICs, with a little practice these can be anticipated when entering programs written on another machine. The difference I've encountered most often is with the INPUT statement; a response to a string INPUT must be enclosed in quotes. Extended B.H. BASIC offers a LINE INPUT statement which doesn't require this.

Heath's BASICs are not the fastest interpreters on the market, but their speed should be sufficient for most applications. Nor are they compatible with other BASICs, because they employ the PAM-8 monitor subroutines.

Heath supplies an extensive software reference manual in a looseleaf binder. The binder is large enough to insert the operating manuals for the H8 and H9 as well, thus creating a single notebook containing all the reference materials you are likely to need.

Separate sections are included in the software reference manual for the PAM-8, BUG-8, TED-8, HASL-8, and BASIC. Individual tables of contents and indexes accompany each section.

The BASIC section of the manual divides statements into three types — those valid only in the command mode (LOAD, DUMP, RUN, etc.); those valid in either the command or the program mode (CLEAR, DIM, FOR/NEXT, GOSUB/RETURN, GOTO, POKE, etc); and those valid only in the program mode (DATA, INPUT, etc.). Predefined functions (INT, PEEK, RND, etc.) are described separately. An appendix briefly summarizes each statement and function.

The statements and functions are organized alphabetically in the subsections and the appendix, but in both cases the breakdown is into the three different types of statements and then functions. The only complete alphabetical listing of all statements and functions together is contained in the index. As a result, working with the statement POKE and the function PEEK, for example, requires flipping back and forth between a number of different pages.

The software reference manual is intended to be just that. Examples are included, as are cross-references to related instructions. However, as the manual's introduction makes clear, it is not designed to teach you programming. Heathkit has an excellent series of continuing education courses available; as of this writing, they include one on BASIC programming. You should be prepared to look there, or to the multitude of books and magazines published by others in the microcomputer field, to learn computer programming. However, the software reference manual does an excellent job of fulfilling the purpose for which it was designed.

Overall, the Heath software provided with the H8 is well-suited to the needs of the user. Like the 50-line bus, the H8 software is unique to Heath — it cannot be used with other systems and the H8 cannot use software designed for those systems. Thus, software support for the H8 is just as critical as the hardware support factor described earlier. However, my conclusion here is the same as before — the current level of software support is excellent, and should continue to be so.

BUILDING THE H8

Building the H8 is certainly not an overnight project, nor should it be undertaken by a first-time kit builder without some supervision and assistance being available. On the other hand, anyone who has (or is willing to acquire) the ability to solder correctly and who approaches the task with normal amounts of patience and attention to detail can expect to successfully complete the kit.

Building the basic H8 took approximately 14½ hours. Of that time, approximately two hours were spent in checking parts against parts lists and performing the prescribed tests of completed subassemblies. Building each 8K RAM board took two hours, including the time required for parts list checks and board checkout. The serial I/O and cassette interface board required approximately 6½ hours to complete, including one-half hour spent in checking parts and testing and aligning the circuit. The complete computer, including 24K RAM and the serial I/O and cassette interface, therefore required approximately 27 hours to assemble. To borrow a phrase from the car ads, your assembly time may vary based upon your level of experience.

The most important investment you can make to assure success in constructing the H8 — and the H9 also — is a good soldering iron, complete with a stand *which includes a cleaning sponge*. Every ten connections or less, be sure and clean the iron tip — and make this a habit which you follow rigorously. If you don't do this, you'll face the exasperating task of locating and resoldering cold solder joints caused by flux buildup on the iron tip. One bad connection can cause a byte of RAM to function improperly, and the problem may only surface when a program is running at full CPU speed.

You should build the basic H8 first, memory boards (or at least one) next, and then the interface board(s). The checkout procedures for each assume they've been built in this order. If you are also building an H9, it should be constructed before the H8 serial board.

A 65-page assembly manual is included with the basic H8; separate assembly manuals cover the RAM and I/O boards. In typical Heathkit fashion, the manuals are comprehensive and clear. Parts are unpacked from separate packages only as needed, and parts lists are supplied at the beginning of each section of assembly.

Pictorial layouts, schematic diagrams and X-ray views are provided, either in the manuals or separately. Not a single part was missing from any of the H8, H9 or accessory board packages — a remarkable record.

The H8 chassis and motherboard are assembled first. The motherboard includes connectors for all ten positions on the bus. Each 50-pin position consists of two 25-pin male plugs. The Heath-recommended procedure, which should be followed here and throughout the kit when installing all plugs, IC sockets and connectors, is to solder one or two pins at each end and then recheck the plug to be sure it's tight against the board and perpendicular to it. It is important to rigorously follow this procedure — unsoldering a 25-pin plug to realign it is, at best, something to avoid!

As the chassis is constructed, the power supply is assembled at the same time. Power supply components not mounted on the chassis are contained on the motherboard.

The left and right cabinet side panels are black plastic. These should be handled with care, as scratching them will remove the black finish. They are mounted via retaining nuts pushed into holes in the panels. Some nuts are mounted flush; others are mounted (using a washer as a guide) extending slightly above the panel surface. If the retaining nuts are not installed precisely as directed, the panels cannot be properly mounted.

The next step is assembling the front panel circuit board. When installing transistors and LEDs, take care to install each lead in the correct hole. Most (but not all) transistors have the emitter, base and collector leads marked on the body. Check that the flat edge of each transistor and LED lamp corresponds with the outline screened on the circuit board.

Disk capacitors should be prepared before inserting them into a board. The leads should be cleaned of insulation with a needle-nose pliers; failure to do so can result in poor (or no) solder connections.

When installing the 16 push button switches, follow a procedure similar to that used with plugs and sockets — position the switch firmly against the board, solder the two pins, and then recheck the alignment and resolder the pins if necessary. After all switches are mounted, knobs are installed. Then, pregummed paper labels are installed on the knobs. Do not attempt to remove a label which has been installed on the wrong knobs; instead, move the knob itself to the correct position. While tedious, care taken here in aligning the switches and installing the labels will pay off in a professional appearance.

Your first exposure to preparing cables and connectors comes at this point. Before soldering the spring connectors to the cable wires, analyze which way — facing up or down — the connectors should be installed. This is best done by matching the cable against the connector shell with the right color wire at the corresponding end of the shell. Spring connectors are then soldered on so that their flat edges will be on the bottom (hole) side of the connector shell when inserted. A large heat sink or a set of spring loaded pliers is very helpful in holding cable wires while soldering on the connectors. Apply solder *very* sparingly — avoid getting solder in the tab or on the spring portion of a connector. If you are building the H9 also, refer to the instructions on page 13 of the H9 manual for a better description of the proper installation procedure and also for a description of how to remove connectors from the shell after they are inserted. If you are building the serial I/O board, look also at page 21 of its manual. It may be easier to hold everything steady if you insert each wire of a cable in the connector shell after its spring connector is attached, rather than soldering all spring connectors on at once.

When installing the 7-segment LED sockets, and later the LEDs themselves, take some time to insure that all nine are aligned parallel. As with the front panel switches, this will enhance the appearance of the completed unit.

When installing ICs, carefully follow the procedure giving for handling the MOS ones. Read the instructions all the way through first and make sure you understand them; failure to follow them can cause destruction of the IC through static electricity.

The CPU board is supplied fully assembled and tested. All that needs to be done is to install it and perform the initial checkout.

Final assembly consists of installing the front panel and some support brackets. I suggest installing the display window, and perhaps the entire front panel, later, after checkout of the H8 with a RAM board installed. This will save removing the panel if any components need to be replaced or wiring errors corrected on the face of the front panel circuit board. Saving the window until after the panel is installed also avoids getting fingerprints on the back of it in the process.

The last step in the assembly manual refers you to the H8 operating manual for the initial test routine. The test routine didn't work — in fact, nothing did! I took the kit back to the local Heathkit store; five days and one red face (mine) later I picked it up. One IC was bad and one LED socket was intermittent; this saved me any service charge. However, the main problem was what is euphemistically called "operator error." Had I analyzed the test routine carefuly, I would have seen that it involves loading data into memory locations. In other words, the routine can't be performed without RAM installed! Once a RAM board was built and inserted, everything was fine.

The end result of the initial test routine is a series of characters on the nine display LEDs. With a little imagination, the message is "YOUR H8 IS UP AND RUNNING (beep beep). I won't tell you how long I let this message repeat itself, or the reactions of other members of my household to this end result of the hours I had spent locked away in my workroom!

PHOTO 10 Underside view of the H9. Keyboard is at left. TPU board is at center top; RAM and counter board is below it. Character generator board is at bottom right.

H8 ACCESSORY CARDS

As I haven't built the parallel I/O board, I will only discuss construction of the RAM and serial I/O and cassette interface boards.

H8 RAM BOARD

Assembling this board is really nothing more than installing IC sockets, bypass capacitors, sockets connecting the board with the H8 motherboard, and jumpers and miscellaneous components in that order.

When installing sockets connecting the board with the motherboard, follow the same procedure as with other sockets — solder the pins at each end, check alignment, and only then solder the rest.

The basic board comes with ICs and sockets for 4K of RAM. Another 4K (ICs and sockets), available as an accessory kit, may be installed initialy or later. The instructions for the board and the accessory kit are coordinated to cover either alternative.

If the board is your first memory board, it is assigned an address of 8K by a jumper. Otherwise, assignment is at 56K. The manual then directs you to the 8K address memory test routine in the H8 operation manual or the 56K address test routine in the board manual itself. If you follow the board manual test routine, memory is then reassigned to the appropriate address. Since memory must be continuous from 8K up, only one 4K board can be installed, and it must be located at the high end of continuous memory.

H8 SERIAL I/O AND CASSETTE INTERFACE BOARD

By this time, you'll be an old hand at assembling H8 cards. I do suggest that you annotate the manual, either at the beginning or on the appropriate pages, as to which jumper options (audio output level, serial and tape receive and transmit baud rates, one or two tape recorders, and EIA/TTY type signals) you have selected.

The board includes a logic probe circuit for adjusting the PLL and space detector. The logic probe LED can later be used (with the H8 top removed) for monitoring tape input data. I found the PLL adjustment, which is accomplished by rotating the potentiometer until the LED completely stops flickering, to be difficult. It requires a very fine hand on the screwdriver! You might try rotating the pot several times to free up its movement if you have the same problem.

After finding the proper settings of the volume and tone controls on the cassette recorder, you should mark those settings on the controls. It's easy to disturb the settings in the process of connecting and disconnecting the motor control line from the recorder.

If you build this card before your terminal is ready, remember to go back and perform the "terminal test" in the checkout section of the board assembly manual later on.

BUILDING THE H9

Assemblying the H9 took a total of 27 hours, the same amount of time as required for the complete H8 with all

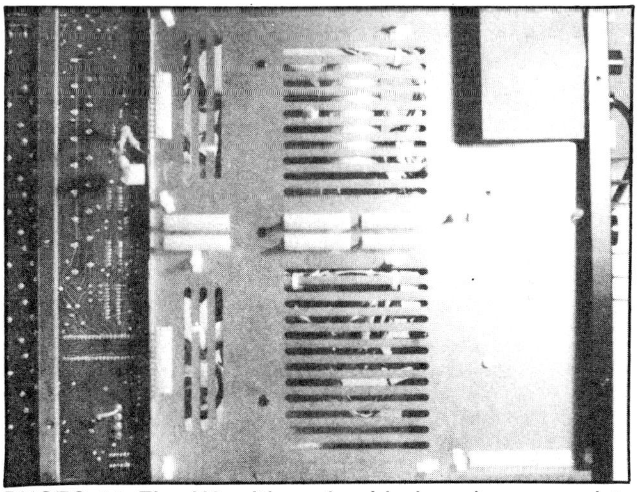

PHOTO 11 The H9 with underside boards removed to show mounting pins. These pass through to wiring harnesses atop the chassis.

PHOTO 12 Rear top view of the H9. I/O board is at left; video board is at right. Controls for focus, brightness and height are visible at the top of the video board.

its accessory cards. The H9 seemed more involved, perhaps because there is no finished cabinet until the end! On reflection, however, building the H9 is just as straightforward, and no more difficult, than building the H8.

The 140-page assembly manual is accompanied by a multitude of separate sheets of pictorials, X-ray views, schematics, etc. My guess is that this manual was prepared after the one for the H8; it has better instructions and pictorials for such things as assembly of cable connectors. The H9 kit also includes a plastic magnifying glass for finding solder bridges, and a better IC puller. If you're building the H8 and H9, you should use these items for both kits.

The H9 contains separate circuit boards for the power supply, character generator, video circuit, keyboard, RAM and counter, I/O interface and the timing and processing unit. The RAM and counter, TPU and character generator boards are mounted underneath the chassis (Photo 10). These boards plug onto connectors which pass through the chassis (Photo 11) and mate with sockets on the main wiring harnesses. The power supply, video and I/O boards mount above the chassis behind the CRT (Photo 12).

In assembling the chassis, follow the same precautions as with the H8 regarding the black plastic side panels. If you liked preparing the H8 cable connectors, you'll love the H9's! Although considerable work is involved in soldering what seems like an endless number of cable spring connectors, the main cabling is precut and assembled. This significantly reduces point-to-point wiring, which would have been a considerable task.

Construction proceeds through the power supply circuit board, character generator board, video circuit board, keyboard, RAM/counter board and I/O circuit board. The last board is the TPU, and the fact that it is supplied assembled and tested is at that point most welcome.

The H9 keyboard, like the H8 keypad, is assembled by installing switches, then blank knobs, and then pre-gummed labels on the knobs. You should follow the same precautions as with the H8 regarding switch alignment and label installation. I found a few of the switches to have high resistance or to be intermittent when depressed; these were quickly replaced by the Heath factory.

Some but not all of the circuit boards in my H9 kit were fully solder masked. The circuit board for the keyboard is only etched on the underside. This requires the builder to install a number of jumpers, some of them several inches long, on top of the board. This could have been eliminated by Heath's using a double sided circuit board here, similar to many of the other boards.

In checking out the video circuit board, a problem developed. Instead of 12 lines of 80 characters per the test procedure, my display was of 12x80 solid blocks. After rechecking all boards then installed, upon turning the unit back on there was no video at all.

Upon the advice of local Heath personnel, I went ahead and assembled the rest of the H9 so it could be checked out as a unit. It developed that the horizontal output transistor was shorted, and there were two bad ICs on the I/O board. However — red-faced time again — I had installed two ICs loose and had connected one main harness wire to the wrong pin of a socket. After the unit was repaired by Heath it functioned perfectly.

After two months of use, the H9 CRT display brightness suddenly dropped significantly. This was quickly repaired by Heath at no charge to me. The problem was caused by a leaky capacitor on the video board which resulted in low voltage on grid 2 of the CRT. I was able to have the terminal repaired while I waited at the local Heath store — you couldn't ask for better service.

SUMMARY

If you want to build your computer yourself, in my opinion Heath must be the standard against which to measure. Although considerable time was involved, I found assembling the H8 and H9 to be straightforward, relatively simple and really enjoyable. After 54 hours of work and over 6,000 solder connections, I had a complete, fully operational, professional-looking computer system which I could say I built myself. (That impresses neighbors no end; don't let them know how simple it really is with instruction manuals of this calibre.)

I am completely satisfied, and indeed delighted, with my H8 system. It does everything Heath says it will, and does it very well. Anyone in the market for a microcomputer should give careful consideration to the H8; it represents a very well thought out approach, from beginning to end.

The remarkable Apple-II

by Robert J. Bishop

Kilobaud Magazine, November 1978 (Reprinted by Permission)

In 1976, after many years of dreaming about it, I finally got my first personal computer. At that time, a rather unknown little company by the name of Apple Computer advertised their Apple-I system for $666.66. It consisted of a 6502 microprocessor, 4K bytes of RAM, power supply and all the other necessary electronics. But most important, it came fully assembled.

I phoned the company to inquire about ordering an Apple-I. It was during this phone conversation that I was told of their upcoming Apple-II computer, a system that would display not only alphanumerics, but also color and high-resolution graphics! But this new computer was not scheduled to be marketed until around November 1976, so I began playing the waiting game.

Then, around late September, I received word that, because of difficulties, the Apple-II would not become available until sometime in 1977. Tired of waiting, I went ahead and bought an Apple-I. Later, in the summer of 1977, when the Apple-II became available, I was able to receive a fair trade-in allowance on my Apple-I system towards the purchase of an Apple-II.

The Hardware

Probably the most impressive feature of the Apple-II computer is its color-graphics capability. This graphics mode can be operated either as a 40 x 40 element display with room at the bottom of the TV screen for four lines of text, or as a 40 x 48 element display with no text. Each raster element can be set to any one of 16 colors. Since the color-graphics display buffer coincides with the text buffer (hex 0400 to about 07FF), a system with as little memory as 4K can utilize this color graphics feature.

In addition to this 16-color low-resolution graphics, the Apple-II also has four-color (black, white, green and purple) higher-resolution graphics. (It was actually this HIRES (high resolution) graphics capability, not the LORES color graphics, that prompted me to get an Apple-II.)

As with the lower-resolution 16-color graphics mode, the HIRES graphics can be operated either with space for four lines of text at the bottom of the TV screen or with no text. Since HIRES graphics requires almost 8K bytes for the display buffer, it cannot be used effectively with systems having less than 12K bytes of memory. (Actually, 16K minimum is *recommended*.)

In its literature Apple Computer, Inc., says, "... Apple-II can generate a high-resolution (280 H x 192 V) graphics display in four colors. ..." This statement is somewhat misleading, if not erroneous. It implies that you can generate a 280 x 192 dot display in which each dot can be set to any one of four colors.

Actually, the computer displays 280 x 192 dots, half of which can be either green or black, while the other half can be either purple or black. Thus, on a color TV the resolution is only 140 x 192 with four colors per raster coordinate; on a black-and-white TV, the resolution is 280 x 192 with only two colors (black or white) per raster coordinate.

The Apple-II can, of course, also display text without graphics. In this mode it has a capacity of 24 40-character lines. Text characters can be displayed as either normal video (white on black), inverse video (black on white) or flashing. And since the display is completely under sofware control, text can be placed anywhere on the screen in any order and in any video mode. (The Apple-I, by comparison, only allowed for a slow serial display of normal video and had no graphics capability at all.)

In addition to visual output, the Apple-II has a built in speaker, which is accessible via software. This is useful for producing games with sound effects, generating computer music, etc.

Also built onto the Apple-II board are eight peripheral board connectors for interfacing to the outside world, and a game-paddle connector capable of handling up to four input paddles. (Two paddles come supplied with the computer system.) The game paddles are, of course, nothing more than potentiometers; but the Apple-II's ability to read resistance values means that you have essentially four built-in A/D converters at your disposal! No other personal computer on the market offers this feature as part of its standard configuration.

The cassette interface,

which is also built right onto the Apple-II board, is capable of 1500 bps. This means you can load or save a 4K byte program in less than 30 seconds. To load a program from tape, connect the line-out (or earphone) jack from the tape recorder to the cassette-in jack on the back of the computer; to save a program on tape, connect the cassette-out jack on the back of the computer to the microphone jack on the recorder. (Note that the line-in jack of the tape recorder is *not* used with the Apple computers. Many dealers who are used to other computers' cassette interfaces often use the wrong jack when recording from an Apple.)

One oversight in the design of the cassette interface is the failure to utilize the remote start/stop jack found on most portable cassette recorders. This implementation would have been useful for data processing, creating and assembling symbolic source code, etc. In other words, it would be nice to be able to read data from an input tape, and then stop the tape while that data is processed.

The Apple-II uses the new 16K dynamic RAM chips. The board contains three rows of memory sockets with eight sockets per row. Thus, the computer has the capacity to hold up to 48K bytes of memory on a single board! In addition, the Apple-II comes with 8K bytes of ROM, which contains the system monitor (2K) and Apple BASIC (6K). Two additional empty ROM sockets are provided for future expansion.

Apple Computer was the first company to produce a computer powered by a small, lightweight switching power supply; most of the other manufacturers' machines have large, bulky power supplies. Consequently, the Apple-II does not even require a cooling fan. In fact, when you take the lid off an Apple-II and look inside, it seems almost empty! By avoiding the use of heavy components and by packaging the unit in a plastic case instead of a steel case, the designers of the Apple-II created a truly portable, lightweight computer.

Apple-II Monitor

Besides allowing you to examine and/or modify memory locations (as you'd expect from a monitor), the 2K ROM monitor also contains many other useful features. One of the handiest routines in the monitor is the miniassembler. It allows you to enter an assembly-language program from the keyboard, and assembles it line by line as you type. You must specify all addresses in absolute hex since the miniassembler does not use a symbol table.

Also built into the monitor is a handy disassembler for converting machine code back into mini-assembly language.

To aid in debugging programs, the monitor also has the ability to either single-step through a program or trace the flow of execution while the program is running. Thus, if a program hangs up, you can determine exactly where it is stuck.

The monitor also contains the routines for reading and writing cassette tapes. The timing and formatting of the tape are done with software, not hardware. This means that, given the right software, it should be possible to read or write tapes in almost any format (Kansas City, Tarbell, etc.). However, Apple-II does not use one of the standard formats . . . it uses a format of its own. The cassette routines in the monitor also utilize a checksum to help insure that tapes are read back correctly. The Apple-I firmware did not use a checksum. (When I first pointed out this deficiency, Apple's reply at that time was that their cassette interface was so reliable it didn't need a checksum!)

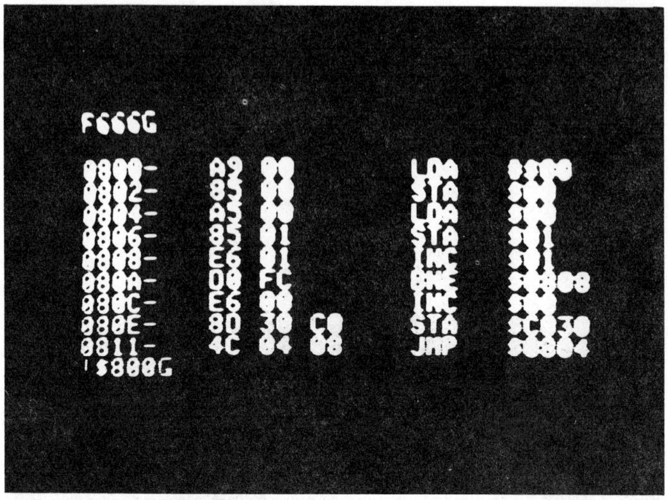

A short program written with the Apple's miniassembler.

Apple-II BASIC

The Apple BASIC interpreter is almost legendary as one of the fastest, if not *the* fastest, interpretive languages on any microcomputer. Of course, one of the reasons for its high speed is that it's an integer-only BASIC. But then, there are many applications (like games) that do not require floating-point operations. In fact, Apple BASIC (which is on ROM) and the Apple-II itself are both ideally suited for creating computer games. The paddle controls, the built-in speaker and the exceptional graphics capability make it easy for you to produce arcade-quality video games.

Apple's integer BASIC turns out to have some powerful features, some of which are not usually found in other BASICs. For example, the TRACE command causes each line number to be displayed as it is executed.

Another handy debugging feature is the DSP command, which allows you to see where and how variables become redefined in your program. PEEK and POKE commands allow access to absolute memory locations and are useful for passing arguments to machine-language subroutines (which can be invoked with the CALL command), among other things.

Not surprisingly, Apple BASIC also supports the low-resolution color-graphics capability of the hardware. For example, the PLOT command allows you to plot points, VLIN allows you to draw vertical lines, etc.

What *is* surprising is that the HIRES graphics capability is *not* supported directly. There are no commands in the language to do any HIRES plotting. (This omission, I was told, occurred because the HIRES routines had not yet been completed at the time the ROMs were made. Future versions of Apple BASIC will support the HIRES feature.)

Apple-II Software

In November 1977, Apple Computer released the floating-point BASIC for their Apple-II systems. Written by Microsoft, the same company that wrote Mits BASIC and the BASIC for Commodore's PET computer, Apple's new BASIC (called AppleSoft) now allows the Apple-II to be used for more serious applications than just playing games. The new BASIC is intended for use in business, scientific and educational applications in which decimal numbers must be manipulated.

The AppleSoft BASIC, like the integer BASIC in ROM, also supports the low-resolution color-graphics capability of the Apple-II, while the HIRES graphics is, again, not supported. But this time the omission is understandable since the floating-point BASIC resides in part of the primary HIRES display area and thus cannot be used for graphics. (HIRES graphics *is* possible with the floating-point BASIC if your Apple-II has at least 24K bytes of memory. But you must call separate machine-language subroutines.)

This HIRES graphics problem is currently being worked on at Apple, and a *new* floating-point BASIC that doesn't have the memory conflict may soon be coming out.

Because they are interpretive languages, all BASICs, including Apple's integer BASIC, are relatively slow. Sometimes it is necessary to produce code that executes as quickly as possible. For these applications the Apple-II has, as part of the system monitor, a miniassembler that is very useful for writing small machine-language programs.

What about writing *large* machine-language programs? Yes, you can also use the mini assembler to produce big programs (it's a lot better than assembling them by hand!). But the main problem with a mini-assembler (not just Apple's) occurs when you have to insert new code in the middle of an already existing program. Your only resort is to patch in the changes (i.e., insert a JUMP instruction to some other part of memory containing the needed code, and then return). This tends to produce confusing program flow.

Assemblers are usually written for microcomputers with source code read from one input tape and object code written onto another output tape. But the Apple-II only supports one cassette unit, which cannot be started or stopped under software control.

To get around this problem, it is necessary to store the source code and/or object code in memory, along with the assembler itself. This approach has actually been used; text editors/assemblers for the Apple-II are currently available from several sources. (I have recently modified Microsoftware Specialists' ASSM/TED program for the KIM to run on the Apple-II. Copies of this modified program are available from: Microproducts, Hermosa Beach CA, (213) 374-1673.)

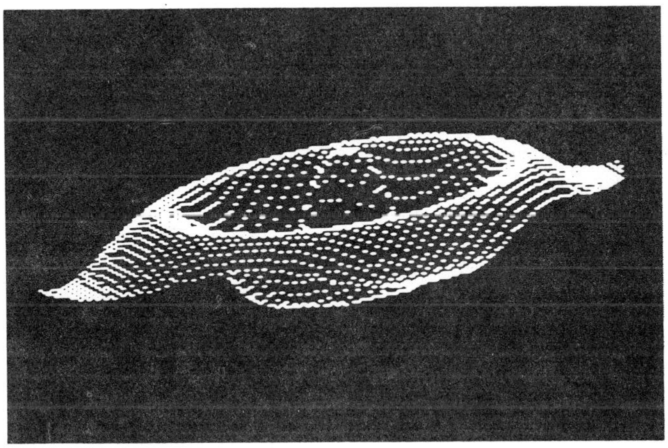

Example of the high-resolution graphics mode.

As more and more Apples get around, more and more Apple software will appear, especially games and applications software. Apple has started a new service called the Apple Software Bank from which Apple owners can receive documented and tested software. And if you've written a worthwhile program, you can submit it to the Bank for others to use.

Apple-II vs the Competition

The Apple-II computer comes completely assembled in an attractive plastic case with a full ASCII keyboard. A vinyl carrying case is also supplied with the unit for ease of portability. Since the machine is easy for almost anyone to set up and use, the Apple-II just might become the leading "appliance" computer of the future.

The original price of an Apple-II, complete with 4K bytes of RAM, was around $1300. In the early days of personal computing, a system like the Apple-II at this price would have been a fantastic bargain. For many years B.C. (Before Commodore), computer *kits* with much less capability than the Apple-II were selling for much more money.

But as we enter the era of cheap computing, the pricing standards of yesterday are becoming obsolete. At least two companies (Commodore and Radio Shack) are each offering completely assembled 4K appliance computers for about $600. Although this price includes both a cassette tape recorder and black-and-white TV display, neither system offers color or high-resolution graphics (however, Radio Shack says they plan to offer a similar capability sometime this year at an additional cost).

Furthermore, both companies seem to be having problems in actually delivering their machines—each is quoting a three-to-four-month waiting period. But you can get an Apple-II *right now*; and with it you'll get a good set of useful documentation.

In early 1978, the price of a 4K Apple-II was lowered to $995. Although this is still a little higher than the price of a PET, you get a lot more computer for your money. I bought my Apple-II (serial number 0013) at the higher original price, but I've never regretted it. Now that the price has been lowered to below $1000, there's no excuse for not getting an Apple-II of your own! ■

VideoBrain: the consumer computer

by Mike Peak

Reprinted by permission of INTERFACE AGE Magazine from the Feb. 1978 issue.

Consumer electronics is one of the oldest industries known as "electronics." Consumer electronics dates as far back as the crystal receiver, and is ever advancing with the state of the art.

During the past three years, a new and exciting generation of consumer-oriented devices has been made available to the American public. These devices have ranged from video games to highly sophisticated video cassette systems. Now as we enter 1978, another new and innovative approach is being taken by the electronics industry.

The industry is now viewing the microprocessor, not only for games, but for viable home computing systems. One company in particular, VideoBrain of Sunnyvale, Calif., has recently developed one of the more exciting entrants to the new field of consumer computers. This new device is named the VideoBrain.

The consumers' interests

According to Dr. David Chung, one of the developers of the system, the VideoBrain was designed to fit five areas of consumer interest.

The first and most obvious is entertainment. The VideoBrain is indeed entertaining. Several off-the-shelf game programs are available with more on the way. The second area is education and self-improvement. With the VideoBrain the user can practice typing or learn music. The third area is personal finance and data storage with hardcopy printouts. The VideoBrain can be used to balance the checkbook or handle the yearly Christmas card list. Fourth, the system is a communication device when used with an audio coupler. Using the VideoBrain as a communications device, the consumer can have the convenience of querying large data bases or depositing information into them for use by others. Finally, the area of home control has been addressed. The system, along with the appropriate application package, can be used to handle the daily mundane tasks of controlling the household environment.

Both developers, Dr. Yu and Dr. Chung, feel that the pesonal computer, up until now, has been in the same class as calculators, chips, and watches. The product is developed and marketed in large volumes, without sufficient thought going into what the consumer really wants. Therefore, to add viability to the VideoBrain, the broad spectrum of the marketplace has been addressed. Consequently the VideoBrain system provides something for everyone in the family, not just the in-house computer enthusiast.

Basic structure

The F8 microprocessor used in the VideoBrain was originally designed for use as a controller, and consequently does not use the typical hobbyist bus structure. However, the bus structure used by the VideoBrain is designed to allow for the addition of a network of microprocessors by simply clipping them on. As Dr. Chung describes it, "The machine uses both a tightly coupled and loosely coupled method of bus architecture. This method of bus design gives the system a great deal of flexibility, when connecting it to other intelligent devices."

The system incorporates a new innovative chip, used to handle the screen housekeeping. Therefore, approximately 100,000 points and 16 bright colors can be defined and displayed. To relate this to conventional systems, it would take 100 4-K RAMs, and possibly two microprocessors to service the RAMs, to perform the same function.

The keyboard used with the system is somewhat unconventional. However, it was designed only after careful consideration of what would be workable for the consumer, and also be cost-effective. The keyboard controls all the computer functions including changing the color displays.

The machine in its basic configuration comes with 1-K of RAM, which allows for five lines of 16 characters of text. Also included is 4-K of ROM for handling the internal working of the machine. The system is expandable, not by adding to the bus, but through the ROM cassettes.

Application development

The area of applications, for the VideoBrain, is by far the most exciting thing about the machine. The applications are designed in the same manner as they would be for a large system. This requires application planning, that is, the need and method are previously defined. Then, the entire program development is handled by a programming team utilizing the best of all possible programming techniques. The result is reliable, efficient software to handle the needs of the consumer.

The programs are run in the machine by popping a ROM cassette into the built-in reader. Therefore, instant communication exists between the computer and the user.

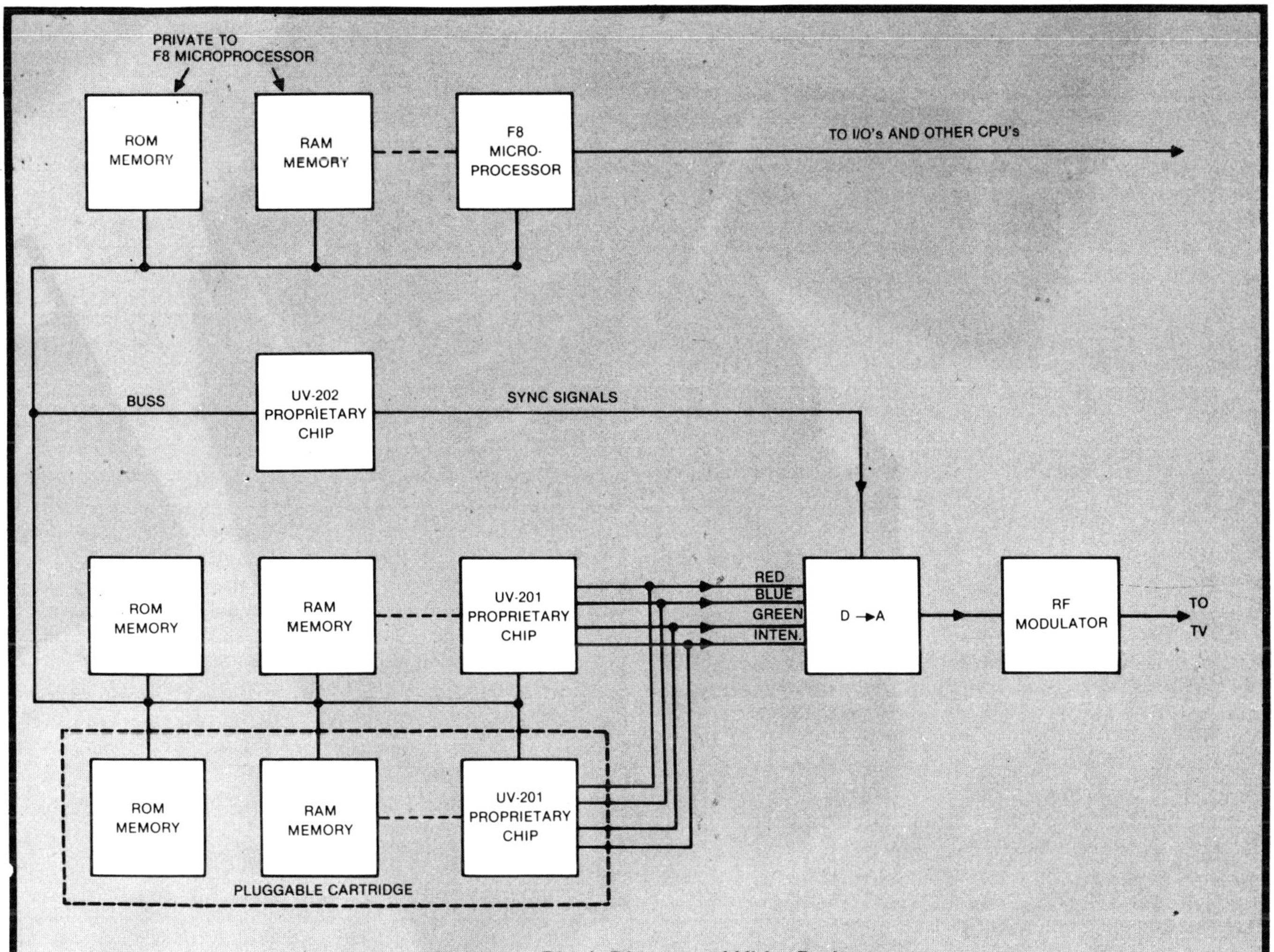

Figure 1. Block Diagram of VideoBrain.

Summary

The Video Brain comes with a spectrum of cassette programs from games to personal finance. The plan for future application development is three programs a month selling in the $20 to $50 range, depending upon the complexity of the program.

The VideoBrain people have addressed the problem of add-ons, and are making available so-called expandables. These expandables will give the user the ability to interface with Teletypes, printers, audio cassettes, and sensing devices.

The VideoBrain is designed to be the very first computer system to take full advantage of current technological know-how, and remove the mystery surrounding computers. The VideoBrain provides for man-machine interface by utilizing familiar objects found in the home, the color TV and telephone. The basic application design provides something for everyone, with the greatest emphasis placed on the homemaker. □

Microcomputer kits

Reprinted with permission from *Mini-Micro Systems*, Dec. 1976.

Hobby electronic kits came on strong shortly after World War I when the Heathkit Co. introduced such consumer products put together out of war surplus parts. Since then, the hobby kit concept has expanded to include, not only high fidelity components in kit form, but also depth finder kits, treasure hunting kits, electronic organ kits, and even a color television kit. The high point in the marketplace undoubtedly occurred in 1926 when the Heathkit Co. introduced a kit airplane at a cost of $199 – minus the engine.

All kits come with step-by-step instructions, of course, so that persons without any formal technical training or experience can assemble them. But, now, the microcomputer kit, first introduced by Cramer Electronics in 1975,

Intel SDK-80 kit assembled

makes the concept a whole new ballgame. When conventional kits are assembled, the builder need have no special skills to operate the completed products, since the controls on a high fidelity set or television receiver are very simple. Not so with the microcomputer kit. Upon its completion, one's work has only begun. To do anything worthwile, the microcomputer needs to be programmed.

NOT FOR JOE, THE TRUCKER

As a result, the microcomputer kit poses a formidable challenge. Assembling and operating a kit in no way appeals to Joe, the truck driver, or Harry, the used car salesman. Indeed, the complex devices are not even likely to be built by Mike, the electronic engineer or Betty, the programmer.

Knowing the content of a typical microcomputer kit explains why this is so. For as little as $100, we can buy a basic microcomputer kit to contain a microprocessor chip, 1K or 2K RAM memory, ROM memory that includes a rudimentary debugging program, input-output buffer, teletypewriter interface circuit, crystal and timing circuits, voltage regulator, DIP sockets, printed circuit board, and other miscellaneous items. Roughly five pounds of literature – assembly instructions, debugging materials, theoretical explanations, and the like – are included in the package.

The $100 budget, however, does not afford a power supply. But no matter. After assembling the kit, we run into many other missing elements. We have no way to communicate with the presumably, powerful computer, and, as a result, we cannot know what tricks the computer can perform. That takes more of an outlay; the cheapest solution is to connect switches and lamps to the computer as basic I/O devices.

GENIUS WANTED

Now, at last, we can communicate with the machine, though only in its own terms – in binary or hexadecimal language. Communicating this way to any substantial extent, unfortunately, is beyond the mental capacity of most mortals. So, we must turn to a more accommodating, human-oriented device if we are to use the computer, and this means still another expenditure to purchase an alphanumeric display and keyboard. Hence, add another $100, at least, to the microcomputer kit budget.

National Semiconductor SC/MP kit and materials

At long last, now, we are on the way. Because an alphanumeric terminal accommodates the 10 numerals and 6 letters required to describe the hexadecimal codes, we can begin to exercise the microcomputer by using the debug

MICROCOMPUTER KITS

Vendor	Microprocessor Type	(Bytes of Mem) RAM	ROM	Peripheral Options	Software	Price
Advanced Micro Devices Sunnyvale, CA	AM 2900	64 Std		No	No	$289
American Microsystems, Inc. Santa Clara, CA	AMI 6800	512	2K ROM 2K EPROM	No	Tiny Basic	$950
	AMI 6800	512	2K ROM 512 EPROM	No	No	$595
	AMI 6800	512	2K ROM	No	No	$295
Compsultants Inc. Huntsville, AL	Intel 8080	256 Std 2K Opt		TTY, Console	No	$175
Cramer Electronics Newton, MA	Intel 8080A	1K Std 13K Opt	1K Std 13K Opt	Terminal, Cassette	Good	$750
	TI TMS 9900	2K Std 13K Opt	2K Std 13K Opt	Same	Same	
	Motorola 6800	Same	1K Std 13K Opt	Same	Same	$495
Fairchild Microsystems San Jose, CA	Fairchild F8	1K Std 64K Opt	1K Std	Minimal	Minimal	$185
General Instrument Hicksville, NY	GI CP 1600	8K Opt	4K Opt	Console, TTY, PT	Adequate	$495
IMS Assoc. Inc. San Leandro, CA	Intel 8080	1K Std 64K Opt	4K Opt	Excellent	Excellent	$599
Intel Corp. Santa Clara, CA	Intel 8080	2K Std 4K Opt	256 Std 1K Opt	Minimal	Minimal	$350
Martin Research Northbrook, IL	Intel 8008	1K Opt	2K Opt	Console	Minimal	$ 95
Microcomputer Associates Santa Clara, CA	MOS Technology MCS 6502	512 Std 8K Opt	1K Std	Minimal	Good	$159
Motorola Semiconductor Phoenix, AZ	Motorola 6800	128 Std 640 Opt		No	Minimal	$149
	Motorola 6800	256 Std		No	Minimal	$795
National Semiconductor Corp. Santa Clara, CA	National SC/MP	256 Std	512 Std	TTY	Minimal	$ 99
Polymorphic Systems Goleta, CA	Intel 8080	512 Std 8K Opt	1K Std 3K Opt	Excellent	Good	$595
Quay Corp. Freehold, NJ	Zilog Z 80	1K Std	1K Std 4K Opt	Minimal	Good, includes PROM Programmer	$450
RCA Solid State Division Somerville, NJ	CDP 1802 Cosmac	256 Std 4K Opt	512 Std	No	No	$249
Signetics Corp. Sunnyvale, CA	Signetics 2650	512 Std	1K Std	No	No	$190

software that is supplied in the ROM and which comes with the kit. What does our $200 capital investment now buy us? Sad to say, nothing but an academic exercise in microprocessor operations. Even the casual hobbyist, it may be assumed, ultimately wants to see his microcomputer perform a useful or entertaining function. But to do this, a kit enthusiast must be able to code an instruction sequence in assembly language and, manually, enter the set of rules into the machine. And he must go through the chore each time he powers up the microcomputer unless he opts to leave the power on all the time.

A KICK IN THE HEAD

So now our recreational budget gets a real kick in the head. To do any serious work, we need a teletypewriter to communicate with the machine easily and to write and debug programs. Or, we can buy a CRT keyboard to do the same job, but in either case, we bring our kit budget up to the $1000 mark.

And if we want to attach the microcomputer to real world devices in an actual application, then we must not forget the cost of either an oscilloscope or a larger test unit to do this work. If we go this route, we have passed the experimental phase and maybe have even developed some computer programs. Any smile of success at this point, however, will not last too long. Almost immediately, another problem arises and a very expensive one: How do we make

RCA evaluation kit

the application programs resident in the microcomputer? Now, our costs can really soar, because this task requires either a punch paper tape, tape cassette, floppy disk, or similar device to input the program into the RAM memory. Alternatively, we could buy a ROM programming unit to do the same job. Whatever the choice, now the micro kit budget is headed toward the $3000 range.

WHO SHOULD BUY KIT?

Most professionals working on an industry project of course, do not bother with a kit. They turn directly to a microcomputer development system to be discussed in the succeeding article. Who then should buy a kit? The credentials one must have to put a microcomputer kit to good use are impressive. First, any prospective builder should be proficient at programming a minicomputer, at least, and preferably have degrees in electronic engineering and computer sciences. Indeed, an IBM-370/135, which uses higher level assembly languages, takes much less training and expertise to program than does a fully assembled $100 microcomputer kit that can be programmed only in machine language – a very difficult task.

Joe the truck driver and Harry the used car salesman, indeed, are some four years of night school away from ever doing anything useful with a microcomputer kit. Moreover, Mike the engineer and Betty the programmer will have to spend many nights at studying manuals before even they can utilize the device, which presumably is "right down their alley."

The most likely person to make use of a microcomputer kit, indeed, would be someone knowledgeable about computers who wants to extend his professional capabilities while, at the same time, trying his hand at automating a home furnace, lights, burglar alarm, TV set, or other household appliances.

Students at the Massachusetts Institute of Technology or other universities may also enjoy a microcomputer kit. They should keep the students harmlessly preoccupied, so that they need not seek entertainment by trying to break privacy codes on local time sharing networks. Still other potential users of kits are small business proprietors or physicians and dentists and other professionals who want to computerize their paperwork. ■

Part 5: Software for Microcomputers and Microprocessors

With the programmability of machines came a whole new problem, called software. Programming microcomputers involves the same problems as programming for big computers. Whether you're writing at the machine level—in assembly-language statements—or in high level like Basic, Pascal, and Fortran, the generation of code is hardly ever simple. This section describes the more popular languages at both levels and some approaches for putting them to use.

A popularity contest for languages

by Andreas S. Philippakis

The theory and practice of computer programming have received wide attention over the last few years. Although the proliferation of new languages in the '60s was followed by a short pause in the early '70s, since then the popularization of structured programming concepts and the concern over software reliability have again heightened the level of activity.

But has the new thinking on structured programming and language design affected language usage? Are new, "structure-oriented" languages replacing "old" ones?

In an attempt to answer at least part of that question, a survey was recently conducted among systems analysts and programmers in commercial data processing installations. A total of 132 respondents replied to questions concerning the percentage of their programming time spent using various languages. (The questionnaire listed seven popular languages and an "other" category.)

Before discussing the results, it should be emphasized that the basic question being investigated is on which language do professional programmers spend their time. No attempt is made here to rank languages in terms of efficiency or suitability.

A summary of current language use is presented in Table 1. The table also compares results from the current survey to those of a similar one conducted by the author in 1972. A *usage index* is included to make that comparison easier; it is computed as follows:

$$\text{index} = \frac{\text{number of users} \times \text{average \% use}}{\text{total respondents}}$$

where "average % use" is actually "average % use *where used*." This index weighs use by the total universe of respondents and to some degree adjusts for the differences in sample size between the 1977 and 1972 data. (Note, however, that this index has the disadvantage that size and type of installation are not being considered in the computation.)

What were the results?

Several observations are worth making regarding the data in Table 1:

1. The most widely and extensively used language for administrative data processing is still COBOL.
2. Assembly languages remain in wide and extensive use, being second only to COBOL.
3. All other languages are used to a far lesser extent.
4. FORTRAN is used by approximate-

PROGRAMMING LANGUAGE USE

	1977			1972			1972-1977
LANGUAGE	NUMBER OF SITES	AVERAGE % USE WHERE USED	USAGE INDEX	NUMBER OF SITES	AVERAGE % USE WHERE USED	USAGE INDEX	USAGE INDEX CHANGE
Assembler	97	22%	16	124	27%	20	−4
APL	4	14%	0.4	1	1%	0.0	+0.4
BASIC	11	15%	1	14	13%	1	0
COBOL	119	70%	63	138	70%	59	+4
FORTRAN	45	9%	3	79	11%	5	−2
PL/1	26	32%	6	26	28%	4	+2
RPG	23	25%	4	49	20%	6	−2
Other	42	16%	5	33	17%	3	+2

Table 1. COBOL is still the most commonly used commercial programming language, if not always the most well liked. It is used for some 70% of all programming at those sites where it is installed, on the average. Its usage index indicates it has slipped very little since 1972. (The usage index reflects "overall" usage of the language, and is intended to compensate for changes in the sample sizes for 1972 and 1977.)

LANGUAGE USE BY INDUSTRY

Language	Banking & Savings (20 sites/ 1280 users): Number of sites	Banking & Savings: Average % use where used	Government Related (27 sites/ 351 users): Number of sites	Government Related: Average % use where used	Health Care (6 sites/ 168 users): Number of sites	Health Care: Average % use where used	Insurance (5 sites/ 135 users): Number of sites	Insurance: Average % use where used	Manufacturing (21 sites/ 735 users): Number of sites	Manufacturing: Average % use where used	Public Utilities (14 sites/ 714 users): Number of sites	Public Utilities: Average % use where used	Retail & Distribution (15 sites/ 195 users): Number of sites	Retail & Distribution: Average % use where used	Other (24 sites/ 456 users): Number of sites	Other: Average % use where used
Assembler	14	30%	16	28%	6	18%	4	7%	16	9%	12	19%	13	39%	16	14%
APL	0		0		0		0		1	10%	1	3%	0		2	21%
BASIC	3	34%	3	17%	0		1	1%	0		3	1%	0		1	10%
COBOL	18	75%	26	67%	6	80%	5	76%	19	81%	13	56%	11	64%	21	68%
FORTRAN	3	1%	13	12%	0		0		8	8%	11	8%	0		10	11%
PL/1	1	2%	7	10%	2	5%	0		4	42%	5	55%	0		7	42%
RPG	1	1%	4	34%	1	5%	0		6	26%	0		3	35%	8	21%
Other	4	28%	10	10%	0		4	24%	2	8%	6	9%	5	35%	11	12%

Table 2. Some industries seem to have less need for a variety of languages. Note, for example, that none of the sites responding for the Retail and Distribution industries claimed to be using any of the analytical languages.

ly one-third of the sample with an average use of 9% of the hourly programming effort.

5. PL/1 is used only by one-fifth of the sample, but those who use it do so extensively, with an average usage of 32%.

6. RPG-type languages compare in use to PL/1, being used by just under one-fifth of the sites responding, with 25% average use.

7. BASIC is used by 8% of the sample. However, the wide use of BASIC with many popular business minicomputers is not reflected in this sample. The sample was biased in favor of larger organizations which have formal data processing departments.)

8. APL is very limited both in number of sites and level of use. (Languages such as APL, FORTRAN, and to some extent BASIC and PL/1, can be categorized as analysis-oriented. One would expect that these terse languages are often used by persons who do their own limited programming for analysis of data and do not submit jobs through a regular dp department. Again, such usage would not be included in the responses to this questionnaire.)

9. The "other" category shows that other languages are used, often extensively, by about one-third of the sample. This category included several low level languages (such as NEAT/3), some very high level languages (such as MARK IV), and two ALGOL sites, each with a 5% usage level.

10. Comparing the 1977 survey results to those of 1972, little change appears. APL, COBOL, PL/1, and the "other" category show increases, while Assembler, FORTRAN, and RPG show small decreases. Taking into account that the responses were only estimates, plus the small size of the changes and the inherent inaccuracies in sampling, it is safe to say that language use has remained practically the same between 1972 and 1977.

Overall, no great variations exist across industry groups either (see Table 2a and 2b), but notice the absence of the more analytic languages, APL and FORTRAN, from the Health Care, Insurance, and Retail & Distribution groups.

Table 3 compares languages by usage level within an organization. It is interesting to see that the majority (51) of sites using Assembler use it for less than 10% of their programming, while on the other hand, 18 others use it for over 90%, and three of the latter use it exclusively. As expected, most COBOL sites polled use it for a large

LANGUAGE USE BY SITES

Language	AVERAGE % USE: ≤10%	11%-50%	51%-90%	>90%	100%
Assembler	51	23	8	15	3
APL	2	1	0	1	0
BASIC	8	1	0	2	1
COBOL	11	15	56	37	7
FORTRAN	32	10	0	3	0
PL/1	13	5	2	6	0
RPG	14	5	2	2	2
Other	22	11	1	8	1

Table 3. Few sites can get by on a single language, but 74 out of the 132 sampled use a single language for over 90% of their work.

WRITING NEW PROGRAMS OR MODIFYING OLD ONES?

LANGUAGE	AVERAGE % USE: WRITING NEW PROGRAMS	MODIFYING OLD PROGRAMS
Assembler	31%	69%
APL	70%	30%
BASIC	55%	45%
COBOL	47%	53%
FORTRAN	55%	45%
PL/1	50%	50%
RPG	40%	60%
Other	56%	44%

Table 4. The data on check-out versus maintenance must be used with the other tables to make sense. For example, the 40/60 split for RPG does not mean that report generators are becoming less popular, but that more work is done in maintenance than in writing new code. The 70/30 split for APL may mean both that the language is becoming more popular **and** that much APL code is thrown away.

portion of their programming: seven used it exclusively. In general, single-language sites are few. One language rarely satisfies all programming needs.

Table 4 distinguishes between use of each language in writing new programs and in the modification of old ones. Note that assembler language, when used, is used primarily to modify old programs. One can infer that about 70% of assembler programming results from Assembler having been used previously to write programs. The APL usage split is just the reverse of Assembler, as would be expected of a new language often used in ad hoc analysis. In the remaining six language categories, the split between new programs and modification of old ones is about even, which goes along with the general observation that about one-half of the computer programming effort is devoted to program maintenance.

What does it prove?

Administrative data processing still is being programmed using just a few languages. COBOL, by far the most commonly used language, has remained so over the past five years. And despite all the literature in recent years about the merits of high-level language programming, assembler programming continues to be a close second. The well-known general purpose language PL/1 appears to be standing still (despite rumors that IBM has been encouraging its use), as do APL, BASIC, FORTRAN, and report generators.

It is safe to predict, based on this study, that the established momentum of currently popular languages will prove difficult to arrest. The merits of newly designed languages may remain academic subjects for some time to come, at least as far as administrative data processing users go. ✻

BASIC's token of good fortune

by Tim Ryan

Reprinted by permission of the Author and of INTERFACE AGE Magazine from the May 1978 issue.

Most readers of hobby computing magazines have by now done some programming in BASIC. Any issue will contain a sample showing just what a program written in the BASIC language looks like. The more sophisticated reader may be wondering by now just how does the computer manage to keep all the statements and variables in a program straight in memory. Particularly, how does BASIC allow the flexibility of changing code so conveniently midstream during the interactive debugging stage of writing a program. Some readers may even be thinking of writing changes to BASIC to give them special features they need.

In order to reach the broad audience of users who have had experience programming in BASIC, but not in other languages, several concepts should be outlined. There are several levels of intricacy constantly occurring and invisible to you as a BASIC user. If you think of turning on a TV set and watching it, you do not have to be aware of the scanning of the beam across the screen and of the drift of the station frequency you have chosen. These are taken care of automatically by the electronics of the set. Likewise, if you are running BASIC, you are not concerned about the signals passing back and forth on the bus, or the translation of instructions by the microcode or logic of your processor. These are handled automatically. If you begin to think of your computer in terms of assembly language rather than just BASIC, there are still several other levels of subtlety that go unseen. These are located in your operating system and your specific flavor of BASIC.

OPERATING SYSTEM

You may be so used to working in BASIC that you don't think much about your operating system. It handles the routines kinds of chores that have to be done regardless of what language you are programming in. The bigger a computer is, the more diverse it must be in order to talk to terminals, printers, communication lines, disks, tapes, and other memory devices. If more than on person can run something on the computer at a time, it must schedule each job depending on its needs. Your operating system may be called the "executive" or the "monitor" but no matter what its name, it is the unseen workhorse that BASIC must communicate with to get certain things done. There are times when the computer may seem to idle but the monitor never sleeps. It "talks to itself" in a diddle pattern during which it is constantly checking (or "polling") to see if someone needs its help.

COMPILERS VS. INTERPRETERS

The operating system should not be fussy about who it's willing to help. It should be able to handle BASIC, FORTRAN, PL/I or any other language that you want to send it. There is nothing mysterious about each language, each is just another program that makes it easier for you to be understood by the computer and still be economical with your own time. One of these programs may translate a high level language into compiled assembly language, essentially casting the code in concrete. Once this is done with a language like FORTRAN, the compiler has done its job and from now on the resulting 'object' code produced by the compiler will function stand alone.

In contrast, BASIC is sometimes another kind of high level program, one called an interpreter. An interpreter translates the high level language it was designed for, statement by statement, symbol by symbol, each time the program is run, even if the statement is executed several times in a loop in the program. This has the advantage of being very flexible to allow for last minute debugging changes, but much slower than a compiled language where everything has been pre-translated. Another disadvantage is that the BASIC must always be present in memory to perform the translation. To combine the best of both worlds, some companies produce two versions of a language, one that runs interactively as an interpreter, and a second that can compile the resulting debugged code. This, of course, doubles their development and maintenance costs.

INTERPRETIVE COMPILER

In an effort to economize on speed and money, a better BASIC will combine the features of a compiler and interpreter to produce an intermediate form of code in memory. This code is more compact and will execute faster than the source code statements you type into the computer. It is not, however, as fast as compiled language and the BASIC must still be present in the memory at all times to translate this intermediate code.

200 \	231 STOP	262 =>	313 PI
201 FOR	232 END OF PROG	263 <>	314 SYS(
202 GOSUB	233 OPEN	264 ><	315 RND(
203 GO TO	234 CLOSE	265 <	316 RND
204 ON	235 OVERLAY	266 >	317 SIN(
205 IF	236 CHAIN	267 =	320 COS(
206 INPUT	237 KILL	270 (	321 SQR(
207 LINPUT	240 NAME	271 "	322 ATN(
210 LET	241 &	272 '	323 EXP(
211 NEXT	242 ^	273 :	324 LOG(
212 PRINT	243 *	274 #	325 LOG10(
213 RETURN	244 /	275 FN	326 ABS(
214 RESTORE	245 +	276 FOR OUTPUT	327 INT(
215 RESET	246 (UNARY)	277 AS FILE	330 SGN(
216 READ	247 -	300 FOR INPUT	331 BIN
217 CALL	250 (TERM)	301 %	332 OCT
220 IF END	251 ,	302 $	333 LEN(
221 LET VS	252)	303 DOUBLE BUF	334 ASC(
222 DIM	253 TO	304 RECORDSIZE	335 CHR$(
223 COMMON	254 STEP	305 FILESIZE	336 POS(
224 RANDOMIZE	255 THEN	306 MODE	337 SEG$(
225 REM	256 .	307 USING	340 VAL(
226 DEF	257 <=	310 LINE	341 TRM$(
227 DATA	260 =<	311 TAB	342 DAT$
230 END	261 >=	312 VF	343 STR$(

Table 1. Statement Tokens for Multi-user BASIC.

The process of compacting the code involved replacing each occurrence of a keyword like PRINT or INPUT in a program by a single character (or byte) called a token. There must be a unique token for each keyword (or verb). Unique tokens may also be set aside for arithmetic operation symbols like +, −, *, / and other special symbols like (,), ", ', and #. Table 1 shows the actual tokens used for one version of BASIC. The resulting compact code exists only in memory, although some versions of BASIC may allow you to store this 'core image' copy from memory onto disk or tape, to allow for a faster response time when a program is brought into memory.

There are also many other things happening during the compacting process that cause some of the memory that has been saved to be used for other purposes. Tables are created containing all line numbers and variables in the program and space is set aside for arrays that may appear in a DIM statement in the program. Once a program is in memory in this reduced form, BASIC must undo the compaction process every time a command like LIST is typed, to allow the program to be printed at a terminal, or when SAVE is typed to preserve the source code for the program on a device like a tape or disk.

Unfortunately, this process of compacting code is also called compiling, so as to confuse the distinction being made here between intermediate level of compilation like a BASIC interpretive compiler. The word compaction has been used temporarily in this section instead of compilation to keep the distinction clear.

A SPECIFIC EXAMPLE

It is not easy to choose a specific manufacturer's version of BASIC for discussion of details at the token level. As most of us are aware, BASIC comes in 57 varieties and 31 flavors. One of the primary advantages of a high level language is that it should be able to run on many different kinds of computers regardless of the manufacturer or hardware attached. Recently, a national minimal standard ANSI BASIC has been adopted. This will help create a minimum set of instructions that must function "the same," but it is unlikely to do away with the many unique features that each company might add above and beyond the standard. Since many of the hobby computers use the same microprocessor chips which have the identical instruction set, and since many hobby firms have only small, in house programming staffs, they are wary to supply listings of source code that would allow users to more easily understand or modify BASIC for a special purpose or enhancement.

One of the more sophisticated versions of BASIC that will run on the recently introduced Heath H-11, can also be purchased with source code. This code is available both on microfiche and on magnetic media to licensed users from the original manufacturer, Digital Equipment Corporation (DEC). DEC manufactures the LSI-11 CPU board used by Heath and furnishes the RT11 operating system along with BASIC-11.

BASIC-11 is really a family of languages meant to run on many different computers with many types of peripherals. The member chosen for this article is MU-BASIC, short for Multi-User BASIC. It needs the RT11 operating system and at least one disk or diskette drive to run. Since there is a large user's group called DECUS that Heath customers may join, they can take advantage of the experience of many sophisticated users who have paved the way by testing the software, lobbying for fancy special features and accumulating programs in the DECUS library.

BASIC	ASSEMBLY
Line number	Address (or Label)
Statement	Instruction
GO TO	Jump (JMP)
GOSUB	Jump to Subroutine (JSR)
RETURN	Return from Subroutine (RTS)
STOP	Halt (HALT)
LET A=0	Clear A (CLR A)
LET B=A	Move A to B (MOV A,B)
LET A=A+1	Increment A (INC A)
LET A=A-1	Decrement A (DEC A)
LET B=A+B	Add A to B (ADD A,B)
LET B=B-A	Subtract A from B (SUB A,B)
IF A=B GO TO	Compare (CMP A,B)
	& Conditional Branch (BEQ)

Branching in an assembly language program can be to an absolute address but the goal is usually to use a label for a destination in a program rather than absolute addresses so that the program can be loaded into memory at varying places and still be able to run. The resulting code is called relocatable or position independent code (PIC)

Table 2. BASIC vs. Assembly Language list of analogous concepts.

MU-BASIC

MU-BASIC allows several different users to be running programs simultaneously. There are not many versions of BASIC that can run on hobby machines that are this powerful. Figure 1, which shows how memory is used, helps you to visualize where BASIC is and how a BASIC program is divided up.

The left portion of Figure 1 shows how the available memory is allocated or 'mapped.' This overall breakdown shows an area called locore that is set aside to furnish the current address of devices, as well as to give addresses to branch to if certain kinds of errors are discovered or 'trapped' during the execution of the program.

The highest address range (141362-157777) is set aside for the operating system. As mentioned earlier, an interpretive language must always be present in memory to translate the BASIC code. The MU-BASIC interpretive compiler is located between locore and program one in memory. Only one copy is needed to handle several different programs written in BASIC simultaneously. The remaining room is divided between the current number of BASIC programs being run. Each BASIC program or job has a fixed amount of memory allotted to it. Jobs do not pool available space to be alternately used by one job, then the other.

A SINGLE BASIC PROGRAM

The right half of Figure 1 is the show and tell guide to the organization of a typical program written in BASIC as it appears in memory. The space shown is exclusively for the use of one program. The upper and lower boundaries of the job space are fixed during a dialogue when MUBAS is started. Typing the command LENGTH will tell the number of words used and the number of words

Addresses		Total Memory	Single Program
Decimal	Octal		
00000	000000	LU CORE	HEADER
00319	000477	~~~~~~~~~~~~	
		~~	
00680	001250	MU-BASIC	USER CODE
25268	061264		
25269	061265	BASIC PROGRAM 1	SYMBOL TABLE
36863	107777		
36864	110000	BASIC PROGRAM 2	STRINGS
49905	141361		
49906	141362	RT11	ARRAYS
57346	157777		

The approximate numbers on the left are called addresses. They are usually shown as octal numbers.

Figure 1. LSI-11 Memory Layout

available at each terminal. The total of these numbers does not include the area labeled *header* but includes the four remaining areas labeled *user code, symbol table, strings,* and *arrays*. The boundaries are not fixed, but shift as the program is altered or run.

The *header* for each user's job contains a list of the exact boundaries of the five areas at any point in time, the address of any free space, the name of the program, and the number of current lines being executed. It also contains work areas (buffers) which hold data input when editing a line in an immediate mode. Many other pointers, counters, and condition flags also can be found there.

The *user code* contains the intermediate form of code stored as tokens, text and references to the symbol table. All line numbers, variable names, numeric constants, and keywords are changed from the form in which they are entered to an altered form. Line numbers and variable names are stored as a two-byte reference to a spot in the symbol table. Numeric constants are stored in three different ways. If the number is an integer between 0 and 255, it is stored as two bytes (byte one is 375). If it is an integer between -32767 and +32767 not in the range 0-255, it is stored as three bytes (byte one is 376), and if it is neither of the first two, it is stored as a first byte of 374, followed by a four-byte floating point number. Keywords are stored as a single byte token. Each statement ends with an end-of-line token regardless of whether this results from a backlash in the code or the termination of a line of code. The last byte of the user code area is an end-of-program token.

The *symbol table* contains one entry for each different line number and variable name in the program regardless of how many times either appears in the program. The line number reference consists of four bytes, two of them hold the line number and the other two point to the location of the beginning of the line in the user code area. The variable name may be numeric, or string, and may also represent an array. The variable entry requires ten bytes, the first two of which identify the type of variable it is, numeric (375 377), array (376 377) or string (377 377). The remaining bytes hold the variable name and either the value of a variable or point to where the value may be found. Every time the user code is scanned during execution, it must go to the symbol table to check out any reference to a line number or to check the current value of a variable.

```
                    Before Translation

10 IF X1<=9 THEN X1=515

                    After Translation

User Code Area (as octal bytes)

   10      IF    X1    <=    9   THEN   X1    =       515      \  END
000 000  205 000 004 257 375 011 255 000 004 267 376 002 003 200 232


Symbol Table (as octal bytes)

   LINE 10              NUMERIC VARIABLE X1
000 012  xxx xxx   375 377  xxx xxx xxx xxx  000 000  130 061
  10     ADDRESS   NUMERIC       VALUE        UNUSED     X1

   All numbers shown in memory are shown in octal.  A line
   number or variable reference in the user code area is a
   relative address in the symbol table.  Address 000 000
   is the first byte of the table and 000 004 is the fifth
   byte.  The first two bytes of the line number in the
   symbol table is the only place the actual line number is
   permanently recorded anywhere in the total job area.
   The address portion (last two bytes) of the line number
   entry is the absolute memory address of the first byte
   of the translated line in the user code area.
```

Figure 2. Sample view of user code and symbol table in memory.

The area containing *strings* holds the data pointed to by the symbol table whenever a string variable is referenced. Elements of string arrays are also contained in the string area. The symbol table data contains the length of a string variable. If much string manipulation is done in the program, the string area will become a scratch pad for string values that will eventually overflow. Then a 'garbage collector' routine will be called to consolidate all strings that are currently in use. This routine will also move the strings to one end of the string area so that free memory can be obtained in order to continue execution.

The values of the elements of numeric *arrays* are held in a separate area. If the array has more than ten elements, it is set up before execution of the user code as part of a preliminary scan of the code. This scan locates any DIM statement, so as to set up and initialize large arrays.

EDITING THE PROGRAM

Typing a line of code into the terminal in immediate mode results in a module known as the editor, calling a routine known as the translator. The translator constructs a new line of code from the line that was input.

This new line will be inserted into the user code area in memory by the editor.

The translator analyzes the line character by character, deciding what token to use and checking the symbol table for line numbers and variable names. Figure 3 shows a simplified flow chart that illustrates the translation process. If the translator does not find that an entry already exists in the table, it creates an entry at the end of the table. It alters the form in which numbers are stored, as mentioned earlier. Special text tokens are also inserted between quotes and text or in a remark statement. If a NEXT statement is found, the translator sets up a ten-byte work area to aid in execution of the code at a later time.

After the translation is complete, control returns to the editor routine. This routine inserts new and modified lines or deletes lines whose line number is typed alone, by updating the translated code in the user code area. The entire symbol table must be moved each time there is a change in size of user code. Because the 'free area' of memory is located between the symbol table and the string area, the boundaries of both areas may float when room is needed during the typing in of code or during the execution of the program.

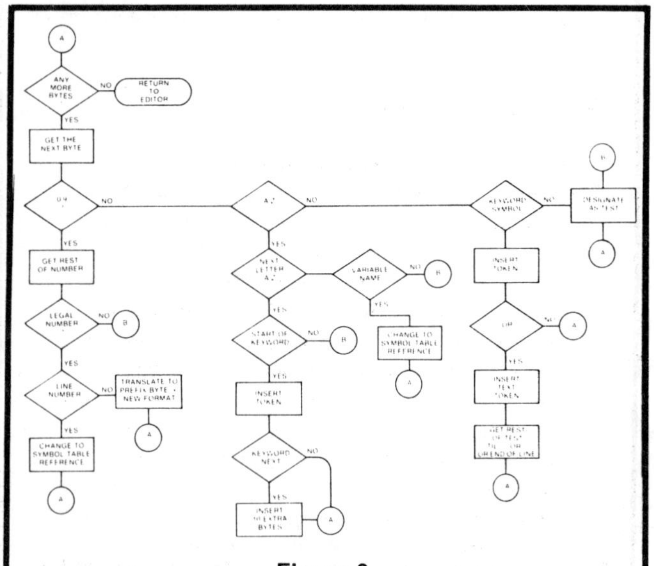

Figure 3.

RUNNING THE PROGRAM

When the command is given to RUN the program, MUBAS will become very busy. We will ignore all the times it might be interrupted by the operating system to process the ticking of a clock, the processing of I/O, and the swapping of control from one user to the next. Instead, we will concentrate on the execution of the translated user code which is waiting in memory. First, the editor has the command translated just as it would for a numbered statement. When it realizes there is no line number, it will look the RUN command up in a table of commands to be sure it is valid. It then passes control to the execution module. This modules makes sure you didn't change your mind and hit control C key (^C) to stop the program, and then dispatches the command to be executed by a RUN routine.

This run routine does two main types of tasks. It cleans up any unfinished business from the last time the program was run (we may have just been in the process of debugging), and sets up new parameters based on the current state of the program. It must tidy up any open files and eliminate the buffer space allotted to such files. It must also clear out the values of any variables both in the symbol table and the string area, and reset any parameters associated with the random number generator or special keyboard characteristics.

After these items have been initialized, the RUN routine then starts to examine the code in the user area to locate any DIM statement. Any DIM statement found is used to allocate room in the array area, if the array is numeric. DEF statements are also examined so as to establish any user defined functions needed in the program. The presence of a RANDOMIZE statement will uniquely initialize the parameters of the RND function, and then control will pass back to the execution routine

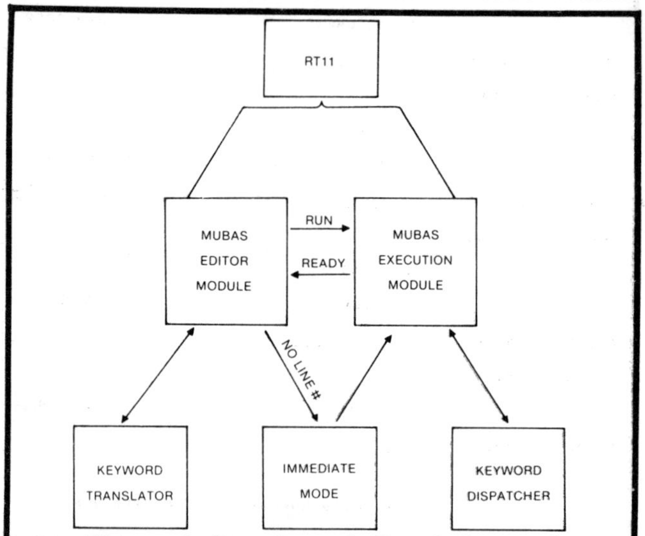

Figure 4. Overview of Translating and Dispatching Keywords.

with the line number pointer set to begin execution at the first statement of the program.

The execution routine will then check for ^C, and if execution is to continue, will start to unravel the tokens in the first statement. Since a large part of the syntax checking has already been done when the token was originally generated, the execution can take place very quickly. However, even the simplest of statements, such as a GOTO statement, would require dozens of instructions to be executed. MUBAS scans the translated line until it finds the GOTO token. This must be checked in a table of tokens and control is passed to the routine that handles GOTO's. This routine calls another routine to get the next two bytes and use them to get the line number address from the symbol table. Some error checking must be done in case the line number address is not in the symbol table, or an end of line token does not follow the code already interpreted. The pointer that indicates the current line being executed must be updated, and control then passes back to the execution module.

We can see from this discussion that an interpretive compiler like MUBAS can not compete, in terms of sheer speed, with a truly compiled language in which a GOTO statement requiring dozens of statements could be replaced by a single jump statement (JMP). However, the convenience factor of the flexibility of the interactive debugging of a program, and the simplicity of use, make BASIC a very powerful language. A second important consideration is that for most applications outside of scientific computing, the issue of speed does not center around the speed of execution in memory, but rather on the slowness of peripherals like disks or printers. In other words, most applications are I/O bound and not compute bound. This can truly turn the tokens in BASIC into tokens of good fortune! □

Pascal becomes software superstar

by John G. Posa

From the mountain fastness of Switzerland there came 10 years ago a programming language called Pascal. For the first few years of its life it created little stir, but then it began to gain popularity in academia and eventually industry. Today, Pascal is finding its way into machines of all shapes and sizes around the world.

Pascal has exercised the hardware of more than 60 families of computing machines, and new ones are being added to the list at this moment. It has been dubbed "PL/1 done right" and "Basic of the future," and it has been made to run on the ubiquitous 8080 microprocessor, Cray Research's giant, superfast Cray-1, and a host of machines in between.

Kenneth Bowles, director of the Institute for Information Systems at the University of California at San Diego, and his colleagues are now a major force pushing for Pascal in the U. S. They have put together a single-user operating system that an increasing number of people are using and even redistributing as part of their own systems.

Looking back, Bowles feels it was just lucky that Pascal was chosen. While using Algol during a seven-year stint as director of UCSD's Computer Center, he became convinced that the benefits of structured programming practices could not be overemphasized. He also realized that microcomputers would not disappear and that they represented a very cost-effective teaching aid.

Now for a language. About four years ago, Bowles looked to Pascal. Algol just was not general enough and Pascal, which was designed to teach programming in the first place, was starting to be used as an academic tool. "We saw industry producing a number of different machines and we didn't want to be locked into any one in particular," he remembers. "We needed software that would last a long time and could also be traded between various institutions." So portability became an underlying factor in their work.

Pascal, drafted in 1968 in Zurich by Niklaus Wirth (see "Obeisance to Pascal," p. 182, was chosen as the starting point, but its memory requirements were excessive. With eyes on the LSI-11 as a target machine, Bowles used frequency-based encoding to squeeze the compiler's requirements down to less than 20 kilobytes. (Simply stated, frequency-based encoding rearranges operators so that the most frequently used are the easiest to access.) He got this working on the PDP-11 and knew it would also go on the LSI-11, so in June of last year he reset his sights on the 8080.

Within eight months, Pascal was running on the 8080, and Bowles was stunned. He recalls saying something like, "We've got something here and we'd better let the world know about it." They did. Soon, Pascal was running on Zilog's Z80, and by the end of this year, the language will be routing electrons in the 6800, TI's 9900, and Rockwell International's 6502. In fact, there doesn't appear to be any machine incapable of handling Pascal.

Bowles and his associates work with Pascal's intermediate code called P-code. Pascal programs are first compiled into the P-code, which in turn gets interpreted on the various target machines. This is one reason why UCSD Pascal comes up so quickly. The only code that needs to be written in the native tongue of the target processor is the small interpreter. From that point on, the UCSD system takes over. At this time, some of the major components of the UCSD operating system package include the Pascal compiler with extensions for strings, disk files, interactive graphics, and system programming, an editor, a file manager, a debugger, and various utilities.

Plans at UCSD are to continue to make Pascal more enticing to prospective users by adding target machines and useful extensions. There is also a chance to put Pascal in read-only memory. "All of the code that our compiler generates is potentially ROMable," says Bowles. "It's position-independent, it doesn't modify itself, and our system itself would make it very straightforward to refer to procedures in ROM." UCSD Pascal also just received another boost in the form of a four-chip, 16-bit microcomputer introduced by Western Digital Corp. that actually interprets P-code in hardware (see p. 155).

"It's serendipitous," admits Bowles, "Somehow we happened to be at the right place at the right time with a Pascal system and the microcomputer industry was hurting for a high-level language—and our system will run on just about all the popular processors."

Happy user. One of the many firms adopting UCSD's Pascal is American Microsystems Inc. AMI plans to offer the language as part of its MDC-100 Microprocessor Development Center. Dick Woodward, manager of microprocessor software development at AMI, says, "For defining data structures, Pascal is much more powerful than Basic, Fortran, PL/1, and certainly assembly language. In conjunction with Pascal's control constructs, we plan to cut programming time by a factor of four to five and reduce the cost of maintenance."

The Pascal User's Group is based at the University of Minnesota in Minneapolis; Andy Mickel, the group's coordinator, says he is swamped with inquiries. After two years, the group comprises some 2,600 members from 41 countries and is growing.

Mickel is also a systems programmer at the university's computer center. "Two years ago, we ran less than 1,000 Pascal jobs," he says. "This year it will reach 262,000." He takes no credit for promoting the language's popularity but rather attributes it to the language itself. "Pascal is good on its own merit. It would have been successful regardless," he says.

Group interest. The Digital Equipment Computer User's Society has its own Pascal Special Interest Group, formed about two years ago. Enrollment now stands at approximately 600 and is climbing. According to John R. Barr, a professor in the computer science department at the University of Montana and spokesman for the group, it is evaluating various implementations of Pascal in DEC computers. Now operational is a two-pass compiler that runs in conjunction with the RSX—11/M, RSX—11/D, IAS, and RSTS operating systems; it is being extended to use RT—11 and Bell Lab's UNIX. Other members are adapting Pascal for DEC's new VAX 11/780 system.

Closer to the commercial world, Pascal has been equally successful. For example, Texas Instruments Inc. uses Pascal extensively, though it stops short of calling it the corporate language. Roger Bate, manager of advanced software at TI, says the company surveyed languages about a year and a half ago and narrowed the choice to C, Pascal, and Bliss. Pascal was chosen, but it was apparent that TI had to make some changes to make it "more for programming than for teaching." So the firm's programmers took Wirth's language (which remains a proper subset) and added fixed-point and decimal arithmetic capabilities to it, as well as more versatile array processing.

Pascal usage at TI is on the rise,

What is Pascal?

Pascal is a block-structured programming language in the style of Algol. Programs consist of two parts: a heading names the program and specifies the variables it will use, and the body of the program, called a block, follows. A block is further subdivided into six sections. The first four declare the labels, constants, data types, and variables. The fifth names and precedes an actual procedure or function. The last section, called the statement section, contains the executable code for the named function or procedure.

Labels identify statements so they can be referenced. Constants equate numbers with names for use throughout a program, like pi = 3.14. Data types are numerous; furthermore, structured types can be defined to include arrays, records, sets, and files. Each named variable must be followed by its type. Procedures can be put within procedures, and the statements for each must be preceded with the keyword "begin" and terminated with the word "end." Operators are defined for multiply, divide, add, subtract, logical, and relational, and numerous control statements are allowed.

with 30% to 40% of the new programs being written in it. Included are those for initial software development, tools like compilers and libraries, and systems programming. In April, TI began offering Pascal for its DS990 disk-based minicomputer systems. The 990 compiler and several 990 system software modules are themselves coded in Pascal. Even Fortran routines can be embedded into TI's Pascal source code.

Another user is Electro Scientific Industries Inc. of Portland, Ore., a manufacturer of instruments and minicomputer-based laser trimmers. "We were coding in assembly language, but realized that we wouldn't be flexible enough to track the needs of our users," says Don Cutler, manager of systems engineering. So, like TI, the company went shopping for a high-level language. Basic and Fortran did not provide the real-time performance sought; PL/1 was too thorny and not benchmarked enough on small machines.

Choice. But Pascal seemed easy enough to understand and implement, so the firm obtained a compiler from the University of Illinois, changed about 99% of it to add things like real-number–processing capabilities, and ESI's software needs were satisfied. "The code generated typically uses only twice the memory and execution time of an assembly version," says Cutler.

But Electro Scientific did not go the P-code route. "When we started about five years ago, there wasn't much being done with P code," says Cutler. Instead, its compiler generates macrocode and a macro assembler generates assembly code. The macrocode gives ESI certain advantages. For efficient execution, complex operations like fast Fourier transforms can be written in macrocode and embedded directly. Also, macro debuggers for the PDP-11 can be utilized. But Cutler does not scoff at P-code. "Given a random processor, P-code is the only way to go because it's so portable. Microprocessor implementations center around it, and it's the way of the future," he says.

The firm's compiler has spawned a separate company called Oregon Minicomputer Software. It has exclusive rights to market the compiler, which sells for $1,500, and has written versions to run on the PDP-11 with the RT-11, RSX—11/M, and RSTS operating systems. Oregon Minicomputer also has developed symbolic and variable editing packages in collaboration with its parent firm, and is about a year away from an optimized compiler that will be even more efficient, although it may not be appropriate for small machines.

Question. But even as the enthusiasm builds, one may reasonably ask, "If Pascal is so wonderful, why is it that every new user has to practically rewrite it?" The answer stems from the fact that all languages have their shortcomings, and Pascal has some too. First, Wirth's definition does not allow for separate compilation, which can be cumbersome. It means that a Pascal program must be compiled in its entirety: if a new routine must be added, it has to be entered into the original source code and recompiled.

Another complaint voiced by some users is that the size of an array must be fixed at the time of compilation. Pascal is very big on type-checking, which means that if a variable is of a certain type (integer, for example) in one part of a program, it must remain that type. This is actually a desirable programming practice, except that if the size of an array changes, it is considered a new type and genuine Pascal will flag it as an error.

In terms of system programming, it can be awkward to introduce modules of the type necessary for concurrent processes. Large arrays must be set up with global variables for the procedures to use, and if one of the variables is altered inadvertently, problems arise.

But complex operating systems can be written in Pascal, as Per Brinch-Hansen proved a few years ago with his Concurrent Pascal. And Wirth himself is now concerned with a new language called Modula that is based on Pascal and aimed at the concurrent-computation problem.

The newer Pascal compilers have all but eliminated some of these headaches. For example, Electro Scientific and others simply insert a dummy header with the variables they will use and add the actual procedure later. And TI has an expression to vary the size of an array without getting reprimanded. The only remaining problem seems to be exactly what extensions should become standard and how they should be implemented. Standards are important not to force their use but to enable those not adhering to them to state in precise terms how they are being different.

Workshop. This summer, UCSD held a workshop to discuss such standard extensions, and over 30 different firms were represented. Many ideas were discussed, including interrupts and the ability to pass procedure and function names as parameters; the report from that meeting will soon be available.

The military, too, began with Pascal to develop its standard language, now in the Steelman phase. For a while, it was believed that the result would be Pascal with standard extensions. However, recent documents reveal a widening gap between the Defense Department's language and Pascal, to the extent that Pascal may not even be a proper subset. Compatibility may be possible, however,through filter programs that would translate one language into the other. □

Obeisance to Pascal

Why Pascal? The programming language apparently was named by its author, Niklaus Wirth, for the French philosopher and mathematician Blaise Pascal (1623–1662) for no reason other than the high esteem in which Prof. Wirth holds his teachings. The language is a relatively young one: a preliminary version was drafted at the Technische Hochschule in Zurich, Switzerland, by Wirth in 1968. Two years later, Urs Ammann, also at Zurich and aided by Wirth and colleagues, developed an accompanying compiler for Control Data Corp.'s CDC 6000 computer, and Pascal was off and running.

PASCAL vs BASIC

by David A. Mundie

Getcha PASCAL here!

David Mundie's discourse explores Pascal by contrasting it to BASIC. For readers with a limited programming background we recommend reading the Pascal listing on page before beginning the article. The object of the Mastermind-like game is for the player to guess a randomly generated array of characters. The last 5 statements are the action part of the program; the preceding statements are the definition part.

The formal definition of Pascal is contained in Pascal: User Manual and Report *by Kathleen Jensen and Niklaus Wirth, published by Springer-Verlag, Berlin 1974. Ken Bowles'* Introduction to Computer Science, *published by Springer-Verlag in late 1977, uses Pascal as its teaching vehicle. Information on implementations of Pascal may be obtained through the* Pascal Newsletter, *available from Andy Mickel, University Computer Center, 227 Exp Engr, University of Minnesota, Minneapolis, MN 55455.*

If someone were to propose that the outdated Z-8888 CPU be retained in preference to the newer, faster, and more powerful 6868A, simply because everyone was already familiar with the older machine, his sanity would probably be questioned. Yet when it comes to the languages used on those machines, the personal computing community seems content to hobble along with a hopelessly inadequate language whose only excuse for existence is that it got there first. This contrast between our compulsiveness with regards to machines and our fetishism with regards to languages is surely one of the more interesting psychological aspects of the current computing scene.

Those with a vested interest in BASIC would have us believe that the situation is irreversible. I personally believe that the market for BASIC is just about saturated, and that if personal computing is to attain its full potential, the many marginally interested members of the general public will have to be won over with a language more suited to their needs than

BASIC. The casual user of the future will demand a language that is simple, powerful, and logical; I am hopeful that he will get it.

Be that as it may, now that microprocessor implementations of my favorite language, Pascal, are becoming available, I think the time has come to examine the two languages side by side, and what follows is my contribution to such a comparison. I am a prototypical applications programmer with no background in computer science, so I shall not attempt to propound the principles of structured programing on which, to a large extent, Pascal is based. Instead I shall concentrate on an actual BASIC program and its Pascal translation. I shall attempt to demonstrate that Pascal, because it offers an adequate repertoire of data types and control structures, allows the programmer to remain on a high level of algorithmic abstraction, where he functions best, whereas BASIC forces him to dirty his hands with improvised tricks and clumsy stopgaps. Pascal expresses algorithms clearly and simply, while BASIC does its best to obscure them altogether.

	BASIC	PASCAL
DATA TYPES		
integer	x	x
real	x	x
character (string)	x	x
boolean		x
defined scalar		x
STRUCTURING METHODS		
array	x	x
record		x
set		x
file		x
pointer		x
OPERATORS		
mixed arithmetic	x	x
integer division		x
modulus		x
exponentiation	x	
relational operators	x	x
set operators		x
logical operators		x
CONTROL STRUCTURES		
if	x	x
case		x
for	x	x
while		x
repeat		x
goto	x	x
SUBPROGRAMS		
recursion		x
local variables		x
parameters		x

CHART 1. Pascal vs. BASIC at a glance. The only feature BASIC has that Pascal doesn't is exponentiation!

I could have made my task easier by examining those features of Pascal which have absolutely no equivalent in BASIC, and which by themselves would justify Pascal's adoption as a standard language: its recursive procedures, for example, or its superb data-structuring facilities. But a binary tree in BASIC, if feasible, would be a painful thing to behold, so I have restricted myself to only the simplest uses of the simples of Pascal's constructs. Furthermore, I could have chosen one of the illegible, amorphous BASIC programs which abound, because BASIC encourages sloppy thinking. Instead, I have chosen one which is carefully written. This is, then, a 'worst possible case' comparison as far as Pascal is concerned.

The sample programs are presented in Listings 1 and 2. The functioning of the programs will be explained below under 'program structure'. It is not my intention to teach Pascal, but the following points may be helpful to the BASIC user seeing a Pascal program for the first time. **Readln(x)** and **writeln(x)** are roughly equivalent to INPUT X and PRINT X — they are mnemonics for 'READ a LiNe' and 'WRITE a LiNe' respectively. Statements are separated by semicolons. Arrays are indexed using square brackets. Type declarations are mandatory for all variables. **Chr** and **ord** are transfer functions; **chr(3)** returns the third element in the character set — usually the character 'c' — while **ord('c')** returns the integer 3.

I shall compare the programs on nine specific points.

1. IDENTIFIERS. I should think the most refreshing aspect of Pascal for a weary BASIC programmer would be its identifiers, which may be of any length. Thus the completely opaque 'T' and 'G' of the BASIC program become the much more transparent 'target' and 'guess'; this is absolutely essential if a program is to be readable as an algorithm. I shall not belabor the point, since I realize that BASIC is at last moving towards longer variable names, but it should be pointed out that in Pascal identifiers name not just variables, but also proce-

```
10   DIM F(9),G(9),T(9),H(18,3)
20   GOSUB 560
30   FOR X = 0 TO A
40   LET T(X) = INT(RND(R)*B)+1
50   NEXT X
60   FOR I = 1 TO A+B+1
70   FOR X = 0 TO A
80   LET F(X) = 0
90   NEXT X
100  LET F1 = 0
110  LET F2 = 0
120  INPUT V
130  IF V<>0 THEN 180
140  FOR X = 1 TO I-1
150  PRINT H(X,0); "," ;H(X,1); "=" ;H(X,2)
160  NEXT X
170  GO TO 120
180  IF V = 1 THEN 480
190  IF V = 2 THEN 670
200  LET T1 = V
210  FOR X = 0 TO A
220  LET G(X) = INT(T1/(10**(A-X)))
230  LET T1 = T1-G(X)*(10**(A-X))
240  IF G(X)<1 THEN 260
250  IF G(X)<B+1 THEN 280
260  PRINT "BAD NUMBER IN"; V
270  GO TO 70
280  IF G(X)<>T(X) THEN 310
290  LET F(X) = 1
300  LET F1 = F1+1
310  NEXT X
320  IF F1 = A+1 THEN 540
330  FOR Y = 0 TO A
340  IF T(Y) = G(Y) THEN 420
350  FOR X = 0 TO A
360  IF G(Y)<>T(X) THEN 410
370  IF F(X) = 1 THEN 410
380  LET F(X) = 1
390  LET F2 = F2+1
400  GO TO 420
410  NEXT X
420  NEXT Y
430  PRINT F1;",";F2
440  LET H(I,0) = F1
450  LET H(I,1) = F2
460  LET H(I,2) = V
470  NEXT I
480  LET V= 0
490  FOR X = 0 TO A
500  LET V = V+T(X)*(10**(A-X))
510  NEXT X
520  PRINT "ANSWER IS";V
530  GO TO 30
540  PRINT "YOU GUESSED IT"
550  GO TO 30
560  PRINT
570  PRINT "   DIGITS & MAX VALUE"
580  INPUT A,B
590  LET A = A-1
600  RETURN
610  END
```

Listing 1. This is a simple number-guessing game of the Mastermind type.

```
program banbasic(input,output);
const maxnumch=10; maxmax=71;
type token=packed array[1..maxnunch] of char;
var target,guess:token; hi,lo,ch:char; oldg:array 1..maxmax of token;
     i,j,try,maxtries,black,white,numchar:integer;
     oldb,oldw:packed array[1..maxmax] of integer;
     endofround,endofgame,wmatch,bad:boolean;
     matched:array[1..maxnumch] of boolean;
procedure newgame;
 begin endofgame:=false;
  for i:=1 to maxnunch do target[i]:=' '; guess:=target;
  writeln(' low character?'); readln(lo);
  writeln(' high character?'); readln(hi);
  writeln(' no. of characters?'); readln(numchar);
  maxtries:=numchar+ord(hi)-ord(lo)
 end;
procedure newround;
 begin endofround:=false; try:=0; for i:=1 to numchar do
  target[i]:=chr(ord(lo)+trunc(random(1)*(ord(hi)-ord(lo))))
 end;
procedure command;
  procedure tally(var i,color:integer);
   begin matched[i]:=true; color:=color+1 end;
 begin writeln(' command?'); readln(ch); case ch of
  'r':for i:=1 to try do writeln(oldb[i],'b',oldw[i],'w',oldg[i]);
  'q':begin writeln(' answer is: ',target); endofround:=true end;
  's': begin endofround:=true; endofgame:=true end;
  'c': begin i:=0; repeat i:=i+1; read(guess[i]);
        bad:=not(guess[i]in[lo..hi]) until (i=numchar)or(bad); readln;
        if bad then writeln(' bad character') else if guess=target then
        begin writeln(' you guessed it!'); endofround:=true
        end else if try=maxtries then
        begin writeln(' you are lost; answer is: ',target);endofround:=true
        end else
        begin black:=0; white:=0; try:=try+1;
         for i:=1 to numchar do matched[i]:=false;
         for i:=1 to numchar do if guess[i]=target[i]then tally(i,black);
         for i:=1 to numchar do if guess[i]≠target[i]then
         begin j:=0; repeat j:=j+1;
          wmatch:= (guess[i]=target[j]) and (not(matched[j]));
          if wmatch then tally(j,white) until (wmatch)or(j=numchar)
         end; writeln(' b',black,' w',white);
         oldg[try]:=guess; oldb[try]:=black; oldw[try]:=white
        end
       end
   end
  end;

begin neugame;
 repeat neuround;
  repeat command until endofround
 until endofgame
end.
```

Listing 2. This is a free Pascal translation of listing 1, using arrays of characters rather than integers. Notice that the algorithm for the entire program is contained in just the last five lines of the listing. Following traditional Pascal practice, reserved words have been underlined.

dures, functions, constants, and types, so that, for example, 'GOSUB 560' becomes 'newgame'.

2. PROGRAM STRUCTURE. Another major difference which immediately strikes the eye is the difference in the structure of the two programs. The structure of the BASIC program is easy to describe: it hasn't any. It is a simple list of statements of equal value. It has been shown time and time again that this is bad news when it comes time to debug, modify, document, or just plain *understand* a program. In contrast, the Pascal program is broken down into a number of manageable parts which may be tested and understood separately. The algorithm for the program as a whole is found at the very end, in five succinct lines:

```
begin newgame;
  repeat newround;
    repeat command until endofround
  until endofgame
end.
```

It is difficult to imagine programming on a higher level of algorithmic abstraction. Even the complete programming novice could intuit that 'newgame' initializes certain game conditions, that 'newround' starts a new round, that a round consists of processing commands until the round is over, and that rounds are played until the game is over. Nothing in the BASIC program gives so much as a hint of what the overall pattern of the game is; instead, the eye wanders aimlessly over the page, desperately looking for a clue as to what is going on.

By looking at the declaration part of the Pascal program (broken down into **const** for constant, **var** for variable and **type** declarations), then at each of the program's subroutines, we can fill in that general algorithm with the details of its operation. The object of the game is for the player to guess an array of characters which the computer generates in the procedure newround using a random number generator. The procedure command prompts the player to enter one of four possible commands by typing one of the four letters 's', 'q', 'r', or 'c'. A S(top) command terminates the round and the game immediately. A Q(uit) command shows the player the answer and terminates the round, while a R(ecap) command shows the player his previous guesses and how well they scored, using the arrays oldg, oldb, and oldw. Lastly, a C(alculate) command reads in a guess from the player, and checks it for correctness; if the player has exceeded the limit on the number of tries (maxtries) or has guessed the target exactly, the round is terminated and a suitable message displayed, otherwise the guess is compared to the target and the player is told how many correct characters he had in the correct positions (black) and how many in incorrect positions (white). The procedure newgame, finally, specifies the number of characters in the target and guess (numchar), the range of acceptable characters (lo to hi), and the maximum number of tries allowed.

The movement from generality to detail which we have just seen is called 'stepwise refinement' by the theoreticians, and it makes a program easier to read because at any step one need only consider those details that are really necessary. Step-wise refinement is possible because Pascal is block-structured, which means that subprograms, like 'command' have the same structure as programs. Without going into detail, we may say that a block in Pascal consists of a definition part, in which constants, types, variables, and subprograms are defined, and an action part, which contains the algorithm of the block. Thus the five lines quoted above constitute the action part of the main program; everything else is its definition part.

3. DATA TYPES. Here's another example of how Pascal allows the programmer to think at a higher level of abstraction than can his BASIC counterpart. Consider the function of the array F in the BASIC program. The elements of this array are initialized to zero (line 80), then whenever a match between the target and the guess is found, the appropriate element of F is set to one. Later the array is used to test whether a given element has already been matched, by testing 'IF F(X) = 1' at line 370. From this it should be clear that on the *algorithmic* level, F(X) is not a *number* at all: it is a Boolean variable taking on the values *true* and *false*. Because BASIC lacks this data type, the programmer has had to leave the algorithmic level and make do with integers, with the result that the intent of his program has become seriously disguised. One's first expectation is that F(X) will *count* something, and only a painstaking examination of the entire program reveals its true function.

In contrast, Pascal provides a Boolean type, so that the programmer can remain on the more abstract level and simply write 'matched[i] := true', where the intention of the statement is perfectly transparent. An incidental advantage of this is that each element of 'matched' takes up just one bit of storage whereas each element in 'F' takes up at least a byte, probably more.

The type Boolean is one of Pascal's four predefined scalar data types, the others being integer, real, and character. In addition, it is possible to define new scalar (i.e. ordered) types by listing their values, as for example 'week = (mo, tu, we, th, fr, sa, su)', thus providing for extremely easy-to-read programs. These scalar types are the fundamental building blocks from which all structured types are derived.

4. STRUCTURING METHODS:
ARRAYS. Not only does BASIC fail to provide one of the most important basic data types, it also fails to provide adequate means of structuring the types it does have. To see this, let us look at the arrays 'T' and 'G'. From a strictly logical point of view, these are simply arrays of characters. But in trying to express this in his program, the BASIC programmer ran up against the fact that BASIC *has* no arrays of characters. Once again, a makeshift solution has been imposed on him: in this case, it is the 'integer' V which is read in and then 'unpacked' into its individual digits by the tortured routine in lines 220 - 230, then repacked in lines 490 - 510. This is bad not just because it is awkward and slow, but also because it completely obscures what is going on.

Now Pascal *also* lacks arrays of characters as a data type. But it does have the character as a basic data type, and the array as a basic structuring method, so that the definition of a type for the target is as simple as saying:

```
token: packed array [1..maxnumch]
    of char
```

This done, the type token may be used just as any of the basic data types may be: in assignment statements (target:= guess), as parameters to subprogram calls (writeln(target)), in expressions (if target = guess) and so on. Two incidental advantages of the Pascal approach are that the player is not restricted to digits, and that the Pascal arrays take up only a fraction of the space occupied by their BASIC equivalents.

The newer kinds of BASIC with string variables may answer this *specific* objection, but not my central point, which is that in Pascal it is possible to define *any* data type built out of the basic units, whereas in BASIC you must take what you are offered.

This is perhaps the place to mention that requiring an array to start at 0 (or at 1), with the resulting awkwardness of line 590 where a variable is read in and then immediately decremented by one, seems barbaric to a Pascaler. In Pascal arrays may have any number of dimensions, and both bounds are chosen at will.

The array is only one of five basic structured types in Pascal. I shall discuss the type **set** below, but the other three (**pointer**, **file**, and **record**) are, as I mentioned above, so far beyond BASIC that discussing them would be pure malice on my part.

5. STRUCTURING METHODS: SETS. For the sake of conciseness I have eliminated most error-checking from the two programs, but suppose we wanted to check that no illegal commands were entered. If the commands were letters, as in the Pascal program, checking them in BASIC would entail the absurd:

```
100 IF C$ = "R" THEN 220
110 IF C$ = "Q" THEN 220
120 IF C$ = "S" THEN 220
130 IF C$ = "C" THEN 220
140 PRINT "ILLEGAL INPUT"
```

where each value must be tested separately. Pascal takes care of this with the structured type **set**, whose utility goes far beyond this simple example, and which in fact allows set manipulation in all its generality. The above test in Pascal would be this simple:

```
if ch in ['r', 'q', 's', 'c'] then . . .
```

where **in** is the relational operator for inclusion; program banbasic uses it to check that the characters in the guess are in the set [hi. .lo]. Thanks to this feature, it would be a trivial matter to rewrite the Pascal program so that the target and guess be composed of *any* set of values, contiguous or not; for example, to make it into a card game, one could use the set ['0'..'9', 'j', 'k', 'q']. In BASIC this would require a completely new program.

6. CONSTANTS. The second line of the Pascal program defines two program constants. 'Maxnumch', for example, is set to 10. This feature of Pascal allows for a more abstract and therefore more meaningful program. Instead of seeing '10' in the program and wondering 'Why 10?', one sees maxnumch and remembers that it represents the maximum number of characters in a token, whatever that number happens to be. In addition, this makes *changing* the value of maxnumch throughout the program simply a matter of changing one line. The BASIC programmer must either type '10' throughout the program, in which case changing its value becomes an ordeal, or else resort to the illogical and wasteful expedient of designing a variable which never varies. Gone forever is the absurdity of a pi 'function' — one simply writes 'pi=3.1415927' at the beginning of the program and forgets about it after that.

7. CONTROL STRUCTURES: ASSIGNMENT AND CONDITIONAL STATEMENTS. We have seen how Pascal outperforms BASIC at setting up meaningful data types. Now let us turn our attention to the other side of the coin, and see how data is manipulated in the two languages.

In Pascal as in BASIC the fundamental kind of statement is of course the assignment statement. But where BASIC lacked the courage to introduce a special symbol for this all-important operation, using instead the awkward LET and the ambiguous equals sign, Pascal (like Algol) clearly distinguishes between the assignment operator (:=) and the relational operator (=).

To control program flow from one part of a program to another, two kinds of branching are essential. In the first, flow is determined by the values (*true* or *false*) of Boolean expressions such as 'X=1'. In both languages, this kind of branching is achieved by the **if** statement, but the Pascal version is far superior for two reasons. For one thing, it has an **else** clause which is so desirable it has begun to show up in certain versions of BASIC. But even more important, it is a much more natural tool for expressing algorithms because it groups statements with the conditions for their execution, rather than the reverse, as BASIC does. Consider for example the following program segment:

```
100 IF X=1 THEN 400
200 LET Y=456
300 GO TO 500
400 LET Y=123
```

It is absurd to place the action to be taken if X equals 1 as far as possible from the expression 'X=1' and instead place alongside 'X=1' the action that will be taken precisely when X is not equal to 1. This kind of thing is well and good for machine languages, but it is not the way we think and has no place in a high-level language used to express our thinking in machine-usable form. It makes far more sense to do as Pascal does:

```
if x=1 then y:=123 else y:=456
```

This is more readable as well as more elegant.

The confusion in BASIC's control structures reaches catastrophic proportions when we come to the second kind of branching, where flow is determined not by Boolean expressions, but by expressions which may take many different values. The particular course of action to be taken depends on the value of the expression. Some versions of BASIC provide a rudimentary version of this feature in the computed GO TO statement but the Pascal **case** statement is incomparably better for the following reasons. First, any scalar type except real may be used as the **case** variable. In the sample program the **case** statement in the procedure command depends on the value of the character ch. Second, the values specified need not be contiguous. In our example, the four values are 'r', 'q', 's', and 'c', whereas in BASIC they could only be the integers 1, 2, 3, and 4. This is an inelegant approach often requiring painful contortions. Third, as with the **if** statement, Pascal groups statements with the conditions for their execution, while BASIC does not. Thus the statement that will be executed if the command is 's' is the compound statement:

```
begin endofround:=true;
endofgame:=true end .
```

If the reader has any doubts as to whether the Pascal version is superior, I would ask him to look at the four commands in the procedure command, then try to trace the same flow of control in the BASIC program given that it depends on the value of V read in at line 120. (Hint: the BASIC program fails to distinguish between data and action, so that V is the player's guess as well as his command.) I think that any fair judge will have to admit that it is easier to follow the Pascal program than to chase all over in the BASIC version.

Pascal's approach to program control is made possible in large part by the compound statement. In Pascal any sequence of statements may be made into a single compound statement simply by bracketing it with the symbols **begin** and **end**. This possibility of grouping statements into meaningful wholes contributes to the structure of Pascal programs; in fact, the action parts of Pascal blocks are nothing more than compound statements.

Before leaving the subject of conditional statements, I must mention BASIC's lack of logical operators. I am sure that BASIC is already sufficiently embarrassed at its deficiency in this area, so I shall tactfully restrict myself to asking which is clearer:

```
100 IF X=1 THEN 500
200 IF Y>=2 THEN 800
300 IF Z=1 THEN 500
```

or

```
if (x=1) or ((y<2) and (z=1))
then . . .?
```

8. CONTROL STRUCTURES: REPETITIVE STATEMENTS. In a high-level language it is essential to provide ways to repeat a given statement until certain end-conditions are met. We may distinguish three cases: (a) The statement is repeated a specific number of times, no matter what. (b) The statement is repeated while (as long as) a certain condition is true. (c) The statement is repeated until a certain condition *becomes* true.

BASIC creates utter algorithmic confusion by providing only one control structure for all three cases, namely the FOR statement. Thus a reader of the BASIC program would quite naturally expect the loop starting at line 60 to be executed A+B+1 times, but this is *wrong*: it will execute until *either* I=A+B+1 *or* the player ends the round *or* the player ends the game *or* the target has been guessed. Once again, BASIC manages to camouflage completely the intended algorithm, which is clearly case (c), not case (a). This algorithm is perfectly expressed by the Pascal version:

```
repeat command until endofround
```

where 'command' sets the Boolean variable 'endofround' to true whenever any of the foregoing conditions occurs. Needless to say, Pascal also supplies a **while** statement for case (b).

9. PROCEDURES AND FUNCTIONS. It would have been nice to conclude with a point on which BASIC did almost as well as Pascal, but unfortunately, BASIC does very poorly with procedures and functions. Indeed, BASIC's miserable handling of subprograms is probably the single strongest argument in favor of ditching the language altogether, whereas Pascal's superb subroutine declaration facilities are a continual source of delight. Considerations of space prevent me from doing more than list some major points of comparison: (a) As already mentioned, Pascal subprograms bear *names*, not numbers, making for self-explanatory programs. (b) In Pascal, subroutines may have parameters, passed either by value or by address; without this feature I am not sure one should speak of subprograms at all. The procedure tally is used to keep track of both white and black by passing these two variables as parameters. (c) Pascal functions can return any scalar type or a pointer, not just numbers. (d) Pascal's block structure means that subprograms may define local constants, types, variables, and subprograms. An example is the procedure tally, which is local to the procedure command. This means that storage may be allocated as efficiently as possible, yet it is easy to guard against unwanted side effects. (f) Machine language programs external to the main program may be called.

IS BASIC EASY TO LEARN? We have seen that Pascal out-performs BASIC right down the line, and before concluding I would like to consider the oft-repeated advertisement that BASIC is an easily learned language closely resembling simple English. I think that even a casual consideration of this statement will reveal its falsity. As far as I know, two-character names and GO TO statements have never been elements of good English writing style. 'And', 'not', and 'or' are surely among the most common words in our language. We do not say, 'If it rains then 400 go to the beach go to 500 400 stay home', we say 'If it rains than stay home else go to the beach'. We do not tell our children to do their homework 999 times when we mean they should do it until they get it right. High-level languages should be judged on the simplicity and flexibility of their basic constructs, not on how much they look like English, but even on the latter score BASIC's claims are pure advertising hype.

Is Pascal harder to learn than BASIC? Frankly, I do not know. But of this I am certain: a Pascal subset consisting only of the four basic scalar types, the array as a structuring method, the five control structures and the subprogram facilities would *still* put BASIC to shame, and would be *easier* to learn than BASIC because it would be more systematic and more flexible. Even the 22 constructs of the full language represent a trivial pedagogical burden given the power of the language. Add to this the fact that in learning Pascal one is learning to think algorithmically and I think we need not fear Pascal's being unsuited for beginning programmers.

CONCLUSION. The radical difference in design philosophy between Pascal and BASIC was driven home to me recently by an item in *Kilobaud*. Some poor BASIC programmer had, quite naturally, felt the need to control program flow depending on whether a 'y' or an 'n' were input from the keyboard. Unable to do this easily in BASIC, he was seriously proposing a new statement of the form ANSWER F1, F2 which would brand to F1 or F2 depending on what was input from the keyboard. To a Pascaler, it is difficult even to imagine that what in Pascal amounts to a simple one-line function declaration (function answer: boolean; begin answer:=input↑='y'; readln end) should be in BASIC a question of redefining the language itself, to be fought out among the implementers and in the halls of ANSI, the American National Standards Institute.

BASIC offers an absolutely minimal set of features and expects you either to devise makeshift solutions or to design a new version of the language when they are not adequate. No wonder there are so many different versions of BASIC! Pascal offers a somewhat wider selection, but avoids the pitfall of trying to incorporate every feature known to man, as PL/I seems to. Instead of trying to foresee every possible application which might arise, Pascal's designers chose just those features which allow the user to expand the language himself to suit his needs. It is this combination of power and simplicity which makes Pascal the perfect choice for a standard microprocessor language. BAN BASIC! □

Assembler, compiler, or interpreter?

by Carol A. Ogdin
Reprinted with permission from *Mini-Micro Systems*, Aug. 1977

In olden days, when time on a computer cost $500 an hour at least, there was immense pressure on programmers to write lots of productive programs quickly to keep the equipment busy. Casual users, like engineers and mathematicians who had an occasional problem to solve, were discouraged from using the computer because they usually did not have the specialized skills to program in assembly language.

With the introduction of early high-level languages like Fortran, the cost to write programs declined. Now, programmers could afford to concentrate on describing algorithms instead of working out instruction sequences. More programs could be completed more quickly to keep a big machine busy. And users having only an occasional need to work a computer could also write their own programs in a fairly familiar notation. Competent programmers increased greatly in number and programming productivity climbed.

"The use of an assembly language imposes some extra requirements on a programmer."

Now, with the advent of the microcomputer, the differences between assembly language and the high-level languages have become the subject of continuing controversy. Which type is best to use? But the answer is not straight forward. Language choice may be influenced by the types of translators, storage capacity, and register quantity available to a systems designer. If execution time is of major importance, for example, the use of an interpreter can be ruled out. However, if a popular high-level language is available, some of the time-dependent code can be written in assembly language while the remaining code can be written in more powerful form.

A designer should also consider programmer productivity. If the software implementors are all relatively new to the field, the use of a high-level language will probably be best. Going this route will serve to give the design team more programming experience, and enable productivity to be compared when assembly language is attempted later.

All such factors influence the selection of a microcomputer language, but trade-offs on life cycle costs dominate any management's final decision. In general, it will be more economical to write programs in a high-level language if only a few of the same computer-based systems are to be built. Assembly language tends to be more economical to employ when more than 200 systems are to be built. A careful evaluation is usually required when production volumes range between 20 to 200 units.

LANGUAGE STYLES

It once was said that high-level languages like Fortran, Basic, and Cobol were "free-form." Statements in these languages could be written freely across the page. In contrast, most assembly languages were called "fixed form" with individual statements written in rigid vertical columns.

Later, high-level languages were called "one-to-many" languages. Each assembly language source code statement represented one computer instruction, but each high-level language statement translated into many equivalent computer instructions. Then macro processors with their vast "one-to-many" capabilities were added to assemblers, again making the distinction unclear.

In place of these historical definitions, perhaps a functional approach to the distinction between assembly language and high-level language would be useful: Let us look at language translators to determine how much work the programmer must do.

Thinking of the computer's hardware registers and storage locations as resources, we may determine where the responsibility and authority for resource allocation lie. If the programmer must allocate all of the registers in detail, then the language is at the assembly level. If the translator, be it interpreter or compiler, takes the responsibility for detailed allocation away from the programmer, then it accepts a high-level language.

The use of an assembly language imposes some extra requirements on a programmer. If there are two nested loops that must share the same index register, for example, a programmer must undertake a difficult, error-prone task: To keep track of which loop variable is in the register at each point in the program. The burden is relieved in a high-level language where the translator takes care of saving and restoring loop variables in index registers for the programmer.

On the other hand, the compiler for a language may have only one safe and predictable way of saving and restoring registers. However, a clever programmer, capitalizing on special knowledge of internal operation of the program,

SPECIAL MICROCOMPUTER LANGUAGES

New languages will continue to be announced. The microcomputer industry is just too large to avoid attracting new ventures in this area. The cautious designer should look at each new offering carefully, asking whether the language will be good enough to warrant the training expense involved, and whether it will be around long enough to justify using it in programs that may require maintenance after many years. Generally, only the popular languages that are also used in minis and large-scale computers will fit those criteria. For all their faults, Fortran and Basic will be with the micro designer for a long time to come.

A user who adopts a standard, popular language has access to the wealth of programs that already exist and the large pool of talent available to write new programs using a host machine-based cross-translator or a translator resident on the target computer itself.

An interpreter, of course, must execute on the micro for which programs are being written. Basic has been implemented on the Intel 8080, Zilog Z80, Motorola 6800 and 2650 microprocessors. Data General has an interpreter for its MicroNova. On DEC's LSI-11, the programmer can debug under the Basic interpreter, turning to the Basic compiler before long production runs.

The more sophisticated the language, the more likely that the compiler will be a cross-translator. As skills in compiler-writing trickle into the microcomputer industry, more and more compilers will be native to their object computers. Fortran compilers are available from Motorola for the 6800, and Texas Instruments for the 9900. Realistic Controls Corp. offers a dialect of Fortran for the 8080, still useful despite its lack of portability. The benefits of portability are generally illusory anyway; rarely will one model microcomputer in an application be replaced with a different model.

PL/M, MPL, PL/Z

These popular languages are not designed to allow access to the important resources of a microcomputer. In most Basic and Fortran environments, a large operating system isolates the program in execution from its peripheral devices. In a micro, on the other hand, a given program may exist just to control individual bits of input and output ports. To provide these facilities, and to provide for ease of structured programming, Intel developed a proprietary language, PL/M. PL/M was followed by similar products like Motorola's MPL and Zilog's PL/Z. All are implemented as compilers. Intel also offers PL/M as a cross-compiler.

Forth, Inc. has a novel language, microForth, implemented as an interpreter for the 8080 and for RCA's Cosmac. Although strange looking at first, microForth allows the designer to use high-level language statements that are implemented as simple assembly-language sequences. The designer builds ever-larger structures to create the eventual final applications program. MicroForth is especially good for the development of lots of little "one-shot" programs. The development of large-volume applications programs, however, would probably rely more heavily on microForth's assembly language subset.

BSAL

Another novel language is muPro's Block Structured Assembly language, BSAL. It looks like a high-level language with IF-statements and loop controls, but it is really an assembly language, producing code as efficient as the output of a traditional assembler. A programmer can, for example, make direct reference to the A-register of an 8080 by name. The language is more readable than conventional assembly language and probably reduces the number of lines written by half.

Although it is possible to construct interpretive assemblers, there is little reason to do so. The source code bears a one-for-one relationship with the object code, so once it is translated it may as well be stored in memory for future execution. Some of the new software debugging aids, like HP's 1610A logic analyzer or Electronic Modules' D9780, use interpreters for assembly language so that complex interaction can be maintained between the programmer and his program. In production form, however, the final program is assembled into target-computer code for execution.

There are many other languages, most of them very special-purpose and destined to be ignored by the majority of users. However, when investigating the alternatives, the designer should at least find out what the computer manufacturer supplies. The more popular the micro, the more likely it is to be supported by a wide variety of languages and translators.

---

may be more efficient in index register allocation, saving the index register's content in a CPU register that is not referenced by the inner loop of the nested pair instead of in main storage. The resulting program is likely to execute faster than the equivalent output produced by a compiler.

The additional programming effort is not worth the savings in execution time for a program that executes only occasionally on a large-scale computer. But if the program is part of a real-time microcomputer task that consumes 90 percent of the CPU horsepower, then the extra effort will be clearly justified.

TRANSLATOR ENVIRONMENTS

Even a program that is to execute in a microcomputer may require another kind of computer for translation. During the first year or so of the microprocessor revolution, the only assemblers available were written for large-scale computers that could accept Fortran. These cross-assemblers were relatively fast, but required some compatible storage medium so the object program could be written on the large computer and read into the micro.

Cross-assemblers are faster than their "native" microprocessor-based counterparts, usually because of the better peripheral devices available on the larger computer. When the only device for printing out the assembly listing is a 10 cps teletypewriter, it may take hours to accomplish a single assembly. If that same listing can be printed out on a high-speed line printer, total assembly time may be less than five minutes. A time-sharing system or a large-scale computer can provide this speed. However, development work limited to assembly on a small microcomputer may have to defer reassembly until a large number of changes have accumulated.

HIGH-LEVEL LANGUAGES

The folklore of computing tells us that a programmer can generate a fixed number of lines of debugged source code each work day. To take advantage of this "law of nature," a project manager should provide his programmers with the most powerful languages available. At a given programmer's productivity rate, this will contribute the maximum amount of finished code in the shortest possible time.

A typical Basic program might consist of a few hundred source lines; an equivalent assembly language program can consume a thousand lines or more. And an assembly language program typically takes up between 100 percent to 1000 percent more lines than does an equivalent program written in a high-level language. The designer saves in program coding and testing cost, and he finishes the program sooner.

INTERPRETERS

An interpreter does not generate the object program for each source statement to be saved for later execution. Instead, an interpreter actually executes some code each time the source statement is encountered. The interpreter is superior to the compiler in that the executing program can be easily interrupted, changed, and resumed. Each source statement is translated anew each time it is to be executed. The disadvantage, of course, is slower execution time. An interpreter may generate results 10 to 20 times more slowly than the equivalent compiled code.

Compilers require more completely defined source code, but they produce programs that are relatively fast. Interpreters, on the other hand, need only have available the actual or condensed source code. In many applications, the combined size of an interpreter and its source code will still be much smaller than the code produced by a compiler from the same language.

Most commercially available Basic translators are interpreters. They are attractive for use in debugging and casual computer use. In many micro-based applications, slower execution time may not even be important. If a typical process is being controlled with thermocouples, relays, and some modest amount of computation, the microcomputer is only "taxed" to perhaps one percent of its capacity; the balance is left for interpreter overhead, and the program still spends most of its time in an idle loop waiting for something important to happen.

ASSEMBLY LANGUAGE

By finding some novel way to describe or process data, a good assembly language programmer can turn a large, complex muddle of a program into a simple, elegant, small, and fast equivalent. A compiler, on the other hand, works on a rote basis, generating code of only limited flexibility. A compiler can be only as clever as the originating author. So, the price paid for using a high-level language is lower efficiency in the object program executed.

This traditional argument in favor of assembly language may be out of date. Most programmers today do not produce highly efficient code. Even good programmers have a hard time beating the efficiency of sophisticated compliers, like IBM's Fortran-H. For micros, though, such optimizing compilers do not yet exist.

Typical compilers produce anywhere from 1.15 to 3 times as much code as a good assembly language program. If only one copy of the system is to be built, there is little justification for increasing programming costs to save money on storage. When production quantities are in the thousands or even hundreds, the potential savings can be worthwhile.

The execution time penalty introduced by a compiler is more complex to quantify, since it is highly dependent on each application: A clever programmer might find a unique algorithm that cannot be efficiently represented in the high-level language. However, if comparisons are based on alternative implementations of the same algorithm, a compiler can produce code that takes 1.15 to 4 times as long to execute as the equivalent assembly-language version.

MAKING THE CHOICE

The designer must make the essential trade-off between the cost of program development and the life-cycle cost in production. In traditional applications, managers have usually opted to sacrifice object-code efficiency to gain that 100 to 1000 percent improvement in programmer productivity.

It is well to note that a significant part of the cost of writing programs – analysis of the applications, algorithm selection, and program design activities – usually is not affected by the language choice.

Some outrageous claims of "10-to-1 reduction in programming cost" have appeared in print, but these refer solely to the coding and testing time, not design effort. In well-designed programs, more than two-thirds of the dollars are spent before code is ever written, so the savings may not be as great as the seller would like to cliam.

In a large centralized computer environment, the cost of development dominates the life-cycle costs of most programs. The most powerful language available is favored. Since each program typically executes on a computer for only a small fraction of the day, the improved execution-time efficiency is not worth the additional programming cost. And, since each program does not normally consume all of the memory resources of the computer, there is little economic incentive to expend programming effort to reduce program size.

With minicomputers, assembly language becomes a more popular option. In dedicated applications, where a single program runs 100 percent of the time, a designer may not be able to afford the execution time penalty imposed by a compiler. However, where only one or a small number of computers will have this software installed, program size will not be a terribly important issue. The savings in memory costs will not warrant developing the entire program in assembly language. To gain the execution time efficiency, the critical part of the software will typically be isolated and written in assembly language, while the bulk of the program will be implemented in a high-level language. Often, when a critical fragment of a program is rewritten in assembly language, performance improves by several hundred percent.

To achieve an overall reduction in program size – not just speed – an entire program should be written in assembly language. Many microcomputer applications demand small program size. A typical single-board computer (SBC), for example, has space for only 4K bytes of program storage. When this limit is exceeded, another memory card will be required to accompany the SBC. If only one or two units will be built, there is no justification for using assembly language. The memory card might cost an additional $500, but the added programming costs to save that money might be $2000. If, however, five or more copies of such a program are required, extra programming effort to save the cost of five or more memory cards may be worthwhile.

The microprocessor application, of course, represents the extreme case. The number of units of production may be in the hundreds or thousands, so the additional software development costs can be recouped rather quickly. If the use of a compiler requires an extra memory chip that costs $20 and 1000 copies will be made, then the end-item manufacturer can afford to spend up to $20,000 to program in assembly language. ■

FORTRAN/BASIC conversions

by Wm. C. Thompson III
Reprinted by permission of INTERFACE AGE Magazine from the Aug. 1977 issue.

A microcomputer, despite its size and cost, is capable of much more than most users realize at purchase time. Through experience, it is soon found that with careful programming and sacrifices in speed of execution, major programs which the user has developed or run on larger machines may be adapted to run on the microcomputer (or mini) even *without* a full complement of floppy disc drives and 64k memory.

The program run time may suffer considerably, but because of the ready access of the microcomputer, the user can have the results hours or days ahead of batch or time-share solutions on large computers. If the program runs are fast enough, or the program is run very infrequently, the microcomputer can entirely replace use of the costly batch or time-share machines. With this in mind, I offer the following tips and outline for conversion of programs from FORTRAN to BASIC. These tips have accumulated from many program conversions from FORTRAN to Hewlett-Packard BASIC but are applicable to virtually any FORTRAN/BASIC conversions with only minor changes.

As an example I shall use the conversion of a Load Flow Circuit Analysis Program run in FORTRAN on a Xerox Sigma 3 computer and an IBM 360 to run in BASIC on a Hewlett-Packard 9830A programmable calculator.

1. First examine the dimension statements in the program and determine the amount of memory necessary to dimension fully the arrays. At this point you must also note what precision most of the variables have. Fortran, and some versions of BASIC allow integer, single and double precision. Single precision on most machines is 6 or 7 significant digits, double precision 12 or more.

```
10 DIM AS[25],BS[25],CS[25,4],DS[25,4],ES[25],FS[25],GS[25],HS[25,7]
20 DIM II[25,2],JS[25],KS[25],LS[25],MS[25],NS[25],OS[25],PS[25],QS[25]
30 DIM RS[25],SS[25],TS[25],US[25,9],VI[25,2],WS[100],XS[25],YS[25]
40 DIM ZS[25],A$[25],B$[40],C$[240]
```

a. BASIC program DIMENSION statements. I and S after an array name indicate integer and split precision. $ indicates a string variable.

```
DIMENSION P(100),Q(100),GS(100),BS(100),EMR(100),JSTR(100),EMB(100),
   ER(100),EI(100),PLOD(100),QLOD(100),QMAX(100),QMIN(100),PDEL(100),
   QDEL(100),ZLR(100),ZLI(100),ZKLR(100),ZKLI(100),QGEN(100)
DIMENSION G(100),B(100),NFTO(100),RATO(100),RATG(100),B2(100),
   QQQ(100)
DIMENSION NAM(5),ITIL(40),LNAM(100,5),NNAM(100,5),CLIN(10,7),
   LLIN(10,7),CBUS(10,9),LBUS(10,5),KBUS(200)
```

b. Fortran program DIMENSION statements.

Figure 1.

Some calculations will require double precision but single precision is adequate for most problems. If the fully dimensioned arrays take up more than one-half your available memory, then you should consider decreasing the array size if possible.

In Figure I is shown the dimension statement for the Load Flow Program. The arrays were dimensioned at only one-fourth their original size.

This limited the size of circuit which could be run to 25 lines and 25 busses but a little checking up had shown that anyway 95% of the cases run were less than 20 busses and 20 lines. If you must have large arrays you may have to break the program into very small segments. Since the HP9830 only allows 26 array names (A to Z), several of the arrays were dimensioned as 25X4 matrices. In these each 25X1 array was used as a separate matrix.

For example, the matrix ZLI (100) in the Fortran source corresponds to C(n,3) in the BASIC version while ZKLI (100) corresponds to C(n,4) in BASIC.

Some of the arrays which were dimensioned were Alphanumeric (A-format). You will have to go through the program to pick these out. They may be handled by using strings (as in the sample) or sometimes may be entirely replaced by print statements (for titles and other functions).

Now we have determined that we will have sufficient space for the variables, let's attack the program head on.

2. The program structure was now examined and it was found that the program naturally broke into five segments. Iterative processes and loops that must cycle repeatedly were retained completely within a segment so that repeated loading of tape files — a slow process at best was avoided. If disc files are available such repeated loads may be tolerable, but are still ideally avoided.

3. With this structure in mind, conversion on a line-to-line basis was begun. Here the question of what to do with the variable names arises. That is, most Basics only allow one letter and one number (such as A1) for variable names so what do you do with RATG or QMAX? The first answer which comes to mind is to abbreviate RATG : "R" (or R1 if R is already used). With some quick thinking you realize that there are undoubtedly going to be *at least* 12 variables that start with R or some letter so that scheme falls apart. Here is where I decided to adopt a different means of shortening variables. I made two columns on a sheet of paper and wrote down the variables from the fortran program, *as I came to them,* in one column and assigned consecutive Basic variables to the other column (consecutive BASIC variables: A;, A1, A2 . . . A9, B0 . . . Z9) The *only* exception to this scheme was to keep the index variables such as I, J, K, M which were used and reused repeatedly. Variables such as A1, A0 in the Fortran program did *not* retain the same names and ended up with such designa-

tions as M9, P0. Any attempt to maintain the same names at this point seems to lead into a confusing and tangled mess. Note that some Fortran programs I have converted have contained both A1 and AONE.

Since my first program I have found ways to speed up greatly this step by using string substitution utility routines available on time sharing and on micro's and mini's via text editing provisions.

Thus using the program as text, you can substitute A7 for QVAR everywhere it occurs in the program with one command (sheer ecstasy!). Beware though of possible problems with substrings. For example, if you also have a variable TQVAR you might end up with TA7. This need not become a problem if you just remember to substitute B3 for TA7 instead of TQVAR.

This is also the time to change other easily replaceable nomenclature such as " < " for ".LT.", " < = " for ".LE.", etc. You could even substitute "FOR" for "DO" and "NEXT" for "CONTINUE" if the Fortran loops seem to warrant it. The FOR-NEXT loops will require more than just this substitution though so you may want to make all the modifications at once.

Setting up the variable conversion table is much easier if you have a variable list from a run of the program. Most Fortran compilers will print some type of variable list or map if requested.

4. In a similar manner, a two column table of line number references will be very valuable in establishing proper program flow.

5. Fortran "IF" statements are replaced by BASIC "IF" or computed "GOTO" statements. For example, the Fortran statement:

```
IF(C*A**B) 500,600,700
```

might be replaced by:

```
GOTO (SGN(C*A↑B) + 2)500,600,700
```

(in some BASICS: ON(SGN(C*A↑B) + 2) GOTO 500,600, 700)

also possible is:

```
Q = C*A↑B
GOTO 1*(Q < 0) + 2*(Q = 0) + 3*(Q > 0) of 500,600,700
```

and if you have many IF statements:

```
DEF FNI(X) = SGN(X) + 2
GOTO FNI(C*A↑B) of 500,600,700
```

Remember, that if the Fortran statement is similar to this,

```
IF X 500,500,510
510 X = X + 1
```

the BASIC statement of this form will normally execute much faster than the above forms:

```
IF X < = 0 THEN 500
510 X = X + 1
```

Execution is faster since most compilers/interpreters will treat a computed GOTO as a nest or series of comparisons, while the simple IF statement requires only one comparison.

6. "FORMAT" (and accompanying READ/WRITE statements) normally will take special considerations. Even if your version of BASIC incorporates FORMAT and WRITE statements similar to Fortran the probability is high that you will want to convert from a 132 character width to a 80 character or 72 character width. And, most BASIC compiler/interpreters allow either PRINT statements or perhaps, PRINT with USING statements. With all the complications that formatting produces, I have found it best to simply enter a statement like:

```
PRINT "FORT. STATEMENT #125";A;A1;B;BL;B2
```

Then when you test the program you will have the values of the variables along with a reference to the Fortran program to aid in verifying proper program execution. Once the program has been debugged you may then experiment with establishing a format for the output, using actual values for the variables.

7. In Fortran programs you will come across statements using H and A formats. Some of these, in WRITE/FORMAT pairs are easily handled, since they simply print a heading or title. Others may actually input, compare and manipulate data. If you have string capabilities in your BASIC, these are usually easily handled, though deciphering the Fortran execution may be complicated. If you do not have string capabilities, you will probably have to change the type of data handled, resorting to some types of numeric coding schemes.

8. At last you're finished with your conversions, except, the results you get just don't agree with those from the original. At this point, before you tear your hair out and resign yourself to a six week step by step debugging run through the program, try this: — Take your Fortran program to your nearest computer which can run it and run a sample set of data through the program. Now, compare these results with your BASIC version on the same data. From my experience at least half the Fortran programs I have converted in which I was furnished sample data and output, did not include the output from the furnished data, including some in which a manual had been prepared which included a sample run of the program.

Now with respect to your results, do not expect exact agreement. The way that numbers, calculations and functions are handled varies enormously between different machines and may result in a build-up of accumulated "errors" — "residuals" may be a better word. The results however, should not be significantly different, so if they vary greatly, closer study is certainly necessary.

Software becomes the real challenge

Microprocessors simplify systems, but not the design process. "Hardware development time drops nearly to zero when you use a microprocessor. With the Intel 8008, we had a machine on the street in six months, and then with the 8080, we went from parts layout directly to final printed-circuit art work. But then the real design job started—writing and debugging the programs," says Frank Trantanella, president of Tranti Systems, a N. Billerica, Mass., maker of electronic cash registers.

Not all microprocessor system designs will involve so little hardware effort, but it is true that software is becoming of major importance in systems based on the device. The extent to which design engineers must immerse themselves in software-design methods depends on the intended uses of the systems they are developing.

For example, programs in a traffic-light controller are a matter of simple logic replacement, and probably would not exceed 500–1,000 bytes, or about two 4,096-bit chips of random-access-memory or read-only-memory. In small business applications, however, data-handling microprocessors masquerade as minicomputers. They require more extensive programs, possibly running close to the 64-kilobyte limit of the 16-bit address bus in most 8-bit microprocessors.

To varying degrees, engineers must become programers when working with processors. For the more complex systems, chances are they will share the work with professional programers—computer-science specialists drawn into the field by the rapid boom in programing. But even then, they will have to learn the basics to take care of the peripheral-control tasks off-loaded from the central processing unit.

Nearly every microprocessor manufacturer offers a complete package of development software programs: editors, simulators, monitors, assemblers, and, in a growing number of cases, compilers (see "Software tools aid program development," p. 196). Generally they are available in three forms: in the manufacturer's development hardware; on magnetic tape for entry into a user-owned larger computer (so-called cross-computer programs), and from time-sharing services. Independent software houses offer programs that are installed

Software packages. Typical of the support available from semiconductor vendors is the Signetics offering—a basic design module to try out programs, manuals to help learn programing, and magnetic tapes with development software that can be run on larger in-house computers.

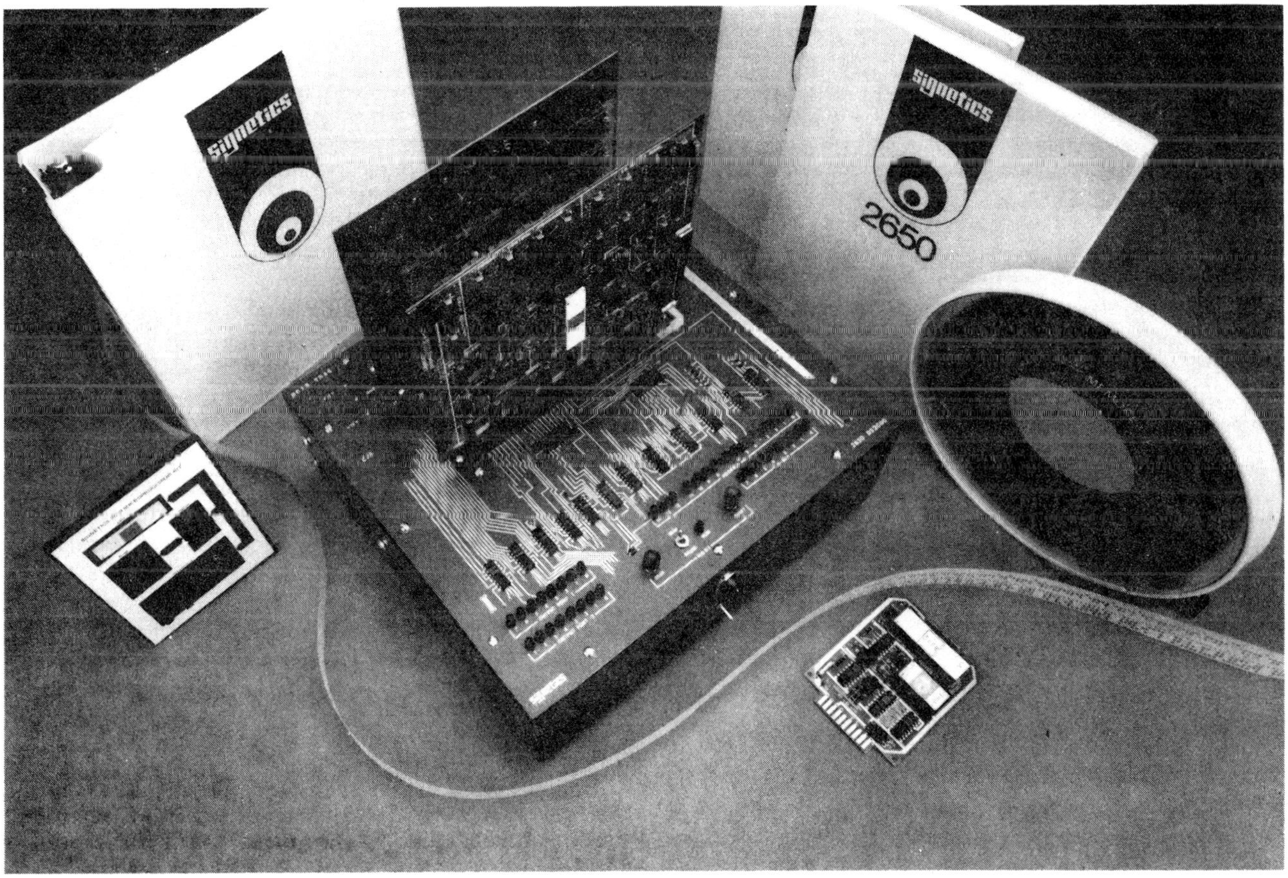

Software tools aid program development

There are five main categories of software programing tools for microcomputers; editors, translators (assemblers and compilers), loaders, simulators, and debuggers—each of which facilitates a stage of the development of the system operating program. The following capsule descriptions of each category are supplied by Irene M. Watson, a microcomputer consultant in Los Altos Hills, Calif.

Editors: programs that take the source program, written by the programer in assembly or high-level language and entered through a keyboard or paper tape, and transfer it to a "file" in the computer's auxiliary memory, such as magnetic disk or tape. The editor also acts on special commands from the user to add, delete, or replace portions of the source program in the auxiliary memory. Editors can vary significantly in the ease with which they permit a user to make changes in the program. For example, some editors can operate only on entire lines in a program, whereas others can add, delete, or replace arbitrary character strings in the program. However, the less-sophisticated editors are usually easier to learn to use.

Assemblers and compilers: programs that translate source programs to object programs—the actual patterns of bits interpreted by the computer. They also print a program listing that displays, side-by-side, the source and object versions of the program while giving error messages and other kinds of diagnostic information useful to the programer.

Loaders: programs that transfer the object program from an external medium, such as paper tape, to the microcomputer random-access memory. Some loaders also convert a relocatable version of the object program to a loadable version. A program might originally be assembled to reside in the microcomputer memory starting at address zero. If the compiler or assembler has allowed the object program to be relocatable, the programer can specify to the loader the program's new base address and the loader will modify all addresses accordingly in the object program.

Another feature that is sometimes available is linkage editing, which establishes the linkages between different object programs that make reference to one another. Linkage editing requires both a compiler or assembler and a loader program that can communicate the appropriate information.

Simulators: cross-computer programs that allow the user to test the object program by simulating the action of the microcomputer when the actual circuitry is unavailable. Simulators often provide certain kinds of diagnostic information unavailable with a debugger program (below) running on the actual microcomputer; warning of the overflow of a processor stack or of an attempt by the program to write into a location in the read-only-memory, for example.

They usually allow manipulation and display of the simulated microcomputer memory and central-processing-unit registers; setting of break points, where processing can be stopped at a certain program address or when the program reads or writes into a specified memory location, and tracing, in which each instruction in a certain address range is printed out as it is executed. Often they provide timing information, such as the number of instructions or machine cycles executed from program start to stop.

The power of a simulator varies from manufacturer to manufacturer, but it cannot completely replace program testing on the microcomputer itself, because the specific timing and external environmental conditions of the actual microcomputer hardware can never be completely simulated.

Debuggers: programs that facilitate the testing of the object program on the microcomputer and its input-output devices. They usually accept commands from the user to perform such functions as displaying or printing out the contents of the microcomputer memories, or the contents of the registers of the central processing unit; modifying the RAM; starting execution of the object program from a specific memory location, and setting a break point or stop execution of the program when the instruction at a specific memory location is reached in the program or when a given condition is met.

on time-sharing systems or sold for installation on an in-house computer.

Several semiconductor companies also have established libraries of programs contributed by users ("for those people opposed to reinventing the wheel," according to Motorola Semiconductor's software manager Wes Patterson). However, care is needed when using such programs, says Jerry L. Ogdin, president of Microcomputer Technique, Reston, Va., a consulting firm.

He recommends novice users of such programs assume the software to be a first draft that must be debugged and tested just as if it were generated in-house. Many of the programs, he says, are "redundant and error-laden, and many are naive solutions to well-understood problems." Nevertheless, the programs are available and could be useful with the proper precautions.

There may be a good argument for the available support software serving as the basis of choice between microprocessors, but the general industry practice is a decision based on how well the devices fit the intended application. Then designers must decide how to program the selected processor so that it fits perfectly.

Their first, tentative efforts probably will involve programing directly in machine language—the actual pattern of bits interpreted by the device to perform its functions. Such programing is done in hexadecimal code, but the inherent tedium in translating instructions into the generally unfamiliar code soon surfaces.

Assembly language offers the engineer the ability to write instructions in mnemonic form, which he or she can associate with the actual function being performed. This is probably the most widely used method.

For such programing, many new hardware aids are coming onto the market—systems that include a keyboard and a cathode-ray-tube display, or a printer, or both, and magnetic tape or disk storage units. These help the programer edit the programs and even to debug them on the particular microprocessor selected for the system (see the following article on design aids).

Not all assembler programs are the same, even if

designed for the same device. Careful study should be devoted to extra features such as the ability to use macroinstructions (a name associated with a sequence of instructions, with the assembler substituting the sequence of instructions every time the programer writes a statement with this name), editing features, and the like.

Comparing assemblers

Irene M. Watson, a microcomputer consultant in Los Altos Hills, Calif., recently completed a study comparing the characteristics of various assemblers. She points out the following major features to look for:

- A format that is easy to use, read, and understand is essential. For example, the programer should be able to set up his own format for the fields in each statement, and the assembler should not reject a statement because a particular field is started in the wrong column.
- The assembler should accept symbols for variable data quantities and addresses, rather than insisting on actual representation. Along with this goes the ability to translate data constants provided in the form most meaningful to the programer—hexadecimal, ASCII code, or whatever.
- It should be able to handle arithmetic or logic expressions as operands, and then evaluate the expression and use the result as the operand value of the statement.
- Assemblers should be able to provide an alphabetical listing of symbols and their numerical values (usually a hexadecimal number). Similarly, they should be able to produce an alphabetically sorted cross-reference listing for each symbol in the program, along with the statement defining the symbol, and the statement refering to each symbol.
- The assembler should flag any source-program statements that violate assembly-language syntax rules. Error statements should, whenever possible, indicate the specific statement or field containing the error. They should not abort at the first error, but should flag it, place a skeleton instruction in the object code with the incorrect field set to zero, and continue as much of the program translation as possible.
- It should provide a macroinstruction facility in which variable parameters can be included in the macro statement and automatically inserted in the proper places in the instructions it defines. Assemblers can be compared on the basis of the number of macroinstructions that can be defined in a program, the total number of characters that can be included in all macroinstructions in the program, the level to which macro calls can be nested in macro bodies, and the number of parameters permitted for each macroinstruction.

The chief advantage of assembly-language programing is that it allows the designer to make maximum use of the microprocessor's capabilities. However, when programs get large—say beyond 2,000 bytes or between 500 or 1,000 program lines—it becomes difficult for any programer to maintain the overall flow without errors inevitably creeping in.

Many subtle errors show up only under rare combinations of conditions, and thus nearly every program must be assumed to have undiscovered bugs that will have to be corrected later. Yet other engineers and maintenance personnel may have difficulty understanding the intentions of the original programer because of the shorthand nature of assembly language. Therefore it is important to keep good documentation of the program-writing process, showing the program in clear, understandable detail.

To forestall unintelligibility and to speed programing, languages appeared that are closer to standard English, the so-called high-level languages such as Fortran and Basic. Although they are widely known, problem-solving languages for use in computer applications involving computations, they have not been often used in designing microprocessor systems. Instead, manufacturers of microprocessors have emphasized systems-programing languages better suited to equipment design—handling inputs and outputs, managing internal resources, and so on.

Enter PL/M

The first such language developed especially for microprocessors was Intel's PL/M, derived from PL/1, a language developed by some IBM-computer users in the mid 1960s for business and scientific calculations.

Intel's PL/M compiler itself is a Fortran IV program, and will run on any 32-bit host processor. It also is available on time-sharing networks. Many new PL/M-type compilers are being designed to run on 16-bit minis, more widely available to engineers.

The language was formulated to help designers using Intel's 8008 chip. When the 8080 appeared, it was modified slightly to cover that device as well. Since its introduction, it has been improved many times—"There's been an average of one revision a month," says Intel's Paul Rosenfeld, software product manager for microcomputer systems.

The major problem with any high-level language is that the compiler takes over the job of optimizing the program by cutting out duplications and so on. Programers, in a sense, get further away from the microprocessor and cannot perform the same tricks of processing that they can with assembly language. Nor can the program be as concise, so memory requirements are larger. It amounts to a tradeoff: less efficiency, but easy use of language and good documentation.

"Each user decides whether it's efficient enough," Rosenfeld says. "Some customers, when they start, generate twice as much code as they would with assembly language, but in six months, they usually are down to 1.5 to 1. Here at Intel, we get in the 10-to-25% range." But programing takes one-fourth to one-fifth the time of assembly-language, according to the firm.

One important factor in the choice between assembly and high-level languages is the number of systems that will be produced. For high volumes, the addition of just one extra memory chip to each system could raise the overall cost to a noncompetitive level. (According to a corollary of Murphy's law, any program written for a high-volume system will turn out to be a few bytes beyond the capacity of a given number of memory chips, so an extra chip is always a possibility.)

With assembly language, it is much easier to redo

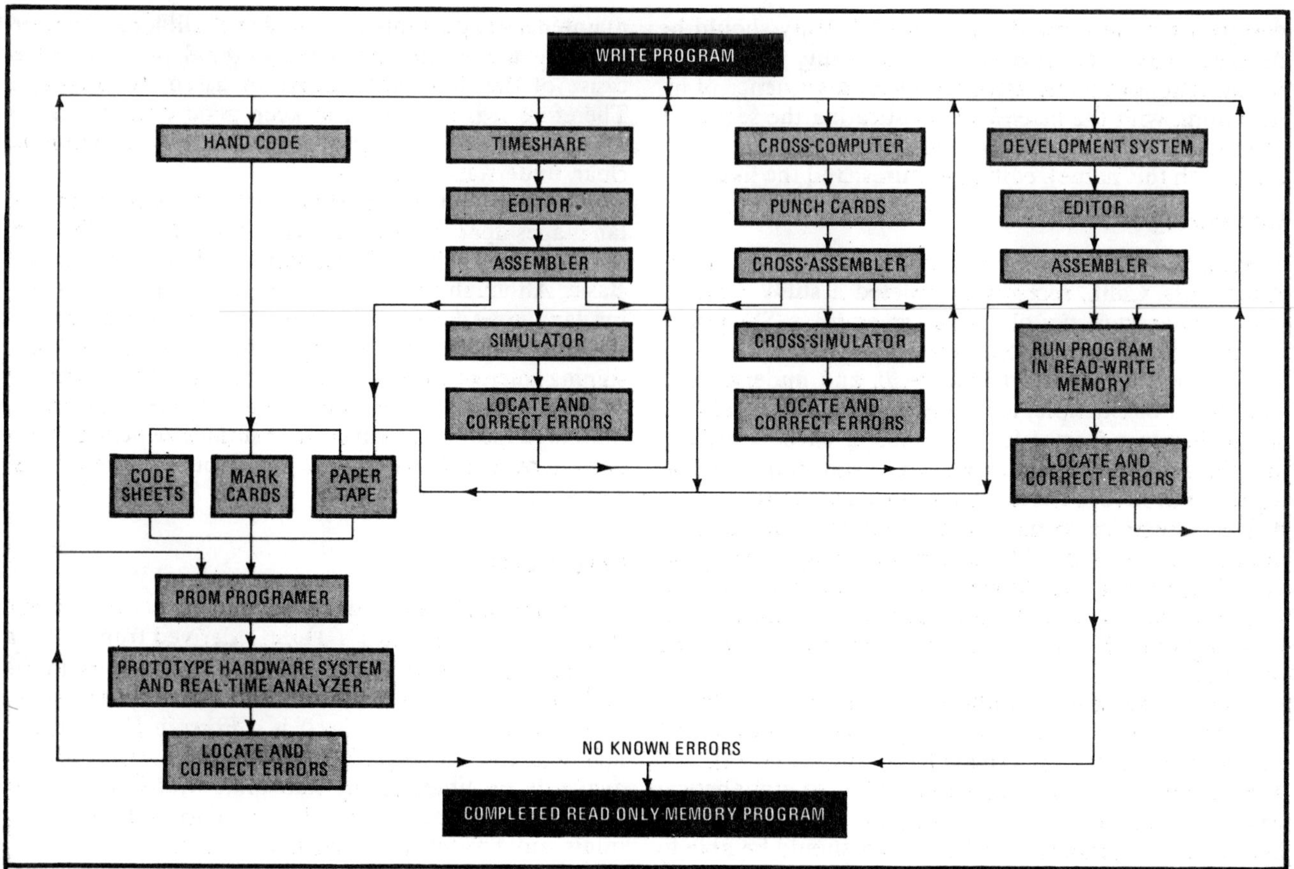

HAND ASSEMBLY

Advantages
- Relatively fast for small programs
- No assembler processing time
- No equipment costs
- Results entered directly into programer for read-only memories

Disadvantages
- Slow and tedious for larger programs
- Very difficult to expand or contract program once written
- Error-prone
- Assembler-tested error conditions go unchecked

When to use
- OK for small jobs
- As an alternative to assembler processing when the assembler is not readily accessible

MACROINSTRUCTIONS

Advantages
- Repeated small groups of instructions replaced by one macro
- Errors in macros need be corrected only once, in the definition
- Duplication of effort reduced
- In effect, new instructions can be created
- Programing is made easier, less error-prone

Disadvantages
- Macros are not subroutines – every time a macro name is used, storage space is required for the defined instructions

When to use
- To replace small groups of instructions not worthy of subroutines
- To create a higher instruction set for specific applications or for compatibility with other computers
- Caution: whenever possible use subroutines, not macros

ASSEMBLY LANGUAGE PROGRAMING

Advantages
- Symbolic references
- Revisions easily incorporated with reassemblies
- Symbolic code easier to read
- Programing aids included
- Values can be parameterized (table sizes, input/output port assignment)
- Error checking included

Disadvantages
- Assembler system required (development hardware, terminal)
- Some assembly processes are slow
- Assembly language rules and formats must be learned

When to use
- Usually recommended for instruction-level coding

HIGH-LEVEL LANGUAGE

Advantages
- Better control of software
- Reduced programing cost
- Faster programing
- Well suited to program solving
- Self-documenting
- Easier maintenance
- Transferability avoids reprograming

Disadvantages
- Bigger programs – compilation efficiency
- Cost of compilation
- Programing experience required for good results

When to use
- For larger programs – 1,000 bytes or more
- For low-volume products or prototype systems
- For production systems when experience warrants

Design routes, pros, cons. There are many approaches to software design, shown by the chart tracing development steps. Similarly, there are advantages and disadvantages for each method of programing. (From course material prepared by Integrated Computer Systems, Inc.)

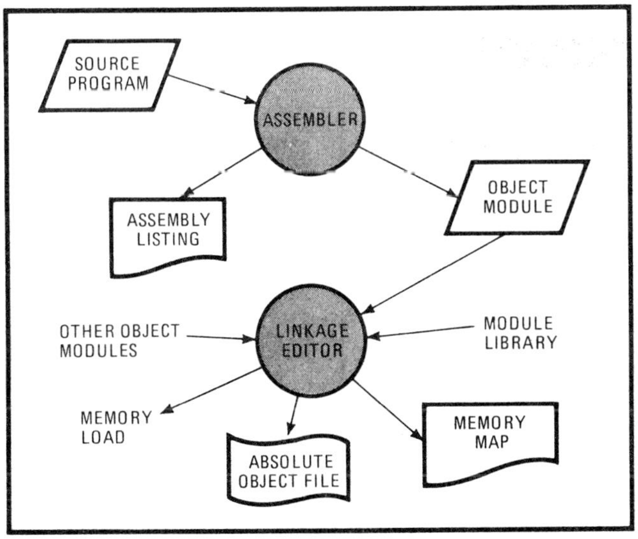

Linking up. Typical of charts describing software is the operation of the macroinstruction assembler and linkage editor from Motorola Semiconductor. Object code produced by the assembler enters linkage editor with other programs to produce the final code.

portions of the program to reduce the memory usage to fit into the desired number of memory chips. High-level language is best for lower-volume products where fast design turnaround is desirable and where the cost of an extra memory chip can be absorbed in favor of competitive advantages.

Making changes in PL/M

One of the largest users of PL/M outside of Intel is Sycor, Inc., Ann Arbor, Mich., a manufacturer of intelligent terminals. Sycor committed itself to the language about a year and half ago, according to software head Geoffrey Leach. But, he says, "in a sense that commitment was somewhat ill-advised, because the state of the Intel PL/M at that point was somewhat less than solid."

So the firm went its own way and made a number of improvements to the compiler. Now, compared with the early versions of the language, Leach says, "we feel we have achieved a 30% reduction in the amount of code the compiler produces."

Sycor uses its home-brewed version almost exclusively for all programing of 8080-based systems and does little in assembly language. "For the amount of software that we produce, the programer productivity in assembly language was not sufficiently high to allow us to make our delivery schedules," Leach says.

These are large programs—typically for a fully configured system, the program runs to about 48 or 56 kilobytes of stored code. "I don't think our programs would be any smaller than if we had the same people do them in assembly language," he says. "I have to admit this is one of my favorite soap boxes.

"Programing in higher-level languages is often faulted on the grounds that much better code can be written in assembly language. But if you ask the person making that criticism to sit down and code a 48-kilobyte system in assembly language, you will find him making compromises, missing organizational structures, generally doing things which introduce extra code. That's why I say that for an average programer over a year I don't think we have necessarily lost anything in using PL/M."

The next system programing language to appear from a semiconductor manufacturer was the recently announced MPL, also a descendant of PL/1, from Motorola Semiconductor. The MPL compiler produces assembly language (the PL/M produces machine-level object language) and must be run through an assembler to generate the object language.

Motorola says this feature allows the user to study the assembly-language program for possible refinements before generating the final object code. This is "both a blessing and a curse" says Motorola's Wes Patterson, because the need to use an assembler results in a longer run on a computer.

MPL also allows the programer to drop down from high-level language to assembly language in those areas where he feels it is important to conserve memory space. This may be useful, but the user must know how fully the compiler can take advantage of the microprocessor's ability to streamline instructions and save memory space.

However, the ability to drop into assembly language can be too much of a temptation for some programers to resist, according to Gary Kildall, the consultant primarily responsible for the original PL/M. He likens it to "having a parachute while flying a plane—you may bail out too soon."

The assembly language pollutes the program, he says, because, when the programer drops into assembly language, chances are others will have difficulty understanding what he was trying to do. With PL/M, Kildall points out, assembly language could be used to simplify particular parts of the program, but it is included as a subroutine, called by a high-level statement. This increases the overhead by the three bytes of the call, but it vastly increases the understandability, he says.

Other PL/M-type high-level-language compilers available, or just over the horizon are:

- SMPL, intended for use on National Semiconductor's IMP-16 devices, with another version due soon for PACE, another of the firm's microprocessors.
- PL/M 6800, written by Intermetrics, Cambridge, Mass., for the 6800.
- PL/W, written by Wintek Corp., Lafayette, Ind., for the 6800.
- PLμS, for the Signetics 2650, developed primarily by Kildall.
- PL/Z, soon to come for the Z-80 of Zilog, Los Altos, Calif.

Various versions of Basic have also been written for the 8080 and other devices. Fortran compilers also are on the way from such sources as Zeno Systems, Santa Monica, Calif., and the Boston Systems Office, Boston, Mass. Many engineers point out that there is greater familiarity with these high-level languages because of their prevalence in minicomputers—so why switch to the PL/1 derivatives? However, there is a noticable bandwagon effect shaping up. Just as the 8080's head start led to its wide adoption, PL/M and its cousins threaten to become a *de facto* standard. □

Developing software for micros

by Chris Hawkins and Alex d'Agapeyeff

Practitioners of commercial data processing, the prime target of the computing industry for the past two decades, have suffered a quiet indignity. The records will show 1977 to be the year in which they ceased to be the main buyers of programmable devices.

The key to this transformation is large scale integration technology, which enables the fabrication of complex electronic circuits, these days of relatively high speed, on a single piece of semiconductor material. These can take a variety of forms, such as a programmable processing circuit (microprocessor chip), a support circuit such as a section of fast memory, or a fixed-logic circuit able to execute predetermined functions. But their most important characteristic is that they can be manufactured in quantity at very low cost, typically retailing at $8 to $80.

The principal market for the new LSI components is currently for the replacement of conventional circuitry in a great variety of engineering products including current computers and their peripherals. They will have a growing impact on the commercial mainframe also, to the extent that the data processing manager cannot merely dismiss them as some enhanced form of transistor.

Many of the latest terminals and remote job entry units are driven by programmable devices; there are devices soon to be announced for voice input which rely heavily on microprocessors for their operation; new mass memory systems will become available, based on LSI technology, which will partially replace rotating magnetic machinery such as discs and drums. The data processing department is unlikely to be able to assess these facilities unless it becomes aware of the concepts and potential of microcomputers and acquires the skills to adapt these developments to its advantage.

Yet this represents the least part of the impending impact of microcomputers on the dp scene. The time is now approaching for the mass exploitation of microcomputers as stand-alone computing devices. This trend has already been established, as seen in the rapidly increasing sales of small business computers, more and more of which are going to be found upon examination to be driven by single-chip microprocessors. But it will be further accelerated when users start to assemble their own microcomputer systems, a radical innovation which has been made possible by two recent developments within the LSI component industry, neither being initially prompted by data processing needs.

> The big majority of microcomputer programs are over 1,000 bytes long.

Standard components

The first of these is the appearance on the market of "standard" boards or so-called "computer" boards, each having the same set of LSI components and being able to act as a miniature central processing unit with some working storage. Even among the engineering community, which is able to configure individual components to its own requirements, such boards have grown in popularity with the fall in prices. They have also stimulated a commonality in simple board interfaces, together with the ready availability of ancillary boards—such as those which provide a working storage extension.

The second important development is found in the design of single circuit "controllers" for the attachment of a wider range of peripherals, notably the floppy disc. It is the availability of file storage which ultimately transforms the microcomputer into a workable dp system. At the same time, the peripherals themselves have been becoming cheaper.

The results are dramatic. It is now possible for a commercial user to configure his own computer system, embracing a processor, 16KB of memory, a visual display unit, a serial printer, and two floppies, for about $12,000. At that price it is probably justified to provide personal computing, such as file storage and inquiry, to the line manager, the very small office, and individual clerical staff members.

Some of the most cherished computing preconceptions have been turned upside down. It may be cheaper to offload dp tasks onto such systems than to upgrade a current mainframe. For the small organization, the cost of getting started in computing can now be found by saving half a man-year of clerical effort.

The result is that now dp departments have a choice. They can wait for their established suppliers, such as IBM or Burroughs or Honeywell, to introduce the latest circuit technology (as they are doing) into existing and revised computers. This will be the simplest and sometimes the most convenient option, but the established computer suppliers may avoid any rush into microcomputer systems both to protect current lines and because of doubts about sustaining their current software.

Alternatively, they can start putting together their own microcomputer configurations, as already outlined. This offers them the possibility of exploiting systems with a startling improvement in cost/performance ratio through the use of the latest system components. It offers them the promise of a new dimension of user configurability and simplicity, to provide single user services for the clerk or manager. It offers them the opportunity to build up experience and understanding on which, eventually, to base choices for future systems.

Acceptance of the latter philosophy may be traumatic. The manufacturer of the original microprocessor chip (and standard board) is a new breed of supplier, who sees business data processing as only a small part of his marketplace. He is attracted to other, less demanding parts, where component sales in millions are possible for inclusion in automobiles, machine tools, domestic equipment, homes, the fast-growing hobbyist market, and educational institutions.

The dp manager cannot dismiss micros as some form of overgrown transistor.

It is left to the packaged systems vendor to assemble and sell complete working systems for the businessman, and even then, a user may find it convenient to have separate suppliers for the microprocessor, for several different peripherals, the maintenance, and the software. Cheap hardware makes bundled services impractical, and when he has to contract separately for his specific needs the user may decide to consider afresh what his particular needs are and how they can best be met.

The deciding factor for many user organizations is likely to be the available methods of programming their selected applications. This is crucial when considering the exploitation of very inexpensive hardware; the cost of producing 10 debugged micro instructions is comparable to the cost of the processor chip on which they will run.

Despite much past criticism, the established computer suppliers (especially the mainframe manufacturers) have a good record in the provision of basic software. This fact readily becomes apparent after actual experience in programming a microprocessor. A recent survey in the U.S. showed that over 36% of the programs for micros were being written in absolute hexadecimal. Even in the better environment of microassembly language, how many programmers are there who are readily capable of programming 64-bit commercial arithmetic on an 8-bit machine?

Programming, therefore, is the essential ingredient in the exploitation of low-cost microcomputers for commercial data processing.

Reinventing programming

The history of software for microprocessors has been a reincarnation of earlier problems and a similar, albeit quicker, learning curve. Staggering improvements in circuitry have been accompanied by a surprise that micro programs grew so large (at least 85% exceed a thousand bytes), are so difficult to debug, and have their own development requirements in both software instrumentation and machine configuration. The need for documentation and ease of modification is being relearned.

And when the manufacturers make changes to the original, imperfect instruction sets, the conversion problems for users are rediscovered, and the phrase "nearly compatible" is reborn, this time with a choice of over 100 microcomputer types. Software development is now an issue of which microprocessor users are much aware.

The microprocessor manufacturer tends to provide development support to a standard sequence (Fig. 1). After announcing his microprocessor chip (Stage 1) he soon announces some "support chips" (Stage 2), a necessary complement to enable an engineer to develop complete hardware systems. At Stage 3, perhaps several months later, he mounts the microprocessor chip on a printed circuit board with 100 or so supporting components, producing what we have referred to as the "standard board," which he mass produces at a unit price which might be $300. A primitive software capability is provided at this juncture, through a small resident monitor.

At Stage 4, to support more serious

The purpose of an In-Circuit Emulation system is not to emulate the operation of a microcomputer, as its name suggests, but to help in debugging a microprocessor program by giving the designer "hooks" into the system which the microprocessor cannot provide. For example, a designer might use one to single-step through a microcomputer program. Here an Intel ICE-80 is being used to exercise an Intel SBC 80/10 "standard" single board computer.

programming, the manufacturer announces some cross-products—cross-assemblers, cross-compilers, simulators. These permit writing programs on conventional computers, using either specialized time-sharing services or in-house mainframes, to generate symbolic source language instructions for the micro.

He then usually creates and markets his own development system board, commonly called a "prototyping system," based around his own microprocessor (Stage 5). This is ultimately equipped with aids which help an engineer to debug his hardware as well as his software.

We shall look at some of these stages in more detail. But it is first useful to note that there are some alternative evolutionary paths. A "minicomputer manufacturer turned micro supplier," such as DEC or Data General, is faced with the problem of moving downwards rather than upwards in complexity, reversing his path of the past decade (Fig. 2).

Then there are the "second source" suppliers, those who sell copies of other manufacturers' components. Initially they will make pin-compatible circuits and leave you with the development support facilities of the prime supplier. They will then see merit in selling rival hardware configurations, and may then start getting their own ideas as to what development software should be.

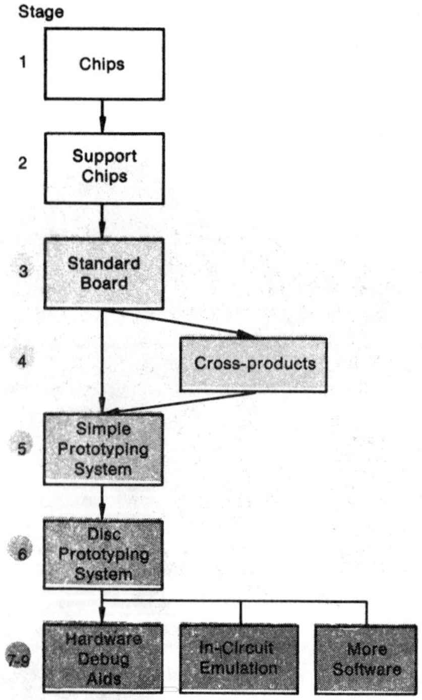

Fig. 1. After developing his microprocessor chip, the semiconductor manufacturer generally goes through this sequence in offering support for it: support chips like memory first, then a standard computer board, cross-products like cross-compilers, then prototyping systems (more expensive boards with specialized debugging aids), and finally in-circuit emulation kits which allow for testing the user's boards in a real-time manner.

A similar path may be followed by those who emulate the instruction sets of larger computers; for instance, the Intersil IM6100 microprocessor reproduces the DEC PDP-8/E instruction set and will run DEC's papertape software.

Three ways to micro software

In essence, the evolution of the industry has provided three main environments for the development of microprocessor software: *the standard board, cross-products*, and *the prototyping system*. Combinations are possible too. For instance, standard boards are sometimes enhanceable to support better resident facilities, or a program can be partially developed using cross-products to produce code for the standard board, and then transferred to a prototyping system for completion.

Examples of standard boards are the Motorola MES6800, the Signetics PC1001, and the Intel 80/10. They are purchased both singly for evaluation purposes, or, where suitable, as a basis for actual systems. The resident monitor normally allows programs to be entered in low level terms, such as in absolute hexadecimal characters. Such an environment is not suitable for applications of any complexity, although users can be found struggling with substantial programs at this level, because any improvement calls for further expenditure.

Cross-products are commonly written in ANSI FORTRAN so as to be relatively transportable between conventional computers. It is inherent to the approach that one uses the large computer's utilities (such as its text editor), and the cross-product package will certainly include a good cross-assembler. Cross-compilers for high level languages are now commonplace: the microprocessor industry leans towards PL/1 derivatives, but BASIC and FORTRAN are gaining favor. There may also be an instruction simulator for each microprocessor simulator to permit testing the micro's software on the host machine.

Cross-products have been improved with the entry of independent vendors. The service bureaus have been particularly active (for instance, National CSS Inc. supports the products of 14 microprocessor manufacturers) and must be pleasantly surprised to be deriving commercial benefit from developments in computer "miniaturization." One can get off the ground speedily using a service bureau and can experiment with different micro architectures.

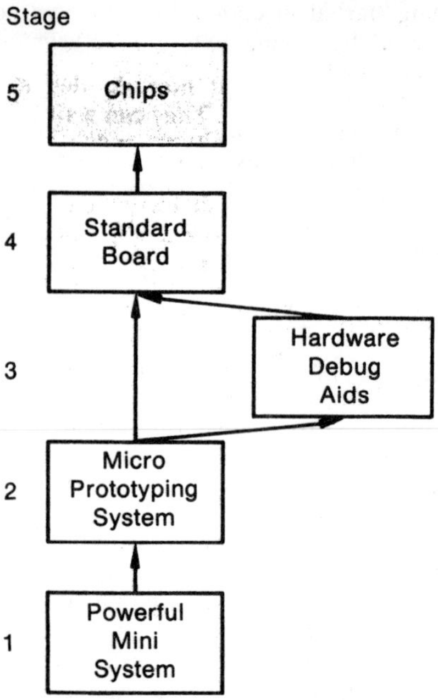

Fig. 2. Existing minicomputer makers "back into" the microcomputer business by delivering more sophisticated products first, and never getting to the point of offering the chips themselves.

Program checkout using simulators can be helpful but expensive, as instruction simulation is processing-intensive. Simulator writers need to be knowledgeable, because microprocessors can have barely announced "eccentricities" and even unannounced instructions. But the most serious constraint is the inability to check out a program in real-time with the actual peripherals and interfaces. Ultimately, the program must be proven on the microcomputer system itself.

Prototyping systems are purchased from the microprocessor manufacturers (and their distributors) as standalone microcomputer systems carrying their own programming aids. Examples are Motorola's "Exorciser," Fairchild's "Formulator," Rockwell's "Assemulator," and Intel's "Intellec."

Initially such systems were papertape-based but soon moved on to the use of discs and other file storage. They are equipped with editors, assemblers (increasingly with subroutine relocation and linking), a debugging package, and a monitor. Resident compilers for high level languages are now available too. But in general, lacking the configuration size and utilities normally found with a conventional computer, prototyping systems may be less convenient than cross-products for initial program preparation.

Prototyping systems are, on the other hand, much better equipped for realistic debugging of user programs, running them on the actual microprocessor, and offer a clever blend of hardware and software weaponry for this purpose. The demand for support of user-constructed target boards has led to novel hardware-oriented features, such as the "in-circuit emulation" technique (Intel's "ICE," Motorola's "USE," and others). On such a system the user's microprocessor chip on its multipin mounting is removed from the user's target board, and replaced by a plug with leads attached to the prototyping system. This enables the user's target board to be checked out in stages.

With these two latter environments available, cross-products and prototyping systems, the micro user can program and test his new applications with much greater ease than was once the case. But dissatisfaction remains. Service bureaus are an incomplete answer, and can be expensive. The manufacturers' prototyping systems are necessary but their high cost (typically $13,000) is a deterrent to many would-be users.

But the most serious problem may be that all the methods discussed so far have been addressed to a specific microprocessor—if you wish to change to a rival microprocessor at any time, you have to scrap your entire investment in development systems and programs, and start again.

Dp software

The first organizations to exploit suitably configured microcomputers for data processing had to rely on some combination of cross-products, prototyping systems, and their own, custom-built, system software. These items were not always satisfactory, but they could suffice for a determined user.

The organizations could use cross-products, but apart from their inherent debugging limitations, these are frequently proprietary and can mean a reliance on service bureaus. Then too, prototyping systems were not designed for, and are seldom very helpful with, file handling on target board configurations, and are nearly always dedicated to the programming of a particular processor. Finally, custom built system software (for instance, to support file handling) also raises a similar doubt over the wisdom of investing in one processor among so many.

For the single installation user, or the user who must program at every site, an attractive alternative may be to purchase a ready-packaged microcomputer system equipped with its own development capability, including a familiar high level language.

The microcomputers which emulate minicomputers provide one source of supply, for instance the LSI-11 from DEC or the Micronova from Data General. These have a great software advantage with their existing languages and libraries, but some have constraints on the peripherals which can be attached.

The second source of supply is the vendor of small business systems who has created such a product around a mass-selling microprocessor. These vendors are often new to this marketplace, leading to price reduction pressures as they have no existing lines to protect, and they are tending to favor BASIC as their resident language. But it may be assumed that they, too, would rather the user bought their selection of peripherals rather than those of anybody else.

But what about the organization which expects to exploit microcomputers on a significant scale at multiple sites? It has an unfortunate choice to make. To go one way means a commitment to a single manufacturer and type of standard board, and to build up specialized expertise and program libraries accordingly. But this is done in the knowledge that new and faster boards are being announced in considerable numbers each year; even processors from the same manufacturer are changing fast, and obsolete lines are unlikely to be indefinitely sustained.

To go the other way is to exploit several different microcomputers on an opportunistic basis, but knowing at the same time from previous experience that software compatibility even at source language level is usually difficult. There is a further source of concern if it is necessary to invest in an endless variety of dedicated prototyping systems for the generation of their programs.

From the hardware cost viewpoint the large user, in particular, must be attracted by the second approach rather than the first. To take full advantage of the reversal of former computing economics, standard microcomputer boards at $300 each or less should be treated as replaceable. Peripherals are

Standard computer boards at $300 or so each should be treated as replaceable.

more expensive and should last longer by being attachable to a sequence of successive processors.

The biggest expense and value is then in the application programs. It is highly desirable that methods are found for the efficient generation of programs for an arbitrary microprocessor, such programs being hardware independent and truly portable from one processor to the next.

Host development systems

The problem just raised has traditionally been regarded by many as insoluble. But this ignores a line of experimentation which has been showing much promise.

An intuitively attractive idea for the generation of microprocessor software is to combine the hardware independence of a host computer configuration (as enjoyed by cross-product users) with the debugging reality of the micro-dependent prototyping system. This can be attempted by physically linking standard microcomputer boards to a permanent host.

A number of users have pursued this approach. They include Oxford Univ. where Intel 8080 programs have been developed with the help of a PDP-11. And Millenium Information Systems

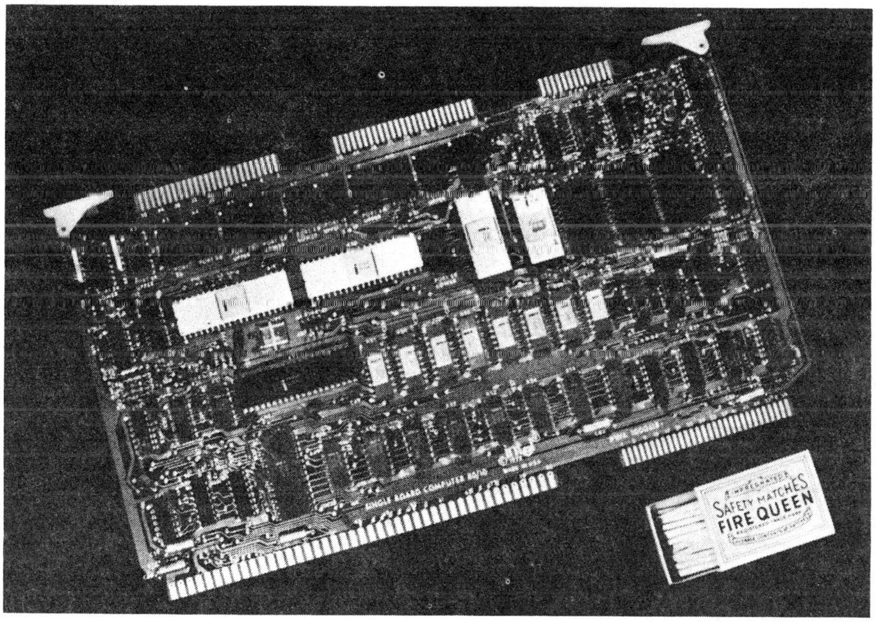

The standard computer board serves several purposes. It allows the user to become familiar with the microprocessor and other components, serves as a test bed for software (which may have to be done at the hexadecimal machine instruction level), and may help in checking out other pieces of the user's application hardware.

has its Universal-One prototyping system, which internally comprises an invariant "host" microprocessor for target-independent functions such as file handling, linked to a more variable microprocessor (the same type as the purchaser's target microprocessor) for functions such as program assembly. And the authors' own organization, CAP MicroSoft, has exploited the concept as the basis for its micro applications development Workshop. And, no doubt, others await announcement.

Fig. 3 shows a schematic of a joint host-target configuration suitable for data processing. It has been found possible to provide software for the host (employing sets of macros) which allows micro source programs to be assembled, then loaded into the target microcomputer board for execution and testing under the overall supervision of the host.

Debugging facilities in the overall system allow the user, sitting at the host's console, to insert breakpoints in the running micro program, to call for trace reports, and to interrogate program locations in terms of the programmer's own symbols.

This general approach requires very little in the way of systems software in the target microcomputer. The manufacturer's own software monitor is used as the basis upon which facilities must be built for the handling of commands received over the host/target link.

In the many cases where the objective is portability of software, this will only be achieved by coming away from assembler source codes and using a common, simple, high-level language.

This host development system at large is currently oriented towards small, simple, single-terminal applications, but is capable of growth as the use of micros develops. Thus it seems very probable that from a set of standalone applications within an office environment will grow a network of office services linked by a communications facility. A host system linked into such a network then becomes the common development facility for the systems on the network. At the same time it can support, through library, editing, and debugging facilities, languages like BASIC offered on some of the machines.

What it means

Both the power of microcomputers and the ease and flexibility with which they can be configured continue to run ahead of their full exploitation in data processing applications. However, programming methods have reached the stage where dp departments can now consider microcomputers as part of their equipment mix. In particular, low microcomputer costs make it feasible to introduce small, local, almost personal forms of office automation.

The hardware, software, and systems are not yet sufficiently mature to think of the early and general replacement of existing computers. Such advances take time. During this time, the same LSI technology will introduce new options into today's conventional machines. But users need to think in terms of a strategy for growth that includes micros, so that they can accumulate experience as a basis for their decisions of the future. ❋

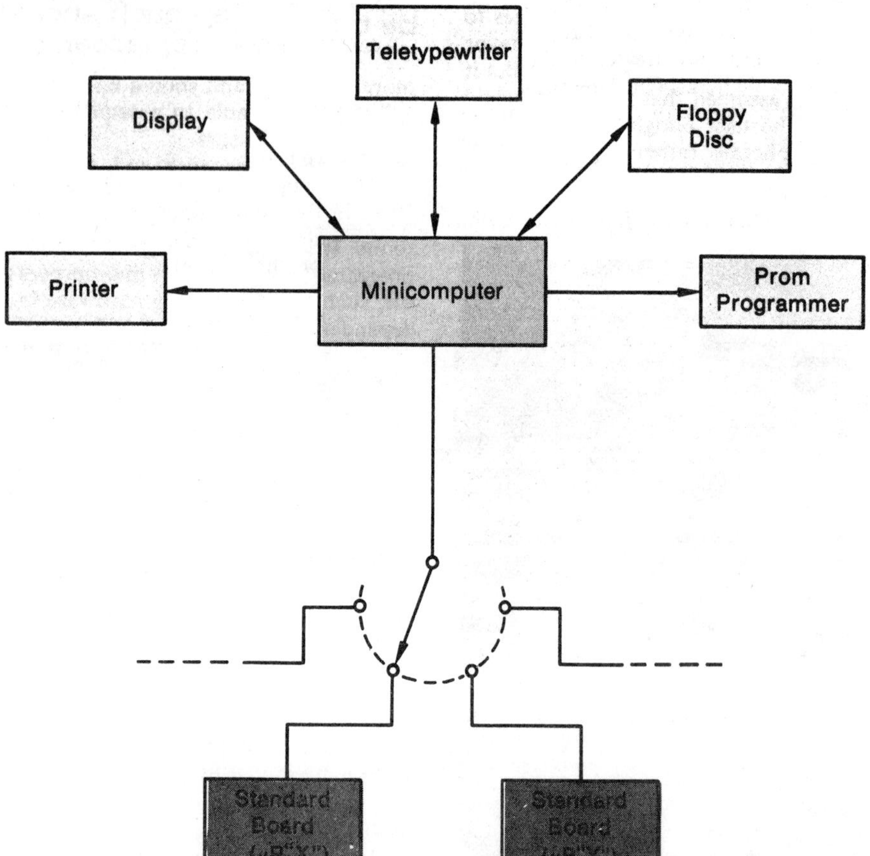

Fig. 3. Host development systems allow the user to test microprocessor boards by attaching them to a minicomputer as a peripheral. One advantage of the method is the low requirement for systems software for the micro.

Microcomputer software makes its debut

by Howard Falk

"We want the microcomputer that offers the most programming power." That's the conclusion of one experienced designer of microcomputer-based CRT terminals, convinced after hard experience that good software is essential to his work.

For the engineer who is a first-time user of microcomputers, software costs can seem almost invisible. The task of learning to program a new machine is so challenging and absorbing that the engineer may find himself looking back on a completed microcomputer-based system design, amazed at the hours of programming that have accumulated.

The long-term experience of computer people is that more than half the design cost of an operating computer system lies in the software portion of the design. For microcomputer applications, with software resources only beginning to develop, programming tends to take up a very large portion of the overall design effort.

That doesn't mean that software-based designs are more difficult than those based on hardwired logic. For example, one Bell Labs test system engineer didn't know anything about microprocessors until he started a project that was to include one of the devices. He and his coworkers soon discovered the tiny computers were easier to work with than their regular logic circuits. Filled with confidence, they wrote their programs, had them "burned" into programmable read-only memory chips, and then wired their test rig together. With very little further effort—it worked!

On the negative side, neophyte users soon discover that the microcomputer world is a Tower of Babel. Every microcomputer manufacturer has invented his own unique machine architecture, and with it goes a unique set of software tools. To switch from one brand of microcomputer to another means that the user has to start from scratch. Previous programs are useless, and there is a whole new language to learn before new programming can begin.

If all this sounds familiar, please notice that history is being relived, with the microcomputer industry now moving through many phases identical to those of the computer industry of the 1950s.

Old computer hands have long known of the language barriers between different computer systems, but they too face some unexpected experiences when they begin to work with microcomputers. Used to working—in large computers and minicomputers—through software operating systems that occupy tens of thousands of bytes of memory, experienced programmers are often surprised to rediscover how much they can accomplish with only 1000 bytes of microcomputer memory.

One group, at RCA, developed a program to simulate a car—on a TV screen—going through a maze, while keeping track of the travel time. The whole program took 800 memory bytes.

A 1000-byte assembly language program takes an experienced microcomputer programmer about a week to write and debug. But the longer the program, the less efficient the process becomes. Thus, it might take two months to write and debug a 4000-byte program.

One of the toughest tasks is defining the techniques to use in writing the program. That is a task somewhat equivalent to laying out a printed circuit board, and it is time-consuming. Some system designers estimate that—including program design, writing, and debugging—about two program instructions per hour can realistically be produced.

Actually, almost everything that can be said of basic microcomputer software concepts and practice holds equally well for minicomputers and large computers. Microcomputers are true computers like any others, and are capable—given a large enough memory, and adequate peripheral equipment—of performing the same kind of computational tasks as minicomputers or large computers. In fact, it is widely believed that computer systems containing multiple microprocessors may eventually be the preferred way to handle complex tasks now performed by large computers.

The programmer who is used to large computers will find that, with microcomputers, he has to be more conscious of minimizing his use of memory space and of meeting strict execution-time requirements. Such optimizing efforts are important because microcomputer systems are often designed to go into mass production.

When software development costs are spread over many systems—in consumer goods, hundreds of thousands of units of a given microcomputer system may be produced—the software design strategy necessarily concentrates on such factors as minimum use of memory space, or maximum speed of operation, and emphasizes the controls that designers must have over the system. Lower design costs for software become a secondary consideration.

In this article, software for microprocessor-based

Some currently available microcomputer software

Microcomputer Systems	Cross-Assembler	Self-Assembler	Editor
Control Logic L-series modules	Batch version, runs on PDP-8 source tape, $120 (object tapes and documentation also available for all programs)	Compatible with cross-assembler source tape, $120	Source tape, $60
Digital Eqpt- Corp. MPS Series Modules	A paper tape system is used to assemble source code on a PDP-8 and proviee binary output for the MPS processor		Editor is PDP-8 based
Intel MCS-4 MCS-8 MCS-80	Written in ANSI standard Fortran IV; source deck, $1250; now used on many systems, including IBM, CDC, and Univac, Time-sharing versions now up on several commercial systems. Offers macro and conditional assembly capabilities	Versions for MCS-8 and -80 are compatible with the cross-assemblers. MCS-4 version is not compatible. Available only to development system users. No charge	Editors run on MCS-8 and -80. Manipulate strings, search, and substitute. Available only to development system users. No charge
Motorola Semiconductor Products MC6800	Runs on Tymshare system; macro capabilities are in development	None	Source statement text editor runs on GE Tymshare system
National Semiconductor IMP-4 IMP-8 IMP-16	Batch version in ANSI Fortran IV for IBM and other computers. Offers conditional assembly. Source deck, $1250. Similar, noninteractive time-sharing version now up on Tymshare, and GE systems	Available for IMP-8, -16. Similar to cross-assembler. No cost; comes with prototyping system purchase	Source editor for paper tape for IMP-16. No charge; comes with prototyping system
Raytheon RP-16	Batch version in Fortran—for Datacraft 6024. No price policy set yet. Time-sharing version in APL up on APL-plus system	Planned	Uses host-computer editing facilities
RCA Cosmac	Batch version in standard, simple Fortran for IBM machines. Has macros and conditional assembly. More powerful time-sharing version up on Tymshare system. No pricing policy yet	In development	Uses host-computer editing facilities. Editor in development
Rockwell International PPS-4 PPS-8	Available for GE time-sharing, Tymshare, IBM batch, and several other systems. No price set yet	Applied Computer Technology, Inc., provides assembler for PPS-4	None
Signetics 2650	Batch version in Fortran II for IBM, Xerox, other machines. Time-sharing version also	None	Uses host-computer editing faciliteis
Toshiba TLCS-12	Batch version only, in Fortran II	Written in Fortran II	Under development

Loader	Debugger	Simulator	Other Programs
Absolute type source tape, $15	Memory dumps and modification source tape, $30	None	PROM programmer, source tape, $45 User's library offers math and other programs
Binary tape bootstrap loader	Resides in MPS memory, used during application program development	None	Program to load, verify, and modify PROM programs is PDP-8 based. Duplicator program copies and verifies eight-channel paper tapes
Part of system "Monitor" program. Available only to development system users. No charge	Part of system "Monitor" program. For MCS-4 and MCS-8: memory dump and modify. For MCS-80: breakpoints; dump and modify for both registers and memory. Available only to development system users. No charge	Simulators written in Std. Fortran IV for MCS-8 and -80. Debugging uses source program symbols, $750	"Monitor" programs offer elementary operating system with I/O capability. No charge to users PL/M, a higher-level language written in Fortran IV for MCS-8, -80, $1250 A user's library offers many programs. Member fee is charged
—	—	Written in Fortran IV. Available on Tymshare system. Allows timing of calculations, and interactive control of execution	In development
Relocatable linking loader offers memory map and error messages; for IMP-16. Absolute loader PROM; includes bootstrap capability; for IMP-8, -16; no cost with system	Debugger offers snapshots, dumps, breakpoints, memory search, alteration of registers, and memory	None	Subroutines include math, code conversion PROM programmer Teletype I/O, and card reader I/O, in PROM for IMP-8, -16. User's library planned
Absolute loader, no charge to users	In development	None	In development
Absolute loader in hardware	Time-sharing package offers symblolic debugging. Dump and modify for memory in stand-along debugger	Time-sharing package offers simulation facility	"Monitor" program in PROM form; others in developmen
None	Debugging comes with cross-assembler facilities	Simulator comes with cross-assembler facilities	Some macros and subroutines No pricing policy yet
Absolute loaders, bootstrap loader	Simulator includes debugging features	In batch and time-sharing versions. Written in Fortran II. No pricing policy yet	About 15 arithmetic and utility routines, including keyboard scanning
Relocatable loader	"Teletypewriter service" program includes some debugging capabilities	Batch-processing version written in Fortran II	Floating-point arithmetic; exponential, trigonometric, and log functions. Higher-level language similar to PL/M is under development

Microcomputer software basics

To program a microcomputer, a list of coded instructions is prepared. Each instruction includes an *operation code* and a memory location where that code is to be stored.

Every microcomputer is designed to accept a specified list of operation codes—usually called an *instruction list* (or set). Based on the accumulated past experience of system designers and computer programmers, these instruction lists include an assortment of operations designed to allow the computer to handle efficiently the diverse tasks expected of it.

In the microcomputer, the instructions exist in binary code form as strings of zeros and ones. It is possible to program a microcomputer in binary code—commonly called *machine language*—but the process is very time-consuming, particularly when almost inevitable program alterations and corrections have to be made.

To speed the programming process, and make the microcomputer a practical system component, an *assembly language* is a necessity.

In assembly language, each operation code is a mnemonic code like ADD, STORE, or JUMP. A special program called an *assembler* converts these mnemonic codes into the binary machine code. The assembler also assigns and keeps track of memory locations. This allows the programmer to use simple reference numbers—like 10, 15, or 20—to identify his instructions, while the assembler program converts these to actual memory locations, as needed.

With the help of an assembly language, the prospective microcomputer user can write down his instructions, telling the computer exactly what sequences of operations to follow. But having in hand a piece of paper with a written assembly-language program, the user is still faced with the task of getting his program into the microcomputer.

Let us assume that his object is to put the program into semiconductor memory chips containing the random-access memory (RAM) used by the microcomputer. A general series of steps to accomplish this goal are shown in Fig. 1. Programs, depicted as rectangles, include an *Editor*—which controls the entry, correction, and tape-recording of the assembly-language program. At the center of the figure is the *Assembler* program, which converts the assembly language statements into machine language. The *Loader* program reads memory addresses and operation codes from the machine language tape and enters them into the semiconductor random-access memory. After the program, in machine language, has been loaded, the *Debugger* is used to make any corrections necessary to assure that operation is satisfactory.

The tapes shown in Fig. 1 are usually punched paper tapes, but other recording media—such as magnetic tape cassettes and floppy disks, as well as conventional computer cards, tape, and disks—can serve equally well. In some systems, editing and assembly are combined, and there is only one, machine language, tape.

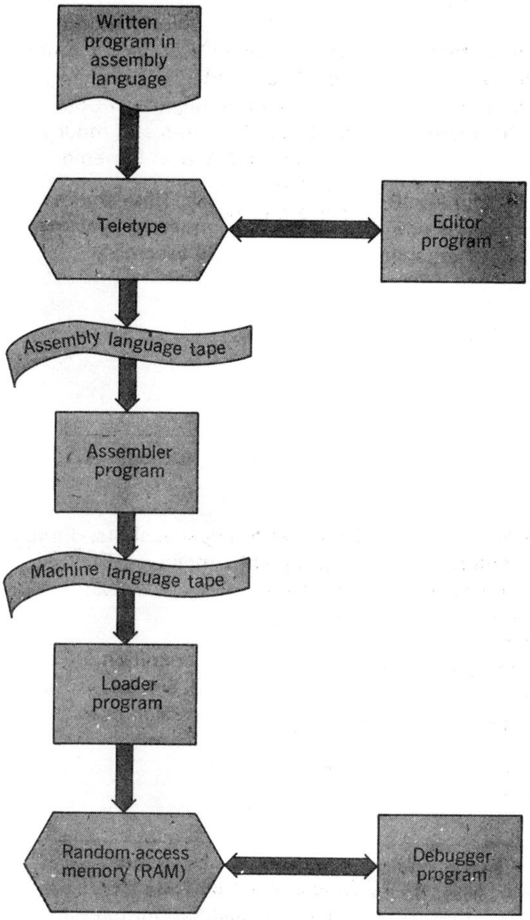

systems is discussed. A step up the computer-size ladder is the one-board minicomputer—the Digital Equipment Corporation PDP-8A, for example, and the General Automation LSI-16, both of which were designed as condensed versions of full-size minicomputers.

The table on pages 206 and 207 displays many of the software resources currently being offered by microcomputer manufacturers. The most important of these to present-day microcomputer users are probably the assembler programs.

The assembler: a basic software tool

Two general types of assembler programs are available for microcomputers: *Cross-assembler* programs run on minicomputers or large computers; *self-assembler* programs run on the microcomputer itself.

Every microprocessor now produced has one or more accompanying cross-assembler program. Often the chip manufacturer writes a cross-assembler even before the microprocessor chips are physically available; this allows programming effort to get under way as soon as the basic microprocessor architecture and instruction list are determined. Using a *simulator* program, a mini- or larger computer can be used to check out and debug many features—but not necessarily all aspects—of assembled microcomputer programs.

Cross-assemblers are often run on time-sharing facilities, and microcomputer manufacturers frequently arrange to make versions of their cross-assemblers available on one, or more, commercial time-sharing services. With a teletype or CRT console, the user can type in his assembly language program, making corrections along the way, as indicated by an interactive editor program. Other cross-assembler versions are written for use with various minicomputers and large computers.

Cross-assemblers are popular because most microcomputers are not configured to handle assembler operations conveniently, while larger computers, equipped with more adequate printers and more memory space, offer the programmer many conveniences.

Like cross-assemblers, self-assemblers are written with a definite computer system in mind. The operation of a self-assembler is highly dependent on the input–output equipment that surrounds the microprocessor. This specific system dependence can sometimes cause problems.

Several features of assemblers are potentially important to microcomputer users. For instance, *relocatable* assemblers allow the memory locations for the machine language program to be transparent to the user. Some assemblers—known as *absolute* assemblers—always start the machine language program storage at the same, fixed memory location; others offer several alternative starting locations and allow some limited linking of program segments in different locations.

Relocatability is a convenience that eases the programmer's task, but it is not an essential feature for many applications.

A *conditional* assembly feature is available with some assembler programs. This allows the user to decide which of the various sections of the program will be assembled and to choose the most efficient order for assembly.

Macro capabilities in an assembler program allow the user to use a single assembly-language instruction to call a specified sequence of machine language instructions. This can be a very powerful tool when certain sequences are repeated during a program. For example, in an instrument operation program, calibration macros can be a great programming time-saver.

Cross-assemblers are generally written in a widely used computer language like Fortran, so that they can be easily adapted to many different time-sharing and batch-processing systems. In general, use of simpler and more standard Fortrans—such as the one specified by the American National Standards Institute (ANSI) minimizes the problem of getting the assembler to run on a new system.

Programs that edit, load, and debug

Editor programs work together with a teletype, or CRT keyboard, to enable the user to type his assembly language statements on the keyboard, while making any needed changes by brief, typed commands. For example, such commands might be used to add a single character, delete a group of lines, or search for a line containing a certain combination of characters. Editor programs are often an integral part of the larger computer systems used to run microcomputer cross-assemblers.

Loader programs accept machine language code, usually in the form of punched cards or punched paper tape. The loader output may go directly into random-access memory (RAM) or into a device that burns the code into a programmable read-only memory (PROM). Sometimes separate programs are used to convert the machine code for PROM burning.

Some loaders are only capable of handling absolute modules of code, destined for prespecified memory locations. Other, more elaborate loaders can link together various code modules and fit them into available memory space in a flexible manner. Then, if an error is found, only the small number of instructions in a single code module need be rewritten.

Along with this linking and relocation capability, these more sophisticated loaders provide such added tools as memory maps—showing where various programs and program-segments are physically located—as well as appropriate error messages, when a faulty program cannot be properly loaded.

Bootstrap loaders can place a program into memory when the microcomputer system is "empty"—in the sense that it contains no previous program information at all. In some systems, a loader program is made available in PROM memory form. To get the system started, it often includes a bootstrap routine that is activated by hitting a reset button or keying in a single instruction. In addition, the program is used for loading and for displaying memory contents and the contents of microprocessor registers.

Display capabilities are important in program debugging. Debugger programs allow the user to manipulate and observe assembled programs. When a program malfunction occurs, debuggers provide such conveniences as printouts, called "dumps," of register contents, or of selected areas of memory.

Snapshot or breakpoint stops may also be provided. With these, the user can specify the conditions under which he wants to examine memory or registers. For example, he may specify that a breakpoint will occur when a given memory location is accessed, or when a specified code appears in a register.

Debugger programs can also allow the user to change the contents of processor registers and memory locations, to start program execution from any point in the program, and to search memory for the location of specified contents.

Simulating microcomputer operation

Even after a microcomputer program is assembled and debugged, the user does not yet know whether it will truly do the job for which it was written. Most users seem to feel that the only practical way to find out is to wire together the integrated circuit packages, connect them to the system equipment, turn on the power, and see if the program will run properly.

Because of the relatively low cost of microprocessors and other microcomputer equipment, this direct approach usually makes good engineering sense.

In some special situations, it may be worthwhile to simulate the system hardware before it is actually produced. Microprocessor manufacturers, concerned about developing effective system architecture, often find simulation programs easier to manipulate and less expensive to alter than MOS chip designs. Similarly, microcomputer system designers who plan to specify their own custom-made microprocessors find use of simulation programs a necessary design step.

Generally, the more accurate the simulation, the more expensive the simulator program, and the longer

If I only had a benchmark!

With so many different architectures and different program instructions, how can one microcomputer's software power ever be compared to another? One way is to select a meaningful problem; program and run it on different, competing machines; and compare the results.

As yet, few benchmarks for microcomputers are available. The most significant to come to our attention is run by Charles Popper of Bell Telephone Laboratories. His benchmark test uses a standard quick-sort algorithm that manipulates a list of values into ascending or descending order. Up to 256 8-bit bytes are sorted using programs that contain the equivalent of about 50 PL/M statements.

The benchmark results found that, with assembly language programs, the RCA Cosmac processor used 181 bytes of memory and the Intel 8080 used 192 bytes, while the Intel 8008 used 347 bytes. Using the PL/M language, the Intel 8008 required 495 bytes.

Even the benchmarking procedure, which sounds eminently fair and equitable, has its drawbacks. The benchmark just cited concentrates on memory operations and character manipulation, but many microprocessor applications are oriented toward input-output and bit manipulation.

Benchmark problems can be chosen so they favor one microcomputer over another, since every machine has its own special strengths and weaknesses. Furthermore, the results depend heavily on the cleverness of the programmers.

The following three examples are not proper benchmarks since they all involve small, simple routines using little code, and can therefore give only a very limited picture of machine performance. We present them as comparison problems that serve to illustrate how very similar results can be obtained with different machines.

Programs were written to implement these problems on the Intel 8080, the Motorola MC6800, and National Semiconductor's IMP-16.

The first comparison problem assumes A and B are positive 8-bit binary numbers. If $A \geq B$, the program is to compute $C = A - B + 2$. If $A < B$, it is to compute $C = B - A + 2$. Random-access memory locations ADDRA, ADDRB, and ADDRC are to contain A, B, and C. The flow chart specified for the solution is shown to the right.

Results for this problem depend on whether $A - B$ is a positive or a negative number. The three machines used from 8 to 15 bytes of memory and from 12 to 39.2 μs to execute the programs.

In the second problem, 8 bits of data (b_8 through b_1) are to be entered into one of the microprocessor's registers, and the one-bit furthest to the left is to be located. If b_8 is the one-bit furthest to the left, the integer 8 is to be entered in a second register; if b_7 is the furthest-left one-bit, integer 7 is to be entered, etc. If b_8 through b_1 are all zeros, the second register should be left with zero.

Solutions for this problem used from 10 to 14 bytes of memory. Execution times varied, depending on the nature of the data, with minimum times ranging from 18.5 μs to 36.4 μs.

The third problem involves a list of consecutive data entries stored in random-access memory. The address of the first list entry in memory is denoted ALIST. A second memory address denoted ENTRY contains a number n—between zero and 255—that signifies the location, in the list, of a desired entry. The entry is to be obtained and added to the microprocessor accumulator.

Memory space used for this problem varied from 6 to 13 bytes, with execution times running from 13 to 34 μs.

Comparison arithmetic problem.

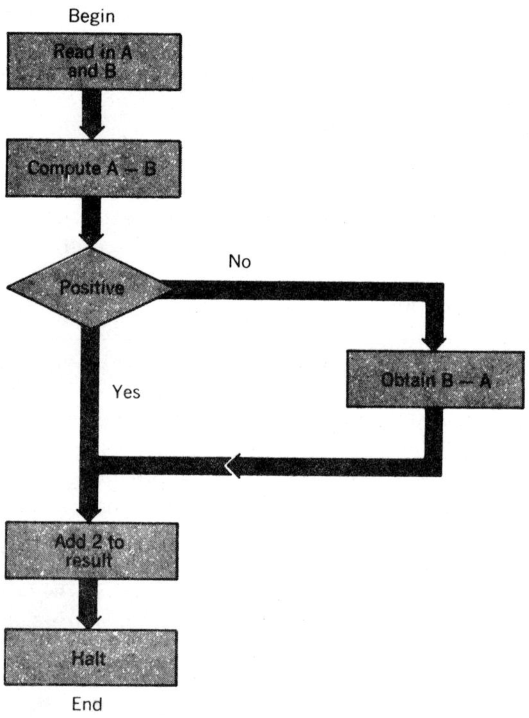

it takes that program to run. Near the point of diminishing returns, the engineer must decide whether he is better off checking his programs on actual hardware, or trying to get more refined simulation.

Simulation of input-output (I/O) operations is particularly difficult. For example, the actual time taken by the processor for any given I/O computation is significant, because peripheral devices—like a tape reader or a disk—require data transfers within strict time limitations if they are to operate efficiently. To simulate these I/O operations, the program must keep track of simulated "real time," and this is difficult and costly to program.

Design control of overall aspects of microcomputer system accuracy can be nicely handled by simulation techniques. Error budgeting is, for example, a potentially spiny problem that is readily handled by simulation. In a given system, the required output accuracy can usually be attained by using more accurate sensors, or more accurate computation, or more accurate A/D conversion, etc. Proper error budgeting finds the mix of component accuracies that will produce the required overall system accuracy at lowest cost.

Microcomputer users generally have to contend with fixed-point arithmetic and 4- or 8-bit words. That is, the program must specify the location of the decimal point in each set of calculation numbers. Floating-point arithmetic moves these decimal points automatically, but this facility is not yet available for most microcomputers. A simulation program known as a fixed-point scaler can help considerably with this decimal point location problem. The output of the program is a matrix that indicates—for each set of computation numbers—the dynamic range of the numbers during the computations, and where the decimal points should be located.

Programming at higher levels

With a higher-level language, the user issues a relatively small number of quite general commands—Fortran statements are of this type—and the microcomputer translates these commands into specific machine code steps, hopefully producing the desired results. This translation process is carried out by a special program called a compiler.

In fact, there is only one higher-level language now available to microcomputer users—the Intel PL/M language.

Tests on sample programs are said to indicate that a PL/M program can be written in less than 10 percent of the time it takes to write the same program in assembly language. The main reason for this savings in time is the fact that PL/M allows the programmer to define his problem in terms natural to him. For a program that selects the largest of two numbers, the PL/M programmer need only write: If $A > B$, then $C = A$; else $C = B$.

But to many hardware designers the notion of higher-level languages seems misplaced and distorted. As one engineer put it, ". . . languages like PL/M have only a marginal value. It is not really difficult to program microcomputers in assembly language. Using PL/M necessarily means supporting a time-sharing terminal, which may be a substantial expense for many small groups and firms." Other users seem to have little confidence that a compiler can produce machine code that does an efficient enough job of bit manipulation to save memory space or speed computation.

Most of the applications software now written for microcomputers is quite naturally being done by users, rather than manufacturers. Some fairly standard routines—like those for scanning a keyboard—are being offered by the manufacturers, mainly as sales incentives to potential customers. Intel (see Box below, left) has organized a cooperative library for user programs.

Users complain that computation on microcomputers is hampered by a lack of mathematical utility routines. Since requirements of different users for such routines vary widely, some microcomputer manufacturers—for example, Signetics—are working on libraries of arithmetic utility routines, such as multiples, variable length multiples, divides, and multiple precision arithmetic. These routines are each being written in several different versions. Some are for maximum speed of execution, others for compactness, so they can be stored in very limited memory space.

Careful records are important

Hardware-oriented engineers tend to discount the importance of careful software documentation. Their first impulse is often to use as little energy as possible to assure that their microcomputer programs will operate correctly. In the debugging stage, this generally means patching a programmable read-only memory to make it do the job.

As Dick Lee, of Boonton Electronics, puts it: "When the original programmer is gone, leaving behind nothing but a program listing, somebody has to sit down and conceptally recreate the program from the listing. That is a difficult, time-consuming job. Until he actually builds up a flow chart, he can't be sure that when he tries to modify the program, he won't introduce some logical fault. Such faults may be subtle and not show up until the system is out in the field. Then, bingo!"

Many users feel that a printed program listing provides an adequate record that can be handled like any other engineering drawing, with revisions and change notices. In truth, only the person who wrote the listing knows the reasoning behind the program, and he may easily forget. To understand a program well enough to make meaningful changes, a programmer needs a flow chart, and a written description of the program strategy can be a great help, as can line-by-line comments on assembly language programs.

The first microcomputer user's library

Users' program libraries have been a familiar part of the computer scene since the SHARE organization began to collect and make available programs written by IBM employees and customers.

Starting early this year, the first microcomputer user's program library was organized by Intel Corporation. The library is divided into three sections, corresponding to use of the three principal Intel microcomputers: the MCS-4, MCS-8, and MCS-80.

Membership in each of these three sections is available "to any interested person or organization" for a yearly fee of $100 per section. The fee will be waived for users who submit a program to the library.

Documentation for each library program includes function, required hardware and software, details of user-program interaction, and a listing of the program.

Among the programs now available through the library for the MCS-4 machines are: AND, OR, and XOR subroutines; an 8-bit multiply, 8-bit divide, decimal addition and subtraction; Chebyshev approximation; 64-bit arithmetic; elementary functions including sin, cos, tan, e^x, and log; conversion of binary code to and from binary-coded-decimal; and teletype read and punch routines. For the MCS-8 machine, there are programs for binary search, floating-point arithmetic, floating-point input-output conversion, processor state restoration in interrupts, 8- and 16-bit multiply and divide, and teletype read and punch. All these MCS-8 programs will also be available for the MCS-80 machine.

A similar library is being planned by National Semiconductor Corp. for users of their IMP-4, -8, and -16 microprocessors.

When to use higher-level languages in microcomputer-based systems

by Jim Gibbons

☐ Unlike other types of computers, microcomputers have seldom been programable by their users. But as soon as they become programable in high-level languages like Fortran or Basic, the users will be free to tailor microcomputer-based systems to their own individual requirements, and the range of microcomputer applications will expand enormously.

The fact is that until now designers have not used microprocessors to build highly flexible systems with many different applications. Rather they have used them to simplify their own job of building complex logic systems intended for high-volume production. For this purpose the compact programs that can be written in the lower-level assembly languages are more than adequate—the undoubted costliness of the process is offset by the high volume of the product and the reduction in memory requirements.

But such an overhead becomes steadily less economical as production runs get shorter. At a certain point it should become much less expensive to use higher-level languages, which make programing quicker and therefore cheaper, even if less efficient in the use of memory.

The obstacle has been a lack of compilers to translate these languages into the machine language of the microprocessor. All microcomputer manufacturers now supply either a cross assembler or a resident assembler or both for programing their products in assembly language. (A cross assembler runs on a large host computer, while the resident assembler runs on the microcomputer itself in its prototyping environment—Intellec, Exorciser, Imp, Assemulator, and so forth.) In contrast, only one compiler—Intel's PL/M—is available, and only in a cross version. Nevertheless, several manufacturers have announced their intention to develop compilers for other high-level languages that will operate on both host and prototyping systems.

In short, designers will soon have to decide when to use a higher-level language in preference to assembly languages. That decision will have to be made on the basis of the time and cost of completing the project and delivering the product. In fact, when the process of programing a product limits its potential sales, it may very well prove best to deliver an unprogramed system and a compiler to the end user and permit him to do the programing—just as other computer users do.

Why use compilers?

The efficacy of compilers is a topic which will draw an hour-long dissertation from just about anyone in the field. In fact there is a rich tradition of pros and cons on the subject which are generally accepted if not thoroughly proven. The first argument usually made in favor of using a compiler is that it reduces the cost of programing. The average output of programers per day is about 10 lines of code, regardless of language. At reasonable salaries and overheads, this can work out to as much as \$10/line programing costs. Since compilers

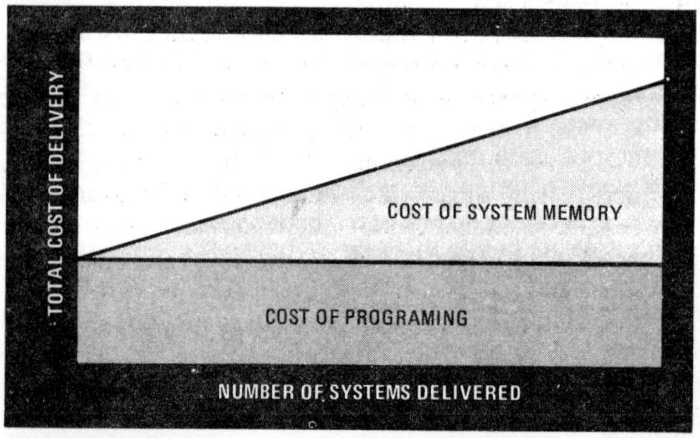

1. Delivery costs. The total cost of delivering a number of systems comprises two factors: a constant programing cost and a variable cost of memory, depending on the number of systems produced.

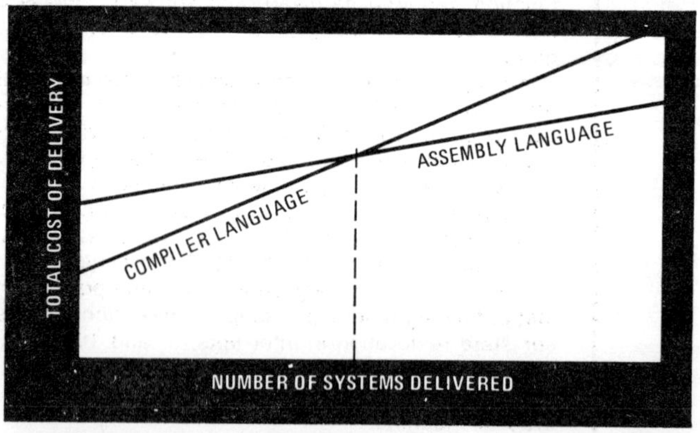

2. Crossover. The total system cost will be lower with compiler-language programing if the number of systems is low, while assembly language leads to lower over-all costs for large numbers of systems.

TRADEOFF POINT FOR COMPILER VERSUS ASSEMBLER					
Memory cost per bit (M)	Expansion factors (E_C)				
	1.0 or less	1.1	1.25	1.5	2.0
$.0005	∞	9,750	3,750	1,750	750
$.001	∞	4,875	1,875	875	375
$.005	∞	975	375	175	75
$.010	∞	488	188	88	38
$.015	∞	325	125	58	25
$.020	∞	244	94	44	19

$$N = \frac{10\,(1/16 - E_C/80)}{(E_C - 1) * M}$$

generate several instructions per statement while assemblers generate only one, a line of compiler code obviously will do more work than a line of assembly code. Thus, both time and the cost of developing a program could be reduced by using a compiler.

Another argument is that programs written in compiler language are easier to read and hence easier to debug and maintain than those written in assembly language. Although incomprehensible programs have been written time and again in Fortran and Cobol, by and large they are easier to read than an equally poor program written in assembly language.

Nevertheless, nearly all the microcomputer programs written today are in assembly language, mainly for efficiency—or so it is alleged. The argument goes something like this: "Compilers are inefficient. They generate more machine language than the bare minimum required for a given function and therefore generate larger and slower programs than can be achieved with assembly language. Cost savings on hardware thus not only justify but require the use of assembly language."

It sounds very persuasive. In fact the only possible comeback is to ask, "What specifically are the cost savings, and do they outweigh the added cost of coding?" These factors must be analyzed a bit more closely.

In most cases speed is irrelevant, since today's microcomputers overpower almost all of their applications. The real question is memory cost. Compilers are accused of increasing memory requirements anywhere from 10% to 100% (depending on the particular compiler and accuser). If "efficiency" is in this range, the costs of hardware and software need to be explored.

A question of volume

Given that programs are less costly to develop and maintain in a higher-level language, whereas programs in assembly language make more efficient use of the computer memory, one must compare the total costs of delivery for each. The key is the number of systems which will be delivered with this program. If this number is very high and significant cost savings are envisioned as a result of careful assembly-language programing, the greater programing costs could be justified. If the number is low, then the cost of programing would dominate total system costs. In this case, the use of compilers could be an important technique in reducing the costs of microcomputer-based products.

Two extreme cases will illustrate this point. First, consider a microcomputer system, such as a digital meat scale, that will be programed once and for all during its design phase and will be delivered by the thousands, always with the same program. Here, programing the system in assembly language may be more expensive at the outset, but could prove to be a good investment, being amortized over all the systems delivered. It is also possible that component costs—most likely memory cost—might be reduced.

On the other hand, consider an automated test station, which will require periodic reprograming to accommodate various testing operations. It would be quite unlikely that any component of the system or even the full system would compare in total cost to the cost of preparing, changing, and maintaining the programs. In this instance the same delivered system is operating several different programs. The cost reductions in programing achievable by using higher-level languages would far outweigh the cost of any additional memory required in the system because of "inefficiency" of the compiler.

It would be helpful to have a better idea of what constitutes a "low" or "high" number of systems to be delivered. A simple linear model of the costs of delivery will express the concepts which underlie the two examples given above. The total cost of delivering a program will comprise the fixed cost of programing plus the variable cost of memory in each system delivered (Fig. 1). Since the cost of programing can be directly related to the number of lines written, it can be expressed as

$$L \times P$$

where L is the number of lines and P is the programing cost per line. It has already been stated that P is about $10 regardless of the language used.

The cost of memory in a single system will be related to L, the number of program lines, B, the number of bits generated by each line of code, and M, the cost per bit of memory:

$$L \times B \times M$$

The total cost of delivering a program in N systems thus will be

$$N \times L \times B \times M + L \times P$$

It is clear from the examples mentioned before that for very large N this cost should be lower when assembly language is used, and that for very small N, this cost will be lower when compiler language is used. Therefore, the two lines must intersect, as shown in Fig. 2. It is this point of intersection that is of interest. It is the boundary between "low" and "high" values of N. This point is defined by the relation

$$N \times L_A \times B_A \times M + L_A \times P = N \times L_C \times B_C \times M + L_C \times P$$

where subscripts A and C refer to assembly language and compiler language, respectively. For a given program, we also know that the total size of the assembly language program and the compiler language program, i.e. the machine language generated by each, will be re-

The hierarchy of computer languages

Computers operate by fetching and executing instructions from their memory. These instructions are nothing more than strings of 1s and 0s arranged by the programer in such a way as to direct the computer to perform some useful task. They are stored as words in the computer's memory. This most fundamental language—the binary patterns actually fetched and executed by the computer—is referred to as "machine" language.

While machine language is the only language recognized by the computer hardware, it has several disadvantages. First, writing programs in machine language can be very tedious since the programer must remember the binary instructions recognized by the machine or continually look them up. Second, after these instructions have been written they are extremely difficult to read, making maintenance difficult. And finally, one computer cannot execute the machine language of another.

The first major advancement in computer languages was the creation of "assembly" language. In assembly language, simple mnemonics indicate the operations to be performed, and memory locations are referred to by symbolic names rather than binary addresses. This language still maintains a one-to-one relationship with the machine language, but it is far easier to read and write. "Macro assembly" languages employ the same techniques of mnemonic instructions and symbolic addressing, but the programer can also develop his own mnemonics, to generate one or more additional instructions.

Since the computer itself recognizes only machine language, assembly language must be translated into binary patterns before it can be executed. A computer program called the assembler performs this task. It accepts assembly language as its input (the "source" code) and produces machine language as its output (the "object" code). While assembly-language programing is far less tedious than machine-language programing, it still requires a knowledge of the architecture and instruction repertoire of the particular computer being programed.

The strict relationship between programing and the particular computer being programed was finally broken when higher level languages such as Fortran, Cobol, PL/I and Basic were introduced. Statements in these languages no longer correspond one-to-one with machine language, but rather generate several machine instructions depending on the exact form and syntax of the statement. Programs are shorter, easier to read, easier to write, and related more closely to what the programer intends to do than to the specific steps the computer will use to accomplish the task. Translation of these languages (from high-level language "source" code to machine-language "object" code) is a somewhat more difficult task than translation of assembly language and is performed by a program called a "compiler."

With a high-level language, a program can be written regardless of the kind of computer that will run it. However, each computer requires its own compiler to translate the program into its own set of instructions.

Another alternative for programing in higher level languages is to use an "interpreter." A high-level language interpreter combines the steps of translation and execution. Machine language is never actually developed. When the program is executed, each line is translated and executed as it is encountered. The translation must be performed each time the line is executed.

Programing languages can most easily be compared by considering a simple example. The one used here is:

P = Q + R

which means: "Take the data from the memory location called Q, add to it the data in location R, and store the result in location P". Below are solutions to this problem in various languages.

	What the programer writes	What it means	Translation	Execution
IN MACHINE LANGUAGE: (8080)	3A 0300	LOAD ACCUMULATOR FROM ADDRESS 300 (Q)	No translation is required since the programer writes in the binary patterns recognized by the processor	Machine language instructions are executed by the processor
	47	MOVE THIS TO STORAGE REGISTER B		
	3A 0560	LOAD ACCUMULATOR FROM ADDRESS 560 (R)		
	80	ADD STORAGE REGISTER B TO ACCUMULATOR		
	32 0100	STORE THE RESULT IN ADDRESS 100 (D)		
(6800)	B6 0300	LOAD ACCUMULATOR A FROM ADDRESS 300 (Q)		
	BB 0560	ADD TO THIS THE CONTENTS OF ADDRESS 560 (R)		
	B7	STORE THE RESULT IN ADDRESS 100 (P)		
(Every other microcomputer would have its own unique machine-language program to solve this problem.)				
IN ASSEMBLY LANGUAGE: (8080)	LDA Q	LOAD ACCUMULATOR FROM LOCATION Q	Assembler program which is executed on the microcomputer or some other computer translates these instructions into the machine language shown above	Machine language instructions are fetched and executed by the processor
	MOV B, A	MOVE THIS TO STORAGE REGISTER B		
	LDA R	LOAD ACCUMULATOR FROM LOCATION R		
	ADD B	ADD STORAGE REGISTER B TO ACCUMULATOR		
	STA P	STORE THE RESULT IN LOCATION P		
(6800)	LDA A Q	LOAD ACCUMULATOR A FROM LOCATION Q		
	ADD A R	ADD TO THIS THE CONTENTS OF LOCATION R		
	STA A P	STORE THE RESULT IN LOCATION P		
(Every other microcomputer would have its own unique assembly-language program to solve this problem.)				
IN COMPILER LANGUAGE:	P = Q + R	P = Q + R	Compiler program which is executed on the microcomputer or some other computer translates this statement into machine language	Machine language instructions are fetched and executed by the processor
(This statement would have the same net effect on any microcomputer for which a compiler is provided.)				
IN INTERPRETIVE LANGUAGE:	P = Q + R	P = Q + R	No translation step is required since the interpreter program will do this at the time of execution	This instruction is fetched, translated and executed under control of the interpreter program
(This statement can be executed on any microcomputer which has an interpreter.)				

lated by the expansion factor, E_C of the compiler:

$$L_A \times B_A \times E_C = L_C \times B_C$$

(For example, if the compiler language program generates 25% more machine language than the assembly language program, E_C will be 1.25).

With the relation for E_C we can now solve for N:

$$N = \frac{P[(1/B_A) - (E_C/B_C)]}{(E_C - 1)M}$$

All that remains is to fit the parameters and calculate N. P has already been given as $10 per line. Values of 16 for B_A (the number of bits of code generated by an assembly language instruction) and 80 for B_C (the number of bits of code generated by a compiler language instruction) are reasonable choices.

The parameters that are hard to fit are E_C, the compiler expansion factor, and M, the cost of memory.

E_C is simply a matter of strong disagreement. People have claimed to observe values anywhere in the range of 1.1 to 2.0 or higher. M is hard to fit because there are so many different types of memory (read-only memory, programable ROM, static random-access memory, dynamic RAM). ROM memory in 16,384-bit packages purchased in large quantities can run as low as 0.05¢/bit, while PROMs in 2,048-bit packages purchased in small quantities can cost as much as 2¢/bit. At the system level, these costs run slightly higher, but for the present the semiconductor costs dominate.

If these ranges of compiler efficiency and memory costs are assumed, a table of crossover N values can be developed (see the table on p.213). Somewhere on that table, everyone should be able to find an entry that corresponds both to his memory costs and to his particular beliefs about compiler efficiency.

When the extreme values are ignored, the crossover works out at about 100 for PROMs and 1,000 for ROMs. If a program is to be delivered in fewer systems, a compiler language program should be used. There are problems with this calculation. Most notably the units of memory one can actually purchase are fairly large—1-k to 16-k bits. This means that the cost of memory in a single system is actually a step function rather than being continuous. This has the effect of distorting the value of E_C. For instance, even if E_C = 1.1, if the assembly-language program exactly fills one memory package, using compiler language will almost certainly force the use of another package. This will make E_C effectively equal to 2.0. Another problem is the nonlinearity of memory cost with the total number of systems purchased. But even with the shortcomings of this cost model, the general conclusion holds up.

These numbers translate into very specific rules. A compiler should be used or delivered whenever:

- Customization is required for each delivery of hundreds of systems (or fewer).
- The total volume of a product is hundreds or fewer.
- The end user will program his own system (his total number of systems is always small—usually one).

Two compiler options

Given that one might want either to use a compiler or deliver one as a system component, what are the options in compiler technology? Choosing the right approach dramatically affects the efficiency of object-code generation. Consider, as an example, a simple statement

(a) 6800
```
*LOAD Q
        LDA   A     Q
        LDA   B     Q+1
*MULTIPLY BY R
        STA   A     TEMP
        STA   B     TEMP+1
        LDX   #17
        CLR   A
        CLR   B
        BRA         LOC3
LOC1    BCC         LOC2
        ADD   B     R+1
        ADC   A     R
LOC2    ROR   A
        ROR   B
LOC3    ROR   TEMP
        ROR   TEMP+1
        DEX
        BNE         LOC1
        LDA   A     TEMP
        LDA   B     TEMP+1
*ADD T
        ADD   B     T+1
        ADC   A     T
*STORE P
        STA   A     P
        STA   B     P+1
        (56 BYTES)
```

(a) 8080
```
*LOAD Q
        LHLD  Q
*MULTIPLY BY R
        XCHG
        LHLD  R
        MOV   A, H
        MOV   C, L
        MVI   B, 8
        LXI   H, 0
LOC1    DAD   H
        RAL
        JNC   LOC2
        DAD   D
LOC2    DCR   B
        JNZ   LOC1
        MOV   A, C
        MVI   B, 8
LOC3    DAD   H
        RAL
        JNC   LOC4
        DAD   D
LOC4    DCR   B
        JNZ   LOC3
*ADD T
        XCHG
        LHLD  T
        DAD   D
*STORE P
        SHLD  P
        (48 BYTES)
```

(b) 6800
```
*LOAD Q
        LDA   A     Q
        LDA   B     Q+1
*MULTIPLY BY R
        LDX   R
        JSR   MULTIPLY
*ADD T
        ADD   B     T
        ADC   A     T+1
*STORE P
        STA   A     P
        STA   B     P+1
        (24 BYTES)

MULTIPLY
        STA   A     TEMP
        STA   B     TEMP+1
        STX         TEMP2
        LDX   #17
        CLR   A
        CLR   B
        BRA   LOC3
LOC1    BCC   LOC2
        ADD   B     TEMP2+1
        ADC   A     TEMP2
LOC2    ROR   A
        ROR   B
LOC3    ROR   TEMP
        ROR   TEMP+1
        DEX
        BNE   LOC1
        LDA   A     TEMP
        LDA   B     TEMP+1
        RTS
        (39 BYTES)
```

(b) 8080
```
*LOAD Q
        LHLD  Q
*MULTIPLY BY R
        XCHG
        LHLD  R
        CALL  MULTIPLY
*ADD T
        XCHG
        LHLD  T
        DAD   B
*STORE  P
        SHLD  P
        (18 BYTES)

MULTIPLY
        MOV   A, H
        MOV   C, L
        LXI   H, 0
        CALL  LOC1
        MOV   A, C

LOC1    MVI   B, 8
LOC2    DAD   H
        RAL
        JNC   LOC3
        DAD   D
LOC3    DCR   B
        JNZ   LOC2
        RET
        (22 BYTES)
```

3. Programs. For the simple operation of "Multiply Q by R, add T, and store results in P," assembly-language programs for the Intel 8080 and the Motorola M6800 are complex (a). Use of subroutines for multiply operation (b) reduces program size but adds to overhead.

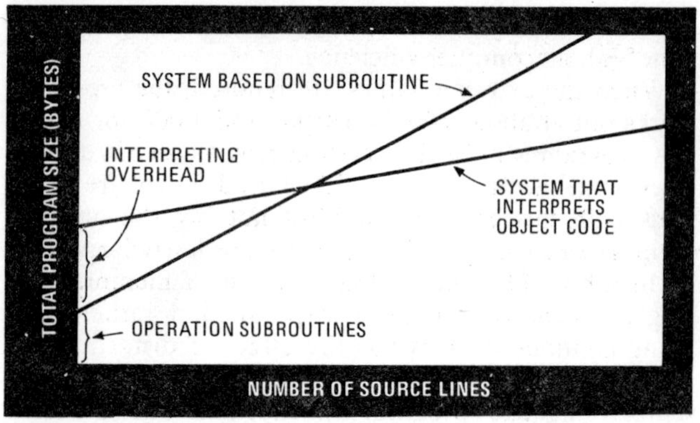

4. Subroutines vs interpreters. Although interpreting systems have a higher overhead, they are more efficient for large numbers of source lines—that is, they result in fewer total program bytes.

that might be written in any higher-level language:

$$P = Q * R + T$$

(Multiply Q by R, add T, and store the results in P.) For a larger machine (some minicomputers and most large mainframe machines), this statement might compile very simply into four instructions:

```
LOAD    Q
MPY     R
ADD     T
STORE   P
```

However, it is not that easy for a microcomputer, since the high-level language statement generates several times more instructions in machine language. For, say, the simplest case—16-bit unsigned binary arithmetic and 16-bit direct addressing—assembly-language programs are shown in Fig. 3(a) for the Intel 8080 and Motorola M6800 microprocessors. Even for the simple case, note that a multiply operation, for example, generates more than 35 bytes of code. With the problem compounded by the more complicated data representations and addressing techniques of most high-level languages, these programs could become much more complex.

One possible solution is to use subroutines for the more complex operations that will probably be repeated. When this is done for the multiply operation, the programs shown in Fig. 3(b) would be generated. However, the support subroutines also shown in that figure would be required as well. (Since subroutines have been introduced anyway, an extra level of subroutining—CALL LOC1—is used in the 8080 version to further reduce the program size.)

What is the tradeoff? Basically, a much smaller program has been generated, but it will run somewhat more slowly because of the transfer of control to the multiply subroutines and the subsequent returns. Also, some system "overhead"—the multiply subroutine—is now inherent in the system. Every compiled program must now include the multiply and other overhead subroutines and will therefore be no longer directly proportional in length to the number of program statements. And, despite the fact that a major portion of the code has been eliminated by the subroutines, it is still not as compact as it was for a large computer.

A second approach can offer much more concise compilation. The principle is simple. Compile for a somewhat "larger" computer designed for the efficient execution of higher-level-language programs, and then do one of two things: either emulate that hypothetical computer by using an interpreter to translate and execute the compiler's object code, or microprogram a central-processing unit built from bit-slice components to "be" the computer that's needed to efficiently execute a program written in the higher-level language.

The major difference in object-code size between this approach and one which relies on subroutines is that the subroutine calls no longer are required. Thus a statement that might be compiled for a subroutine-based execution system as

```
LOAD    DATA1
CALL    OPERA
LOAD    DATA2
CALL    OPERB
```

would not require the subroutine CALL and would be compiled this way for the hypothetical computer:

```
OPERA   DATA1
OPERB   DATA2
```

The definition of the hypothetical computer and its emulation should turn out to be simple. But, if either does prove to be complex, then the definition probably is wrong. In fact, this approach has been used to design Fortran systems for minicomputers that require only 32 operations. Even for a more complex language, complete specification of all required operations and address modes should always be possible in single bytes.

When object-code interpreting systems are compared to subroutine-based systems, the only real differences in the overhead required at runtime are the interpreter's address-mode routines and decoding section. All of the operation routines are common to both.

Figure 4 shows the relation of total program size, including overheads, to the number of executable source program lines for object-code interpreting and subroutine-based systems. Not surprisingly, the graph indicates that the former, higher-overhead approach is more efficient when large programs must be compiled. It should also be noted that overheads will not necessarily cost as much per byte as object code, since they can be committed to ROMs and purchased in high volume.

Thus, one of the key parameters in selecting a compiler technology must be the expected size of programs to be written in the higher-level language. If the programs are expected to be several hundred lines or more, an object-code interpreting system or one which has been microprogramed for the correct set of operators will produce the shortest programs.

An extra benefit to compiling for an "ideal" machine and then emulating it is the independence gained for the CPU. The programs generated by such a compiler could be executed on any CPU for which the appropriate interpreter or microcode had been written.

This CPU independence could prove to be the most important technological consideration. The rapid changes in semiconductor technology make it important not to be "trapped" by software. Transferability of microcomputer software is therefore more than just a desirable feature, it is a necessity. □

Say it in a high-level language with 64-K read-only memories

by Rudy Langer and Thomas Dugan

□ A new era is dawning in the world of solid-state memories as very-large-scale integration boosts read-only-memory chips to 64-K size, with 256-K devices standing in the wings. These chip capacities make the ROM a full-blown program-storage medium with a cost, convenience, and durability never before possible. Such silicon software—that is, complex, complete software packages in plug-in ROMs—will change the way memory is used, the way microprocessor systems are designed, and the way software is implemented, developed, and distributed.

Right on the horizon is the lodestar of this momentous development: the availability to microcomputers of high-level programming languages. Basic, Fortran, and PL/M, which now require expensive disk-based systems for their effective use, will be accessible for no more than the cost of a $15 or $20 integrated circuit.

Indeed, with programmed ROMs, high-level languages will be at last cheap enough for even the smallest microcomputer systems. Moreover, encapsulating software in ROMs means that a large variety of commonly used routines and subroutines can be packaged in readily available off-the-shelf families. Such firmware will be seen as simply a resource of the microcomputer system, nothing more than another peripheral chip.

Bit patterns to programs

Read-only memories have come a long way since their first use as pattern storage on a bit-by-bit basis. Such applications—code-conversion tables like those converting EBCDIC to ASCII, for example—typically require 1,000 to 2,000 bits. As ROM capacity grew, so did its uses. With 4-K chips, it was possible to store a complete font of 5-by-7 dot-matrix characters.

Now, with 65,536-bit ROMs available, extended bit-pattern storage can be achieved. The most immediate

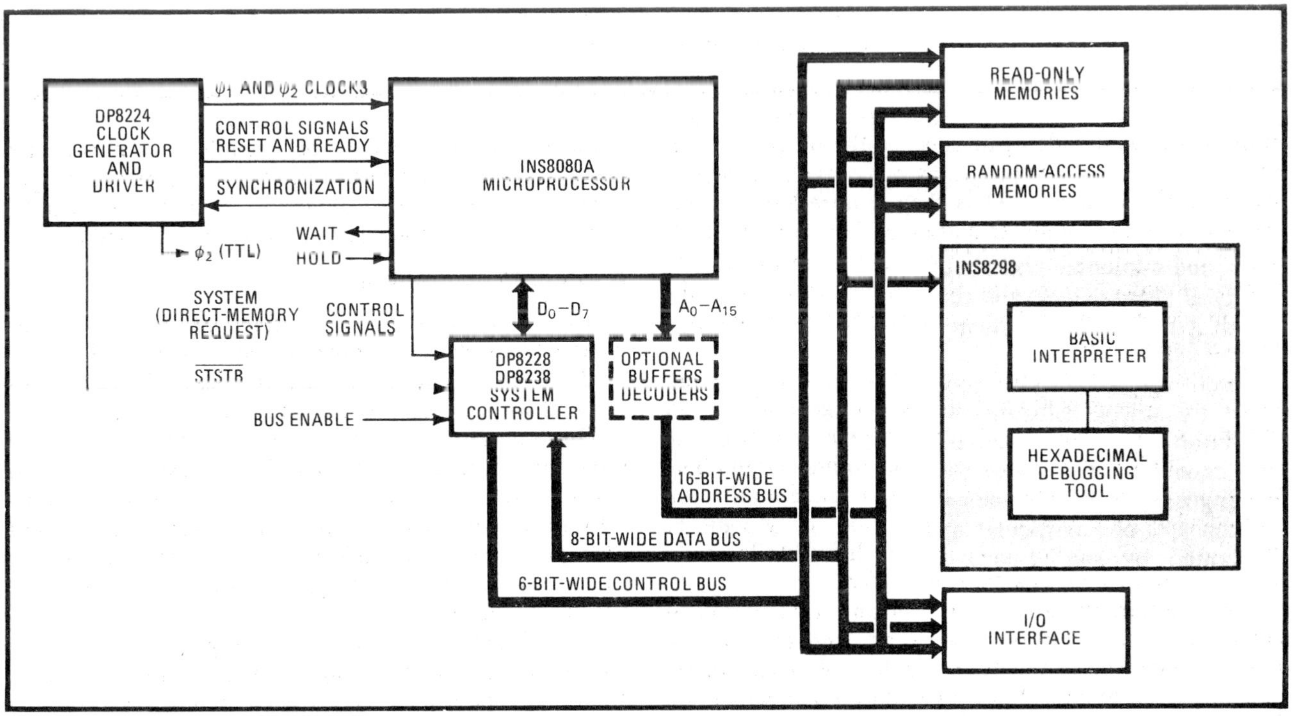

1. Basic microcomputer. Few components are needed to build an 8080-based microcomputer that programs in Basic. Besides the usual ROM, RAM, and system-control chips, the 64-K 8298 ROM is connected to the system's address and data buses. It stores an LLL Basic interpreter and a handy hexadecimal debugging tool, which allows the user to examine and internal registers and memory location.

TABLE 1: BASIC STATEMENTS AND CONTROL COMMANDS

Statement	Function
CALL	Calls user-written assembly-language routines.
DIM	Declares an array. (Indexing is from zero).
END	Terminates a program and returns control to the Basic subsystem.
FOR	Causes program to iterate through a loop a designated number of times.
GET expression	Reads input data from a specified port.
GOSUB nn	Transfers control to a subroutine beginning at line nn.
GOTO nn	Transfers control to line nn.
IF expression THEN nn	Transfers to line nn if the condition of the expression is met.
INPUT list	Allows the user to supply numeric data to a program directly from the terminal.
LET identifier=expression	Assigns the value of an expression to the identifier on the left side of the equal sign.
NEXT	Signals the end of a loop.
PRINT	Allows numeric data and character strings to be printed on the terminal.
PUT expression	Writes output data to a specified port.
REM	Allows comments to be inserted in the program listing.
RETURN	Returns control to the line after the last GOSUB.
STOP	Suspends program execution and returns.

Command	Function
CONTROL/H (backspace)	Deletes the previous character typed during input.
CONTROL/S	Interrupts program during execution and returns to immediate mode.
DEBUG	Transfers control to the hexadecimal debugger program (HDT).
LIST	Prints out all or part of a program at the terminal.
PACK	Frees memory locations in RAM to allow the user more working space.
PLIST	Punches paper-tape copy of a program.
PTAPE	Reads in paper-tape copy of program using high-speed reader.
RUN	Begins execution of the program currently in memory.
SCR	Erases the program in memory.

impact will be in video games, since the bit patterns for the most part are not programs but actually represent patterns on the screen. Thus they require less development time than computer software. The availability of 1-, 2-, and 4-kilobyte ROMs is largely responsible for the variety of video games, and the development now under way of games using 8-kilobyte memories promises even greater sophistication.

Accordingly, consumer product design is a prime target for silicon software. Advanced general-purpose calculators with basic computation keys and programming capability now require the user to understand both the language of the machine and the detailed mathematical concepts of a particular application. They could be supplanted by special-purpose machines tailored to specific applications by a change of ROMs.

For example, the groundspeed of an airplane may be calculated from windspeed, airspeed, and direction of flight, if one knows the fundamentals of trigonometry and vector arithmetic. Most pilots do not and would not have the time to do it anyway. But anyone could solve the problem using a calculator with appropriately designated input keys and a groundspeed answer key. Such a dedicated machine would be feasible only if the same basic hardware were used for, say, a realtor's, photographer's, or carpenter's calculator, with the personality formed simply by the insertion of a programmed ROM.

A future in computers

Soon ROMs will begin to affect the ways in which computer software is implemented, stored, and distributed. In fact, system software that is exclusively ROM-resident will be the norm in systems of the future.

The benefits of such software are many. First, programs need not be loaded from cassettes, disks, or paper tape. ROM chips will be the cheapest storage medium in the long run, as well as being the smallest. Moreover, they are as indestructible as the machine that uses them, in terms of the nonvolatility of the information they contain.

The advantages a high-level language brings to a microcomputer system using silicon software are many:

■ Ease of operation. High-level languages are easy to learn because of their English-like statements and their conversational nature. Compared with assembly language, it takes a relatively short training time to become

```
10   REM "THIS IS A SIMPLE BENCHMARK PROGRAM. IT"
15   REM "MULTIPLIES, DIVIDES, ADDS AND SUBTRACTS."
20   REM
30   INPUT A
40   INPUT B
50   LET C = A + B
60   LET A = A + 1
70   LET E = B/C
80   LET F = A * E
90   LET C = C - F
100  IF A = 1001, THEN 200
110  GO TO 50
200  PRINT "THE LOOP IS DONE AT"
210  END
```

2. Benchmark program. A simple program written in LLL Basic compares run times in compilers and interpreters. The loop in the program carries out addition, subtraction, multiplication, and division, all of which execute 1,000 times. The compiled code runs about 3½ times faster than interpreted code.

proficient in Fortran, and even less time for Basic. Of course, proficiency in the language of a system will simplify the job of operating and maintaining that system.

- Reduced programming time. One high-level statement does the work of about 10 assembly-language statements. Yet, writing a statement in Fortran, for example, takes the same amount of time as writing one in assembly language. High-level languages are also easier to debug, so programs are completed faster.
- Reduced development time. Because the user does not have to convert a high-level development program written for the prototype system into the machine- or assembly-level program for the production unit, development time from concept to market is much reduced.
- Reduced documentation costs. It is easier to write out explanations of high-level programs because they are more natural in their syntax and hence more straightforward in their expression of what is being done.
- Program-language commonality. Assembly language statements vary from computer to computer, but a high-level language can provide a common way of encoding programs for use with different types of computers.
- Elimination of the specialist. Programming in a high-level language lessens the need for a highly trained programming specialist. This brings the system's operation closer to the people who understand the application, not necessarily the computer. With assembly language, the opposite is often true: programs end up adjusting the application to the computer's convenience.

To use high-level languages on a microcomputer system requires either interpreters, which translate and execute each source (high-level) statement into machine language, or compilers, which translate entire high-level programs into machine language before execution. Compilers are much larger programs than interpreters, but generate native machine code that executes significantly faster, having substantially less lines.

TABLE 2: MEMORY MAP FOR BASIC INTERPRETER

ROM Address (hexadecimal)	Function
1000 – 1047	Basic entry points for initialization
1048 – 1291	Basic I/O (standard for INS8251 at ports EC and ED)
1292 – 12CC	PACK routine
12CD – 27FF	Basic interpreter
2800 – 2EFF	Hexadecimal debugging tool and loaders
2F00 – 2FFF	I/O jump routines
RAM Address (hexadecimal)	**Function**
3D00 – 3DFF	Basic RAM scratch area (printers, stack, etc.)
3E00 upward	Basic user program space

Since an interpreter translates and executes individual statements essentially in their source form, the programmer can make immediate alterations to the source programs during checkout. Many interpreters also can detect programming syntax errors as statements are being typed in. With assembly-level programs, errors often go undetected as far as the prototype system.

High level for microcomputers

With lots of program space in the new large ROMs, extremely space-efficient code need no longer be written for every microprocessor application. Although high-level languages may produce four or more times as much assembly code when compiled, they can now filter down to production-level microcomputer systems—unless the execution-speed requirement demands a tightly written assembly program.

With a high-level language running directly in a final production system, the designer may pay penalties in execution time of as much as 10 times over that obtained by using optimized machine languages. But of the range of microprocessor applications, the vast majority are not very time-critical. Most instrumentation, data-acquisition, and process-control jobs can be done by a microprocessor configuration that operate at just a tenth the speed of an 8080A.

Already, several versions of Basic interpreters are available that take up less than 8 kilobytes of memory and could fit in a single integrated circuit. One version, for example, is LLL Basic, developed at the Lawrence Livermore Laboratory in Livermore, Calif., and tailored for data-acquisition and process-control applications. The LLL Basic interpreter requires 6 kilobytes of memory, and therefore fits comfortably in an 8-kilobyte ROM.

Nearly all interpreters, and even some compilers, will be accommodated by the 16-kilobyte ROMs under development, and forthcoming ROMs as large as 64 kilobytes will be large enough for a whole family of compilers and compiled programs that are already in the public domain. Thus the era of silicon software is well on the way to being launched.

Software packaged in ROMs has additional benefits of its own. Immediately apparent is the impetus it adds to

ASSEMBLY-LANGUAGE PROGRAM

```
ORG 37400Q
    SCR E QU 30Q
    PAG EQU 4400Q
    PRESS EQU 4Q
    TEMP EQU PRES +4
    VOL EQU 0Q

                    ; READ VOLUME
LXI H, PAG          ; PAGE 11 LOC 0
MVI C, SCR          ; SCRATCH AREA
CALL INPUT          ; READ VOLUME FROM TTY TO
                    ; MEMORY BUFFER
MVI L, PRESS        ; READ PRESSURE
MVI C, SCR          ; SCRATCH
CALL INPUT          ; READ AND STORE IT
MVI L, TEMP         ; READ TEMP
MVI C, SCR          ; SCRATCH
CALL INPUT          ; READ AND STORE IT
MVI L, TEMP+4       ; CALCULATE STD PRESSURE
MOV B, L            ; SAVE IN B
MVI M, 276Q         ; LOAD 760 INTO MEMORY
INR L
MVI M, 000Q
INR L
MVI M, 110Q
INR L
MVI M, 012Q
MVI I, PRES         ; DIVIDED
MVI C, TEMP+8       ; RESULT
CALL LDIV
MVI L, TEMP+4       ; STORE 273.15
MOV B, L            ; SAVE IN B
MVI M, 210Q
INR L
MVI M, 223Q
INR L
MVI M, 063Q
INR L
MVI M, 0111Q
MVI L, TEMP
MVI C, SCR          ; SCRATCH
CALL LADD           ; ADD TO GET DEGREES KELVIN
MOV C, L            ; STORE RESULT PTR IN C
MOV L, B            ; 273.15 IN B
MOV B, C            ; TEMP IN DEGREES K
MVI C, TEMP+12      ; RESULT
CALL LDIV           ; DIVIDE THEM
MOV B, C
MOV L, TEMP+8       ; PRESSURE
MVI C, PRES         ; TEMPORARY RESULT
CALL LMUL
MOV L, C            ; RESULT PTR TO L
MOV B, VOL
MUI C, TEMP+12      ; FINAL VOL AT STD PARD GING
CALL LMUL
MVI L, C            ; FINAL RESULT
MVI C, SCR
CALL CVRT           ; WRITE ANSWER TO TTY
END
```

(a)

LLL BASIC PROGRAM

```
10REM "THIS IS A TEST TO COMPARE PLM
        ASSEMBLY AND"
20REM "BASIC LANGUAGES FOR WRITING FAST AND
        EASY"
30REM "TO DEBUG PROGRAMS FOR MICROPROCESSORS."
35REM
40REM "CALCULATE VOLUME USING THE IDEAL GAS
        LAW"
45REM "VOL2−VOL1*(P1/P2)*(T2/T1)"
50REM
60PRINT "ORIGINAL VOLUME"
65INPUT V1
75PRINT "ORIGINAL PRESSURE"
80INPUT P1
85PRINT "ORIGINAL TEMPERATURE"
90INPUT T1
100REM "NOW THAT THE VALUES ARE INPUTED LET'S
        DO THE CALCULATION."
105LET A=T1+273.15
115REM "T1 IS IN DEGREES C"
116REM "A IS IN DEGREES KELVIN."
120LET B=P1/760.0
125REM "P1 IS IN MM OF HG."
127REM "P2=760.0 WHICH IS 1 ATM."
130LET C=273.15/A
135REM "C IS T2/T1"
136LET E=C*B
137REM "E=(T2/T1)*(P1/P2)"
140LET V2=E*V1
150PRINT "THE VOLUME AT STD PRESS AND TEMP IS";V2
200END
READY
```

(b)

3. Assembly vs Basic. A program that performs the ideal-gas-law calculation is written in assembly language (a) and in LLL Basic (b). While the Basic-generated code occupies 2½ times as much memory, the program took only an hour to write and debug; the assembly language program took more than four days.

program modularity. A concept widely used in computing circles, application-program modularity is just coming into vogue with microcomputers. It allows the design of software packages or modules that can eliminate redundant programming efforts.

Such modules are at present sold, rented, and swapped in paper-tape, magnetic-tape, and disk form and are ready-to-go application packages designed so that the user merely specifies which options or special requirements are needed and what particular values must be used. If designed and inserted into ROMs, these packages become truly modular, since small plug-in units incorporate the program function.

Interchangeable languages

Another ROM software advantage is in language interchangeability. Using silicon software, a microcomputer-system designer can change the language of his system by simply swapping chips. A single-board computer could be turned into a Basic machine by dropping a ROM-resident interpreter into the proper socket. The board could subsequently be changed to an APL, Fortran, Pascal, or Cobol machine merely by substituting the proper plug-compatible programmed device.

An example of silicon software is the INS8298 Basic interpreter for the 8080A microprocessor. Few additional components are needed with the microprocessor and the 8-kilobyte ROM interpreter to build the complete Basic microcomputer system shown in Fig. 1.

The LLL Basic interpreter in the 8298 can translate, debug, and execute ASCII-coded programs written into random-access memory by the user. Each statement is interpreted from its basic ASCII format and then executed line by line. Since the interpreter works directly from user-written source statements in memory, the user can easily manipulate source code and instantly revise the program when errors are detected. If the application needs more efficient assembly code than can be generated by an interpreter, a Fortran program that compiles LLL Basic programs is available in the public domain.

Basic interpreter in action

The 8298 accepts both the program statements and control commands listed in Table 1. Program statements describe operations to be performed on program data, while control commands specify actions that alter the status of the user's program by directing the execution, saving, and retrieval of programs.

All program statements, except those preceded by a line number, are executed immediately and then discarded. Called the immediate or direct mode, this is especially valuable for program checkout. Those statements preceded by a line number are inserted into the program for later execution at a spot determined by the line number.

The memory map for the Basic interpreter is shown in Table 2. Hexadecimal ROM addresses cover from 1000_{16} to $2FFF_{16}$, and the interpreter assumes its working RAM starts at $3D00_{16}$. All input/output routines used by the 8298 are in the upper 256 bytes of address space so that a simple address-decoding circuit can allow the substitution of special user-supplied input/output packages if necessary. As an alternative scheme allowing the user to tailor I/O to his own needs, entry points to the interpreter are provided that allow the page-0 initialization program to route all Basic input/output through its own routines by preinitializing the RAM I/O jump table used in all 8298 programs.

A hexadecimal debugging and utility tool (HDT) is also included in the 8298. The HDT allows the user to examine internal registers and memory locations and to modify their contents. It is called from the Basic interpreter to help debug user-developed software. Input and output data representation is in hexadecimal format. In addition, HDT also has commands that test a specified range of memory locations, load programs in hexadecimal, NSC, and LLL binary formats, and save the contents of a specified range of memory locations.

The benchmark program shown in Fig. 2 was used to compare the Basic interpreter with a compiler. Running the program took 75 seconds with the interpreter. When it was compiled into 8080 machine code, it ran in 22 seconds. Thus, an application that calls for stringent speed requirements may warrant the extra effort required to program in assembly code rather than in a high-level language.

Gas-law program

For comparative purposes, a program that performs simple mathematical routines—the ideal gas-law calculation—has been written in both LLL Basic and assembly language (Fig. 3). The assembly language routine is 100 bytes long and took four to five days to program and debug on an 8080-based system. The LLL Basic version occupies an estimated 250 bytes, exclusive of comments. But it took only one hour to program and debug into a state suitable for input into a compiler. Of course, an 8298-based system, using the capabilities of its HDT package, could immediately punch the program

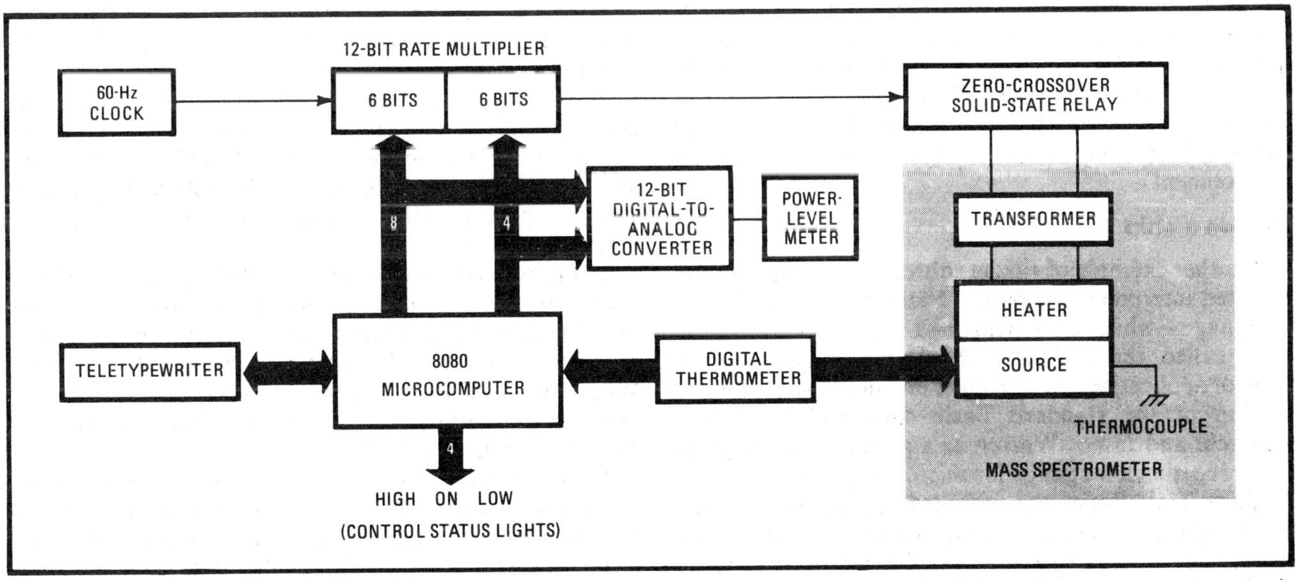

4. Temperature controller. A microcomputer-based temperature controller for the inlet probe of a high-resolution mass spectrometer is programmed in LLL Basic. The system hardware took 1½ months to complete, while the Basic programming required just 1½ weeks. If the program were implemented in assembly language, a period of at least three months would be needed for to carry out the tasks of writing and debugging. In operation, the Basic program calls a small assembly-language routine that performs calculations quickly.

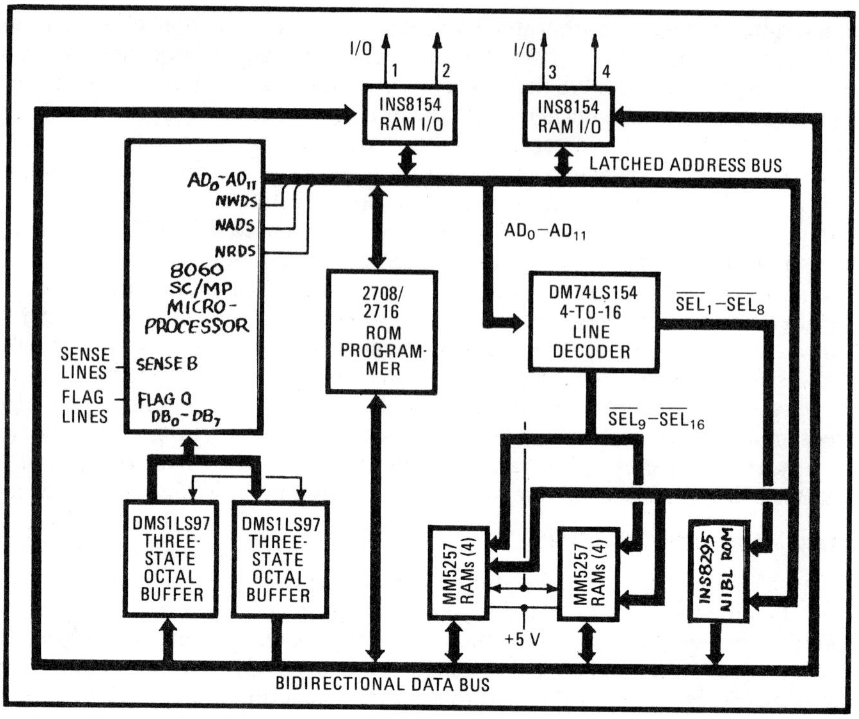

5. Nibl Board. The 9295 32-K read-only memory contains an intepreter for the National Industrial Basic Language (Nibl), which is evaluated in this SC/MP-based microcomputer system. Hooking a teletypewriter to the input/output line, the user can develop his application program in Nibl in on-board random-access memory and then burn it into the PROM once it is debugged.

out in a format suitable for a programmable ROM.

A typical application using LLL Basic is for temperature control of the inlet probe of a high-resolution mass spectrometer (Fig. 4). A digital temperature is obtained from a thermocouple, which is connected to a digital panel meter with a binary-coded-decimal output.

In operation, the LLL Basic program calls a small assembly-language routine to read the temperature. The program then operates on the reading, calculating the deviation of the actual temperature from the desired temperature variation curve, and applies an appropriate amount of heat to keep the inlet temperature tracking correctly.

The hardware for the system took about six weeks to design and debug, and the software effort took about half as long. If assembly language had been used, the software would have taken about twice as long as the hardware. This example shows how high-level languages can greatly reduce the time required for overall system development.

Nibl on a chip

Another example of silicon software is an 8060 SC/MP-oriented interpreter for Nibl—National Industrial Basic Language—which is implemented in a single 32,768-bit ROM called the INS8295. Nibl, aimed at industrial control applications, is a relative of Tiny Basic, a limited version of the standard Basic developed by Robert Albrecht and James Warren as a general-purpose game and educational language for microprocessors.

Since Tiny Basic was intended for adaptation with many different types of microprocessors, it was written in a highly interpretive language designed expressly for the construction of translators. It requires, therefore, only a simple interpreter for the 8060 microprocessor. Since Nibl is intended for industrial applications, significant improvements have been made over Tiny Basic in the areas of I/O, program control, and device control.

The interpreter is broken into two blocks: a program written in the intermediate language that does the actual interpretation, and a collection of 8060 machine-language subroutines invoked by the intermediate language.

The organization of a prototype Nibl-evaluation board is shown in Fig. 5. Its purpose is to aid users of the 8060 in assessing the usefulness of Nibl in their particular applications. The board contains the 8295 Nibl ROM, two random-access memory I/O chips, eight 4-K static RAMs, an 8060, and two PROM sockets, one of which may be used as a 2708 ROM programmer and the other as a 2716 programmer during program development. Once the user programs are developed, both sockets can be used to run them.

A roughly equivalent system—the 8060 low-cost development system—typically requires at least four boards: a central-processing-unit board, a 4-kilobyte ROM/PROM programming board, a 2-kilobyte RAM board, and a special Nibl board containing eight 4-K programmed ROMs.

With the board, users can enter Nibl programs with a teletypewriter or some other RS-232-C link into the on-board ROM. Once developed and debugged, the programs may be loaded into the ROM programmer for burn-in. When the same board is plugged into a user system, the Nibl-based program stored in ROM or PROM is executed directly through the 8295.

The 4 kilobytes of RAM user space allow a minimum of about 120 average Nibl statements, more than adequate for most operator interfacing and for a variety of industrial-control applications. And although Nibl does not have the speed to handle video interfacing or direct control of fast peripherals, the algorithms can easily be proved out in Nibl and translated into 8060 machine code for installation in the final system. □

High-level language simplifies microcomputer programming

by Gary A. Kildall

☐ The microcomputer is being applied to more and more tasks that are not economically feasible for a minicomputer, with its larger instruction set and higher speed and cost. Although the microprocessor is slower than the central processor of a minicomputer, it can easily perform many tasks that are complex enough to require extensive digital processing.

What's more, microprocessors, which serve as central processors of microcomputers and are generally made with MOS large-scale integration, are constantly attaining higher speeds and higher circuit density per chip. As the capabilities of microcomputers are being ever extended, programing aids are being developed to simplify their use, while minimizing design and development time. These aids sometimes require use of a larger computer; when this is the case, they can be used either on commercial time-sharing networks or on a user's own large in-house computer.

The microcomputer may be viewed as a ROM-driven LSI logic chip because the microcomputer can execute complicated sequences of instructions stored in an external memory. Thus, the microcomputer chip connected to a read-only memory containing the proper data can appear to be a single custom chip. In this way, the system designer can substitute microcomputer programing for traditional hard-wired logic design or custom chip fabrication, gaining advantages in reduced development time, ease of design change, and reduced production costs.

The application of microcomputers points up the common ground between software and hardware designers. While software-system designers can use microcomputers most effectively when they are aware of the hardware environment, the hardware designer is well advised to learn the basic techniques of the programer.

These techniques include how to use assemblers, compilers, and processor simulators, which are effective tools in developing and debugging large and small microcomputer programs. This article introduces these programing tools to the hardware designer and specifically examines the advantages of the PL/M language, which make possible rapid design of systems around the MCS-8 microcomputer, made by Intel Corp.

The MCS-8 is based on the 8008 microprocessor, one of a new class of devices being offered by several manu-

1. Symbolic. This simple program for choosing the larger of two numbers takes nine lines of code in symbolic or assembly language, but typically only one line in a higher-level language, such as PL/M.

LABEL	INSTRUCTION	COMMENT
TEST	SHL B	LOAD ADDRESS OF B
	LAM	LOAD B INTO ACCUM
	SHL A	LOAD ADDRESS OF A
	CPM	COMPARE B WITH A
	JFC L1	JUMP TO L1 IF B ≤ A
	LAM	LOAD A INTO ACCUM
L1	SHL C	LOAD ADDRESS OF C
	LMA	STORE ACCUM INTO C
	END	END OF PROGRAM

facturers as a result of recent advances in semiconductor electronics. The PL/M programing aid is a good example of the service that these manufacturers can offer to simplify the use of their products.

Minimizing software costs

Like other programing tools, the PL/M approach automates the production of programs to counteract the rapidly increasing cost of software production at a time when hardware costs are decreasing. And, in addition to rapid production turnaround, the programs can be fully checked out early in the design process. What's more, the self-documentation of PL/M programs enables one programer to readily understand the work of another, which dramatically reduces program-maintenance costs and provides transportability of software between programers and to other Intel processors as they are introduced.

Additional cost reductions will also result from standardization of parts and modules, and alterability of the final program often outweighs benefits of random-logic designs or custom-chip fabrication.

The PL/M compiler, which is another program, translates the PL/M program into machine language. This compiler, which can be run on a medium- or large-scale computer, is available from several nationwide time-sharing services.

Last but not least, PL/M programs can be recompiled as improved optimizing versions of the compiler are released, as Intel has recently done. A recent revision of the PL/M compiler, for example, makes possible reduction of generated code by about 15%.

Although PL/M requires a cross-compiler—one that runs only on a larger machine—a resident compiler that uses the microcomputer itself to produce its programs is technically feasible with the advanced state of microcomputer development and today's inexpensive peripherals. Such a compiler would require several passes to reduce a PL/M source program to machine language, using the developmental system itself, and eliminating the need for large-system support.

A program for the Intel 8008 microprocessor is a sequence of instructions from its normal instruction set that performs a particular task.

Given no programing aids, the designer must determine the machine codes that represent each of the instructions in his program and store these codes into program memory. This approach to programing quickly becomes unwieldy, in all but the most trivial projects.

Nearly all manufacturers of microprocessors (and mini- and maxicomputers as well) provide symbolic assemblers—programs that ease the programing task by eliminating the need to translate instructions manually into machine-readable form. The designer can express his program in terms of mnemonics, which are abbreviations that suggest individual instructions. Then the assembler translates each mnemonic instruction into its binary representation.

Symbolic addresses

In addition, the programer can refer to memory locations by symbolic name, rather than actual numeric address; the assembler translates these, as well as the instructions. The assembler usually runs on a larger computer, although both Intel Corp. and National Semiconductor Corp. have assemblers that run directly on their microcomputer-based development systems, and symbolic programs for Rockwell microcomputers can be assembled on a machine built around that unit by Applied Computer Technology Inc. The assembler requires significantly less development and check-out time than manual translation, and there are fewer coding errors.

STATEMENT

```
DECLARE MESSAGE DATA ('WALLA WALLA WASH'),
    (CHAR, I, J, SENDBIT) BYTE;

/* SEND EACH CHARACTER FROM MESSAGE VECTOR TO TELEPRINTER */
    DO I = 0 TO LAST(MESSAGE);
    CHAR = MESSAGE(I);
    SENDBIT = 0;

    /* SEND EACH BIT FROM CHAR TO TELEPRINTER */
        DO J = 1 TO 11;
        OUTPUT(0) = SENDBIT:
        CALL TIME (91); /* WATTS 9.1 MS */
        SENDBIT = CHAR AND 1;
        /* ROTATE CHAR FOR NEXT ITERATION */
        CHAR = ROR (CHAR OR 1, 1);
        END;
    END;
```

2. Serial sender. To print a short message on a Teletype, this routine in PL/M transmits 11 pulses at 9.1-millisecond intervals for each character in the message, stopping after the last one. The pulse train consists of one start pulse, eight data pulses, and two stop pulses.

Hardware for PL/M

The Intel MCS-8 microcomputer consists of the 8008 microprocessor plus a collection of standard read/write and read-only memories and shift registers. The 8008 is a single-chip MOS device with

- 8-bit parallel word size
- Seven 8-bit general-purpose registers
- 16,384-word address capability, in either read-only or read/write memory
- Up to 32 8-bit latched input and output ports

The MCS-8 instruction set includes register-to-register, register-to-memory, and memory-to-register transfers, along with arithmetic, logic, and comparison instructions. Conditional and unconditional transfers and subroutine calls are also provided. Input and output instructions read data from input ports and set data into output-port latches. Each of these instructions is represented in program memory by a sequence of one, two, or three 8-bit words.

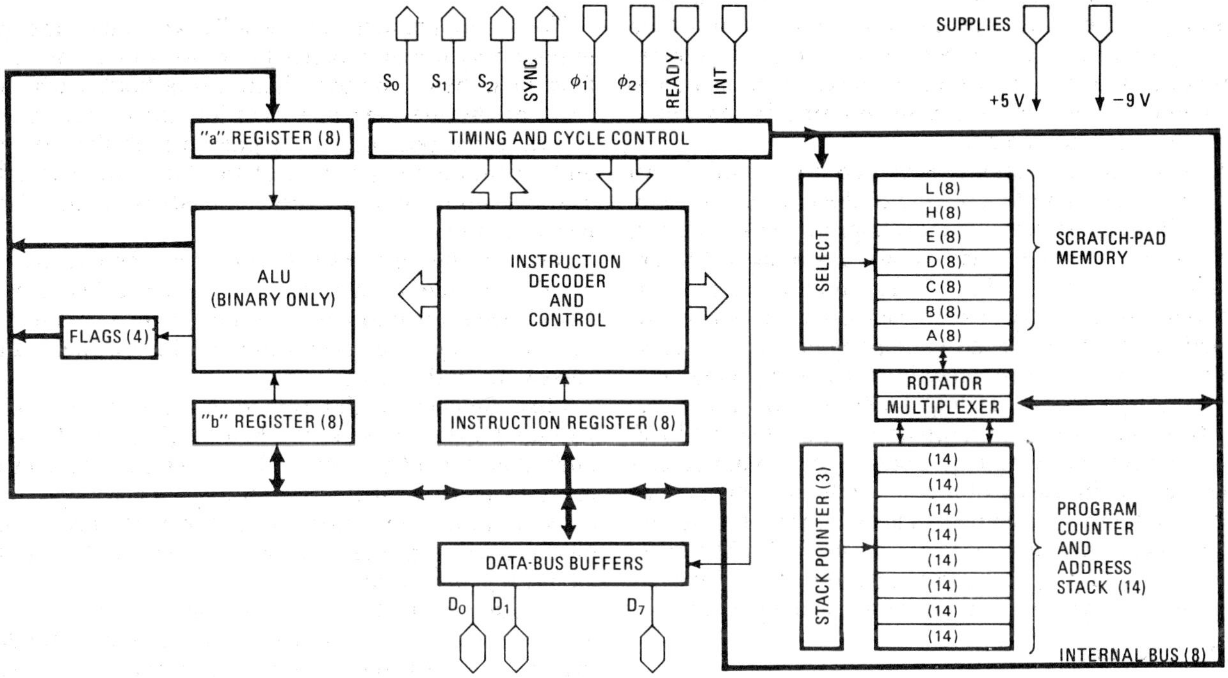

Assembly-language programing, however, is necessarily closely related to the machine architecture because instructions in symbolic code have a one-to-one correspondence with those in machine code. As a result, the programer must spend much more time keeping track of the location of data elements and proper register usage than actually conceptualizing the solution to his problem.

On large-scale computers, high-level languages have been developed to provide important facilities independently of particular machine architectures, while eliminating the trivialities of assembly languages. These facilities include program-control structures, data types, and primitive operations suitable for concise expressions of programs in particular problem environments. For example, a problem environment may be one of numerical computation, in which application-oriented programing languages like Basic and Fortran are appropriate. Or the environment may be the control of a particular class of computer and all its functions, for which system languages, which are necessarily closely related to the machine architecture, are useful.

In a system language, program statements generally correspond directly with machine-level instructions, and conversely, every machine operation is reflected in a high-level language statement. Because of this corre-

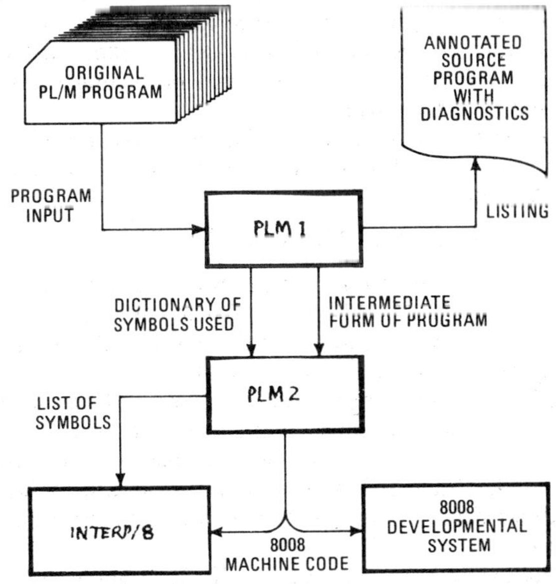

3. Compiler. Translating PL/M programs into machine language takes two passes with programs called PLM1 and PLM2, run by a larger machine. A third pass, with Interp/8, simulates the microprocessor on the big machine to check out the program.

spondence, system-language programs usually translate efficiently to the machine-language level, and the programer finds all the machine's facilities directly available to him. PL/M, an example of such a language, was designed for use with the 8008 microprocessor, and is also usable with Intel's newer 8080 microprocessor which has more useful machine-level instructions and a considerably faster instruction cycle than its predecessor.

Nevertheless, some hardware designers, particularly those newly introduced to software systems, may prefer to work at a comfortable level, which may mean programing in absolute machine code initially and then moving to assembly language as more capability is required. Similarly, they can easily make the transition to a high-level language when programing in assembly-language becomes tedious.

In any case, the designer soon becomes familiar with various programing levels. One of these levels can then be intelligently selected as most appropriate for a given application. Each level has its own advantages. For example, a program in PL/M that compiles into about 500 bytes of memory space when using the 8008's instruction set might require perhaps as much as 30% less space if it were coded directly in assembly language. But larger programs running 1,000 bytes or more usually turn out to be more compact when written in PL/M than in assembly language because the compiler can keep track more easily of memory-reference areas, registers, and other resources. The amount of machine code generated in assembly language or PL/M varies, of course, with program complexity and style. Thus, an absolute comparison between the two is not possible.

Simple coding

The PL/M language consists of a number of basic statement types in which complicated arithmetic, logical, and character operations on 8-bit and 16-bit quantities can be expressed in a form resembling usual algebraic notation. Relational tests can be expressed in a natural way to control conditional branching throughout the PL/M program.

For example, to move the larger of two numbers in locations A and B into the location called C, either the PL/M statement,

```
IF A > B, THEN C=A; ELSE C=B
```

or the nine-instruction assembly-language program shown in Fig. 1 can be used. The statement reads, "If the value of A is greater than the value of B, then set C to equal A; otherwise set C to equal B."

Additional language structures provide iteration control to permit program segments to be "looped," or executed repeatedly a prescribed number of times. Subroutine facilities include mechanisms that are useful for modular programing and construction of subroutine libraries.

The over-all structure of the PL/M language is most easily demonstrated by a simple example. Suppose a teleprinter is connected to the least-significant bit of an output port of the Intel 8008. A PL/M program that sends a short message to the teleprinter is shown in Fig. 2; it individually times the transmission of the bits through the output port. This program can be translated into machine code loaded into the memory of the MCS-8, and then it is executed.

The program begins with a data declaration that defines a string of Ascii characters—the words "Walla Walla Wash" as shown in line 1. The 16 individual characters of this string are labeled from 0 to 15 so that they can be addressed by the program (spaces are characters, too). Four variables, or 8-bit memory locations, CHAR, I, J, and SENDBIT, are defined on line 2.

Any names

These designations are wholly arbitrary; the programer may use any names he wants, so long as he defines them before he uses them. CHAR holds each character of the message in succession for transmission, I identifies the position of the character in the message, and J controls the position of the bit in the character. The right-most bit of location SENDBIT is the next bit to be transmitted.

Since the instructions between lines 5 and 17 are executed repetitively, they are collectively called a loop. Before each repetition, the variable I is incremented until its value indicates the position of the last character in MESSAGE—in this case, 15.

First, the value of all bits in SENDBIT is set to 0 on line 7 to send a start pulse as the first bit (line 11). Then the individual bits of the selected character are sent in the inner loop between lines 10 and 16. This loop is executed 11 times, corresponding to the start pulse, 8 data bits, and 2 stop pulses, during each passage through the outer loop, beginning on line 5.

Each successive bit is sent on line 11, followed by a 9.1-millisecond time-out. This time delay is a standard feature in PL/M; the compiler implements it by inserting a wait loop in the program. The wait loop stores an appropriate number in a counter, decrements it once each processor cycle, and allows the program to continue when the counter reaches zero.

On each inner-loop iteration, the right-most bit of CHAR is selected on line 13 by the AND function, and it is stored in SENDBIT. The operation on line 15 places a 1 in the right-most position of CHAR and then rotates the result one step to the right. This step gradually fills CHAR with 1s, working from left to right in each iteration, so that two stop pulses, which are 1s, are sent properly on the 10th and 11th iterations.

The operation of the PL/M compiler and its PLM1 and PLM2 subdivisions is shown graphically in Fig. 3. PLM1 accepts a PL/M source program from a card reader, time-sharing console, or other input device. This first pass produces a listing of the source program, along with any error diagnostics, and analyzes the program structure. An intermediate file that contains a linearized version of the original program is written, and the symbols used in it are listed.

Although the linearized version does not resemble either an assembly language or PL/M, it has been reduced to a highly simplified form of the original program. PLM2 uses this intermediate file as input and generates machine code for the 8008 microcomputer.

A PL/M program can often be checked out by simulating the 8008 microcomputer's actions on a larger ma-

```
STRING COMPARISON PROGRAM
TYPE SOURCE STRING:  A  B  C  D
TYPE TEST STRING:
  A  B  C  D
*  *  *  *
TYPE SOURCE STRING:  666 666 666
TYPE TEST STRING:  6
666 666 666
*** *** ***
TYPE SOURCE STRING:  AAAAAAAABABABA
TYPE TEST STRING: AB
AAAAAAAABABABA
       * * *
TYPE SOURCE STRING:  XXXXXXX$
TYPE TEST STRING:  XXXX
XXXXXXX
****
TYPE SOURCE STRING:  WALLA WALLA WASH
TYPE TEST STRING:  WALLA$
WALLA WALLA WASH
*     *
```

4. Test run. Sample PL/M program produced this printout. Manually entered data is underlined, and machine output is not underlined. Technique is valuable debugging tool.

chine. A third program, called Interp/8, is available for this purpose. The three programs PLM1, PLM2, and Interp/8 are written in ANSI standard Fortran IV, and will run on most larger computer systems.

A new version of the PL/M compiler is available for use with the extended instruction set of the 8080. Consisting of sections PLM81 and PLM82, it is accompanied by a new simulator called Interp/80. New coding is not required for the 8080. Working with old PL/M programs written for the 8008, the compiler can produce binary code requiring 10% to 20% less storage than the 8008 requires, and having the advantages of new interrupt and decimal arithmetic capabilities.

Experience with PL/M will enable designers of future Intel microprocessors to incorporate new machine-level instructions that will make more efficient use of the PL/M language. Furthermore, if Intel so chooses, it can alter its processor architecture in future designs, as it did between the 8008 and 8080, without affecting the user of PL/M at all, except possibly to improve the performance of this application.

A number of microcomputer manufacturers are considering the use of high-level languages to augment their assembly-language products, although none have been announced yet. Several minicomputer producers, however, offer high-level applications languages, and at least one minicomputer company, Microdata Corp., provides a systems language. In fact, Microdata's MPL language closely resembles PL/M; both of them, in fact, were derived from the same basic system language.

Once the PL/M program is written and checked out, the machine code is punched on paper tape (Fig. 3) and loaded into memory of a microcomputer developmental system. Again, the program is verified, and all real-time and environmental considerations are checked out. Final production systems can then be developed from this prototype. The production system, for example, may use read-only memory for the program when the developmental system's memory is read/write.

How to go on the air

Given a PL/M program and an MCS-8 microcomputer, how does a programer actually go through the compilation and execution process? As mentioned previously, the PL/M compiler is available from several nationwide time sharing services. These are the General Electric, Tymshare, National CSS, Applied Logic Corp., and United Computing Services facilities. Documentation for general programing is available from Intel Corp., and the time-sharing services provide system-dependent operating instructions.

Once the programer has a contract with the commercial service, he is assigned a work area in the host system in which he can store PL/M programs. These programs are created on line by using the time-sharing service's editor, which allows the programer to enter and alter program files. When a particular program is created, it is saved in a permanent file for compilation.

In the compilation process, PLM1 is executed first, using the saved PL/M program as input. Any diagnostic messages are printed at the time-sharing console. If no program errors are detected during the PLM1 pass, then the programer can call for PLM2. This second pass leaves code in MCS-8 machine language, which corresponds to the original program in the user's work area.

With this code, the programer may execute the Interp/8 program, which reads the machine code and simulates the actions of the MCS-8, as previously discussed. If execution errors appear during simulation, the programer can alter the original PL/M program and repeat the compilation and simulation process. When the programer is convinced the program is correct, he can punch the machine language on paper tape or other medium at his local console.

Programing at home

When a large amount of development work is to be done, the user may find it feasible to purchase the PL/M compiler and CPU simulator directly from Intel and run them on an in-house computer system. The user, at his option, can program either in batch or time-sharing mode.

The machine code produced by the compiler can be executed in several different ways. The easiest method is with a developmental system, such as the Intel SIM8-01 or Intellec 8 or equivalent prototyping hardware. These systems include hardware and software for Teletype, as well as facilities for loading and checking out programs.

The machine code is loaded into the SIM8-01 from the Teletype into erasable read-only memories. These chips are then inserted into sockets on the prototype board, and the program is executed. With the Intellec 8 developmental system, the machine code is entered from the Teletype into read/write memory, where the program can be subsequently executed and tested. Both approaches bypass the simulation stage.

After testing the program on a developmental system, a production model making use of MCS-8 and a mixture of read-only and read/write memory can be tailored closely to the final application. Although the hardware is minimized in the production system to reduce costs, the programs remain the same as in the prototype.

Developing systems

Intel Corp. has completed a number of projects using PL/M, including an assembler that runs on the Intellec 8 developmental system. This assembler's characteristics show the effectiveness of the PL/M approach to system development. For example, it has full macro capabilities, which means that a programer can define special pseudo-instructions that cause the assembler to insert sequences of instructions in the main program during the assembly process. Macros are like subroutines, except that the main program executes them as it comes to them, instead of branching out of the main stream and then returning, as it does with subroutines.

The assembler is also capable of conditional assembly, which means that it can react to such external signals as the positions of console switches at the time of assembly. Such signals indicate conditions that are not necessarily known to the programer at the time he writes the code—such as the availability of particular output equipment to which the assembler's results are to be sent.

Another useful characteristic of the assembler is evaluation of expressions at assembly time, which permits the programer to specify certain parameters algebraically instead of numerically or symbolically. Then when a program is assembled, the assembler evaluates the algebraic expressions and inserts the correct values in the machine-language program. The process requires the variables to be specified ahead of time, but it permits the programer to alter these variables by changing their specification only once, rather than every time they are used in the program. It's a great time-saver and bug-killer.

While these characteristics are not uncommon in advanced assembly languages, high-level languages that can handle them are quite rare. Yet by using PL/M, the assembler was coded in approximately 100 man-hours, and it requires 6,000 bytes of program storage—equivalent to 3,000 words on a minicomputer with a 16-bit word size. Intel estimates that the project would have taken five times as long to code and debug directly in assembly language, with little or no reduction in program-memory space. The resulting assembler is easy to maintain and alter, and, equally important, it can be recompiled for Intel's new 8080 microprocessor without alteration.

A practical example

PL/M permits many programing shortcuts, such as dividing a complex task into individual subtasks, or procedures, that are called upon when needed to simplify the job of writing the program itself. These procedures are conceptually simple and therefore easy to formulate and express in PL/M, as well as easy to check out before being incorporated in a larger program.

For example, consider a simple program for character manipulation—one that might be part of the work of a more comprehensive word-processing system. The function is relatively simple: the program asks the keyboard for two input-character strings, scans the first string for all occurrences of the second, echoes the first string, and types an asterisk under the starting position in the first string of each occurrence of the second string. A sample interaction with this program is shown in Fig. 4; all lines typed by the operator are underlined.

Stated in this way, this example may seem to have little or no practical value. But it is almost identical to a program needed to fetch the strings from two different data-entry devices and do something more sophisticated than printing an asterisk when it finds a match.

This suggests a practical application—a teleprinter to check out a routine before it is embedded in a larger program. When all the bugs are out of the routine, the procedures that transfer data to and from the teleprinter can be replaced with other procedures that, for example, check sensors and turn indicators on and off. The new procedures, of course, have to be checked out in a real environment, but that's much easier when the main routine is known to be bug-free. □

Cross-assemblers

by Ken Falor
Reprinted with permission from *Mini-Micro Systems*, Sept. 1977.

For several years, microprocessor manufacturers have offered cross-assembler programs that will execute on an IBM 370, DEC PDP-10, or other host machines to generate machine code that can, in turn, be executed on a particular microprocessor. Such packages have not worked entirely satisfactorily, partly because the chip makers have not had sufficient software development skills in-house and partly because the manufacturers have deliberately sacrificed efficiency to achieve portability and generality in the application of their cross-assemblers to a variety of host computers.

"There are ample reasons why a software house builds a more cost-effective cross-assembler."

Now, The Boston Systems Office in Waltham, MA, Innovonics Corp. in Silver Spring, MD, and other independent vendors have begun to introduce cross-assemblers that come with better credentials: Speed advantages over manufacturer products that go as high as 20:1; more power, especially in macro handling; better use of core; and so on. At the same time, the independents render on-going software support to accommodate operating system enhancements and other changes.

There are ample reasons why a software house builds a more cost effective cross assembler. A manufacturer achieves cross-assembler portability typically by writing it once and in a reduced set of ANSI Fortran. This compromises the product's efficiency. The independent software house, on the other hand, employs assembly language instead, and this alone improves running time by an order of magnitude (Table 1). Beyond the speed advantage, an assembler-written cross-assembler also conserves core – 24K to 65K bytes of memory for a Fortran-written assembler vs. 8K to 12K bytes for one written in assembly language. If still more core is available, the vendor can then prepare larger symbol and macro tables to make the cross-assembler run still faster.

Most independently developed cross-assemblers also adhere to an ironclad law: That they be compatible with the manufacturer's assemblers so that any program developed on a resident microprocessor can also be assembled on the cross-assembler, and vice versa, regardless of the method used by a particular assembler to get from op code to the machine language. Such universality is achieved because the manufacturer specifies the op code and also the machine language that is to result.

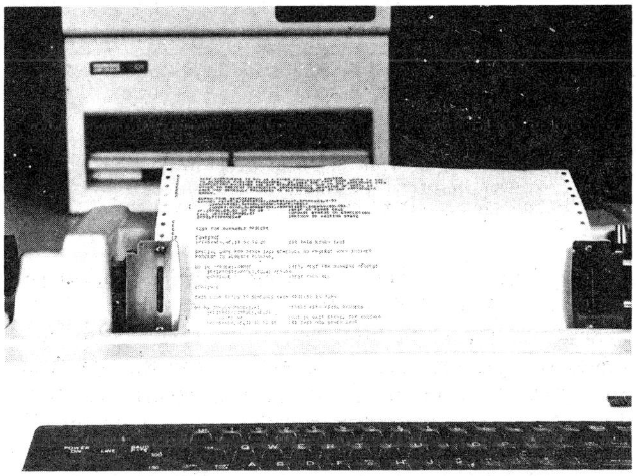

A minicomputer system can be used with cross-assemblers to create a dedicated development system.

EXTENDED FEATURES

Capabilities not found in a manufacturer's own software – so-called extended features – however, often can be introduced into independent cross-assemblers as well, though the codes will be incompatible. For example, certain cross-assemblers marketed by the software house, The Boston Systems Office, can generate files either in ASCII or BNPF. A BNPF file is defined simply by adding a "/B" at the end of an object file name. The assembler outputs the machine code to disk, then the code can be punched on paper tape, loaded into a PROM burner, or down-loaded into memory, depending on the user's facilities. BSO even has a cross-assembler that will accept both 8080 and/or Z80

A CROSS-ASSEMBLER DEFINED

A cross-assembler is a program that executes on a *host* computer that accepts input source statements written in the assembly language of a *target* computer. Its output is an object module that consists of machine language code stored in a *medium* acceptable to the target computer. In a typical case, the host is a large data processing facility, the target is the micro-based system under development, and the machine language medium is punched paper tape or cassette tape.

TABLE 1

Microprocessor	Source of Cross-Assembler	Language	Average Cost of Benchmark Studies
Intel 4040	General Electric	Fortran	$134.00
	United Corp.	Fortran	32.00
	Tymshare	Fortran	28.00
	Boston Systems Office	Assembler	2.00
Intel 8080	General Electric	Fortran	$ 44.00
	United Corp.	Fortran	27.00
	National CSS	Fortran	24.00
	Boston Systems Office	Assembler	1.90
Motorola 6800	General Electric	Fortran	$ 12.00
	Boston Systems Office	Assembler	.44

Source: First Data Corp. Waltham, MA.

Table 1: Average cost of benchmark studies based on the Intel 4040 and 8080 and Motorola 6800. The program was assembled on cross-assemblers written in Fortran, supplied by four different time-sharing vendors, and on cross-assemblers written in assembly language, supplied by the Boston Systems Office and used at First Data Corp. Other benchmarks were collected by First Data Corp. through its clients.

assembly language – even in the same program – and generate the appropriate 8080 or Z80 object code.

Some vendors go even further. They provide better techniques for replacing macro arguments – expressions, instruction mnemonics, comments, or statement labels – to render the coder greater flexibility and the function greater efficiency. Not only can arguments be data fields, they can also be op codes, labels, or even comments. For maximum efficiency, the arguments are actually replaced in the affected string of machine code. Finally, software houses can offer extended trace and debug capabilities, with negligible risk of later incompatibility problems.

Nor do the advantages stop here. Some assemblers are designed to produce dummy object code even when a statement is in error; lines in the object program can be patched without the need to repunch the entire tape. Some assemblers sold by the independents incorporate such extras as conditional assembler instructions, pseudo-ops, free-form instruction option, relocation, and special user-definable operation codes. In addition, certain micro software houses will furnish an assembler or compiler to be run on nonstandard host computers or configurations and even on new microprocessors, and they will support the resulting software.

PURCHASE, INSTALLATION, AND SUPPORT

Pricing on a cross-assembler by a micro manufacturer ranges from $250 to $1750 compared to a software house's charge that can vary from $30 to $2500. Second and third installations typically cost considerably less. But even for a single development project, savings in computer time alone can cover the costs of an assembler.

Installation of a cross-assembler is usually a snap. Typically, the purchased assembler arrives in the mail in whatever form the user has specified – paper tape, cards, mag tape, or floppy. However, a supplier will probably install the assembler himself if the program is to be tailored to a unique hardware configuration.

"A cross-assembler supplier will frequently sell a dedicated minicomputer-based development system that comes complete with the required cross-assemblers and other standard mini software."

In any case, a supplier must know the exact configuration of the target and host systems. A user must identify the model number of the target micro, individual components in the host-installation, and release number on the operating system. If any of these elements ever change, a new assembler, or at least a fix, may be necessary. The maintenance charge – typically $200 a year after an initial 90-day or one-year warranty – usually covers such modifications.

Purchase simplicity, however, may be best for some users. In this case, a cross-assembler supplier will frequently sell a dedicated minicomputer-based development system that comes complete with the required cross-assemblers and other standard mini software. One such system that is marketed by The Boston Systems Office, for example, is the Datasystem-310, based on the PDP-11/03; it contains 16K bytes of memory and a DECwriter terminal with prices starting at $13,300. The unit is equipped with an interactive program development (edit) system that can run in foreground concurrently with, say, compilations in the background partition. The system is also modular. A user can acquire a minimum system and then add assemblers as he or she takes on the different micros. ■

Part 6: Specifications and Other Useful Information

To prevent you from becoming too easily discouraged by the jargon, symbols, and multitudes of different microprocessors, this final section presents some handy reference material. Glossaries, a list of microprocessor specifications for quick information and comparisons, and other material will be invaluable once your interest reaches the workings—both hardware and software—of the computer.

Hints for beginners in microprocessors

by Alan Bloch

Because microprocessors are usually designed to meet the widest possible market, the one chosen for any specific application probably will not fit the application's requirements exactly. Inevitably, it will be slower than was expected, and its instruction set, however powerful it may be, will have gaps. At some point, the engineer will be tempted to start over again with a minicomputer, but he should hang on and remember that he is working with a processor—not a computer.

Given the right help in the form of programing and peripherals, the processor can do a lot. At Chestel, for example, a private automatic branch exchange (PABX) is controlled by a single Intel 8008. For successful design, it is important to use the processor properly. The following guidelines for proper use may be helpful to those applying a microprocessor for the first time.

■ Arithmetic. The typical microprocessor is not a particularly good number-cruncher. If the application involves extensive arithmetic operations, adding a calculator chip as a peripheral device may be desirable.

■ Programs. Programing is simplified by avoiding interruptible subroutines. The program should be arranged so that the microprocessor finishes a task and then looks around to see what needs to be done next. In general, this approach requires first-in/first-out memories at input/output ports that interface with the real world.

It may also be desirable to provide specialized peripheral devices to carry out some tasks in real time. The Chestel PABX, for example, uses tone decoders to put dial-entry data into a processor-acceptable format. The processor could do this job, but it would entail a lot of waiting time (the subscriber's dialing finger can't be scheduled), and during that time the processor wouldn't be available for executing extended subroutines.

■ Peripherals. Design of peripheral devices is facilitated if the various information paths that run between the microprocessor and the rest of the system are separated. The Intel 8008, for example, uses a time-shared 8-bit-wide bus to carry 14-bit memory addresses, 5-bit I/O addresses, and 8-bit data bytes in both directions. It is convenient to separate these information streams as early as possible.

The diagram shows how to do this by capturing address bits and storing them in latches, which then control dedicated address buses. The separation process

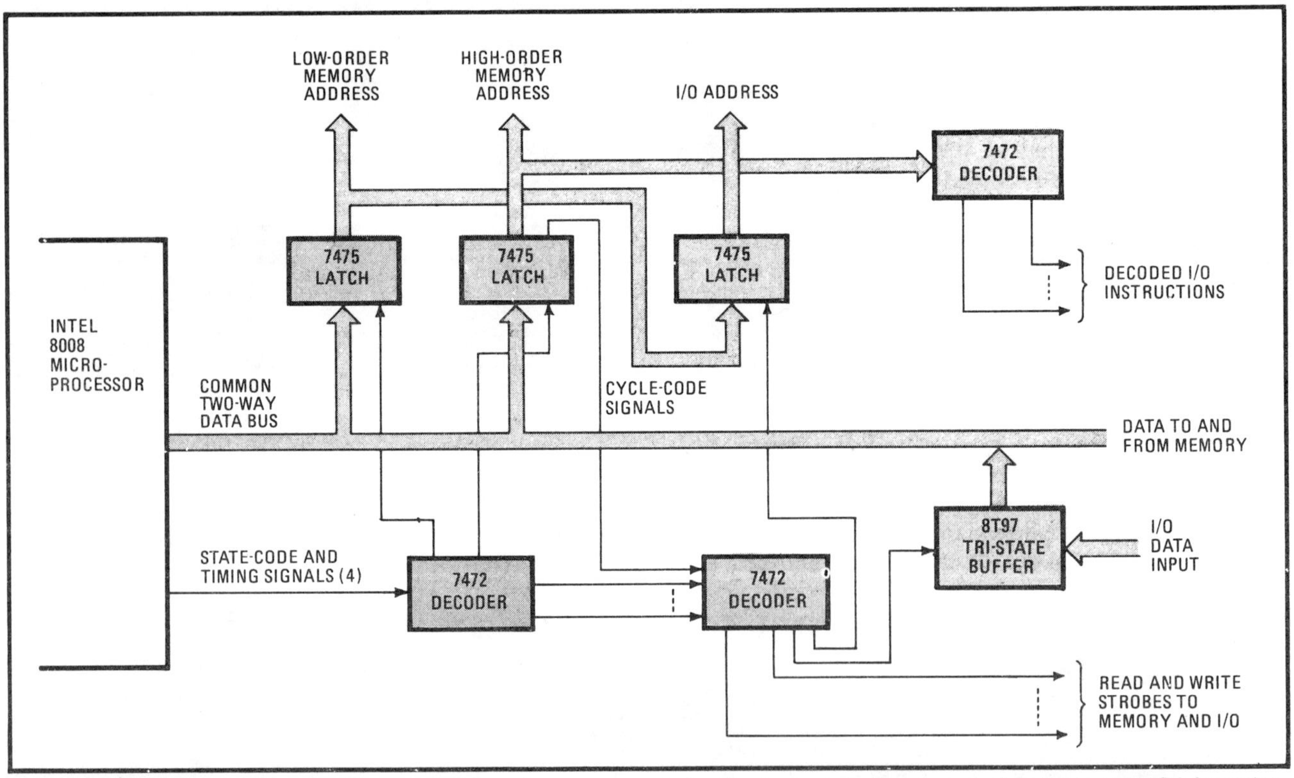

Separate data streams. Peripheral hardware helps a microprocessor do its job. To separate the streams of memory and I/O information, addresses, and data, the information on the common bus of an 8008 microprocessor is demultiplexed, latched, and put on dedicated buses. Timing signals and signals indicating microprocessor states are decoded to control the latches and provide strobes.

is carried even further, using one multiple bus for memory addresses, another for I/O addresses, a third for data transmission to and from the memory, and a fourth for incoming data from I/O ports.

Output instructions to I/O ports are not ordinarily transmitted in an 8-bit format; instead, the instructions are decoded and sent out on dedicated buses, some of which are only 1 or 2 bits wide. The diagramed system also decodes information carried by a number of state buses, which are driven by the microprocessor, and it generates read and write strobes that are sent to the memory and to the I/O ports.

■ Debugging. After the program has been written, it is put on magnetic tape or punched-paper tape and loaded into random-access memory. The engineer must, of course, debug it. He should resist the temptation to go home at the end of the day without dumping the updated program. Otherwise, Murphy's Law guarantees a power failure and a day's work lost.

Debugging will be simplified if the operating program is structured as a simple executive routine and a number of discrete subroutines. The subroutines should be broken down into smaller modules, if possible; an hour spent in modularizing the program structure will save about a day of debugging time.

Above all, software must be documented in detail. Otherwise, development of the next generation of the system will have to start from scratch.

When the program is up and running, the engineer should resist the temptation to order a masked read-only memory. Instead, he should put the program in a programable ROM and live with it for a while. Someone, somewhere, will find something wrong with it.

■ Talents. Designing a system around a microprocessor calls for a mix of hardware and software talent. Programing a microprocessor, though, is different from programing a minicomputer or a full-size computer. The instruction set is limited, and the system usually has only a small memory capacity. Good software people for microprocessors are hard to find, and their expertise usually must be developed in-house. Hiring a consultant would probably turn out to be a wise investment. □

A microcomputer course for professionals

by Gary K. Holt
Reprinted with permission from *Mini-Micro Systems*, Sept. 1977

The microprocessor's rapid evolution has forced system designers to make revolutionary changes in their design approaches. And it has left design education lagging. Like a rock thrown through a beehive, the micro impact has caused a mass swarming, not by bees, but by professional engineers, scientists, software specialists, big computer experts, logic designers, managers, and computer system builders who yearn to learn about the micro. What can it do? How can I use it? Where is it headed?

The questions are hard to answer beyond suggesting formal college courses and reading the technical literature. Professionals may take one-, two-, or three-day intensive courses, but these necessarily lack depth. Then, there are the few pioneers who prefer the school of hard knocks; they buy a microcomputer kit and assemble the components to see what makes them tick.

"Mitre wanted the course to benefit both hardware- and software-oriented professionals."

Most technical professionals, however, do not have this leisure. And yet, they need to know about microprocessors. The challenge to an organization then becomes: How can it introduce its professionals to this fast growing field so they may have sufficient knowledge and confidence to make informed decisions on microprocessor use. Last year, we at Mitre Corp. decided to find a way, and our experiences in doing so should be useful to other organizations and technical professionals.

GENESIS

To understand our program, it is necessary to know something about Mitre itself. The Bedford (MA)-based firm, which employs some 1400 persons total, provides comprehensive systems engineering support to a wide range of military and civilian clients. The technical programs cover systems design in applications that range from energy management and state government operations to military surveillance and warning and battlefield communications.

Hence, Mitre's technical staff runs the gamut of specialties, with electrical and mechanical engineering, mathematics, and physics serving as core disciplines. Over a period of years, any single professional is likely to work on two or three different programs whose scope is broad and whose demands are diverse. To meet this need for qualified systems engineers, Mitre established an in-house training facility some four years ago. The Mitre Institute (TMI), as it is called, trains students simultaneously while they continue to work at their regular jobs.

Micro Excitement: Intensity in the classroom.

Last year the TMI staff wanted to add course offerings on integrated circuits and large scale integration that would emphasize microprocessors, but we found that courses elsewhere did not suit our needs. Typically, they lacked what we consider paramount: hands-on experience. Existing courses tend to be too commercial having been designed to sell a product, too application-oriented having little or no technology, or too inflexible to accommodate working professionals.

Other objectives also prompted the TMI to set up its own program. Mitre wanted the course to benefit both hardware- and software-oriented professionals and to be useful to the engineering assistant working in the field as well as

A MICRO HANDS-ON TRAINER

When setting up the microprocessor course, the toughest challenge we encountered was to select and implement a training vehicle to provide hands-on experience. The trainer that we sought had to have an 8-bit processor, ASCII keyboard entry, CRT readout, hardcopy capability, cassette interface, 512 to 1K bytes RAM, parallel I/O, and a resident monitor/debug program. No doubt any of several processors would have been satisfactory, but I, as the course manager, was already familiar with the Motorola 6800. So, that is what we used.

In sum, the final system resembled a keyboard/CRT terminal connected to a large computer – much like a time-share terminal – but it was much more than this. The trainer (Fig. 1) uses a WINCE MICRO module made by Wintek Corp. It is a microcomputer on a card, based on the American Microsystems S6800, which in turn, is a Motorola 6800 second source. The capabilities include 512 bytes of RAM, asynchronous interface (ACIA), parallel interface (2 PIAs), 1K bytes monitor/debug program, and an onboard clock.

The CT-1024 alphanumeric terminal system made by Southwest Technical Products Corp. provided the keyboard interface (110-1200 baud RS232) between the WINCE MICRO module and the CRT. The terminal can display the full upper case 64-character ASCII set as 16 lines, with each containing 32 characters on either a standard video monitor or, as we used, a slightly modified standard TV receiver. The terminal can also store a second page of 16x32 characters in addition to hardware/software carriage return/line feed, home-up, erase to end of line, erase to end of frame, and four-way cursor movement.

In addition, we added an inexpensive cassette interface to the system using the Kansas City standard that enables us to store and reload programs by means of a standard audio cassette. This format calls for data to be recorded serially according to the standard UART format at 300 baud. Logic ONEs are represented by a 2400-Hz sine wave and ZEROs by a 1200-Hz sine wave, and this allows for variance in recorder speed by as much as 30 percent.

The cassette interface turned out to be a must item. Students saved many hours by not having to manually re-enter their programs in machine language each time they used the trainer. Any trainer built without this capability will wind up orienting a student to machine language entry via a keyboard rather than serving as a microprocessor trainer.

Fig. 1. The Mitre trainer set-up.

We also tried a psychological ploy. We did not put the WINCE MICRO module into a case even though plenty of room was available for one. The approach allowed free access to the parallel I/O. As important, it also reminded the students that the computational power all resided in a small board in front of their eyes.

We put together five systems of this kind to be used in class, and also built a larger, sixth system that employed a Southwest Technical Products 6800 computer having 16K bytes of RAM memory, resident assembler, and editor. Finally, an additional option enabled a student to use a teletype for hard copy and paper tape interface.

the desk-bound theoretical Ph.D. The idea behind the course structure is to expose the inexperienced employee to the basics and a familiarity with the buzzwords at the minimum. More advanced students should be challenged, on the other hand, to use the hands-on trainers so that they can make a microprocessor perform a task. In short, we wanted to provide something for everyone and to expose all students to a broad spectrum of expert insights and viewpoints.

Thus, the course that evolved set out to:

- Give students a perspective on application tradeoffs for LSI, microprocessors, and microcomputers.
- Review current LSI/microprocessor technology.
- Introduce students to microprocessor theory and use.
- Provide hands-on experience with a current microprocessor.

TEACHING LINE UP

The core of the teaching staff included four Mitre professionals who used a team-instruction approach. As course manager, I set up the program, handled the administrative chores, and ran the microprocessor laboratory. I also designed the hands-on trainer and lectured. Michael J. Flanagan helped to design interface hardware and provided application lectures, among other chores. Charles W. Kleekamp held seminars on technology overview, digital logic, and applications; and Andrew G. Malis, TMI's resident software expert, taught programming. Other Mitre professionals participated as needed.

"Most technical professionals do not have leisure. And yet, they need to know about microprocessors."

Visiting experts included Andrew Perlowski at Honeywell's Solid State Electronics Center in Plymouth, MN, who lectured on microprocessor architectures and system components; David Millett at NEC Microcomputers in Lexington, MA, who compared microprocessor technologies; Jasper Norris at Motorola-Phoenix who spoke on the M6800 MPU and instruction set; and Gary Sawyer at Motorola-Lexington who gave a class on support devices and development aids.

Consultants Richard Brisk from Boston and Richard Morely from Greenville, NH, introduced the students to interfacing techniques. Vendors that made presentations included Texas Instruments, Intel, NEC Microcomputers, and National Semiconductor. Nor did the course cover technical matters alone. Indeed, students were especially enthused over a market analysis by Dr. Richard Petritz at New Business Resources in Dallas, TX.

COURSE CONSTRAINTS

The course was designed on the basis of TMI's experiences over four years in shaping similar offerings. The material had to be covered in about three months to avoid changes in job assignments that would begin to seriously interfere with student attendance. We also had to set class hours. Previous experience had shown that two classes a week during working hours, each 2-1/2 hours long, is ideal – with each session composed of a one-hour lecture, a break to include informal conversation, and a second hour session. Altogether, the course structure came to 24 sessions.

In the laboratory.

The response to the course announcement was enthusiastic, beyond expectation. A class of about 25 students had been envisioned. But the 125 applicants made this the Institute's most popular course, and two simultaneous classes had to be offered instead.

SELECTING THE STUDENTS

But even enlarging the class did not resolve the question: How should we select students? It is imperative that any screening be rigorously fair. Accordingly, high priority was given to employees who could demonstrate a job-related need to take the course; Mitre's interests were also taken into account, of course. This, and other data, were gathered by means of a questionnaire that asked:

- Why do you wish to take the course?
- What area of the course interests you most?
- Have you attended a course on microprocessors before? (List.)
- Have you worked with microprocessors before? (Which?)
- If the class is filled, could you attend a later offering?

Applications were then accepted into the course on a first-come, first-served basis.

Motivation was high. Inevitably, one worries about the dropout rate in courses of this kind. Twelve of the original 50 students did not complete the course, but we could not trace this to any loss of interest. Rather, they dropped the course because their job responsibilities had changed, and all said they wanted to be considered for later classes.

The institute is also well equipped to deal with another perennial worry: absenteeism. We maintain a videotape file on all sessions, and when a student cannot attend a class, he or she can readily catch up by screening the videotape at his or her convenience.

COURSE CONTENT

To create a setting, the course started out by giving an overview of what was to come and introducing the method of instruction – a "learn-by-doing" approach. We defined terms reviewed digital logic, programming techniques, and introduced the basic technology.

Once the instructors covered the basic architectural subjects, the students turned to the hands-on part – seven sessions spread throughout the course. The students worked on projects that entailed use of either a hands-on trainer or Mitre's special reference library. During these sessions the real education occurred – applying the material. In addition, each student had the option to work either in a structured workshop or on his own. Thus, those who needed guidance got it, and others who preferred worked alone. In any case, all students had to complete a project and present the results as a paper or briefing at the course end.

Working on the microcomputer trainer.

Some students tackled simple projects, such as internal data manipulation, point-of-sale terminal applications, and mini/micro data base applications. Others pursued highly complex control and simulation applications using sophisticated hardware interfaces to the processor. And still others wrote extensive reports comparing microprocessors.

As for the hands-on trainer, our budget at $12,000 did not permit us to have one for each student. Each system cost $2000, so we built six trainers out of individual components and kits. (See box.) The six systems proved adequate. We kept the lab open on evenings and weekends to accommodate the students. Conflicts did not cause any problems, nor did crowding occur. And, as the course progressed, students began to spend more and more time on the machine. In an end-of-course evaluation, some students said that the trainer had become very habit-forming. Others commented that the course experience would now enable them to recognize opportunities for microprocessor use, evaluate micro specifications, and so on. Here's the best measure of the course's success: We are repeating it! ■

Where to get bargains in used computer equipment

by Sol Libes

Once they have their computers up and running, computer experimenters start hunting around for peripherals. They look for things like Teletypes (usually ASR-33s), video terminals, printers, paper tape readers and punches, etc. The big problem here is cost. In fact, those electronic and electromechanical IO gadgets can often cost several times the price of the processor itself. New video terminals can cost you $1500 and up. Printers can cost as much as $2000. What can a hobbyist do to save money? One way is to buy used equipment. The question is, where do you find it?

The big market in used computer equipment is due to many factors, one being that the state of the art is changing rapidly and companies frequently obsolete working equipment to keep up. Thus, there is a great deal of equipment available that may not be up to the latest speed or have the latest features, but is fully operational. For example, you can buy a used video terminal (ASR-33 compatible) for less than $500, or a video terminal that requires some rewiring for under $200. Hard copy terminals range from $300 (for an untested unit) to $1000 for guaranteed units with extra features.

There are even minicomputers available at bargain prices. Digital Equipment Corporation PDP-8s with 4 K words of core memory and serial interface start at $750 and go up to $3000 for newer models.

New dealers in used equipment are appearing all the time. The list that accompanies this report is not complete by any means, but it does include the larger dealers in the country. Most used equipment dealers publish catalogs and maintain mailing lists. A simple postcard will usually get you their latest equipment listing and put you on their mailing list. Most of these companies are eager to deal with computer experimenters.

Many dealers refurbish the used equipment they sell and restore it to manufacturer's specifications to the point where it is often indistinguishable from new equipment. For example, several dealers refurbish Teletypes to "as new" condition. This means a complete cleaning, replacement of defective or worn components, replacement of items such as plastic covers, repainting exposed metal enclosures, running the machine for at least 5 hours to insure its performance, and guaranteeing it for 90 days. A new Model ASR-33 Teletype

Used Computer Equipment Vendors	Equipment
American Used Computer Corporation POB 68 Kenmore Sta Boston MA 02215 (617) 261-1100	Used minicomputers, printers video terminals, modems, Teletypes, etc. Also new equipment for personal computing via the Computer Warehouse Store.
Atlantic Surplus Sales 3730 Nautilus Av Brooklyn NY 11224 (212) 372-0349	Teletypes, parts, supplies and miscellaneous.
Computer Warehouse Store 584 Commonwealth Av Boston MA (617) 261-2701	(See American Used Computer Corporation)
Data Access Systems 100 Route 46 Mountain Lakes NJ 07046 (201) 335-3322	Used Teletypes, DECwriters, video terminals, modems, parts.
Data-Lease 700 N Valley St #A Anaheim CA 92801	Minicomputers, video terminals, Teletypes, etc.
Data Processing Design Inc 6980 Aragon Cir, Suite B Buena Park CA 90620 (714) 994-4971.	PDP-11s, printers, terminals, etc.
Federal Communications Corporation Suite 107 11105 Shady Trl Dallas TX 75229 (214) 620-0644	Used Teletypes, data phones and TWX units
Herback & Rademan Inc 401 E Erie Av Philadelphia PA 19134 (215) 426-1700	Used computer gear and parts.

costs approximately $1200, while an "as new" reconditioned unit typically sells for $700 and an "as is" nonreconditioned machine goes for as little as $500.

Particularly good buys can be obtained on equipment no longer being manufactured or from a manufacturer who is no longer in business. Prices are often considerably less than those for equipment still being manufactured.

The largest and oldest used computer equipment dealer is American Used Computer Corporation, which was started in 1968. Second largest is Newman Computer Exchange, which was founded in 1972.

In addition to equipment dealers, used equipment is often advertised in publications such as *On-Line, Electronics News, Computerworld* and *Computer Hotline.* These should be consulted regularly for current "buys" and new companies in the market.

Another excellent source of used computer equipment is amateur radio flea markets. Ham radio operators are big users of Teletypes and other printers, tape readers and punches, etc. These flea markets are held locally and regionally. The largest is held in April in Dayton OH, and draws over 10,000 attendees. There are acres of flea marketers. To find out when and where the ham flea markets are being held, consult the ham magazines such as *QST, CQ* and *Ham Radio.*

Good hunting!■

Used Computer Equipment Vendors	**Equipment**
JM Associates 80 Emerald Av Westmont NJ 08108	Used computer peripherals, etc.
ICC Computer Corporation 1115 Security Dr Dallas TX 75247 (214) 630-1401	Used Teletypes and TWX units.
MiniComputer Exchange 154 San Lazaro Sunnyvale CA 94086 (408) 733-4400	Miniperipherals.
National Teletypewriter Corporation 207 Newtown Rd Plainview NY 11803 (516) 293-0444	Used Teletypes, parts and supplies.
Newman Computer Exchange 3960 Varsity Dr Ann Arbor MI 48104 (313) 994-3200	Used minicomputers, peripherals, Teletypes, etc.
PMR Canada Ltd 94 Hyde Av Toronto, Ontario CANADA (416) 653-4842	Used processors, memories, controllers, etc.
RCA Service Company Bldg 204-2 Camden NJ 08101 (609) 779-4129	Used Teletypes
Rondure Company 1224 Security Dr Dallas TX 75247 (214) 630-4621	Miniperipherals, modems, parts, etc.
Van't Slot Enterprises 550 Springfield Av Berkeley Heights NJ 07922 (201) 464-5310	Used Teletypes, parts and supplies.

Microprocessor specifications

The full report of "Microprocessor Specifications," from which this data has been drawn, is available for $12 from Datapro Research Corp., Delran, NJ 08075.

MANUFACTURER & MODEL	Fairchild Semiconductor F8	Fairchild Semiconductor F38E70	Fairchild Semiconductor F9440	Intel 4004	Intel 4040	Intel 8008/8008-1
Type	8-bit CPU	Single chip, 8-bit CPU	16-bit CPU	4-bit CPU	4-bit CPU	8-bit CPU
Chip technology	NMOS	NMOS	I^2L	PMOS	PMOS	PMOS
Number of chips in CPU	1	1	1	1	1	1
Number of pins	40	40	40	16	24	18
Voltages required	+5, +12	+5	+5	+5, −10	+5, −10	+5, −9
Power dissipation—milliwatts	500 (max)	325	750 (5V), 180 (1V)	450	600	420
Clock	On CPU chip	On CPU chip	On CPU chip	Standard	Standard	Standard
Memory interface	3853 (static) 3852 (dynamic)	No	9441	Standard	Standard	Standard
Random access memory	64 bytes on chip	64 bytes on chip	Static RAM or 73481	Optional	Optional	Optional
Read only memory	3851-1K ROM 3856/57-2K ROM	—	Static ROM	Optional	Optional	Optional
Programmable ROM	93426-1K PROM 93496-2K PROM	2K bytes of EPROM on chip	Sep. avail.	Optional	Optional	Optional
Input/output interface	3861 PIO	32 latched I/O lines on chip	Sep. avail. (9442)	Optional	Optional	Optional
CPU second sourced by	Mostek	—	None	National Semiconductor	—	—
Prototyping system	F8 formulator	F8 formulator F8 emulator	Flame 16	Intellec 4/Mod 4	Intellec 4/Mod 40	Intellec 8/Mod 8
Data word size—bits	8	8	16	4	4	8
Instruction word size—bits	8, 16, 24	8, 16, 24	16	4, 8, 16	4, 8, 16	8, 16, 24
Maximum clock frequency	2 MHz	3 MHz	12 MHz	740 KHz	740 KHz	500 KHz/800 KHz
Number of phases per cycle	1	1	1	8	8	2
Number of instructions	70	70	21	46	60	48
Number of registers						
Arithmetic registers	1	1	4	1	1	1
Index registers	0	0	—	0	0	0
General purpose registers	64 8-bit	64 8-bit	4	16	24	6
Number of directly addressable instruction words	64K		32K	4K	8K	16K
Hardware BCD arithmetic	Standard	Standard	No	Standard	Standard	No
I/O word size—bits	8	8	16	4	4	8
Direct memory access	Optional	No	Standard	No	No	No
Interrupt capability	Standard	Standard	Standard	No	Standard	Standard
Type of interrupt system	Vectored, internal	Vectored, internal	Daisy chain	—	Single-level, basic vector	Vectored, 8 levels

MANUFACTURER & MODEL	**Intel 8035/8035L**	**Intel 8039**	**Intel 8080A**	**Intel 8085A**	**Intel 8748/8048**	**Intersil IM6100**
Type	8-bit CPU	8-bit CPU	8-bit CPU	8-bit CPU	8-bit CPU	12-bit CPU
Chip technology	NMOS	NMOS	NMOS	NMOS	NMOS	CMOS
Number of chips in CPU	1	1	1	1	1	1
Number of pins	40	40	40	40	40	40
Voltages required	+5	+5	+5,-5, +12	+5	+5	+5
Power dissipation—milliwatts	325 typical	375 typical	780	780	500	12.5
Clock	On chip	On chip	Standard	Standard	On chip	On chip
Memory interface	On chip	On chip	Standard	On chip	On chip	Not required
Random access memory	On chip (64 x 8)	On chip (128 x 8)	Optional	8155-2 (256 x 8) with I/O	On chip	1024 x 1, 256 x 4—sep. avail.
Read only memory	No	No	Optional	8355-2 (2K x 8) with I/O	On chip (8048)	1024 x 12—sep. avail.
Programmable ROM	No	No	Optional	8755-2 (2K x 8) with I/O	On chip (8748)	64 x 12, 256 x 4—sep. avail.
Input/output interface	On chip	On chip	Optional	Serial I/O on chip; 8-bit parallel	On chip	Sep. avail.
CPU second sourced by	—	—	Texas Instr., Advanced Micro Devices	AMD, NEC, Siemens	AMD	Harris
Prototyping system	Intellec MDS	Intellec MDS	MOS	Intellec MDS	MDS	Intercept Jr. I & II
Data word size—bits	8	8	8	8	8	12
Instruction word size—bits	8	8	8, 16, 24	8, 16, 24	8, 16	12
Maximum clock frequency	6 MHz	6 MHz	2 MHz	3.0 MHz	6 MHz	3.3, 4.0, 8.0 MHz
Number of phases per cycle	5	5	2	1	—	10
Number of instructions	90+	90+	78	80	90+	70+
Number of registers						
Arithmetic registers	16	16	1	1	16	2
Index registers	—	—	0	0	—	8
General purpose registers	64	128	6	6	16 to 64	128 (page 0)
Number of directly addressable instruction words	4K	4K	65K	64K	4K	32K (with extended mem.)
Hardware BCD arithmetic	Standard	Standard	Optional	Optional	Standard	No
I/O word size—bits	8	8	8	8	8	12
Direct memory access	No	No	Standard	Standard	No	Standard
Interrupt capability	Standard	Standard	Standard	Standard	Standard	Standard
Type of interrupt system	2 vectored, single levels	2 vectored, single levels	Vectored, 8 levels	Vectored, 12 levels	2—single level	Vectored, 64 priorities

MANUFACTURER & MODEL	**MOS Technology MCS6502/6502A**	**Motorola 6800**	**National Semiconductor INS8060**	**National Semiconductor MM5782**	**National Semiconductor SCAMP**	**RCA COSMAC CDP1802C**
Type	8-bit CPU	8-bit CPU	8-bit CPU	4-bit CPU	8-bit CPU	8-bit CPU
Chip technology	NMOS Si-gate	NMOS Si-gate	NMOS	PMOS	PMOS	CMOS
Number of chips in CPU	1	1	1	1	1	1
Number of pins	40	40	40	28	1	40
Voltages required	+5	+5	+5	+9	+5, −7 or gnd	+4 to +6
Power dissipation—milliwatts	250 (typ), 700 (max)	600	200	135	800	6
Clock	On chip	MC6870A/ MC6871A	On CPU chip	NM8664	Not required	On CPU chip or ext.
Memory interface	No	None required	On CPU chip	MM5785	Not required	On CPU chip
Random access memory	Standard (1K bits)	MCM6604, -05, -10	Separately available	100 x 4 on chip (expandable)	2102/5260	External std.
Read only memory	Standard (8K, 16K, 32K)	MCM6830, -32, MCM68308, -17	Standard	2K x 8—MM5781; 4K x 8—MM57129	5213/5214	External std.
Programmable ROM	No	—	Standard	—	5203/5204	External std.
Input/output interface	Standard	MC6820, MC6850	Separately available	Printer—MM5788	LS or CMOS	On CPU chip
CPU second sourced by	Synertek	AMI, Hitachi, Fairchild	Signetics	—	Rockwell	Hughes, SSS
Prototyping system	MDT650	Exorciser, M6800B Eval. Module, MEK 6800D1 Eval. Kit	LCDS (ISP-8P/301N)	IMP16P	LCDS	COSMAC Devel. Sys., Eval. Kit
Data word size—bits	8	8	8	4	8	8
Instruction word size—bits	8, 16, 24	8, 16, 24	8, 16	8	8, 16	8
Maximum clock frequency	1 MHz/2 MHz	1 MHz	4 MHz	400 KHz	1 MHz	DC−3.2 MHz
Number of phases per cycle	2	2	—	4	—	8
Number of instructions	—	72 (7 addressing modes)	46	—	46	91
Number of registers						
Arithmetic registers	1	2 8-bit	1	10 x 16 digits	1	1
Index registers	2	1 16-bit	3	0	1	Up to 16
General purpose registers	7	2 8-bit	5	3	5	16
Number of directly addressable instruction words	65,536	Up to 64 K	64K	8K or 16 K	4K	65K
Hardware BCD arithmetic	Standard	Standard	Standard	Yes	Standard	No
I/O word size—bits	8	8	8	24	8	1 and 8
Direct memory access	Standard	No (can be added)	Standard	NA	Standard	On CPU chip
Interrupt capability	Standard	Standard	Standard	No	Standard	On CPU chip
Type of interrupt system	2 levels, polled	Vectored	Vectored, 1 level	—	Vectored, 1 level	One level maskable

MANUFACTURER & MODEL	**Rockwell MP-16**	**Rockwell PPS-4**	**Rockwell PPS-8**	**Signetics 2650A/2650A-1**	**Texas Instruments TMS 9900**	**Zilog Z80/Z80A**
Type	16-bit CPU	4-bit CPU	8-bit CPU	8-bit CPU	16-bit CPU	8-bit CPU
Chip technology	PMOS	PMOS	PMOS	NMOS	NMOS, Si-gate	N-channel Si-gate
Number of chips in CPU	2	1	1	1	1	1
Number of pins	42, 52	42	42	40	64	40
Voltages required	17 (can be +5, −12)	17 (can be +5, −12)	17 (can be +5, −12)	+5	+12, +3, −5	+5
Power dissipation—milliwatts	500	230	400	500 (750 max.)	1200	1000 (max.)
Clock	Not required	Standard (10706)	Standard (10706)	Standard	Standard	Separately available
Memory interface	Standard (256 x 4)	Not required	Not required	Standard	Not required	On CPU
Random access memory	Standard (16K-bit)	Standard (256K x 4)	Standard (256K x 8)	Standard	TMS4050/60/36-39/42	Z6104, Z6116
Read only memory	Optional	Standard (16K-bit)	Standard (16K-bit)	Standard	TMS4700	Separately available
Programmable ROM	Standard	Optional	Optional	Standard	74S473	Separately available
Input/output interface	Standard	Standard	Standard	Standard	Standard TTL	Separately available
CPU second sourced by	—	—	—	AMS	None	Mostek, Sharp, SGS
Prototyping system	Evaluator Board and Assemulator	Evaluator Board and Assemulator	Evaluator Board and Assemulator	TWIN	990/4	Z80
Data word size—bits	16	4	8	8	16	8
Instruction word size—bits	8	8	8	8, 16, 24	16, 32, 48	8, 16
Maximum clock frequency	200 KHz	200 KHz	200 KHz	To 2 MHz	3 MHz	2.5 or 4.0 MHz
Number of phases per cycle	4	4	4	3	4	1
Number of instructions	76	50	109	75	69	158
Number of registers						
Arithmetic registers	2	2	2 8-bit	Use any GP reg.	—	14
Index registers	—	2 12-bit	2 14-bit	Use any GP reg.	—	2 16-bit
General purpose registers	2	2	1 8-bit	7	—	Two sets of 6 each
Number of directly addressable instruction words	4K	4K	16K	32K	32K	64K bytes
Hardware BCD arithmetic	Standard	Standard	Standard	Standard	No	Standard
I/O word size—bits	16	4	8	8	4096	8
Direct memory access	No	No	Standard	Standard	Standard	Standard
Interrupt capability	No	Standard	Standard	Standard	Standard	Standard
Type of interrupt system	Single-level	Single-level	3 levels, 15 prioritized sublevels	Vectored	Vectored, 16 priority levels	Vectored

An abbreviated guide to electronics abbreviations

by John C. McKechnie

The use of abbreviations and acronyms in electronics literature enhances the reading, the writing, and the comprehensibility of information exchange. However, the pervasiveness of such terms has made understanding more difficult for many readers who are not familiar with specialized aspects of the technology under discussion. This alphabetized list of more than 150 terms has been compiled during recent months from a large group of technical periodicals. Since new abbreviations are constantly being generated, readers can add new definitions as they are encountered.

a-d	analog to digital
ADS	address data strobe
AIM	avalanche-induced migration
ALU	arithmetic/logic unit
ANSI	American National Standards Institute
AOI	AND/OR invert
ASCII	American Standard Code for Information Interchange
ATE	automatic test equipment
ATS	automatic test system
BBD	bucket-brigade device
BCD	binary-coded decimal
Boram	block-oriented random-access memory
b/s	bits per second
CAD	computer-aided design
CAM	content-addressable memory
CATT	controlled avalanche transit time
CCD	charge coupled device
CML	current-mode logic
C-MOS	complementary-metal-oxide semiconductor
CMRR	common-mode rejection ratio
CPU	central processing unit
CROM	control read-only memory
CRT	cathode-ray tube
CRC	cyclic redundancy check
CVD	chemical-vapor deposition
CVT	constant-voltage transformer
d-a	digital to analog
DAS	data-acquisition system
DFA	digital fault analysis
DI	dielectric isolation
DIP	dual in-line package
DMA	direct memory access
DMAC	direct-memory-access control
DMM	digital multimeter
D-MOS	double-diffused metal-oxide semiconductor
DMS	dynamic mapping system
DMUX	demultiplexer
DPM	digital panel meter
DTL	diode-transistor logic
DVM	digital voltmeter
Earom	electrically alterable read-only memory
EBCDIC	extended binary-coded-decimal interchange code
ECL	emitter-coupled logic
EDP	electronic data processing (or processor)
EFL	emitter-follower logic
EFTS	electronic funds-transfer system
EOC	end of conversion
EPROM	erasable programable read-only memory
EROM	erasable read-only memory
ESS	electronic switching system
Extnd	extended data transfer
FDM	frequency-division multiplex
FET	field-effect transistor
FFT	fast Fourier transform
FIFO	first in, first out
FPLA	field-programable logic array
F-PROM	field-programable read-only memory
GDS	graphic data system
HiNIL	high-noise-immunity logic
HTL	high-threshold logic
IC	integrated circuit
ICE	in-circuit emulator
IDS	input-data strobe
IEC	infused emitter coupling
I^2L	integrated injection logic
I/O	input/output
J-FET	junction field-effect transistor
JI	junction isolation
Laput	light-activated programable unijunction transistor
LASCR	light-activated silicon controlled rectifier
LCD	liquid-crystal display
LED	light-emitting diode
LIC	linear integrated circuit
LIFO	last in, first out
LNA	low-noise amplifier
LPTTL	low-power transistor-transistor logic

LRU	least recently used
LSB	least significant bit
LSI	large-scale integration
MDS	microprocessor-development system
MESFET	metalized semiconductor field-effect transistor
MHL	microprocessor host loader
MIS	metal insulator silicon
MLA	microprocessor language assembler
MLB	multilayer board
MLE	microprocessor language editor
MNCS	multipoint network control system
MNOS	metal-nitride-oxide semiconductor
Modem	modulator/demodulator
MOS	metal-oxide semiconductor
MOSFET	metal-oxide-semiconductor field-effect transistor
μP	microprocessor
MPU	microprocessor unit
MSB	most significant bit
MSI	medium-scale integration
MTBF	mean time before failure
MTD	mass tape duplicator/verifier
MTTF	mean time to failure
MUX	multiplexer
NAND	inverted AND gate
NDRO	nondestructive readout
n-MOS	n-channel metal-oxide semiconductor
NOR	inverted OR gate
NRZ	non-return to zero
NRZI	non-return to zero inverted
OCR	optical character recognition
ODS	output data strobe
OEM	original-equipment manufacturer
OPAL	operational performance-analysis language
PAR	program-aid routine
pc	printed circuit
pcb	printed-circuit board
PDP	plasma display panel
PIA	peripheral interface adapter
PLA	programable logic array
PLL	phase-locked loop
PM	phase modulation
PMG	permanent-magnet generator
p-MOS	p-channel metal-oxide semiconductor
POS	point of sale
PPI	plan-position indicator also, programable peripheral interface
PRACL	page-replacement algorithm and control logic
PROM	programable read-only memory
PTH	plated-through holes
PUT	programable unijunction transistor
RALU	register and arithmetic/logic unit
RAM	random-access memory
RIM	read-in mode
RMM	read-mostly mode
ROM	read-only memory
RTL	resistor-transistor logic
R/W	read/write
SBS	silicon bilateral switch
SC	semiconductor
SCA	subchannel adapter
SCR	silicon controlled rectifier
SDLC	synchronous data-link control
S/H	sample and hold
SIP	single in-line package
SOS	silicon-on-sapphire
SSI	small-scale integration
SUS	silicon unilateral switch
TBMT	transmitter buffer empty
TTL	transistor-transistor logic
T^2L	transistor-transistor logic
TTY	teletypewriter
TWT	traveling-wave tube
UART	universal asynchronous receiver/transmitter
URCLK	universal receiver clock
Usart	universal synchronous/asynchronous receiver/transmitter
USRT	universal synchronous receiver/transmitter
UTCLK	universal transmitter clock
UUT	unit under test
VCO	voltage-controlled oscillator
VIL	vertical injection logic
VTR	video-tape recorder
XOR	exclusive-OR gate

□

Microprocessor "buzz words"

Reprinted with permission of Schweber Electronics Corp., Westbury, NY 11590.

A

ABBREVIATED ADDRESSING: A modification of the Direct Address mode which uses only part of the full address and provides a faster means of processing data because of the shortened code.

ACCUMULATOR: One or more registers associated with the ALU which temporarily store sums and other arithmetical and logical results of the ALU.

ACIA (Asynchrous Communications Interface Adapter): A Motorola device which interfaces the microprocessor's bus-organized system with incoming serial synchronous communication information. The parallel data of the multi-bus system is serially transmitted by the asynchronous data terminal. The ACIA interfaces directly with low-speed Modems to enable microprocessor communication over telephone lines.

ADAPTER: A device used to effect operative capability between different parts of one or more systems or subsystems.

ADDRESS: An address is a coded instruction designating the location of data or program segments in storage. The address may refer to storage in registers or memories or both. The address code itself may be stored so that a location may contain the address of data rather than the data itself. This form of addressing is common in microprocessors. Addressing modes vary considerably because of efforts to reduce program execution time.

ALGORITHM: Any mechanical computational procedure. As applied to microprocessors, the meaning can be narrowed down to: "A set of rules for getting a specific output from a specific input."

ALU (Arithmetic and Logic Unit): The ALU is one of the three essential components of a microprocessor . . . the other two being the registers and the control block. The ALU performs various forms of addition and subtraction; the logic mode performs such logic operations as ANDing the contents of two registers, or masking the contents of a register.

ARCHITECTURE: Any design or orderly arrangement perceived by man: the architecture of the microprocessor. Since the extant microprocessors vary considerably in design, their architecture has become a bone of contention among specialists.

ASCII: ASCII* is a standardized 7-bit binary code of which various combinations of 1's and 0's correspond to 128 different keyboard characters and control symbols. Most microcomputers are able to communicate to terminals by reading and writing ASCII symbols via this 7-bit code.

*ASCII stands for United States of America Standard Code for Information Interchange.

ASSEMBLER PROGRAM: The Assembler Program translates man readable source statements (mnemonics) into machine understandable object code.

ASSEMBLY LANGUAGE: A machine oriented language. Normally the program is written as a series of source statements using mnemonic symbols that suggest the definition of the instruction and is then translated into machine language.

ASYNCHRONOUS: Operation of a switching network by a free-running signal which signals successive instructions, the completion of one instruction triggering the next. There is no fixed time per cycle.

B

BAUD RATE: A measure of data flow. The number of signal elements per second based on the duration of the shortest element. When each element carries one bit, the Baud rate is numerically equal to bits per second (bps). The Baud rates on UART data sheets are interchangeable with bps.

BCD (Binary Coded Decimal): Each decimal digit is binary coded into 4-bit words. The decimal number 11 would become 0001 0001 in BCD. Also known as the 8421 code.

BENCHMARK: Originally a surveyor's mark used as a reference point in surveys. In connection with microprocessors, the benchmark is a frequently used routine or program selected for the purpose of comparing different makes of microprocessors. A flow chart in assembly language is written out for each microprocessor and the execution of the benchmark by each unit is evaluated on paper. It is not necessary to use hardware to measure capability by benchmark.

BIDIRECTIONAL: A term applied to a port or bus line that can be used to transfer data in either direction.

BINARY: A system of numbers using 2 as a base in contrast to the decimal system which uses 10 as a base. The binary system requires only two symbols, 0 and 1. Two is expressed in binary by the number 10 (read one, zero). Each digit after the initial 1 is multiplied by the base 2. Hence the following table expresses the first ten numbers in decimal and binary:

Decimal	Binary	Decimal	Binary
0	0	5	101
1	1	6	110
2	10	7	111
3	11	8	1000
4	100	9	1001

BRANCH: Refers to the capability of a microprocessor to modify the function or program sequence. Such modification depends on the actual content of the data being processed at any given instant.

BREAKPOINT: A program point indicated by a breakpoint flag which invites interruption to give the user the opportunity to check his program before continuing to its completion.

BUFFER: A circuit inserted between other circuit elements to prevent interactions, to match impedances, to supply additional drive capability, or to delay rate of information flow. Buffers may be inverting or non-inverting.

BUS DRIVER: An integrated circuit which is added to the data bus system to facilitate proper drive to the CPU when several memories are tied to the data bus line. These are necessary because of capacitive loading which slows down the data rate and prevents proper time sequencing of microprocessor operation.

BUS SYSTEM: A network of paths inside the microcomputer which facilitate data flow. The important busses in a microprocessor are identified as Data Bus, Address Bus, and Control Bus.

BYTE: Indicates a pre-determined number of eight consecutive bits treated as an entity. "Word" and "Byte" are used interchangeably.

C

CLOCK: A generator of pulses which controls the timing of switching circuits in a microprocessor. Clock frequency is not the only criterion of data manipulation speed. Hardware architecture and programming skill are more important. Clocks are a requisite for most microprocessors and multiple phased clocks are common in MOS processors.

COMBINATIONAL LOGIC: A circuit arrangement in which the output state is determined by the present state of the input. Also called Combinatorial logic. (See also Sequential Logic.)

COMPILERS: Compilers translate higher-level languages into machine code.

CONDITION CODE: Refers to a limited group of program conditions such as carry, borrow, overflow, etc., which are pertinent to the execution of instructions. The codes are contained in a Condition Codes Register. (See also Status Word Register.)

CONTROL BLOCK: This is the circuitry which performs the control functions of the CPU. It is responsible for decoding microprogrammed instructions, and then generating the internal control signals that perform the operations requested.

CONTROL BUS: Conveys a mixture of signals which regulate system operation. These "traffic" signals are commands which may also originate in peripherals for transfer to the CPU or the reverse.

CONTROL PROGRAM: The Control Program is a sequence of instructions that will guide the CPU through the various operations it must perform. This program is stored permanently in ROM memory where it can be accessed by the CPU during operations.

CPU (Central Processing Unit): The heart of any computer system. Basically the CPU is made up of storage elements called registers, computational circuits in the ALU, the Control Block, and I/O. As soon as LSI technology was able to build a CPU on an IC chip, the microprocessor became a reality. The one-chip microprocessors have limited storage space, so memory implementation is added in modular fashion. Most current microprocessors consist of a set of chips, one or two of which form the CPU.

CROM (Control Read Only Memory): This is a major component in the control block of some microprocessors. It is a ROM which has been microprogrammed to decode control logic.

CROSS-ASSEMBLER: When the program is assembled by the same computer that it will run on, the program that performs the assembly is referred to as the resident or native or self-assembler. If the program is assembled by some other computer, the process is referred to as cross-assembly.

CYCLE STEALING: A technique used to transfer data between microprocessor memory and external bulk memory. Data transfer is accomplished without stopping MPU operation by using microcycle time between data fetch and instruction fetch time in an instruction cycle. Creates a virtually infinite memory storage for MPUs. Applicable for 3-state output memories and MPUs. (See also DMA.)

D

DAISY CHAIN: A bus line which is interconnected with units in such a way that the signal passes from one unit to the next in serial fashion. The architecture of the Fairchild F-8 provides an example of daisy-chained memory chips. Each chip connects to its neighbors to accomplish daisy-chaining of interrupt priorities beginning with the chip closest to the CPU.

DATA: Information in numerical code which is assigned an address in memory that the CPU uses when storing or fetching the information.

DATA BUS: The microprocessor communicates internally and externally by means of the data bus. It is bidirectional and can transfer data to and from the CPU, memory storage, and peripheral devices.

DATA COUNTER: (See Program Counter)

DATA FIELD POINTER: (See Stack Pointer)

DEBUG: As used in connection with microprocessor software, debugging involves searching for and eliminating sources of error in programming routines. Finding a bug in software routine is said to be as difficult as finding a needle in the proverbial haystack. A single step tester is the suggested method, so that each instruction operation can be checked individually.

D-BUS: (See Data Bus)

DECREMENT: A programming instruction which decreases the contents of a storage location. (See also increment and decrement.)

DEDICATED: To set apart for some special use. A dedicated microprocessor is one that has been specifically programmed for a single application such as weight measurement by scale, traffic light control, etc. ROMs by their very nature (Read-Only) are "dedicated" memories.

DIRECT ADDRESSING: This is the standard addressing mode. It is characterized by an ability to reach any point in main storage directly. Direct addressing is usually restricted to the first 256 bits in main storage for microprocessors.

DISASSEMBLER: A computer program which translates object code back to source (mnemonics) statements. (See also Assembler Program.)

DMA (Direct Memory Access): A method of gaining direct access to main storage to achieve data transfer without involving the CPU. The manner in which CPU is disabled while DMA is in progress differs in different models and some use several methods to accomplish DMA.

DYNAMIC MEMORY: Dynamic memories are faster than static and use less power, but must be refreshed periodically to maintain their programmed state. Available predominantly in MOS technology.

E

EXECUTION TIME: Usually expressed in clock cycles necessary to carry out an instruction. Since the clock frequency is known, the actual time can be calculated. Clock frequencies can be varied.

EXTENDED ADDRESSING: Refers to an addressing mode that can reach any place in memory and requires more than one byte to locate the data in memory.

F

FETCH: To go after and return with things or objects. In a microprocessor, the "objects" fetched are instructions and data which are entered in the Instruction and Data Registers. The next, or a later step in the program will cause the machine to execute what it was programmed to do with the fetched instructions and data

FIELDS: A source statement is made up of a number of code fields, usually four, which are acceptable by the assembler. The four fields may connote Label, Operator, Operand, and Comment. Fields are also applicable to data storage. The eight bits stored in a memory location might contain two 4 bit fields, or eight 1-bit fields, etc.

FIRMWARE: (See Solid State Software.)

FLAG BIT: An information bit which indicates some form of demarcation has been reached such as overflow or carry. Also an indicator of special conditions such as interrupts.

FLOW CHART OR FLOW DIAGRAM: A sequence of operations charted with the aid of symbols, diagram or other representations to indicate an executive program. Flowcharts enable the designer to visualize the procedure necessary for each item on the prograr A complete flowchart leads directly to the final code.

G

GARBAGE COLLECTION: As programs lapse into disuse, these memory segments must be freed for the storage of new programs. Usually the word lengths of new programs do not match the available space. Small chunks of unused, but programmed memory accumulate. Aside from the waste of memory space, these programmed locations can often hang up a machine's operation. Hence the technique employed to clean these memory segments for efficient use is called garbage collection.

H

HANDSHAKING: A colloquial term which describes the method used by a modem to establish contact with another Modem at the other end of a telephone line. Often used interchangeably with buffering and interfacing, but with a fine line of difference in which handshaking implies a direct package to package connection regardless of functional circuitry.

HARDWARE: The individual components of a circuit, both passive and active, have long been characterized as hardware in the jargon of the engineer. Today, any piece of data processing equipment is informally called hardware.

HARD-WIRED LOGIC: Random Logic design solutions require interconnection of numerous integrated circuits representing the logic elements. An example of hard-wired logic is the use of a hand-wired diode matrix instead of a ROM. These interconnections, whether done with soldering iron or by printed circuit board, are referred to as hard-wired logic in contrast to the software solutions achieved by a programmed ROM or Microprocessor.

HIGH LEVEL LANGUAGE: This is a problem-oriented programming language as distinguished from a machine-oriented programming language. The former's instruction approach is closer to the needs of the problems to be handled than the language of the machine on which they are to be implemented.

HEXADECIMAL: Whole numbers in positional notation using 16 as a base. (See Octal and compare.) Since there are 16 hexadecimal digits (0 through 15) and there are only ten numerical digits (0 through 9) an additional six digits representing 10 through 15 must be introduced. Recourse is had to the alphabet to provide the extra digits. Hence, the least significant hexadecimal digits read: 0, 1, 2, 3, 4, 5, 6, 7, 8, 9, A, B, C, D, E, F. The decimal number 16 becomes the hexadecimal number 10. The decimal number 26 becomes the hexadecimal number 1A.

I

IMMEDIATE ADDRESSING: In this mode of addressing,

the operand contains the value to be operated on, and no address reference is required.

INCREMENT (and Decrement): These two words are software operations most often associated with the stack and stack pointer. Bytes of information are stored in the stack register at the addresses conained in the stack pointer. The stack pointer is decremented after each byte of information is entered into the stack; it is incremented after each byte is removed from the stack. The terms can also refer to any addressable register.

INDEX REGISTER: The Index Register contains address information subject to modification by the Control Block without affecting the instruction in the memory. The IR information is available for loading onto the stack pointer when needed.

INDIRECT ADDRESSING: Addressing a memory location which contains the address of data rather than the data itself.

INITIALIZE: The reset control unit is used to start execution of program for initial startup. At the beginning of each new program, initialization requires re-setting all hardware controls to starting values.

INSTRUCTION: One of a number of computer operations stored in memory that may, when called upon, command the CPU to perform arithmetic and logic functions, control peripheral devices, or indicate succeeding instructions.

INSTRUCTION SET: Constitutes the total list of instructions which can be executed by a given microprocessor and is supplied to the user to provide the basic information necessary to assemble a program.

INTERFACE: Indicates a common boundary between adjacent components, circuits, or systems enabling the devices to yield and/or acquire information from one another. In the face of common usage, one must regretfully add that the words Buffer, Handshake, and Adapter are interchangeable with Interface.

INTERPRETER: A method or program that translates high level langauge into machine assembleable information. (See also Machine and High Level Language.)

INTERRUPT: An interrupt involves the suspension of the normal programming routine of a microprocessor in order to handle a sudden request for service. The importance of the interrupt capability of a microprocessor depends on the kind of applications to which it will be exposed. When a number of peripheral devices interface the microprocessor, one or several simultaneous interrupts may occur on a frequent basis. Multiple interrupt requests require the processor to be able to accomplish the following: to delay or prevent further interrupts; to break into an interrupt in order to handle a more urgent interrupt; to establish a method of interrupt priorities; and, after completion of interrupt service, to resume the interrupted program from the point where it was interrupted.
(See also Vector Interrupt.)

INTERRUPT MASK BIT: The Interrupt Mask Bit prevents the CPU from responding to further interrupt requests until cleared by execution of programmed instructions. It may also be manipulated by specific mask bit instructions.

I/O (Input/Output): Package pins which are tied directly to the internal bus network to enable I/O to interface the microprocessor with the outside world.

J

JUMP: The Jump operation, like the Branch operation is used to control the transfer of operations from one point to a more distant point in the control program. Jumps differ from Branching in not using the Relative Addressing mode.

L

LABEL: A label may correspond to a numerical value or a memory location in the programmable system. The specific absolute address is not necessary since the intent of the label is a general destination. Labels are a requisite for jump and branch instructions.

LIBRARY: A collection of complete programs written for a particular computer, minicomputer, or microprocessor. For example, Second Order Differential Equation may be the name of a program in the Library of a particular computer; this program will contain all the subroutines necessary to perform the solution of second order differential equations written in machine language and using the instruction set of this machine.

LIFO: Last-In-First-Out. (See PUSH-POP Stack.)

LINK REGISTER: This is a register of 1 bit (sometimes called the Carry register) which acts as an extension of the Accumulator during rotation or carry operations.

LOGIC: A mathematical treatment of formal logic in which a system of symbols is used to represent quantities and relationships. The symbols or logical functions are called AND, OR, NOT, to mention a few examples. Each function can be translated into a switching circuit, more commonly referred to as a "gate." Since a switch (or gate) has only two states — open or closed — it makes possible the application of binary numbers for the solution of problems. The basic logic functions obtained from gate circuits is the foundation of complex computing machines.

LOOK AHEAD: 1.) A feature of the CPU which allows the machine to mask an interrupt request until the following instruction has been completed. 2.) A feature of adder circuits and ALUs which allow these devices to look ahead to see that all carrys generated are available for addition.

LOOPING: Repetition of instructions at delayed speeds until a final value is determined (as in a weight scale indication) is called looping. The looped repetitions are usually frozen into a ROM memory location and then jumped to when needed. Looping also occurs when the CPU is in a wait condition.

LSB: Least Significant Bit. (See Significant Bits.)

LSI (Large Scale Integration): At the beginning of the LSI era a count of 100 gates qualified for LSI. Today an 8-bit CPU can be fabricated on a single chip.

M

MACHINE LANGUAGE: The only language the microprocessor can understand is binary. All other programming languages must be translated into binary code before entering the processor and decoded back into the original language after leaving it.

MACRO COMMAND: A program entity formed by a string of standard, but related, commands which are put into effect by means of a single macro command. Any group of frequently used commands can be combined into a macro command. The many become one.

MACROLOGIC™: A group of LSI chips which, when combined, will form a microprocessor. These devices can be arranged to permit the user to microprogram his own microprocessor. In such an arrangement he is not limited to a fixed instruction set and is able to build his own instruction set.

MAIL BOX: The Mail Box is a set of locations in a common RAM storage area reserved for data addressed to specific peripheral devices as well as other microprocessors in the immediate environment. Such an arrangement enables the co-ordinator CPU and the supplementary microprocessors to transfer data among themselves in an orderly fashion with minimal hardware.

MNEMONIC CODE: These are designed to assist the human memory. The microprocessor language consists of binary words which are a series of O's and I's making it difficult for the programmer to remember the instructions corresponding to a given operation. To assist the human memory, the binary numbered codes are assigned groups of letters (or mnemonic symbols) that suggest the definition of the instruction. LDA for load accumulator, etc. Source statements can be written in this symbolic language and then translated into machine language.

MICROPROGRAM: This word pre-dates the microprocessor and refers to computer instructions which do not reference the main memory storage. It is a computer technique which performs subroutines by manipulating the basic computer hardware and is often referred to as "computer within computer." The word has not changed its basic meaning when used in connection with microprocessors, but is not to be construed as native to microprocessors. A series of instructions stored in a ROM, any portion of which can implement a higher language program, is labeled a microprogram.

MICROINSTRUCTION: (See Microprogram)

MEMORY: The part of a computer system into which information can be inserted and held for future use. Storage and memory are interchangeable expressions. Memories accept and hold binary numbers only. Memory types are core, disk, drum, and semiconductor.

MOS (Metal Oxide Semiconductor): The structure of an MOS Field Effect Transistor (FET) is metal over silicon oxide over silicon. The metal electrode is the gate; the silicon oxide is the insulator; and carrier doped regions in the silicon substrate become the drain and source. The result is a sandwich very much like a capacitor, which explains why MOS is slower than bipolar since the 'capacitor sandwich' must charge up before current can flow. The three great advantages of MOS are its process simplicity because of reduced fabrication stages; the savings in chip real estate resulting in functional density; and the ease of interconnection on chip. These qualities enabled MOS to break the LSI barrier, something bipolar is just beginning to achieve. The hand-held calculator and the microprocessor are triumphs of MOS-LSI technology.

MICROCOMPUTER: (See microprocessor.)

MICROPROCESSOR: The microprocessor is a Central Processing Unit fabricated on one or two chips. While no standard design is visible in existing units, a number of well-delineated areas are present in all of them: Arithmetic & Logic Unit, Control Block, and Register Array. When joined to a memory storage system and peripheral I/O's, the resulting combination is referred to in today's usage as a Microcomputer. It should be added that each microprocessor is supplied with an Instruction Set listing the basic operations which the processor performs.

MSB: Most Significant Bit. (See Significant Bits.)

MULTIPLEXING: Multiplexing describes a process of transmitting more than one signal at a time over a single link, route, or channel. Of the two methods in use, one frequency-shares the bandwidth of a channel in the same way hurdlers run and jump in their assigned lanes thus permitting many contestants to compete simultaneously on the same track. The second way is to time-share multiple signals in the same way that pole vaulters jump over the same bar one after the other. The two methods may be described as parallel and serial processing. Time-sharing may not seem "simultaneous," but it should be remembered that the signal speed is so fast that it is possible to multiplex four different numbers through a single decoder driver and have them appear on four different displays without a flicker to disturb the eye.

N

NESTING: Nesting is referred to when a subroutine is enclosed inside a larger routine, but is not necessarily part of the outer routine. A series of looping instructions may be nested within each other.

O

OBJECT PROGRAM: The end result of the source language program after it has been translated into machine language.

TM—Macrologic is a Fairchild trademark.

OCTAL: Whole numbers in positional notation using 8 as a base. The decimal or base 10 number, 125, becomes 175 in octal or base 8. Here is a convenient way to convert a decimal number into an octal number:

1 7	Divide the decimal number by 8. The answer is 15 and 5 left over.
8/15 5	
8/125	Divide the answer, 15, by 8 again. The answer is 1 and 7 left over.
	The octal number is 175.

To prove your answer is correct, do the following:

5 x 1 = 5	Arrange the octal number vertically with the least significant digit on top.
7 x 8 = 56	
1 x 64 = 64	The least significant digit represents one's, so multiply 5 x 1 = 5.
125	The next digit in the octal number represents 8's, so multiply 7 x 8 = 56.
	The third digit of the octal number represents 64's, so multiply 1 x 64 = 64.
	The sum is the decimal number 125.

OPERAND: A quantity on which a mathematical operation is performed. One of the instruction fields in an addressing statement. Usually the statement consists of an operator and an operand. The operator may indicate an "add" instruction; the operand will indicate what is to be added.

OVERFLOW: Overflow results when an arithmetic operation generates a quantity beyond the capacity of the register. Also referred to as arithmetical overflow. An overflow status bit in the condition code register can be checked to determine if the previous operation caused an overflow.

OPERATING CODE (Opcode): Source statements which generate machine codes after assembly are referred to as operating codes.

P

PAGE: A natural grouping of memory locations by higher-order address bits. In an 8-bit MPU, $2^8 = 256$ consecutive bytes may constitute a page. Then words on the same page only differ in the lower order 8 address bits.

PAGE MODE ADDRESSING: A technique used in MPU's to directly address memory locations stored within the page. (See Page.)

PARALLEL OPERATION: Processing all the digits of a word or byte simultaneously by transmitting each digit on a separate channel or bus line.

PARITY CHECK: A method of determining the validity of information word by word. The total number of binary 1's and 0's in a word is always even or odd. Each word contains a so-called parity bit whose value is a function of the number of digits. Thus, this parity bit can check whether the word is true or false.

PARTY-LINE: Party-line as used in its telephone sense to indicate a large number of devices connected to a single line originating in the CPU.

PIPELINE REGISTER: A register placed on the output of the microprogram memory to essentially split the system in two. This allows the micro-instruction fetch to occur in parallel with the data operation rather than serially, allowing the clock frequency to be doubled. Stack processing is done on a last-in-first-out basis while pipeline processing is first-in-first-out.

PLA (Programmed Logic Arrays): The PLA is an orderly arrangement of logical AND and logical OR functions. Its application is very much like a glorified ROM. It is primarily a combinational logic device.

POINTER: A register which serves as a reference point to a memory location.

POLLING: Polling is the method used to identify the source of interrupt requests. When several interrupts occur at one time, the control program decides which one to service first.

PORT: Device terminals which provide electrical access to a system or circuit. The point at which the I/O is in contact with the outside world.

PRIORITY INTERRUPT: (See Interrupt.)

PROGRAM: A procedure for solving a problem and frequently referred to as Software.

PROGRAM COUNTER: One of the registers in the CPU which holds addresses necessary to step the machine through the program. During interrupts, the program counter value containing the address of the next instruction is saved. Branching also requires loading of the return address in the program counter.

PROM: (See ROM.)

PUSH-POP STACK: A register that receives information from the Program Counter and stores the address locations of instructions on a last-in-first-out basis. Two operations are involved in stack processing: "Pushing" describes the filling of the stack from registers; "Popping" involves emptying the stack for transfer to registers.

P-STACK: (See PUSH-POP Stack.)

R

RALU (Register, Arithmetic, and Logic Unit): Unlike the discrete ALU package which functions as an Arithmetic and Logic unit only, the ALU in the microprocessor is equipped with a number of registers.

RAM (Random Access Memory): Random in the sense of providing access to any storage location point in the memory immediately by means of vertical and horizontal co-ordinates. Information may be "written" in or "read" out in the same rapid way.

RANDOM LOGIC DESIGN: Designing a system using discrete logic circuits. Numerous gates are required to implement the logic equations until the problem is solved. Even then, the design is not completed until all redundant gates are weeded out. Random logic design is no guarantee of optimum gate count.

REAL TIME OPERATION: Data processing technique used to allow the machine to utilize information as it becomes available, as opposed to batch processing at a time unrelated to the time the information was generated.

REFRESH: Because electrical charges momentarily

applied to Dynamic memory circuits (representing data or instructions) leak off rapidly, periodic recharging is necessary to keep memory voltage levels intact and determinable.

REGISTER: A register is a memory on a smaller scale. The words stored therein may involve arithmetical, logical, or transferral operations. Storage in registers may be temporary, but even more important is their accessibility by the CPU. The number of registers in a microprocessor is considered one of the most important features of its architecture.

RELATIVE ADDRESSING: The relative addressing mode specifies a memory location referenced to the CPU's Program Location Counter register. This addressing mode is mainly used for Branch instructions in which case an opcode is added to or subtracted from the Program Counter to complete the branching instruction.

RESIDENT ASSEMBLER: (See Cross-Assembler.)

ROM (Read Only Memory): In its virgin state the ROM consists of a mosaic of undifferentiated cells. One type of ROM is programmed by mask pattern as part of the last manufacturing stage. Another, more popular type better known as P/ROM, is programmable in the field with the aid of programmer equipment. Program data stored in ROMs are often called firmware because they cannot be altered. However, another type of P/ROM is now on the market called EPROM which is erasible by ultra violet irradiation and electrically reprogrammable.

S

SCRATCHPAD: This term is applied to information which the Processing unit stores or holds temporarily. It is a memory containing subtotals for various unknowns which are needed for final results.

SEQUENTIAL LOGIC: A circuit arrangement in which the output state is determined by the previous state of the input. (See also Combination Logic.)

SIGNED NUMBERS: (See Two's Complement Numbers.)

SIGNIFICANT BITS: The most significant bit (MSB) in a byte of 8 numbers is on the extreme left. The least significant bit (LSB) is on the extreme right. The remaining bits are weighted according to their position in the byte between the MSB and the LSB.

SIMULATOR: A special program that simulates the logical operation of the microprocessor. It is designed to execute object programs generated by a cross-assembler on a machine other than the one being worked on and is useful for checking and debugging programs prior to committing them to ROM firmware.

SLICE: A type of chip architecture which permits the cascading or stacking of devices to increase word bit size.

SNAPSHOT: A CRT representation of a contiguous portion of a machine's memory addresses and data contained therein. A series of snapshots can capture the entire state of a machine including memory contents, registers, flags, etc.

SOFTWARE: What sheet music is to the piano, software is to the computer. Looked at from a practical point of view, one might say that software is the computer's instruction manual. The name, software, was obviously chosen to contrast with the formidable hardware which confronted the first programmers. Software is the language used by a programmer to communicate with the computer. Since the only language spoken by a computer is mathematical, the programmer must convert his verbal instructions into numbers. In the case of microprocessors, which vary from maker to maker, software libraries are assembled by the manufacturer for the benefit of the user.

SOLID STATE SOFTWARE Off-the-shelf software permanently fixed in PROM memory.

SOURCE STATEMENT: A program written in other than machine language, usually in three-letter mnemonic symbols, that suggest the definition of the instruction. There are two kinds of source statements: "executive instructions" which translate into operating machine code (opcode); and "assembly directives" which are useful in documenting the source program, but generate no code.

STACK: The stack is a block of successive memory locations which is accessible from one end on a last-in-first-out basis (LIFO). The stack is co-ordinated with the stack pointer which keeps track of storage and retrieval of each byte of information in the stack. A stack may be any block of successive information locations in the read/write memory.

STACK POINTER: The stack pointer is co-ordinated with the storing and retrieval of information in the stack. The stack pointer is decremented by one immediately following the storage in the stack of each byte of information. Conversely, the stack pointer is incremented by one immediately before retrieving each byte of information from the stack. The stack pointer may be manipulated for transferring its contents to the Index register or vice versa.

STATIC MEMORY: Static memories retain their programmed state as long as power is applied. Available in MOS and Bipolar technologies.

STATUS WORD REGISTER: A group of binary numbers which informs the user of the present condition of the microprocessor. In most microprocessors, the Status Register provides the following five pieces of information: plus or minus sign of the value in Accumulator, overflow indication, carry bit, all zero's in accumulator, and interrupt bit status.
(See also Condition Code Register.)

STORAGE: The word storage is used interchangeably with memory. In fact, it has been recommended as the preferred term by people who would rather not imply that the computer has any relationship with the human brain.

SUBROUTINE: Part of a master routine which may be used at will in a variety of master routines. The object of a Branch or Jump command.

T

THROUGHPUT: The speed with which problems or segments of problems are performed is called Throughput. Defined in this way, it is obvious that throughput will vary from application to application. As an index of speed, throughput is meaningful only in terms of your own application.

TWO'S COMPLEMENT NUMBERS: The ALU performs standard binary addition using the 2's complement numbering system to represent both positive and negative numbers. The positive numbers in 2's complement representation are identical to the positive numbers in standard binary.

+127 in standard binary = 01111111 +127 in 2's complement = 01111111. Note that the eighth or most significant digit indicates the sign: 0 = plus;
1 = minus.
However, the negative 2's complement is the reverse of the negative standard binary plus 1.

−127 in standard binary = 11111111. To form the 2's complement of −127.
First reverse all the digits except the sign
= 10000000
Then add 1   1
10000001 = −127 in 2's complement.

U

UART (Universal Asynchronous Receiver Transmitter): This device will interface a word parallel controller or data terminal to a bit serial communication network.

V

VECTOR INTERRUPT: This term is used to describe a microprocessor system in which each interrupt, both internal and external, have their own uniquely recognizable address. This enables the microprocessor to perform a set of specified operations which are pre-programmed by the user to handle each interrupt in a distinctively different manner.

VOLATILE: Semiconductor Read/Write memories are volatile since they cannot retain a program unless power is continually applied. Power failure will wipe out the contents of Read/Write memories. This does not apply to PROMs.

W

WORD: A group of "characters" treated as a unit and given a single location in computer memory. Presumably a byte is a group of 8 bits in contrast to a word which is a group of numeric and/or alphabetic characters and symbols, but the two words are used interchangeably more often than not.

Glossary of digital-computer terms

absolute: Pertaining to an address fully defined by a memory address number, or to a program which contains such addresses (as opposed to one containing symbolic addresses).

accumulator: A register in which numbers are totaled, manipulated, or temporarily stored for transfers to and from memory or external devices.

ADD: Restrictive: "two's complement" addition of binary numbers. General: any arithmetic addition.

address: (noun) A number which identifies one location in memory. (verb) To direct the computer to read a specified memory location (synonymous with "reference").

address modification: A programming technique of changing the address specified by a memory-reference instruction, so that each time that particular instruction is executed, it will affect a different memory location.

address word: A computer word which contains only the address of a memory location.

Algol: (Algebraic-Oriented Language) An international algebraic procedural language for a computer programming system.

algorithm: A prescribed set of well-defined rules or processes for the solution of a problem in a finite number of steps.

alphanumeric: Pertaining to a character set that contains both letters and numerals, and usually other characters.

alter: A modification of the contents of an accumulator or extend bit, e.g., clear, complement, or increment.

AND: A logical operation in which the resultant quantity (or signal) is true if all of the input values are true, and is false if at least one of the input values is false.

argument: 1) A variable or constant which is given in the call of a subroutine as information to it. 2) A variable upon whose value the value of a function depends. 3) The known reference factor necessary to find an item in a table or array, i.e., the index.

arithmetic logic: The circuitry involved in manipulating the information contained in a computer's accumulators.

arithmetic operation: Restrictive: a mathematical operation involving fundamental arithmetic (addition, subtraction, multiplication, division), specifically excluding logical and shifting operations. General: any manipulation of numbers.

array: A set of lists of elements, usually variables or data.

ASCII: An abbreviation for American Standard Code for Information Interchange.

assemble: To translate from a symbolic program to a binary program by substituting binary operation codes for symbolic operation codes and absolute or relocatable addresses for symbolic addresses.

assembler: A program for a computer which converts a

program prepared in symbolic form (i.e., using defined symbols and mnemonics to represent instructions, addresses, etc.) to binary machine language.

assembly language: The source language used as input to an assembler and translated by the assembler into machine language.

auxiliary storage: Storage that supplements core memory, such as disk tape.

background processing: The automatic execution of a low-priority computer program when higher priority programs are not using the system resources.

base: The quantity of different digits used in a particular numbering system. The base in the binary numbering system is two; thus there are two digits (0 and 1). In the decimal system (base 10), there are ten digits (0 through 9).

base address: A given address from which an absolute address is derived by combination with a relative address.

base page: The lowest numbered page of a computer's memory. It can be directly addressed from any other page.

binary: Denoting the numbering system based on the radix two. Binary digits are restricted to the values 0 and 1.

binary-coded decimal (bcd): coding method for representing each decimal digit (0–9) by specific combinations of four bits. For example, the 8–4–2–1 bcd code commonly used with computers represents "1" as 0001 and "9" as 1001.

binary program: A program (or its recording form) in which all information is in binary machine language.

bistable: Pertaining to an electronic circuit having two stable states, controllable by external switching signals, analogous to an on–off switch.

bit (b): A single digit in a binary number, or in the recorded representation of such a number (by hole punches, magnetic states, etc). The digit can have one of only two values, 0 or 1.

bit density: A physical specification referring to the number of bits which can be recorded per unit of length or area.

bit serial: One bit at a time, as opposed to bit parallel, in which all bits of a character can be handled simultaneously.

block: A set of consecutive machine words, characters, or digits handled as a unit, particularly with reference to I/O.

bootstrap: A technique or device designed to bring itself into a desired state by means of its own action, e.g., a routine whose first few instructions are sufficient to bring the rest of itself into the computer from an input device.

branch: A point in a routine where one of two or more choices is made under control of the routine.

breakpoint: A point in a computer program at which conditional interruption is made to permit visual check, printouts, or other debugging aids.

buffer: A register used for intermediate storage ot information in the transfer sequence between the computer's accumulators and a peripheral device or a designated area of memory used to temporarily hold data.

bug: A mistake in the design or implementation of a program resulting in erroneous results.

bulk memory: Storage in addition to the main memory of the computer, e.g., magnetic tape, disk, or drum.

bus: A major electrical path connecting two or more electrical circuits.

byte: A group of binary digits usually operated upon as a unit, frequently 8 b.

calling sequence: A specified set of instructions and data necessary to set up and call a given routine.

carry: A digit, or equivalent signal, resulting from an arithmetic operation which causes a positional digit to equal or exceed the base of the effective numbering system.

central processing unit: The unit of a computing system that includes the circuits controlling the interpretation and execution of instructions—the computer proper, excluding I/O and other peripheral devices.

character: The general term to include all symbols such as alphabetic letters, numerals, punctuation marks, mathematical operators, etc. Also, the coded representation of such symbols.

checkpoint: A point in time during a program run at which processing is momentarily halted to make a record, on an external storage medium, of the condition of the variables of the program being executed.

clear: To erase the contents of a storage location by replacing the contents, normally with zeros or spaces; to set to zero.

code: A system of symbols which can be used by machines, such as a computer, and which in specific arrangements have a special external meaning.

coding: Writing instructions for a computer using symbols meaningful to the computer, or to an assembler, compiler, or other language processor.

compatibility: The ability of an instruction or source language to be used on more than one computer.

compile: To produce a binary-coded program from a program written in source (symbolic) language, by selecting appropriate subroutines from a subroutine library, as directed by the instructions or other symbols of the source program. The linkage is supplied for combining the subroutines into a workable program, and the subroutines and linkage are translated into binary code.

compiler: A language translation program, used to transform symbols meaningful to a human operator into codes meaningful to a computer. More restrictively, a program which translates a machine-independent source language into the machine language of a specific computer, thus excluding assemblers.

complement: (one's) To replace all 0 bits with 1 bits and vice versa. (two's) To form the one's complement and add 1.

computation: The processing of information within the computer.

computer (digital): An electronic instrument capable of accepting, storing, and arithmetically manipulating information, which includes both data and the controlling program. The information is handled in the form of coded binary digits (0 and 1), represented by dual voltage levels, magnetic states, punched holes, etc.

computer word: See "word."

conditioned assembly: Assembly of certain parts of a symbolic program only if certain conditions have been met.

configuration: The arrangement of either hardware instruments or software routines when combined to operate as a system.

console: Usually the external front side of a device, where controls and indicators are available for manual operation of the device.

constant: Numeric data used but not changed by the program.

contents: The information stored in a register or a memory location.

convert: 1) To change numeric data from one radix to another. 2) To transfer data from one recorded format to another.

core: The smallest element of a core-storage memory module.

It is a ring of ferrite material that can be magnetized in clockwise or counterclockwise directions to represent the two binary digits, 0 and 1.

core memory: The main high-speed storage of a computer, in which binary data are represented by the switching polarity of magnetic cores.

current location counter: A counter kept by an assembler to determine the address assigned to an instruction or constant being assembled.

current page: The memory page comprising all those locations which are on the same page as a given instruction.

cycle time: The length of time it takes the computer to reference one word of memory.

data: A general term used to denote any or all facts, numbers, letters, and symbols. It connotes basic elements of information which can be processed or produced by a computer.

data acquisition: The gathering, measuring, digitizing, and recording of continuous-form (analog) information.

data reduction: The transformation of raw information gathered by measuring or recording equipment into a more condensed, organized, or useful form.

data word: A computer word consisting of a number, a fact, or other information which is to be processed by the computer.

debug: To check for and correct errors in a program.

decimal: Denoting the numbering system based on the radix ten.

decrement: To change the value of a number in the negative direction. If not otherwise stated, a decrement by one is usually assumed.

delimiter: A character that separates, terminates, and organizes elements of a statement or programs.

device: An electronic or electromechanical instrument. Most commonly implies measuring, reading, or recording equipment.

diagnostic: (adjective) Relating to test programs for detection of errors in the functining of hardware or software, or the messages resulting from such tests. (noun) The test program or message itself

digit: A character used to represent one of the nonnegative integers smaller than the radix, e.g., in binary notation, either 0 or 1.

direct address: An address that specifies the location of an instruction operand.

direct memory access: A means of transferring a block of information words directly between an external device and the computer's memory, bypassing the need for repeating a service routine for each word. This method greatly speeds the transfer process.

disable: A signal condition which prohibits some specific event from proceeding.

disk storage: A means of storing binary digits in the form of magnetized spots on a circular metal plate coated with a magnetic material. The information is stored and retrieved by READ–WRITE heads which may be positioned over the surface of the disk either by moving the heads or the disk itself.

documentation: Manuals and other printed materials (tables, listings, diagrams, etc.) which provide instructive information for usage and maintenance of a manufactured product, including both hardware and software.

double-length word: A word which, due to its length, requires two computer words to represent it. Double-length words are normally stored in two adjacent memory locations.

double-precision: Pertaining to the use of two computer words to represent one number.

downtime: The time interval during which the device is inoperative.

dummy: Used as an adjective to indicate an artificial address, instruction, or record of information inserted solely to fulfill prescribed conditions, as in a "dummy" variable.

dump: To copy the contents of all or part of core memory, usually onto an external storage medium.

dynamic relocation: The ability to move programs or data from auxiliary memory into main memory at any convenient location. Normally the addresses of programs and data are fixed when the program is compiled.

effective address: The address of a memory location ultimately affected by a memory reference instruction. It is possible for one instruction to go through several indirect addresses to reach the effective address.

enable: A signal condition which permits some specific event to proceed, whenever it is ready to do so.

EXCLUSIVE-OR: A logical operation in which the resultant quantity (or signal) is true if at least one (but not all) of the input values is true, and is false if the input values are all true or all false.

execute: To fully perform a specific operation, such as would be accomplished by an instruction or a program.

exit sequence: A series of instructions to conclude operation in one area of a program and to move to another area.

external storage: A separate facility or device on which data usable by the computer are stored (such as paper tape, tape, or disk).

field: 1) One or more characters treated as a unit. 2) A specified area of a record used for a single type of data.

file: A collection of related records treated as a unit.

file name: Alphanumeric characters used to identify a particular file.

fixed point: A numerical notation in which the fractional point (whether decimal, octal, or binary) appears at a constant predetermined position. (Compare with "floating point.")

flag: A variable or register used to record the status of a program or device—in the latter case, sometimes called "device flag."

flip-flop: An electronic circuit having two stable states, and thus capable of storing a binary digit. Its states are controlled by signal levels at the circuit input and are sensed by signal levels at the circuit output.

floating point: A numerical notation in which the integer and the exponent of a number are separately represented (frequently by two computer words), so that the implied position of the fractional point (decimal, octal, or binary) can be freely varied with respect to the integer digits. (Compare with "fixed point.")

flow chart: A diagram representing the operation of a computer program.

foreground processing: Higher priority processing that takes precedence over "background processing" and can interrupt such processing. It results from real-time events or enquiries.

format: A predetermined arrangement of bits and characters.

Fortran: A programming language (or the compiler which

translates this language) which permits programs to be written in a form resembling algebra, rather than in detailed instruction by instruction format.

forward referencing: The need to refer to a symbol in a program prior to its definition (i.e., trying to assemble the instruction JUMP PLACE, where PLACE is a location symbol further down in the program code).

full-duplex: Describing a communication channel capable of simultaneous and independent transmission and reception.

gate: An electronic circuit capable of performing logical functions such as AND, OR, NOR, etc.

half-duplex: Describing a communication channel capable of transmission and/or reception, but not both simultaneously.

hardware: Electronic or electromechanical components, instruments, or systems.

high core: Core-memory locations having high-numbered addresses.

INCLUSIVE-OR: A logical operation in which the resultant quantity (or signal) is true if at least one of the input values is true, and is false if the input values are all false.

increment: To change the value of a number in the positive direction. If not otherwise stated, an increment by one is usually assumed.

incremental magnetic tape: A form of magnetic tape recording in which the recording transport advances by small increments (e.g., 0.005 in), stopping the tape advancement long enough to record one character at the spot located under the recording head.

index register: A memory device containing an index. (See "address modification.")

indirect address: The address initially specified by an instruction when it is desired to use that location to redirect the computer to some other location to find the "effective address" for the instruction.

information: A unit or set of knowledge represented in the form of discrete "words," consisting of an arrangement of symbols or (so far as the digital computer is concerned) binary digits.

inhibit: To prevent a specific event from occurring.

initialize: The procedure for setting various parts of a stored program to starting values, so that the program will behave the same way each time it is repeated. The procedures are included as part of the program itself.

input: Information transferred from a peripheral device into the computer. Also applied to the transfer process itself.

input/output (I/O): Relating to the equipment or method used for transmitting information into and out of the computer.

input/output channel: The complete input or output facility for one individual device or function, including its assigned position in the computer, the interface circuitry, and the external device.

instruction: A written statement or the equivalent computer-acceptance code, which tells the computer to execute a specified single operation.

instruction code: The arrangement of binary digits which tells the computer to execute a particular instruction.

instruction logic: The circuitry involved in moving binary information between registers, memory, and buffers in prescribed manners, according to instruction codes.

instruction word: A computer word containing an instruction code. The code bits may occupy all or (as in the case of memory reference instruction words) only part of the word.

interface: The connecting circuitry which links the central processor of a computer system to its peripheral devices.

internal storage: The storage facilities forming an integral physical part of the computer and directly controlled by the computer. Also called "main memory" and "core memory."

interpreter: A program which translates and executes source language statements at run time.

interrupt: The process, initiated by an exteranl device, which causes the computer to interrupt a program in progress, generally for the purpose of transferring information between that device and the computer.

interrupt location: A memory location whose contents (always an instruction) are executed upon interrupt by a specific device.

iteration: Repetition of a group of instructions.

job: A unit of code which solves a problem, i.e., a program and all its related subroutines and data.

jump: An instruction which breaks the strict sequential location-by-location operation of a program and directs the computer to continue at another specified location anywhere in memory.

K: One thousand and twenty-four. For example, 4 K words of memory means 4096 words.

label: Any arrangement of symbols, usually alphanumeric, used in place of an absolute memory address in computer programming.

language: The set of symbols, rules, and conventions used to convey information, either at the human level or at the computer level.

leader: The blank section of tape at the beginning of the tape.

least significant digit: The rightmost digit of a number.

library routine: A routine designed to accomplish some commonly used mathematical function and kept permanently available on a library program tape (e.g., Fortran Library).

line feed: The Teletype operation which advances the paper by one line.

line number: In source languages such as Focal, Basic, and Fortran, a number which begins a line of the source program for purposes of identification. A numeric label.

linkage: In programming, code that connects two separately coded routines.

list: 1) A set of items. 2) To print out a listing on the line printer or Teletype. 3) See "pushdown list."

literal: A symbol which defines itself.

load: To put information into (memory, a register, etc.). Also (e.g., loading tape), to put information medium into the appropriate device.

load time: That time at which an assembled program is placed in the computer and readied for execution.

loader: A program designed to assist in transferring information from an external device into a computer's memory.

location: A group of storage elements in the computer's memory which can store one computer word. Each such location is identified by a number ("address") to facilitate storage and retrieval of information in selectable locations.

logical operation: A mathematical process based on the principles of truth tables, e.g., AND, INCLUSIVE-OR, and EXCLUSIVE-OR operations.

logic diagram: A diagram which represents the detailed internal functioning of electronic hardware, using binary logic symbols rather than electronic component symbols.

logic equation: A written mathematical statement, using

symbols and rules derived from Boolean algebra. Specifically (hardware design), a means of stating the conditions required to obtain a given signal.

loop: A sequence of instructions in which the last instruction is a jump back to the first instruction.

low core: Core-memory locations having low-numbered addresses.

machine: Pertaining to the computer hardware (e.g., machine timing, machine language).

machine language: The form of coded information (consisting of binary digits) which can be directly accepted and used by the computer. Other languages require translation to this form, generally with the aid of translation programs (assemblers and compilers).

machine timing: The regular cycle of events in the operation of internal computer circuitry. The actual events will differ for various processes, but the timing is constant through each recurring cycle.

macro: An assembly-time facility that allows lines of text to be named and saved by the assembler, to be retrieved and modified by the substitution of text for dummy names in the saved text. The resulting modified text is assembled at the point of retrieval.

macroinstruction: An instruction, similar in binary coding to the computer's basic machine-language instructions, which is capable of producing a variable number of machine-language instructions.

magnitude: That portion of a computer word which indicates the absolute value of a number, thus excluding the sign bit.

mask: A bit pattern which selects those bits from a word of data which are to be used in some subsequent operation.

mass-storage: Pertaining to a device, such as tape or disk, which stores large amounts of data readily accessible to the central processing unit.

media conversion: The transferral of recorded information from one recording medium (e.g., punched paper tape, magnetic tape, etc.) to another recording medium.

memory: An organized collection of storage elements (e.g., ferrite cores) into which a unit of information consisting of a binary digit can be stored and from which it can later be retrieved. Also, a device not necessarily having individual storage elements, but which has the same storage and retrieval capabilities (e.g., magnetic disks).

memory cycle: That portion of the computer's internal timing during which the contents of one location of memory are read out (into the transfer register) and written back into that location.

memory module: A complete segment of core storage, capable of storing a definable number of computer words (e.g., 4096 or 8192 words). Computer storage capacity is incremental by modules and is frequently rounded off and abbreviated as "4K" (i.e., 4096 or approximately 4000 words), "8K" (8192 or 8000), "16K," etc.

memory protect: A means of preventing inadvertent alteration of a selectable segment of memory.

memory reference: The address of the memory location specified by a memory-reference instruction, i.e., the location affected by the instruction.

microinstruction: An instruction which forms part of a larger composite instruction.

minicomputer: A general term used to describe small computers. In this sense, small usually implies both the computer's physical size and its word size (data-path width). Most minicomputers are designed with a 16-b word size, but sizes from 8 to 18 b are considered in the minicomputer range.

monitor: An operating programming system which provides a uniform method for handling the real-time aspects of program timing, such as scheduling and basic input/output functions.

most significant digit: The leftmost nonzero digit.

multilevel indirect: Indirect addressing using two or more indirect addresses in sequence to find the effective address for the current instruction.

multiple-precision: Referring to arithmetic in which the computer, for greatest accuracy, uses two or more words to represent one number.

multiprocessing: Utilization of several computers or processors to logically or functionally divide jobs or processes and to execute them simultaneously.

multiprogramming: A system of execution of two or more programs kept in core at the same time. Execution cycles between the programs.

normalize: To adjust the exponent and fraction of a floating-point quantity so that the fraction appears in a prescribed format.

object programming: The binary coded program which is the output after translation from the source language; the binary program which runs on the computer.

octal: Denoting a numbering system based on the radix eight. Octal digits are restricted to the values 0 through 7.

octal code: A notation for writing machine-language programs with the use of octal numbers instead of binary numbers.

off-line: Pertaining to the operation of peripheral equipment not under control of the computer.

one's complement: A number so modified that the addition to the modified number and its original value, plus one, will equal an even power of two. A one's complement number is obtained mathematically by subtracting the original value from a string of 1's, and electronically by inverting the states of all bits in the number.

on-line: Pertaining to the operation of peripheral equipment under computer control.

operand: That which is effected, manipulated, or operated upon. The address or symbolic-name portion of an assembler instruction.

operating system: An integrated collection of routines for supervising the sequencing of programs by a computer, e.g.: debugging, input/output, operation, compilation, and storage assignment.

operation (OP) code: That part of an instruction designating the operation to be performed.

operator: That symbol or code which indicates an action (or operation to be performed.

optimum code: A set of machine language instructions which is *particularly efficient with regard to a particular aspects*, e.g., minimum time to execute or minimum or efficient use of storage space.

OR: (inclusive) A logical operation such that the result is true if either or both operands are true, and false if both operands are false. (exclusive) A logical operation such that the result is true if either operand is true, and false if both operands are either true or false.

origin: The absolute address of the beginning of a section of code.

output: Information transferred from the computer to a peripheral device. Also applied to the transfer process itself.

overflow: A condition that occurs when a mathematical operation yields a result whose magnitude is larger than the program is capable of handling.

overlay: The operation of bringing into main memory and executing a segment which is a subprogram (i.e., a more or less separate entity) of a larger program.

packed word: A computer word containing two or more independent units of information. This is done to conserve storage when information requires relatively few bits of the computer word.

page: An artificial division of memory consisting of a fixed number of locations, dictated by the direct addressing range of memory reference instructions.

page zero: The memory page which includes the lowest numbered memory addresses.

parity bit: A supplementary bit added to an information word to make the total number of one bits always odd or even. This permits checking the accuracy of information transfers.

pass: The complete process of reading a set of recorded information (one tape, one set of cards, etc.) through an input device, from beginning to end.

patch: To modify a routine in a rough or expedient way.

peripheral device: An instrument or machine electrically connected to the computer, but which is not part of the computer itself.

plane: An arrangement of ferrite cores on a matrix of control and sensing wires. Several planes stacked together form a "memory module."

pointer address: Address of a core-memory location containing the actual (effective) address of desired data.

power-failure control: A means of sensing primary power failure so that a special routine may be executed in the finite period of time available before the regulated dc supplies discharge to unusable levels. The special routine may be used to preserve the state of a program in progress, or to shut down external processes.

priority: The automatic regulation of events so that chosen actions will take precedence over others in cases of timing conflict.

procedure: The course of action taken for the solution of a problem; also called "algorithm."

process control: Automatic control of manufacturing processes by use of a computer.

processor: The central unit of a computer system (i.e., the device which accomplishes the airthmetic manipulations), exclusive of peripheral devices. Frequently (when used as adjective) also excludes interface components, even though normally contained within the processor unit; thus "processor" options exlcude interface ("input/output") options.

program: A plan for the solution of a problem by a computer, consisting of a sequence of computer instructions.

program listing: A printed record (or equivalent binary-output program) of the instructions in a program.

programmer: A person who writes computer programs. Also (hardware), an interface card or instrument which sets up (or "programs") the various functions of one measuring instrument.

programming: The process of creating a program.

pseudoinstruction: A symbolic statement, similar to assembly-language instructions in general form, but meaningful only to the program containing it, rather than to the computer as a machine instruction.

punched tape: A string of tape, usually paper, on which information is represented by coded patterns of holes punched in columns across the width of the tape. There are commonly 8 hole positions (channels) across the tape.

pushdown list: A list that is constructed and maintained so that the next item to be retrieved is the item most recently sorted in the list.

queue: A waiting list. In time sharing, the monitor maintains a queue of user programs waiting for processing time.

radix: The base of a number system, the number of digit symbols required by a number system. See "binary," "octal."

random-access: Pertaining to a storage device in which the accessibility of data is effectively independent of the location of the data (synonomous with "direct-access").

read: The process of transferring information from an input device into the computer. Also, the process of taking information out of the computer's memory. (See "memory cycle.")

real time: The time elapsed between events occurring externally to the computer. A computer which accepts and processes information from one such event and is ready for new information before the next event occurs is said to operate in a "real-time environment."

record: A collection of related items of data, treated as a unit.

recursive subroutine: A subroutine capable of calling itself and returning at some later point to the program which initially called it.

reentrant code: A program segment (e.g., subroutine) which can be executed (i.e., reentered) by more than one other program simultaneously. This mode of operation requires a separate storage area for storing information that varies for each instance of execution.

register: An array of hardware binary circuits (flip-flops, switches, etc.) for temporary storage of information. Unlike mass-storage devices such as memory cores, registers can be wired to permit flexible control of the contained information, for arithmetic operations, shifts, transfers, etc.

relative address: The number that specifies the difference between the actual address and a base address.

relocatable: Pertaining to programs whose instructions can be loaded into any stated area of memory.

relocating loader: A computer program capable of loading and combining relocatable programs (i.e., programs having symbolic rather than absolute addresses).

reset: A signal condition representing a binary "zero."

response time: The time between initiating some operation from a terminal and obtaining results. Includes transmission time to the computer, processing time, access time to file records needed, and transmission time back to the terminal.

restart: To measure the execution of a program.

rotate: A positional shift of all bits in an accumulator (and possibly an extend bit as well) with those bits lost off one end of the accumulator "rotated" around to enter vacated positions at the other end.

routine: A program or program segment designed to accomplish a single function.

run time: The time in which a progran is executed.

segment: 1) That part of a long program which may be

resident in core at any one time. 2) To divide a program as in 1), or into two or more segments, or to store part of a program or routine on an external storage device to be brought into core as needed.

serial-access: Pertaining to the sequential or consecutive transmission of data to or from core, for example, paper tape. Contrast with "random-access."

service routine: A sequence of instructions designed to accomplish the transfer of information between a particular device and the computer.

set: A signal condition representing a binary "one."

shift: Restrictive (arithmetic shift): to multiply or divide the magnitude portion of a word by a power of two, using a positional shift of these bits. General: any positional shift of bits.

sign: The algebraic plus or minus indicator for a mathematical quantity. Also, the binary digit or electrical polarity representing such an indicator.

significant digit: A digit so positioned in a numeral as to contribute a definable degree of precision to the numeral. In conventional written form, the most significant digit in a numeral is the leftmost digit, and the least significant digit is the rightmost digit.

simulate: To represent the functioning of a device, system, or computer program with another system or program.

skip: An instruction which causes the computer to omit the instruction in the immediately following location. A skip is usually arranged to occur only if certain specified conditions are sensed and found to be true, thus allowing various decisions to be made.

snapshot dump: A dynamic printout during execution, at breakpoints and checkpoints, of selected areas in storage.

software: Computer programs. Also, the tapes or cards on which the programs are recorded.

software package: A complete collection of related programs, not necessarily combined as a single entity.

source program: A program (or its recorded form) written in some programming language other than machine language and thus requiring translation. The translated form is the "object program."

starting address: The address of a memory location in which is stored the first instruction of a given program.

statement: An instruction in any computer-related language other than machine language.

storage allocation: The assignment of blocks of data and instructions to specified blocks of storage.

storage capacity: The amount of data that can be entered, retained, and retrieved.

storage device: A device in which data can be entered, retained, and retrieved.

store: To put information into a memory location, register, or device capable of retaining the information for later access.

string: A connected sequence of entities, such as characters in a command string.

subroutine: A sequence of instructions designed to perform a single task, with provisions included to allow some other program to cause execution of the task sequence as if it were part of its own program.

subscript: A value used to specify a particular item in an array.

swapping: In a time-sharing environment, the action of either temporarily bringing a user program into core or storing it on the disk or other system device.

switch: A device of programming technique for making selections.

symbol table: A table in which symbols and their corresponding values are recorded.

symbolic address: A label assigned in place of absolute numeric addresses, usually for purposes of relocation. (See "relocatable.")

symbolic coding: Broadly, any coding or programming system in which symbols other than actual machine operations and addresses are used.

symbolic instruction: An instruction which is the basic component of an assembly language (input to assembler) and is directly translatable into machine language.

syntax: 1) The structure of expressions in a programming language. 2) The rules governing the structure of a programming language.

table: A collection of data stored for ease of reference, generally an array.

temporary storage: Storage locations reserved for immediate results.

terminal: A peripheral device in a system through which data can either enter or leave the computer.

time sharing: A method of allocating central-processor time and other computer services to multiple users so that the computer, in effect, processes a number of programs simultaneously.

time slicing: A method of job scheduling in a multiprogrammed system. This refers to the allocation of fixed amounts of computing time among users on a round-robin basis. Interrupts are generated by a fixed interval timer causing control to pass to the next waiting service request.

toggle: (adjective) Using switches to enter data into the computer memory.

transfer vector: A table, usually at a fixed location in memory, containing jump instructions and/or indirect addresses for jump instructions. A jump to a particular routine or the address of the routine is placed in a particular place in the table. Other routines can call this routine without necessarily knowing the actual location of this routine in memory. This technique is used frequently when a relocatable assembler is not available for a particular machine.

truncation: The reduction of precision by dropping one or more of the least significant digits; e.g., 3.141592 truncated to 4 decimal digits is 3.141.

truth table: A table listing of all possible configurations and resultant values for any given Boolean algebra function.

two's complement: A number so modified that the addition of the modified number and its original value will equal an even power of two. Also, a kind of arithmetic which represents negative numbers in two's-complement form so that all addition can be accomplished in only one direction (positive incrementation). A two's-complement number is obtained mathematically by subtracting the original value from an appropriate power of the base two, and electronically by inverting the states of all bits in the number and adding one (complement and increment).

underflow: A condition that occurs when a floating-point operation yields a result whose magnitude is smaller than the program is capable of handling.

updated program: A program to which additions, deletions, or corrections have been made.

user: The person or persons who program and operate a particular computer.

utility routine: A standard routine to assist in the operation of the computer (e.g., device drivers, sorting routines, etc.) as opposed to mathematical ("library") routines.

variable: A symbol whose value changes during the execution of a program.

waiting loop: A sequence of instructions (frequently only two) which are repeated indefintely until a desired external event occurs, such as the receipt of a flag signal.

word: A set of binary digits handled by the computer as a unit of information. Its length is determined by hardware design, e.g., the number of cores per location and the number of flip-flops per register.

word length: The number of bits in a word.

working register: A register whose contents can be modified under control of a program. Thus a register consisting of manually operated switches is not considered a working register.

write: The process of transferring information from the computer to an output device. Also, the process of storing (or restoring) information into the computer's memory. (See "memory cycle.")

Graphic symbols for electronics diagrams

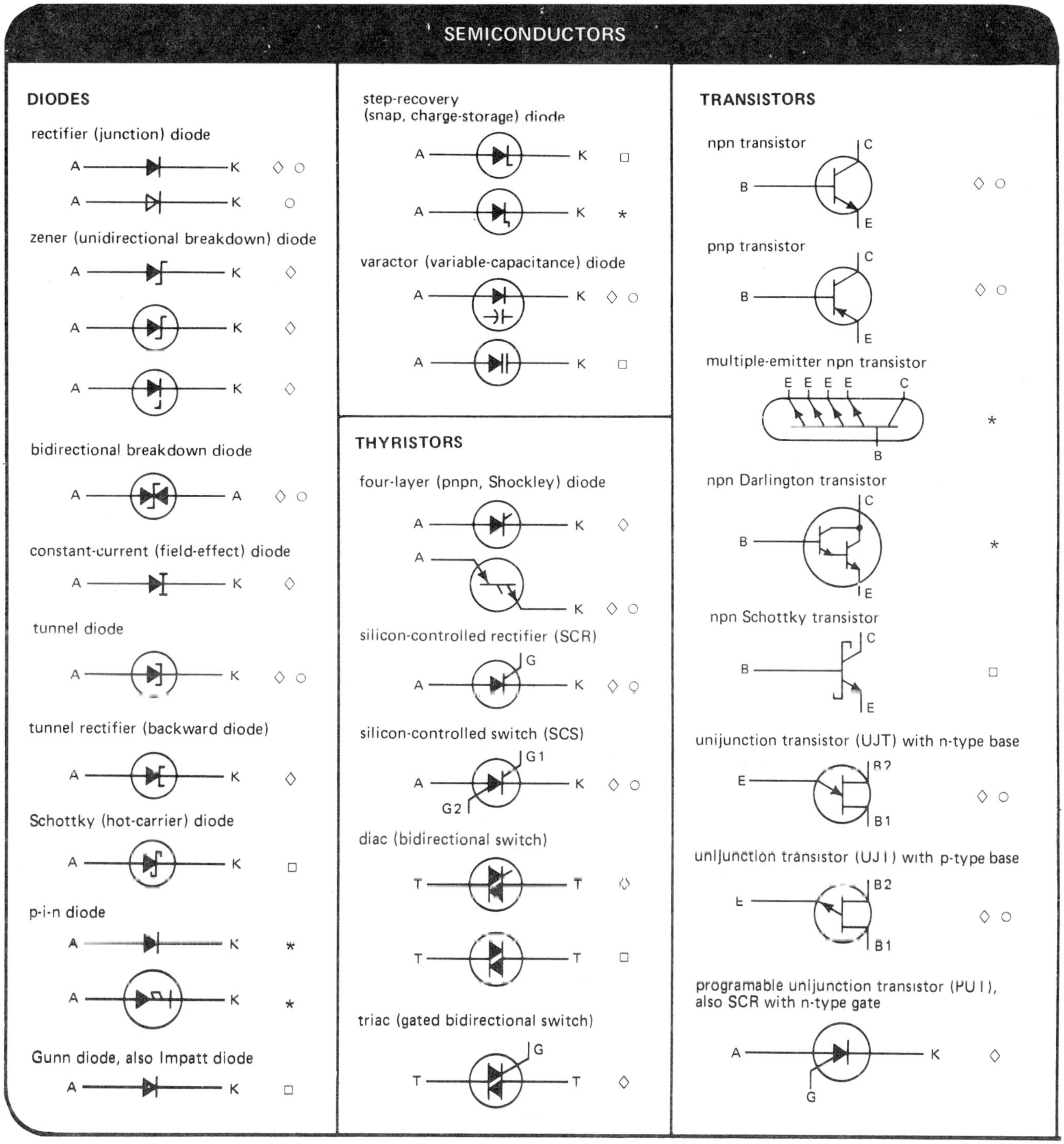

* = Proposed IEEE revision

◇ = IEEE/ANSI approval
○ = IEC approval

□ = Popular industry usage
√ = NARM approval

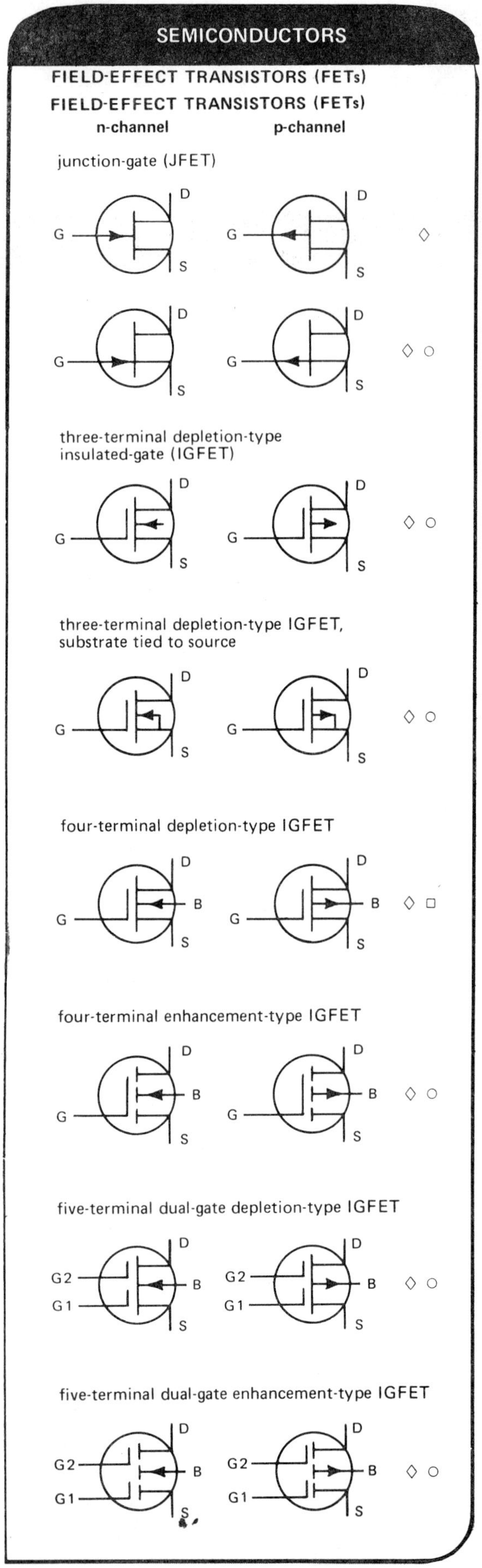
SEMICONDUCTORS
FIELD-EFFECT TRANSISTORS (FETs)
FIELD-EFFECT TRANSISTORS (FETs)
n-channel
p-channel
junction-gate (JFET)
three-terminal depletion-type insulated-gate (IGFET)
three-terminal depletion-type IGFET, substrate tied to source
four-terminal depletion-type IGFET
four-terminal enhancement-type IGFET
five-terminal dual-gate depletion-type IGFET
five-terminal dual-gate enhancement-type IGFET
D
S
G
B
G1
G2

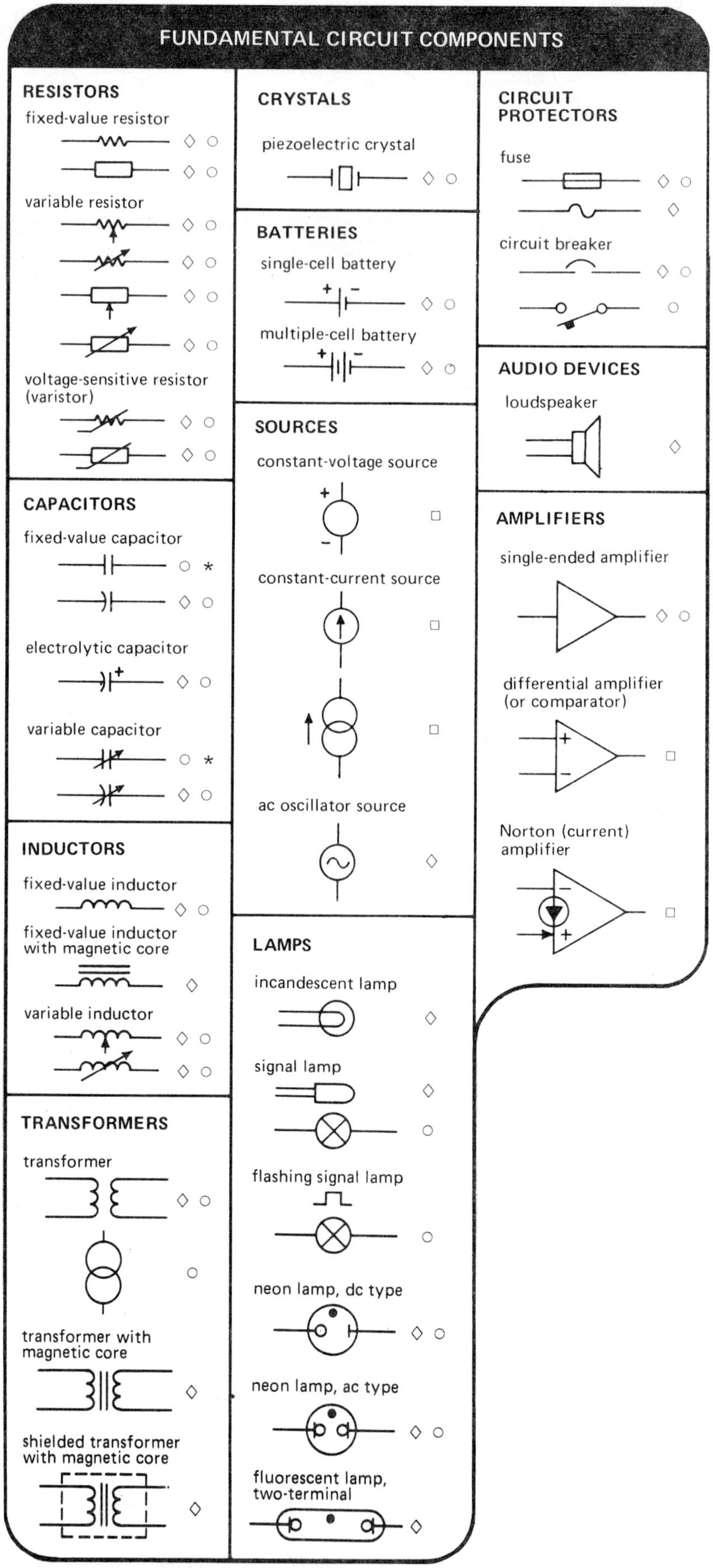
FUNDAMENTAL CIRCUIT COMPONENTS
RESISTORS
fixed-value resistor
variable resistor
voltage-sensitive resistor (varistor)
CAPACITORS
fixed-value capacitor
electrolytic capacitor
variable capacitor
INDUCTORS
fixed-value inductor
fixed-value inductor with magnetic core
variable inductor
TRANSFORMERS
transformer
transformer with magnetic core
shielded transformer with magnetic core
CRYSTALS
piezoelectric crystal
BATTERIES
single-cell battery
multiple-cell battery
SOURCES
constant-voltage source
constant-current source
ac oscillator source
LAMPS
incandescent lamp
signal lamp
flashing signal lamp
neon lamp, dc type
neon lamp, ac type
fluorescent lamp, two-terminal
CIRCUIT PROTECTORS
fuse
circuit breaker
AUDIO DEVICES
loudspeaker
AMPLIFIERS
single-ended amplifier
differential amplifier (or comparator)
Norton (current) amplifier

OPTOELECTRONIC DEVICES

DIODES

light-emitting diode (LED)

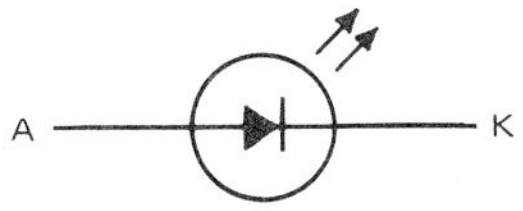

◇ ○

photodiode

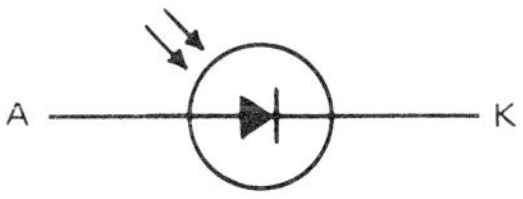

◇ ○

npn bidirectional photodiode
(photo-duo-diode)

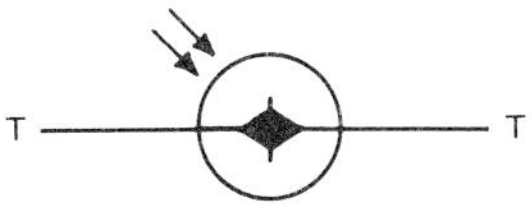

*

pnp bidirectional photodiode
(photo-duo-diode)

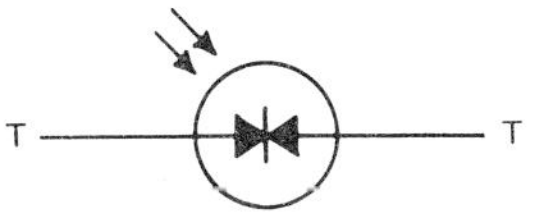

*

pnp two-segment photodiode,
with common cathode

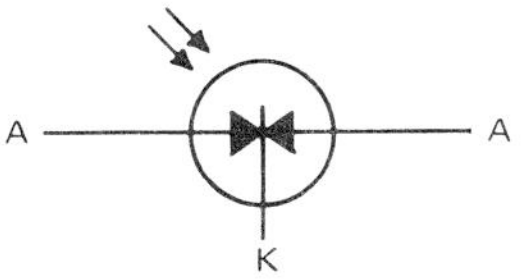

*

pnp four-quadrant photodiode,
with common cathode

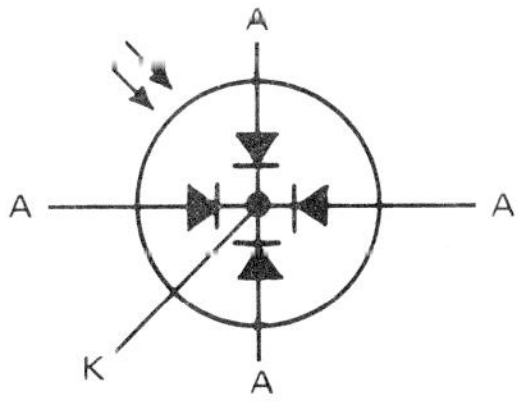

*

TRANSISTORS

npn phototransistor,
no base connection

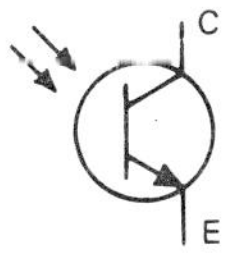

◇

npn phototransistor,
with base connection

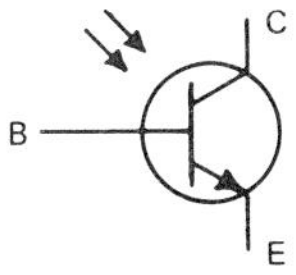

◇ ○

OPTICALLY COUPLED ISOLATORS

with photodiode output

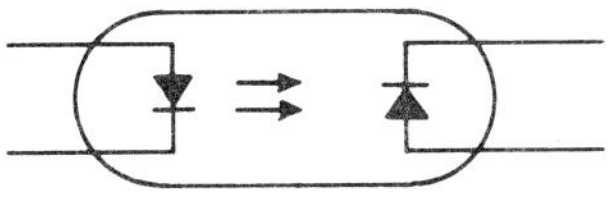

◇

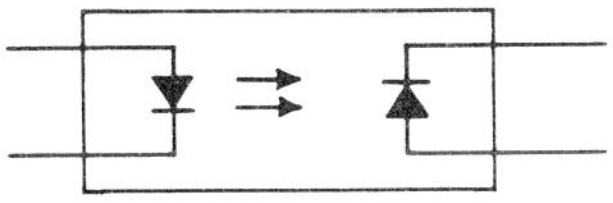

□

with phototransistor output,
no base connection

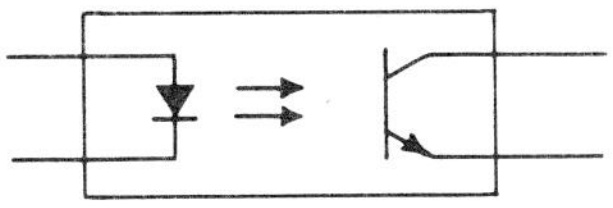

□

with phototransistor output,
and base connection

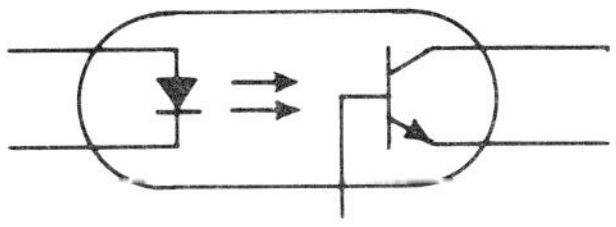

◇

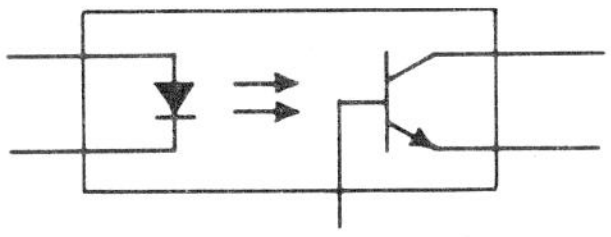

□

with photo-Darlington output, no base

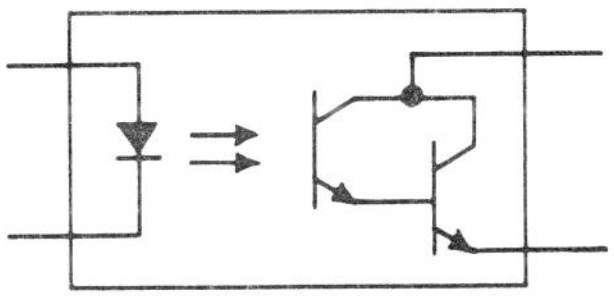

□

with photo-Darlington output, and base

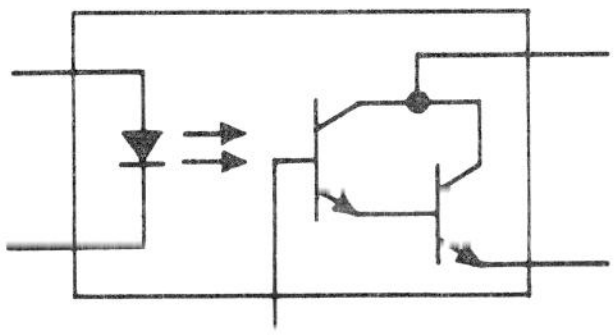

□

with photodiode and amplifier-
transistor output

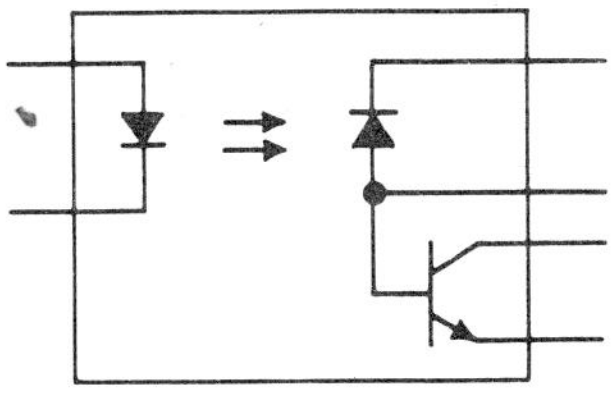

□

with NAND-gate-photodetector output

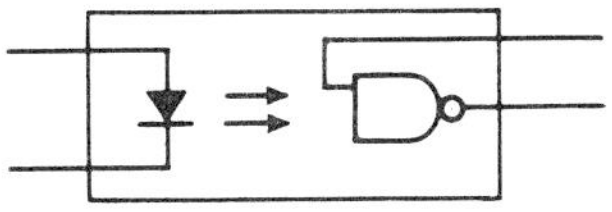

□

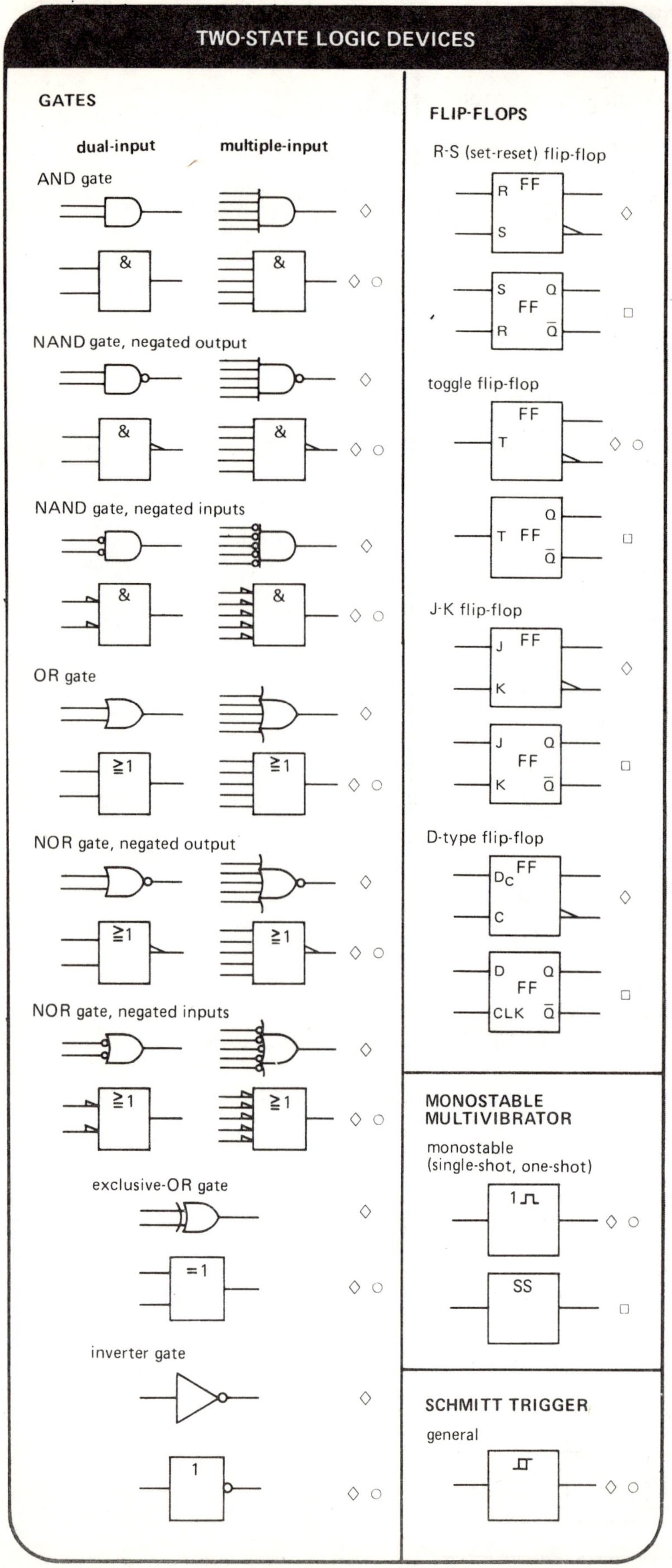
TWO-STATE LOGIC DEVICES
GATES
dual-input
multiple-input
AND gate
&
NAND gate, negated output
NAND gate, negated inputs
OR gate
≧1
NOR gate, negated output
NOR gate, negated inputs
exclusive-OR gate
=1
inverter gate
1
FLIP-FLOPS
R-S (set-reset) flip-flop
R FF S
S Q FF R Q̄
toggle flip-flop
FF T
Q T FF Q̄
J-K flip-flop
J FF K
J Q FF K Q̄
D-type flip-flop
DC FF C
D Q FF CLK Q̄
MONOSTABLE MULTIVIBRATOR
monostable (single-shot, one-shot)
1
SS
SCHMITT TRIGGER
general

Index